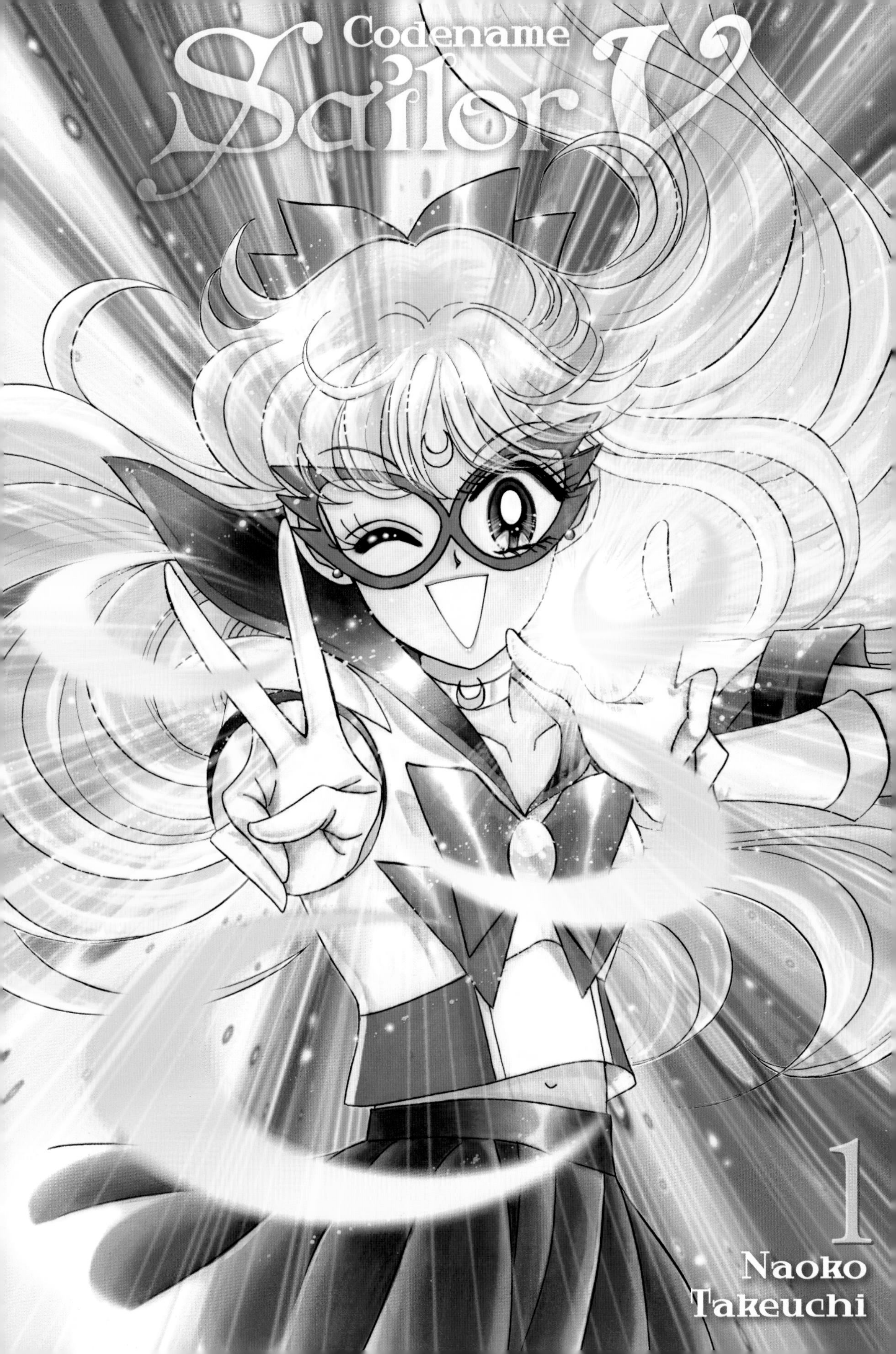
Codename
Sailor V
1
Naoko
Takeuchi

CONTENTS

Codename Sailor V

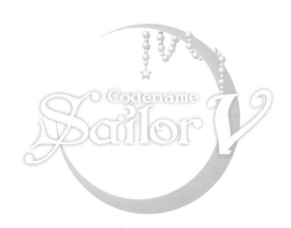

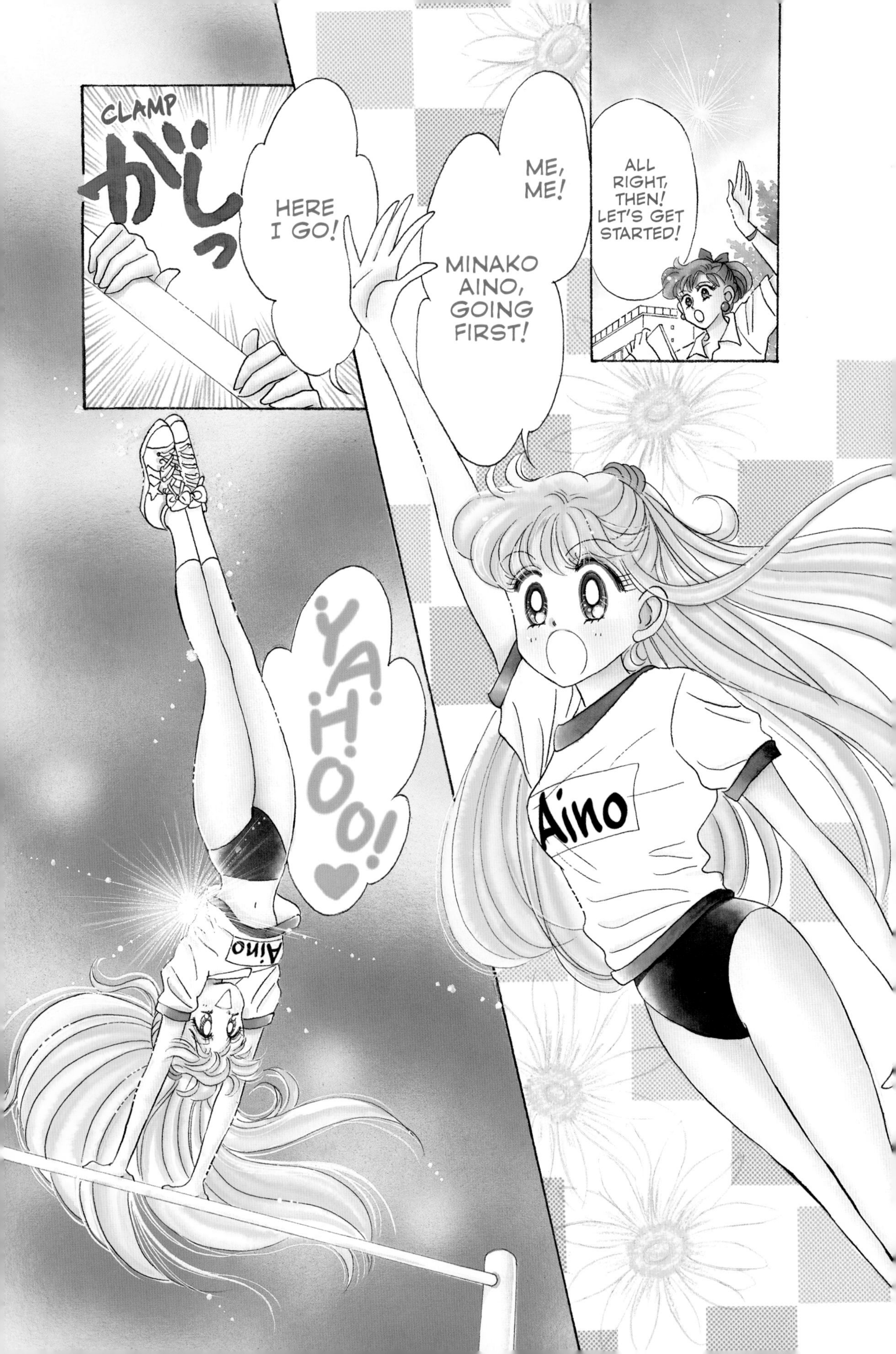

ALL RIGHT, THEN! LET'S GET STARTED!
ME, ME!
MINAKO AINO, GOING FIRST!
Aino
HERE I GO!
CLAMP
がしっ
YAHOO!♥
Aino

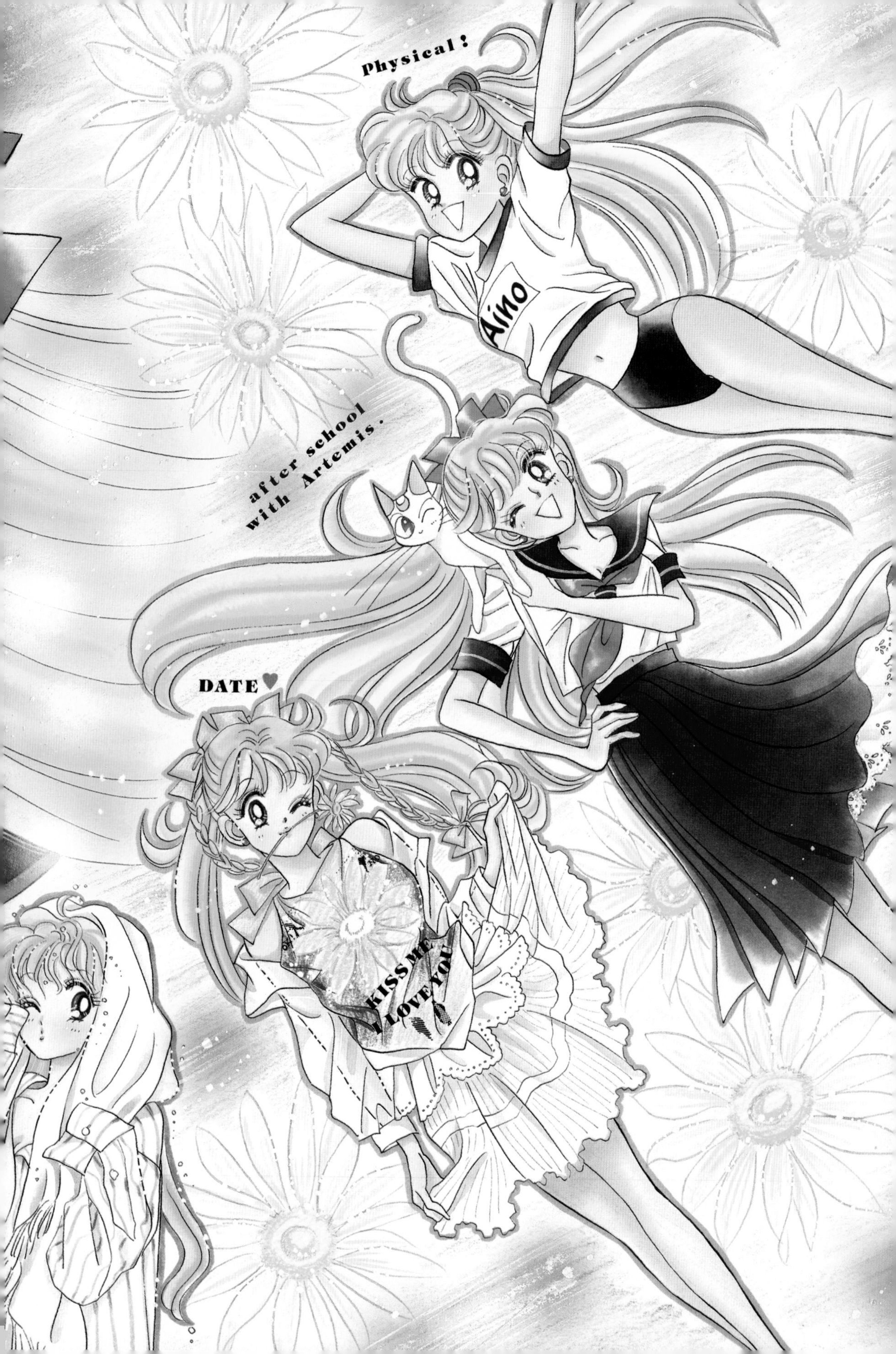
Physical!
Aino
after school
with Artemis.
DATE♥
KISS ME
I LOVE YOU

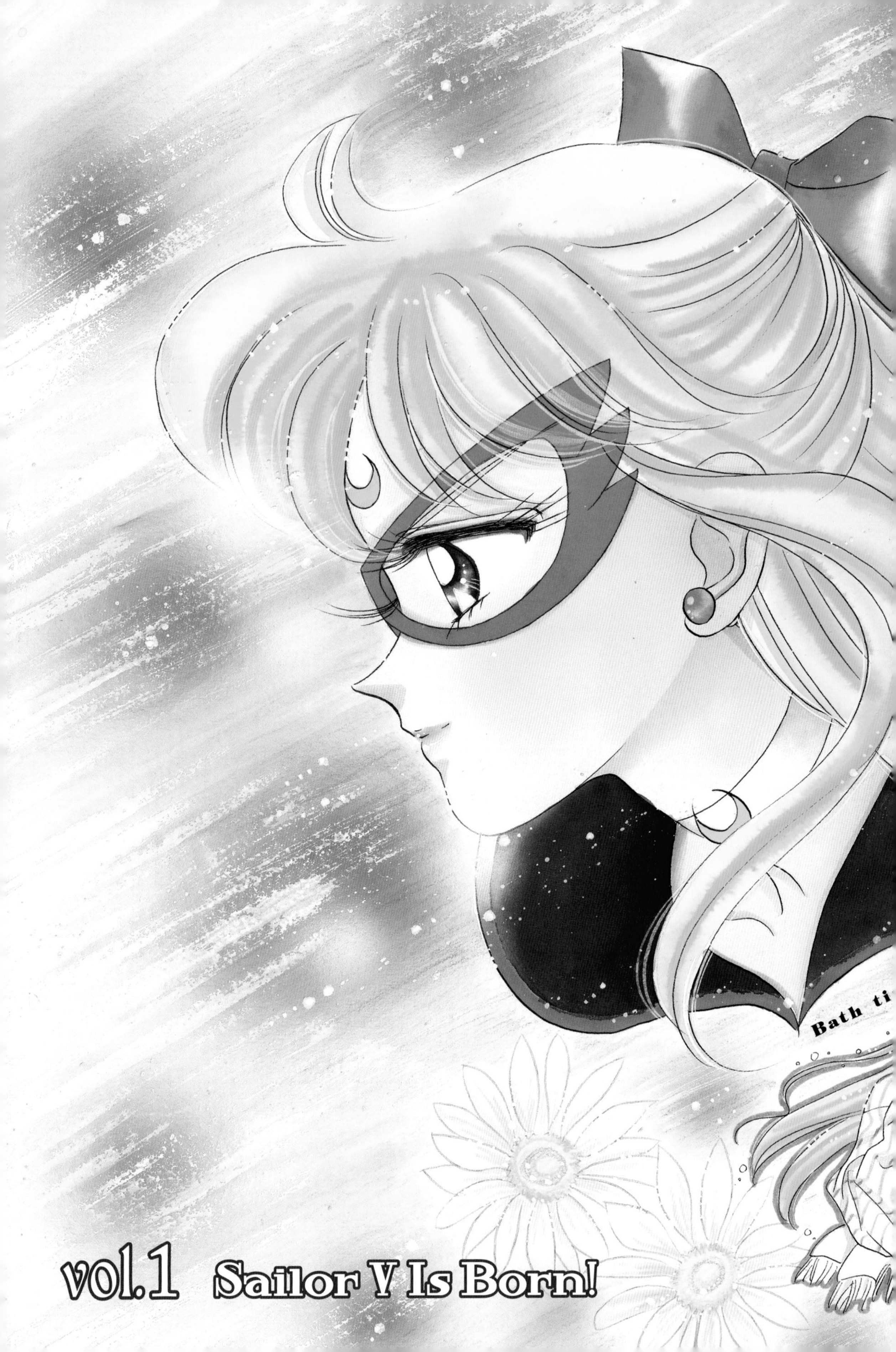
vol.1 Sailor V Is Born!

Codename

Sailor V

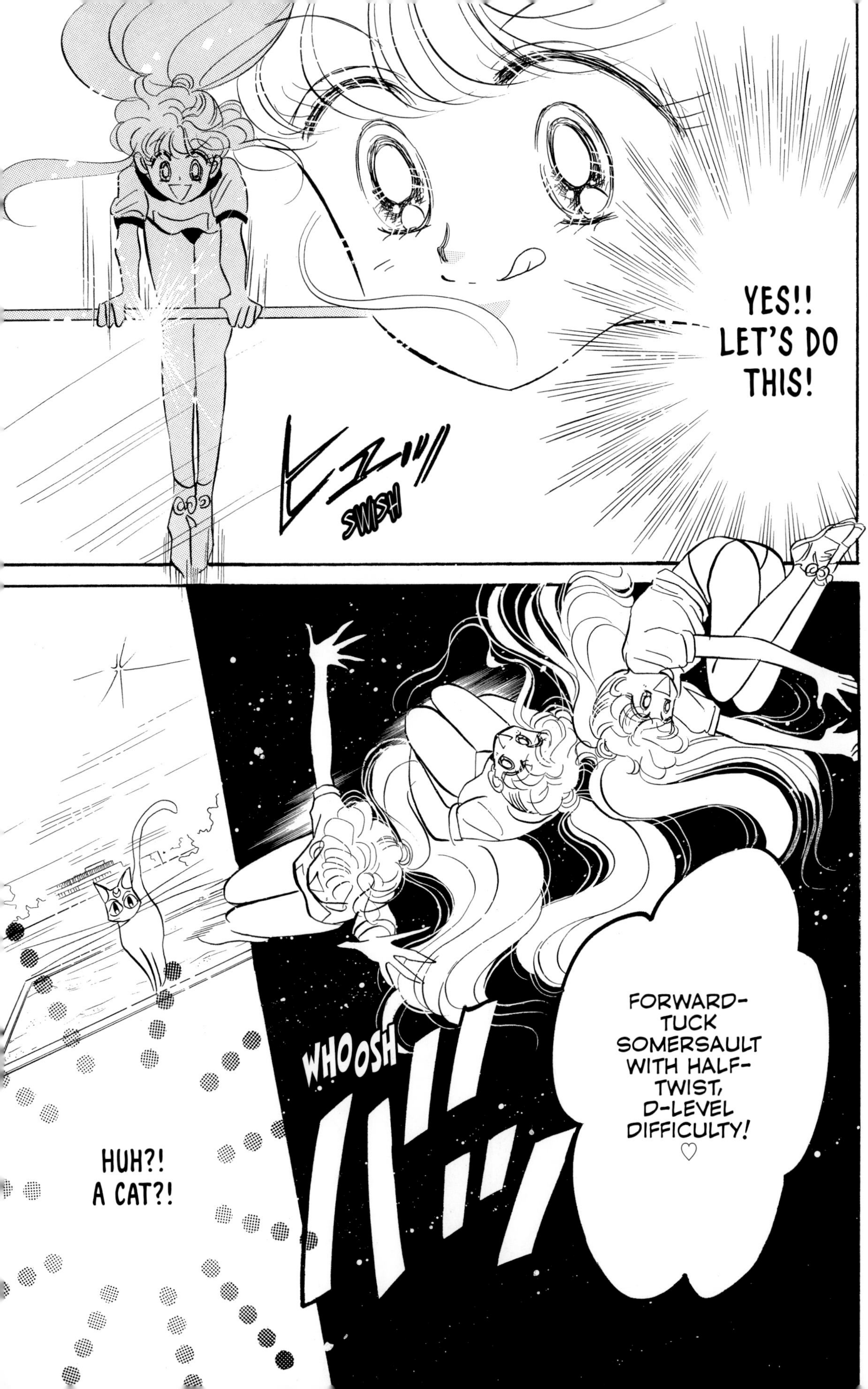
YES!! LET'S DO THIS!
SWISH
FORWARD-TUCK SOMERSAULT WITH HALF-TWIST, D-LEVEL DIFFICULTY! ♡
WHOOSH
HUH?! A CAT?!

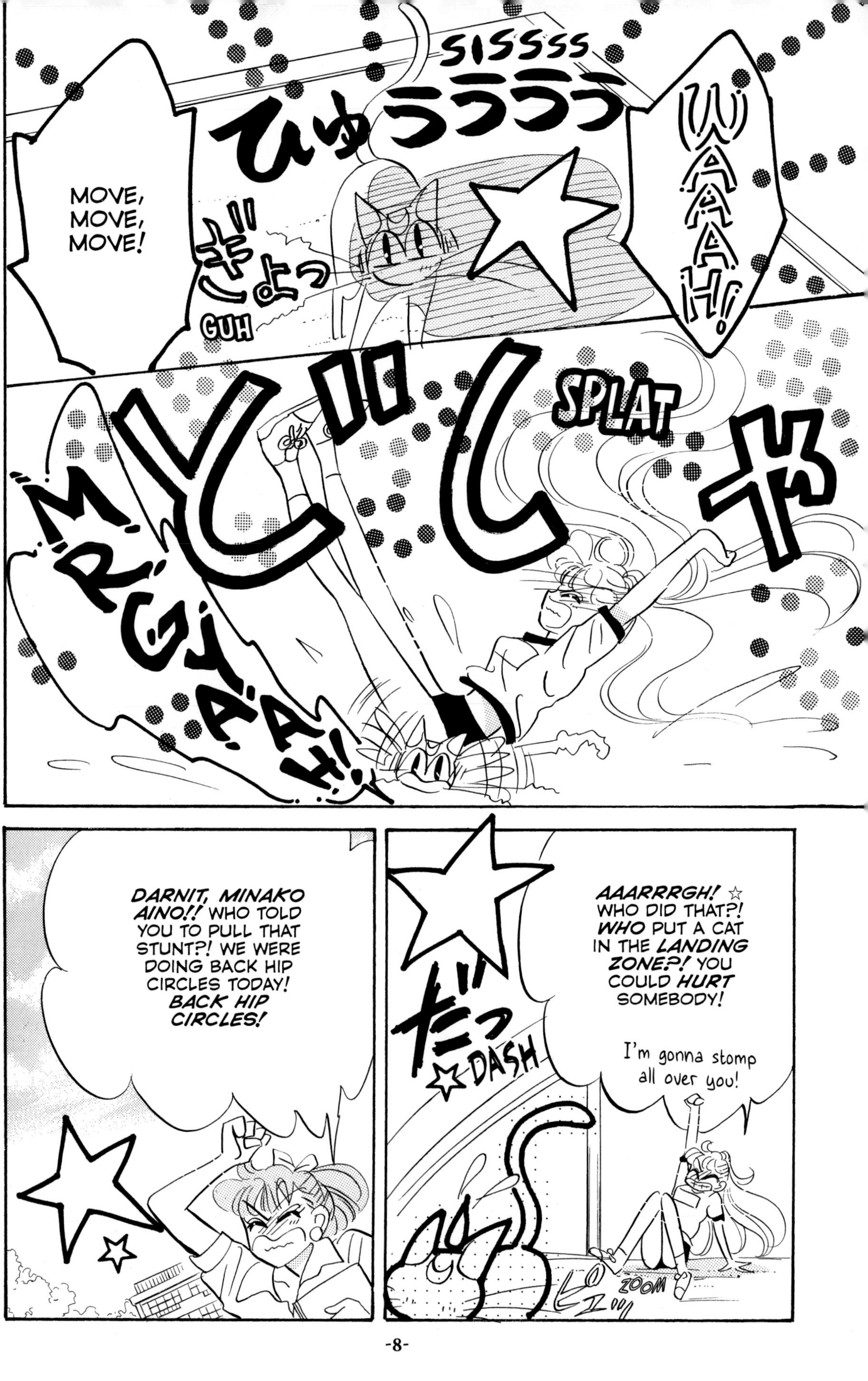
ひゅううううう
SISSSS
WAAAH!
ぎょっ
GUH
MOVE, MOVE, MOVE!
びしゃ
SPLAT
MRGYAAH!
AAARRRGH! ☆ WHO DID THAT?! WHO PUT A CAT IN THE LANDING ZONE?! YOU COULD HURT SOMEBODY!
I'm gonna stomp all over you!
だっ
DASH
ZOOM
DARNIT, MINAKO AINO!! WHO TOLD YOU TO PULL THAT STUNT?! WE WERE DOING BACK HIP CIRCLES TODAY! BACK HIP CIRCLES!

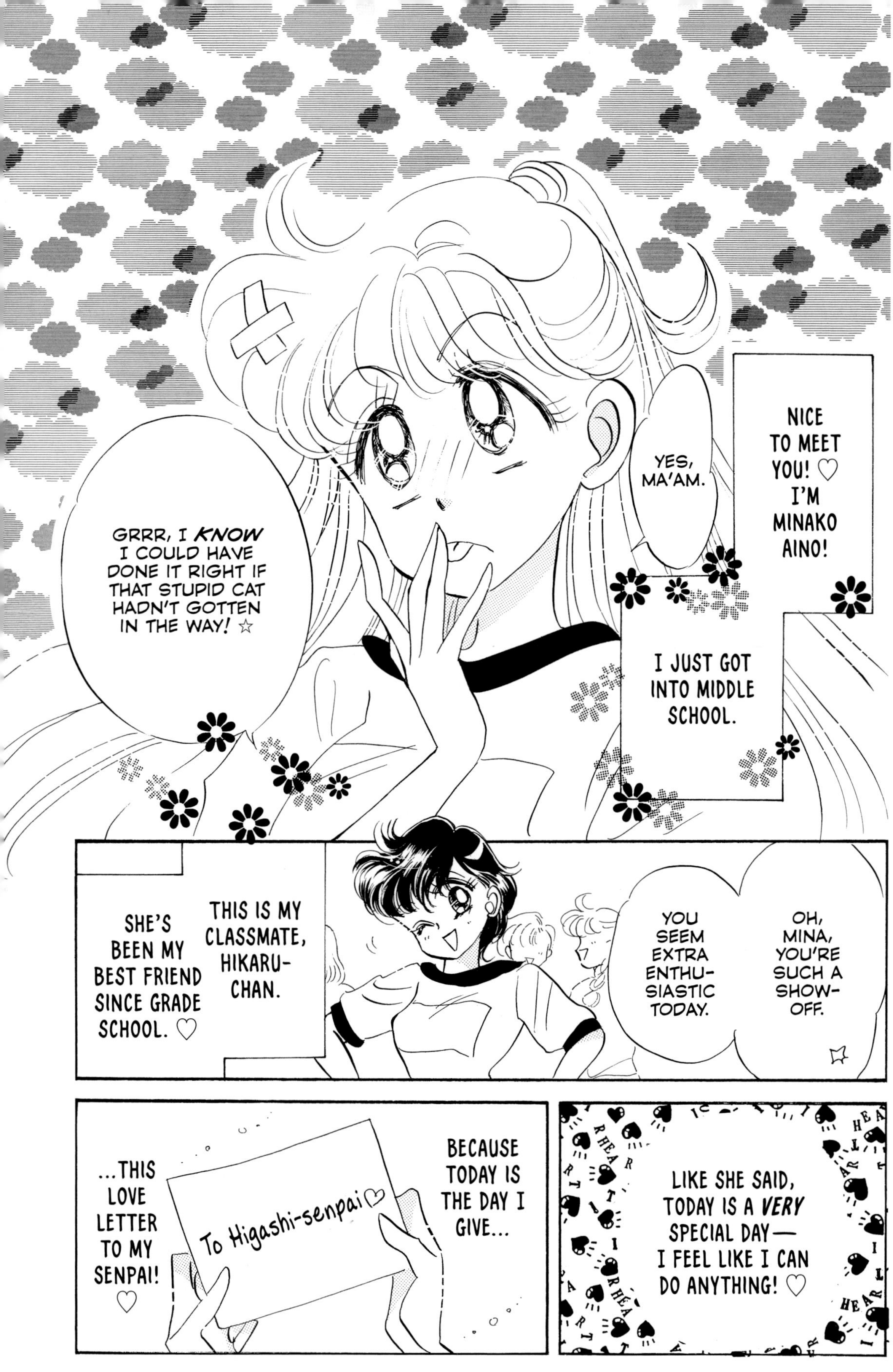
NICE TO MEET YOU! ♡ I'M MINAKO AINO!
YES, MA'AM.
I JUST GOT INTO MIDDLE SCHOOL.
GRRR, I *KNOW* I COULD HAVE DONE IT RIGHT IF THAT STUPID CAT HADN'T GOTTEN IN THE WAY! ☆
OH, MINA, YOU'RE SUCH A SHOW-OFF.
YOU SEEM EXTRA ENTHUSIASTIC TODAY.
THIS IS MY CLASSMATE, HIKARU-CHAN.
SHE'S BEEN MY BEST FRIEND SINCE GRADE SCHOOL. ♡
LIKE SHE SAID, TODAY IS A *VERY* SPECIAL DAY— I FEEL LIKE I CAN DO ANYTHING! ♡
BECAUSE TODAY IS THE DAY I GIVE...
To Higashi-senpai♡
...THIS LOVE LETTER TO MY SENPAI! ♡

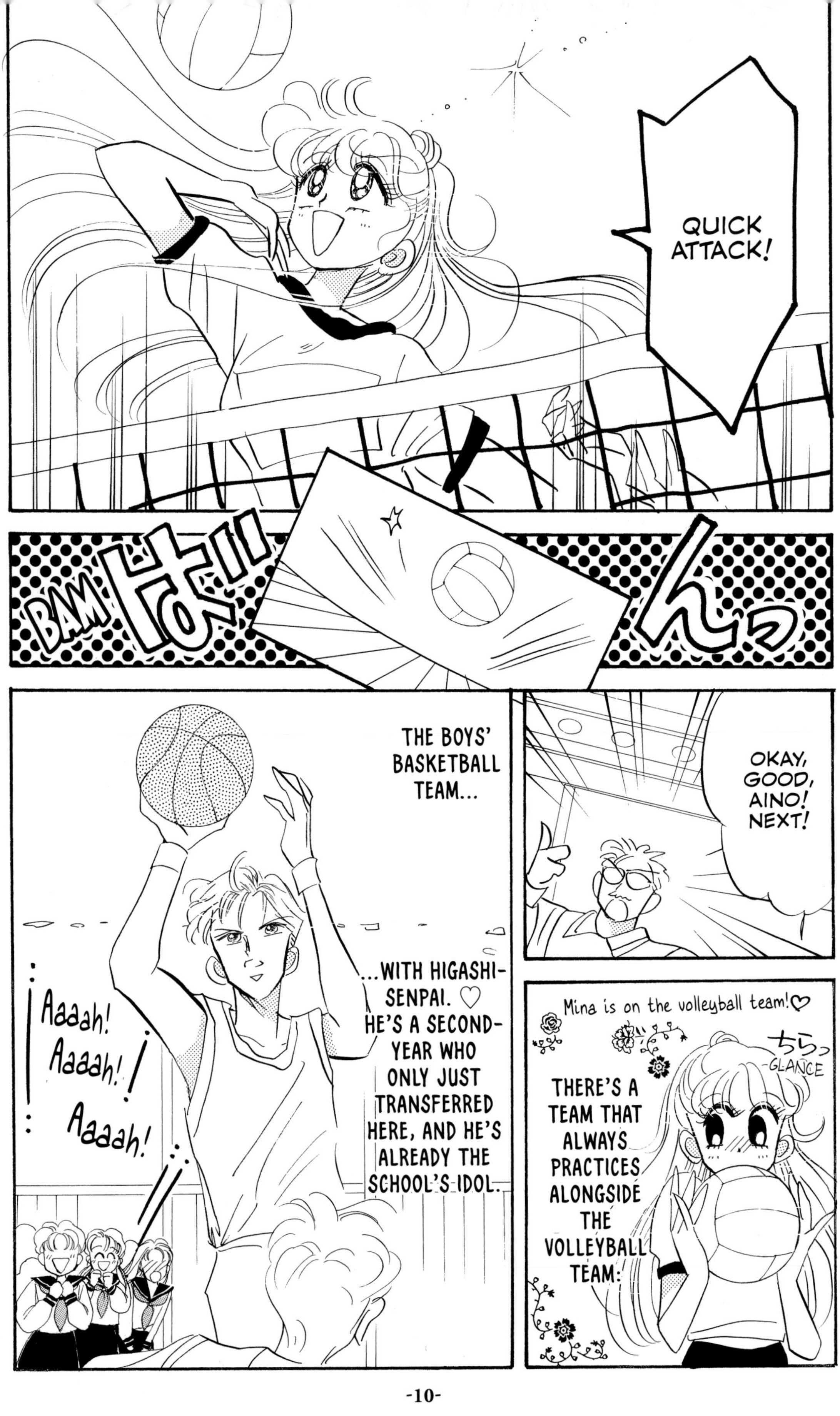
QUICK ATTACK!
BAM
はっ!! んっ
OKAY, GOOD, AINO! NEXT!
Mina is on the volleyball team!♡
ちらっ
GLANCE
THERE'S A TEAM THAT ALWAYS PRACTICES ALONGSIDE THE VOLLEYBALL TEAM:
THE BOYS' BASKETBALL TEAM...
...WITH HIGASHI-SENPAI. ♡ HE'S A SECOND-YEAR WHO ONLY JUST TRANSFERRED HERE, AND HE'S ALREADY THE SCHOOL'S IDOL.
Aaaah! Aaaah! Aaaah!

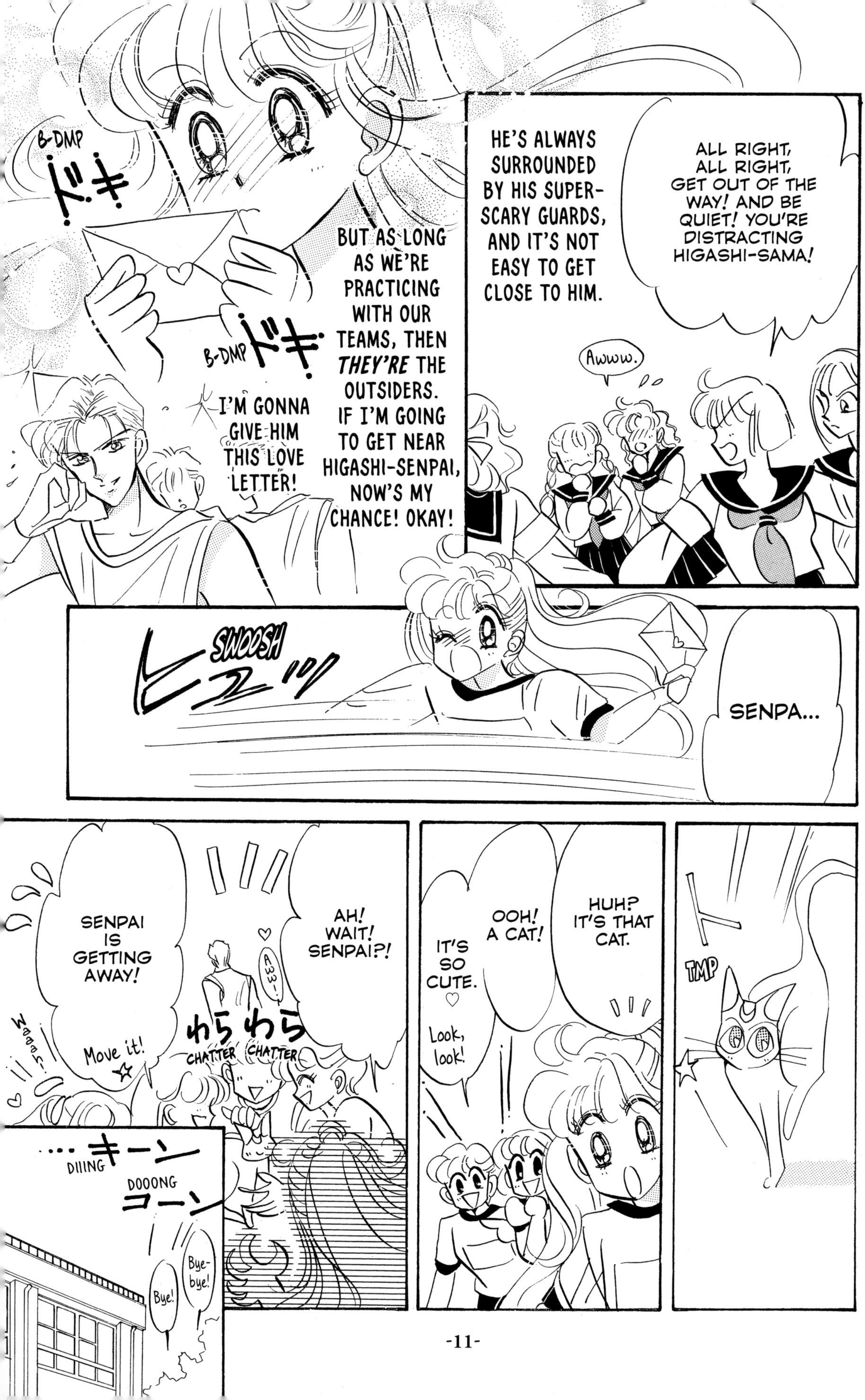

ALL RIGHT, ALL RIGHT, GET OUT OF THE WAY! AND BE QUIET! YOU'RE DISTRACTING HIGASHI-SAMA!
HE'S ALWAYS SURROUNDED BY HIS SUPER-SCARY GUARDS, AND IT'S NOT EASY TO GET CLOSE TO HIM.
Awww.
BUT AS LONG AS WE'RE PRACTICING WITH OUR TEAMS, THEN *THEY'RE* THE OUTSIDERS. IF I'M GOING TO GET NEAR HIGASHI-SENPAI, NOW'S MY CHANCE! OKAY!
ドキ
B-DMP
ドキ
B-DMP
I'M GONNA GIVE HIM THIS LOVE LETTER!
SENPA...
ヒュッ
SWOOSH
TMP
HUH? IT'S THAT CAT.
OOH! A CAT!
IT'S SO CUTE.
Look, look!
AH! WAIT! SENPAI?!
SENPAI IS GETTING AWAY!
わらわら
CHATTER CHATTER
Move it!
Waaah!
キーン
DIIING
コーン
DOOONG
Bye-bye!
Bye!

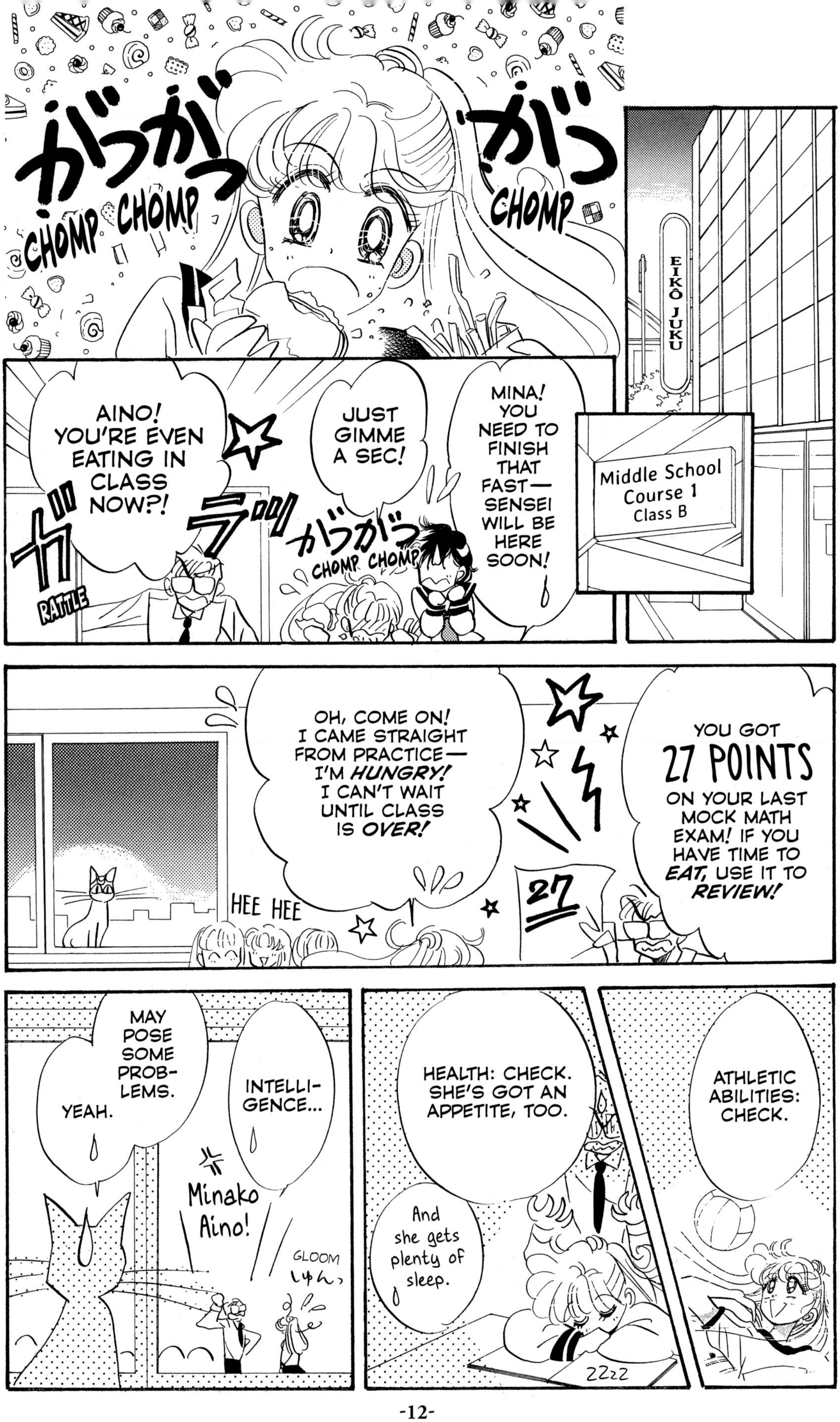

EIKÔ JUKU
Middle School Course 1 Class B
がつがつ
CHOMP CHOMP
がつ
CHOMP
MINA! YOU NEED TO FINISH THAT FAST—SENSEI WILL BE HERE SOON!
JUST GIMME A SEC!
がつがつ
CHOMP CHOMP
AINO! YOU'RE EVEN EATING IN CLASS NOW?!
ガラッ
RATTLE
YOU GOT 27 POINTS ON YOUR LAST MOCK MATH EXAM! IF YOU HAVE TIME TO EAT, USE IT TO REVIEW!
27
OH, COME ON! I CAME STRAIGHT FROM PRACTICE—I'M HUNGRY! I CAN'T WAIT UNTIL CLASS IS OVER!
HEE HEE
ATHLETIC ABILITIES: CHECK.
HEALTH: CHECK. SHE'S GOT AN APPETITE, TOO.
And she gets plenty of sleep.
ZZzz
INTELLIGENCE...
MAY POSE SOME PROBLEMS.
Minako Aino!
YEAH.
GLOOM
しゅんっ

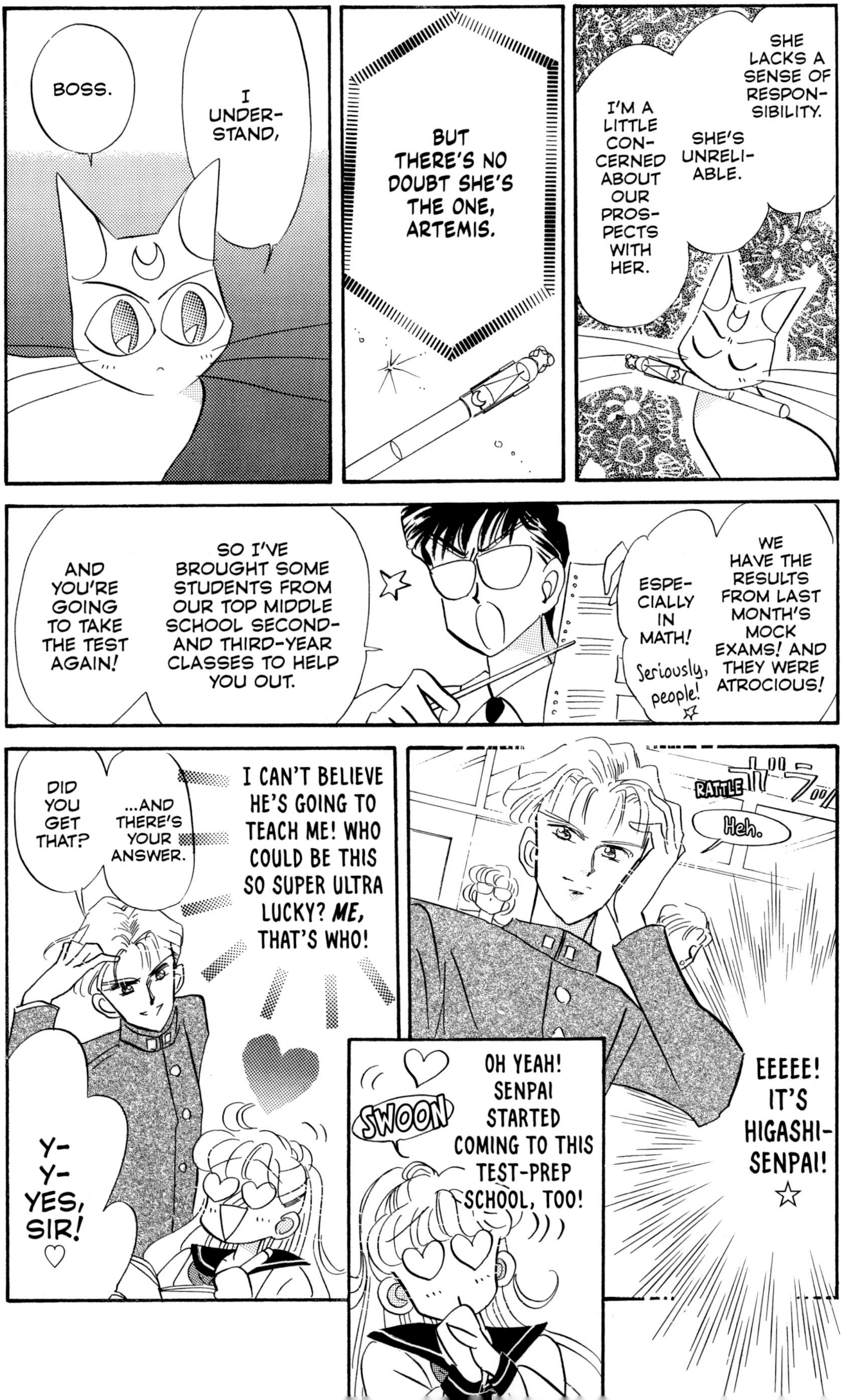
SHE LACKS A SENSE OF RESPONSIBILITY.
SHE'S UNRELIABLE.
I'M A LITTLE CONCERNED ABOUT OUR PROSPECTS WITH HER.
BUT THERE'S NO DOUBT SHE'S THE ONE, ARTEMIS.
I UNDERSTAND,
BOSS.
WE HAVE THE RESULTS FROM LAST MONTH'S MOCK EXAMS! AND THEY WERE ATROCIOUS!
ESPECIALLY IN MATH!
Seriously, people! ☆
SO I'VE BROUGHT SOME STUDENTS FROM OUR TOP MIDDLE SCHOOL SECOND- AND THIRD-YEAR CLASSES TO HELP YOU OUT.
AND YOU'RE GOING TO TAKE THE TEST AGAIN!
RATTLE
Heh.
EEEEE! IT'S HIGASHI-SENPAI! ☆
OH YEAH! SENPAI STARTED COMING TO THIS TEST-PREP SCHOOL, TOO!
SWOON
...AND THERE'S YOUR ANSWER.
DID YOU GET THAT?
I CAN'T BELIEVE HE'S GOING TO TEACH ME! WHO COULD BE THIS SO SUPER ULTRA LUCKY? ME, THAT'S WHO!
Y-Y-YES, SIR! ♡

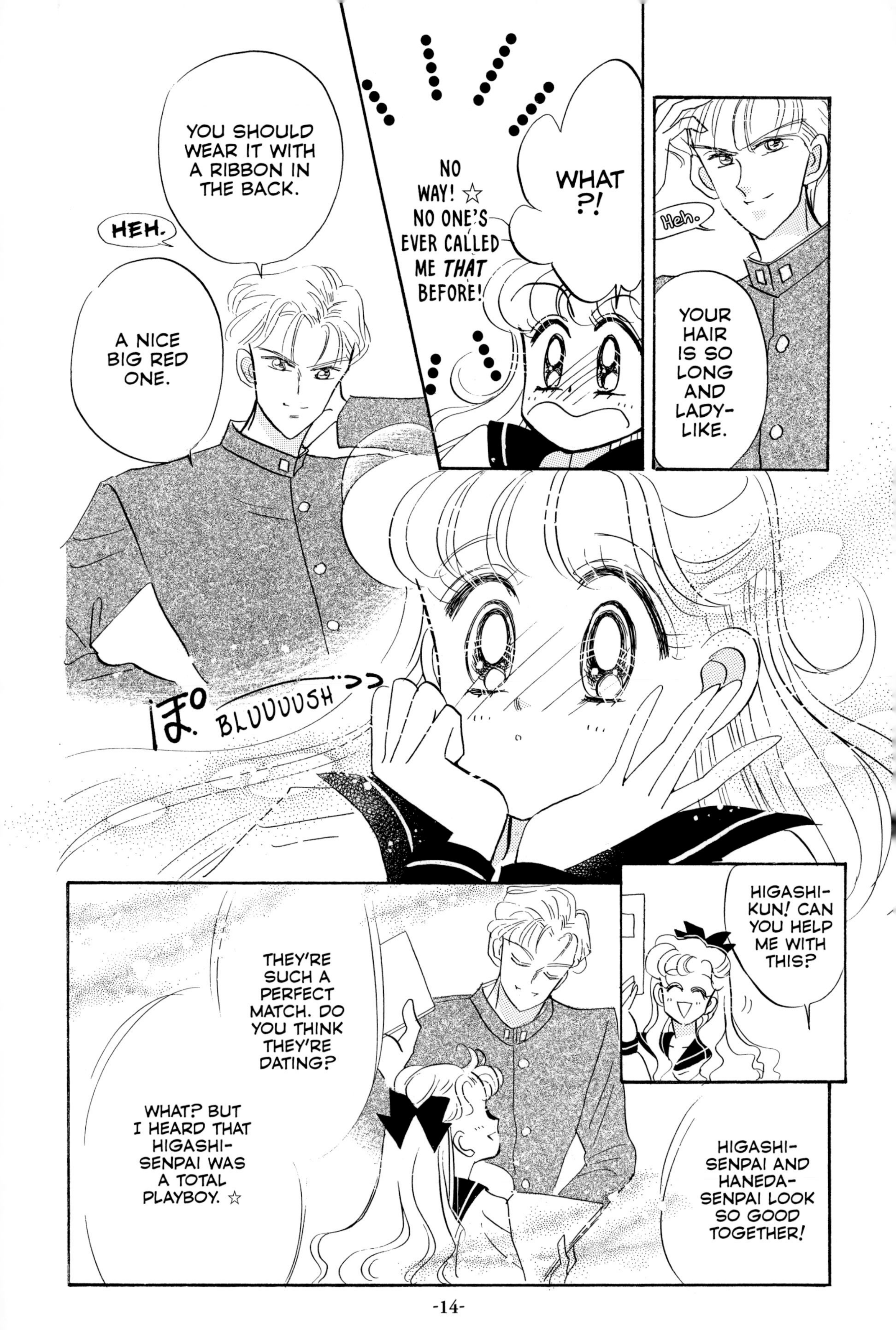
Heh.
YOUR HAIR IS SO LONG AND LADY-LIKE.
WHAT ?!
NO WAY! ☆ NO ONE'S EVER CALLED ME *THAT* BEFORE!
HEH.
YOU SHOULD WEAR IT WITH A RIBBON IN THE BACK.
A NICE BIG RED ONE.
ぽ。 BLUUUUSH
HIGASHI-KUN! CAN YOU HELP ME WITH THIS?
HIGASHI-SENPAI AND HANEDA-SENPAI LOOK SO GOOD TOGETHER!
THEY'RE SUCH A PERFECT MATCH. DO YOU THINK THEY'RE DATING?
WHAT? BUT I HEARD THAT HIGASHI-SENPAI WAS A TOTAL PLAYBOY. ☆

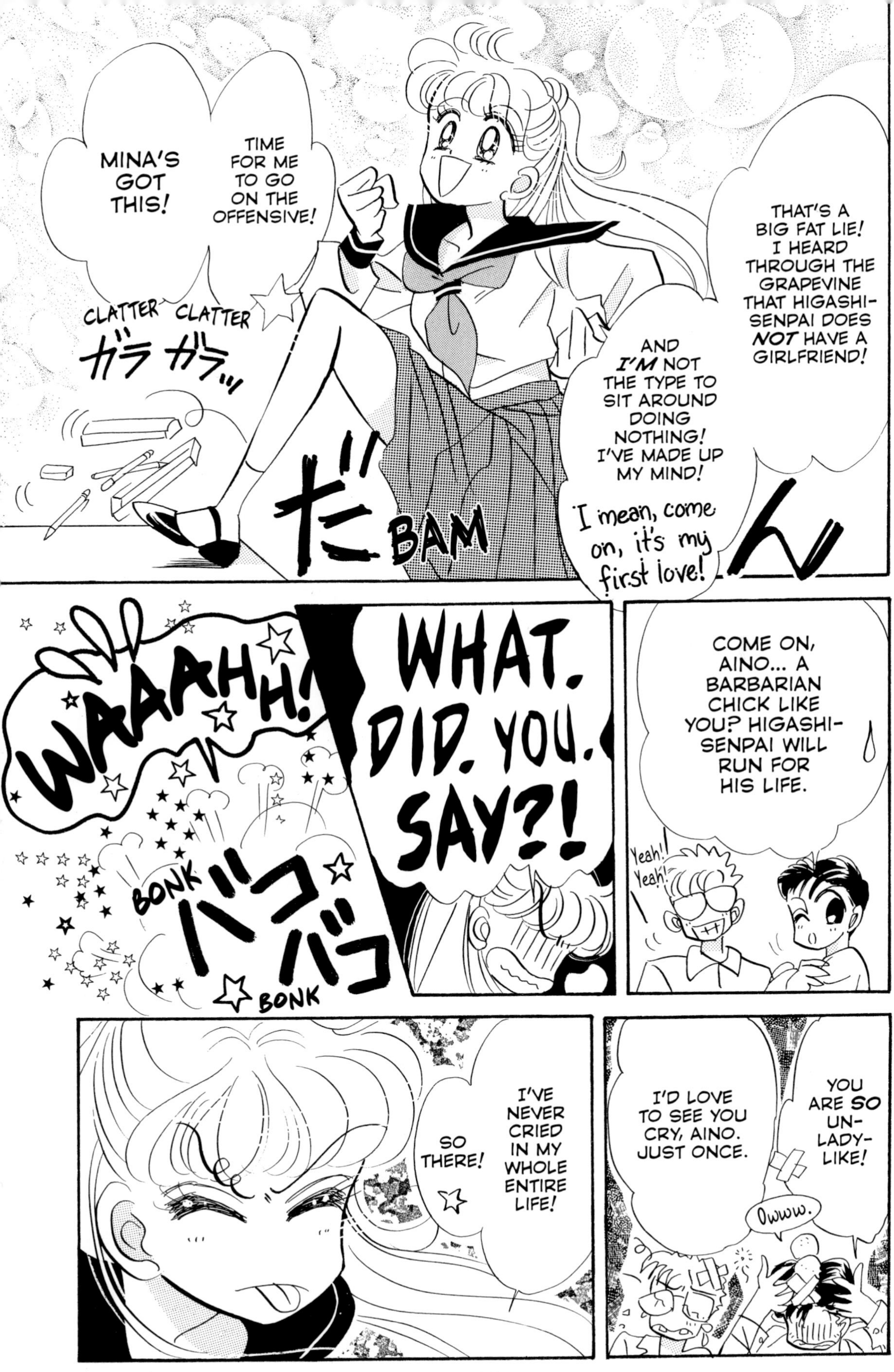
THAT'S A BIG FAT LIE! I HEARD THROUGH THE GRAPEVINE THAT HIGASHI-SENPAI DOES NOT HAVE A GIRLFRIEND!
AND I'M NOT THE TYPE TO SIT AROUND DOING NOTHING! I'VE MADE UP MY MIND!
I mean, come on, it's my first love!
ん
TIME FOR ME TO GO ON THE OFFENSIVE!
MINA'S GOT THIS!
CLATTER CLATTER
ガラガラッ
だ
BAM
COME ON, AINO... A BARBARIAN CHICK LIKE YOU? HIGASHI-SENPAI WILL RUN FOR HIS LIFE.
Yeah! Yeah!
WHAT. DID. YOU. SAY?!
WAAAHH!
BONK
バコバコ
BONK
YOU ARE SO UN-LADY-LIKE!
I'D LOVE TO SEE YOU CRY, AINO. JUST ONCE.
Owww.
I'VE NEVER CRIED IN MY WHOLE ENTIRE LIFE!
SO THERE!

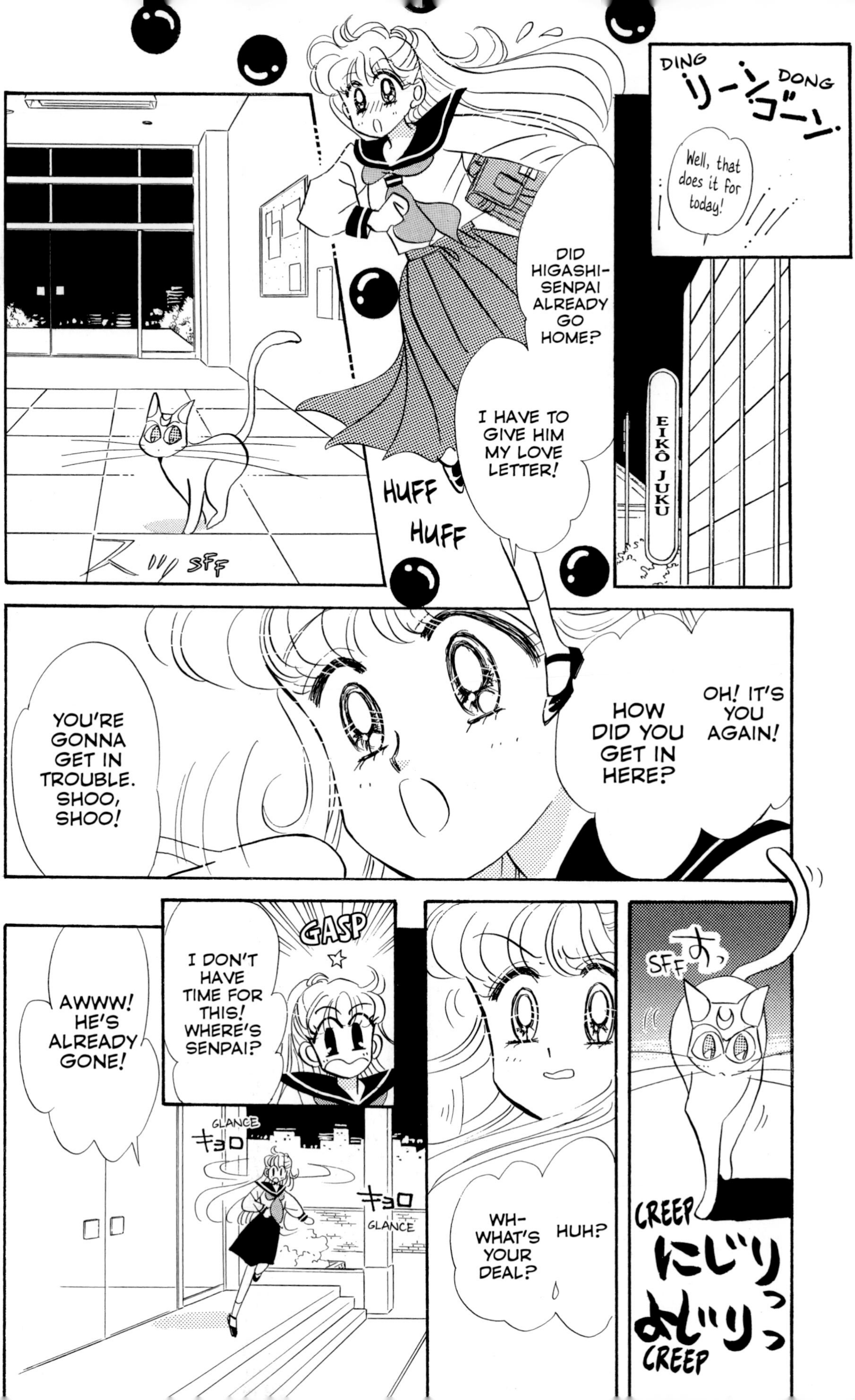

DING DONG
リーンゴーン
Well, that does it for today!
EIKÔ JUKU
DID HIGASHI-SENPAI ALREADY GO HOME?
I HAVE TO GIVE HIM MY LOVE LETTER!
HUFF HUFF
スッ SFF
OH! IT'S YOU AGAIN!
HOW DID YOU GET IN HERE?
YOU'RE GONNA GET IN TROUBLE. SHOO, SHOO!
SFF
CREEP にじりっ よじりっ CREEP
HUH?
WH-WHAT'S YOUR DEAL?
GASP
I DON'T HAVE TIME FOR THIS! WHERE'S SENPAI?
GLANCE キョロ
キョロ GLANCE
AWWW! HE'S ALREADY GONE!

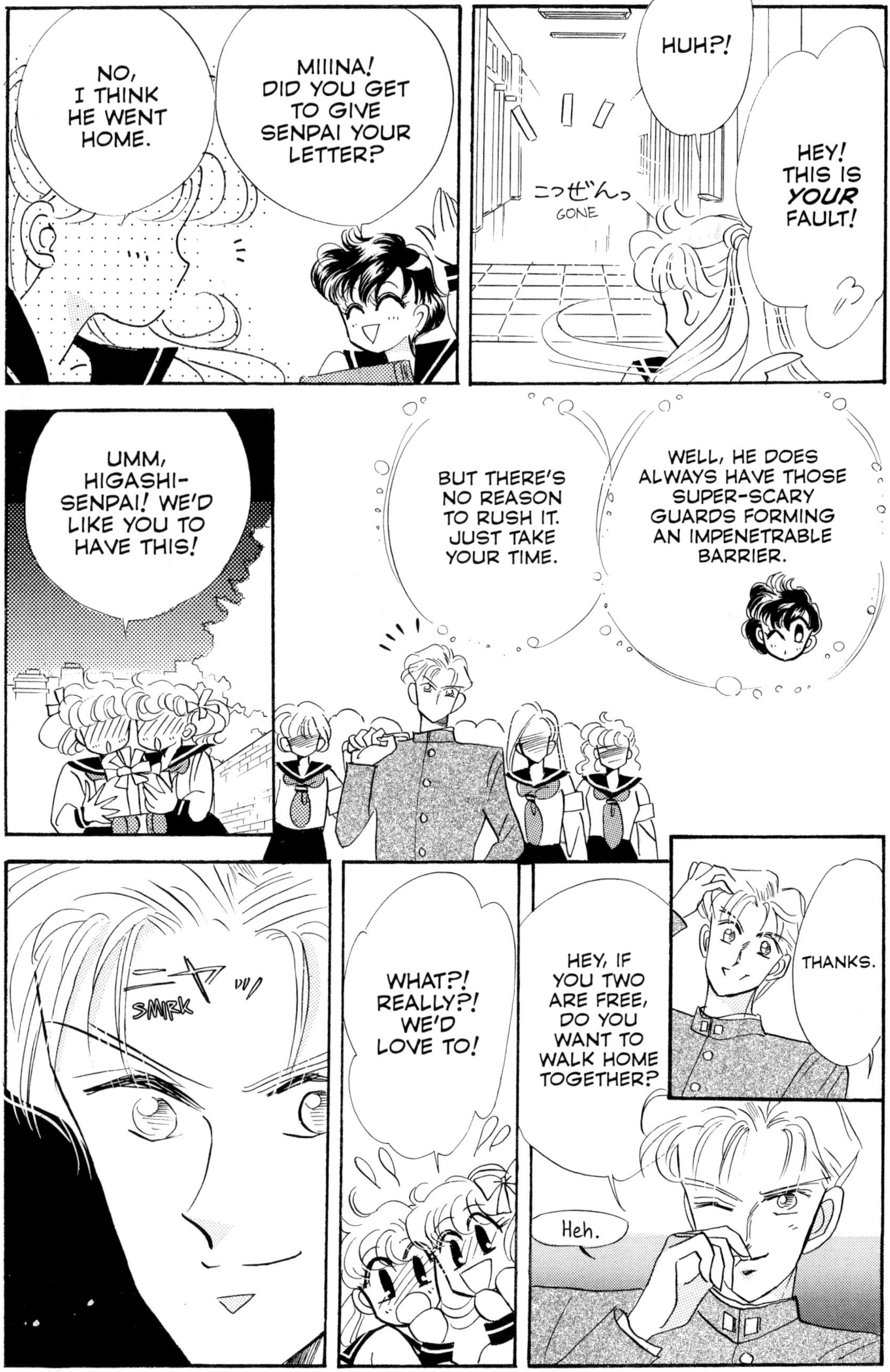
HUH?!
HEY! THIS IS ***YOUR*** FAULT!
こっぜんっ
GONE
MIIINA! DID YOU GET TO GIVE SENPAI YOUR LETTER?
NO, I THINK HE WENT HOME.
WELL, HE DOES ALWAYS HAVE THOSE SUPER-SCARY GUARDS FORMING AN IMPENETRABLE BARRIER.
BUT THERE'S NO REASON TO RUSH IT. JUST TAKE YOUR TIME.
UMM, HIGASHI-SENPAI! WE'D LIKE YOU TO HAVE THIS!
THANKS.
HEY, IF YOU TWO ARE FREE, DO YOU WANT TO WALK HOME TOGETHER?
Heh.
WHAT?! REALLY?! WE'D LOVE TO!
SMIRK

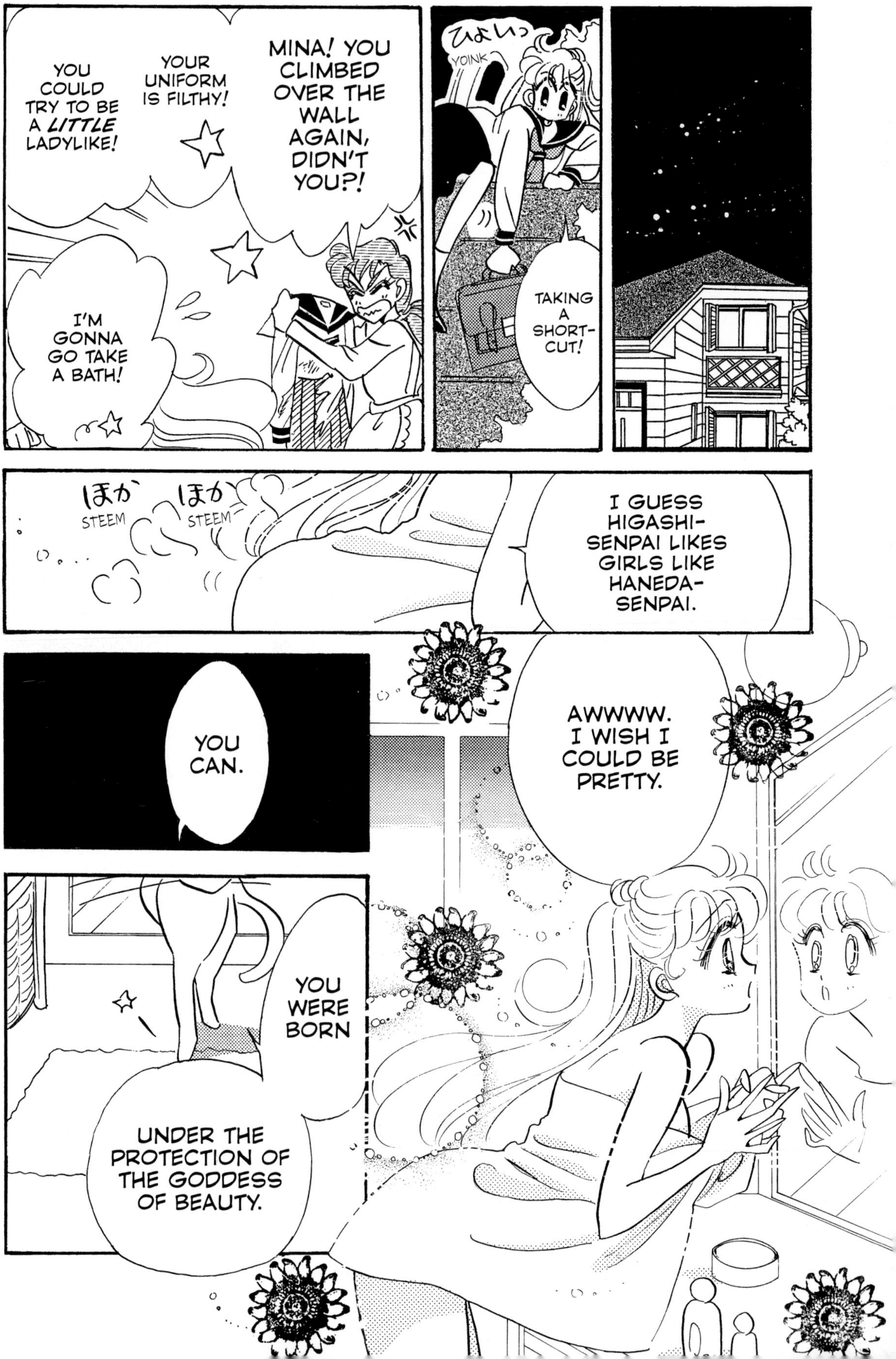
ひょいっ
YOINK
TAKING A SHORTCUT!
MINA! YOU CLIMBED OVER THE WALL AGAIN, DIDN'T YOU?!
YOUR UNIFORM IS FILTHY!
YOU COULD TRY TO BE A *LITTLE* LADYLIKE!
I'M GONNA GO TAKE A BATH!
I GUESS HIGASHI-SENPAI LIKES GIRLS LIKE HANEDA-SENPAI.
ほか
STEEM
ほか
STEEM
AWWWW. I WISH I COULD BE PRETTY.
YOU CAN.
YOU WERE BORN
UNDER THE PROTECTION OF THE GODDESS OF BEAUTY.

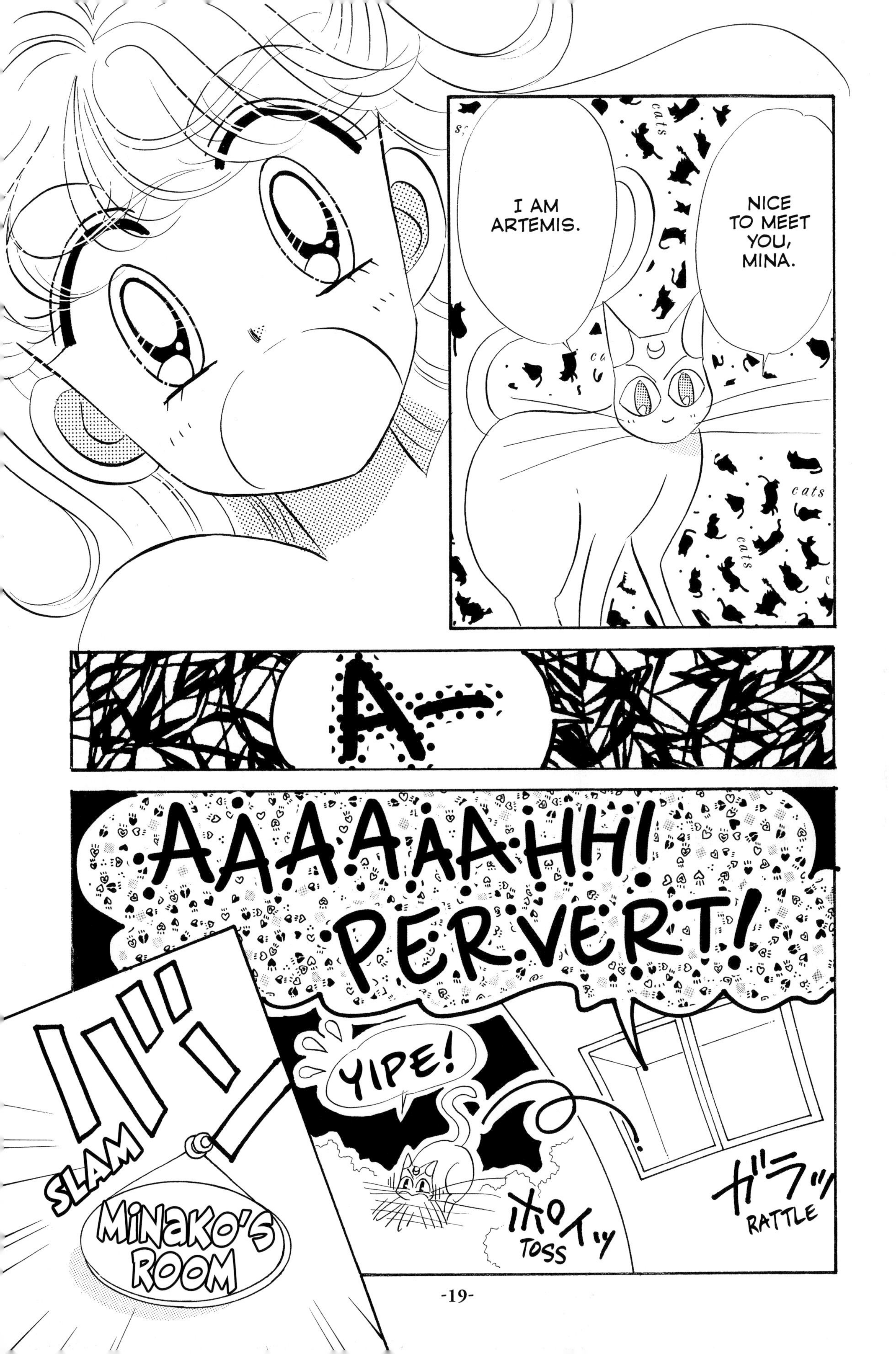

I AM ARTEMIS.
NICE TO MEET YOU, MINA.
A—
AAAAAHH! PERVERT!
ガラッ
RATTLE
YIPE!
ポイッ
TOSS
SLAM
Minako's ROOM

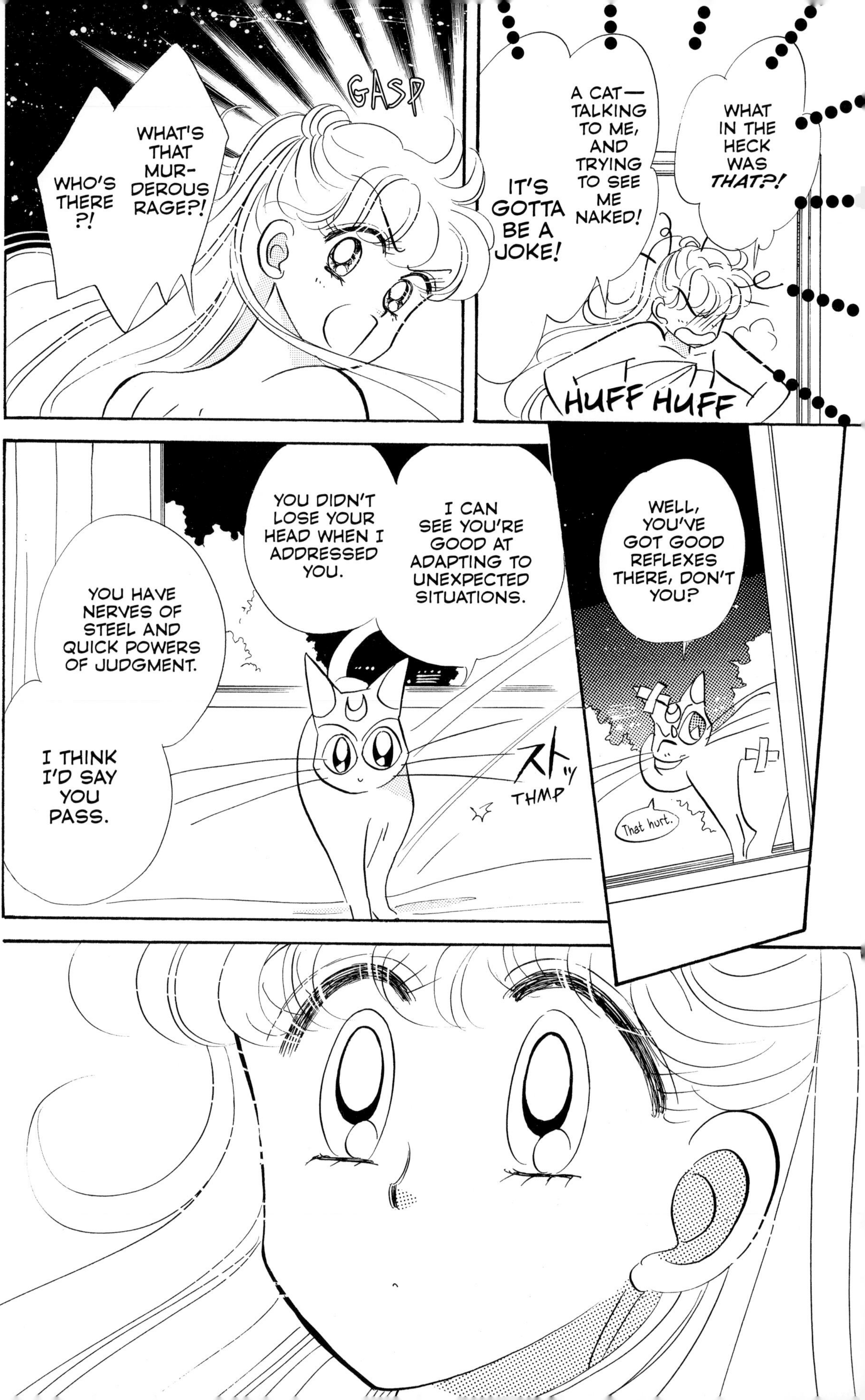
WHAT IN THE HECK WAS *THAT?!*
A CAT— TALKING TO ME, AND TRYING TO SEE ME NAKED!
IT'S GOTTA BE A JOKE!
HUFF HUFF
GASP
WHAT'S THAT MUR- DEROUS RAGE?!
WHO'S THERE ?!
WELL, YOU'VE GOT GOOD REFLEXES THERE, DON'T YOU?
That hurt.
I CAN SEE YOU'RE GOOD AT ADAPTING TO UNEXPECTED SITUATIONS.
YOU DIDN'T LOSE YOUR HEAD WHEN I ADDRESSED YOU.
THMP
YOU HAVE NERVES OF STEEL AND QUICK POWERS OF JUDGMENT.
I THINK I'D SAY YOU PASS.

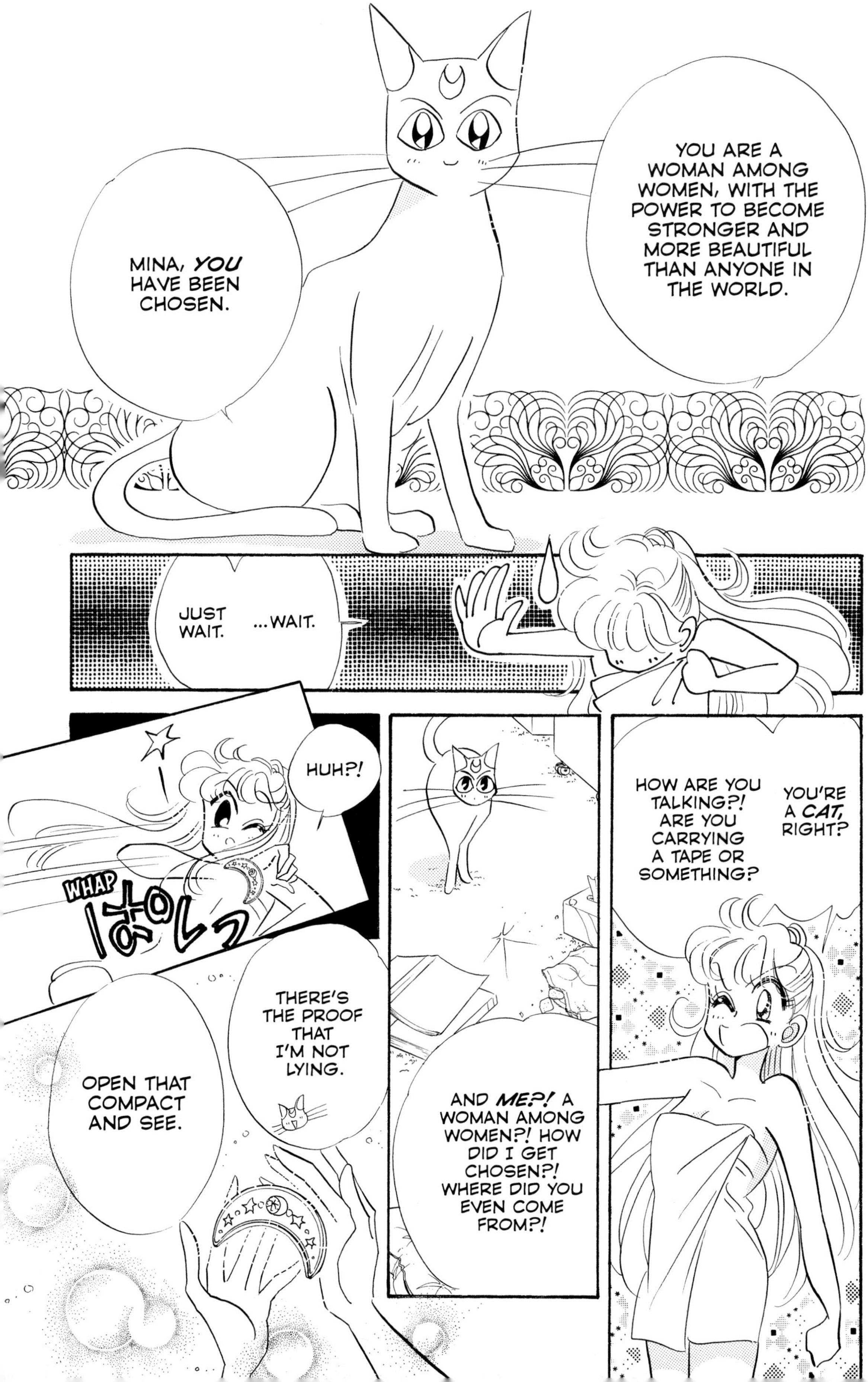
YOU ARE A WOMAN AMONG WOMEN, WITH THE POWER TO BECOME STRONGER AND MORE BEAUTIFUL THAN ANYONE IN THE WORLD.
MINA, *YOU* HAVE BEEN CHOSEN.
JUST WAIT. ...WAIT.
YOU'RE A *CAT,* RIGHT?
HOW ARE YOU TALKING?! ARE YOU CARRYING A TAPE OR SOMETHING?
AND *ME?!* A WOMAN AMONG WOMEN?! HOW DID I GET CHOSEN?! WHERE DID YOU EVEN COME FROM?!
HUH?!
WHAP
ぱしっ
THERE'S THE PROOF THAT I'M NOT LYING.
OPEN THAT COMPACT AND SEE.

WHAT'S THAT CRESCENT MARK?

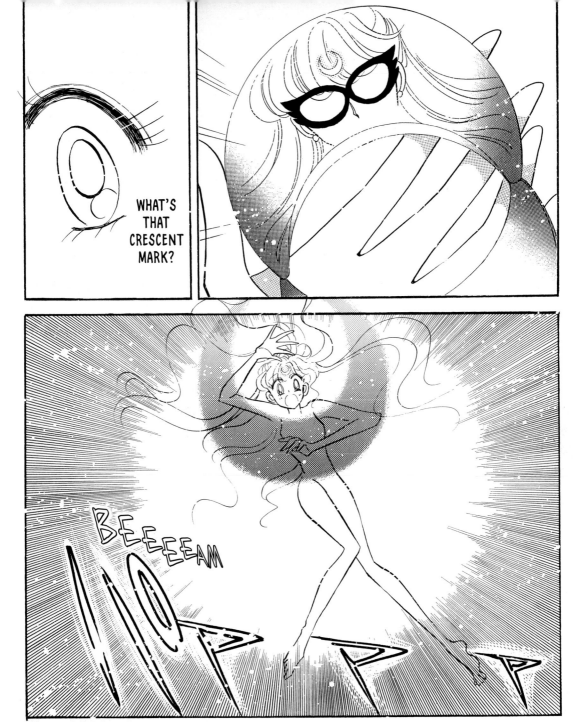

BEEEEEAM

SFF

!!

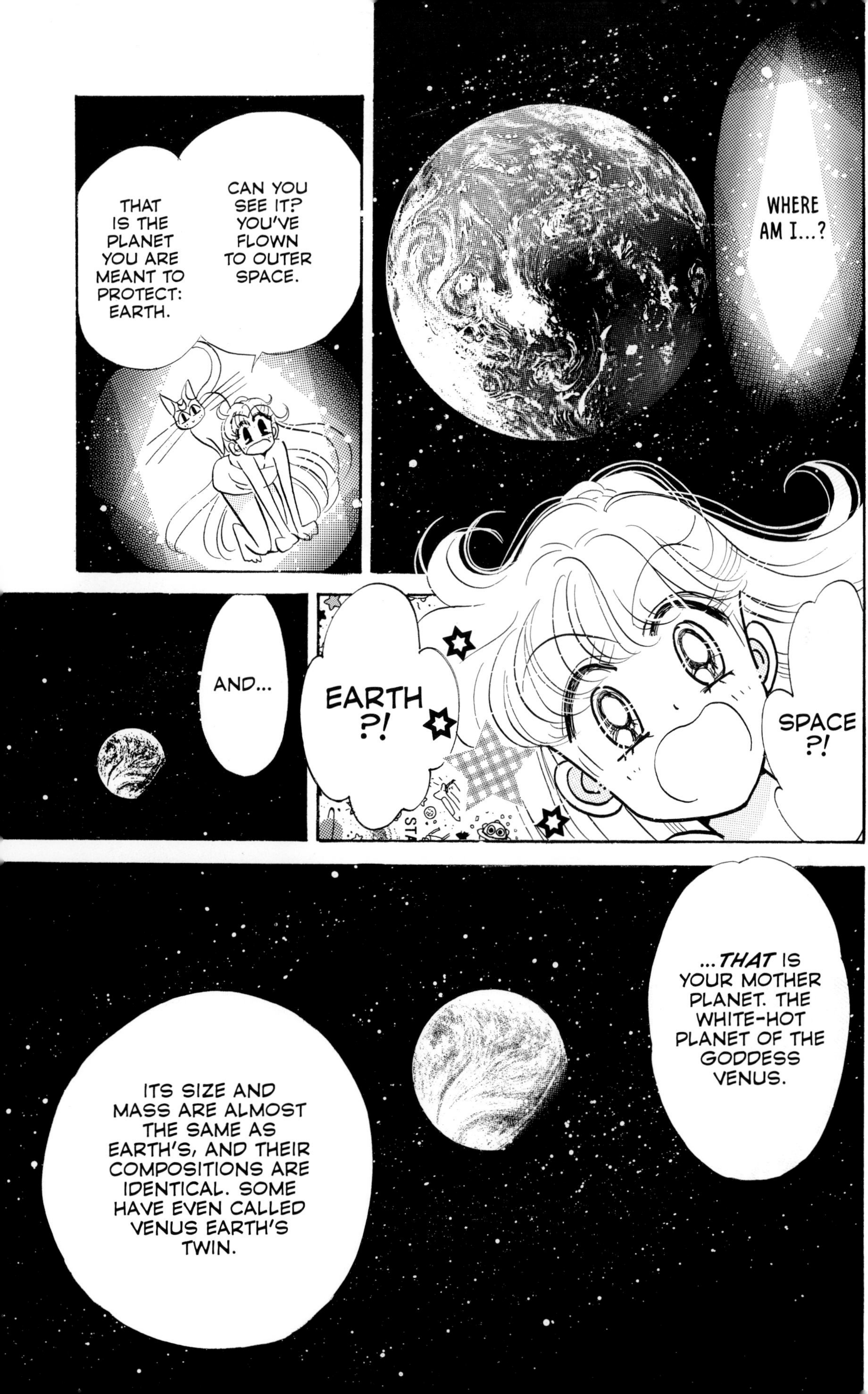
WHERE AM I...?
CAN YOU SEE IT? YOU'VE FLOWN TO OUTER SPACE.
THAT IS THE PLANET YOU ARE MEANT TO PROTECT: EARTH.
SPACE ?!
EARTH ?!
AND...
...*THAT* IS YOUR MOTHER PLANET. THE WHITE-HOT PLANET OF THE GODDESS VENUS.
ITS SIZE AND MASS ARE ALMOST THE SAME AS EARTH'S, AND THEIR COMPOSITIONS ARE IDENTICAL. SOME HAVE EVEN CALLED VENUS EARTH'S TWIN.

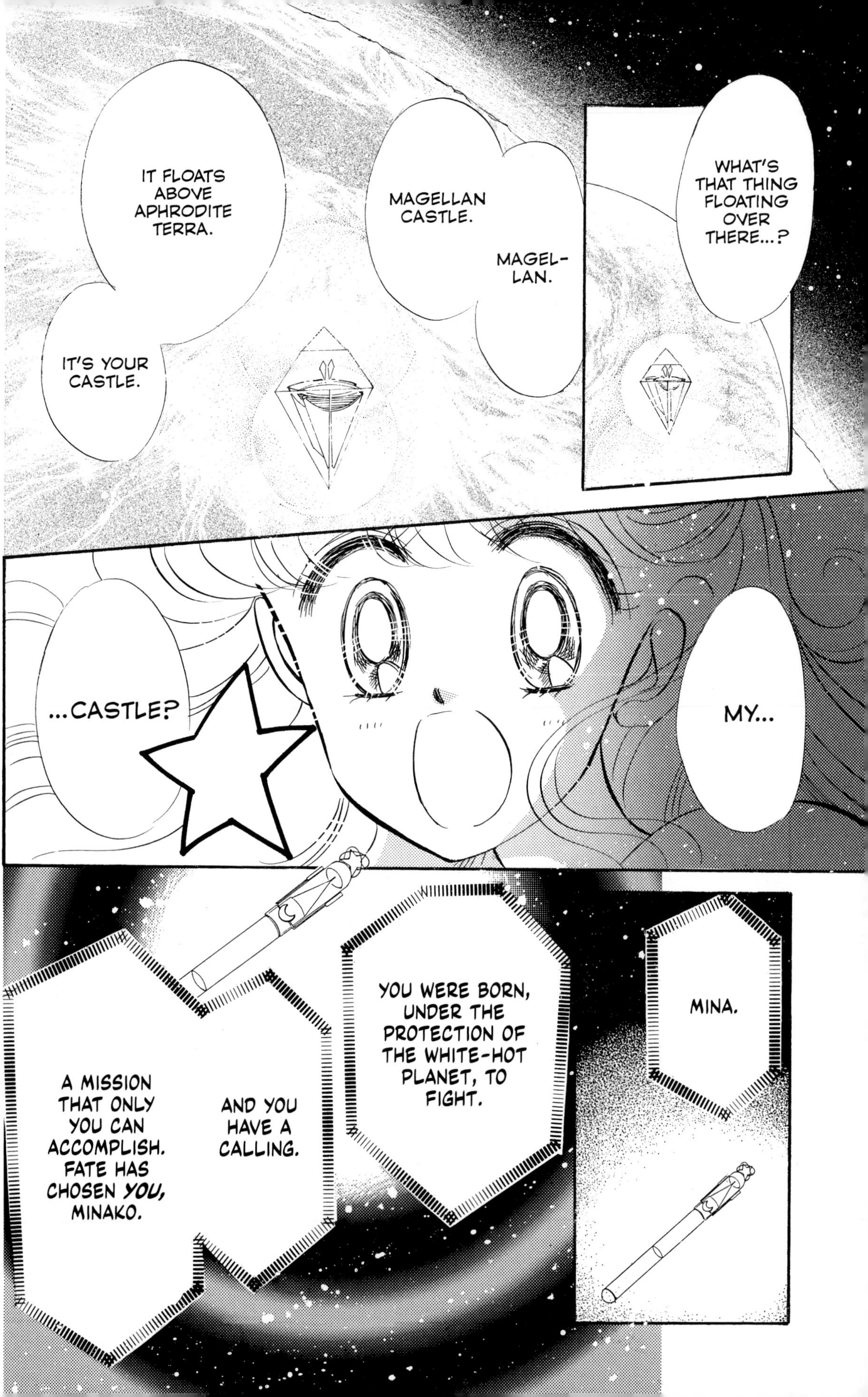
WHAT'S THAT THING FLOATING OVER THERE...?
MAGEL-LAN.
MAGELLAN CASTLE.
IT FLOATS ABOVE APHRODITE TERRA.
IT'S YOUR CASTLE.
MY...
...CASTLE?
MINA.
YOU WERE BORN, UNDER THE PROTECTION OF THE WHITE-HOT PLANET, TO FIGHT.
AND YOU HAVE A CALLING.
A MISSION THAT ONLY YOU CAN ACCOMPLISH. FATE HAS CHOSEN *YOU,* MINAKO.

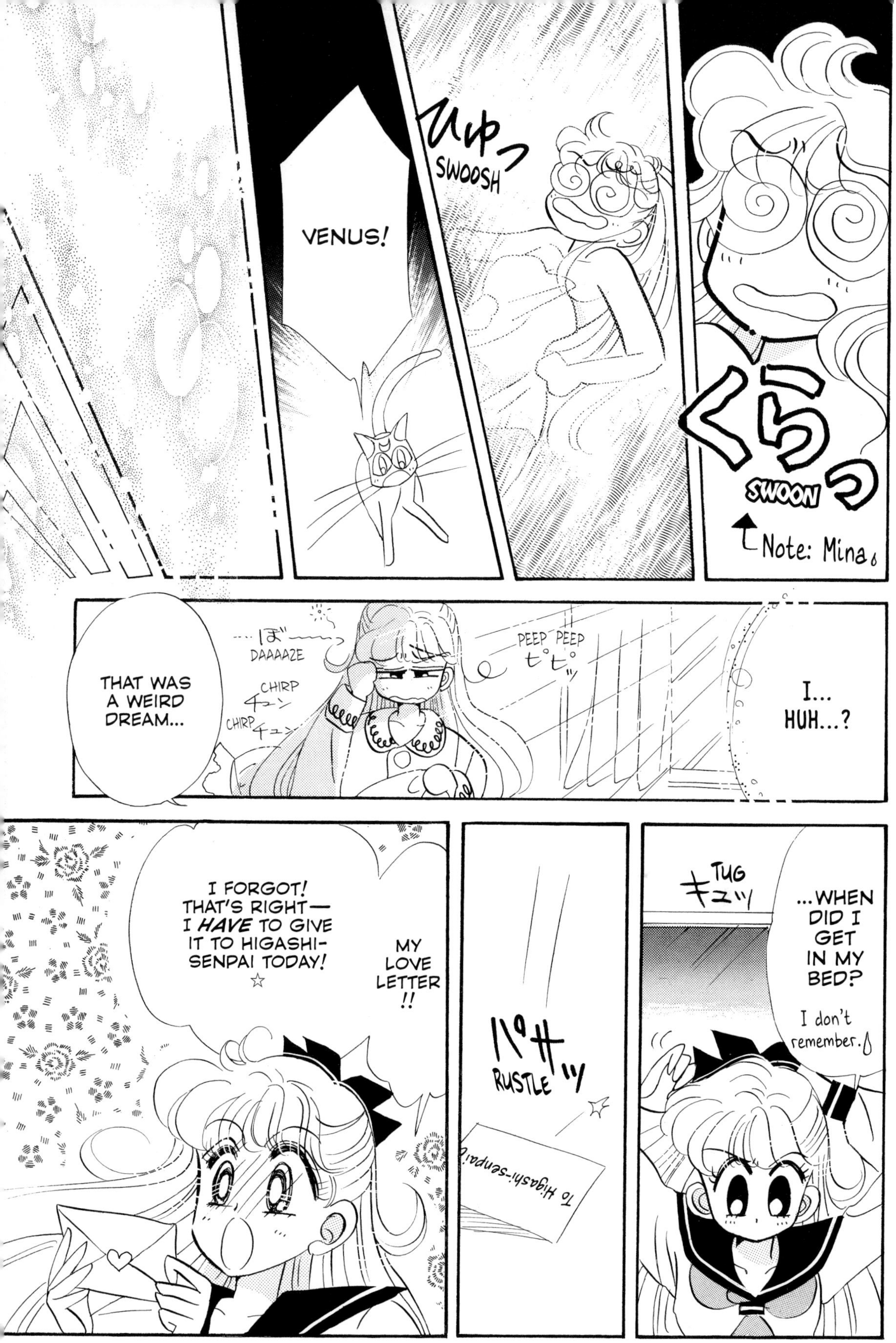
くらっ
SWOON
Note: Mina.
ひゅっ
SWOOSH
VENUS!
I... HUH...?
PEEP PEEP
ピピッ
...ぼ~
DAAAAZE
CHIRP
チュン
CHIRP
チュン
THAT WAS A WEIRD DREAM...
TUG
キュッ
...WHEN DID I GET IN MY BED?
I don't remember.
パサッ
RUSTLE
To Higashi-senpai
MY LOVE LETTER!!
I FORGOT! THAT'S RIGHT— I HAVE TO GIVE IT TO HIGASHI-SENPAI TODAY! ☆

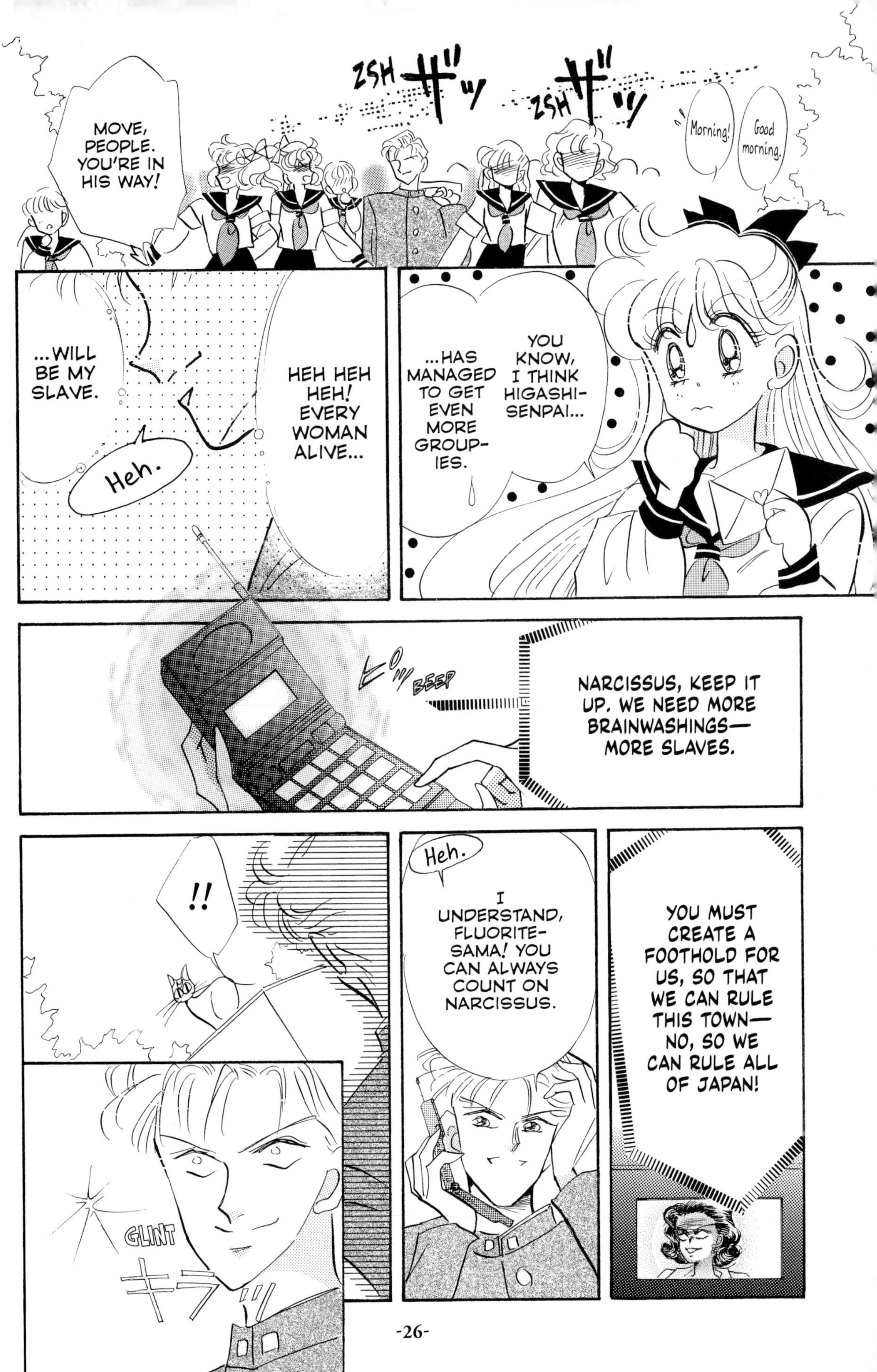
Good morning.
Morning!
ZSH ザッ
ZSH ザッ
MOVE, PEOPLE. YOU'RE IN HIS WAY!
YOU KNOW, I THINK HIGASHI-SENPAI...
...HAS MANAGED TO GET EVEN MORE GROUPIES.
HEH HEH HEH! EVERY WOMAN ALIVE...
...WILL BE MY SLAVE.
Heh.
NARCISSUS, KEEP IT UP. WE NEED MORE BRAINWASHINGS—MORE SLAVES.
BEEP
YOU MUST CREATE A FOOTHOLD FOR US, SO THAT WE CAN RULE THIS TOWN—NO, SO WE CAN RULE ALL OF JAPAN!
Heh.
I UNDERSTAND, FLUORITE-SAMA! YOU CAN ALWAYS COUNT ON NARCISSUS.
!!
GLINT
キラッ

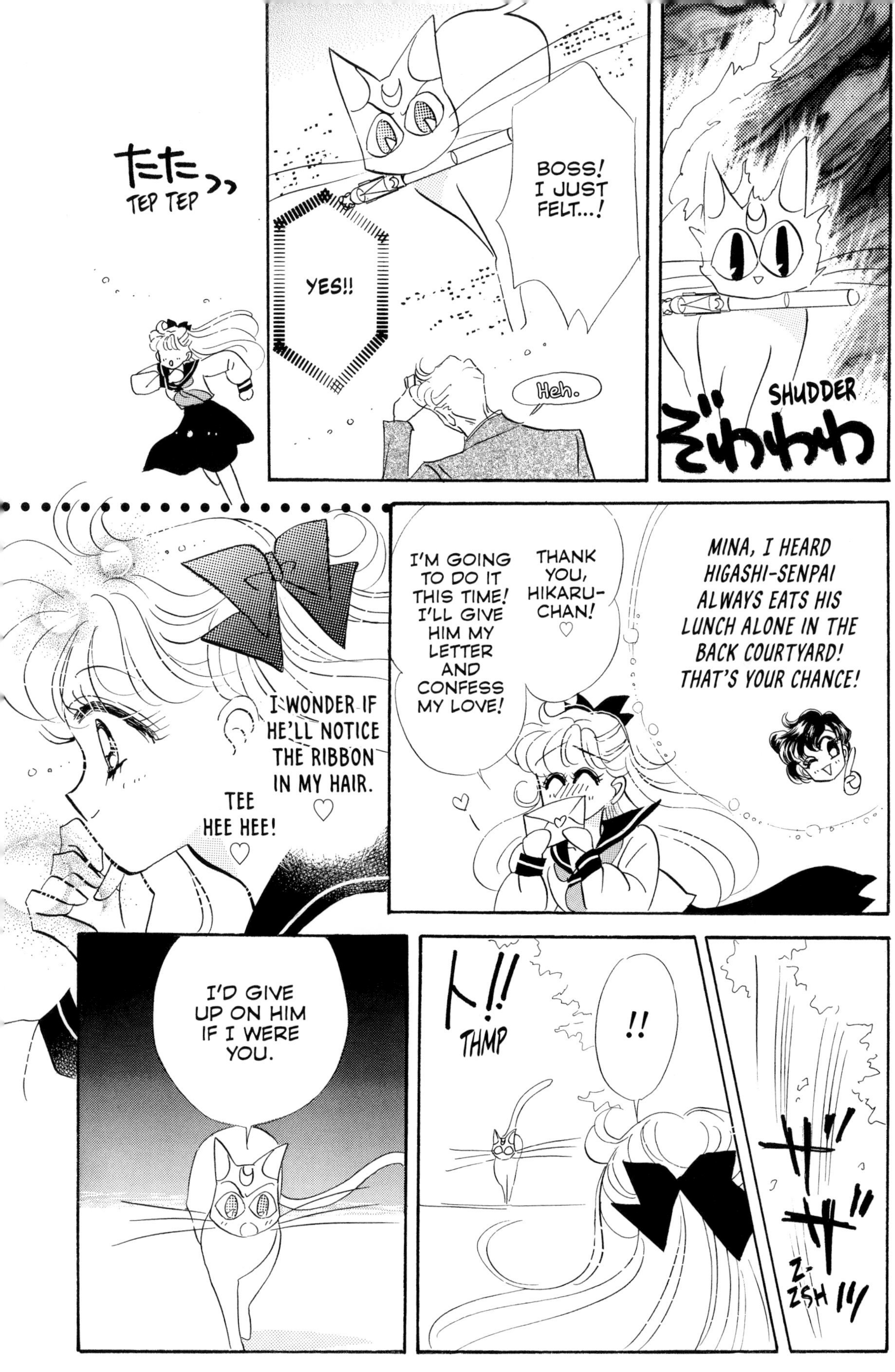

SHUDDER
ざわわ
BOSS! I JUST FELT...!
YES!!
Heh.
たたっっ
TEP TEP
MINA, I HEARD HIGASHI-SENPAI ALWAYS EATS HIS LUNCH ALONE IN THE BACK COURTYARD! THAT'S YOUR CHANCE!
THANK YOU, HIKARU-CHAN! ♡
I'M GOING TO DO IT THIS TIME! I'LL GIVE HIM MY LETTER AND CONFESS MY LOVE!
I WONDER IF HE'LL NOTICE THE RIBBON IN MY HAIR. ♡
TEE HEE HEE! ♡
ザッ
ザッ
Z-ZSH
ト!!
THMP
!!
I'D GIVE UP ON HIM IF I WERE YOU.

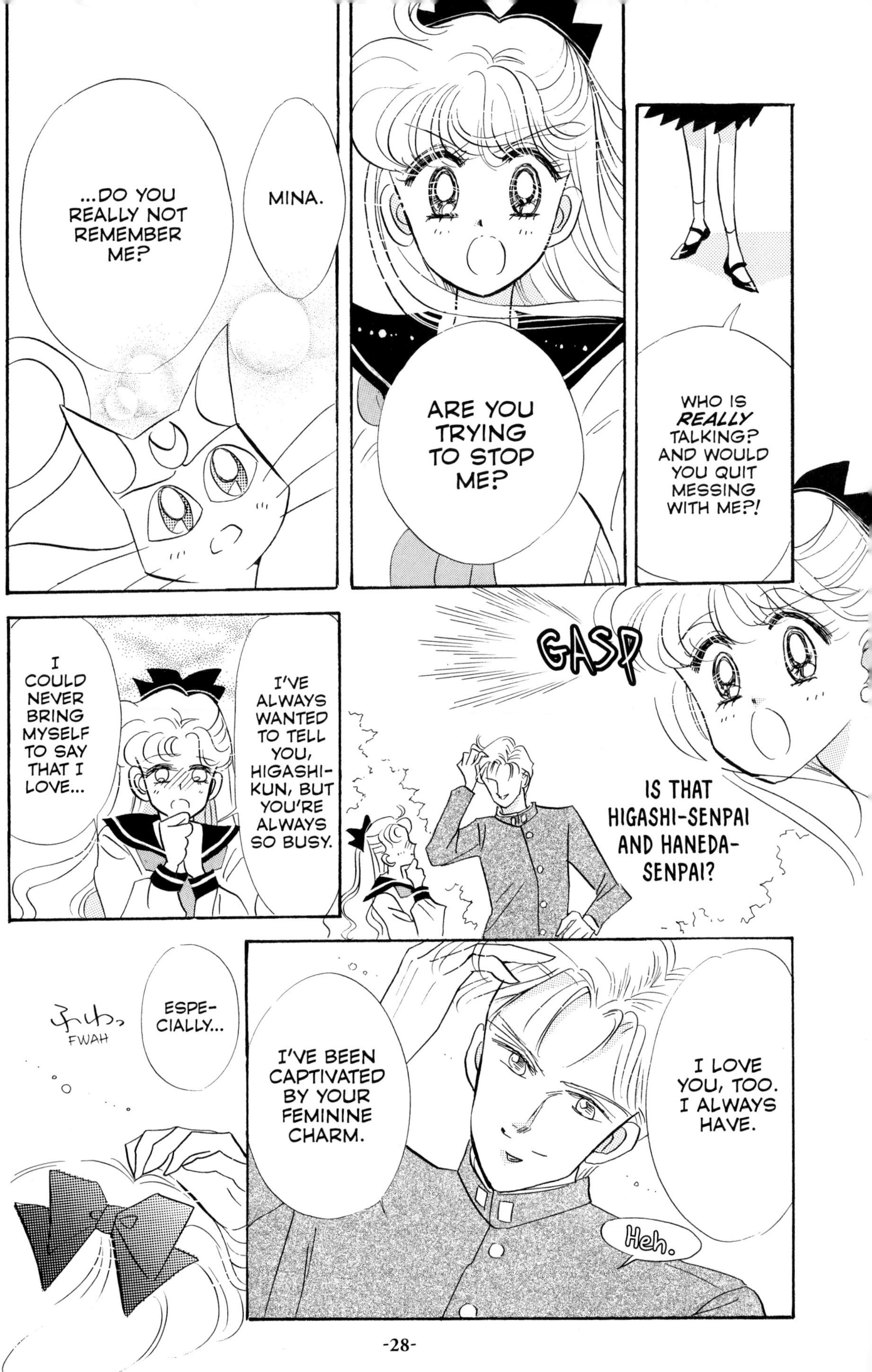
WHO IS *REALLY* TALKING? AND WOULD YOU QUIT MESSING WITH ME?!
ARE YOU TRYING TO STOP ME?
MINA.
...DO YOU REALLY NOT REMEMBER ME?
GASP
IS THAT HIGASHI-SENPAI AND HANEDA-SENPAI?
I'VE ALWAYS WANTED TO TELL YOU, HIGASHI-KUN, BUT YOU'RE ALWAYS SO BUSY.
I COULD NEVER BRING MYSELF TO SAY THAT I LOVE...
I LOVE YOU, TOO. I ALWAYS HAVE.
I'VE BEEN CAPTIVATED BY YOUR FEMININE CHARM.
Heh.
ESPE-CIALLY...
ふわっ
FWAH

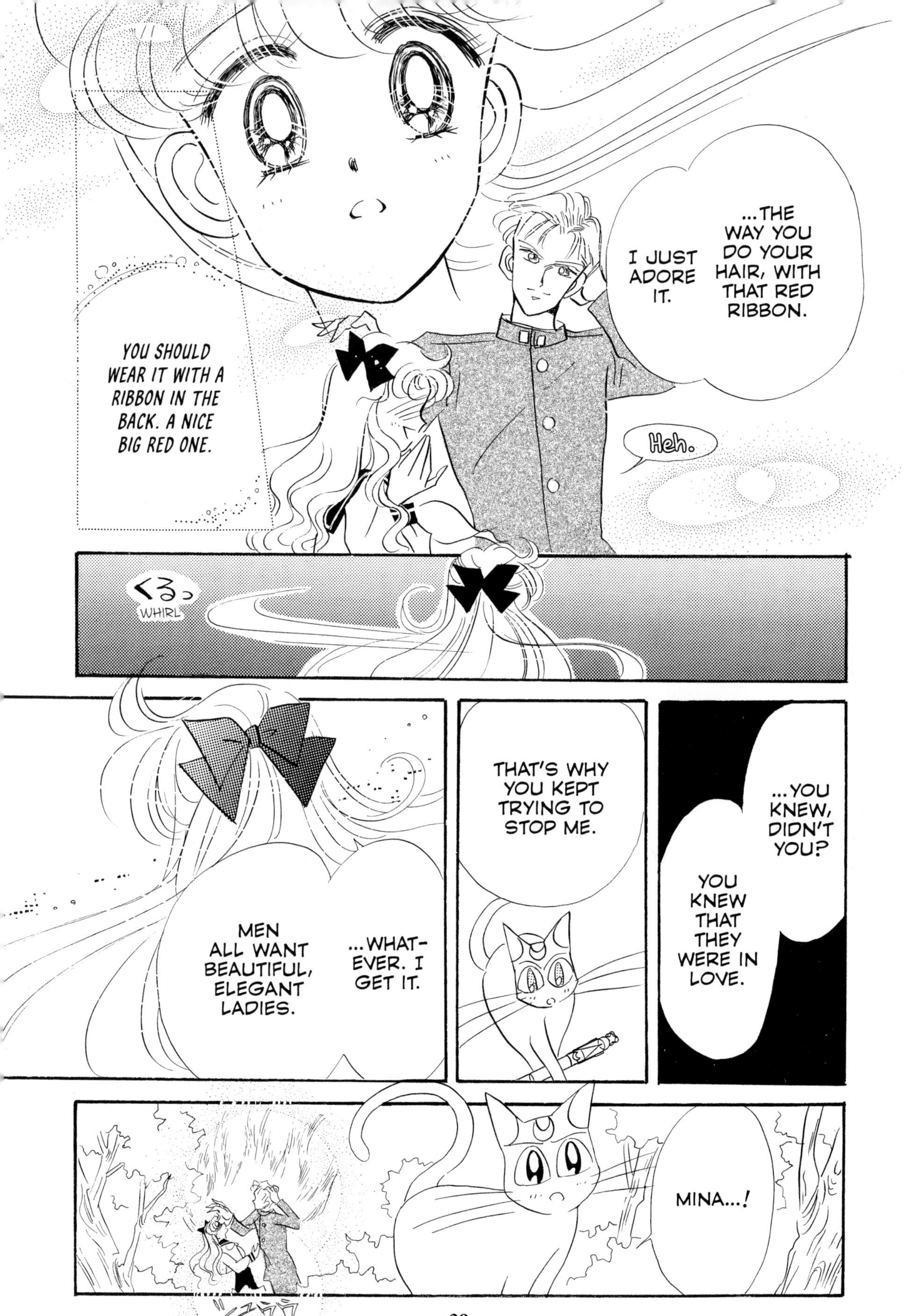
...THE WAY YOU DO YOUR HAIR, WITH THAT RED RIBBON.
I JUST ADORE IT.
Heh.
YOU SHOULD WEAR IT WITH A RIBBON IN THE BACK. A NICE BIG RED ONE.
くるっ
WHIRL
...YOU KNEW, DIDN'T YOU?
YOU KNEW THAT THEY WERE IN LOVE.
THAT'S WHY YOU KEPT TRYING TO STOP ME.
...WHATEVER. I GET IT.
MEN ALL WANT BEAUTIFUL, ELEGANT LADIES.
MINA...!
シュララ
FSHHH

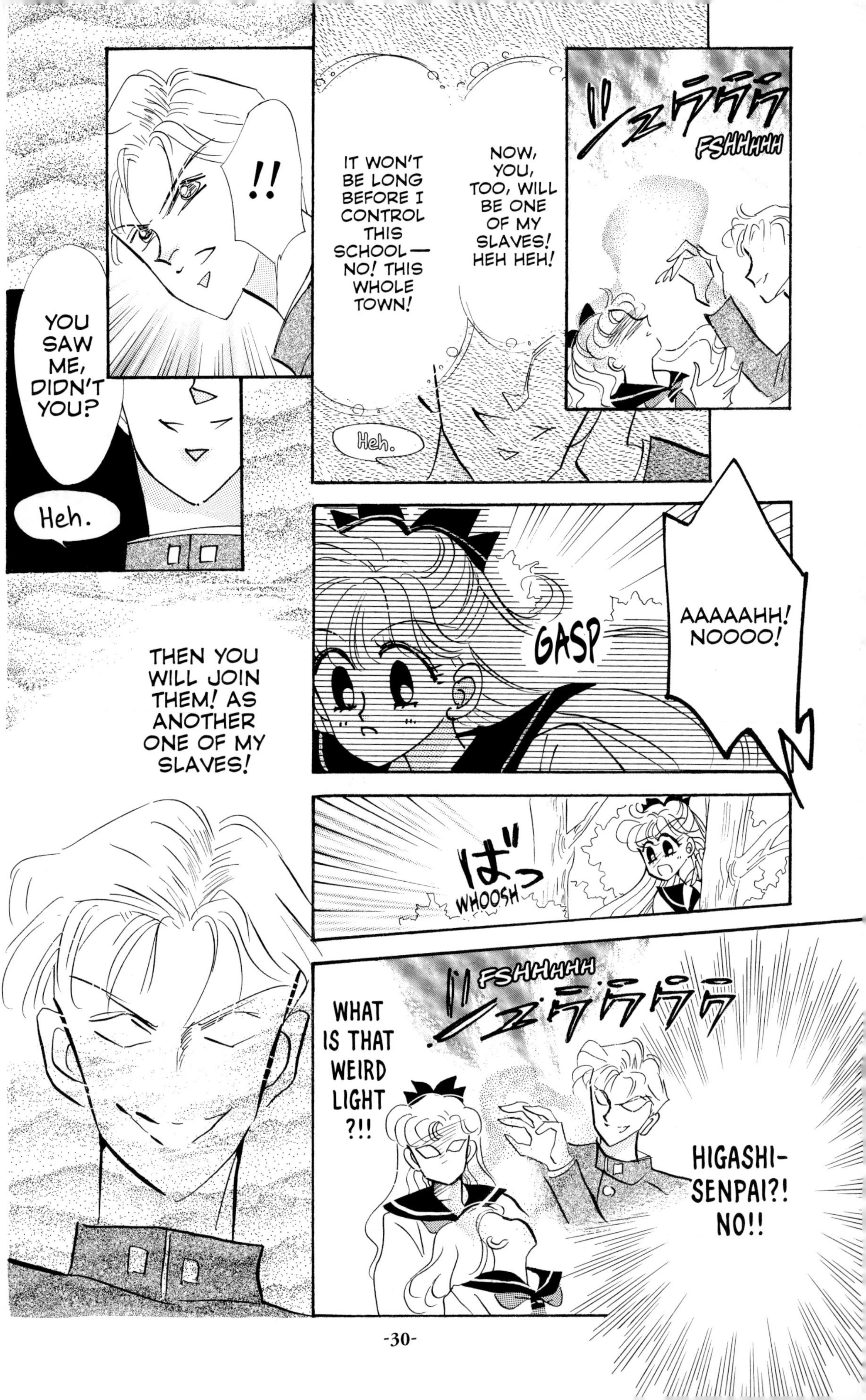
シュワワワ
FSHHHHH
NOW, YOU, TOO, WILL BE ONE OF MY SLAVES! HEH HEH!
IT WON'T BE LONG BEFORE I CONTROL THIS SCHOOL— NO! THIS WHOLE TOWN!
Heh.
!!
YOU SAW ME, DIDN'T YOU?
Heh.
AAAAAHH! NOOOO!
GASP
ばっ
WHOOSH
THEN YOU WILL JOIN THEM! AS ANOTHER ONE OF MY SLAVES!
FSHHHHH
シュワワワワ
HIGASHI-SENPAI?! NO!!
WHAT IS THAT WEIRD LIGHT?!!

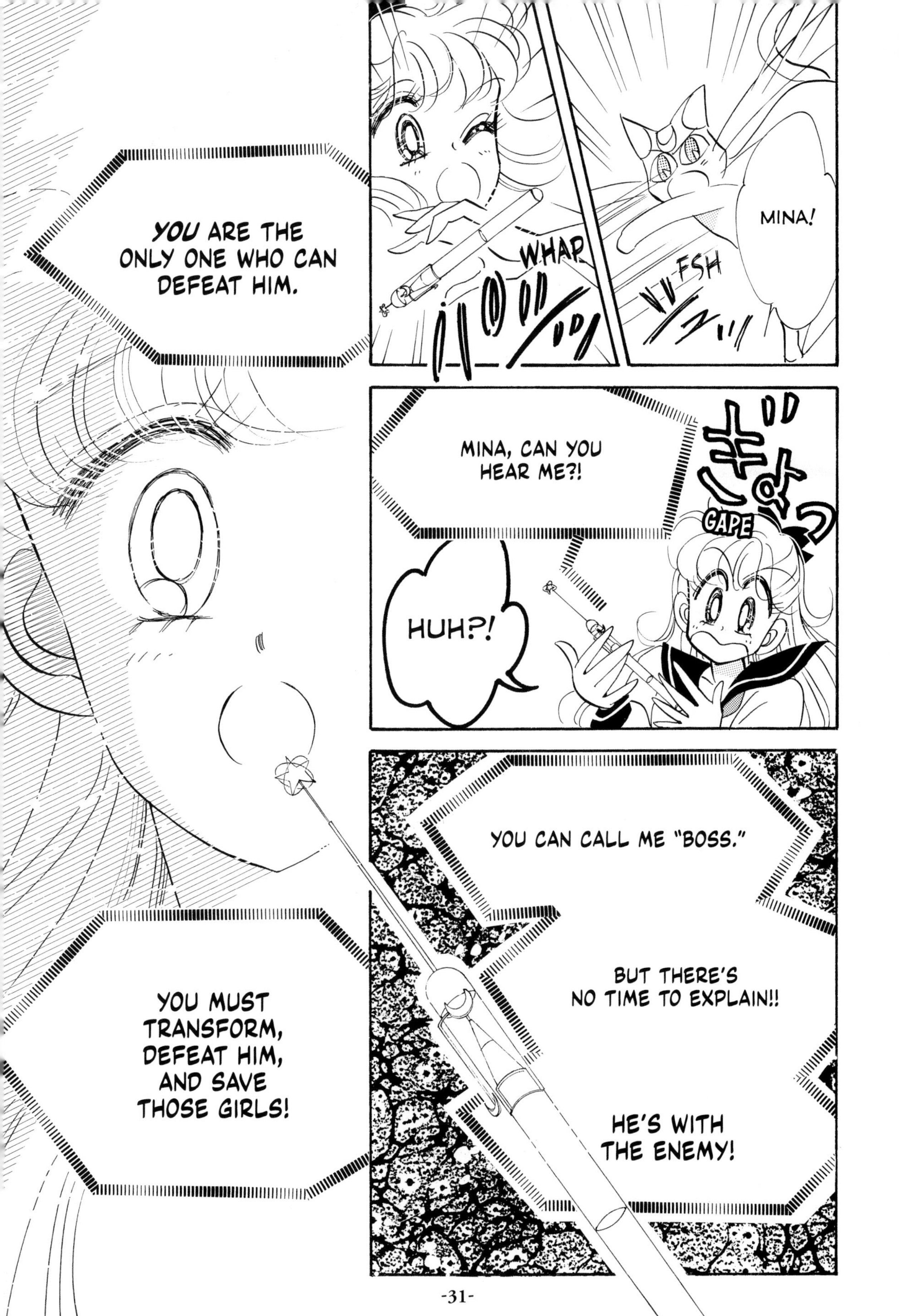
MINA!
FSH
WHAP
GAPE
MINA, CAN YOU HEAR ME?!
HUH?!
YOU CAN CALL ME "BOSS."
BUT THERE'S NO TIME TO EXPLAIN!!
HE'S WITH THE ENEMY!
YOU ARE THE ONLY ONE WHO CAN DEFEAT HIM.
YOU MUST TRANSFORM, DEFEAT HIM, AND SAVE THOSE GIRLS!

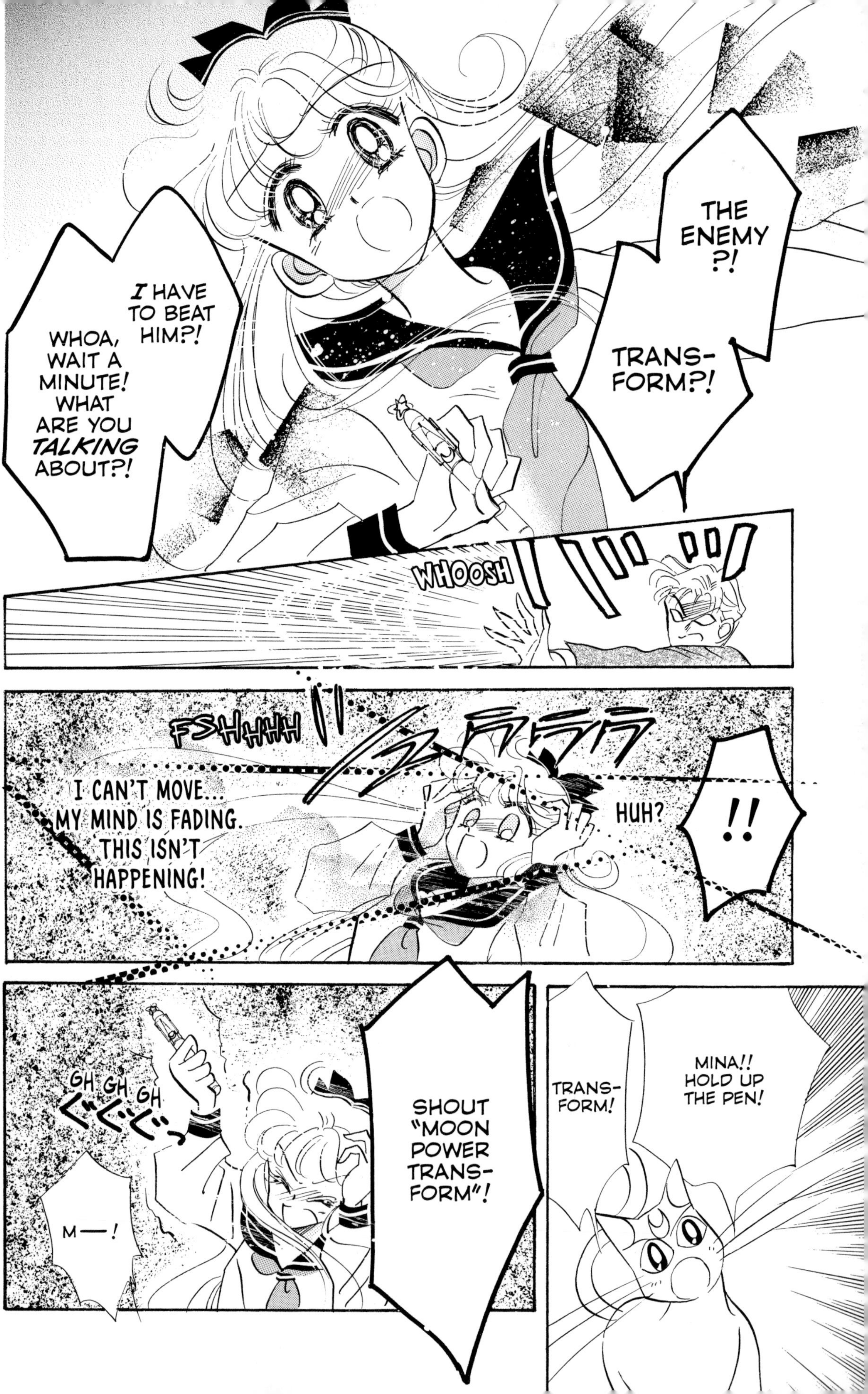
THE ENEMY?!
TRANS-FORM?!
WHOA, WAIT A MINUTE! WHAT ARE YOU *TALKING* ABOUT?!
I HAVE TO BEAT HIM?!
WHOOSH
!!
HUH?
FSHHHH
I CAN'T MOVE... MY MIND IS FADING. THIS ISN'T HAPPENING!
MINA!! HOLD UP THE PEN!
TRANS-FORM!
SHOUT "MOON POWER TRANS-FORM"!
GH GH GH
M—!

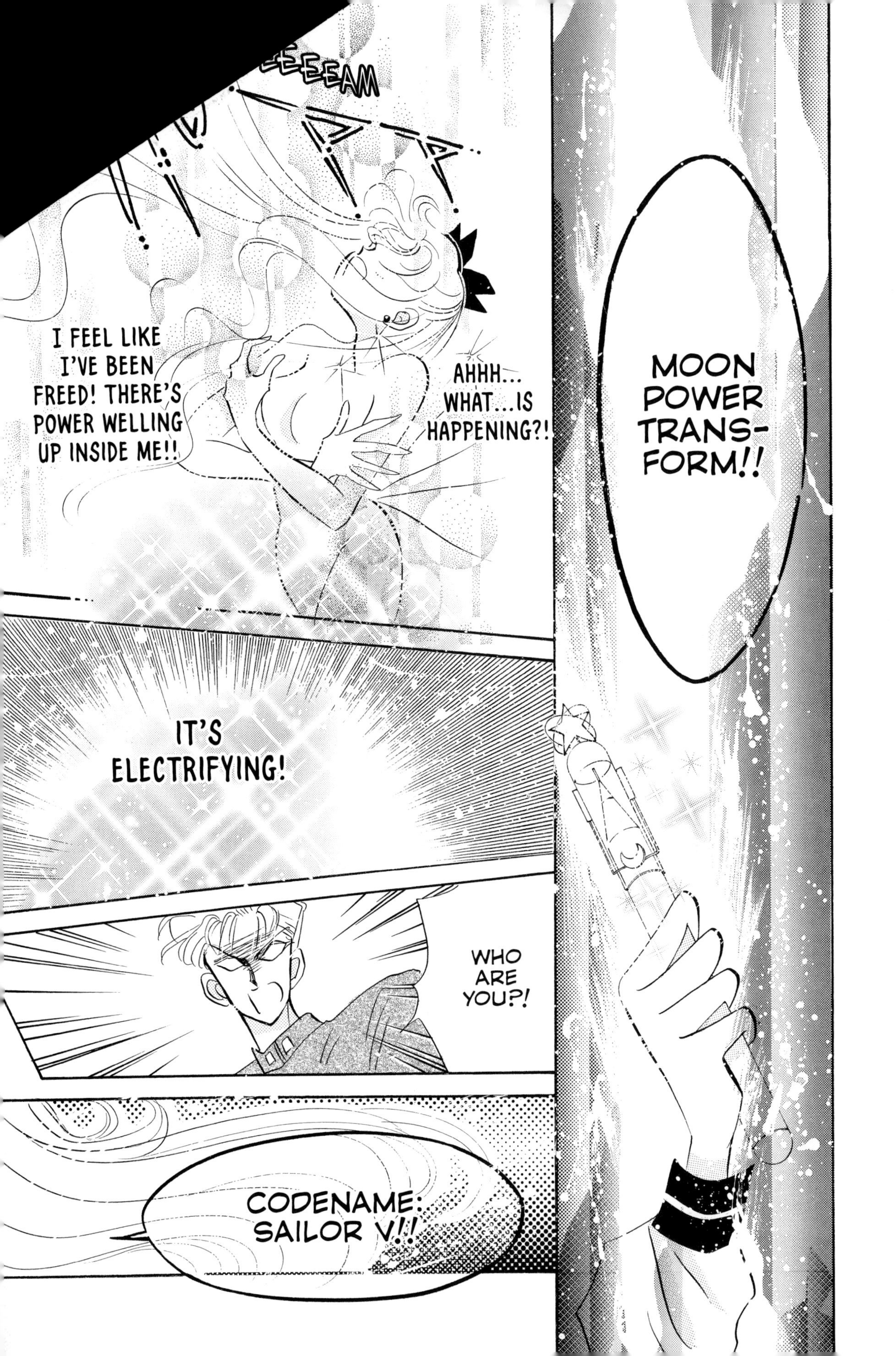
MOON POWER TRANSFORM!!
AHHH... WHAT...IS HAPPENING?!
I FEEL LIKE I'VE BEEN FREED! THERE'S POWER WELLING UP INSIDE ME!!
IT'S ELECTRIFYING!
WHO ARE YOU?!
CODENAME: SAILOR V!!

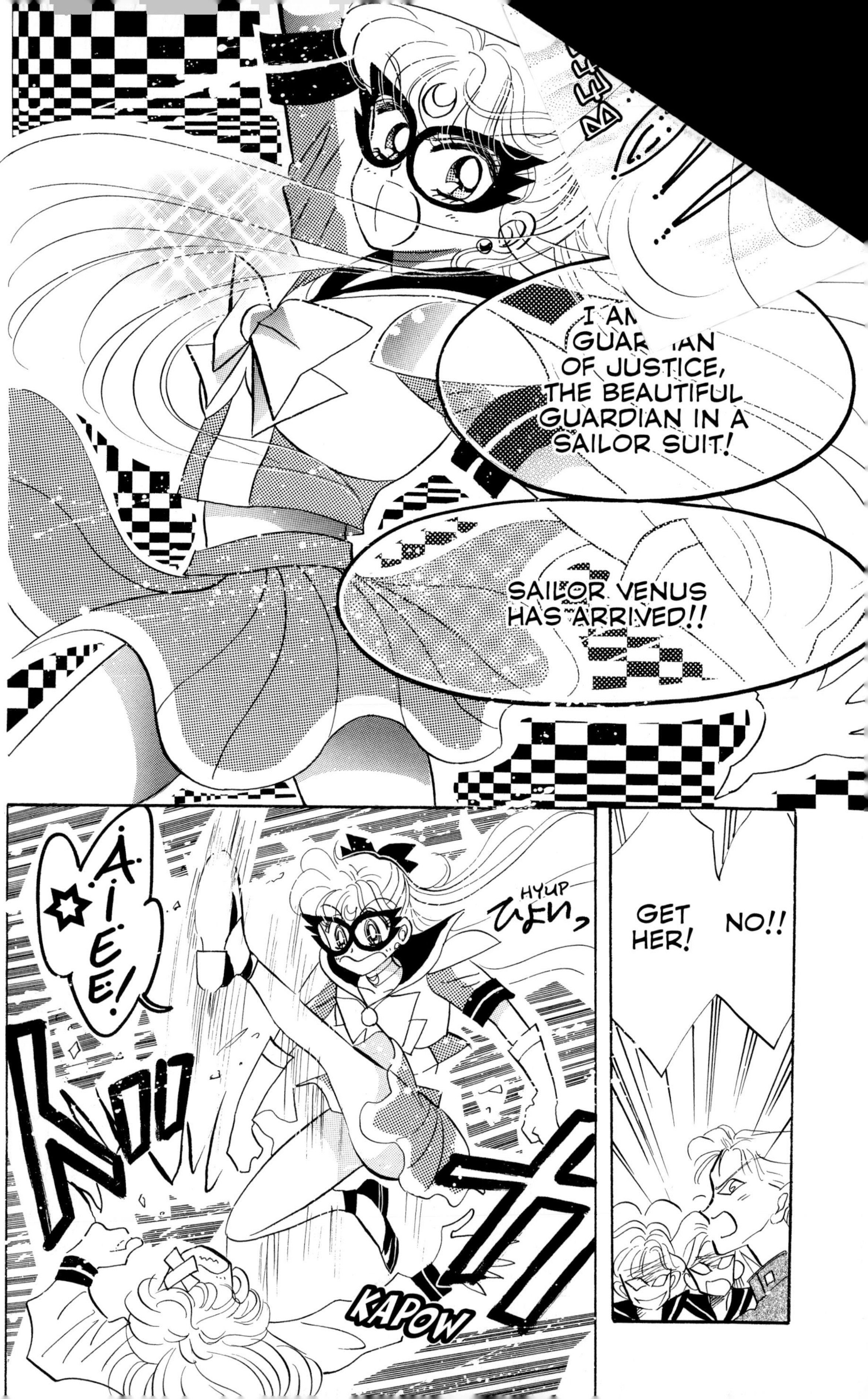
I AM GUAR IAN OF JUSTICE, THE BEAUTIFUL GUARDIAN IN A SAILOR SUIT!
SAILOR VENUS HAS ARRIVED!!
NO!!
GET HER!
HYUP
ひょい
AIEEE!
KAPOW

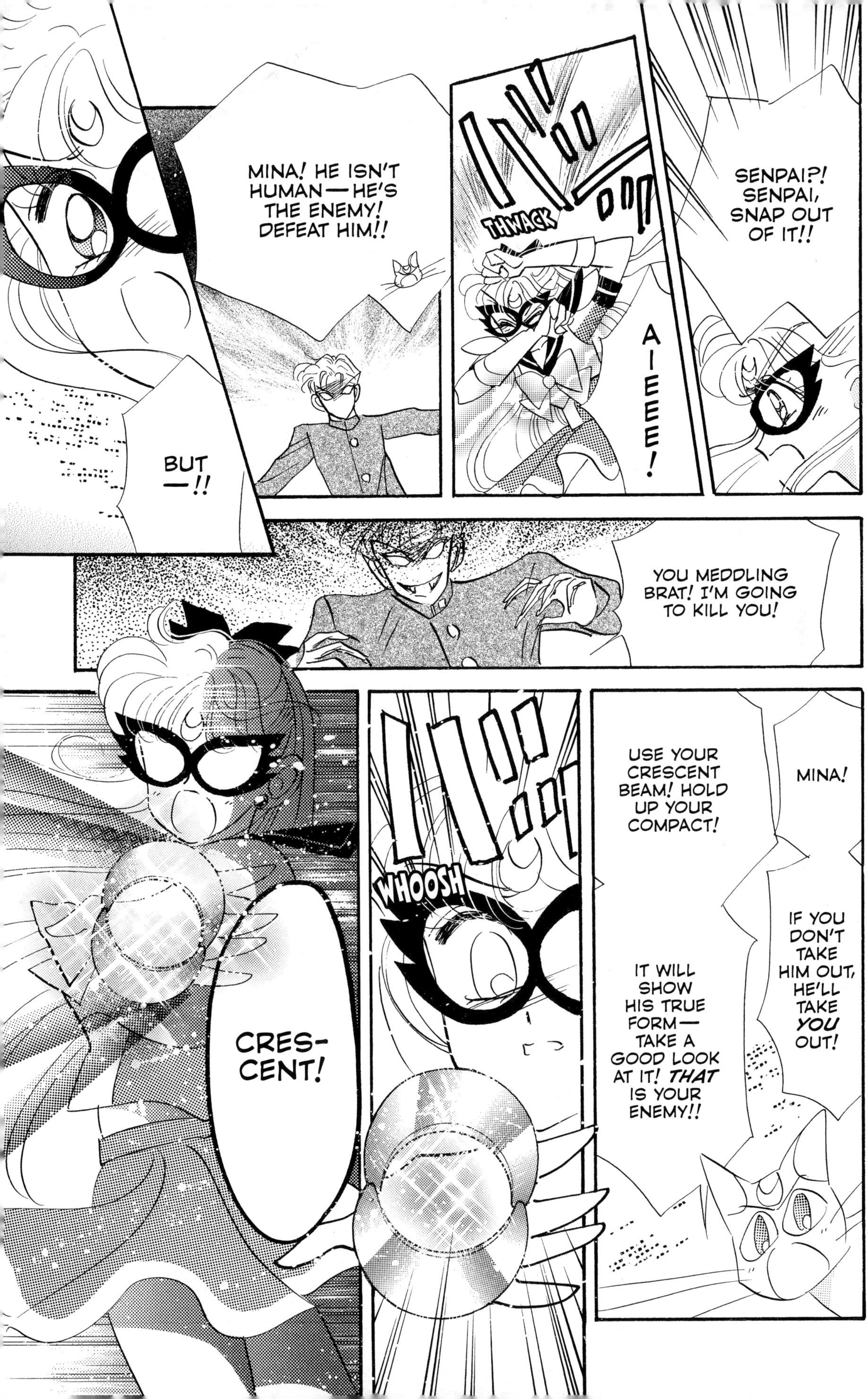
SENPAI?! SENPAI, SNAP OUT OF IT!!
THWACK
AIEEE!
MINA! HE ISN'T HUMAN—HE'S THE ENEMY! DEFEAT HIM!!
BUT—!!
YOU MEDDLING BRAT! I'M GOING TO KILL YOU!
MINA!
USE YOUR CRESCENT BEAM! HOLD UP YOUR COMPACT!
IF YOU DON'T TAKE HIM OUT, HE'LL TAKE *YOU* OUT!
IT WILL SHOW HIS TRUE FORM—TAKE A GOOD LOOK AT IT! *THAT* IS YOUR ENEMY!!
WHOOSH
CRES-CENT!

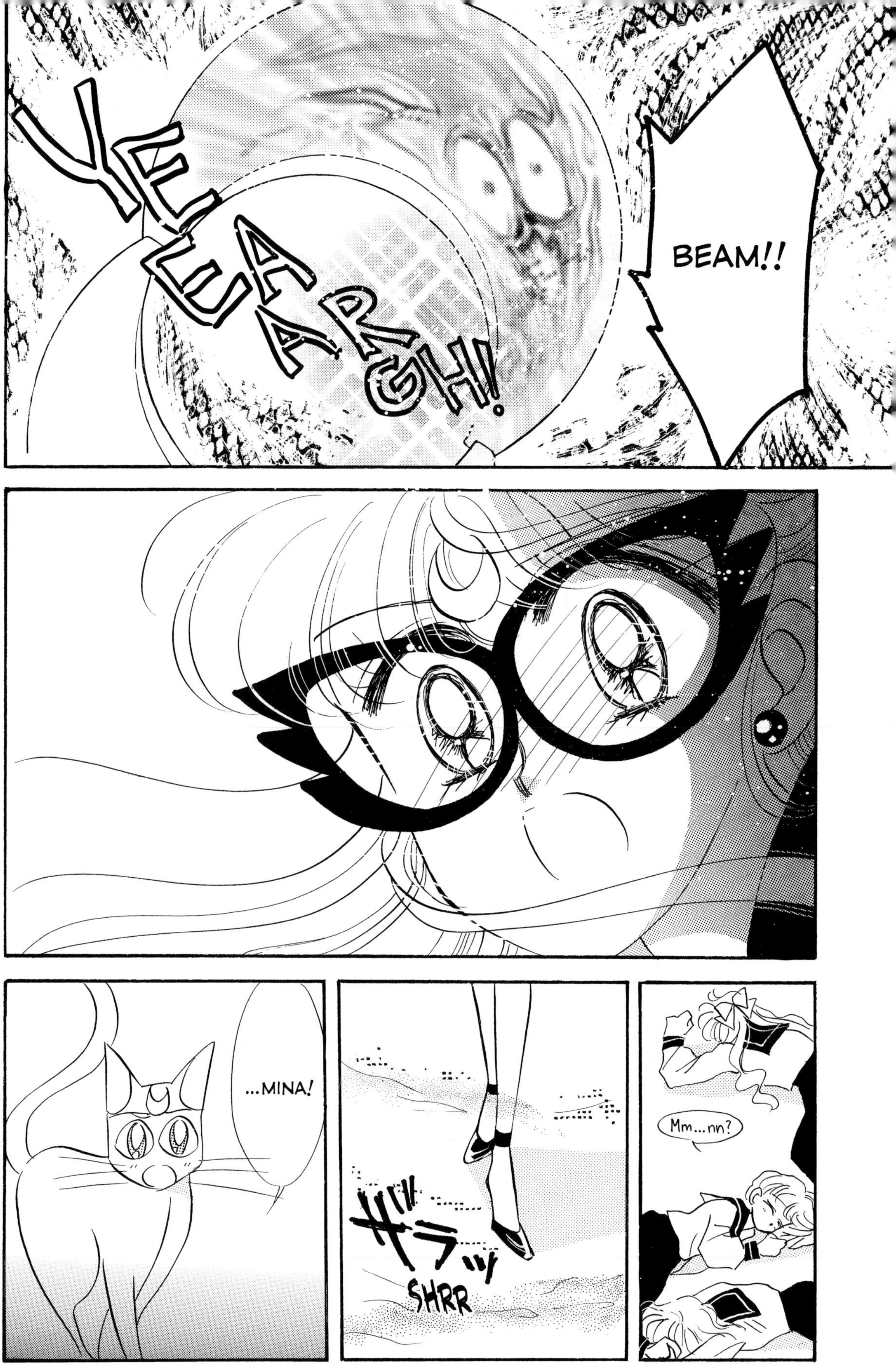
BEAM!!
YEEAARGH!
Mm...nn?
ザラッ
SHRR
...MINA!

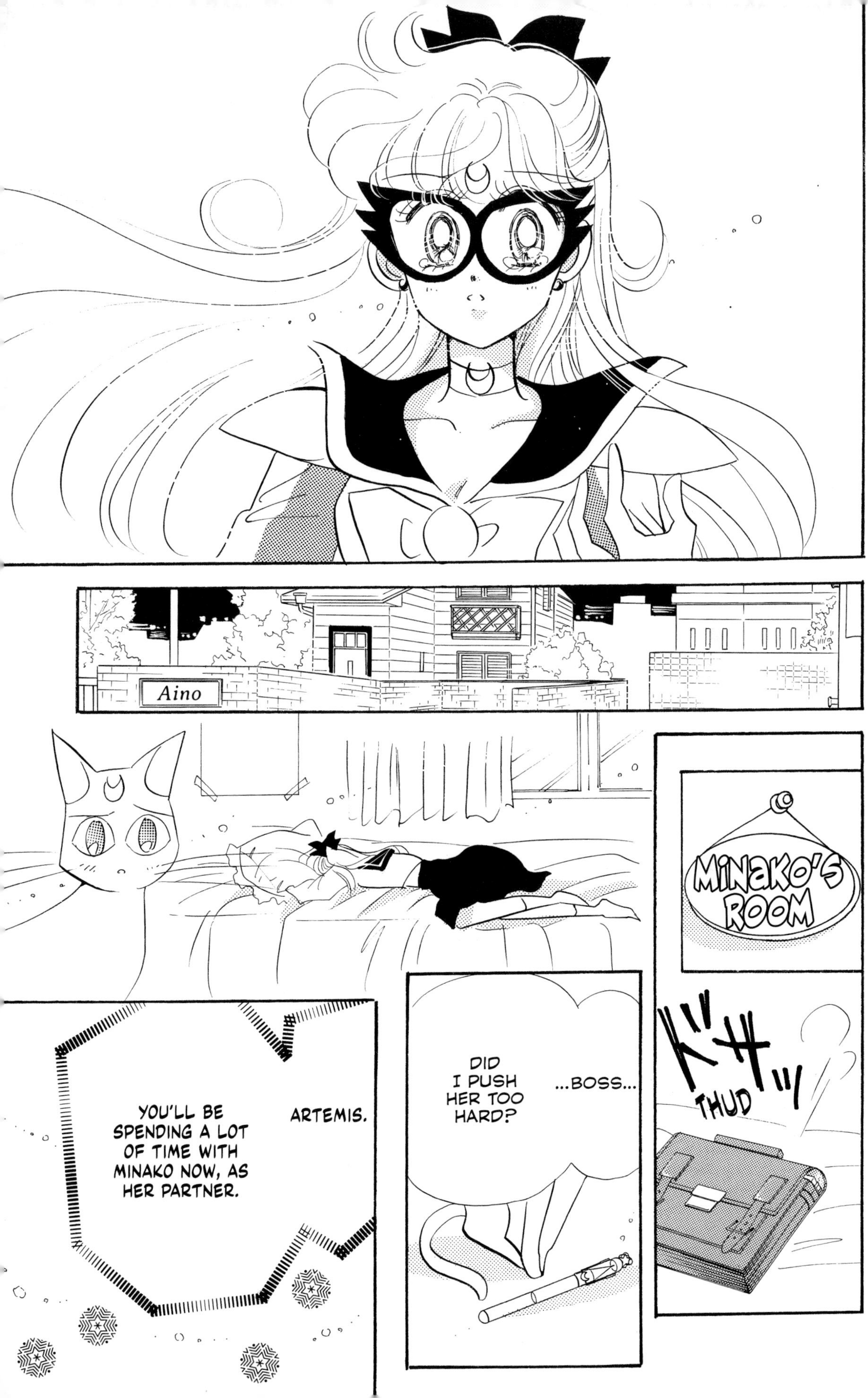

Aino
MINAKO'S ROOM
ドサッ
THUD
...BOSS...
DID I PUSH HER TOO HARD?
ARTEMIS.
YOU'LL BE SPENDING A LOT OF TIME WITH MINAKO NOW, AS HER PARTNER.

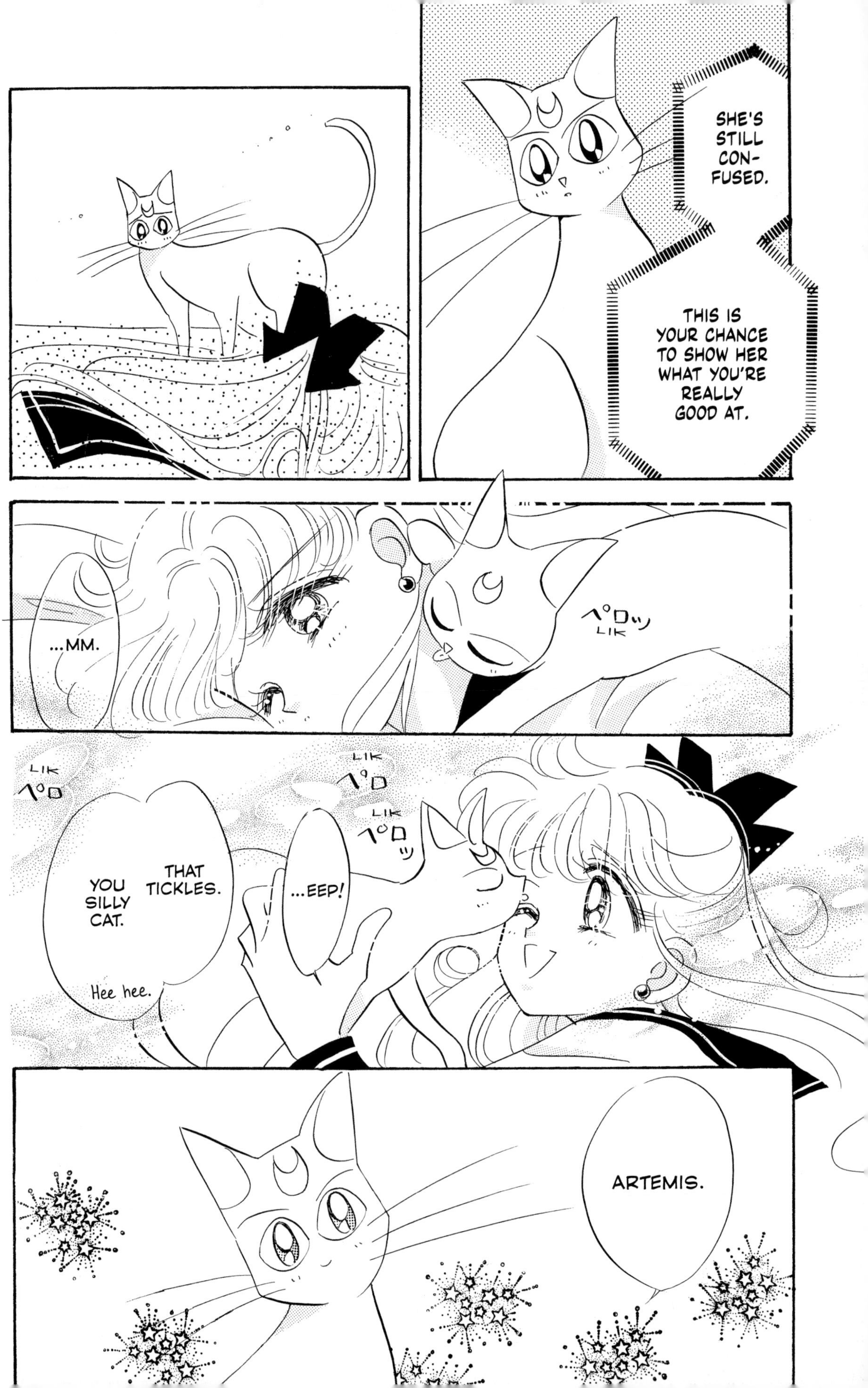
SHE'S STILL CON-FUSED.
THIS IS YOUR CHANCE TO SHOW HER WHAT YOU'RE REALLY GOOD AT.
ペロッ
LIK
...MM.
LIK
ペロッ
LIK
ペロ
...EEP!
THAT TICKLES.
YOU SILLY CAT.
Hee hee.
LIK
ペロ
ARTEMIS.

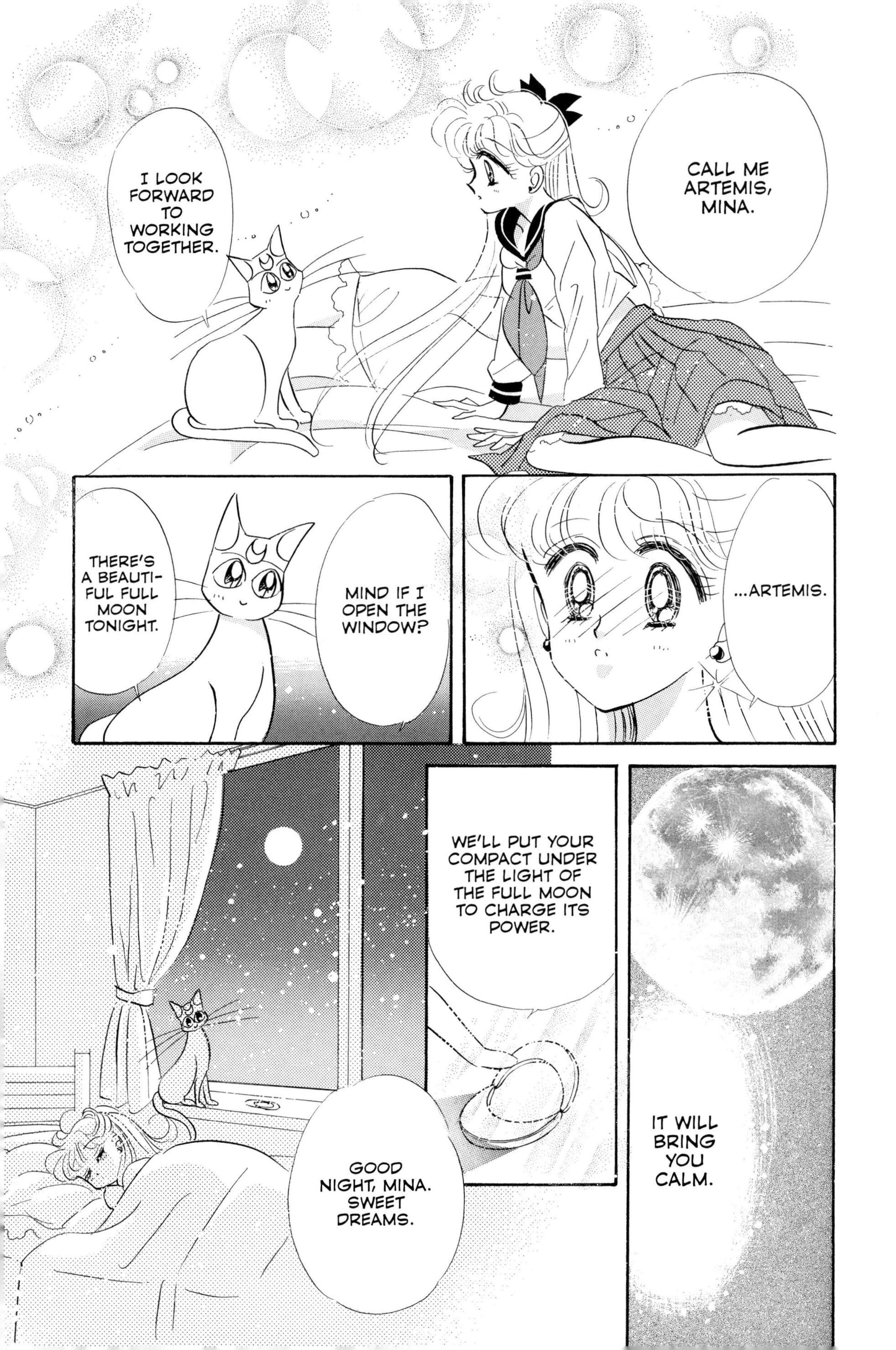
CALL ME ARTEMIS, MINA.
I LOOK FORWARD TO WORKING TOGETHER.
...ARTEMIS.
MIND IF I OPEN THE WINDOW?
THERE'S A BEAUTI-FUL FULL MOON TONIGHT.
IT WILL BRING YOU CALM.
WE'LL PUT YOUR COMPACT UNDER THE LIGHT OF THE FULL MOON TO CHARGE ITS POWER.
GOOD NIGHT, MINA. SWEET DREAMS.

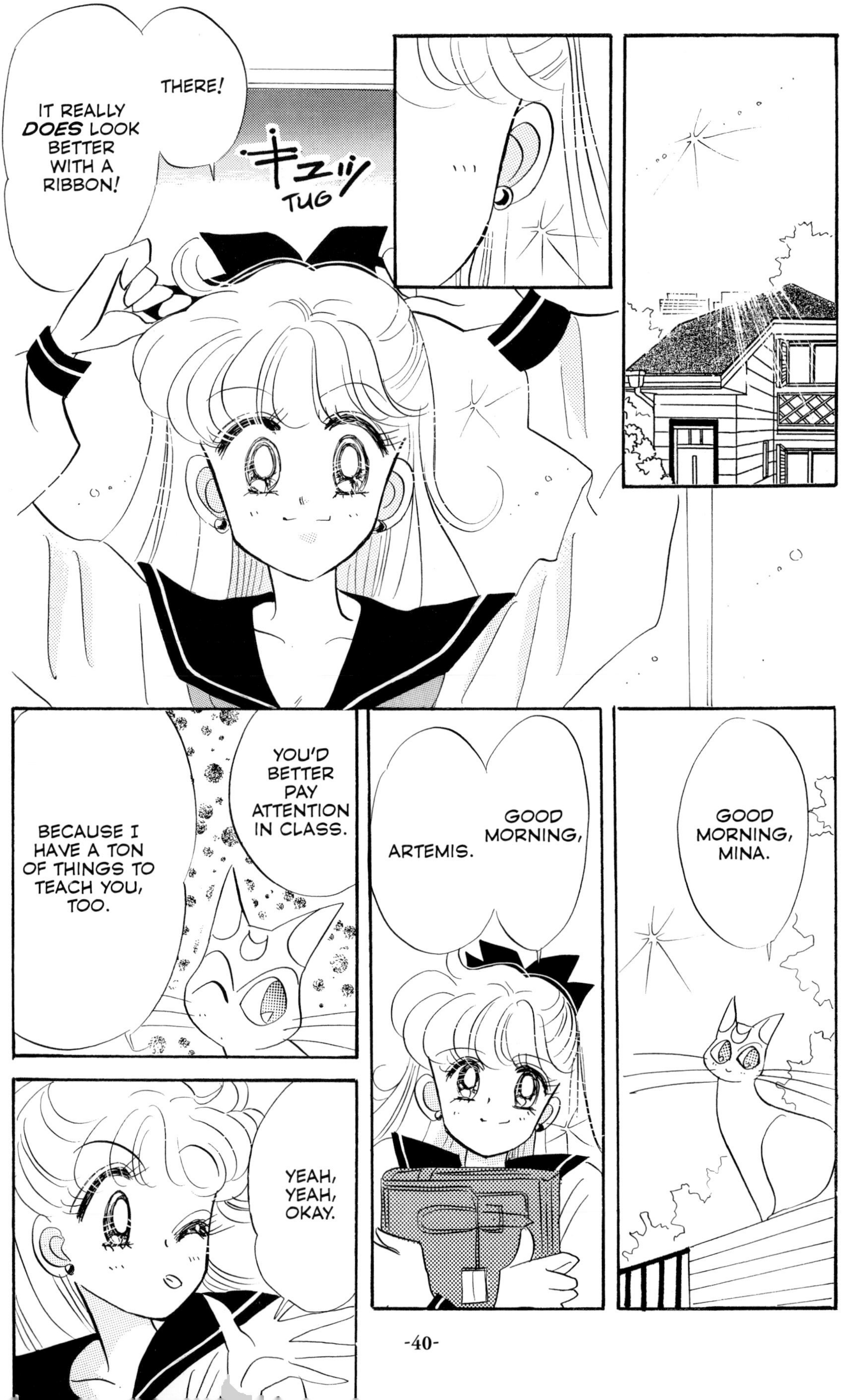
THERE!
IT REALLY DOES LOOK BETTER WITH A RIBBON!
キュッ
TUG
GOOD MORNING, MINA.
GOOD MORNING, ARTEMIS.
YOU'D BETTER PAY ATTENTION IN CLASS.
BECAUSE I HAVE A TON OF THINGS TO TEACH YOU, TOO.
YEAH, YEAH, OKAY.

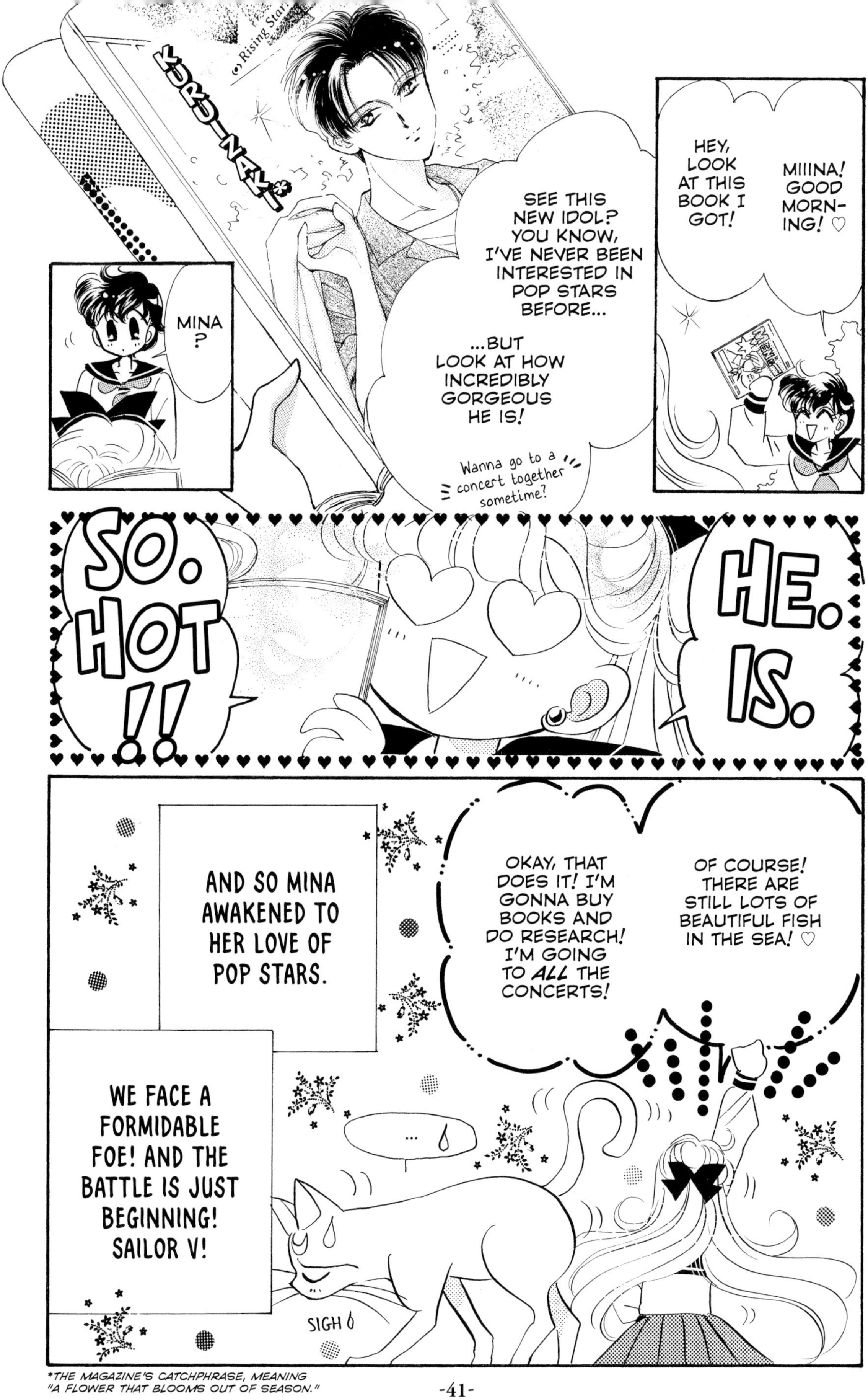
MIIINA! GOOD MORNING! ♡
HEY, LOOK AT THIS BOOK I GOT!
KURU-NAKI*
Rising Star
SEE THIS NEW IDOL? YOU KNOW, I'VE NEVER BEEN INTERESTED IN POP STARS BEFORE...
...BUT LOOK AT HOW INCREDIBLY GORGEOUS HE IS!
Wanna go to a concert together sometime?
MINA ?
HE. IS.
SO. HOT!!
OF COURSE! THERE ARE STILL LOTS OF BEAUTIFUL FISH IN THE SEA! ♡
OKAY, THAT DOES IT! I'M GONNA BUY BOOKS AND DO RESEARCH! I'M GOING TO *ALL* THE CONCERTS!
AND SO MINA AWAKENED TO HER LOVE OF POP STARS.
...
SIGH
WE FACE A FORMIDABLE FOE! AND THE BATTLE IS JUST BEGINNING! SAILOR V!

*THE MAGAZINE'S CATCHPHRASE, MEANING "A FLOWER THAT BLOOMS OUT OF SEASON."

Codename Sailor V

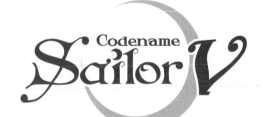

vol. 2 Minako in "Crown Game Center"

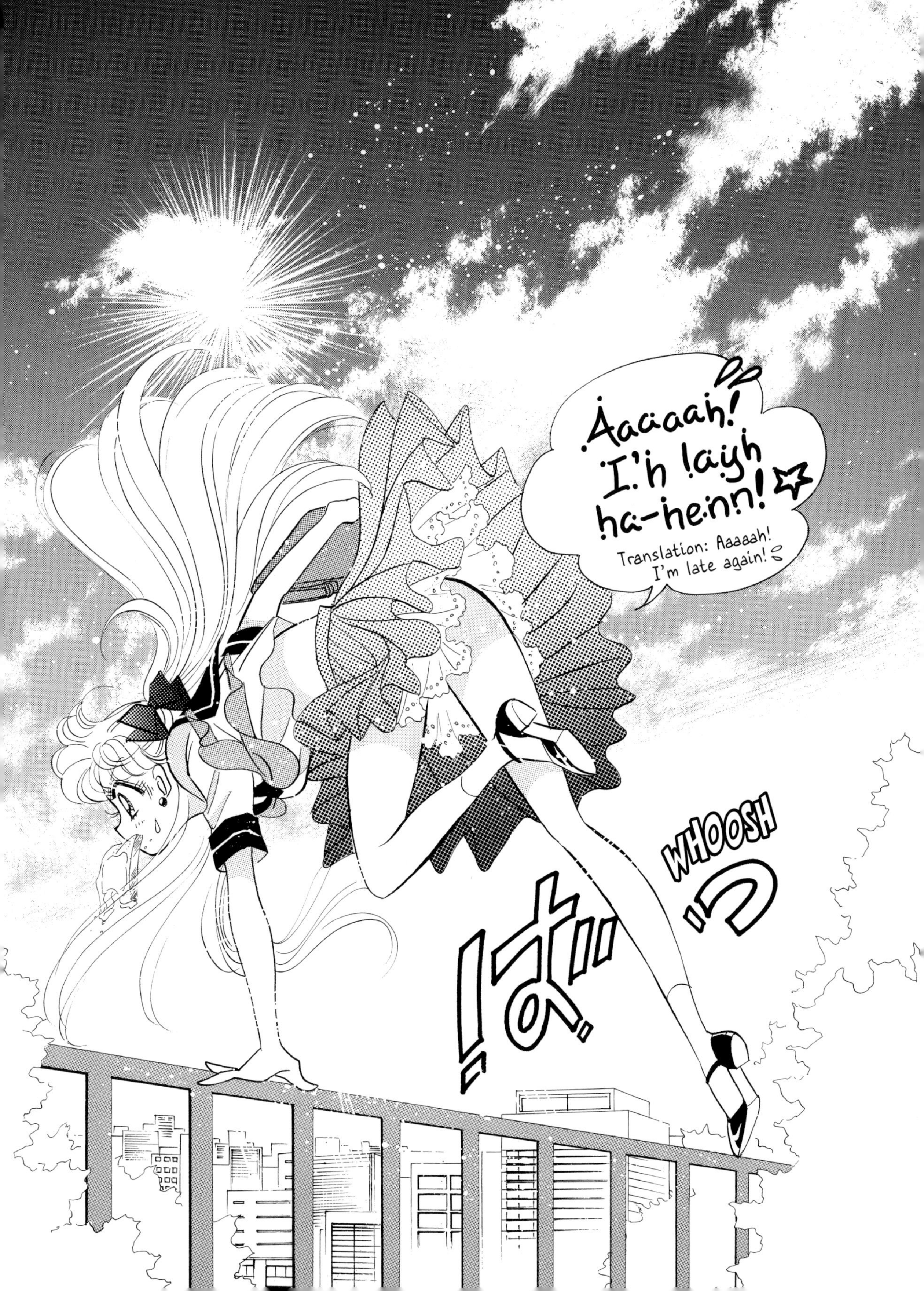
Aaaaah! I'n layh ha-henn! ☆
Translation: Aaaaah! I'm late again!
WHOOSH
ばっ

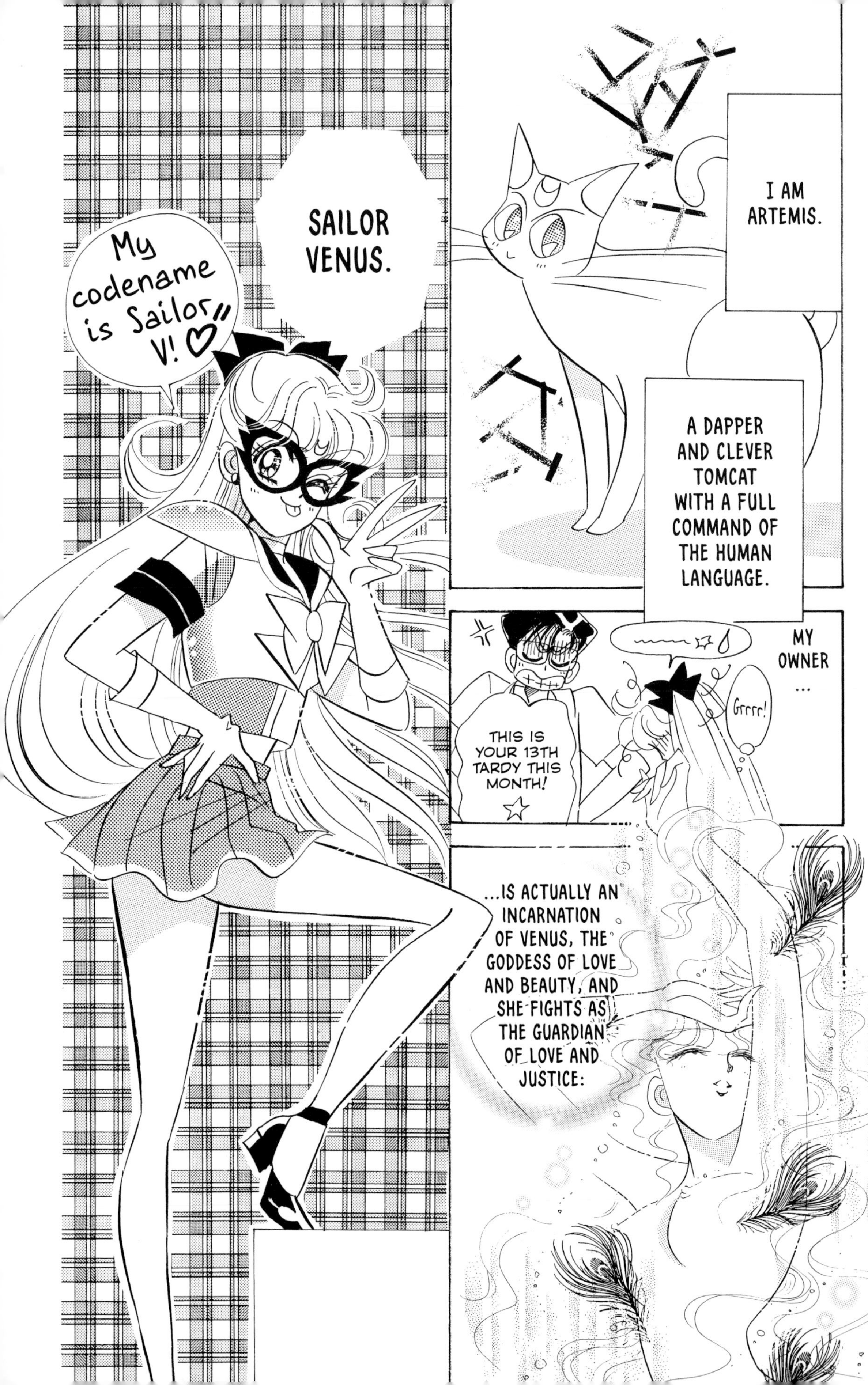

I AM ARTEMIS.
A DAPPER AND CLEVER TOMCAT WITH A FULL COMMAND OF THE HUMAN LANGUAGE.
MY OWNER ...
Grrrr!
THIS IS YOUR 13TH TARDY THIS MONTH! ☆
...IS ACTUALLY AN INCARNATION OF VENUS, THE GODDESS OF LOVE AND BEAUTY, AND SHE FIGHTS AS THE GUARDIAN OF LOVE AND JUSTICE:
SAILOR VENUS.
My codename is Sailor V! ♡

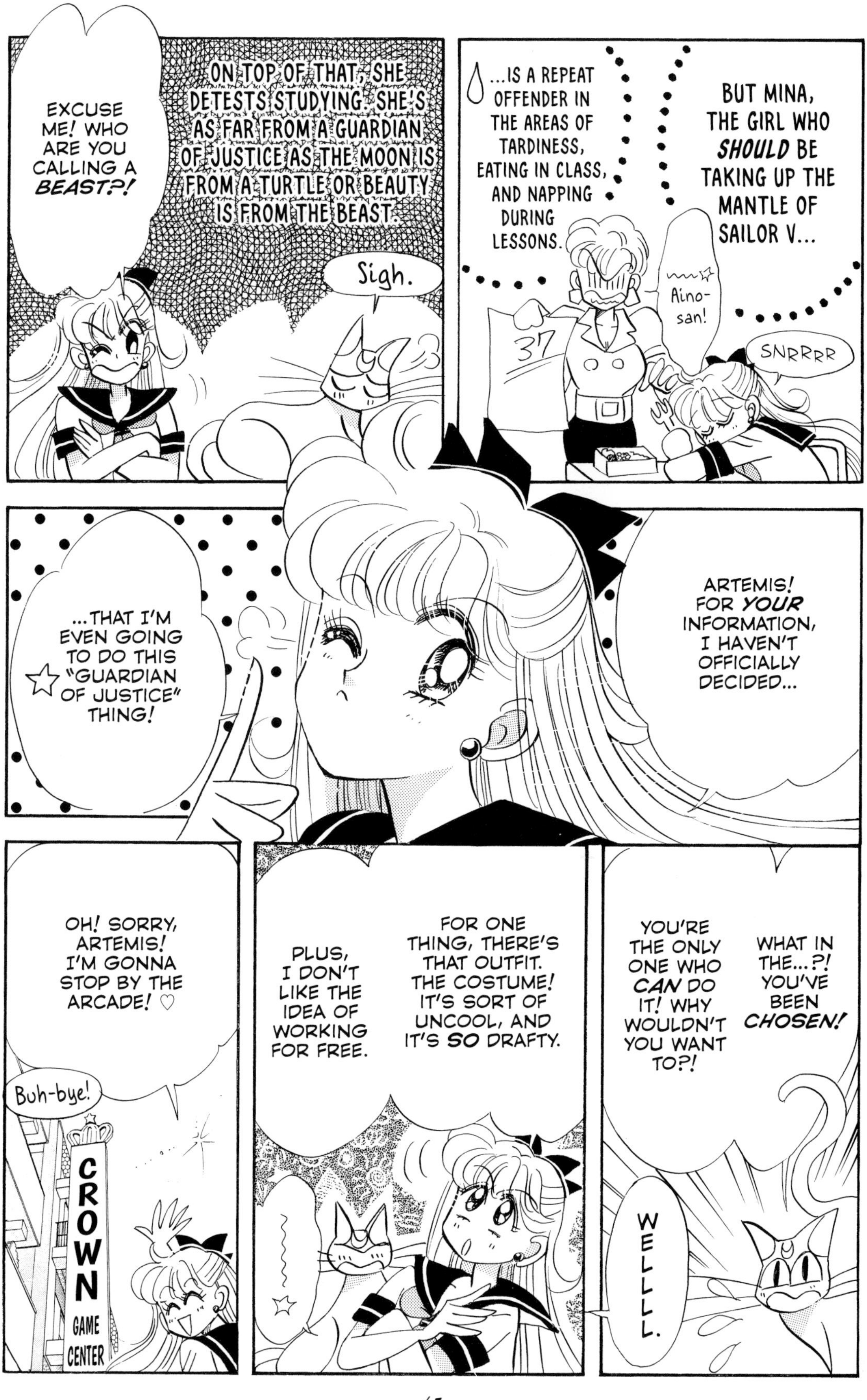
BUT MINA, THE GIRL WHO SHOULD BE TAKING UP THE MANTLE OF SAILOR V...
...IS A REPEAT OFFENDER IN THE AREAS OF TARDINESS, EATING IN CLASS, AND NAPPING DURING LESSONS.
Aino-san!
37
SNRRRR
ON TOP OF THAT, SHE DETESTS STUDYING. SHE'S AS FAR FROM A GUARDIAN OF JUSTICE AS THE MOON IS FROM A TURTLE OR BEAUTY IS FROM THE BEAST.
Sigh.
EXCUSE ME! WHO ARE YOU CALLING A BEAST?!
ARTEMIS! FOR YOUR INFORMATION, I HAVEN'T OFFICIALLY DECIDED...
...THAT I'M EVEN GOING TO DO THIS "GUARDIAN OF JUSTICE" THING!
WHAT IN THE...?! YOU'VE BEEN CHOSEN!
YOU'RE THE ONLY ONE WHO CAN DO IT! WHY WOULDN'T YOU WANT TO?!
WELLL.
FOR ONE THING, THERE'S THAT OUTFIT. THE COSTUME! IT'S SORT OF UNCOOL, AND IT'S SO DRAFTY.
PLUS, I DON'T LIKE THE IDEA OF WORKING FOR FREE.
OH! SORRY, ARTEMIS! I'M GONNA STOP BY THE ARCADE! ♡
Buh-bye!
CROWN GAME CENTER

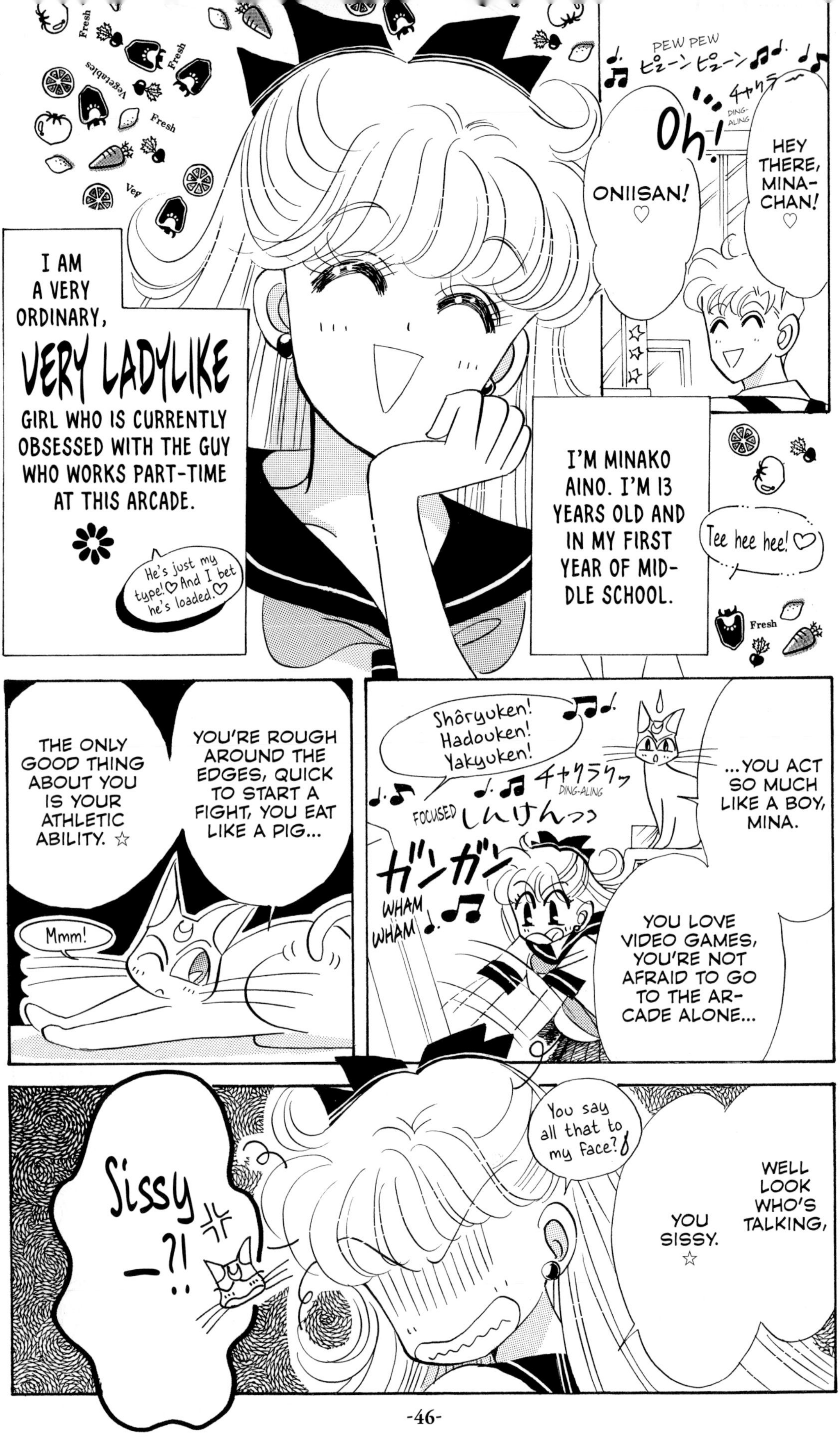
PEW PEW
ピューンピューン
DING-ALING
チャララ～
Oh!
ONIISAN! ♡
HEY THERE, MINA-CHAN! ♡
I'M MINAKO AINO. I'M 13 YEARS OLD AND IN MY FIRST YEAR OF MID-DLE SCHOOL.
Tee hee hee! ♡
I AM A VERY ORDINARY, VERY LADYLIKE GIRL WHO IS CURRENTLY OBSESSED WITH THE GUY WHO WORKS PART-TIME AT THIS ARCADE.
He's just my type! ♡ And I bet he's loaded. ♡
...YOU ACT SO MUCH LIKE A BOY, MINA.
YOU LOVE VIDEO GAMES, YOU'RE NOT AFRAID TO GO TO THE AR-CADE ALONE...
Shôryuken! Hadouken! Yakyuken!
DING-ALING
チャラララッ
FOCUSED
しんけんっっ
WHAM WHAM
ガンガン
YOU'RE ROUGH AROUND THE EDGES, QUICK TO START A FIGHT, YOU EAT LIKE A PIG...
THE ONLY GOOD THING ABOUT YOU IS YOUR ATHLETIC ABILITY. ☆
Mmm!
WELL LOOK WHO'S TALKING,
YOU SISSY. ☆
You say all that to my face?
Sissy—?!

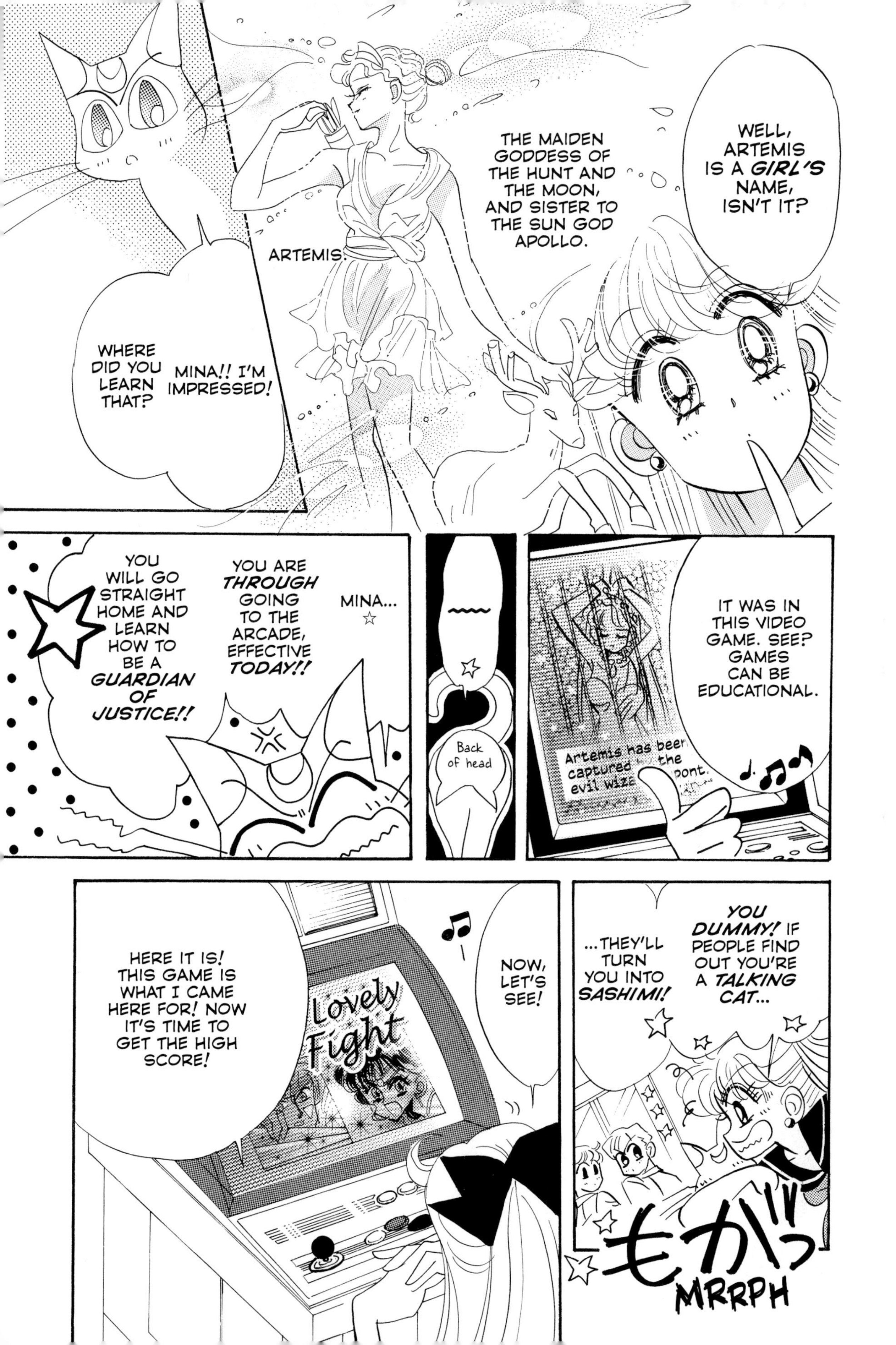
WELL, ARTEMIS IS A *GIRL'S* NAME, ISN'T IT?
THE MAIDEN GODDESS OF THE HUNT AND THE MOON, AND SISTER TO THE SUN GOD APOLLO.
ARTEMIS.
MINA!! I'M IMPRESSED!
WHERE DID YOU LEARN THAT?
IT WAS IN THIS VIDEO GAME. SEE? GAMES CAN BE EDUCATIONAL.
Back of head
MINA... ☆
YOU ARE *THROUGH* GOING TO THE ARCADE, EFFECTIVE *TODAY!!*
YOU WILL GO STRAIGHT HOME AND LEARN HOW TO BE A *GUARDIAN OF JUSTICE!!*
YOU DUMMY! IF PEOPLE FIND OUT YOU'RE A *TALKING CAT...*
...THEY'LL TURN YOU INTO *SASHIMI!*
もがっ
MRRPH
NOW, LET'S SEE!
HERE IT IS! THIS GAME IS WHAT I CAME HERE FOR! NOW IT'S TIME TO GET THE HIGH SCORE!
Lovely Fight

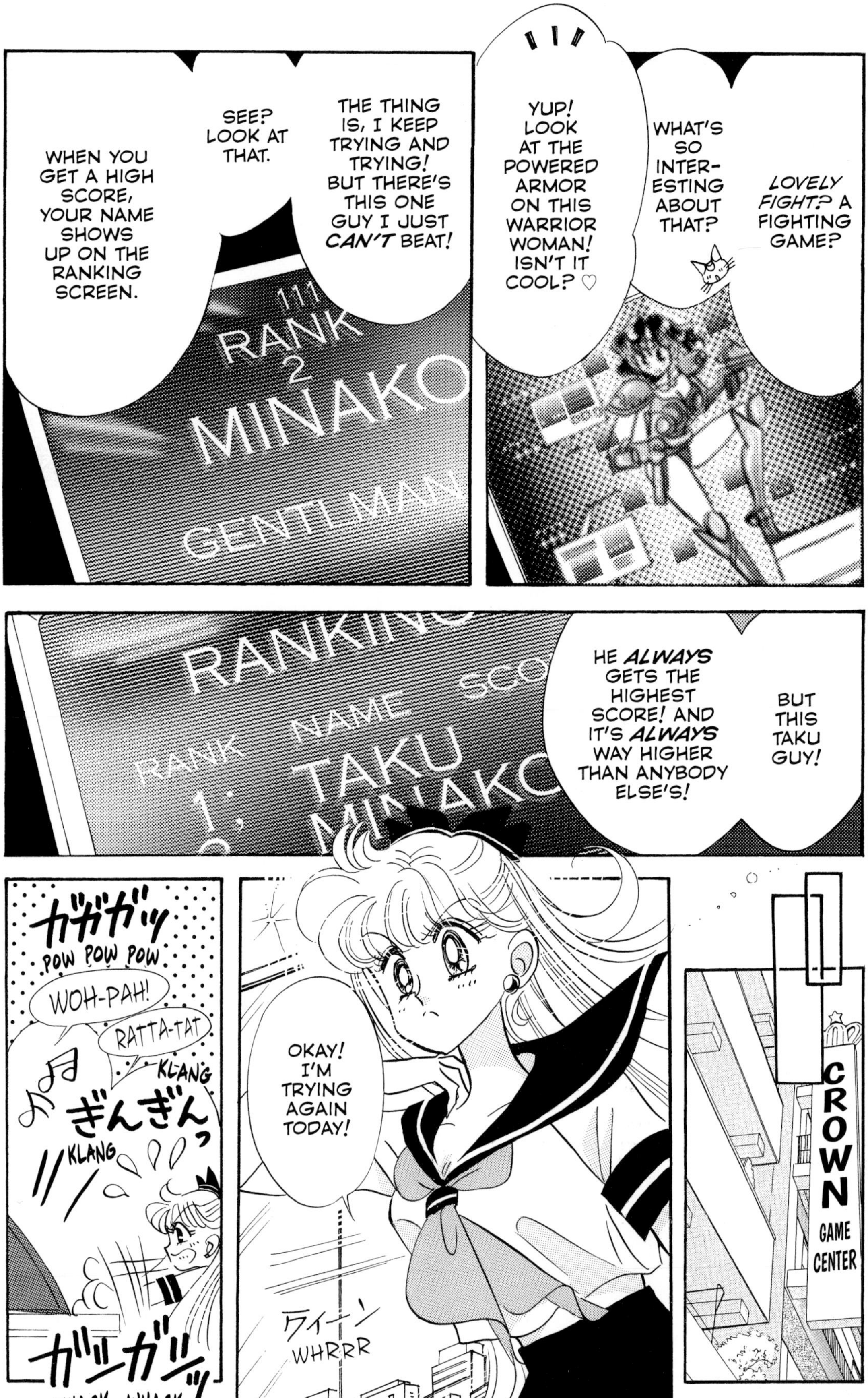

!!!
LOVELY FIGHT? A FIGHTING GAME?
WHAT'S SO INTER-ESTING ABOUT THAT?
YUP! LOOK AT THE POWERED ARMOR ON THIS WARRIOR WOMAN! ISN'T IT COOL? ♡
THE THING IS, I KEEP TRYING AND TRYING! BUT THERE'S THIS ONE GUY I JUST ***CAN'T*** BEAT!
SEE? LOOK AT THAT.
WHEN YOU GET A HIGH SCORE, YOUR NAME SHOWS UP ON THE RANKING SCREEN.
111
RANK
2
MINAKO
GENTLMAN
BUT THIS TAKU GUY!
HE ***ALWAYS*** GETS THE HIGHEST SCORE! AND IT'S ***ALWAYS*** WAY HIGHER THAN ANYBODY ELSE'S!
RANK NAME
1; TAKU
CROWN
GAME CENTER
OKAY! I'M TRYING AGAIN TODAY!
ワイーン
WHRRR
ガガガッ
POW POW POW
WOH-PAH!
RATTA-TAT
KLANG
ぎんぎんっ
KLANG
ガッガッ
WHACK WHACK

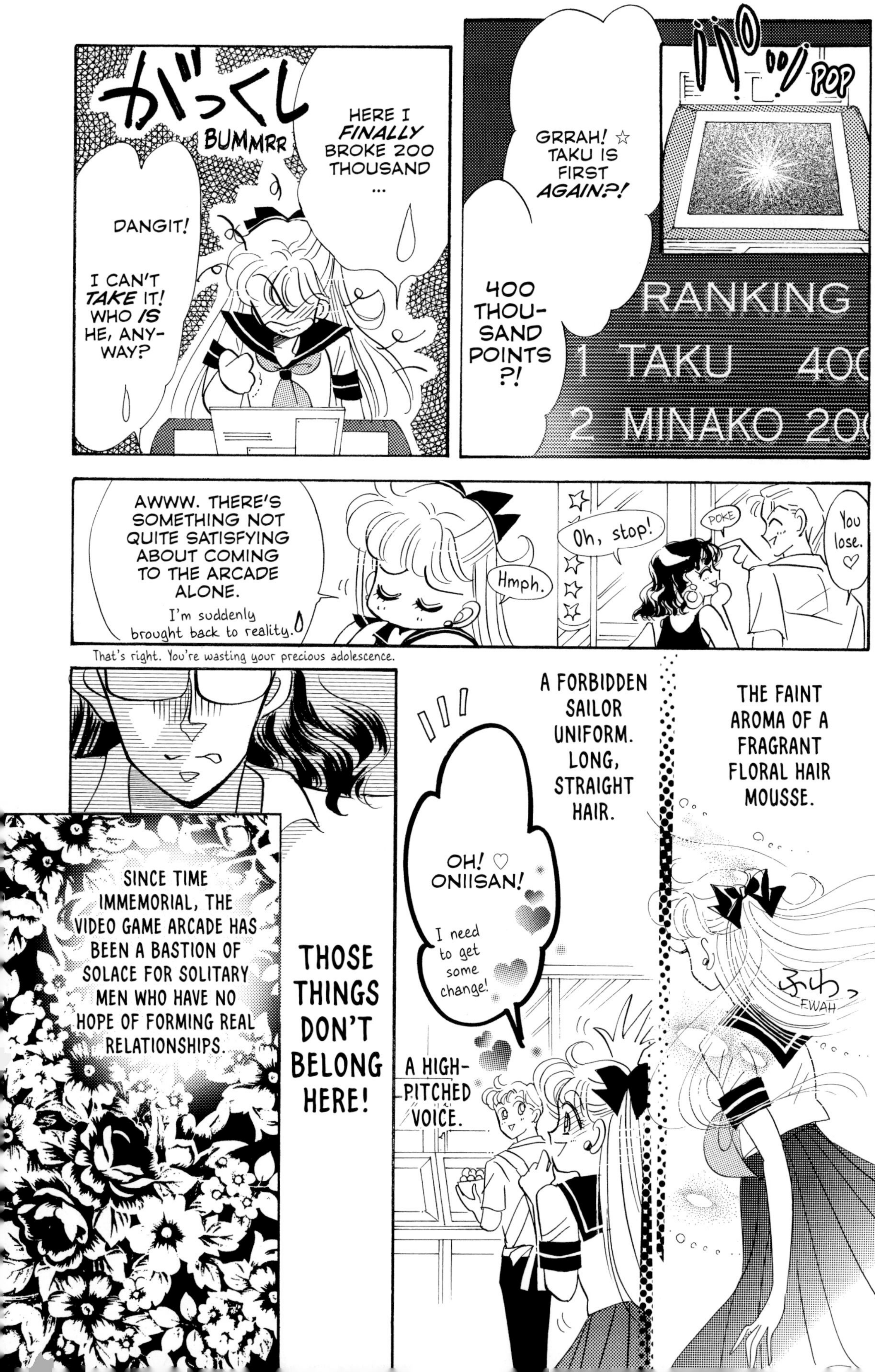
POP
GRRAH! ☆ TAKU IS FIRST AGAIN?!
400 THOUSAND POINTS?!
RANKING
1 TAKU 400
2 MINAKO 20
がっくし
BUMMRR
HERE I FINALLY BROKE 200 THOUSAND ...
DANGIT!
I CAN'T TAKE IT! WHO IS HE, ANYWAY?
You lose. ♡
POKE
Oh, stop!
Hmph.
AWWW. THERE'S SOMETHING NOT QUITE SATISFYING ABOUT COMING TO THE ARCADE ALONE.
I'm suddenly brought back to reality.
That's right. You're wasting your precious adolescence.
THE FAINT AROMA OF A FRAGRANT FLORAL HAIR MOUSSE.
ふわっ
FWAH
A FORBIDDEN SAILOR UNIFORM. LONG, STRAIGHT HAIR.
OH! ♡ ONIISAN!
I need to get some change!
A HIGH-PITCHED VOICE.
THOSE THINGS DON'T BELONG HERE!
SINCE TIME IMMEMORIAL, THE VIDEO GAME ARCADE HAS BEEN A BASTION OF SOLACE FOR SOLITARY MEN WHO HAVE NO HOPE OF FORMING REAL RELATIONSHIPS.

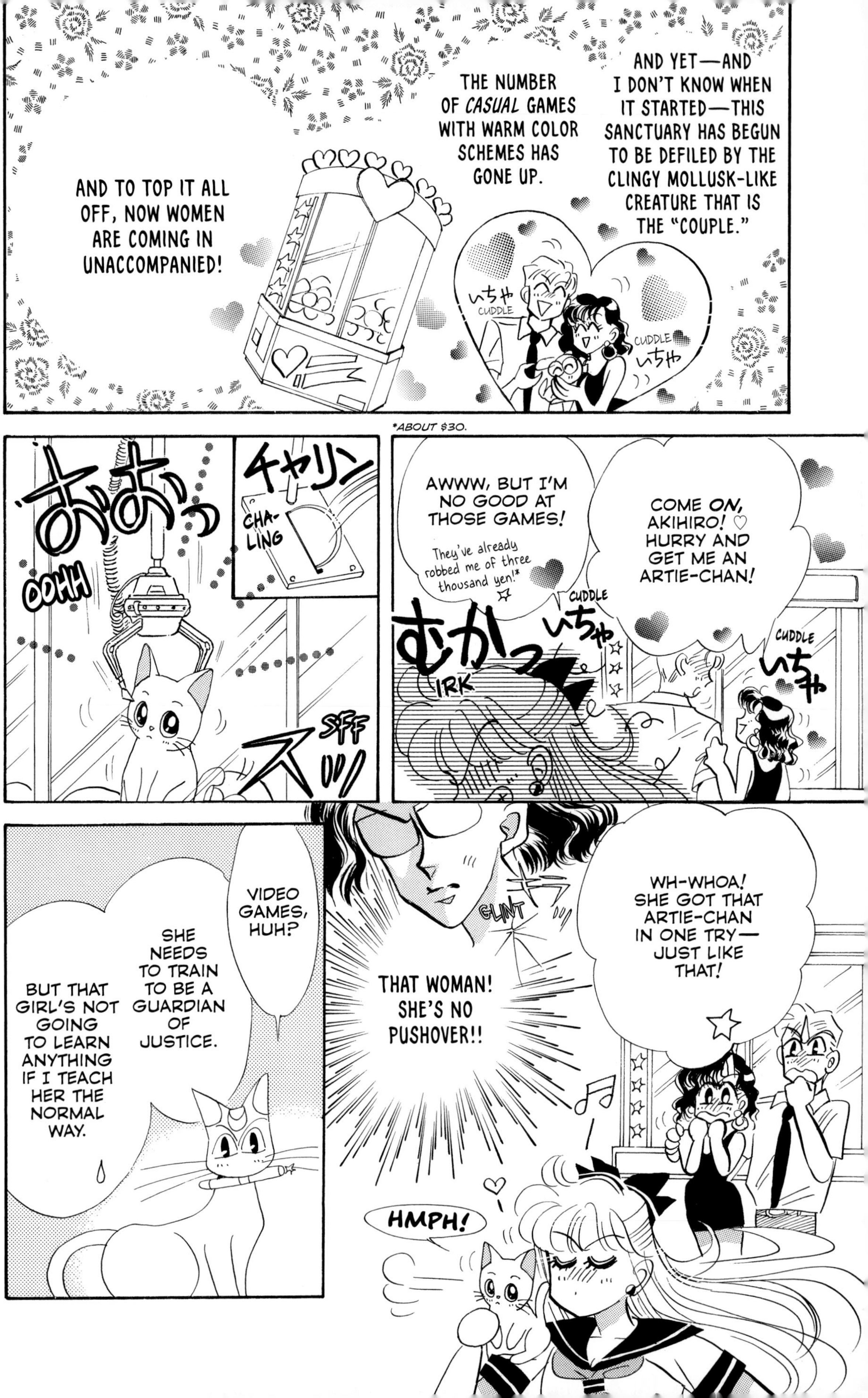
AND YET—AND I DON'T KNOW WHEN IT STARTED—THIS SANCTUARY HAS BEGUN TO BE DEFILED BY THE CLINGY MOLLUSK-LIKE CREATURE THAT IS THE "COUPLE."
THE NUMBER OF *CASUAL* GAMES WITH WARM COLOR SCHEMES HAS GONE UP.
いちゃ CUDDLE
CUDDLE いちゃ
AND TO TOP IT ALL OFF, NOW WOMEN ARE COMING IN UNACCOMPANIED!
COME *ON*, AKIHIRO! ♡ HURRY AND GET ME AN ARTIE-CHAN!
CUDDLE いちゃ
AWWW, BUT I'M NO GOOD AT THOSE GAMES!
They've already robbed me of three thousand yen!*
CUDDLE いちゃ
むかっ IRK
チャリン CHA-LING
おおっ OOHH
ス SFF
WH-WHOA! SHE GOT THAT ARTIE-CHAN IN ONE TRY—JUST LIKE THAT!
HMPH!
キラ GLINT
THAT WOMAN! SHE'S NO PUSHOVER!!
VIDEO GAMES, HUH?
SHE NEEDS TO TRAIN TO BE A GUARDIAN OF JUSTICE.
BUT THAT GIRL'S NOT GOING TO LEARN ANYTHING IF I TEACH HER THE NORMAL WAY.

*ABOUT $30.

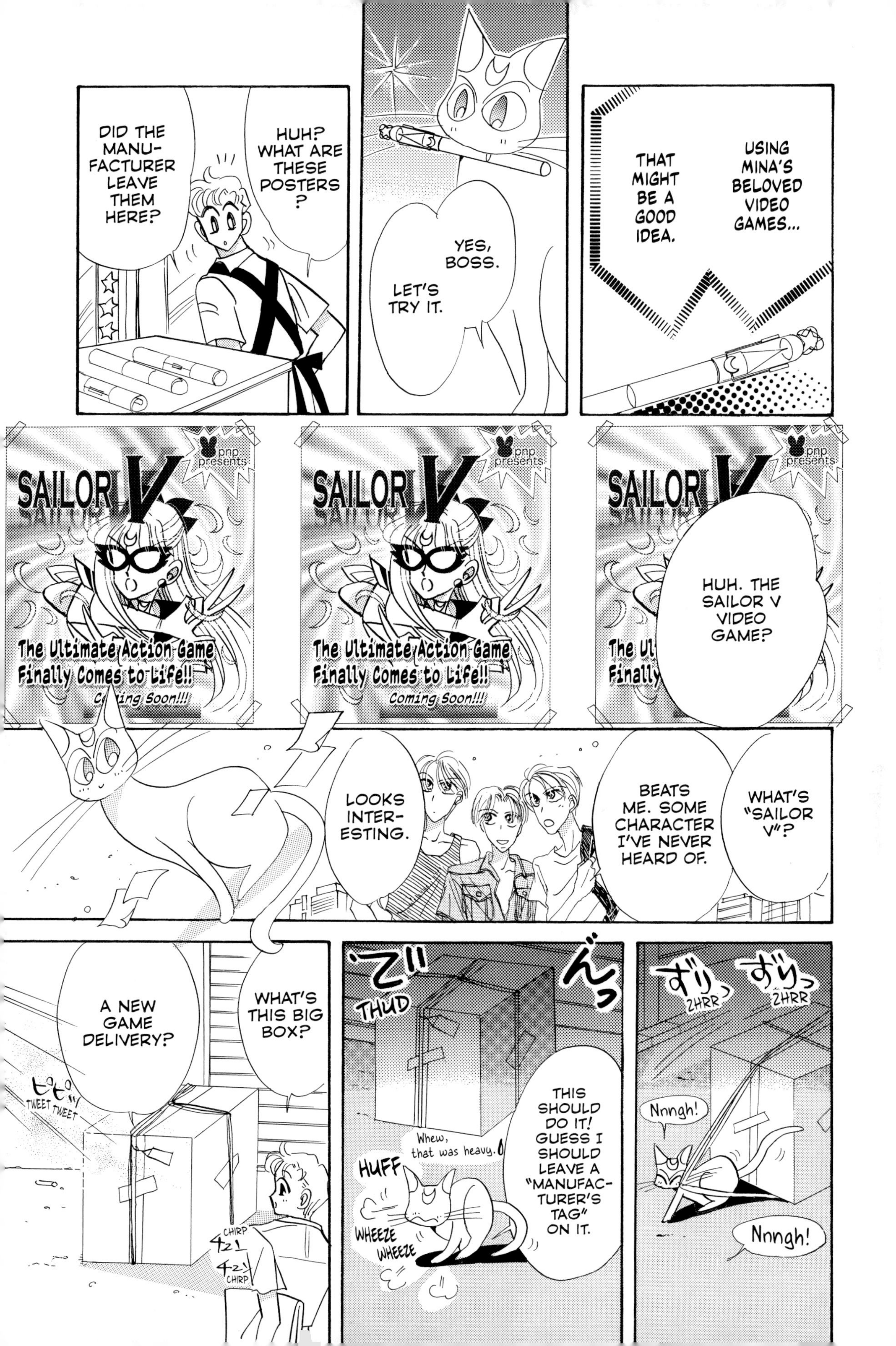
USING MINA'S BELOVED VIDEO GAMES...
THAT MIGHT BE A GOOD IDEA.
YES, BOSS.
LET'S TRY IT.
HUH? WHAT ARE THESE POSTERS?
DID THE MANUFACTURER LEAVE THEM HERE?
pnp presents
SAILOR V
HUH. THE SAILOR V VIDEO GAME?
The Ultimate Action Game Finally Comes to Life!!
Coming Soon!!!
WHAT'S "SAILOR V"?
BEATS ME. SOME CHARACTER I'VE NEVER HEARD OF.
LOOKS INTERESTING.
ずりっ ZHRR
ずりっ ZHRR
Nnngh!
Nnngh!
でんっ THUD
THIS SHOULD DO IT! GUESS I SHOULD LEAVE A "MANUFACTURER'S TAG" ON IT.
Whew, that was heavy.
HUFF
WHEEZE WHEEZE
WHAT'S THIS BIG BOX?
A NEW GAME DELIVERY?
TWEET TWEET
CHIRP CHIRP

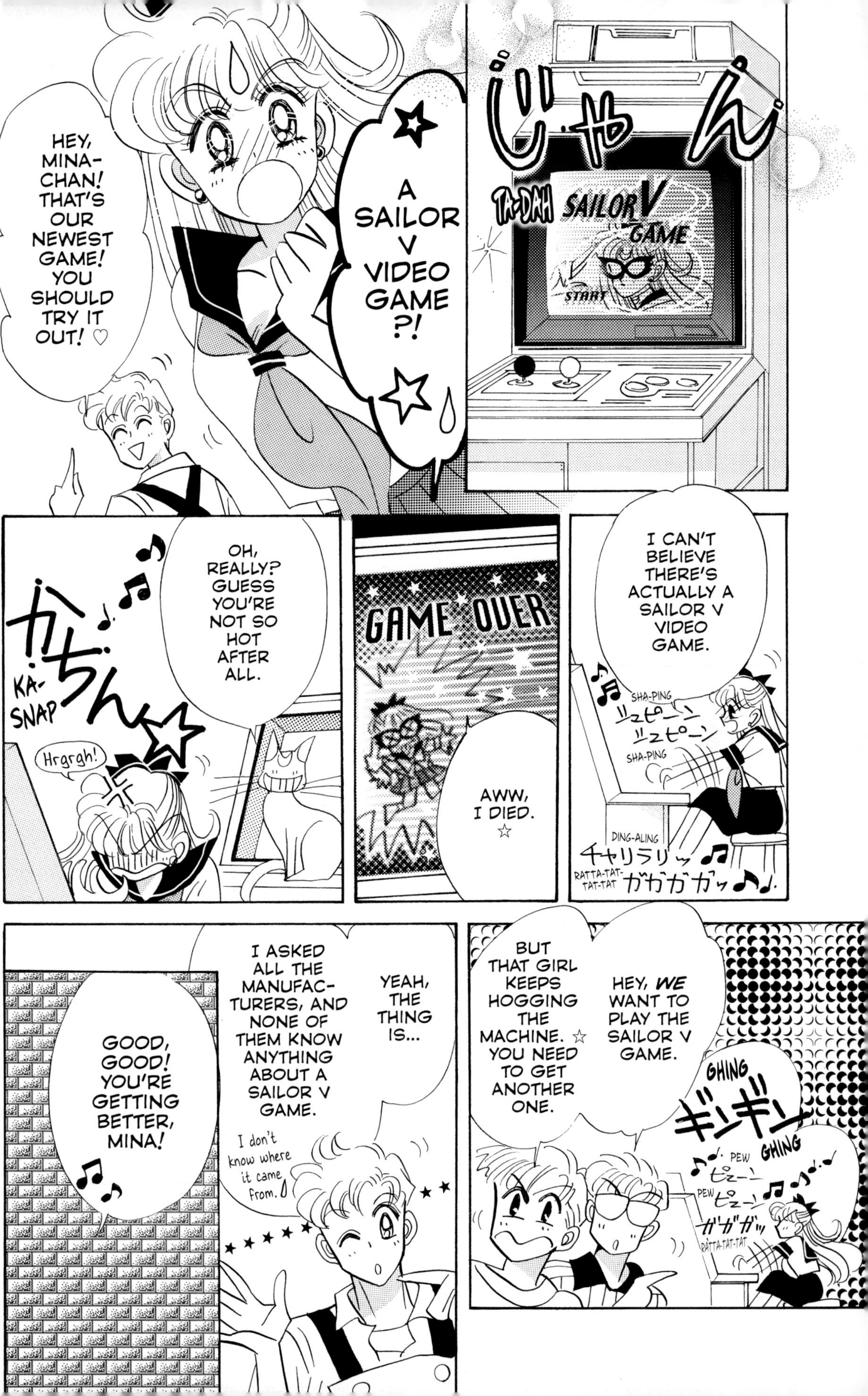
じゃん
TA-DAH
SAILOR V GAME
START
A SAILOR V VIDEO GAME?!
HEY, MINA-CHAN! THAT'S OUR NEWEST GAME! YOU SHOULD TRY IT OUT! ♡
I CAN'T BELIEVE THERE'S ACTUALLY A SAILOR V VIDEO GAME.
SHA-PING
ジュピーン ジュピーン
SHA-PING
DING-ALING
チャリラリッ
RATTA-TAT-TAT-TAT
ガガガガッ
GAME OVER
AWW, I DIED. ☆
OH, REALLY? GUESS YOU'RE NOT SO HOT AFTER ALL.
かちん
KA-SNAP
Hrgrgh!
HEY, WE WANT TO PLAY THE SAILOR V GAME.
BUT THAT GIRL KEEPS HOGGING THE MACHINE. ☆ YOU NEED TO GET ANOTHER ONE.
GHING
ギンギン
GHING
PEW
ピューン
PEW
ピューン
ガガガッ
RATTA-TAT-TAT
YEAH, THE THING IS...
I ASKED ALL THE MANUFAC-TURERS, AND NONE OF THEM KNOW ANYTHING ABOUT A SAILOR V GAME.
I don't know where it came from.
GOOD, GOOD! YOU'RE GETTING BETTER, MINA!

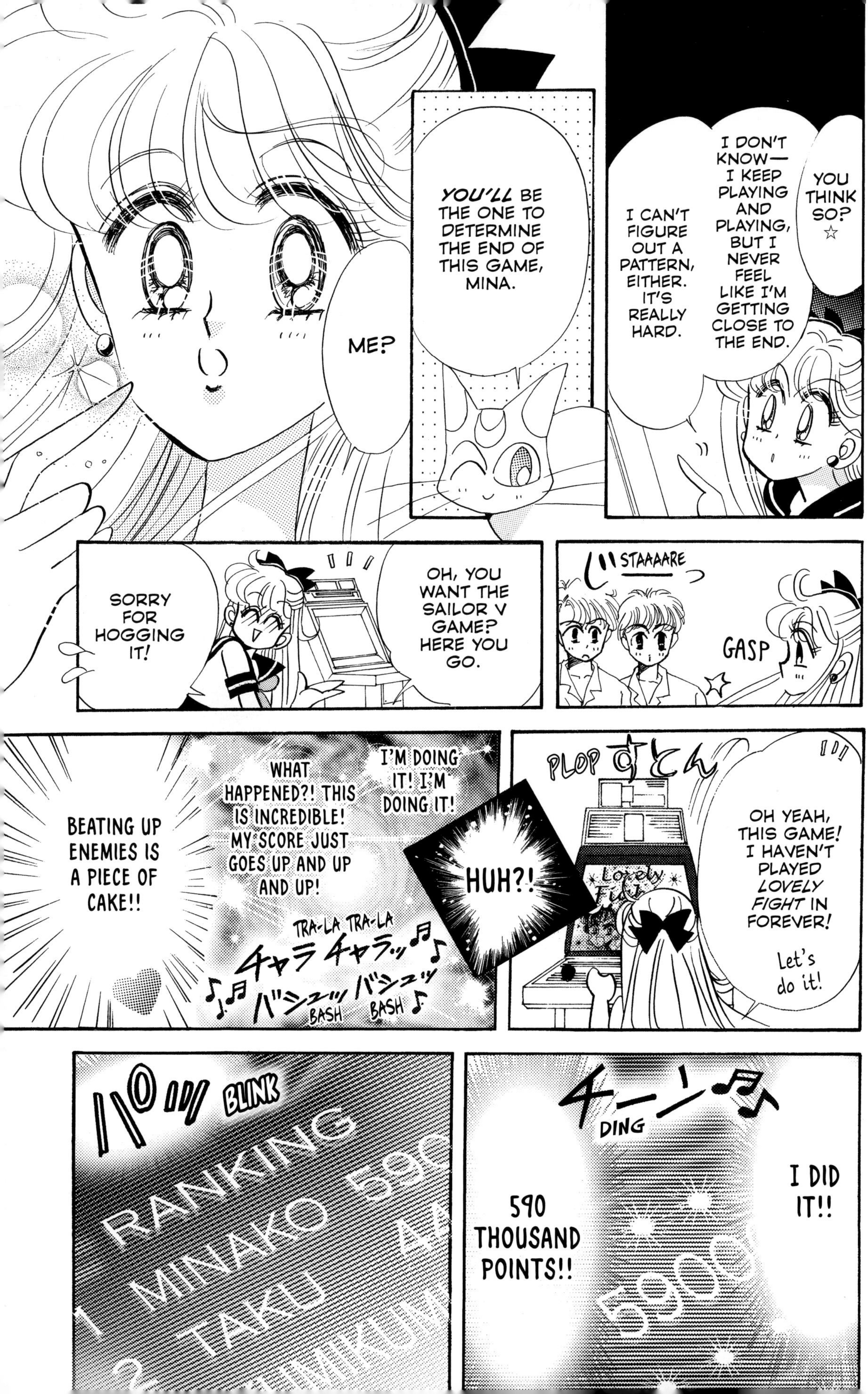
YOU THINK SO? ☆
I DON'T KNOW— I KEEP PLAYING AND PLAYING, BUT I NEVER FEEL LIKE I'M GETTING CLOSE TO THE END.
I CAN'T FIGURE OUT A PATTERN, EITHER. IT'S REALLY HARD.
YOU'LL BE THE ONE TO DETERMINE THE END OF THIS GAME, MINA.
ME?
STAAAARE
GASP
OH, YOU WANT THE SAILOR V GAME? HERE YOU GO.
SORRY FOR HOGGING IT!
PLOP すとん
OH YEAH, THIS GAME! I HAVEN'T PLAYED *LOVELY FIGHT* IN FOREVER!
Let's do it!
HUH?!
I'M DOING IT! I'M DOING IT!
WHAT HAPPENED?! THIS IS INCREDIBLE! MY SCORE JUST GOES UP AND UP AND UP!
TRA-LA TRA-LA
チャラ チャラッ
バシュッ バシュッ
BASH BASH
BEATING UP ENEMIES IS A PIECE OF CAKE!!
チーン
DING
I DID IT!!
590 THOUSAND POINTS!!
パッ
BLINK
RANKING
1 MINAKO 590
TAKU

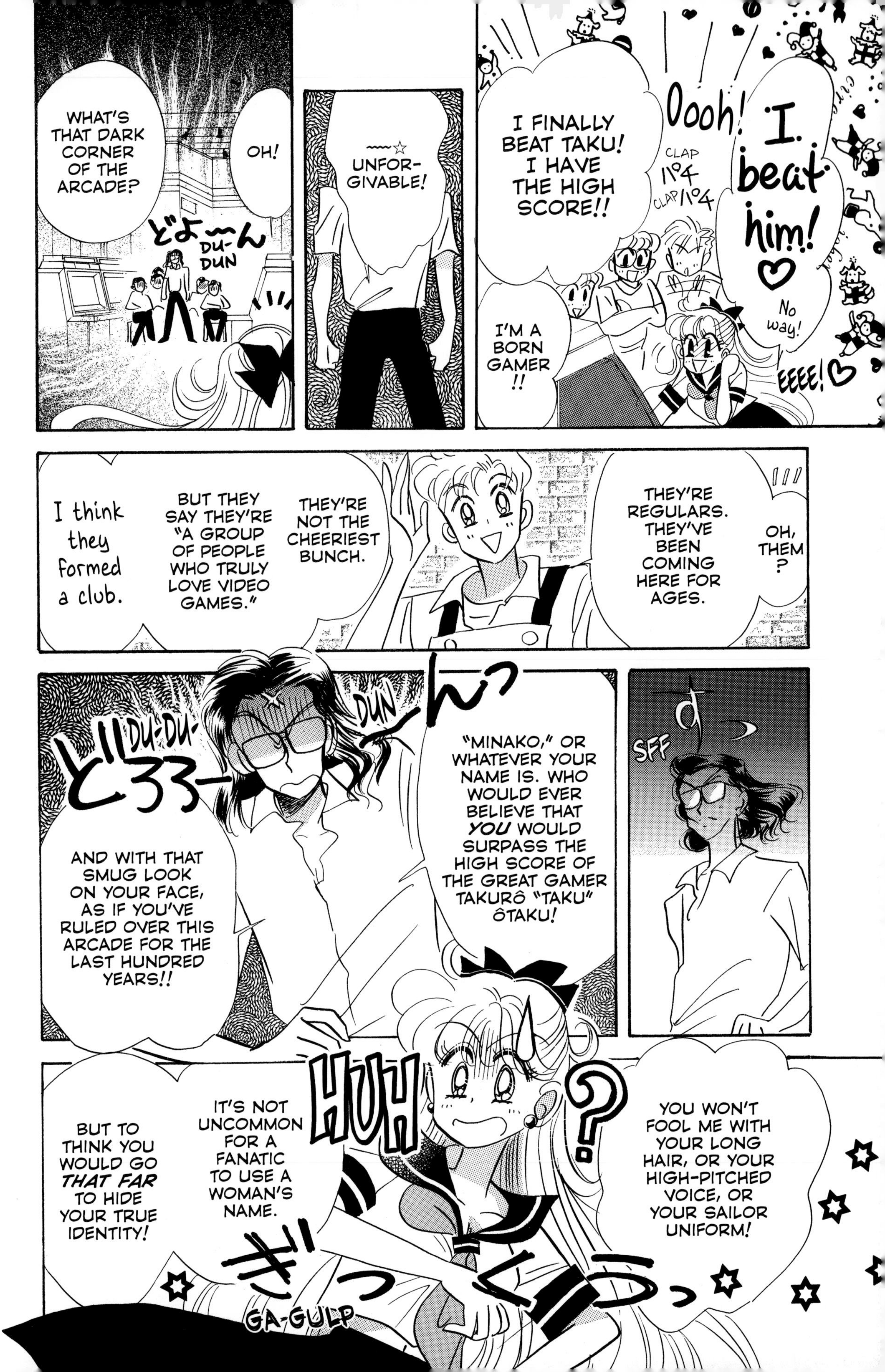
I. beat him! ♡
Oooh!
CLAP パチ CLAP パチ
I FINALLY BEAT TAKU! I HAVE THE HIGH SCORE!!
No way!
EEEE! ♡
I'M A BORN GAMER!!
~~~☆ UNFORGIVABLE!
OH!
WHAT'S THAT DARK CORNER OF THE ARCADE?
どよ〜ん DU-DUN
OH, THEM?
THEY'RE REGULARS. THEY'VE BEEN COMING HERE FOR AGES.
THEY'RE NOT THE CHEERIEST BUNCH.
BUT THEY SAY THEY'RE "A GROUP OF PEOPLE WHO TRULY LOVE VIDEO GAMES."
I think they formed a club.
すっ SFF
DU-DU-DUN
"MINAKO," OR WHATEVER YOUR NAME IS. WHO WOULD EVER BELIEVE THAT *YOU* WOULD SURPASS THE HIGH SCORE OF THE GREAT GAMER TAKURÔ "TAKU" ÔTAKU!
AND WITH THAT SMUG LOOK ON YOUR FACE, AS IF YOU'VE RULED OVER THIS ARCADE FOR THE LAST HUNDRED YEARS!!
YOU WON'T FOOL ME WITH YOUR LONG HAIR, OR YOUR HIGH-PITCHED VOICE, OR YOUR SAILOR UNIFORM!
HUH?
IT'S NOT UNCOMMON FOR A FANATIC TO USE A WOMAN'S NAME.
BUT TO THINK YOU WOULD GO *THAT FAR* TO HIDE YOUR TRUE IDENTITY!
GA-GULP
~~~

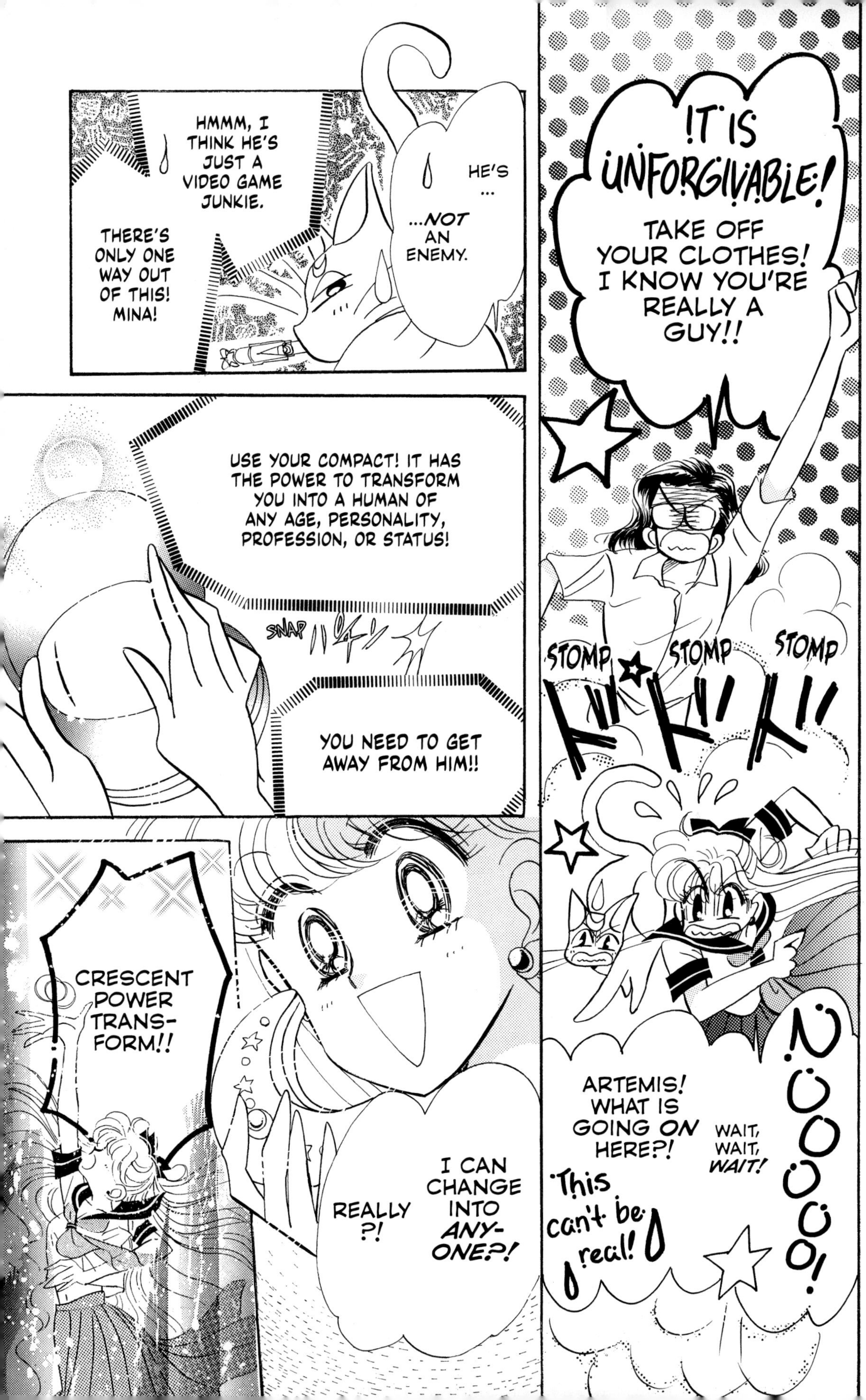
IT IS UNFORGIVABLE!
TAKE OFF YOUR CLOTHES! I KNOW YOU'RE REALLY A GUY!!
STOMP
STOMP
STOMP
NOOOOO!
WAIT, WAIT, WAIT!
ARTEMIS! WHAT IS GOING ON HERE?!
This can't be real!
HE'S ...
...NOT AN ENEMY.
HMMM, I THINK HE'S JUST A VIDEO GAME JUNKIE.
THERE'S ONLY ONE WAY OUT OF THIS! MINA!
USE YOUR COMPACT! IT HAS THE POWER TO TRANSFORM YOU INTO A HUMAN OF ANY AGE, PERSONALITY, PROFESSION, OR STATUS!
SNAP
YOU NEED TO GET AWAY FROM HIM!!
I CAN CHANGE INTO ANY-ONE?!
REALLY?!
CRESCENT POWER TRANS-FORM!!

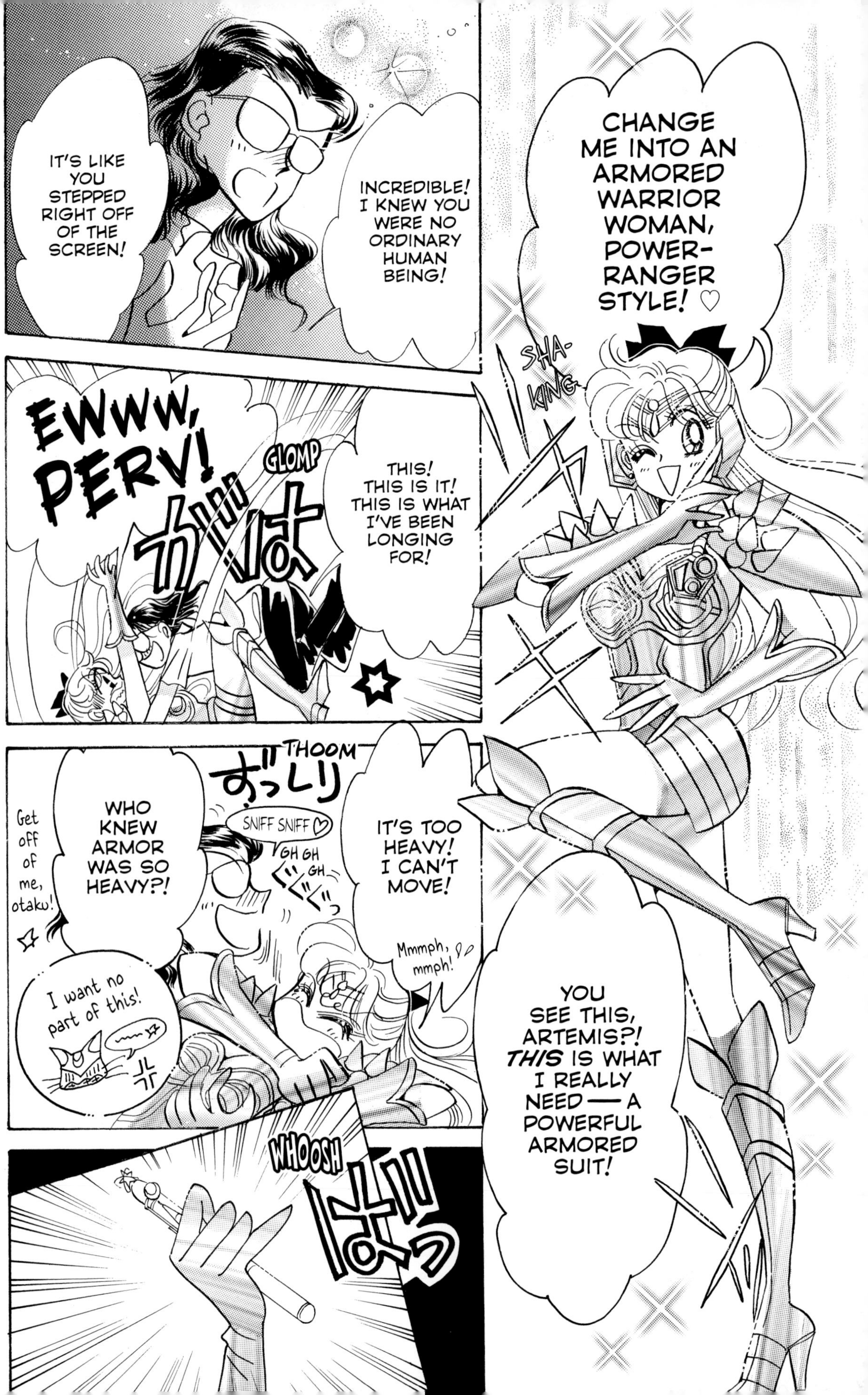
CHANGE ME INTO AN ARMORED WARRIOR WOMAN, POWER-RANGER STYLE! ♡
SHA-KING
YOU SEE THIS, ARTEMIS?! THIS IS WHAT I REALLY NEED — A POWERFUL ARMORED SUIT!
INCREDIBLE! I KNEW YOU WERE NO ORDINARY HUMAN BEING!
IT'S LIKE YOU STEPPED RIGHT OFF OF THE SCREEN!
THIS! THIS IS IT! THIS IS WHAT I'VE BEEN LONGING FOR!
GLOMP
がばっ
EWWW, PERV!
IT'S TOO HEAVY! I CAN'T MOVE!
THOOM
ずっしり
SNIFF SNIFF ♡
GH GH GH
ぐぐぐっ
Mmmph, mmph!
WHO KNEW ARMOR WAS SO HEAVY?!
Get off of me, otaku!
I want no part of this!
WHOOSH
ばっ

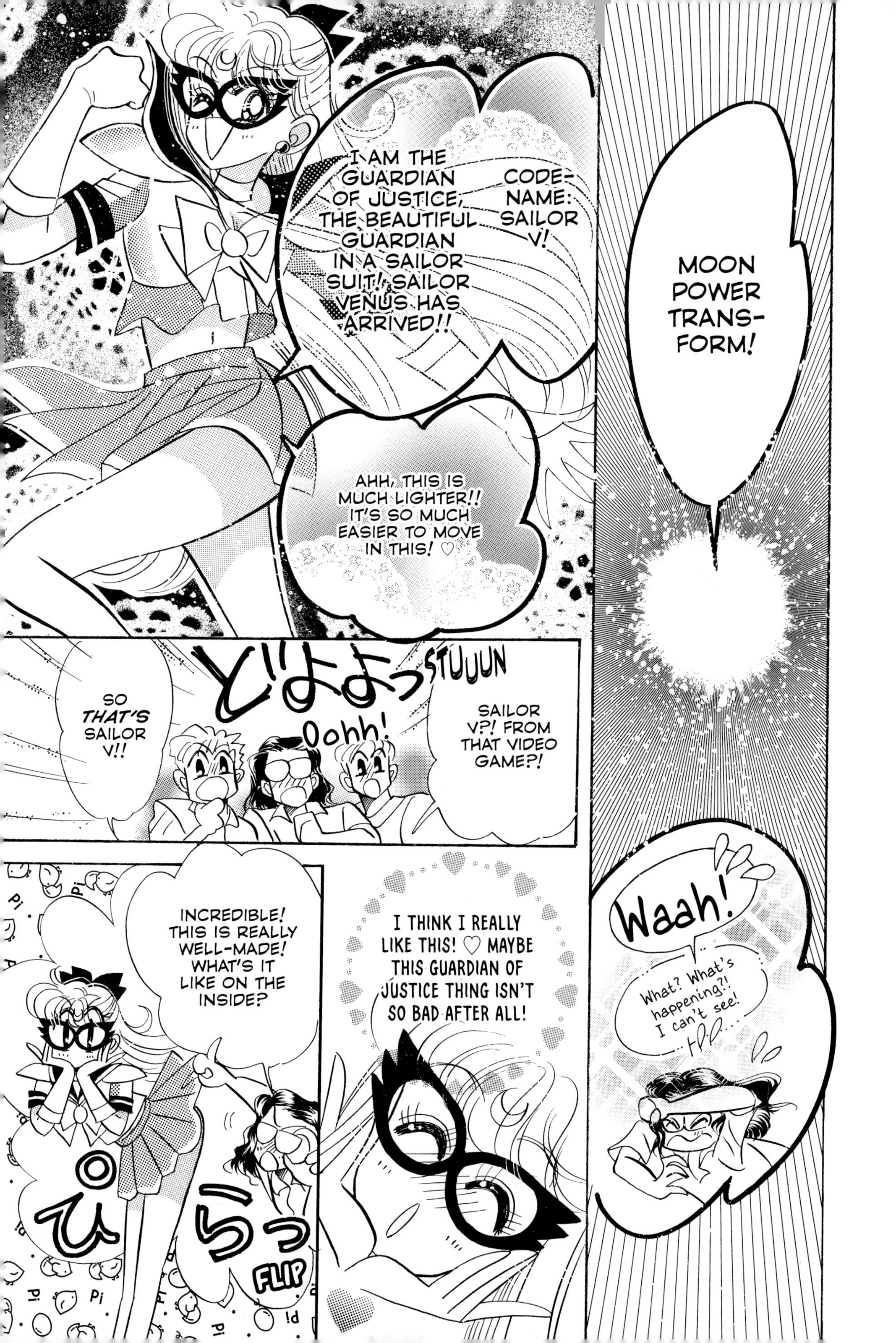
MOON POWER TRANSFORM!
I AM THE GUARDIAN OF JUSTICE, THE BEAUTIFUL GUARDIAN IN A SAILOR SUIT! SAILOR VENUS HAS ARRIVED!! CODE-NAME: SAILOR V!
AHH, THIS IS MUCH LIGHTER!! IT'S SO MUCH EASIER TO MOVE IN THIS! ♡
どよよっ STUUUN
SAILOR V?! FROM THAT VIDEO GAME?!
Oohh!
SO *THAT'S* SAILOR V!!
Waah!
What? What's happening?! I can't see!
I THINK I REALLY LIKE THIS! ♡ MAYBE THIS GUARDIAN OF JUSTICE THING ISN'T SO BAD AFTER ALL!
INCREDIBLE! THIS IS REALLY WELL-MADE! WHAT'S IT LIKE ON THE INSIDE?
ぴらっ FLIP
Pi

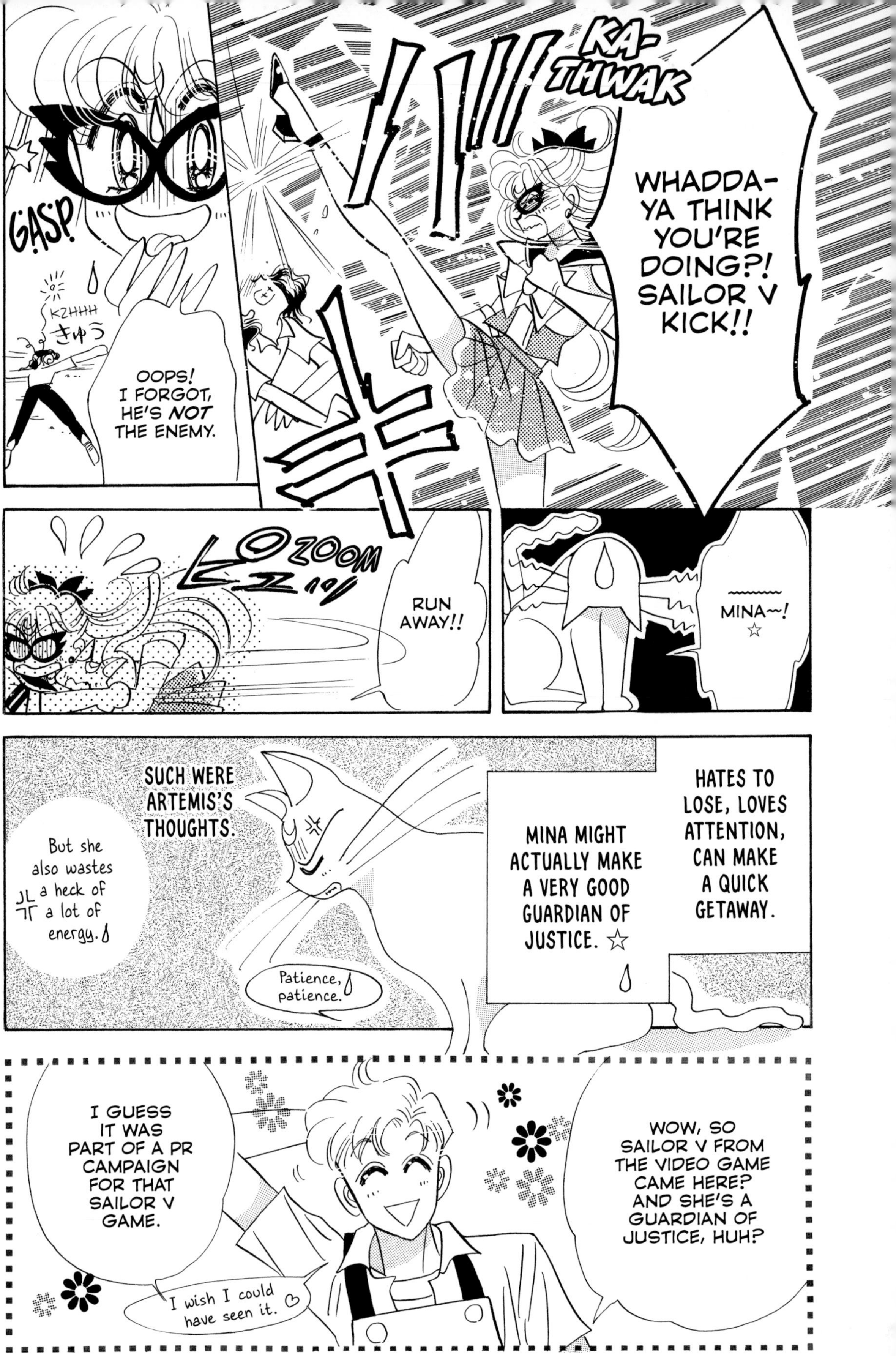
KA-THWAK
WHADDA-YA THINK YOU'RE DOING?! SAILOR V KICK!!
GASP
KZHHH
OOPS! I FORGOT, HE'S *NOT* THE ENEMY.
MINA~! ☆
ZOOM
RUN AWAY!!
HATES TO LOSE, LOVES ATTENTION, CAN MAKE A QUICK GETAWAY.
MINA MIGHT ACTUALLY MAKE A VERY GOOD GUARDIAN OF JUSTICE. ☆
SUCH WERE ARTEMIS'S THOUGHTS.
But she also wastes a heck of a lot of energy.
Patience, patience.
WOW, SO SAILOR V FROM THE VIDEO GAME CAME HERE? AND SHE'S A GUARDIAN OF JUSTICE, HUH?
I GUESS IT WAS PART OF A PR CAMPAIGN FOR THAT SAILOR V GAME.
I wish I could have seen it. ♡

Sailor V's Big Debut!
Channel 44: Pandora's Ambition

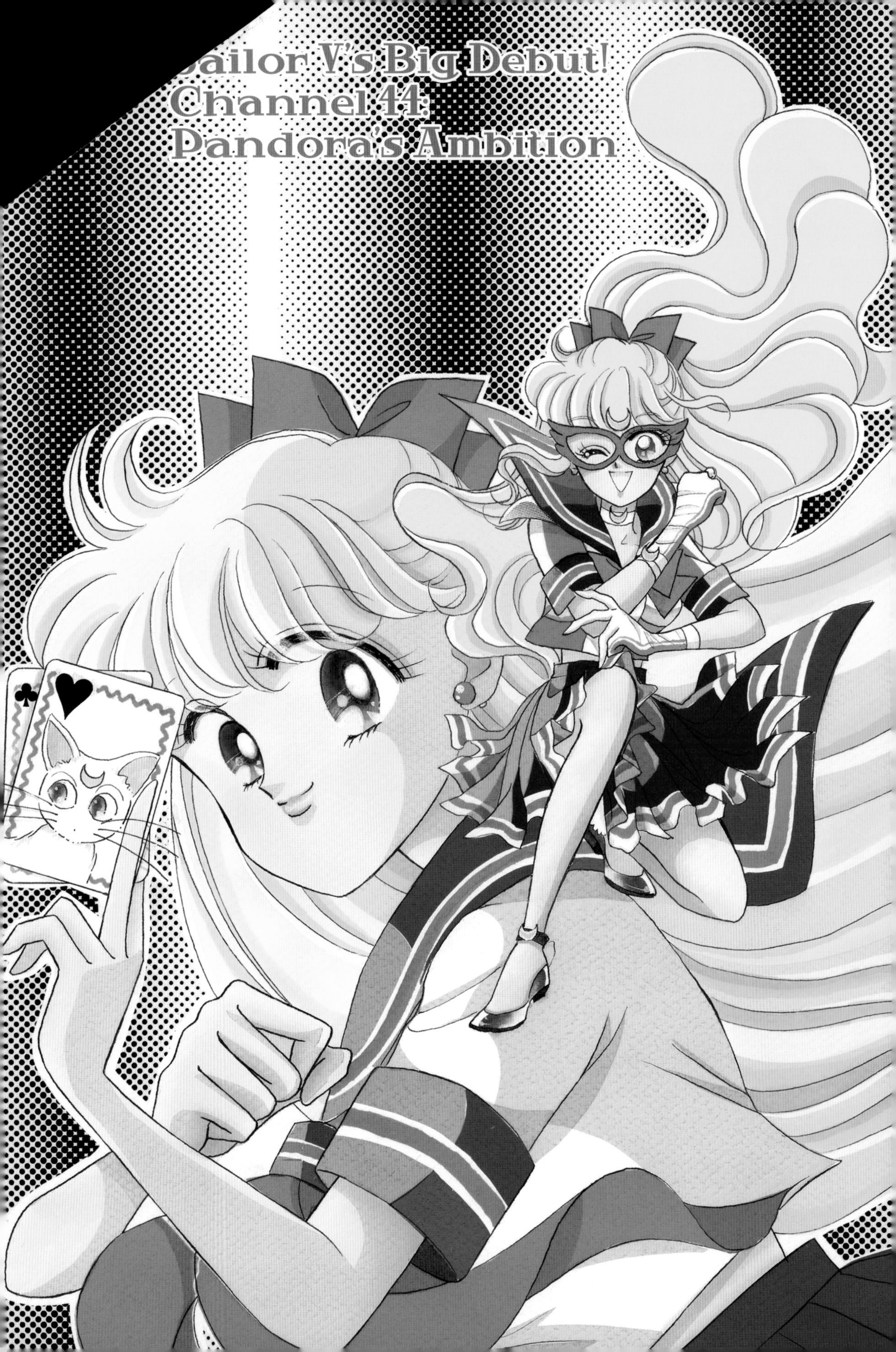

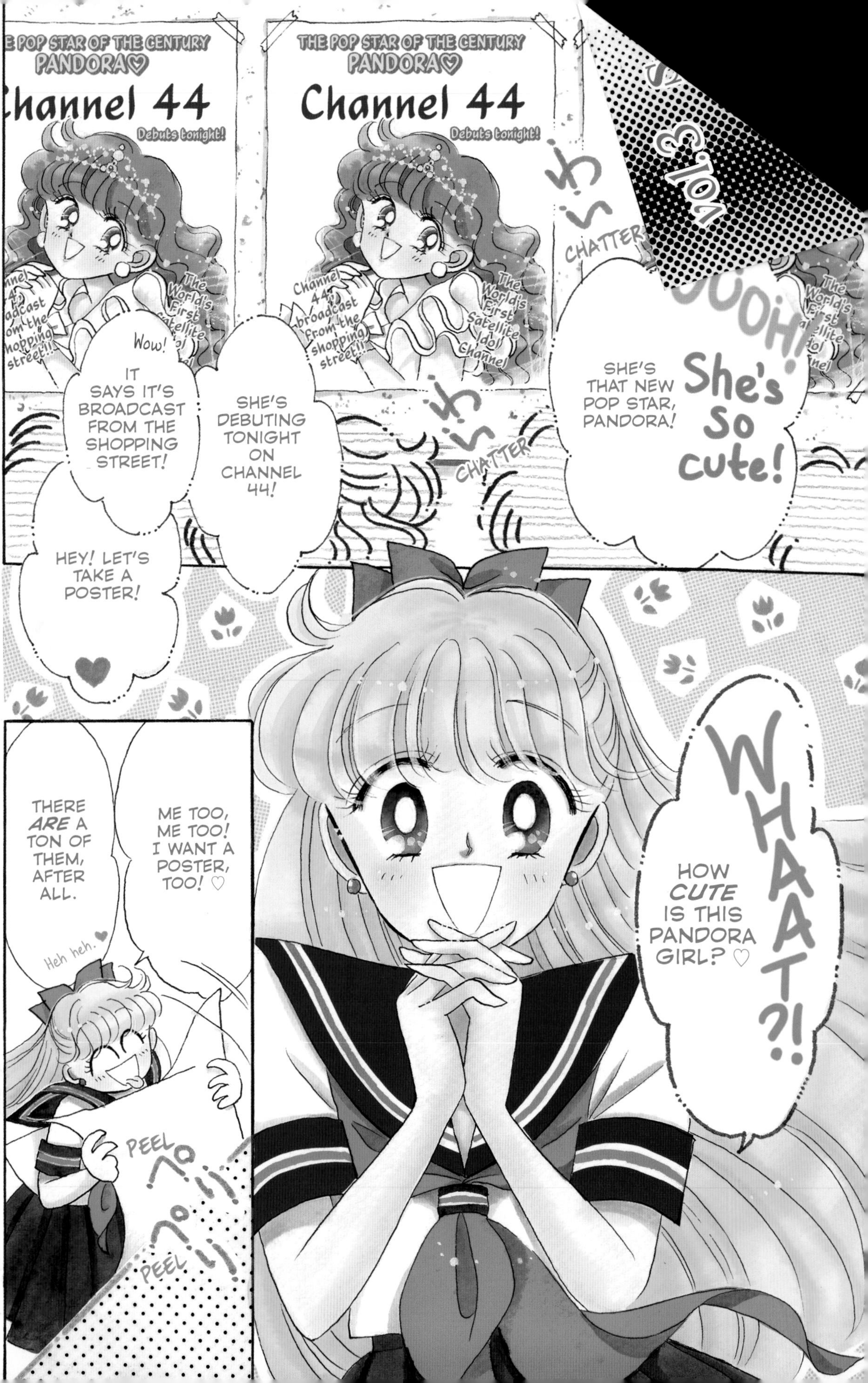
Vol. 3
OOOH!
She's so cute!
SHE'S THAT NEW POP STAR, PANDORA!
CHATTER
THE POP STAR OF THE CENTURY
PANDORA♡
Channel 44
Debuts tonight!
The World's First Satellite Idol Channel
Channel 44 broadcast from the shopping street!!
CHATTER
SHE'S DEBUTING TONIGHT ON CHANNEL 44!
Wow!
IT SAYS IT'S BROADCAST FROM THE SHOPPING STREET!
HEY! LET'S TAKE A POSTER!
WHAAAT?!
HOW CUTE IS THIS PANDORA GIRL? ♡
ME TOO, ME TOO! I WANT A POSTER, TOO! ♡
THERE ARE A TON OF THEM, AFTER ALL.
Heh heh.
PEEL
PEEL

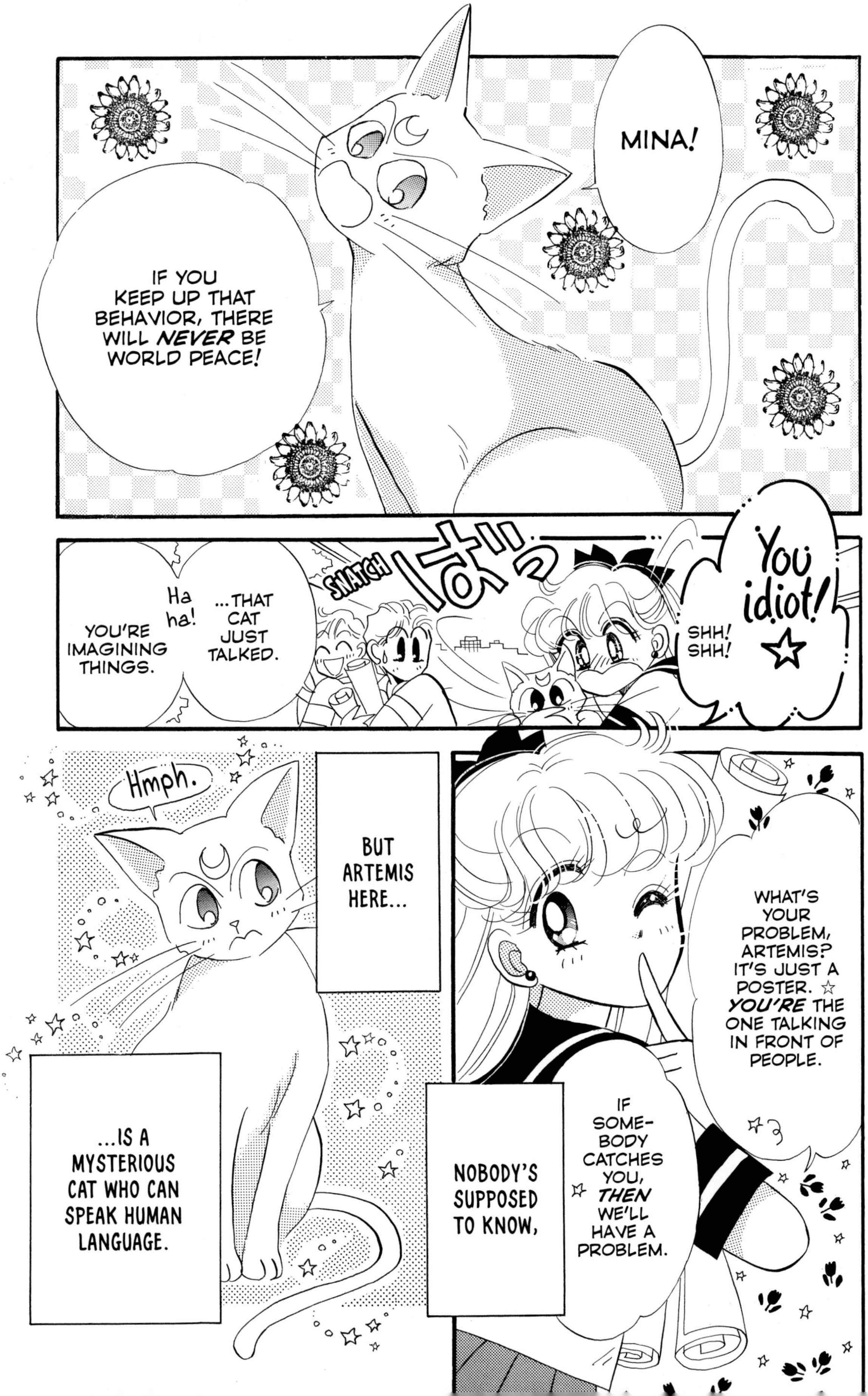
MINA!
IF YOU KEEP UP THAT BEHAVIOR, THERE WILL *NEVER* BE WORLD PEACE!
You idiot! ☆
SHH! SHH!
ばっ
SNATCH
...THAT CAT JUST TALKED.
Ha ha!
YOU'RE IMAGINING THINGS.
WHAT'S YOUR PROBLEM, ARTEMIS? IT'S JUST A POSTER. ☆ *YOU'RE* THE ONE TALKING IN FRONT OF PEOPLE.
IF SOMEBODY CATCHES YOU, *THEN* WE'LL HAVE A PROBLEM.
NOBODY'S SUPPOSED TO KNOW,
BUT ARTEMIS HERE...
Hmph.
...IS A MYSTERIOUS CAT WHO CAN SPEAK HUMAN LANGUAGE.

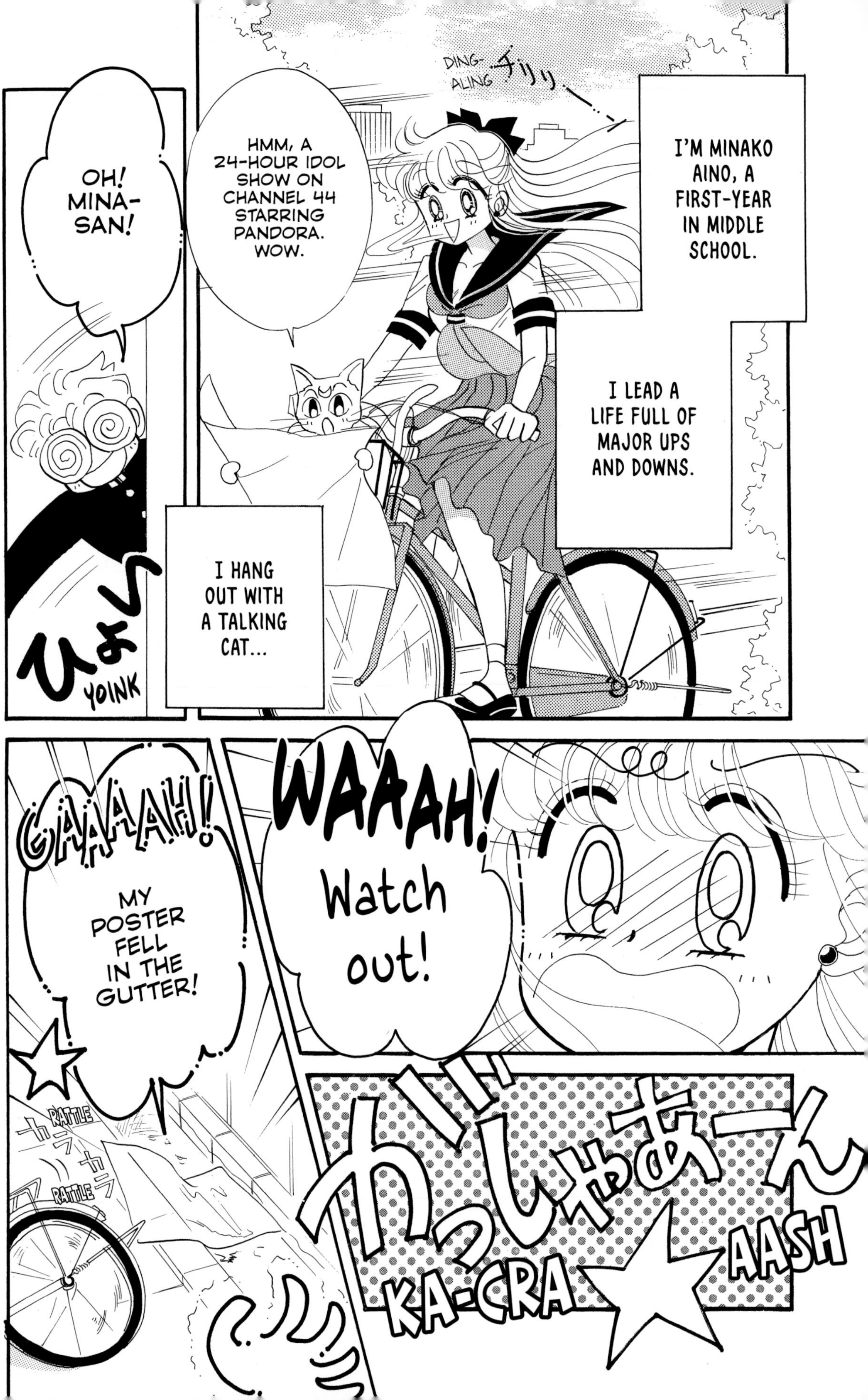
DING-ALING チリリ
I'M MINAKO AINO, A FIRST-YEAR IN MIDDLE SCHOOL.
HMM, A 24-HOUR IDOL SHOW ON CHANNEL 44 STARRING PANDORA. WOW.
I LEAD A LIFE FULL OF MAJOR UPS AND DOWNS.
I HANG OUT WITH A TALKING CAT...
OH! MINA-SAN!
ひょい YOINK
WAAAH! Watch out!
かっしゃあーん
KA-CRA★AASH
GAAAAH!
MY POSTER FELL IN THE GUTTER!
カラ RATTLE
カラ RATTLE

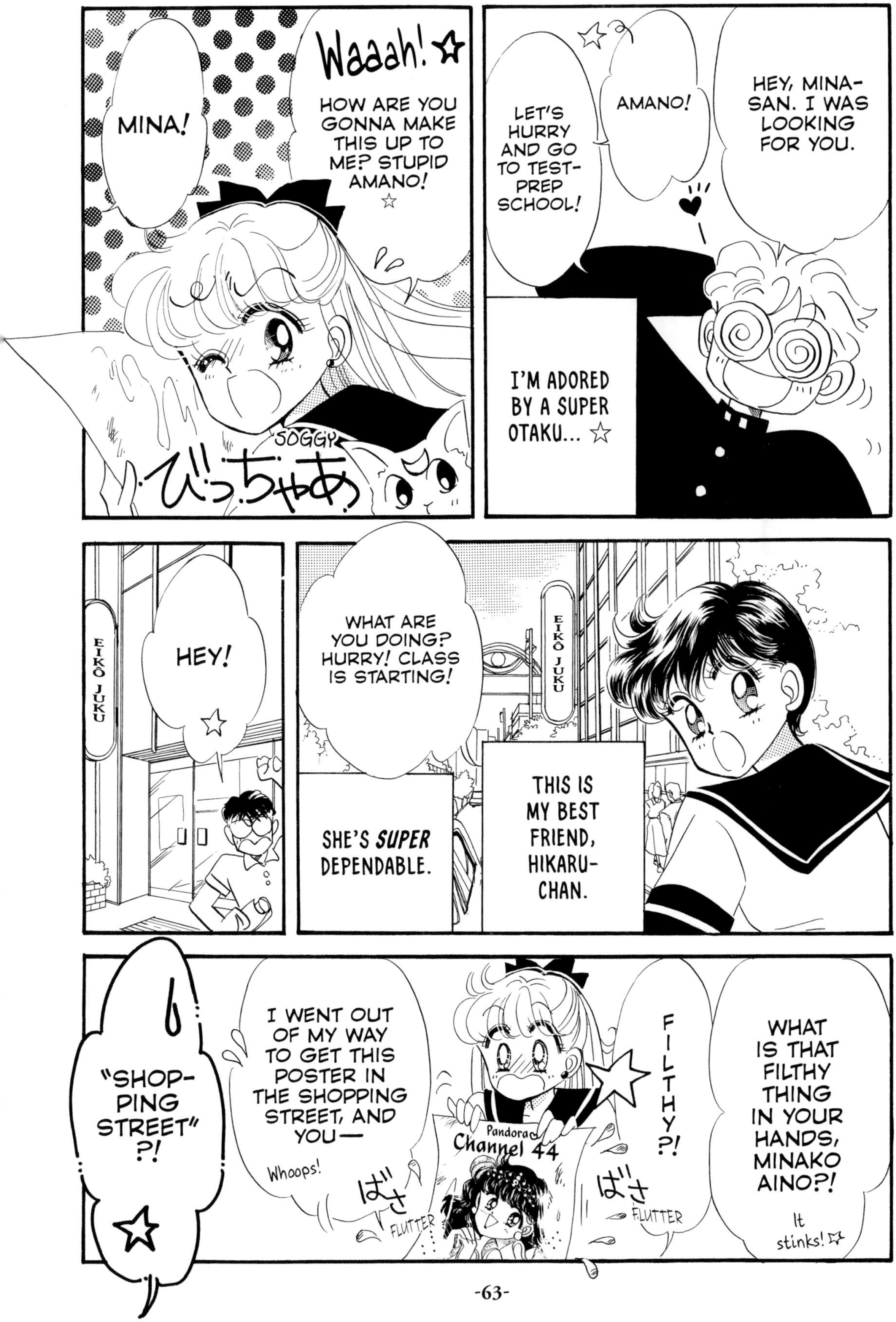

HEY, MINA-SAN. I WAS LOOKING FOR YOU.
AMANO!
LET'S HURRY AND GO TO TEST-PREP SCHOOL!
I'M ADORED BY A SUPER OTAKU... ☆
Waaah! ☆
HOW ARE YOU GONNA MAKE THIS UP TO ME? STUPID AMANO! ☆
MINA!
SOGGY
びっちゃあ
EIKÔ JUKU
THIS IS MY BEST FRIEND, HIKARU-CHAN.
WHAT ARE YOU DOING? HURRY! CLASS IS STARTING!
SHE'S *SUPER* DEPENDABLE.
EIKÔ JUKU
HEY! ☆
WHAT IS THAT FILTHY THING IN YOUR HANDS, MINAKO AINO?!
It stinks! ☆
FILTHY?!
ばさ
FLUTTER
Pandora
Channel 44
I WENT OUT OF MY WAY TO GET THIS POSTER IN THE SHOPPING STREET, AND YOU—
Whoops!
ばさ
FLUTTER
"SHOPPING STREET"?! ☆

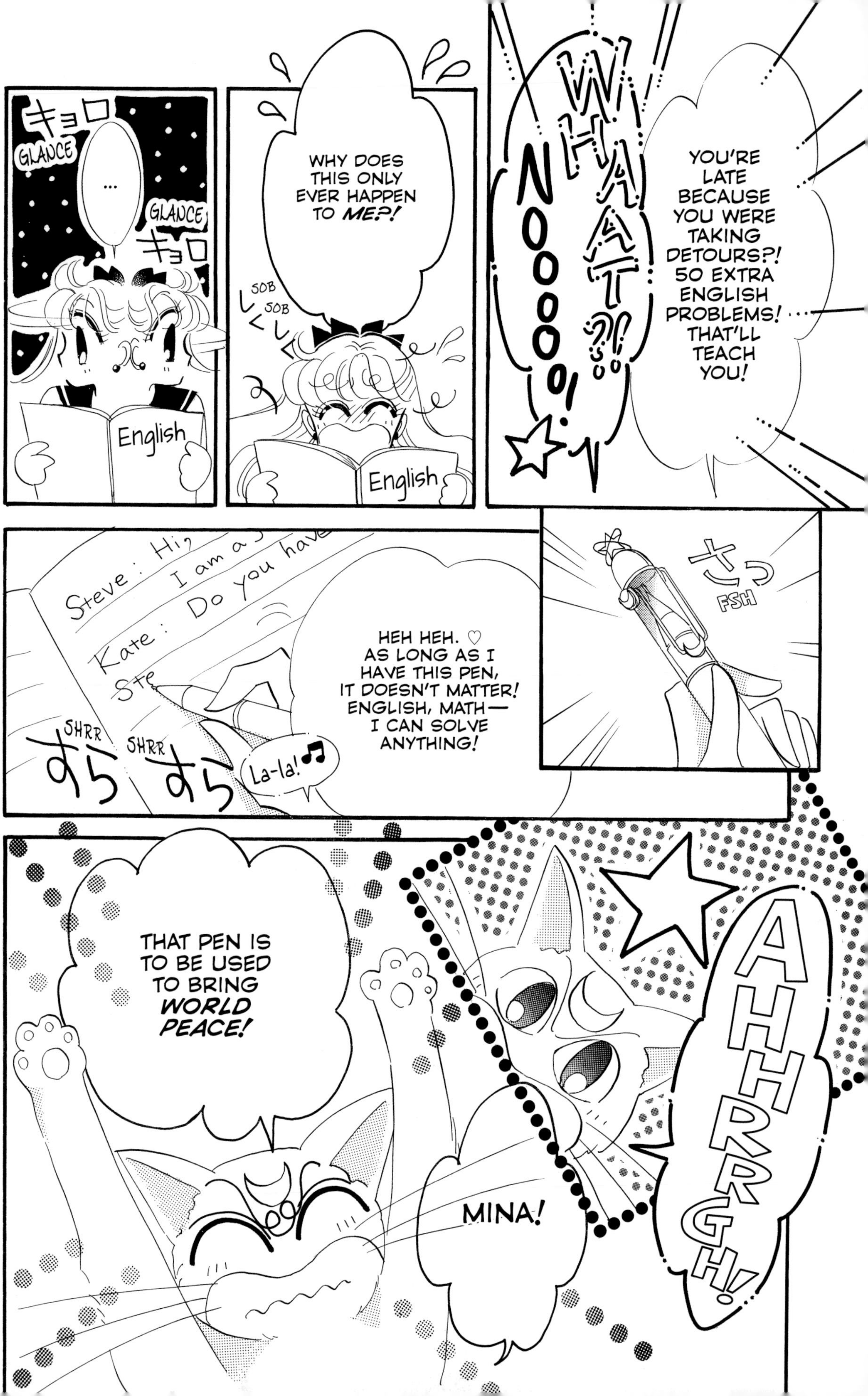
YOU'RE LATE BECAUSE YOU WERE TAKING DETOURS?! 50 EXTRA ENGLISH PROBLEMS! THAT'LL TEACH YOU!
WHAT?!
NOOOOO!
WHY DOES THIS ONLY EVER HAPPEN TO *ME?!*
しくしく
SOB SOB
English
キョロ
GLANCE
...
キョロ
GLANCE
English
さっ
FSH
HEH HEH. ♡ AS LONG AS I HAVE THIS PEN, IT DOESN'T MATTER! ENGLISH, MATH— I CAN SOLVE ANYTHING!
Steve: Hi,
I am a
Kate: Do you have
Ste
La-la!♫
すら
SHRR
すら
SHRR
AHHHRRGH!
MINA!
THAT PEN IS TO BE USED TO BRING *WORLD PEACE!*

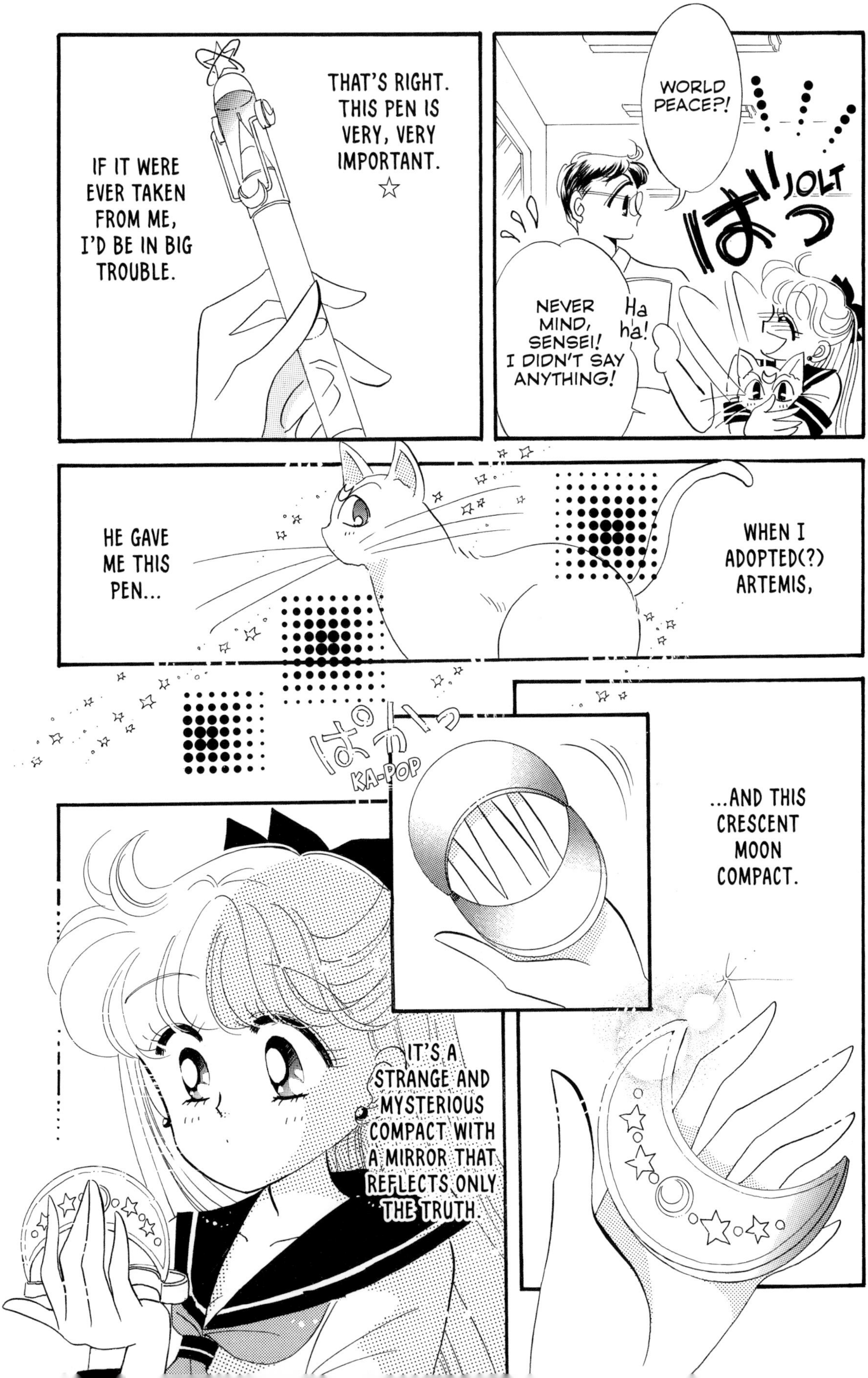
WORLD PEACE?!
はっ
JOLT
NEVER MIND, SENSEI! I DIDN'T SAY ANYTHING!
Ha ha!
THAT'S RIGHT. THIS PEN IS VERY, VERY IMPORTANT. ☆
IF IT WERE EVER TAKEN FROM ME, I'D BE IN BIG TROUBLE.
WHEN I ADOPTED(?) ARTEMIS,
HE GAVE ME THIS PEN...
...AND THIS CRESCENT MOON COMPACT.
ぱかっ
KA-POP
IT'S A STRANGE AND MYSTERIOUS COMPACT WITH A MIRROR THAT REFLECTS ONLY THE TRUTH.

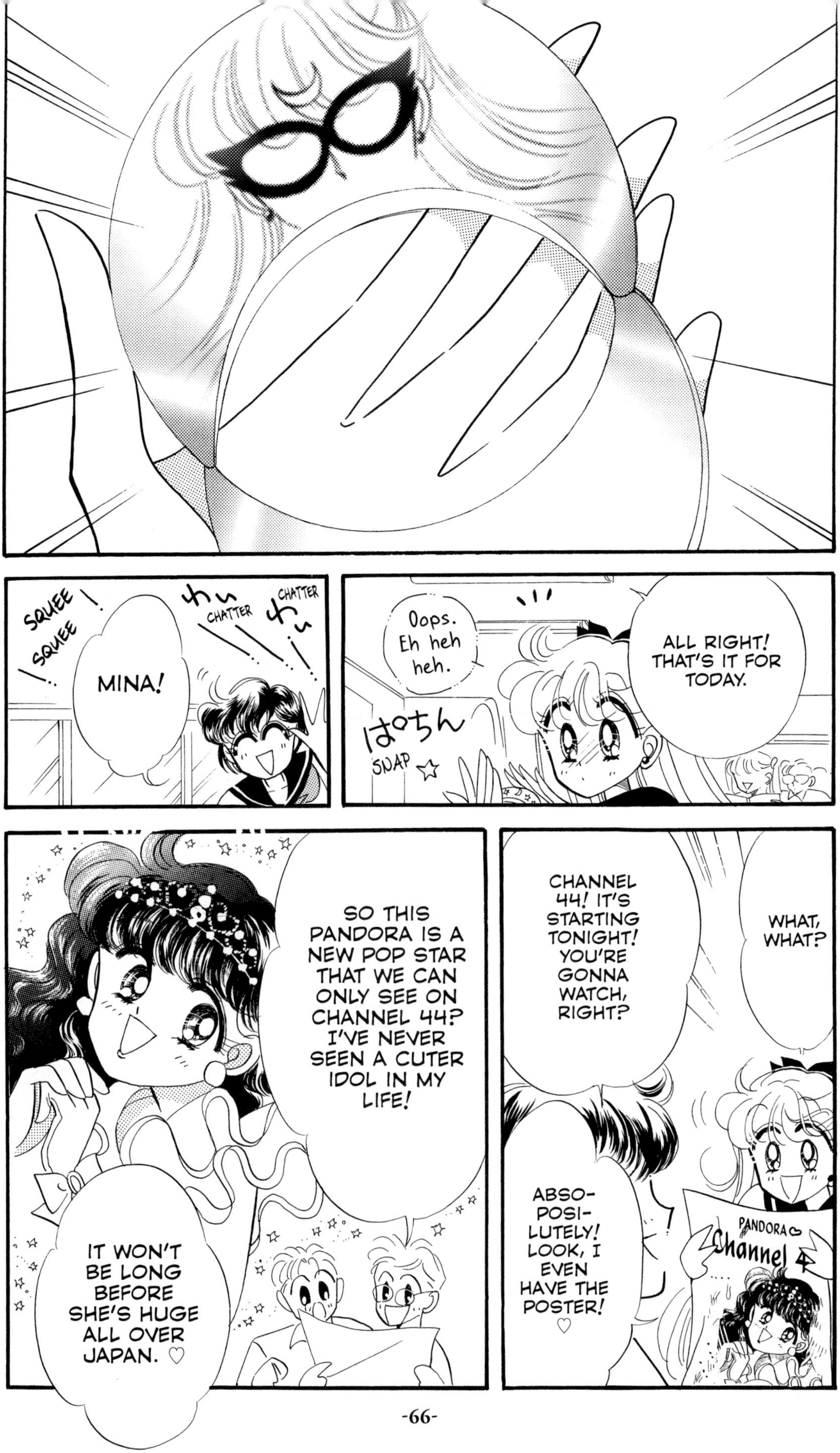
ALL RIGHT! THAT'S IT FOR TODAY.
ぱちん SNAP
Oops. Eh heh heh.
わい CHATTER わい CHATTER
MINA!
SQUEE SQUEE
WHAT, WHAT?
CHANNEL 44! IT'S STARTING TONIGHT! YOU'RE GONNA WATCH, RIGHT?
ABSO-POSI-LUTELY! LOOK, I EVEN HAVE THE POSTER! ♡
PANDORA Channel 4
SO THIS PANDORA IS A NEW POP STAR THAT WE CAN ONLY SEE ON CHANNEL 44? I'VE NEVER SEEN A CUTER IDOL IN MY LIFE!
IT WON'T BE LONG BEFORE SHE'S HUGE ALL OVER JAPAN. ♡

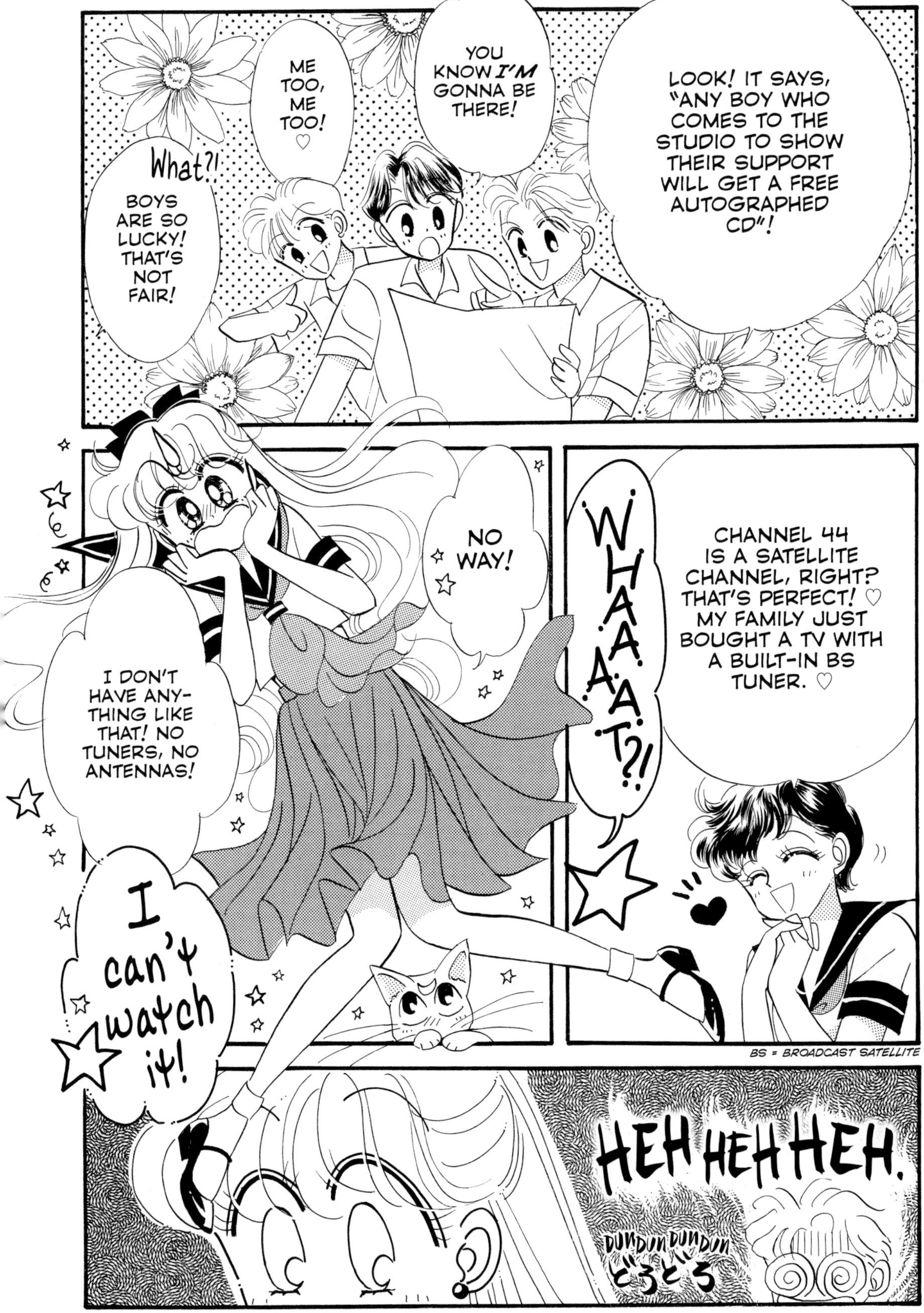
LOOK! IT SAYS, "ANY BOY WHO COMES TO THE STUDIO TO SHOW THEIR SUPPORT WILL GET A FREE AUTOGRAPHED CD"!
YOU KNOW *I'M* GONNA BE THERE!
ME TOO, ME TOO! ♡
What?!
BOYS ARE SO LUCKY! THAT'S NOT FAIR!
CHANNEL 44 IS A SATELLITE CHANNEL, RIGHT? THAT'S PERFECT! ♡ MY FAMILY JUST BOUGHT A TV WITH A BUILT-IN BS TUNER. ♡
WHAAAAT?!
NO WAY!
I DON'T HAVE ANY-THING LIKE THAT! NO TUNERS, NO ANTENNAS!
I can't watch it!
BS = BROADCAST SATELLITE
HEH HEH HEH.
DUNDUN DUNDUN
どろどろ

CS = COMMUNICATION SATELLITE

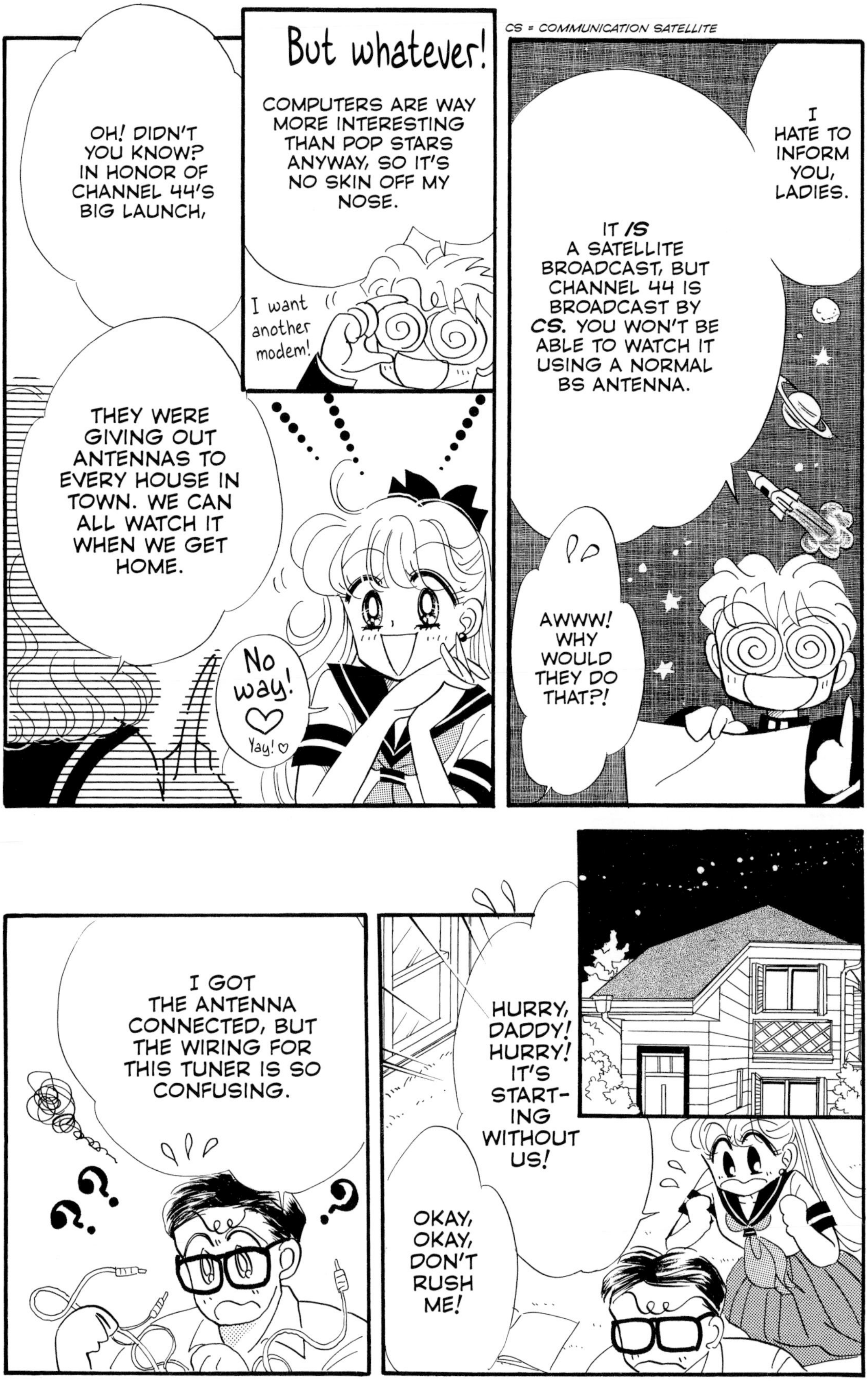
I HATE TO INFORM YOU, LADIES.
IT IS A SATELLITE BROADCAST, BUT CHANNEL 44 IS BROADCAST BY CS. YOU WON'T BE ABLE TO WATCH IT USING A NORMAL BS ANTENNA.
AWWW! WHY WOULD THEY DO THAT?!
But whatever!
COMPUTERS ARE WAY MORE INTERESTING THAN POP STARS ANYWAY, SO IT'S NO SKIN OFF MY NOSE.
I want another modem!
OH! DIDN'T YOU KNOW? IN HONOR OF CHANNEL 44'S BIG LAUNCH,
THEY WERE GIVING OUT ANTENNAS TO EVERY HOUSE IN TOWN. WE CAN ALL WATCH IT WHEN WE GET HOME.
No way! ♡
Yay! ♡
HURRY, DADDY! HURRY! IT'S STARTING WITHOUT US!
OKAY, OKAY, DON'T RUSH ME!
I GOT THE ANTENNA CONNECTED, BUT THE WIRING FOR THIS TUNER IS SO CONFUSING.

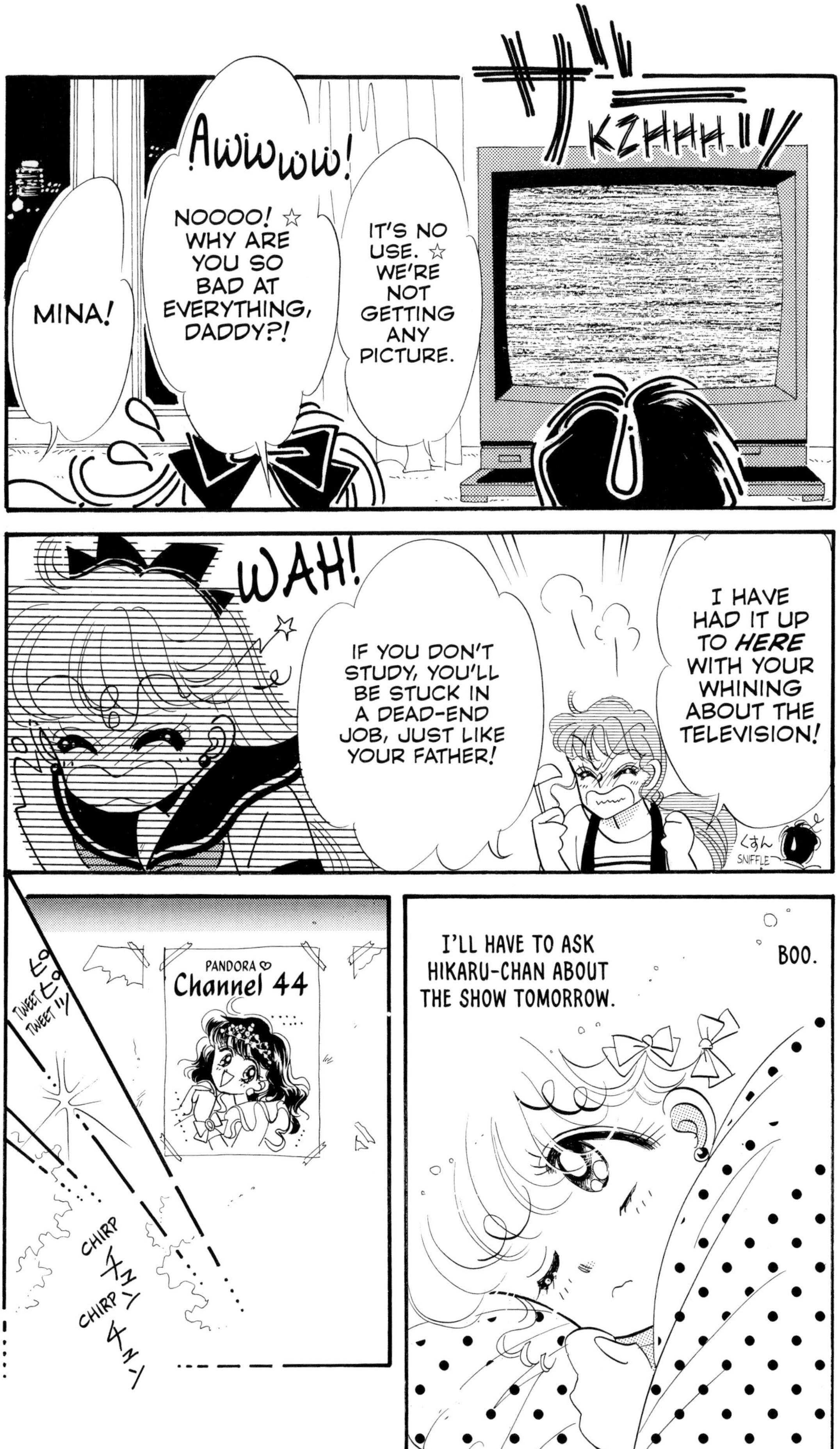
KZHHH!!
IT'S NO USE. ☆ WE'RE NOT GETTING ANY PICTURE.
AWWWWW!
NOOOO! ☆ WHY ARE YOU SO BAD AT EVERYTHING, DADDY?!
MINA!
I HAVE HAD IT UP TO *HERE* WITH YOUR WHINING ABOUT THE TELEVISION!
くすん
SNIFFLE
IF YOU DON'T STUDY, YOU'LL BE STUCK IN A DEAD-END JOB, JUST LIKE YOUR FATHER!
WAH!
BOO.
I'LL HAVE TO ASK HIKARU-CHAN ABOUT THE SHOW TOMORROW.
PANDORA
Channel 44
ピピッ
TWEET TWEET
CHIRP
チュン
CHIRP
チュン

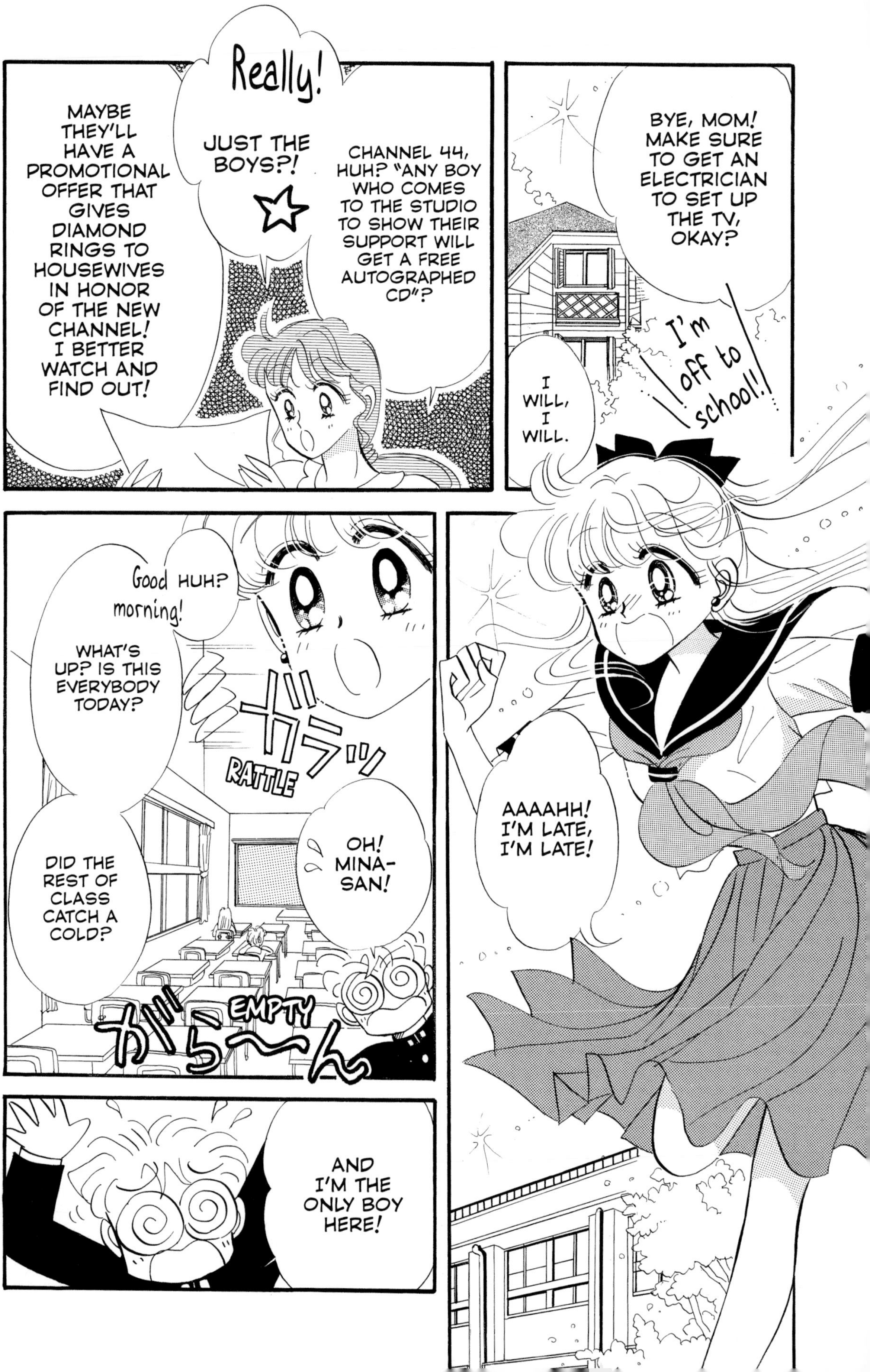
BYE, MOM! MAKE SURE TO GET AN ELECTRICIAN TO SET UP THE TV, OKAY?
I'm off to school!
I WILL, I WILL.
CHANNEL 44, HUH? "ANY BOY WHO COMES TO THE STUDIO TO SHOW THEIR SUPPORT WILL GET A FREE AUTOGRAPHED CD"?
Really!
JUST THE BOYS?!
MAYBE THEY'LL HAVE A PROMOTIONAL OFFER THAT GIVES DIAMOND RINGS TO HOUSEWIVES IN HONOR OF THE NEW CHANNEL! I BETTER WATCH AND FIND OUT!
AAAAHH! I'M LATE, I'M LATE!
ガラッ
RATTLE
HUH?
Good morning!
WHAT'S UP? IS THIS EVERYBODY TODAY?
OH! MINA-SAN!
DID THE REST OF CLASS CATCH A COLD?
がら～ん
EMPTY
AND I'M THE ONLY BOY HERE!

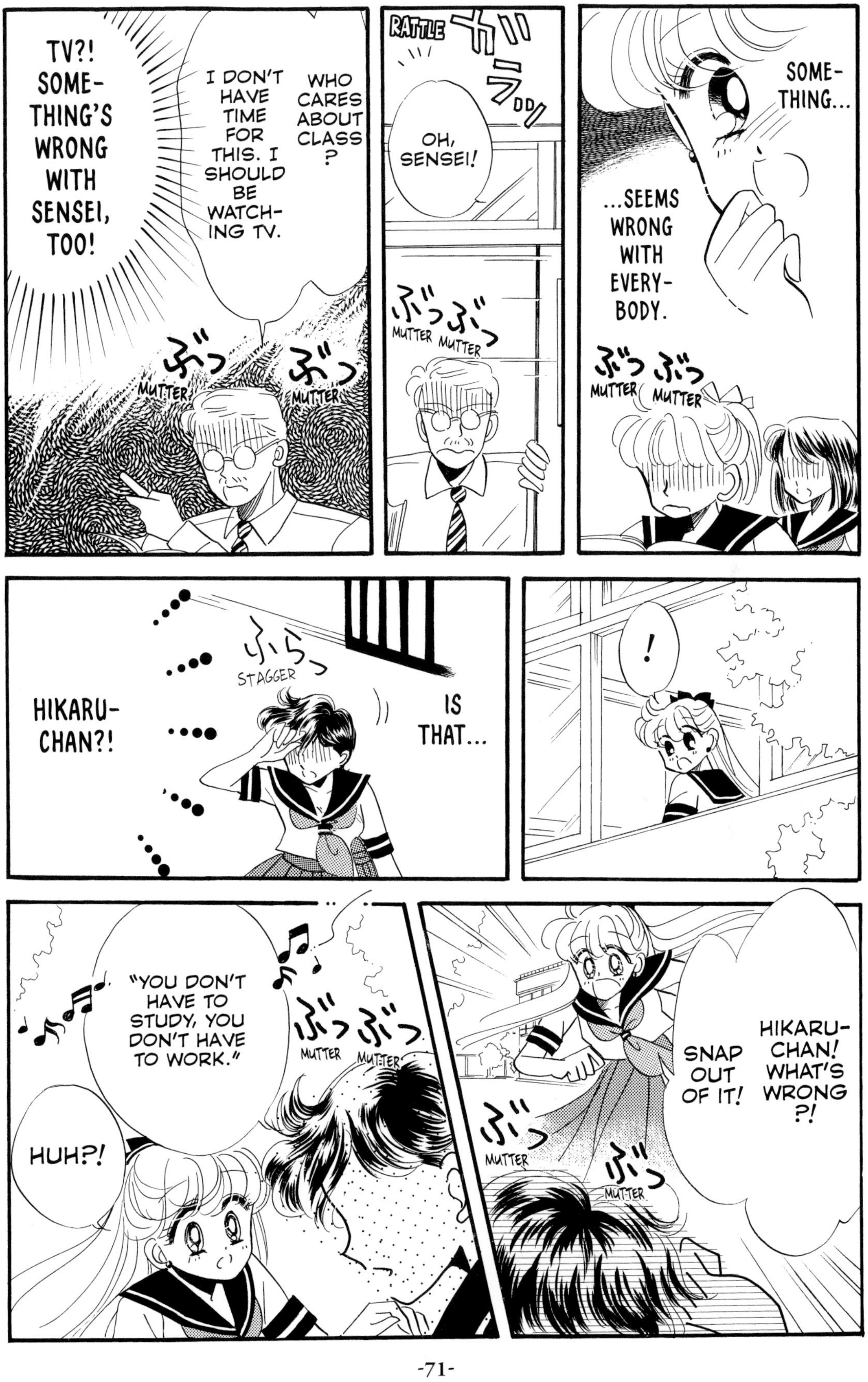
SOMETHING...
...SEEMS WRONG WITH EVERYBODY.
MUTTER MUTTER
RATTLE
OH, SENSEI!
MUTTER MUTTER
WHO CARES ABOUT CLASS?
I DON'T HAVE TIME FOR THIS. I SHOULD BE WATCHING TV.
TV?! SOMETHING'S WRONG WITH SENSEI, TOO!
MUTTER MUTTER
!
IS THAT...
STAGGER
HIKARU-CHAN?!
HIKARU-CHAN! WHAT'S WRONG?!
SNAP OUT OF IT!
MUTTER MUTTER
"YOU DON'T HAVE TO STUDY, YOU DON'T HAVE TO WORK."
MUTTER MUTTER
HUH?!

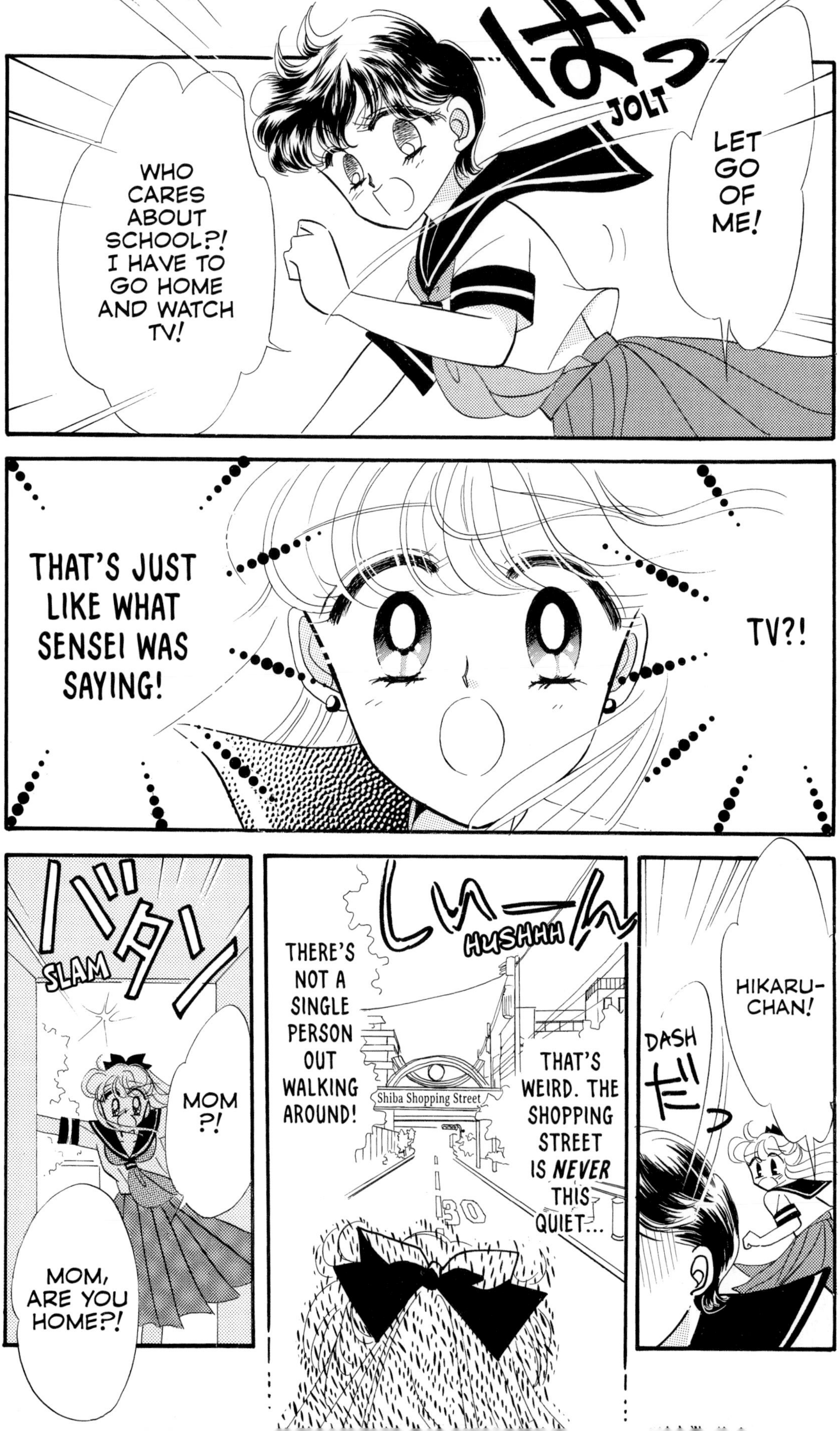
ばっ
JOLT
LET GO OF ME!
WHO CARES ABOUT SCHOOL?! I HAVE TO GO HOME AND WATCH TV!
TV?!
THAT'S JUST LIKE WHAT SENSEI WAS SAYING!
HIKARU-CHAN!
だっ
DASH
しいーん
HUSHHH
THAT'S WEIRD. THE SHOPPING STREET IS *NEVER* THIS QUIET...
Shiba Shopping Street
30
THERE'S NOT A SINGLE PERSON OUT WALKING AROUND!
バタン
SLAM
MOM ?!
MOM, ARE YOU HOME?!

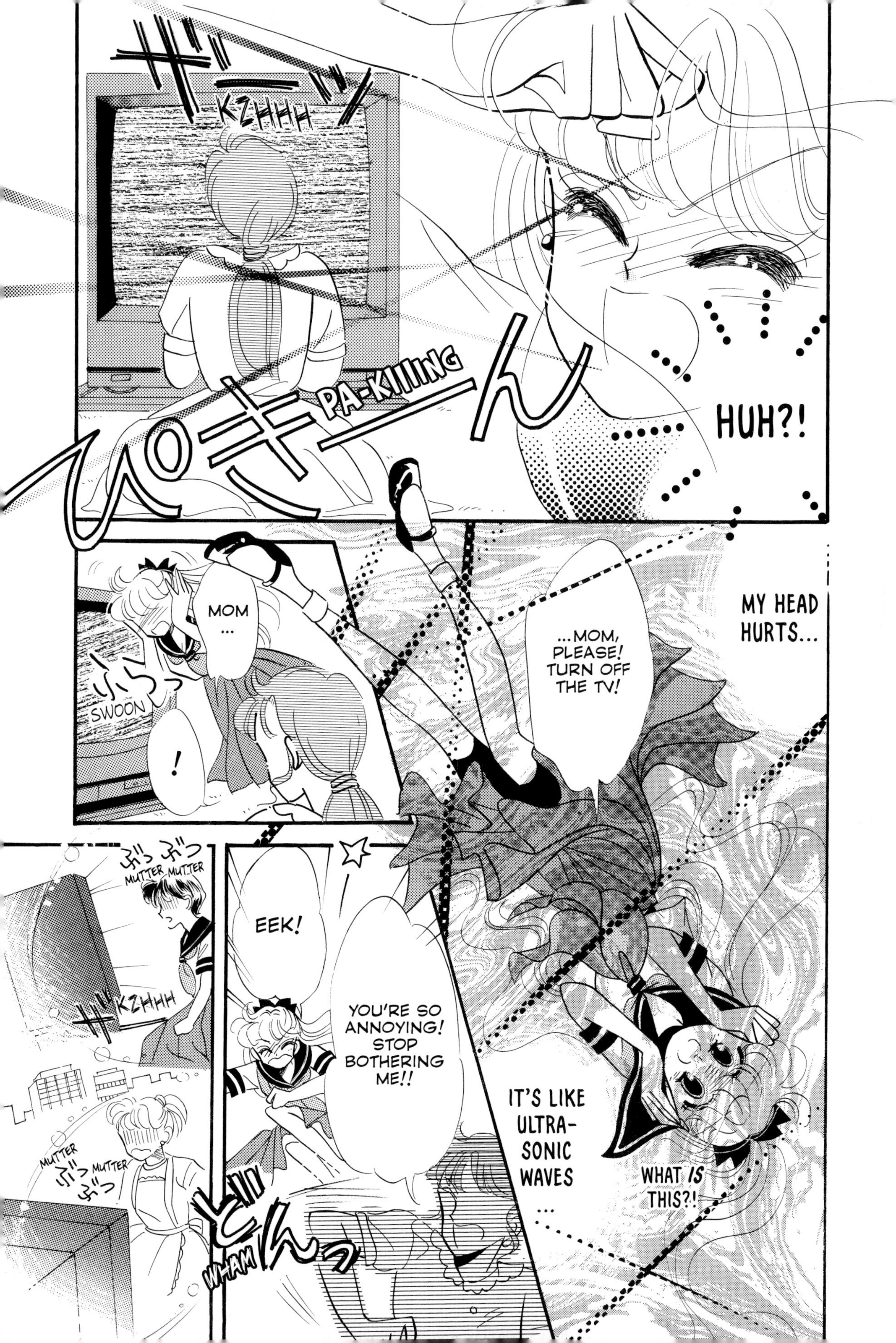
ザーーー KZHHH
HUH?!
ピキーん PA-KIIING
MY HEAD HURTS...
...MOM, PLEASE! TURN OFF THE TV!
MOM ...
ふらっ SWOON
!
IT'S LIKE ULTRA-SONIC WAVES ...
WHAT *IS* THIS?!
EEK!
YOU'RE SO ANNOYING! STOP BOTHERING ME!!
どかんっ WHAM
ぶつぶつ MUTTER MUTTER
ザー KZHHH
ぶつぶつ MUTTER MUTTER

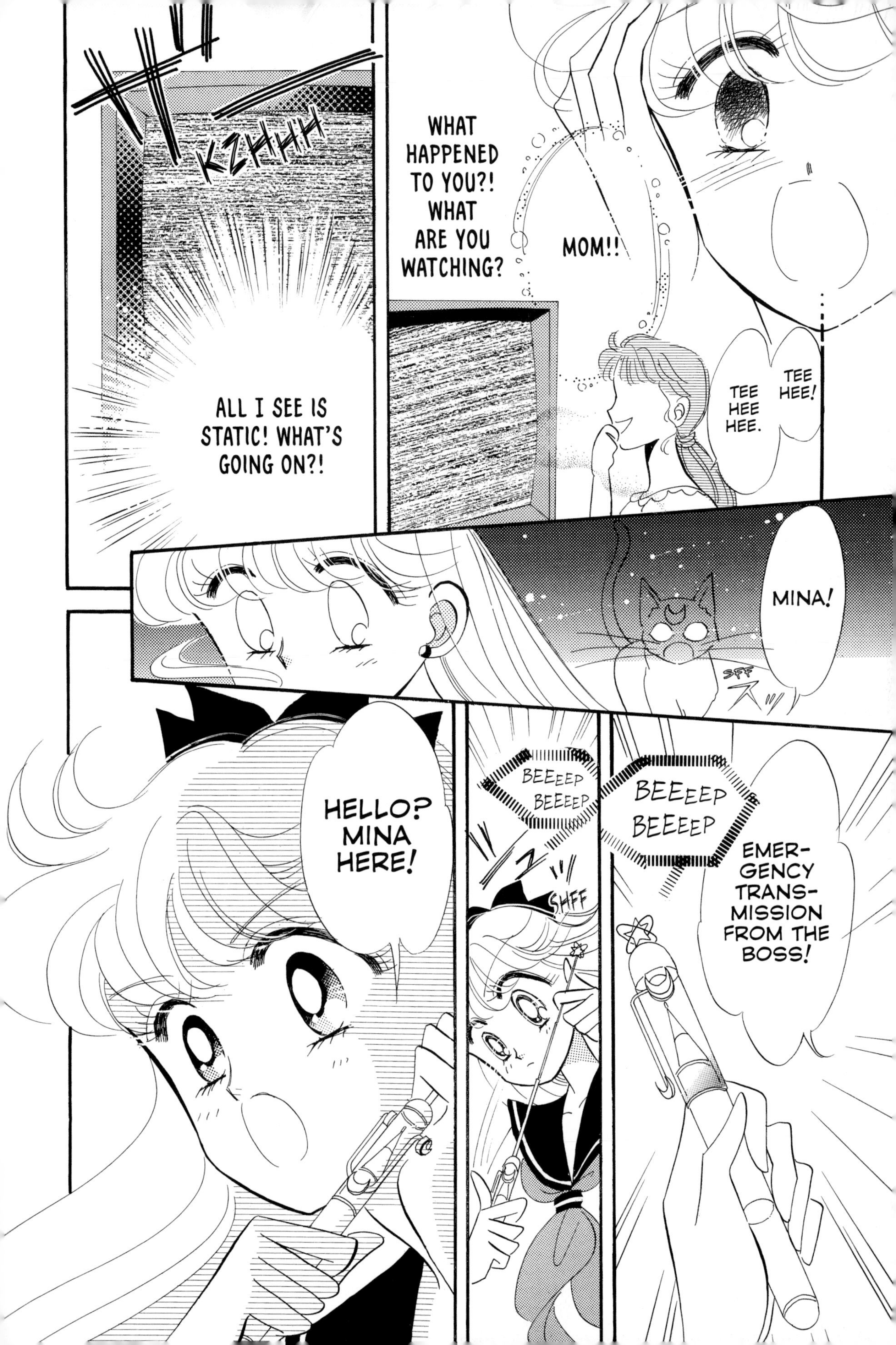
MOM!!
WHAT HAPPENED TO YOU?! WHAT ARE YOU WATCHING?
TEE HEE!
TEE HEE HEE.
KZHHHH
ALL I SEE IS STATIC! WHAT'S GOING ON?!
MINA!
SFF
BEEEEP BEEEEP
EMERGENCY TRANSMISSION FROM THE BOSS!
BEEEEP BEEEEP
SHFF
HELLO? MINA HERE!

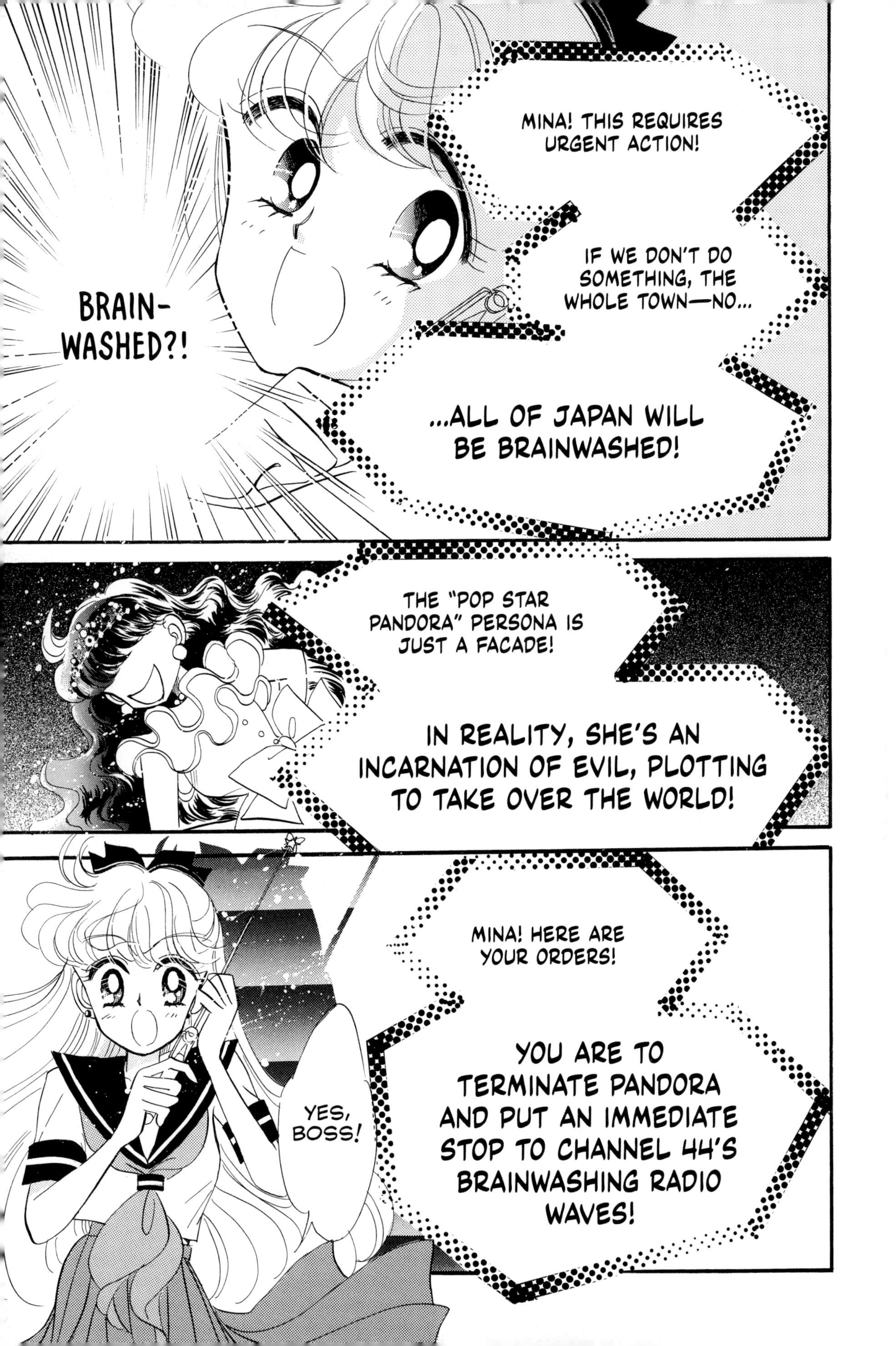
MINA! THIS REQUIRES URGENT ACTION!
IF WE DON'T DO SOMETHING, THE WHOLE TOWN—NO...
...ALL OF JAPAN WILL BE BRAINWASHED!
BRAIN-WASHED?!
THE "POP STAR PANDORA" PERSONA IS JUST A FACADE!
IN REALITY, SHE'S AN INCARNATION OF EVIL, PLOTTING TO TAKE OVER THE WORLD!
MINA! HERE ARE YOUR ORDERS!
YOU ARE TO TERMINATE PANDORA AND PUT AN IMMEDIATE STOP TO CHANNEL 44'S BRAINWASHING RADIO WAVES!
YES, BOSS!

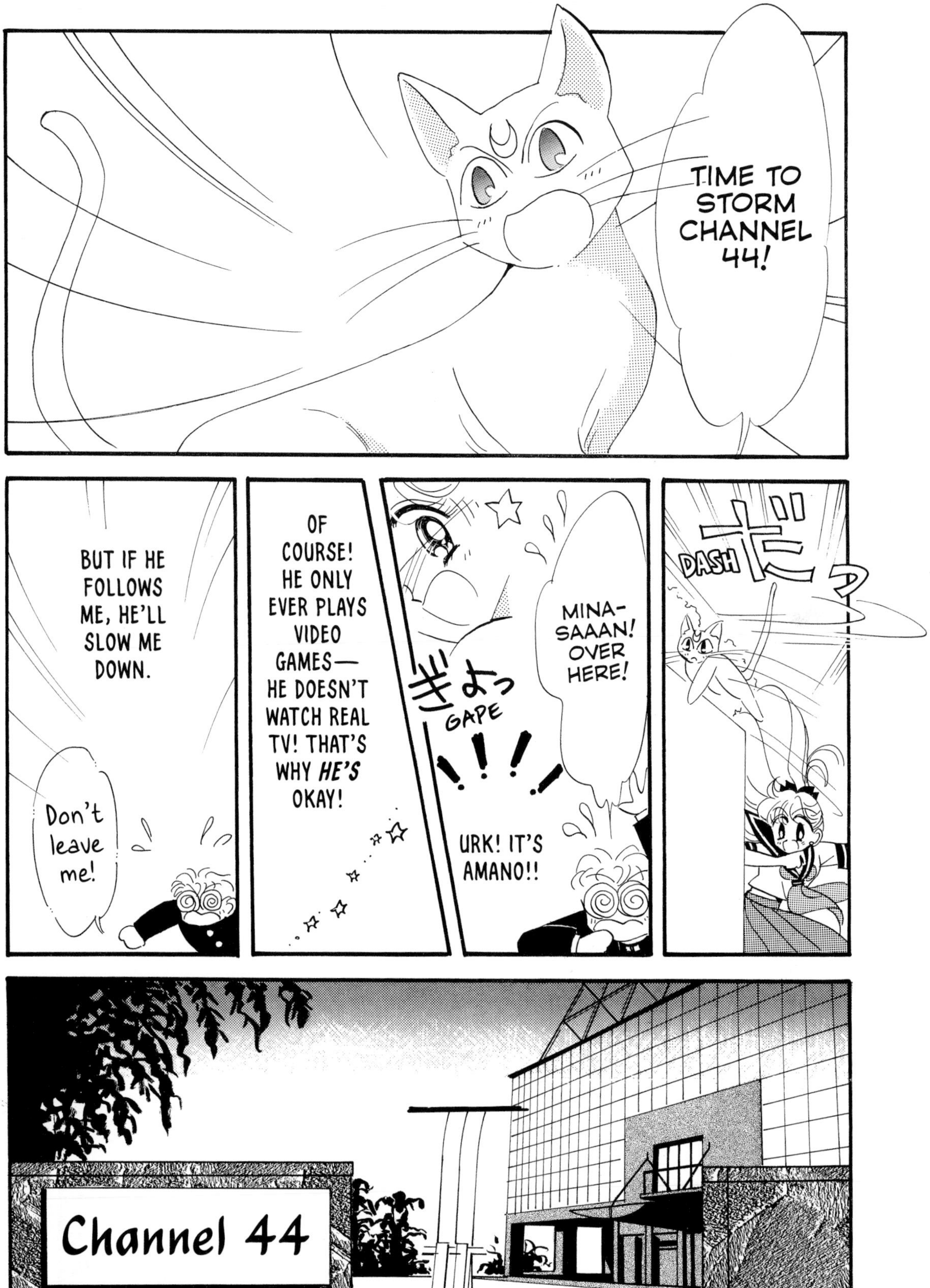

TIME TO STORM CHANNEL 44!
だっ
DASH
MINA-SAAAN! OVER HERE!
ぎょっ
GAPE
URK! IT'S AMANO!!
OF COURSE! HE ONLY EVER PLAYS VIDEO GAMES—HE DOESN'T WATCH REAL TV! THAT'S WHY *HE'S* OKAY!
BUT IF HE FOLLOWS ME, HE'LL SLOW ME DOWN.
Don't leave me!
Channel 44

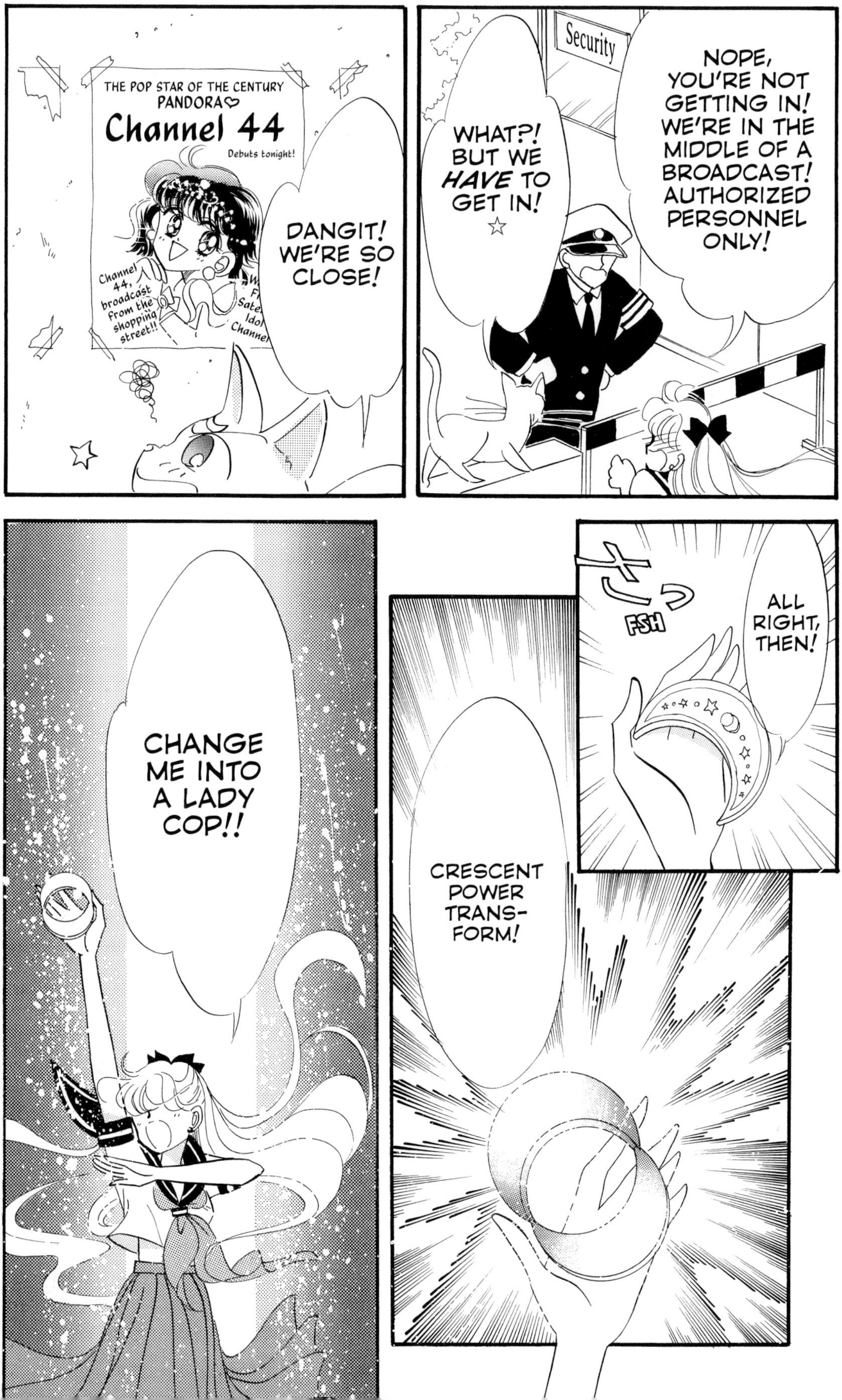
NOPE, YOU'RE NOT GETTING IN! WE'RE IN THE MIDDLE OF A BROADCAST! AUTHORIZED PERSONNEL ONLY!
WHAT?! BUT WE *HAVE* TO GET IN!
Security
THE POP STAR OF THE CENTURY PANDORA♡
Channel 44
Debuts tonight!
Channel 44, broadcast from the shopping street!!
DANGIT! WE'RE SO CLOSE!
ALL RIGHT, THEN!
FSH
CRESCENT POWER TRANS-FORM!
CHANGE ME INTO A LADY COP!!

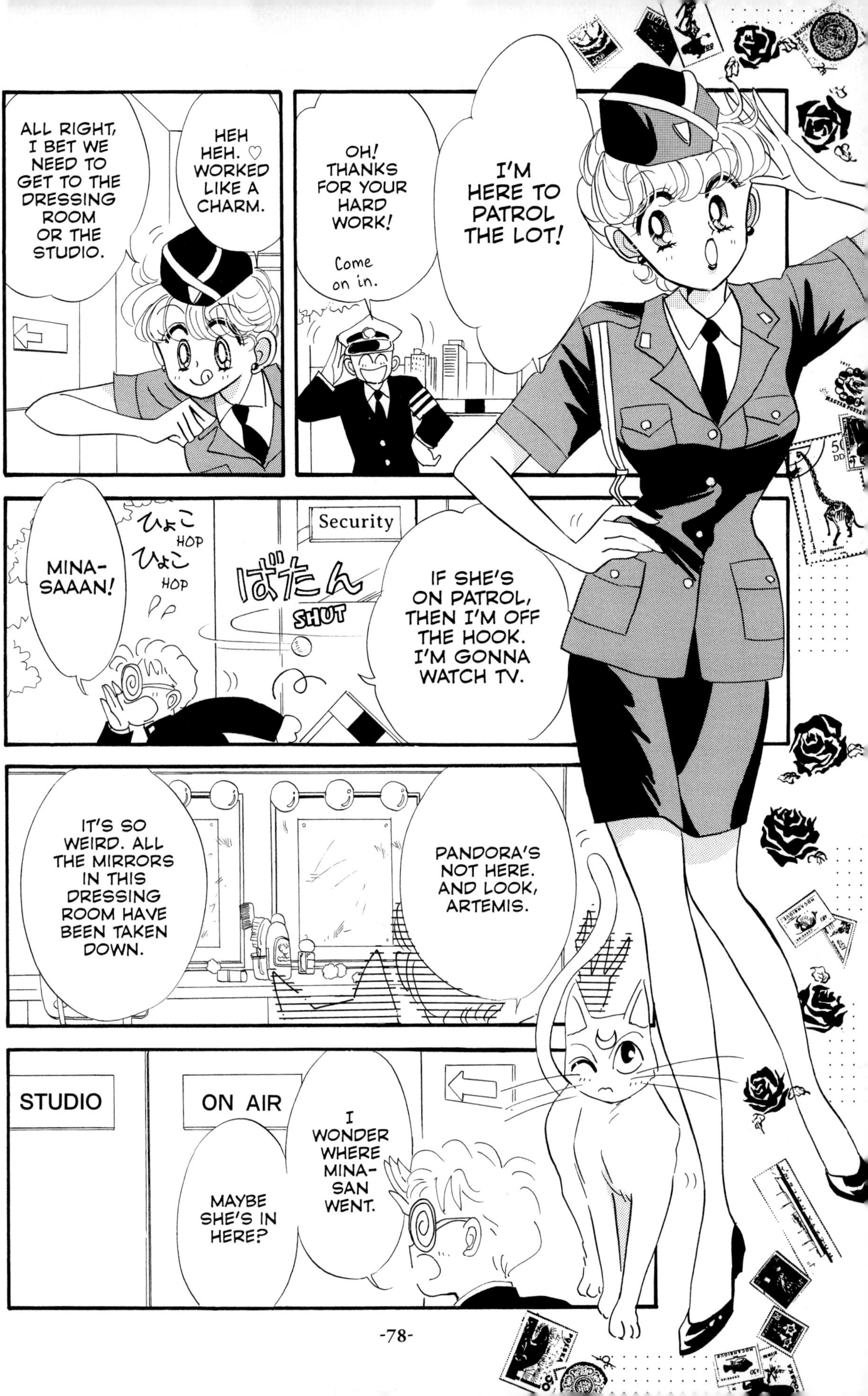
I'M HERE TO PATROL THE LOT!
OH! THANKS FOR YOUR HARD WORK!
Come on in.
HEH HEH. ♡ WORKED LIKE A CHARM.
ALL RIGHT, I BET WE NEED TO GET TO THE DRESSING ROOM OR THE STUDIO.
Security
IF SHE'S ON PATROL, THEN I'M OFF THE HOOK. I'M GONNA WATCH TV.
ばたん SHUT
ひょこ HOP ひょこ HOP
MINA-SAAAN!
PANDORA'S NOT HERE. AND LOOK, ARTEMIS.
IT'S SO WEIRD. ALL THE MIRRORS IN THIS DRESSING ROOM HAVE BEEN TAKEN DOWN.
I WONDER WHERE MINA-SAN WENT.
MAYBE SHE'S IN HERE?
ON AIR
STUDIO

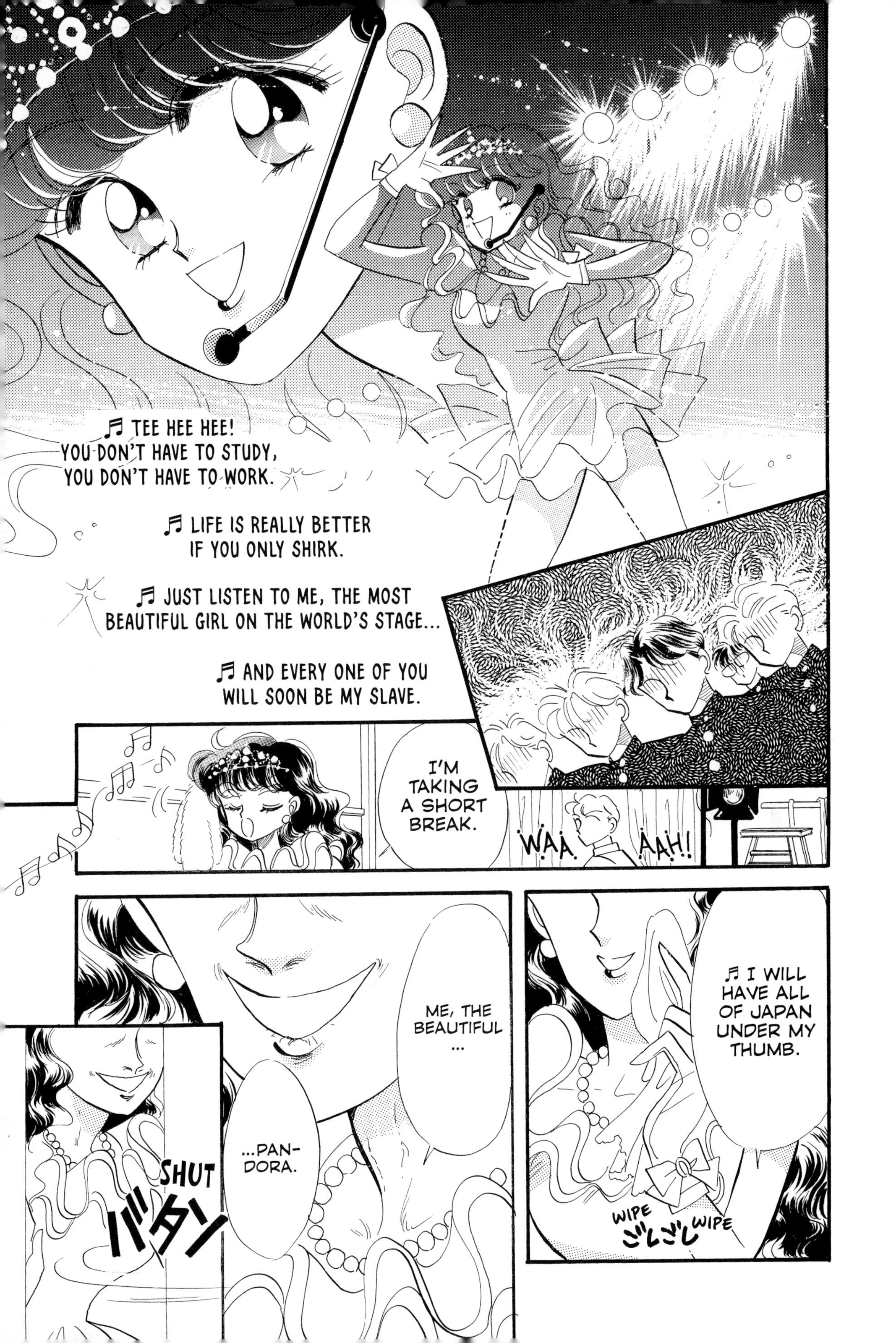
♬ TEE HEE HEE! YOU DON'T HAVE TO STUDY, YOU DON'T HAVE TO WORK.
♬ LIFE IS REALLY BETTER IF YOU ONLY SHIRK.
♬ JUST LISTEN TO ME, THE MOST BEAUTIFUL GIRL ON THE WORLD'S STAGE...
♬ AND EVERY ONE OF YOU WILL SOON BE MY SLAVE.
WAA AAH!
I'M TAKING A SHORT BREAK.
♬ I WILL HAVE ALL OF JAPAN UNDER MY THUMB.
WIPE ごしごし WIPE
ME, THE BEAUTIFUL ...
...PAN-DORA.
SHUT バタン

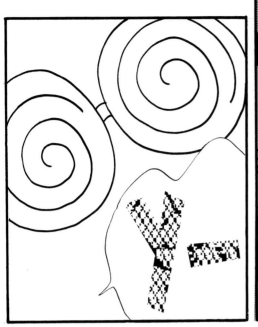

YEEEAARGH!

AI! EE! AI! EE!

MINA-SAAAN!

HELP MEEEEE!

YOU SAW MY REAL FACE.

Ay-yi-yi!

YOU... SAW... ME...

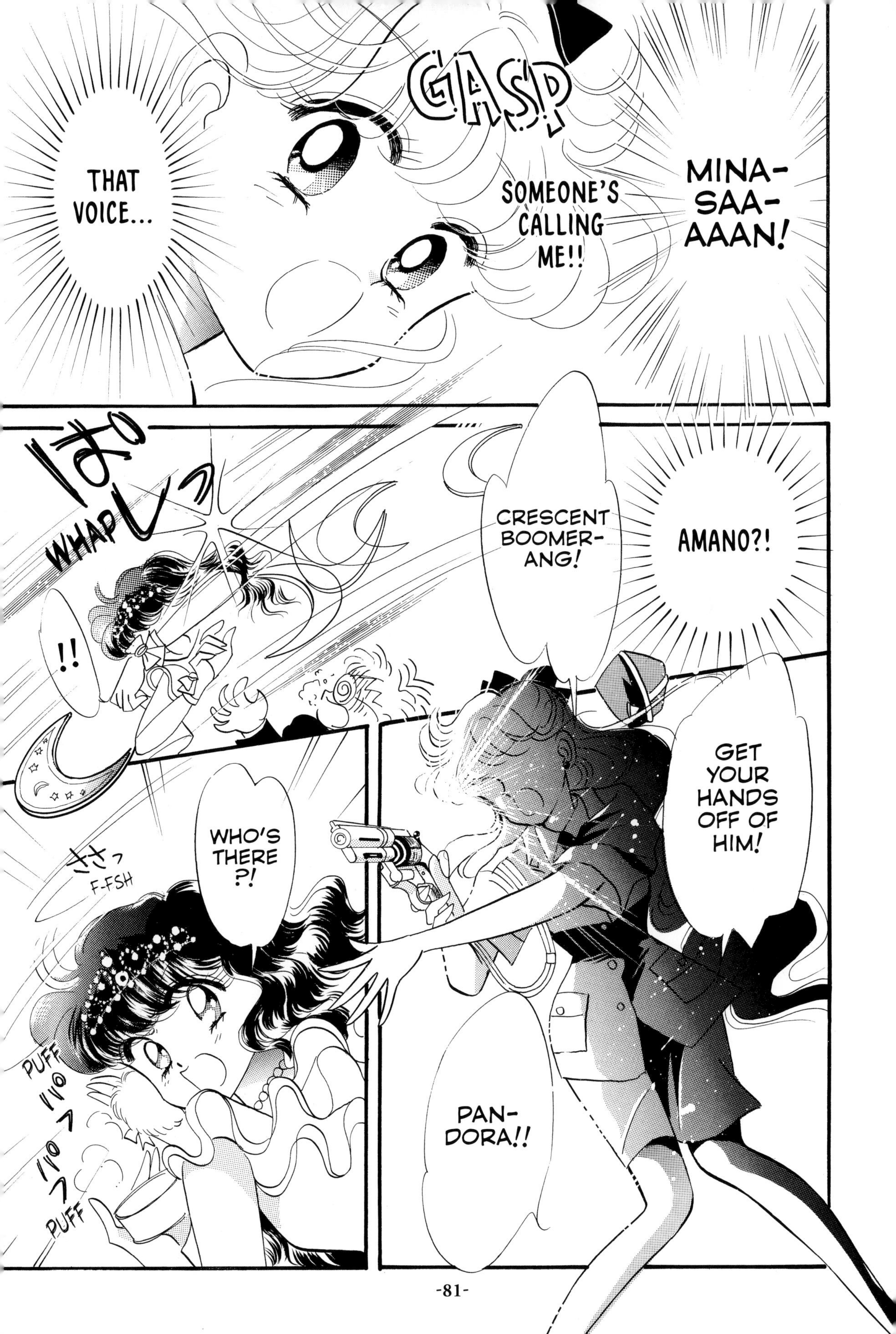
GASP
MINA-SAAA-AAAN!
SOMEONE'S CALLING ME!!
THAT VOICE...
AMANO?!
CRESCENT BOOMER-ANG!
ぱしっ
WHAP
!!
GET YOUR HANDS OFF OF HIM!
PAN-DORA!!
WHO'S THERE?!
ささっ
F-FSH
PUFF
パフ
パフ
PUFF

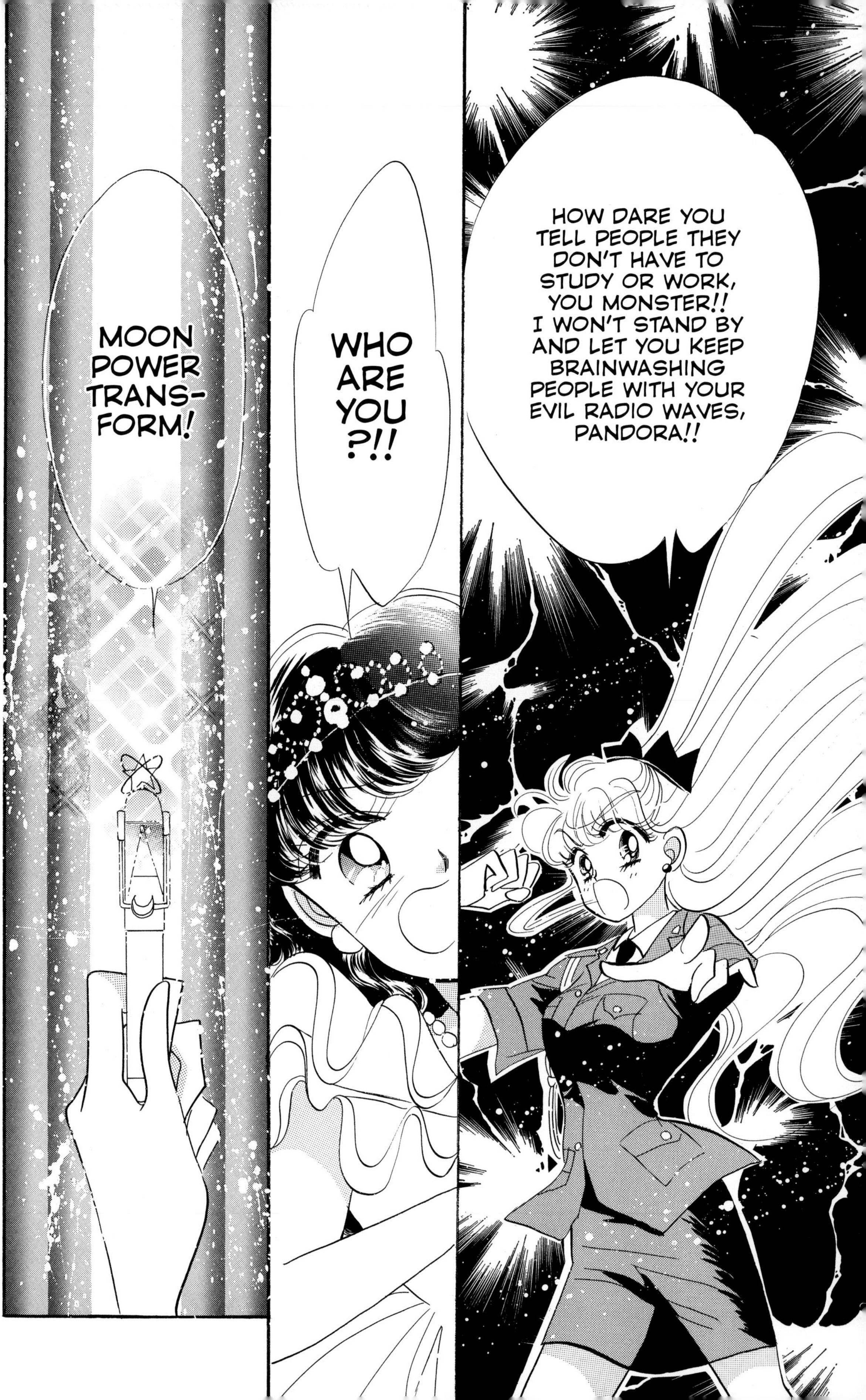
HOW DARE YOU TELL PEOPLE THEY DON'T HAVE TO STUDY OR WORK, YOU MONSTER!! I WON'T STAND BY AND LET YOU KEEP BRAINWASHING PEOPLE WITH YOUR EVIL RADIO WAVES, PANDORA!!
WHO ARE YOU?!!
MOON POWER TRANS-FORM!

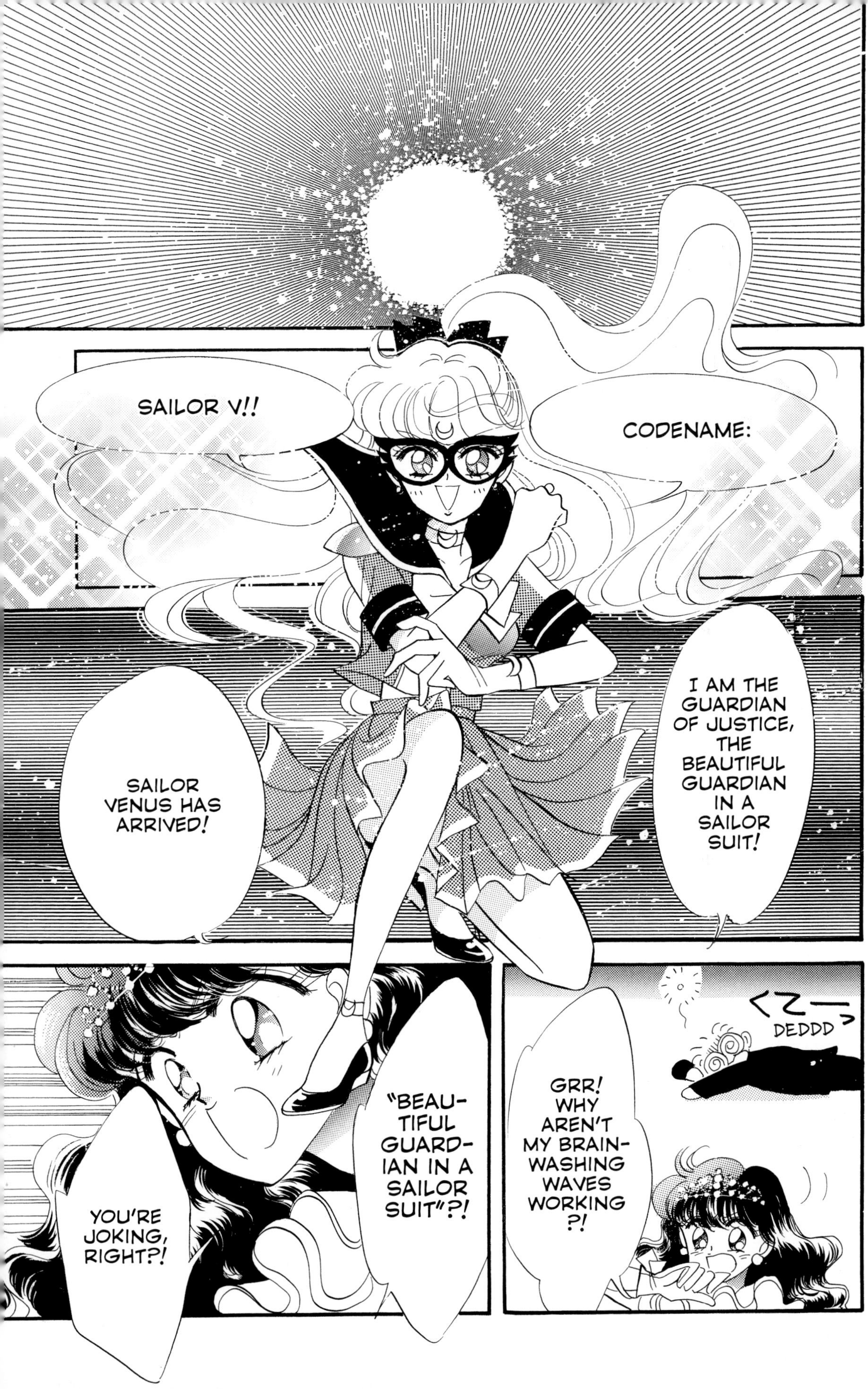
CODENAME:
SAILOR V!!
I AM THE GUARDIAN OF JUSTICE, THE BEAUTIFUL GUARDIAN IN A SAILOR SUIT!
SAILOR VENUS HAS ARRIVED!
くてー
DEDDD
GRR! WHY AREN'T MY BRAIN-WASHING WAVES WORKING?!
"BEAU-TIFUL GUARD-IAN IN A SAILOR SUIT"?!
YOU'RE JOKING, RIGHT?!

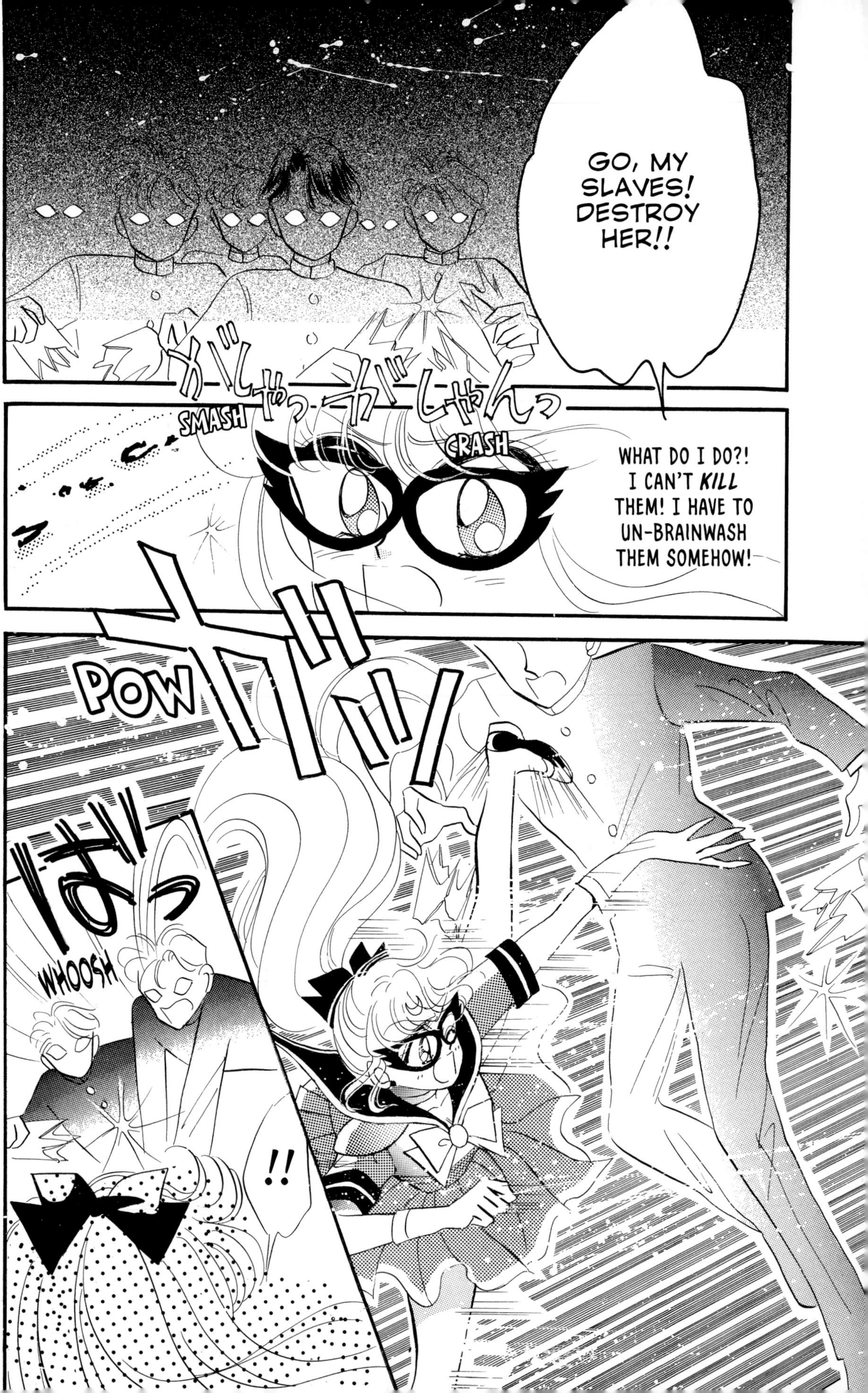
GO, MY SLAVES! DESTROY HER!!
SMASH
CRASH
WHAT DO I DO?! I CAN'T *KILL* THEM! I HAVE TO UN-BRAINWASH THEM SOMEHOW!
POW
WHOOSH
!!

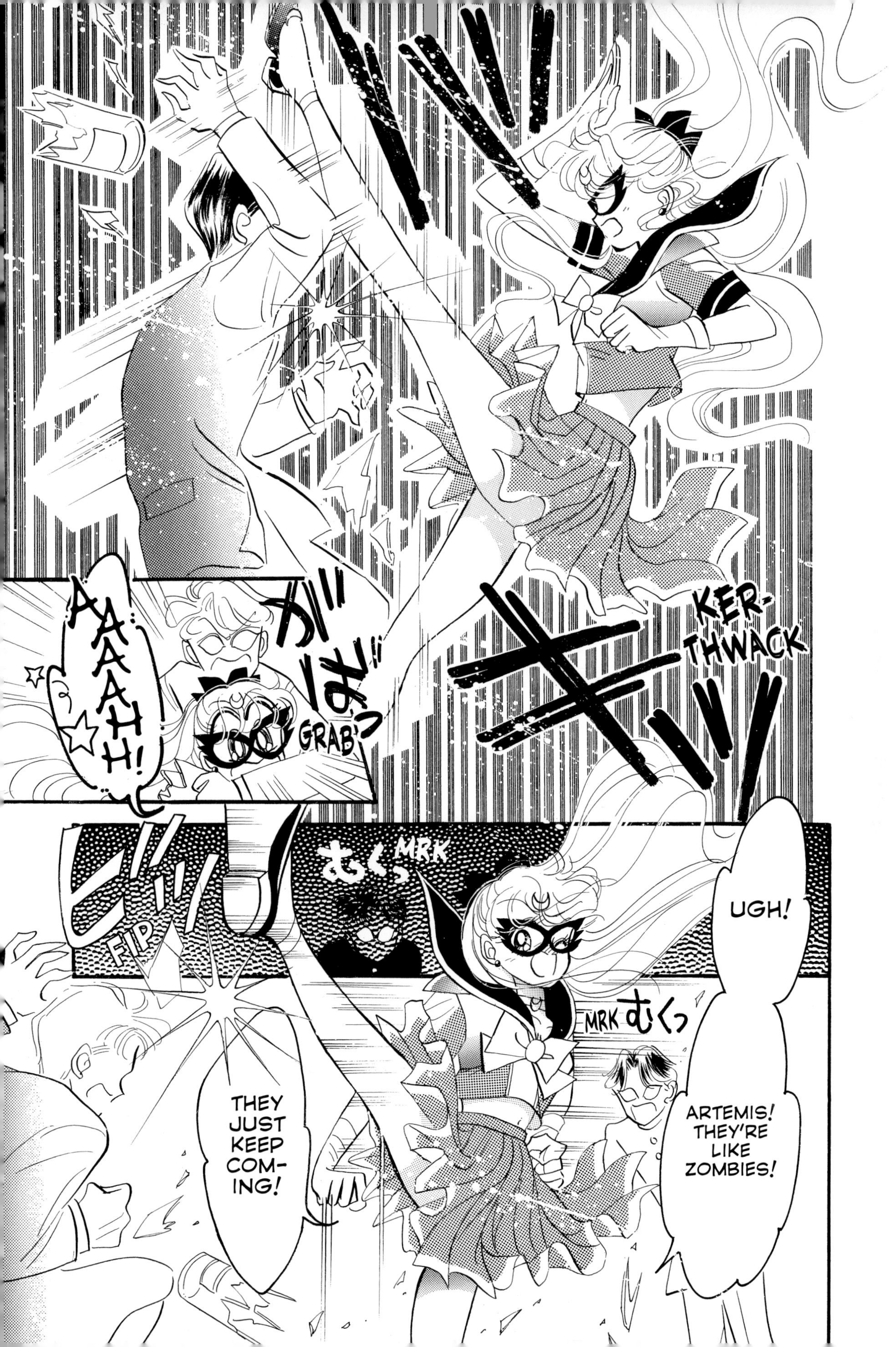
KER-THWACK
AAAAH!
がばっ
GRAB
UGH!
むくっ
MRK
ARTEMIS! THEY'RE LIKE ZOMBIES!
MRK
むくっ
THEY JUST KEEP COMING!
FIP

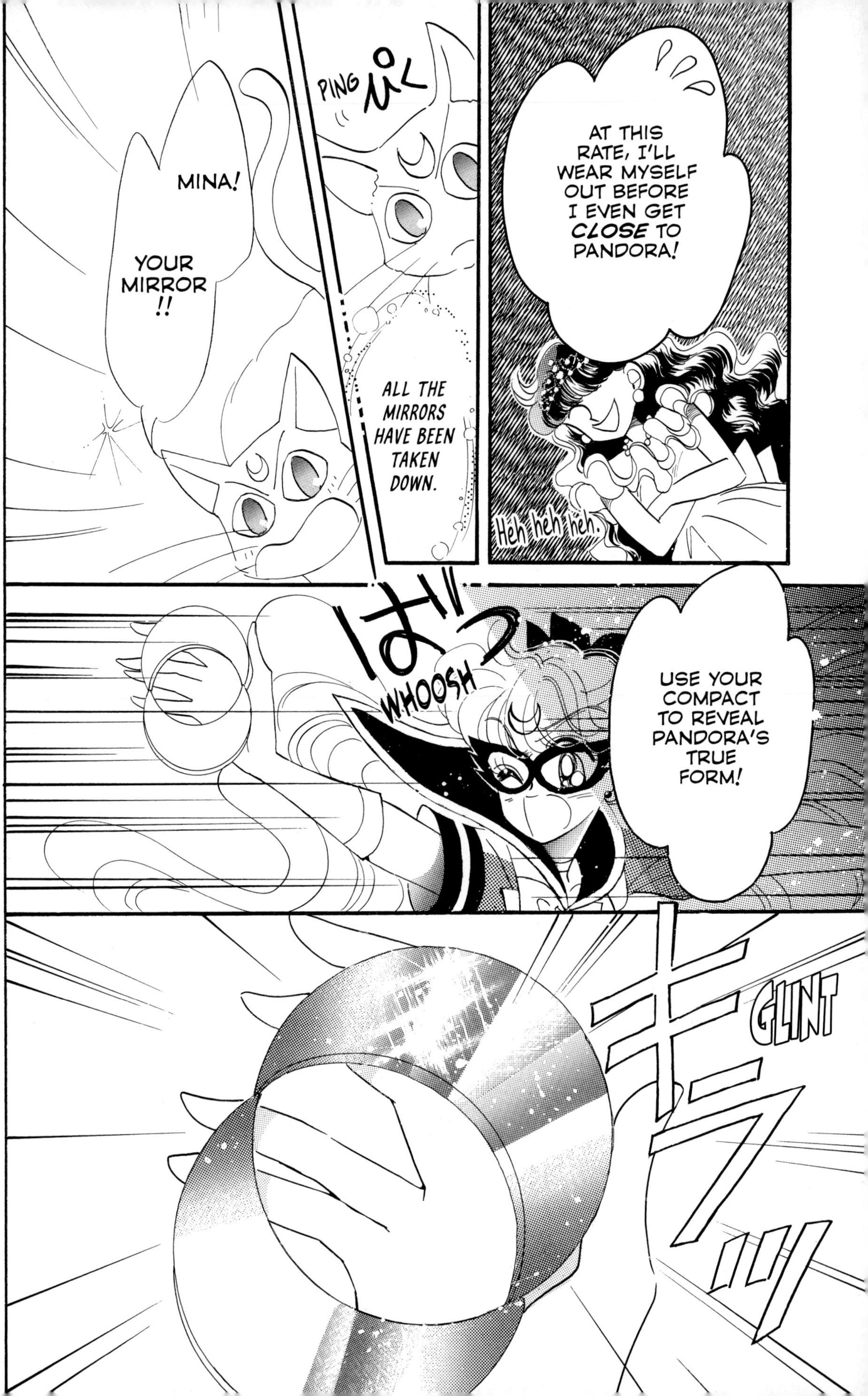
AT THIS RATE, I'LL WEAR MYSELF OUT BEFORE I EVEN GET CLOSE TO PANDORA!
Heh heh heh.
PING ぴく
ALL THE MIRRORS HAVE BEEN TAKEN DOWN.
MINA!
YOUR MIRROR!!
USE YOUR COMPACT TO REVEAL PANDORA'S TRUE FORM!
はっ
WHOOSH
キラッ
GLINT

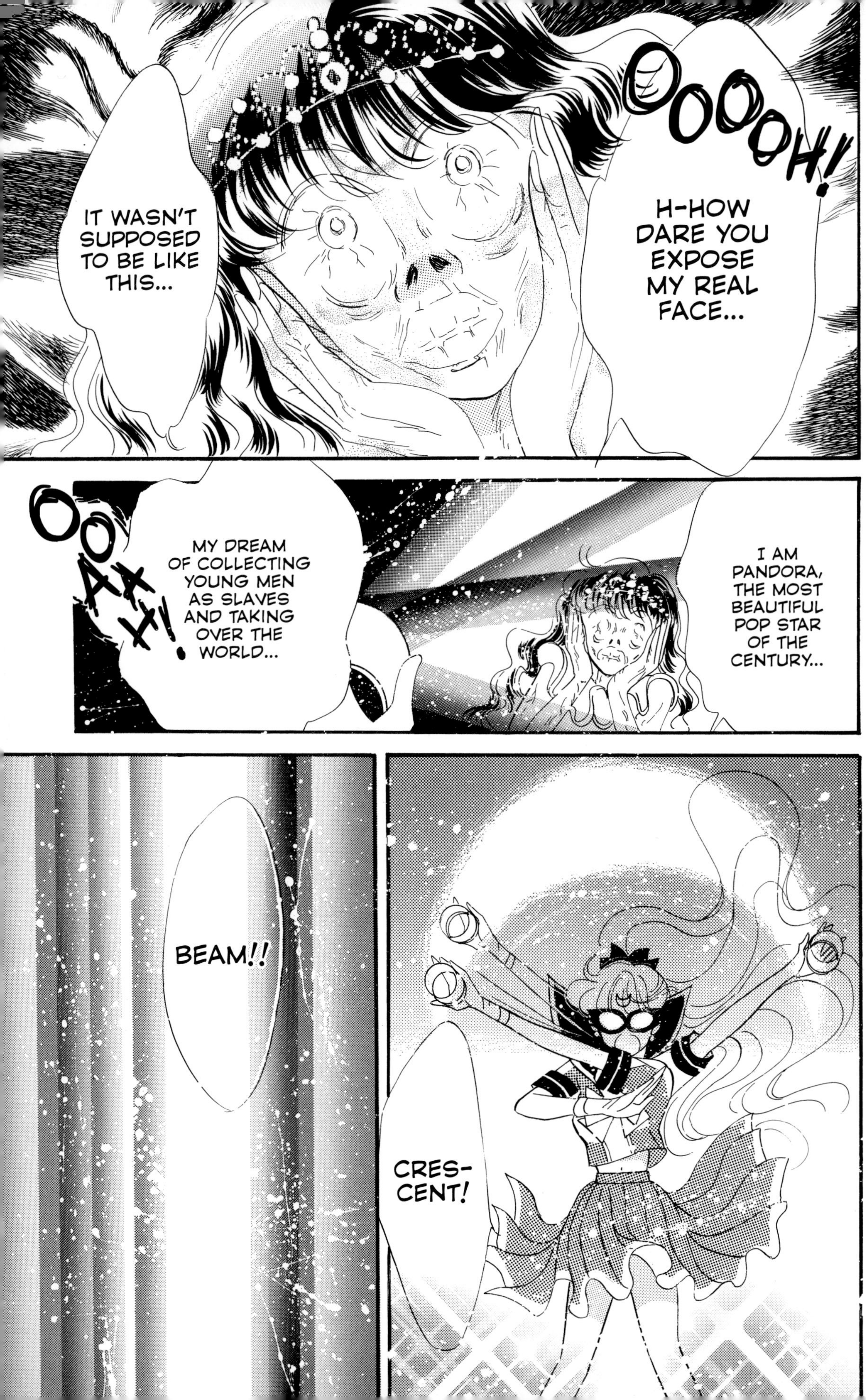
OOOOOH!
H-HOW DARE YOU EXPOSE MY REAL FACE...
IT WASN'T SUPPOSED TO BE LIKE THIS...
I AM PANDORA, THE MOST BEAUTIFUL POP STAR OF THE CENTURY...
MY DREAM OF COLLECTING YOUNG MEN AS SLAVES AND TAKING OVER THE WORLD...
OOAAH!
CRES-CENT!
BEAM!!

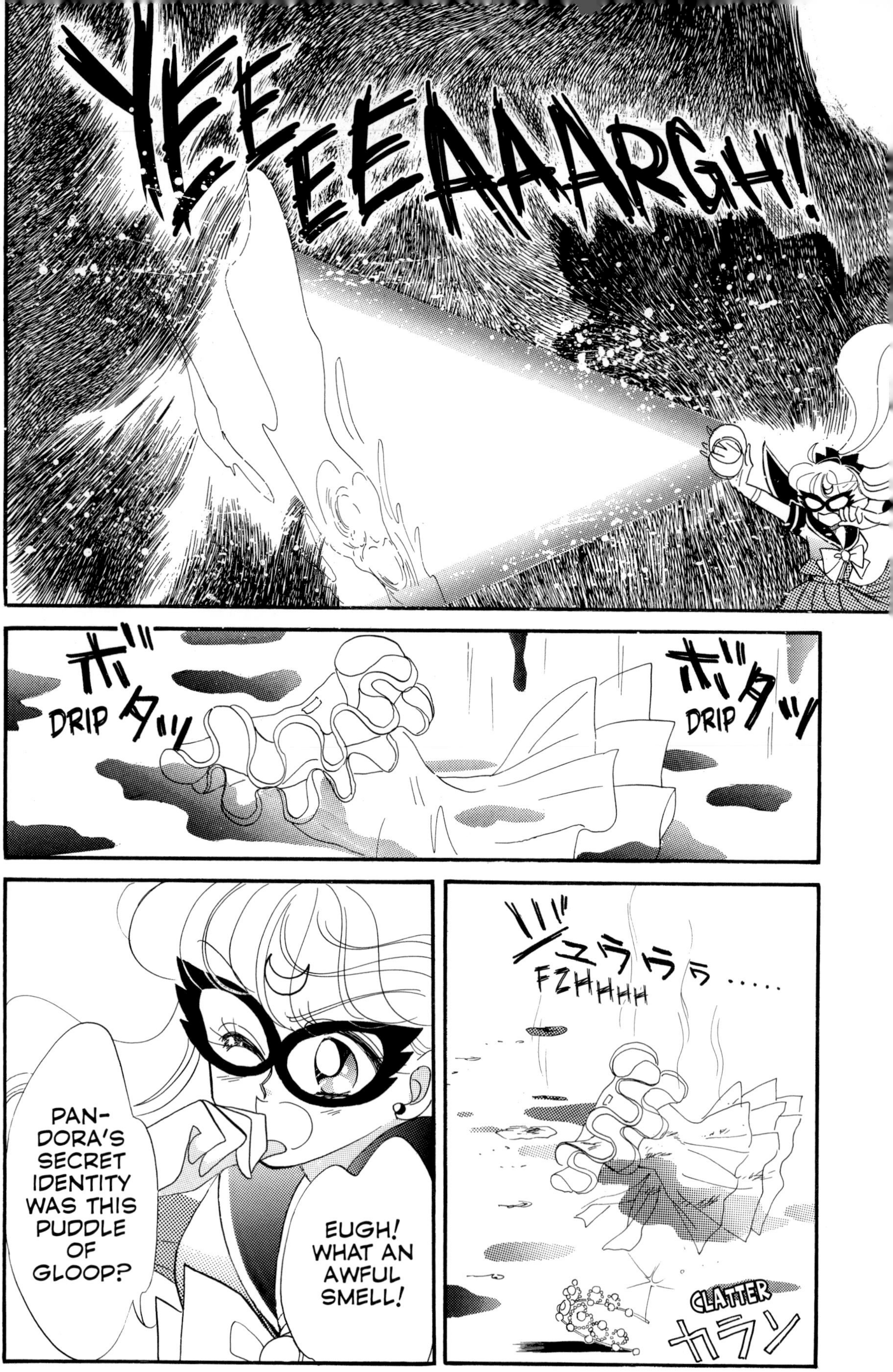
YEEEEAAARGH!
ボタッ
DRIP
ボタッ
DRIP
ジュラララ.....
FZHHHH
CLATTER
カラン
EUGH! WHAT AN AWFUL SMELL!
PAN-DORA'S SECRET IDENTITY WAS THIS PUDDLE OF GLOOP?

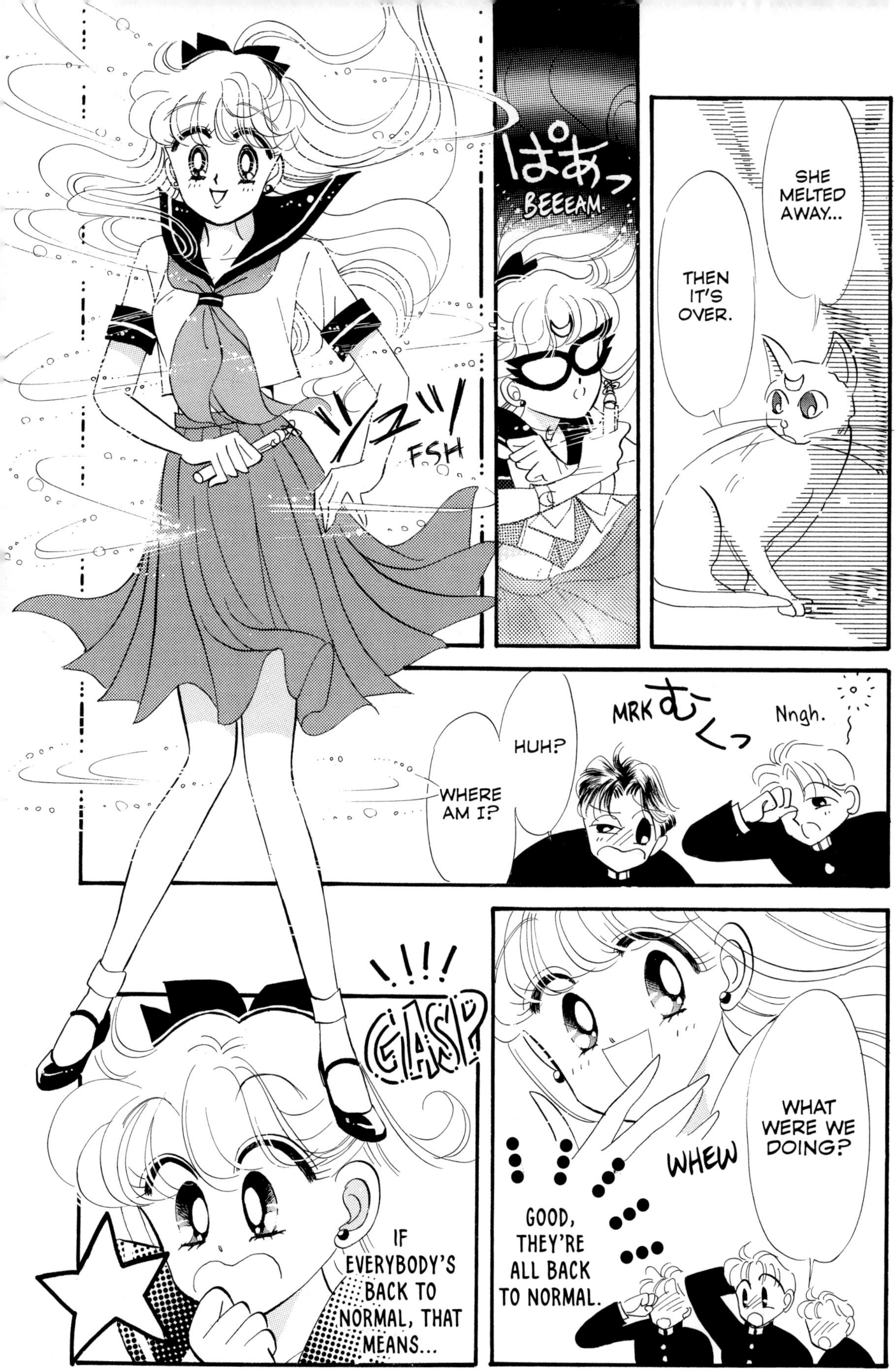
SHE MELTED AWAY...
THEN IT'S OVER.
ぱあっ
BEEEAM
FSH
Nngh.
MRK むくっ
HUH?
WHERE AM I?
WHAT WERE WE DOING?
WHEW
GOOD, THEY'RE ALL BACK TO NORMAL.
GASP
IF EVERYBODY'S BACK TO NORMAL, THAT MEANS...

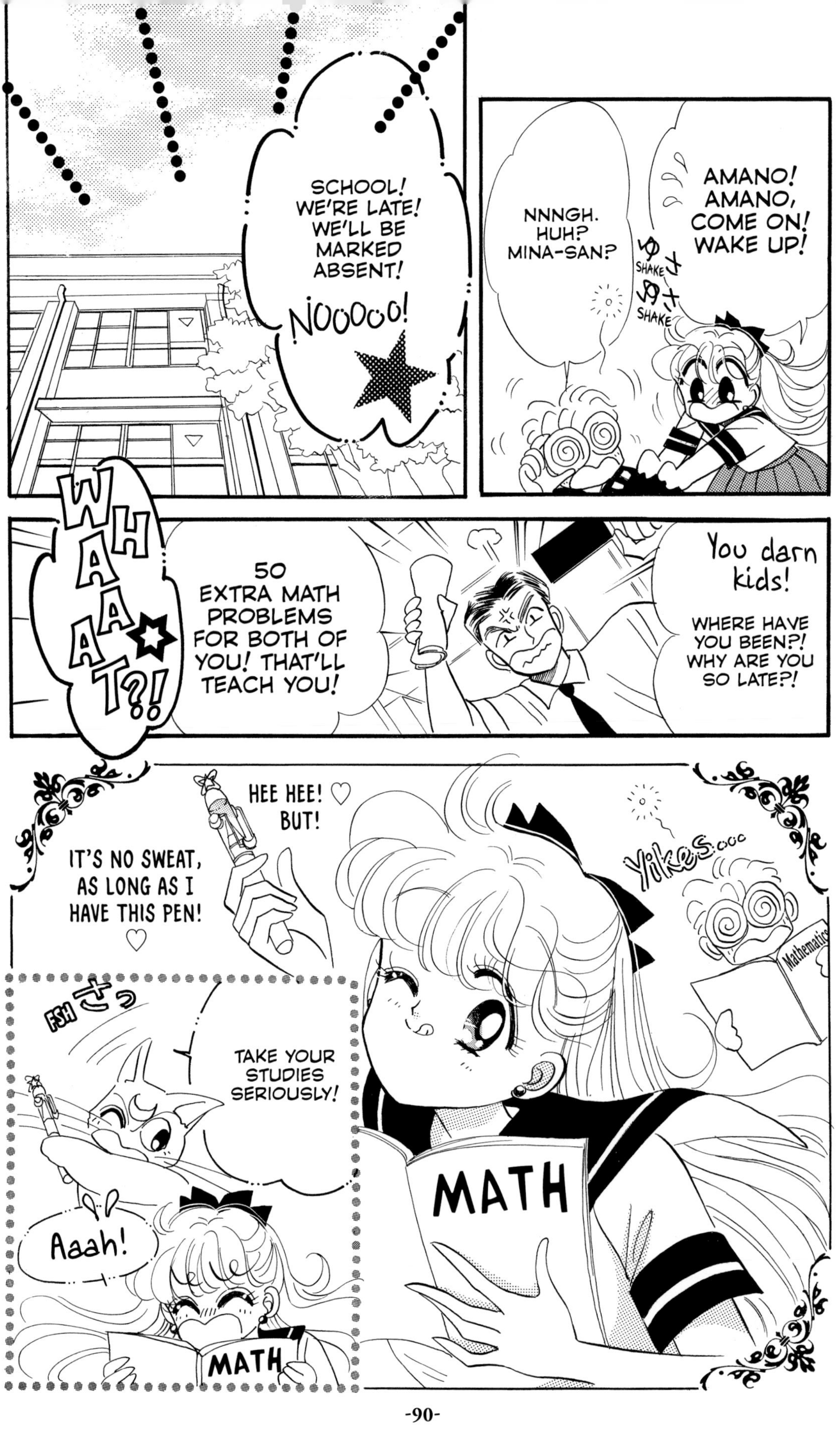

AMANO! AMANO, COME ON! WAKE UP!
SHAKE
SHAKE
NNNGH. HUH? MINA-SAN?
SCHOOL! WE'RE LATE! WE'LL BE MARKED ABSENT!
NOOOOO!
You darn kids!
WHERE HAVE YOU BEEN?! WHY ARE YOU SO LATE?!
50 EXTRA MATH PROBLEMS FOR BOTH OF YOU! THAT'LL TEACH YOU!
WHAAAAT?!
Yikes...
Mathematics
HEE HEE! BUT!
IT'S NO SWEAT, AS LONG AS I HAVE THIS PEN!
MATH
FSH
TAKE YOUR STUDIES SERIOUSLY!
Aaah!
MATH

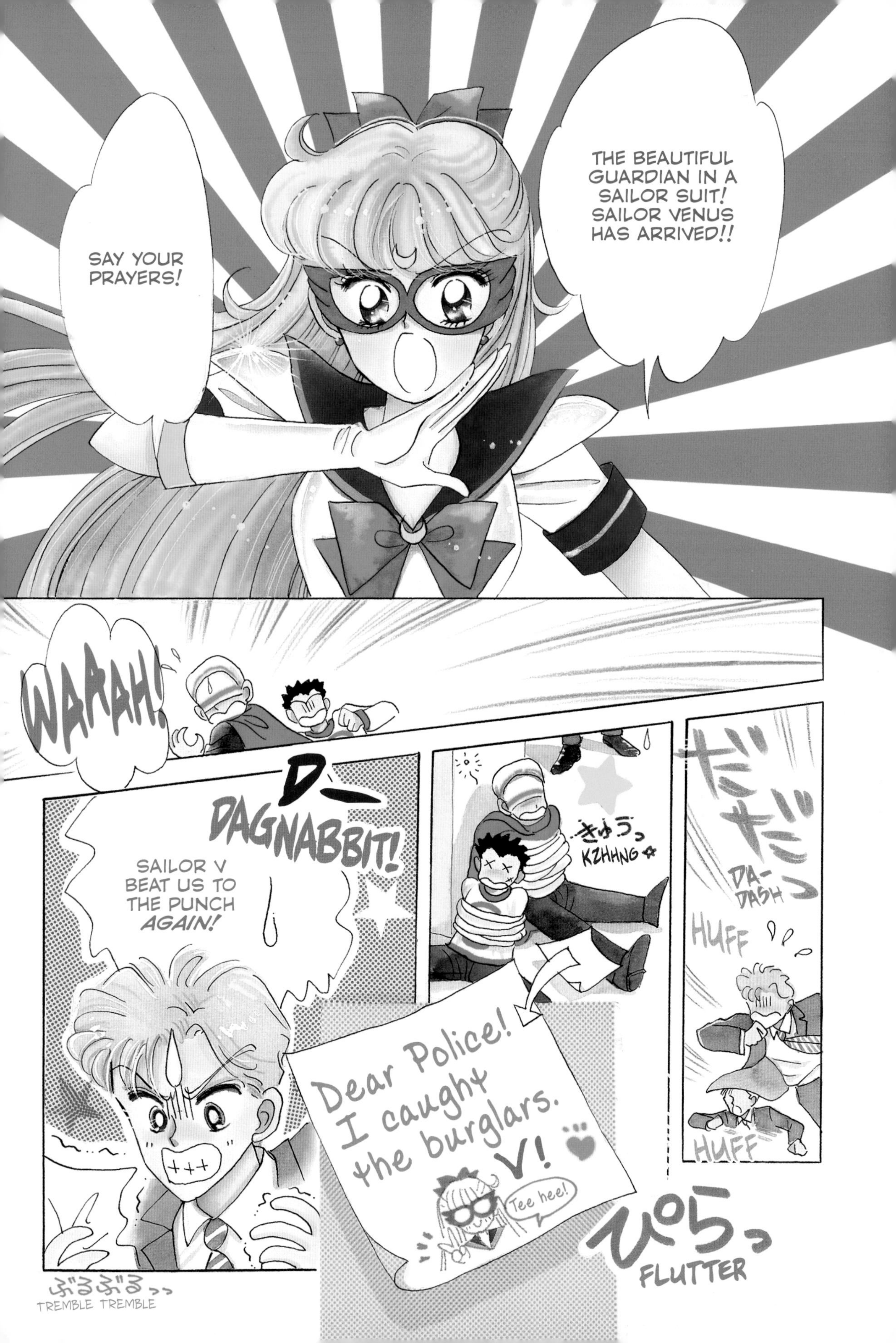
THE BEAUTIFUL GUARDIAN IN A SAILOR SUIT! SAILOR VENUS HAS ARRIVED!!
SAY YOUR PRAYERS!
WAAAH!
だだっ
DA-DASH
HUFF
HUFF
きゅうっ
KZHHNG
D— DAGNABBIT!
SAILOR V BEAT US TO THE PUNCH AGAIN!
ぶるぶるっっ
TREMBLE TREMBLE
Dear Police! I caught the burglars. V!
Tee hee!
ぴらっ
FLUTTER

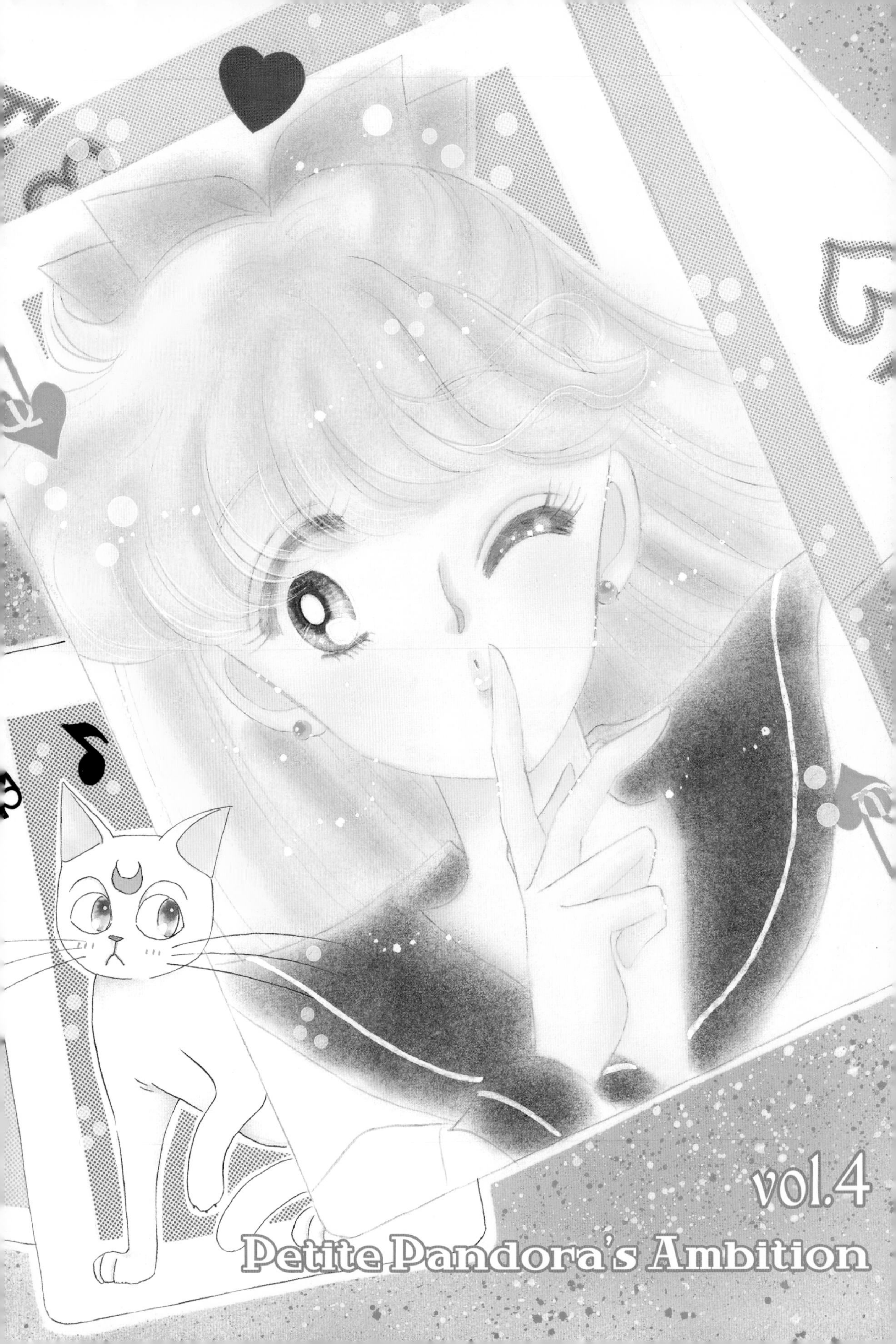

vol.4
Petite Pandora's Ambition

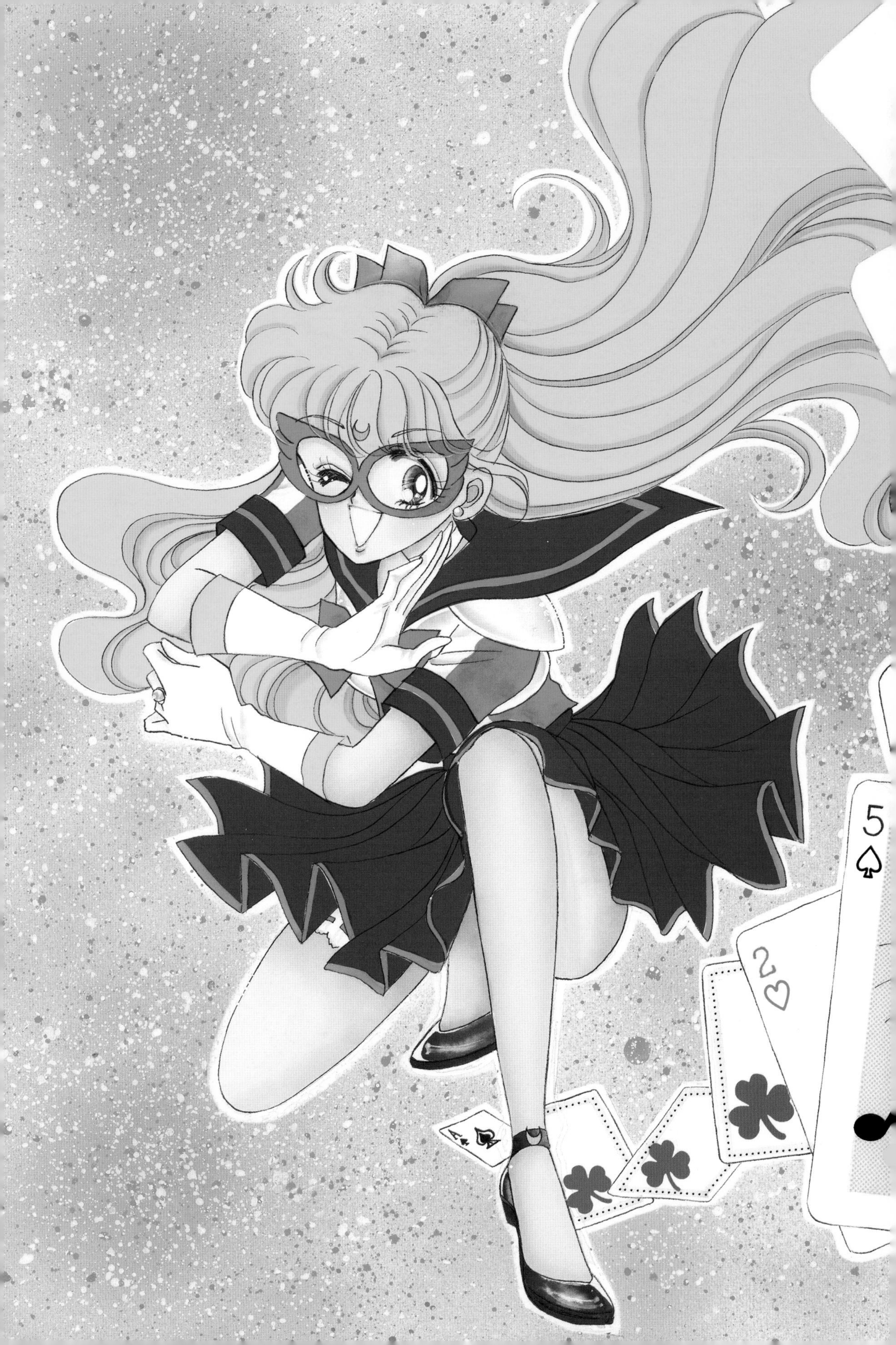

Codename Sailor V

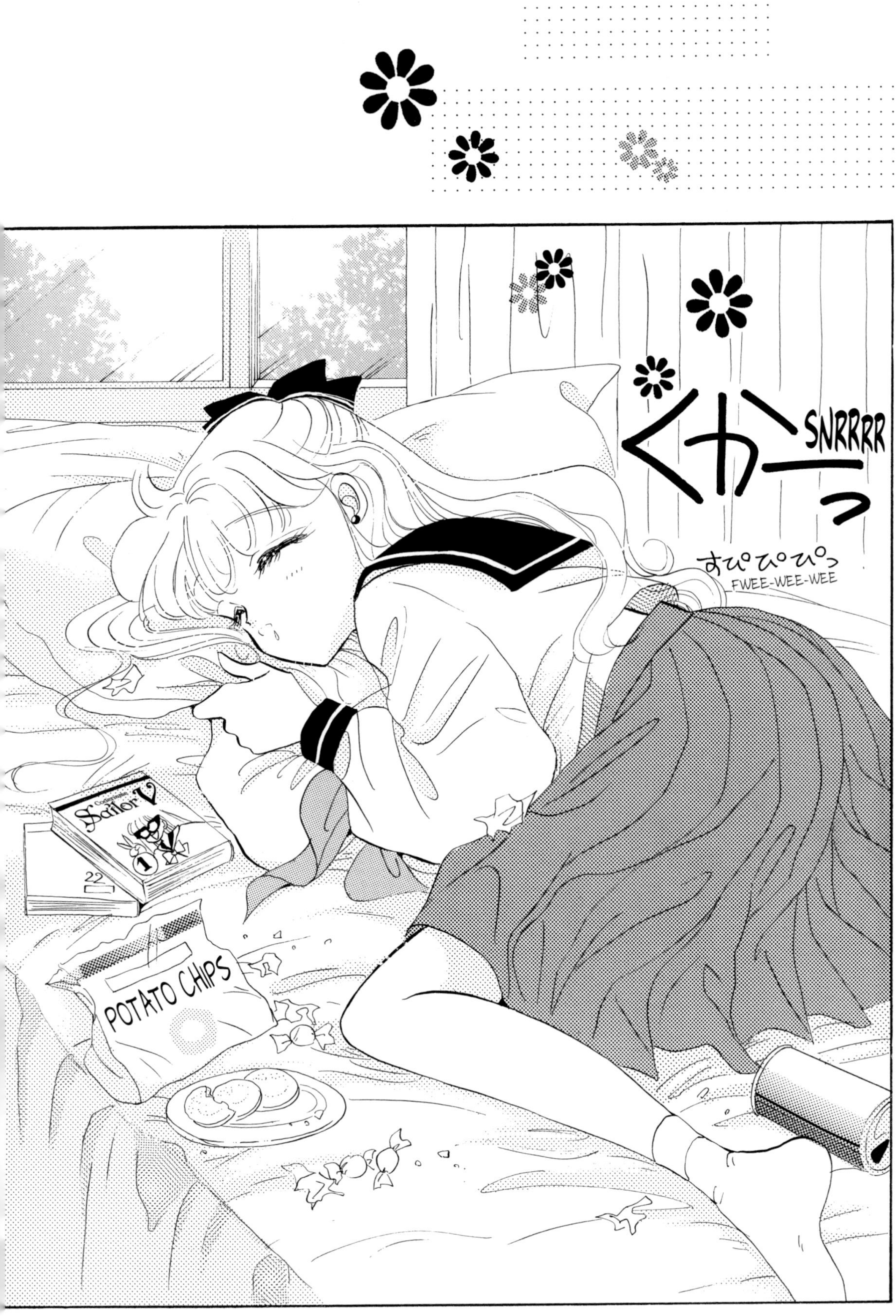
くかーっ
SNRRRR
すぴぴぴっ
FWEE-WEE-WEE
Sailor V
POTATO CHIPS

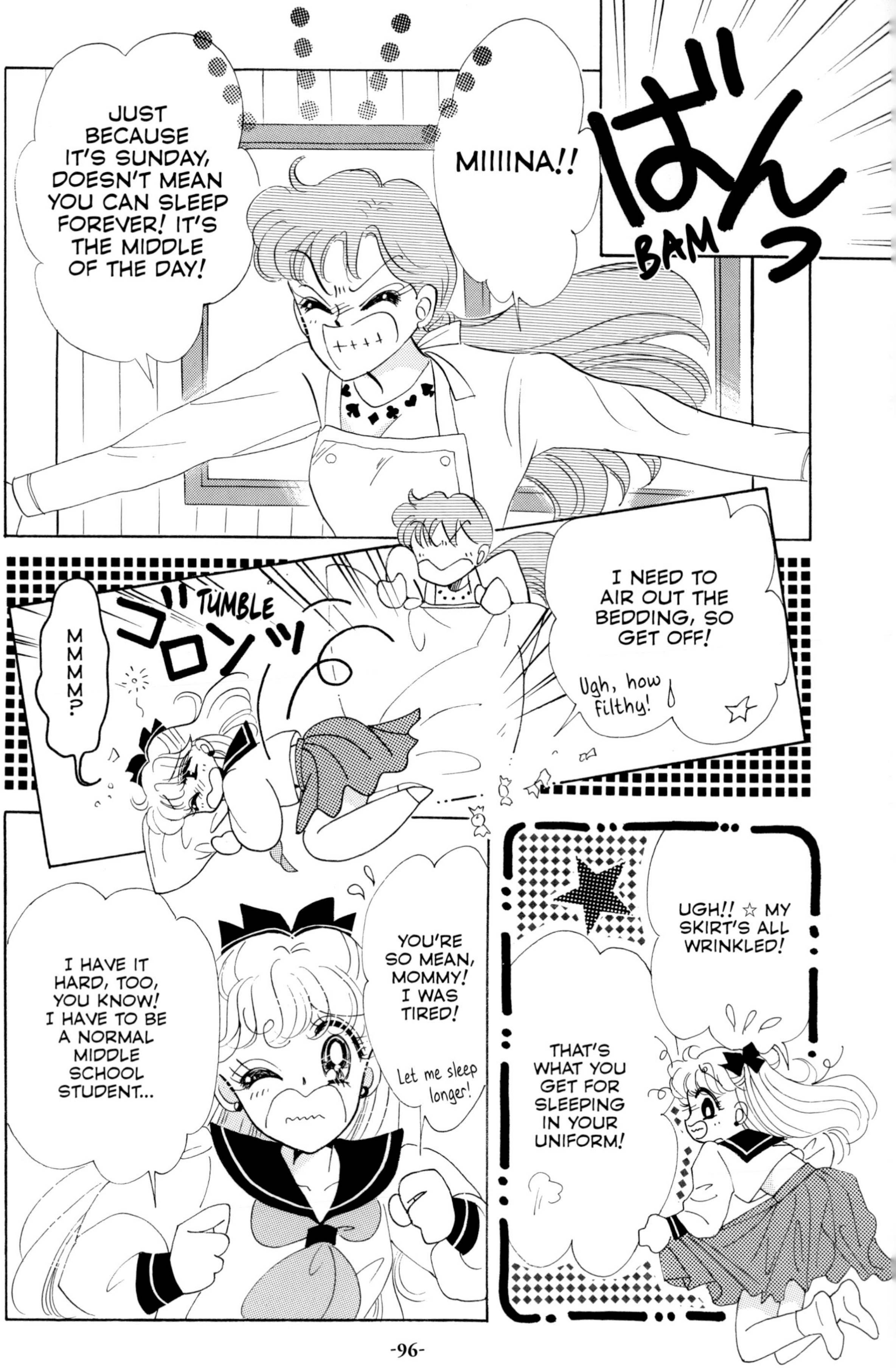
ばんっ
BAM
MIIIINA!!
JUST BECAUSE IT'S SUNDAY, DOESN'T MEAN YOU CAN SLEEP FOREVER! IT'S THE MIDDLE OF THE DAY!
I NEED TO AIR OUT THE BEDDING, SO GET OFF!
Ugh, how filthy!
コロンッ
TUMBLE
MMMM?
UGH!! ☆ MY SKIRT'S ALL WRINKLED!
THAT'S WHAT YOU GET FOR SLEEPING IN YOUR UNIFORM!
YOU'RE SO MEAN, MOMMY! I WAS TIRED!
Let me sleep longer!
I HAVE IT HARD, TOO, YOU KNOW! I HAVE TO BE A NORMAL MIDDLE SCHOOL STUDENT...

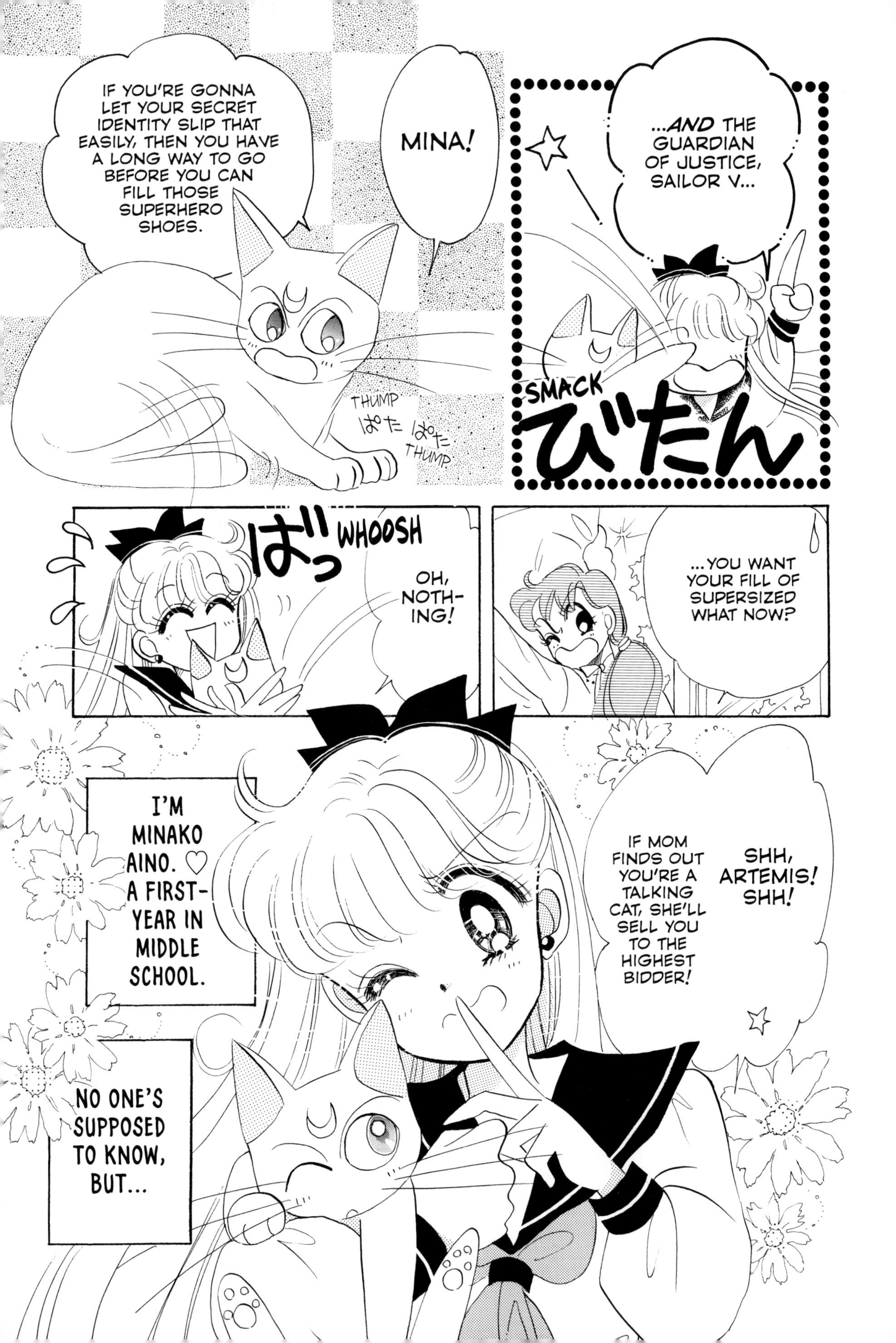
...AND THE GUARDIAN OF JUSTICE, SAILOR V...
SMACK
びたん
MINA!
IF YOU'RE GONNA LET YOUR SECRET IDENTITY SLIP THAT EASILY, THEN YOU HAVE A LONG WAY TO GO BEFORE YOU CAN FILL THOSE SUPERHERO SHOES.
THUMP
ぱた ぱた
THUMP
...YOU WANT YOUR FILL OF SUPERSIZED WHAT NOW?
ばっ
WHOOSH
OH, NOTH-ING!
SHH, ARTEMIS! SHH!
IF MOM FINDS OUT YOU'RE A TALKING CAT, SHE'LL SELL YOU TO THE HIGHEST BIDDER!
I'M MINAKO AINO. ♡ A FIRST-YEAR IN MIDDLE SCHOOL.
NO ONE'S SUPPOSED TO KNOW, BUT...

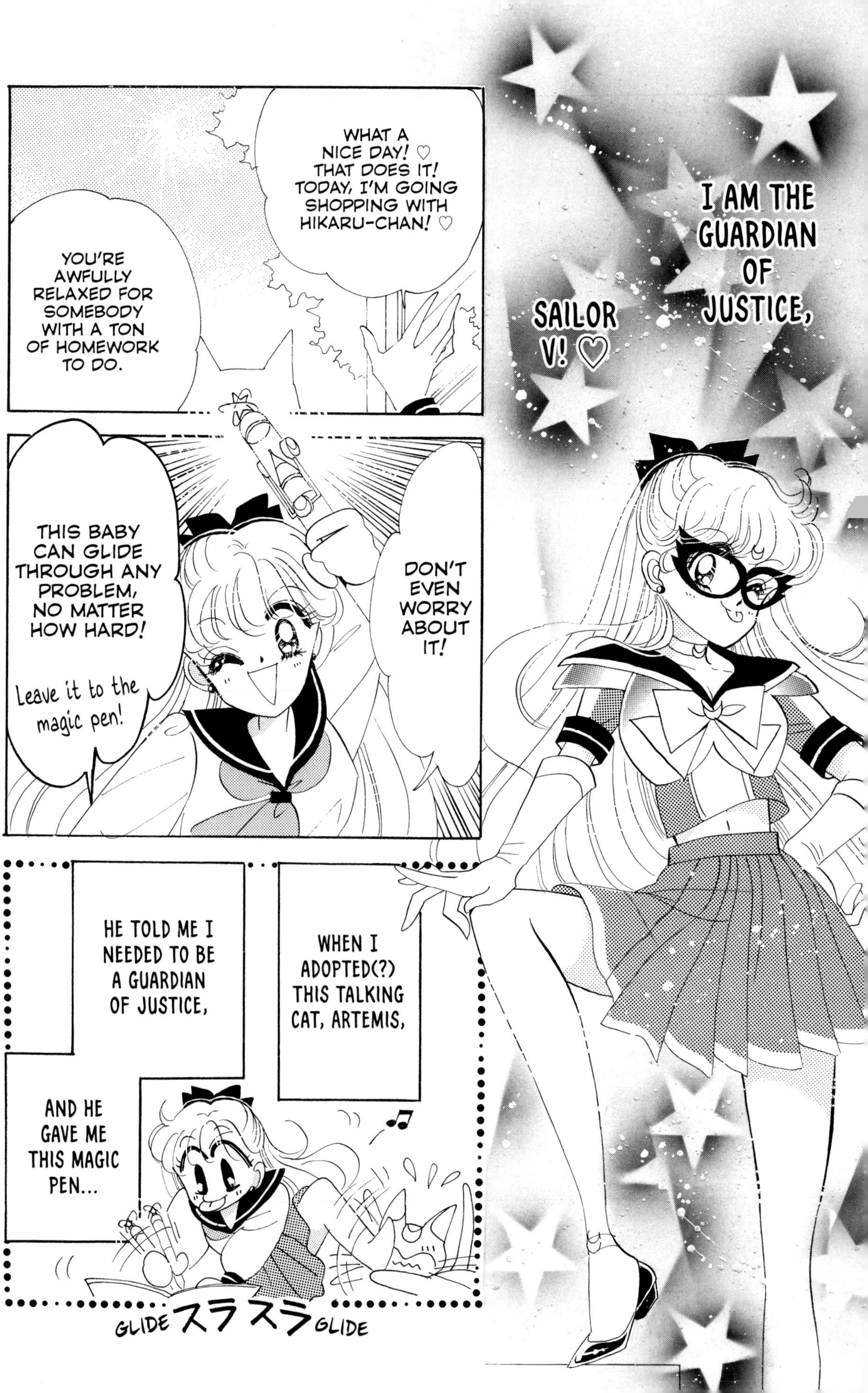
I AM THE GUARDIAN OF JUSTICE,
SAILOR V! ♡
WHAT A NICE DAY! ♡ THAT DOES IT! TODAY, I'M GOING SHOPPING WITH HIKARU-CHAN! ♡
YOU'RE AWFULLY RELAXED FOR SOMEBODY WITH A TON OF HOMEWORK TO DO.
DON'T EVEN WORRY ABOUT IT!
THIS BABY CAN GLIDE THROUGH ANY PROBLEM, NO MATTER HOW HARD!
Leave it to the magic pen!
WHEN I ADOPTED(?) THIS TALKING CAT, ARTEMIS,
HE TOLD ME I NEEDED TO BE A GUARDIAN OF JUSTICE,
AND HE GAVE ME THIS MAGIC PEN...
GLIDE スラスラ GLIDE

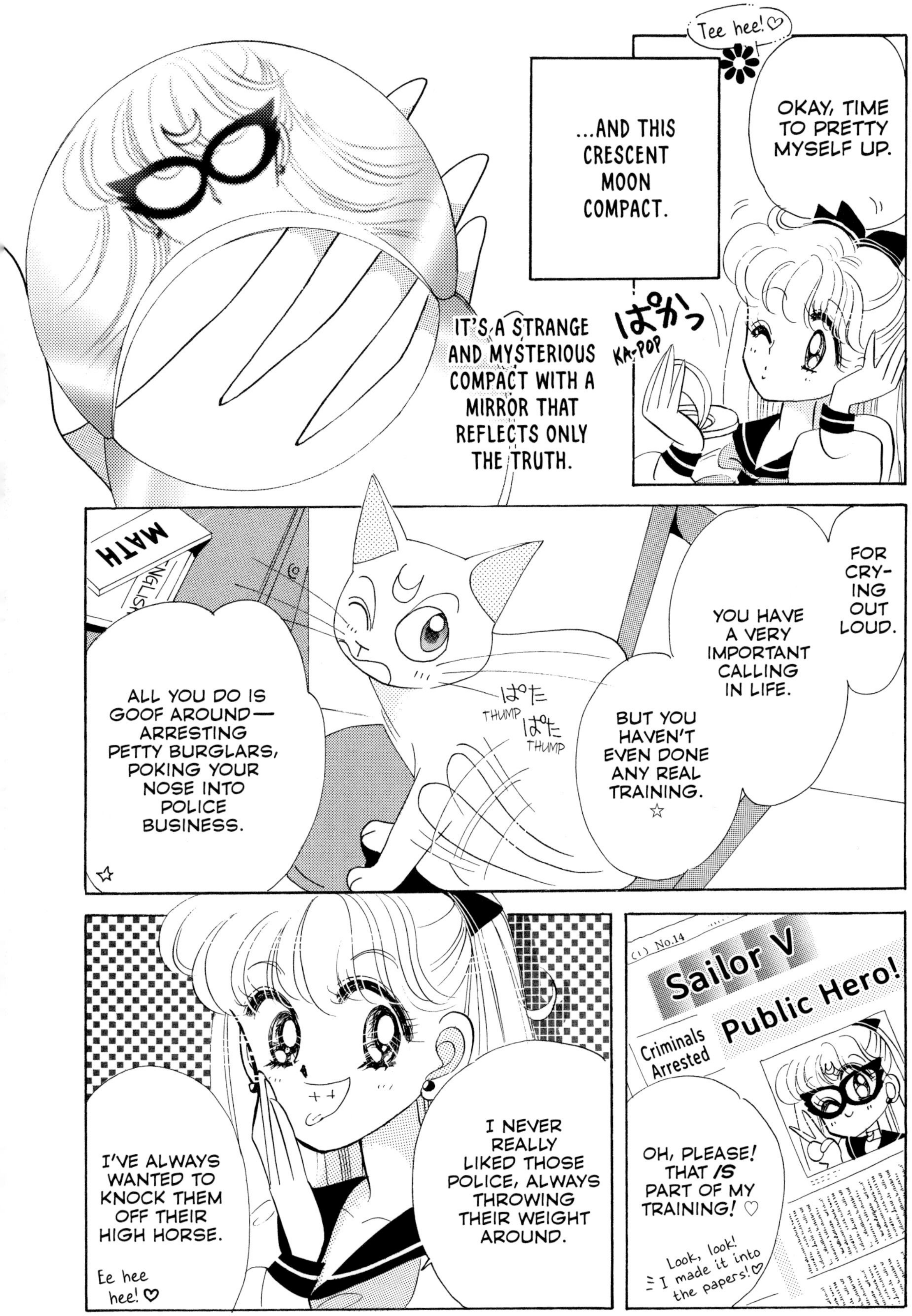
Tee hee!♡
OKAY, TIME TO PRETTY MYSELF UP.
...AND THIS CRESCENT MOON COMPACT.
ぱかっ KA-POP
IT'S A STRANGE AND MYSTERIOUS COMPACT WITH A MIRROR THAT REFLECTS ONLY THE TRUTH.
FOR CRY-ING OUT LOUD.
YOU HAVE A VERY IMPORTANT CALLING IN LIFE.
BUT YOU HAVEN'T EVEN DONE ANY REAL TRAINING. ☆
ぱた THUMP ぱた THUMP
MATH
ENGLISH
ALL YOU DO IS GOOF AROUND— ARRESTING PETTY BURGLARS, POKING YOUR NOSE INTO POLICE BUSINESS. ☆
(1) No.14
Sailor V Public Hero!
Criminals Arrested
OH, PLEASE! THAT IS PART OF MY TRAINING! ♡
Look, look! I made it into the papers!♡
I NEVER REALLY LIKED THOSE POLICE, ALWAYS THROWING THEIR WEIGHT AROUND.
I'VE ALWAYS WANTED TO KNOCK THEM OFF THEIR HIGH HORSE.
Ee hee hee!♡

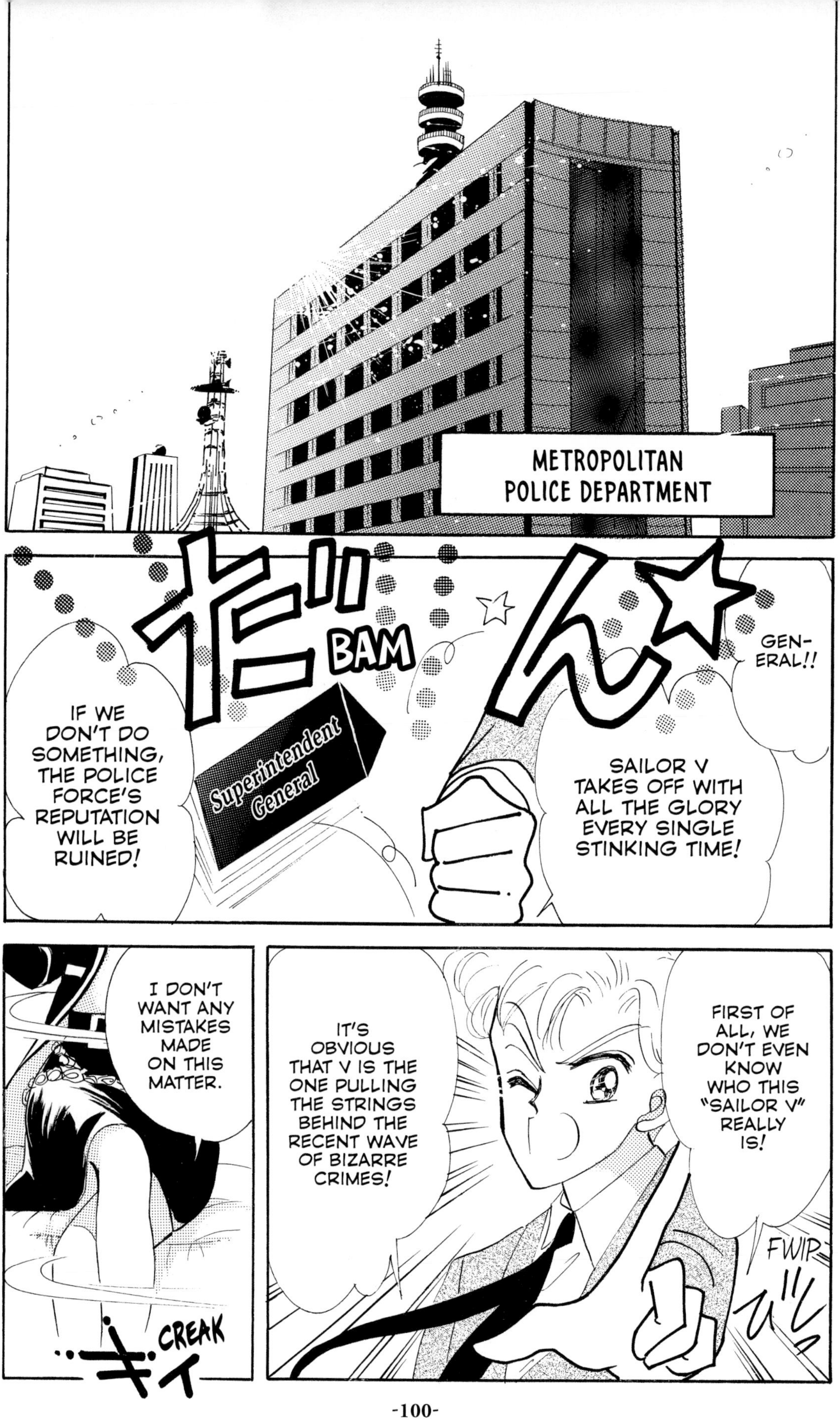
METROPOLITAN POLICE DEPARTMENT
GEN-ERAL!!
SAILOR V TAKES OFF WITH ALL THE GLORY EVERY SINGLE STINKING TIME!
BAM
Superintendent General
IF WE DON'T DO SOMETHING, THE POLICE FORCE'S REPUTATION WILL BE RUINED!
FIRST OF ALL, WE DON'T EVEN KNOW WHO THIS "SAILOR V" REALLY IS!
IT'S OBVIOUS THAT V IS THE ONE PULLING THE STRINGS BEHIND THE RECENT WAVE OF BIZARRE CRIMES!
FWIP
I DON'T WANT ANY MISTAKES MADE ON THIS MATTER.
CREAK

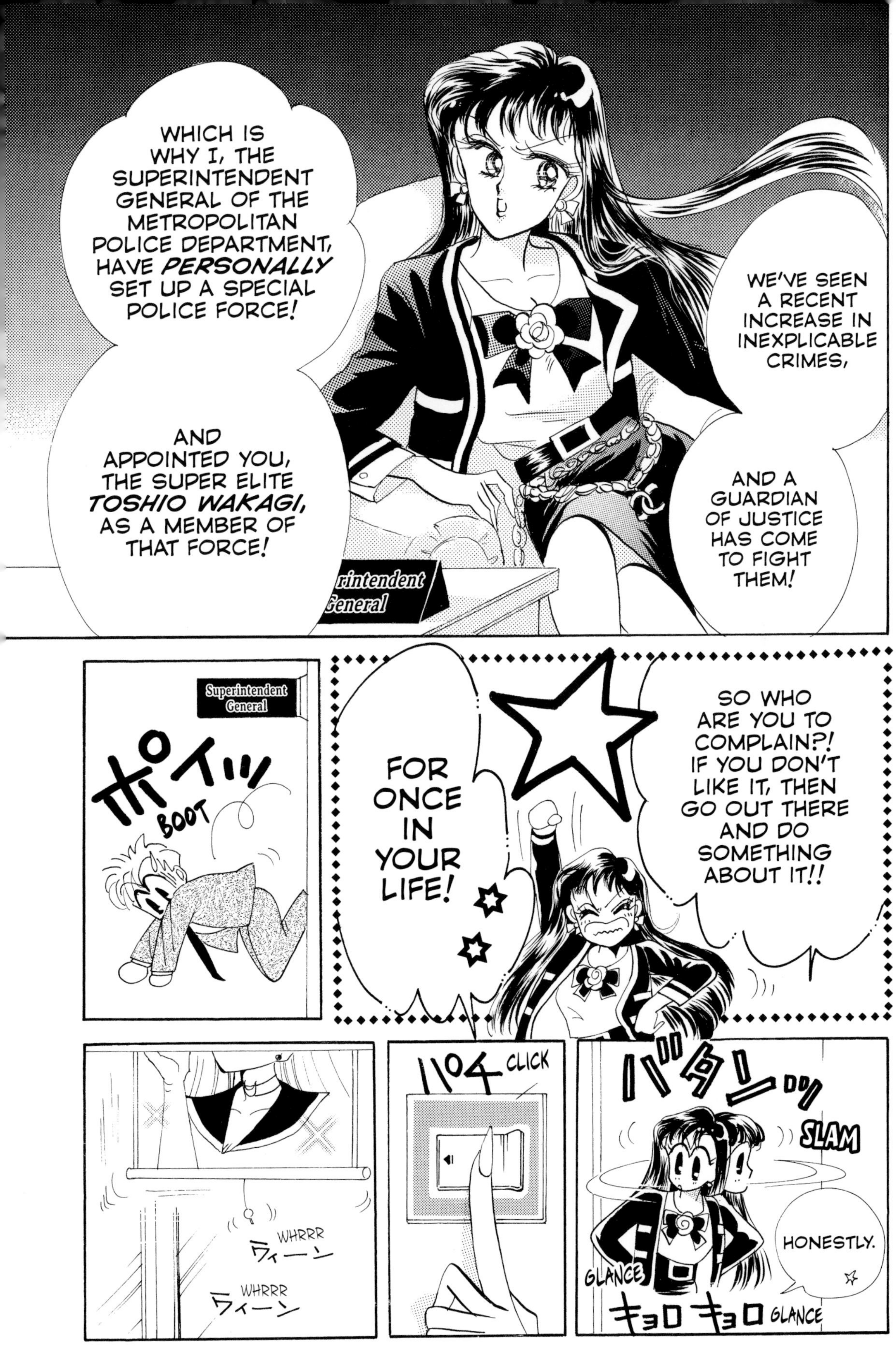
WE'VE SEEN A RECENT INCREASE IN INEXPLICABLE CRIMES,
AND A GUARDIAN OF JUSTICE HAS COME TO FIGHT THEM!
WHICH IS WHY I, THE SUPERINTENDENT GENERAL OF THE METROPOLITAN POLICE DEPARTMENT, HAVE *PERSONALLY* SET UP A SPECIAL POLICE FORCE!
AND APPOINTED YOU, THE SUPER ELITE *TOSHIO WAKAGI*, AS A MEMBER OF THAT FORCE!
rintendent General
SO WHO ARE YOU TO COMPLAIN?! IF YOU DON'T LIKE IT, THEN GO OUT THERE AND DO SOMETHING ABOUT IT!!
FOR ONCE IN YOUR LIFE!
Superintendent General
ポイッ
BOOT
バタンッ
SLAM
HONESTLY.
GLANCE
キョロ キョロ
GLANCE
パチ
CLICK
WHRRR
ウィーン
WHRRR
ウィーン

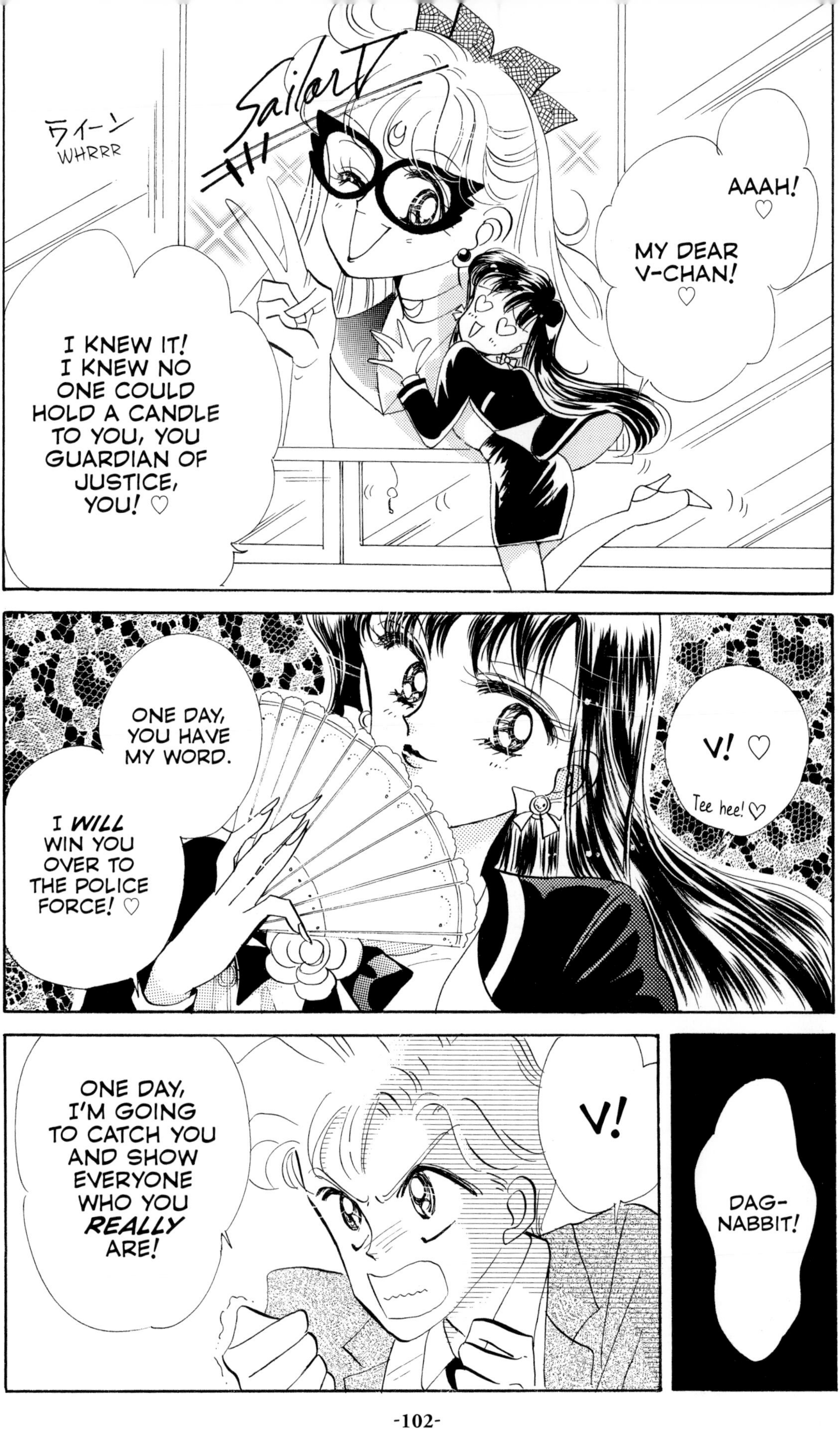
AAAH! ♡
MY DEAR V-CHAN! ♡
Sailor V
ライーン WHRRR
I KNEW IT! I KNEW NO ONE COULD HOLD A CANDLE TO YOU, YOU GUARDIAN OF JUSTICE, YOU! ♡
V! ♡
Tee hee! ♡
ONE DAY, YOU HAVE MY WORD.
I *WILL* WIN YOU OVER TO THE POLICE FORCE! ♡
DAG-NABBIT!
V!
ONE DAY, I'M GOING TO CATCH YOU AND SHOW EVERYONE WHO YOU ***REALLY*** ARE!

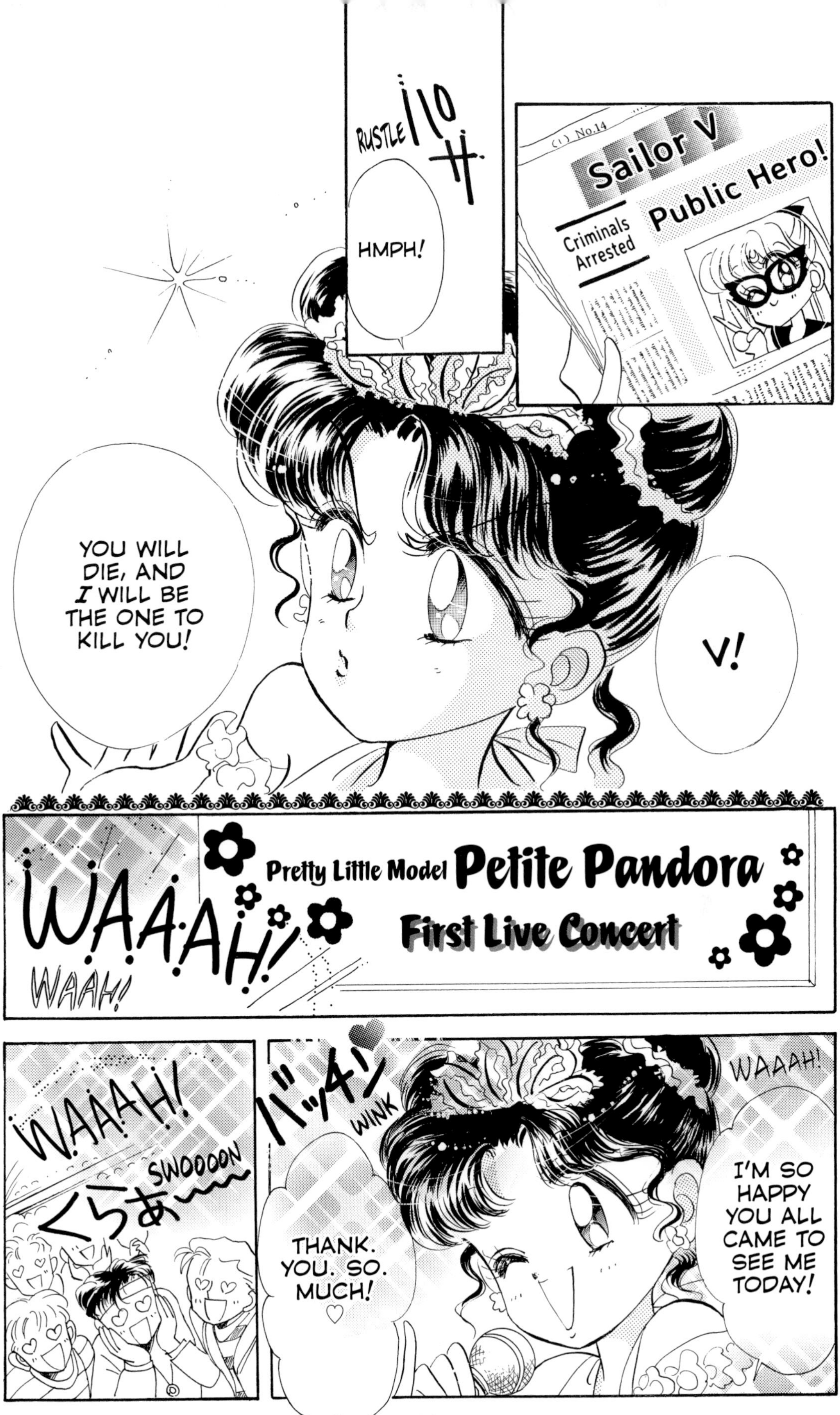
(1) No.14
Sailor V
Public Hero!
Criminals Arrested
RUSTLE
HMPH!
V!
YOU WILL DIE, AND *I* WILL BE THE ONE TO KILL YOU!
WAAAH!
WAAH!
Pretty Little Model Petite Pandora
First Live Concert
WAAAH!
I'M SO HAPPY YOU ALL CAME TO SEE ME TODAY!
バッチン
WINK
THANK. YOU. SO. MUCH!
WAAAH!
くらあ~~
SWOOOON

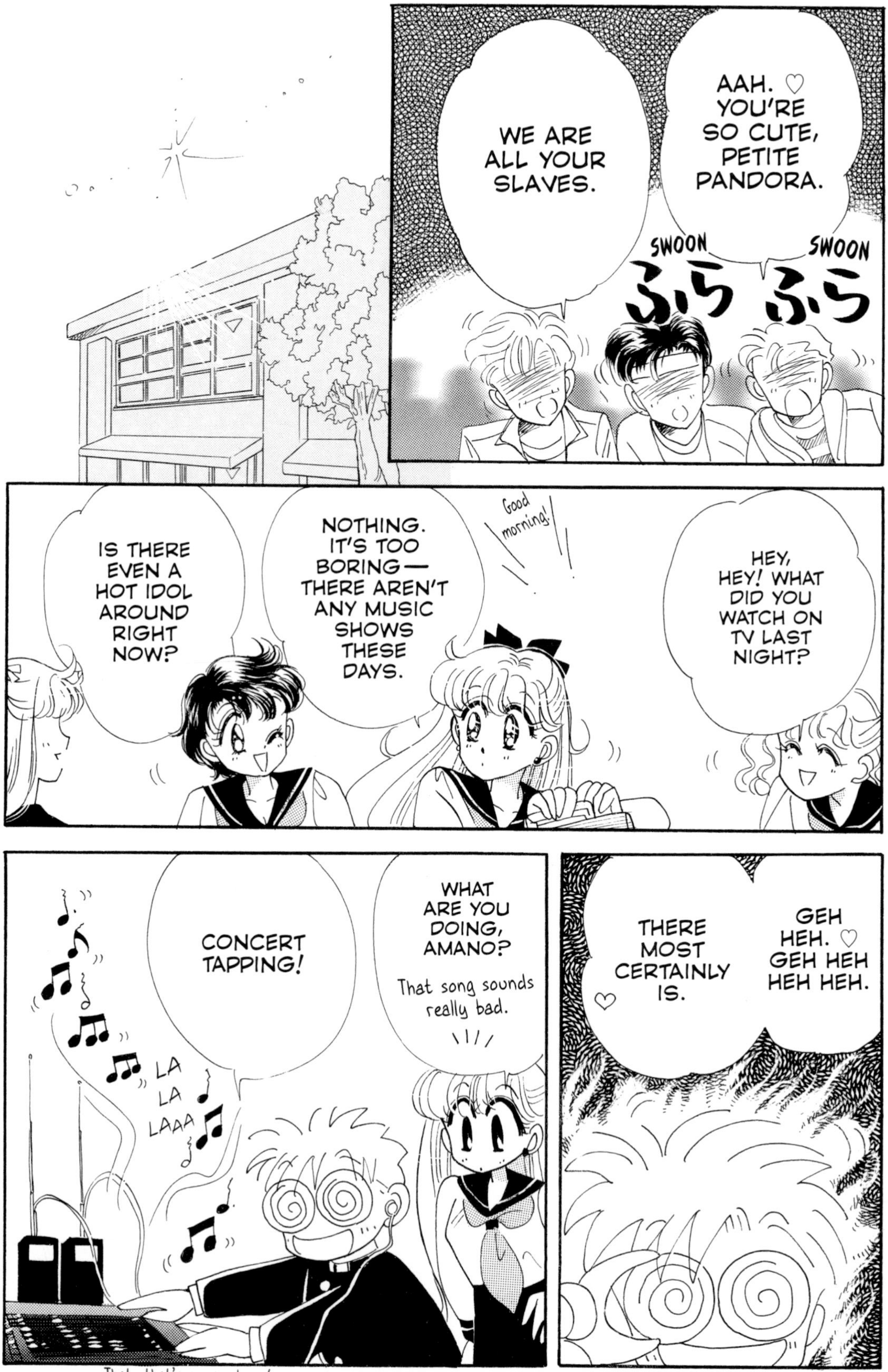
AAH. ♡ YOU'RE SO CUTE, PETITE PANDORA.
WE ARE ALL YOUR SLAVES.
SWOON ふら
SWOON ふら
HEY, HEY! WHAT DID YOU WATCH ON TV LAST NIGHT?
Good morning!
NOTHING. IT'S TOO BORING—THERE AREN'T ANY MUSIC SHOWS THESE DAYS.
IS THERE EVEN A HOT IDOL AROUND RIGHT NOW?
GEH HEH. ♡ GEH HEH HEH HEH.
THERE MOST CERTAINLY IS. ♡
WHAT ARE YOU DOING, AMANO?
That song sounds really bad.
CONCERT TAPPING!
LA LA LAAA
That...that's some setup. ♪

Apparently you have to be near the concert venue for it to work.
Don't try this at home if you want to stay out of trouble!

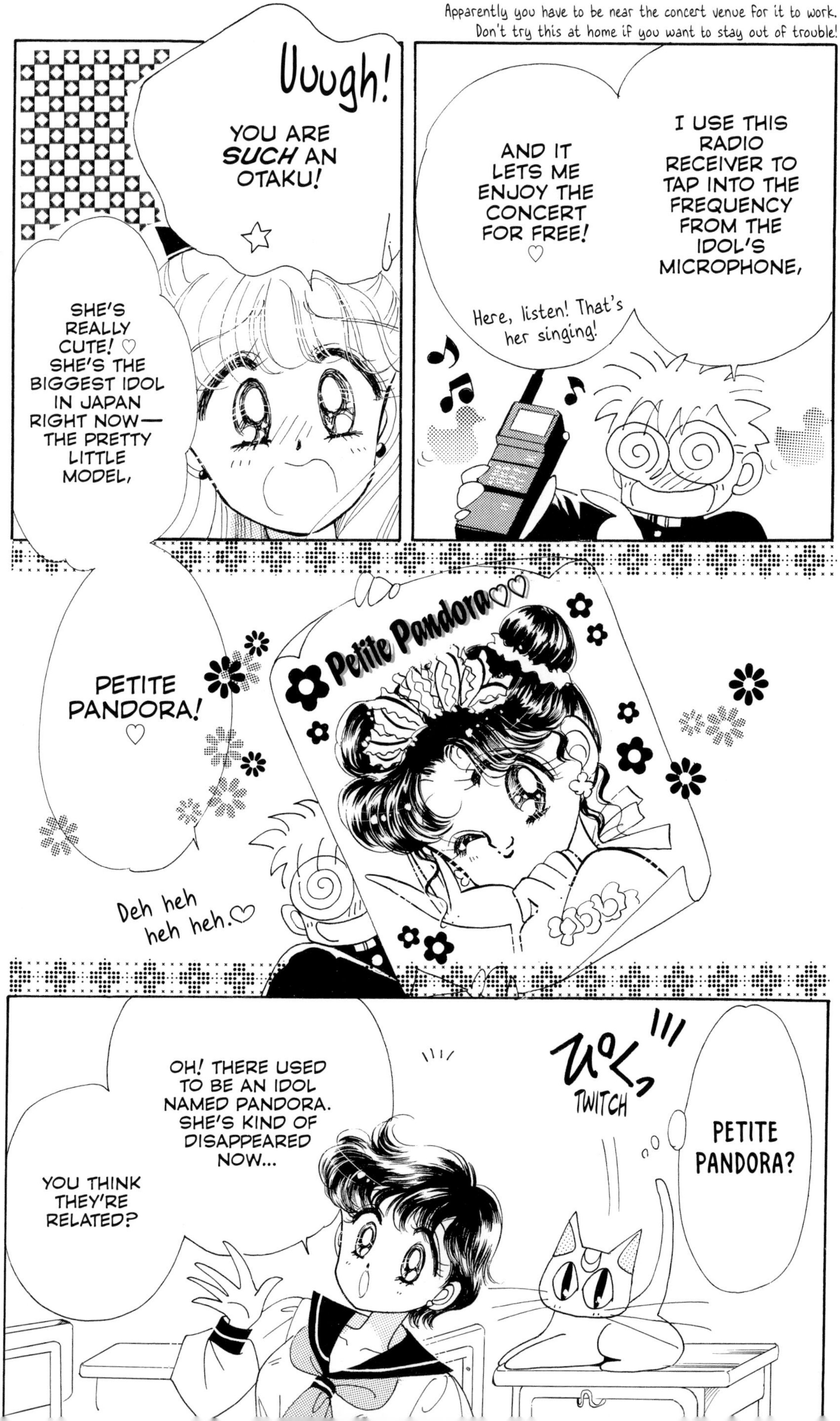

I USE THIS RADIO RECEIVER TO TAP INTO THE FREQUENCY FROM THE IDOL'S MICROPHONE,
AND IT LETS ME ENJOY THE CONCERT FOR FREE! ♡
Here, listen! That's her singing!
Uuugh!
YOU ARE *SUCH* AN OTAKU!
SHE'S REALLY CUTE! ♡ SHE'S THE BIGGEST IDOL IN JAPAN RIGHT NOW—THE PRETTY LITTLE MODEL,
PETITE PANDORA! ♡
Petite Pandora♡♡
Deh heh heh heh.♡
PETITE PANDORA?
ぴくっ
TWITCH
OH! THERE USED TO BE AN IDOL NAMED PANDORA. SHE'S KIND OF DISAPPEARED NOW...
YOU THINK THEY'RE RELATED?

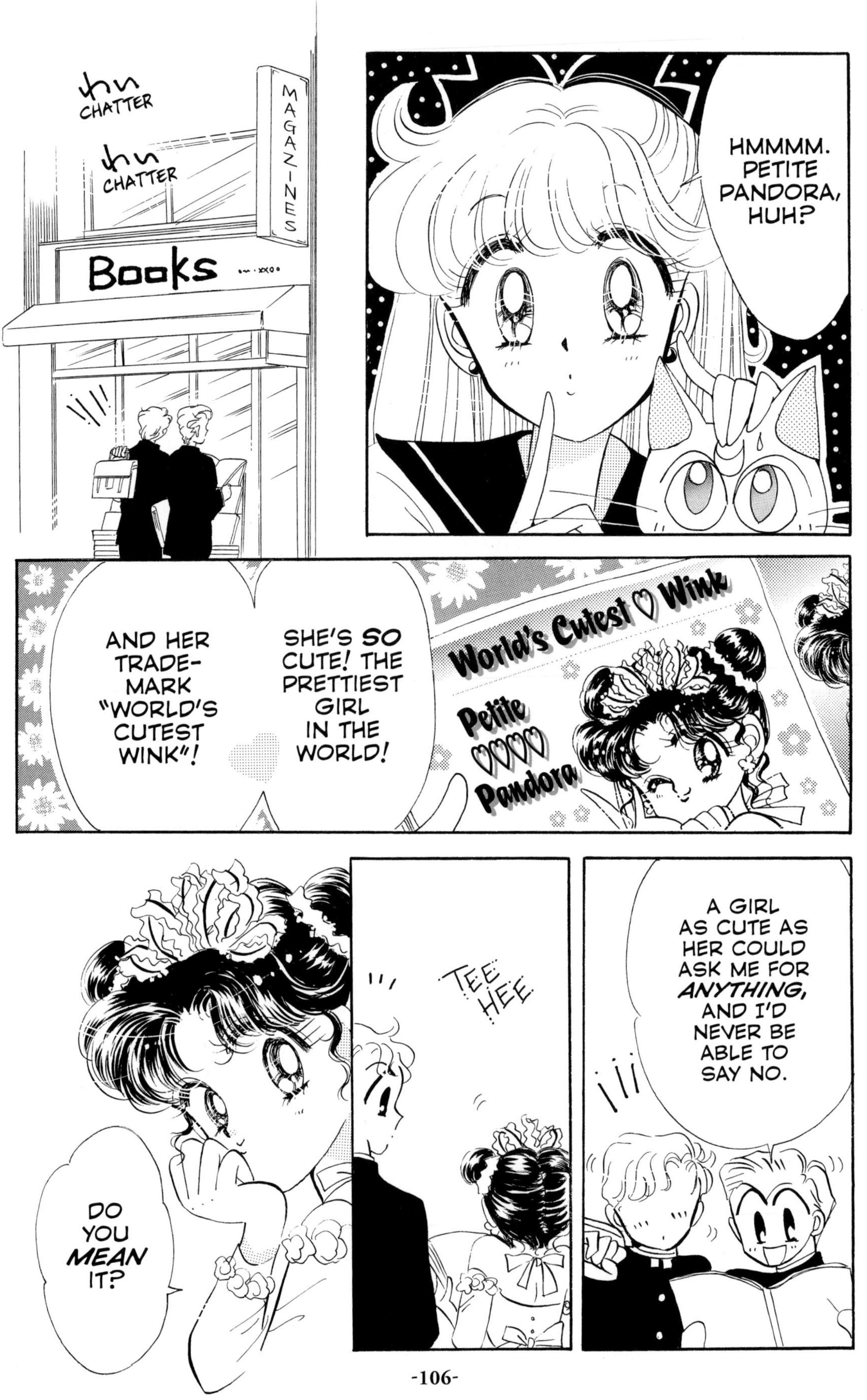

HMMMM. PETITE PANDORA, HUH?
CHATTER
CHATTER
MAGAZINES
Books
World's Cutest ♡ Wink
Petite ♡♡♡♡ Pandora
SHE'S **SO** CUTE! THE PRETTIEST GIRL IN THE WORLD!
AND HER TRADE-MARK "WORLD'S CUTEST WINK"!
A GIRL AS CUTE AS HER COULD ASK ME FOR ***ANYTHING,*** AND I'D NEVER BE ABLE TO SAY NO.
TEE HEE
DO YOU ***MEAN*** IT?

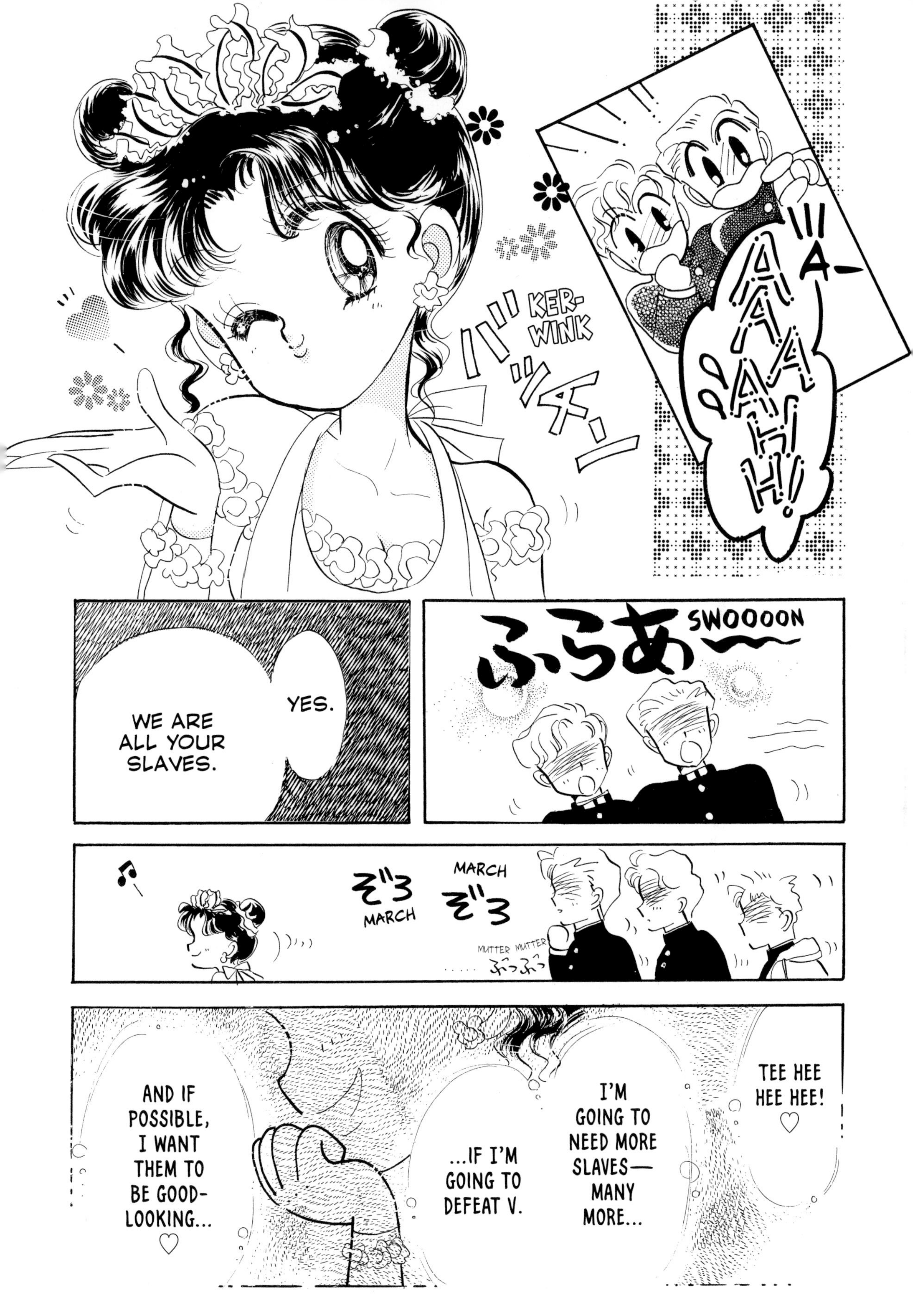

A-AAAAHH!
ハッチン
KER-WINK
ふらあ〜
SWOOOON
YES.
WE ARE ALL YOUR SLAVES.
ぶつぶつ
MUTTER MUTTER
ぞろ
MARCH
ぞろ
MARCH
TEE HEE HEE HEE! ♡
I'M GOING TO NEED MORE SLAVES—MANY MORE...
...IF I'M GOING TO DEFEAT V.
AND IF POSSIBLE, I WANT THEM TO BE GOOD-LOOKING... ♡

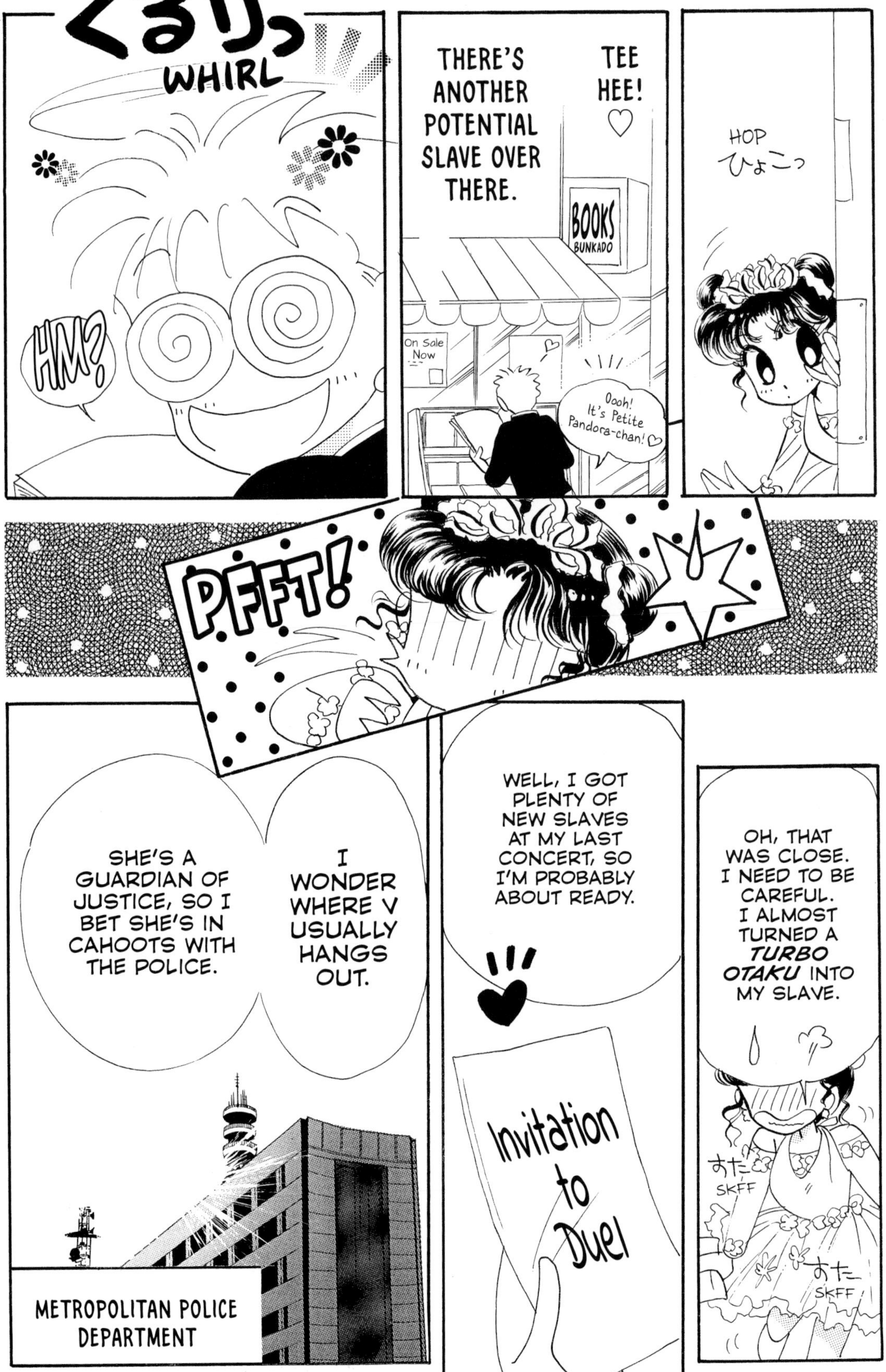
HOP
ひょこっ
TEE HEE! ♡
THERE'S ANOTHER POTENTIAL SLAVE OVER THERE.
BOOKS
BUNKADO
On Sale Now
Oooh! It's Petite Pandora-chan! ♡
くるりっ
WHIRL
HM?
PFFT!
OH, THAT WAS CLOSE. I NEED TO BE CAREFUL. I ALMOST TURNED A *TURBO OTAKU* INTO MY SLAVE.
すた
SKFF
すた
SKFF
WELL, I GOT PLENTY OF NEW SLAVES AT MY LAST CONCERT, SO I'M PROBABLY ABOUT READY.
Invitation to Duel
I WONDER WHERE V USUALLY HANGS OUT.
SHE'S A GUARDIAN OF JUSTICE, SO I BET SHE'S IN CAHOOTS WITH THE POLICE.
METROPOLITAN POLICE DEPARTMENT

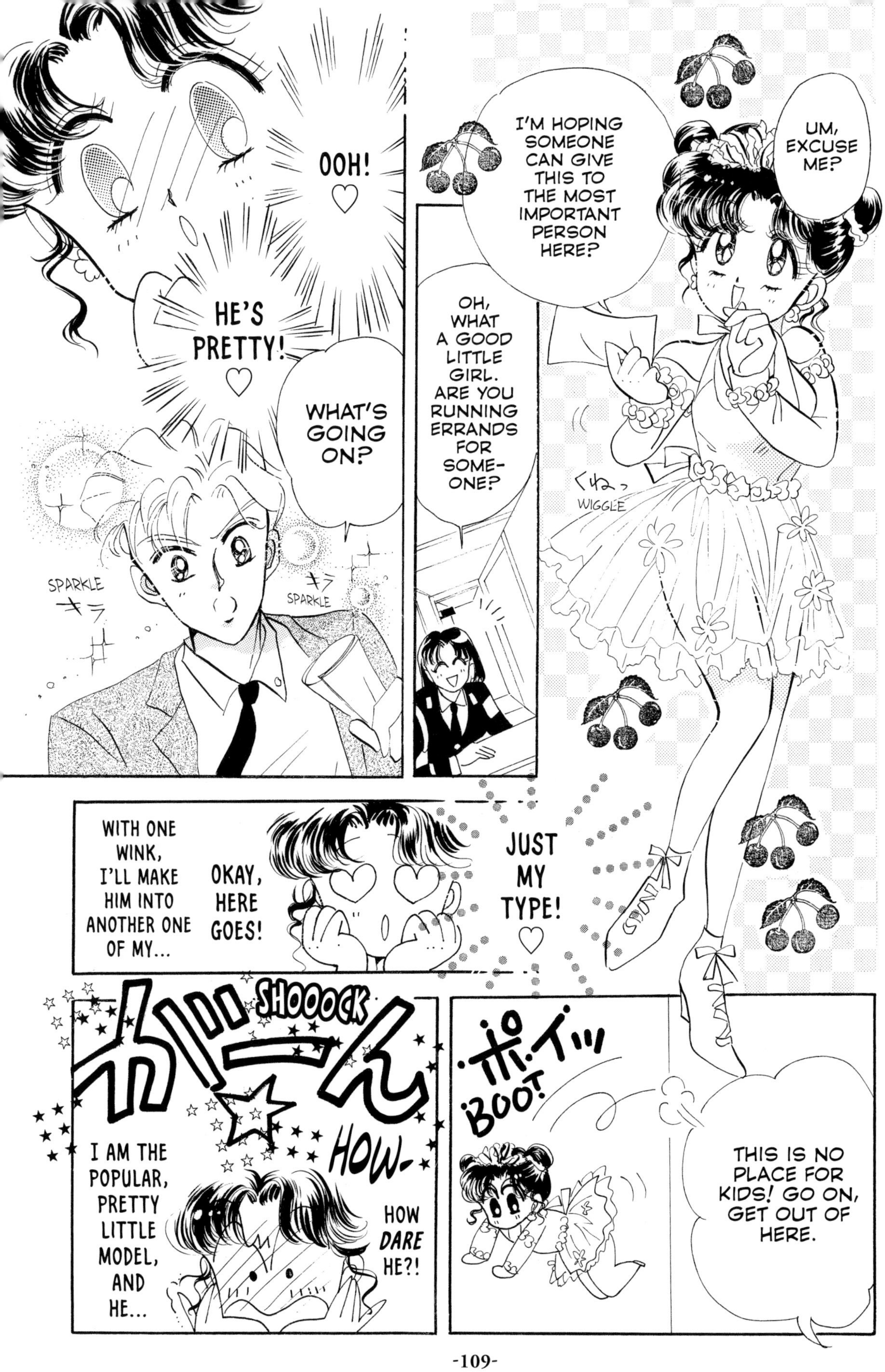
UM, EXCUSE ME?
I'M HOPING SOMEONE CAN GIVE THIS TO THE MOST IMPORTANT PERSON HERE?
くねっ
WIGGLE
OH, WHAT A GOOD LITTLE GIRL. ARE YOU RUNNING ERRANDS FOR SOME-ONE?
OOH! ♡
HE'S PRETTY! ♡
WHAT'S GOING ON?
キラ
SPARKLE
SPARKLE
キラ
JUST MY TYPE! ♡
OKAY, HERE GOES!
WITH ONE WINK, I'LL MAKE HIM INTO ANOTHER ONE OF MY...
ポイッ
BOOT!
THIS IS NO PLACE FOR KIDS! GO ON, GET OUT OF HERE.
がーん
SHOOOCK
HOW-
HOW DARE HE?!
I AM THE POPULAR, PRETTY LITTLE MODEL, AND HE...

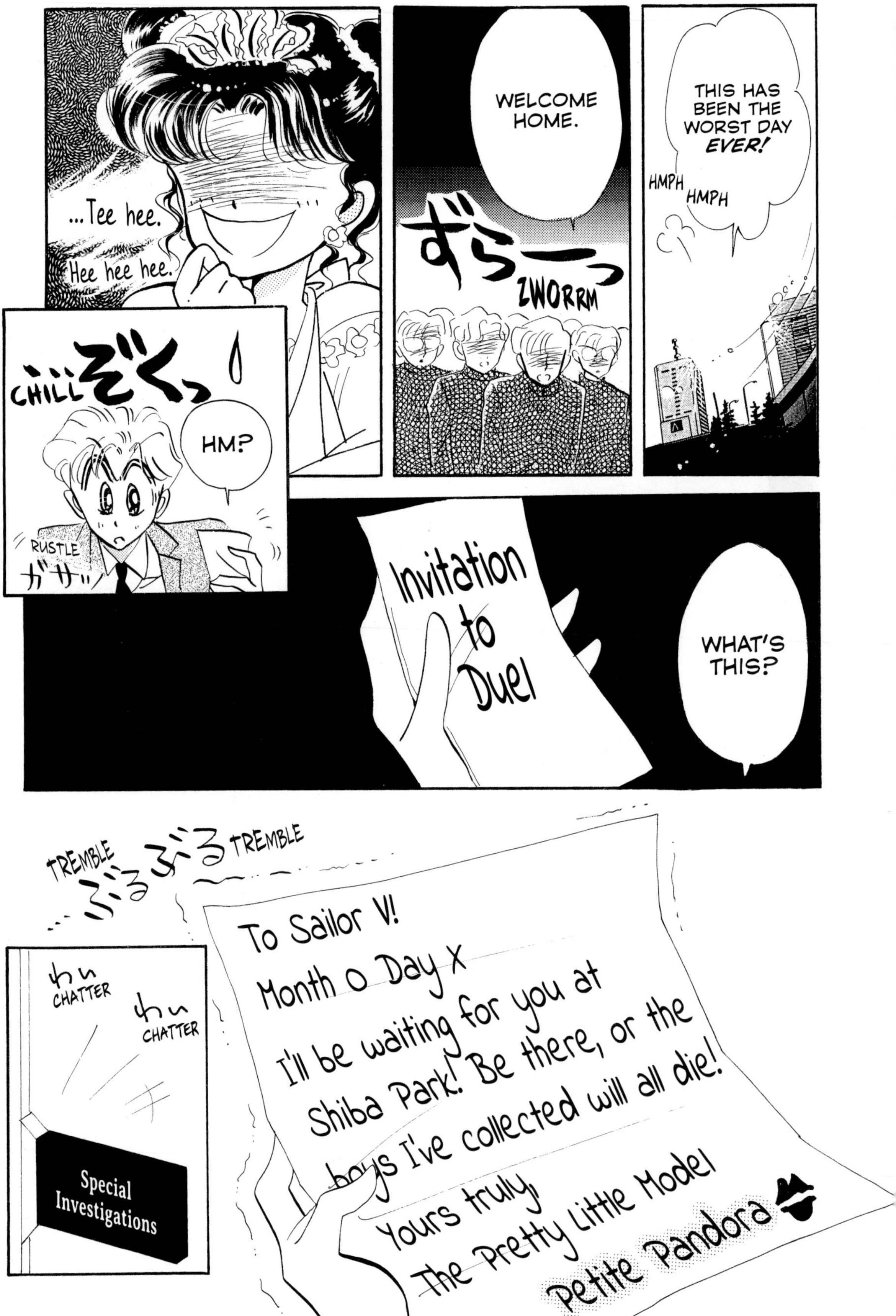
THIS HAS BEEN THE WORST DAY *EVER!*
HMPH HMPH
WELCOME HOME.
ずらーっ ZWORRM
...Tee hee.
Hee hee hee.
CHILL ぞくっ
HM?
RUSTLE ガサッ
WHAT'S THIS?
Invitation to Duel
TREMBLE ぶるぶる TREMBLE
To Sailor V!
Month ○ Day X
I'll be waiting for you at Shiba Park! Be there, or the boys I've collected will all die!
Yours truly,
The Pretty Little Model
Petite Pandora
わい CHATTER
わい CHATTER
Special Investigations

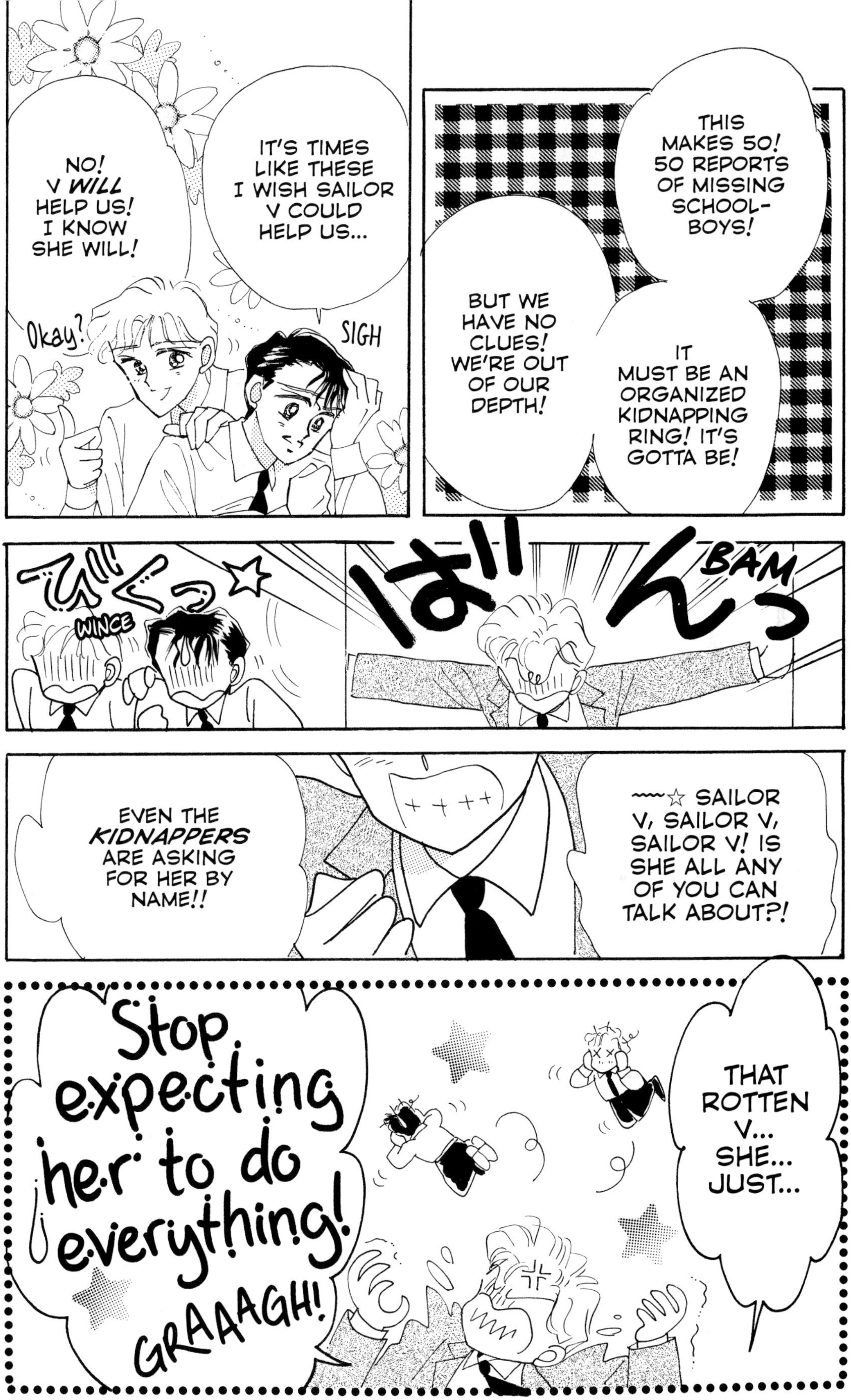
THIS MAKES 50! 50 REPORTS OF MISSING SCHOOL-BOYS!
BUT WE HAVE NO CLUES! WE'RE OUT OF OUR DEPTH!
IT MUST BE AN ORGANIZED KIDNAPPING RING! IT'S GOTTA BE!
IT'S TIMES LIKE THESE I WISH SAILOR V COULD HELP US...
SIGH
NO! V *WILL* HELP US! I KNOW SHE WILL!
Okay?
ばんっ
BAM
びくっ
WINCE
~~~☆ SAILOR V, SAILOR V, SAILOR V! IS SHE ALL ANY OF YOU CAN TALK ABOUT?!
EVEN THE *KIDNAPPERS* ARE ASKING FOR HER BY NAME!!
THAT ROTTEN V... SHE... JUST...
Stop expecting her to do everything!
GRAAAGH!
~~~

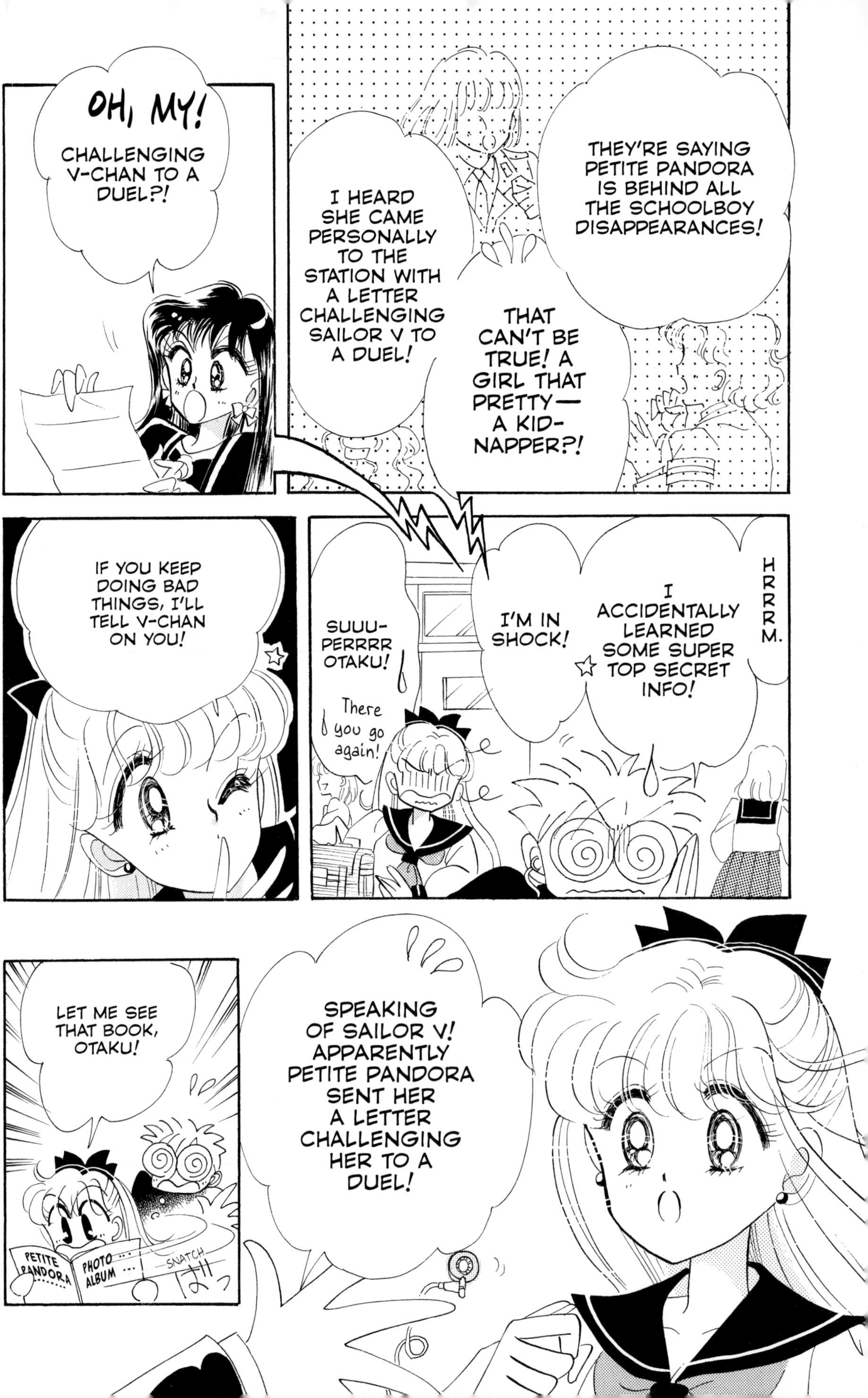
THEY'RE SAYING PETITE PANDORA IS BEHIND ALL THE SCHOOLBOY DISAPPEARANCES!
I HEARD SHE CAME PERSONALLY TO THE STATION WITH A LETTER CHALLENGING SAILOR V TO A DUEL!
THAT CAN'T BE TRUE! A GIRL THAT PRETTY— A KID-NAPPER?!
OH, MY! CHALLENGING V-CHAN TO A DUEL?!
HRRRM.
I ACCIDENTALLY LEARNED SOME SUPER TOP SECRET INFO!
I'M IN SHOCK!
SUUU-PERRRR OTAKU!
There you go again!
IF YOU KEEP DOING BAD THINGS, I'LL TELL V-CHAN ON YOU!
SPEAKING OF SAILOR V! APPARENTLY PETITE PANDORA SENT HER A LETTER CHALLENGING HER TO A DUEL!
LET ME SEE THAT BOOK, OTAKU!
PETITE PANDORA
PHOTO ALBUM ...
SNATCH

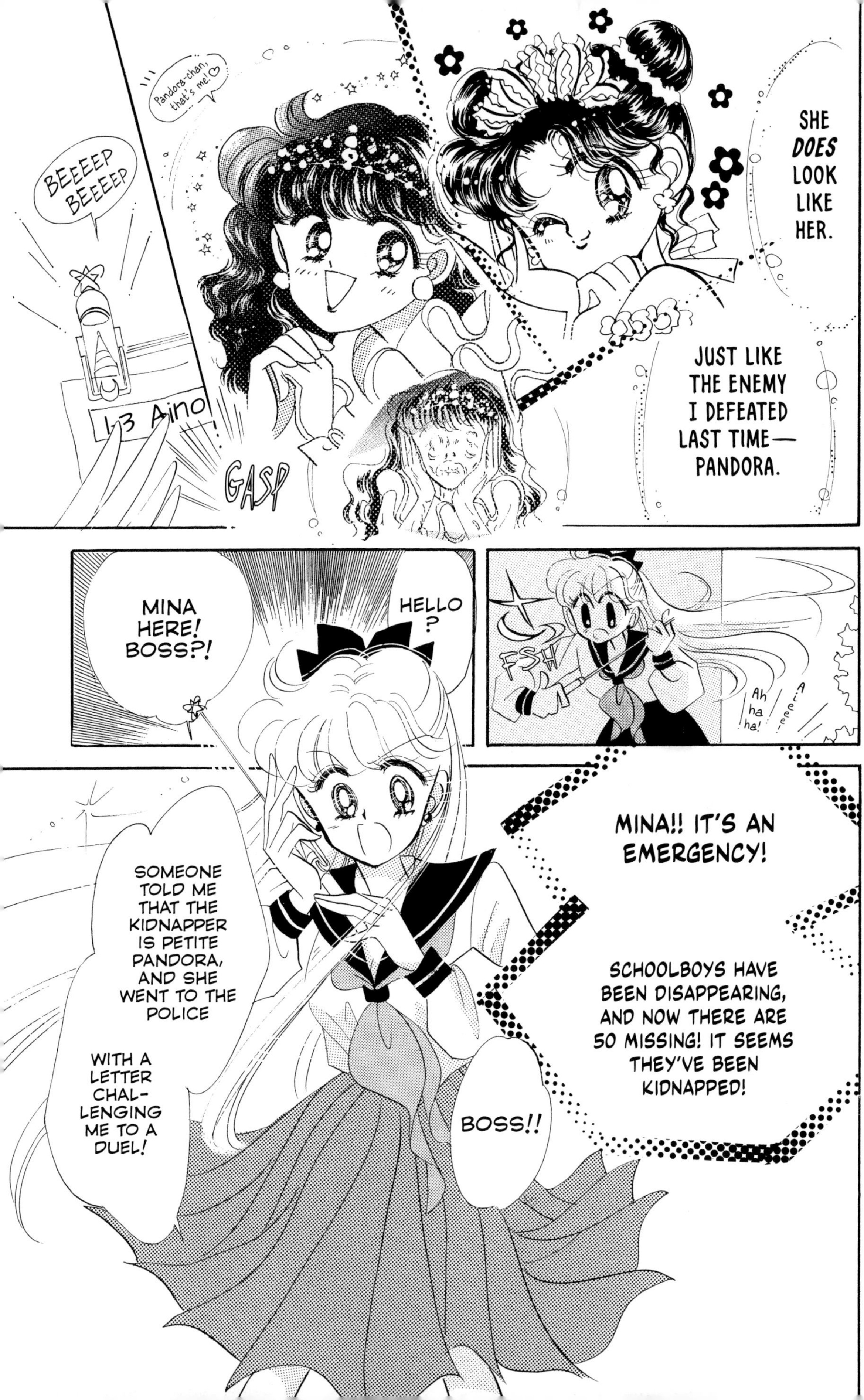
SHE DOES LOOK LIKE HER.
JUST LIKE THE ENEMY I DEFEATED LAST TIME— PANDORA.
Pandora-chan, that's me!♡
GASP
BEEEEP BEEEEP
1-3 Aino
Aieee!
Ah ha ha!
FSH
HELLO?
MINA HERE! BOSS?!
MINA!! IT'S AN EMERGENCY!
SCHOOLBOYS HAVE BEEN DISAPPEARING, AND NOW THERE ARE 50 MISSING! IT SEEMS THEY'VE BEEN KIDNAPPED!
BOSS!!
SOMEONE TOLD ME THAT THE KIDNAPPER IS PETITE PANDORA, AND SHE WENT TO THE POLICE
WITH A LETTER CHAL-LENGING ME TO A DUEL!

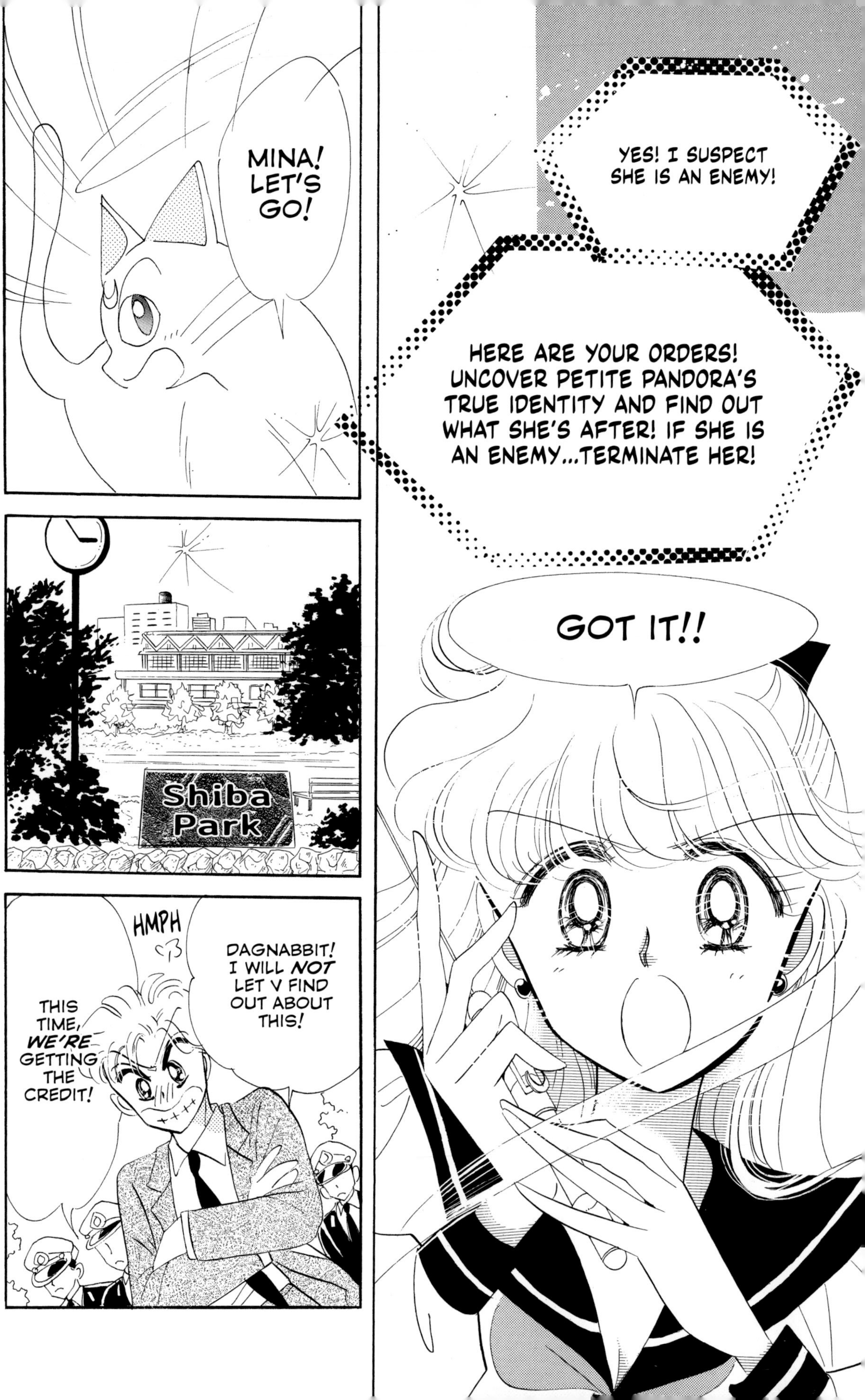
YES! I SUSPECT SHE IS AN ENEMY!
HERE ARE YOUR ORDERS! UNCOVER PETITE PANDORA'S TRUE IDENTITY AND FIND OUT WHAT SHE'S AFTER! IF SHE IS AN ENEMY...TERMINATE HER!
GOT IT!!
MINA! LET'S GO!
Shiba Park
HMPH
DAGNABBIT! I WILL *NOT* LET V FIND OUT ABOUT THIS!
THIS TIME, ***WE'RE*** GETTING THE CREDIT!

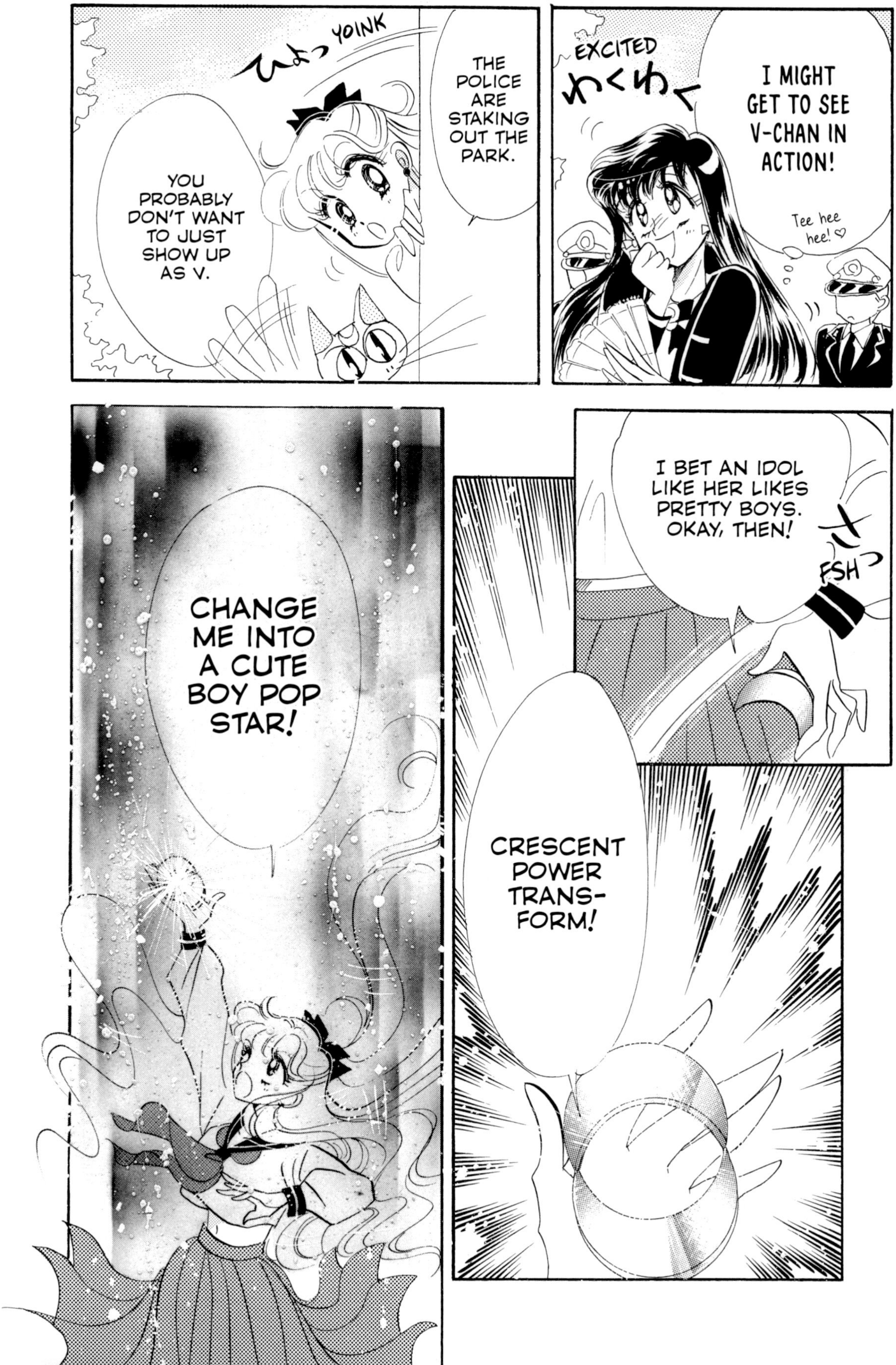
EXCITED
わくわく
I MIGHT GET TO SEE V-CHAN IN ACTION!
Tee hee hee! ♡
THE POLICE ARE STAKING OUT THE PARK.
ひよっ YOINK
YOU PROBABLY DON'T WANT TO JUST SHOW UP AS V.
I BET AN IDOL LIKE HER LIKES PRETTY BOYS. OKAY, THEN!
さっ FSH
CRESCENT POWER TRANS-FORM!
CHANGE ME INTO A CUTE BOY POP STAR!

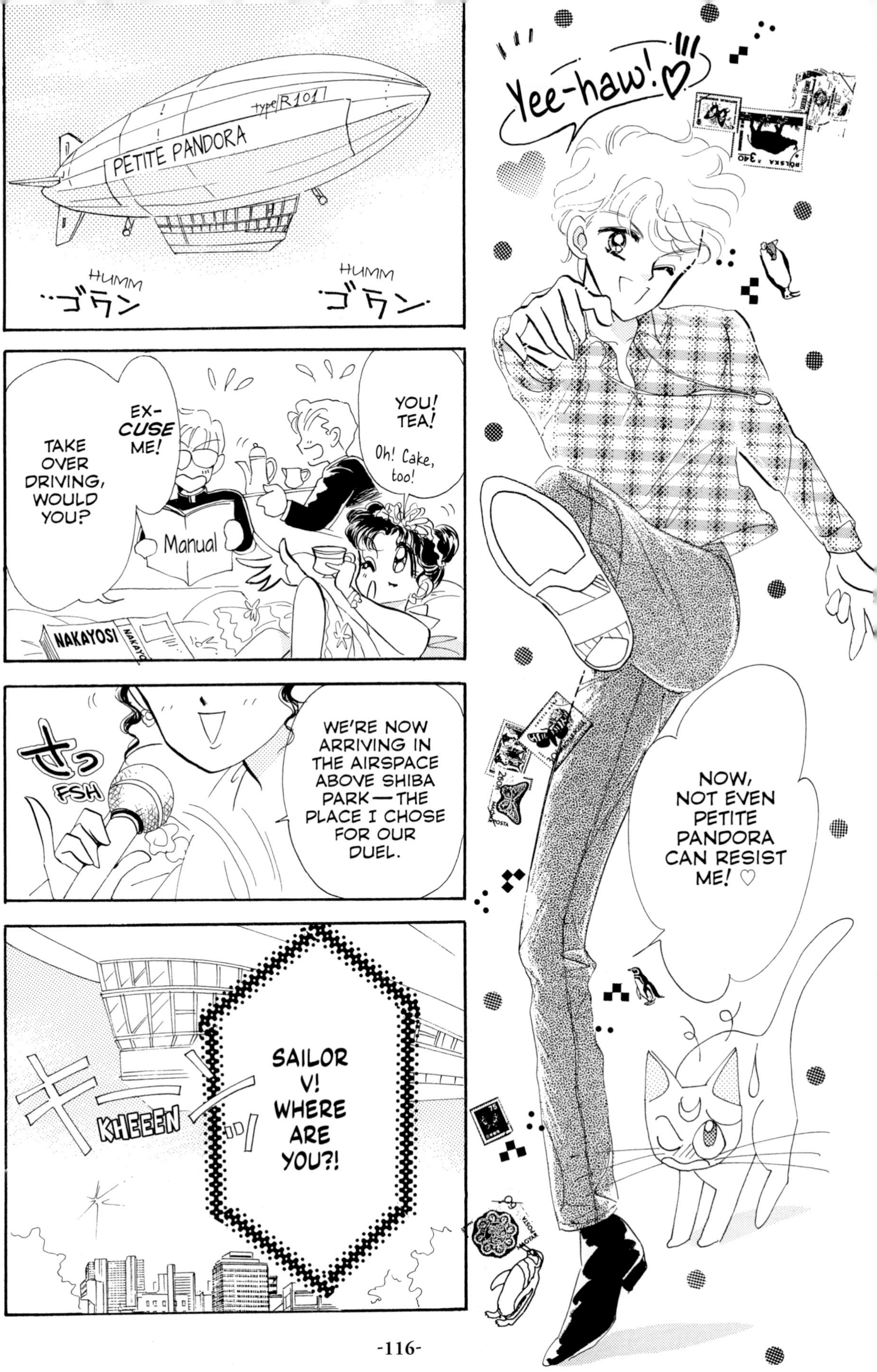
Yee-haw! ♡
NOW, NOT EVEN PETITE PANDORA CAN RESIST ME! ♡
type R101
PETITE PANDORA
HUMM
ゴウン
HUMM
ゴウン
YOU! TEA!
Oh! Cake, too!
EX-CUSE ME!
TAKE OVER DRIVING, WOULD YOU?
Manual
NAKAYOSI
WE'RE NOW ARRIVING IN THE AIRSPACE ABOVE SHIBA PARK—THE PLACE I CHOSE FOR OUR DUEL.
さっ
FSH
SAILOR V! WHERE ARE YOU?!
キーン
KHEEEN

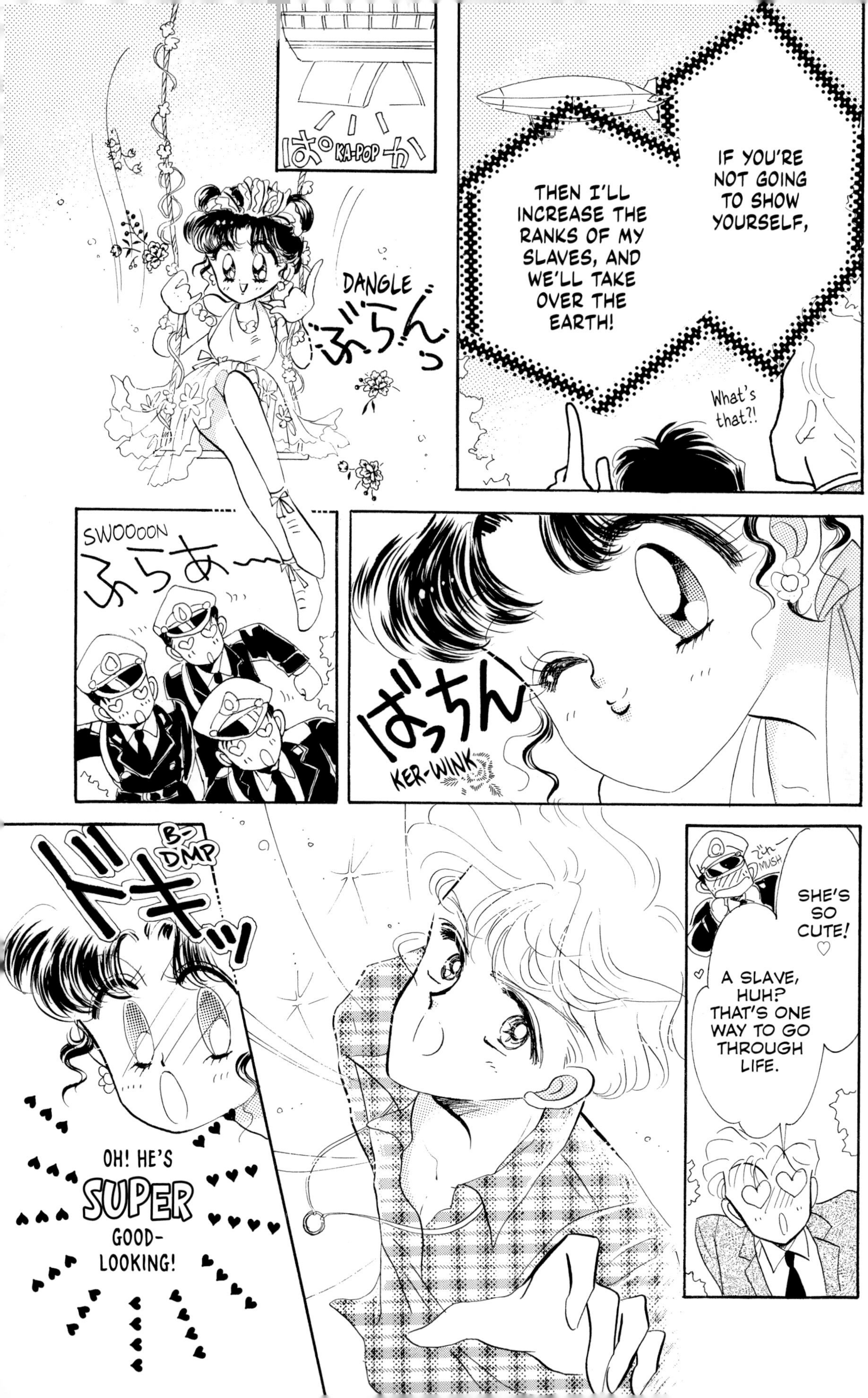

IF YOU'RE NOT GOING TO SHOW YOURSELF,
THEN I'LL INCREASE THE RANKS OF MY SLAVES, AND WE'LL TAKE OVER THE EARTH!
What's that?!
KA-POP
DANGLE
ぶらんっ
ばっちん
KER-WINK
SWOOOON
ふらあ〜
MUSH
SHE'S SO CUTE! ♡
A SLAVE, HUH? THAT'S ONE WAY TO GO THROUGH LIFE.
ドキッ
B-DMP
OH! HE'S SUPER GOOD-LOOKING!

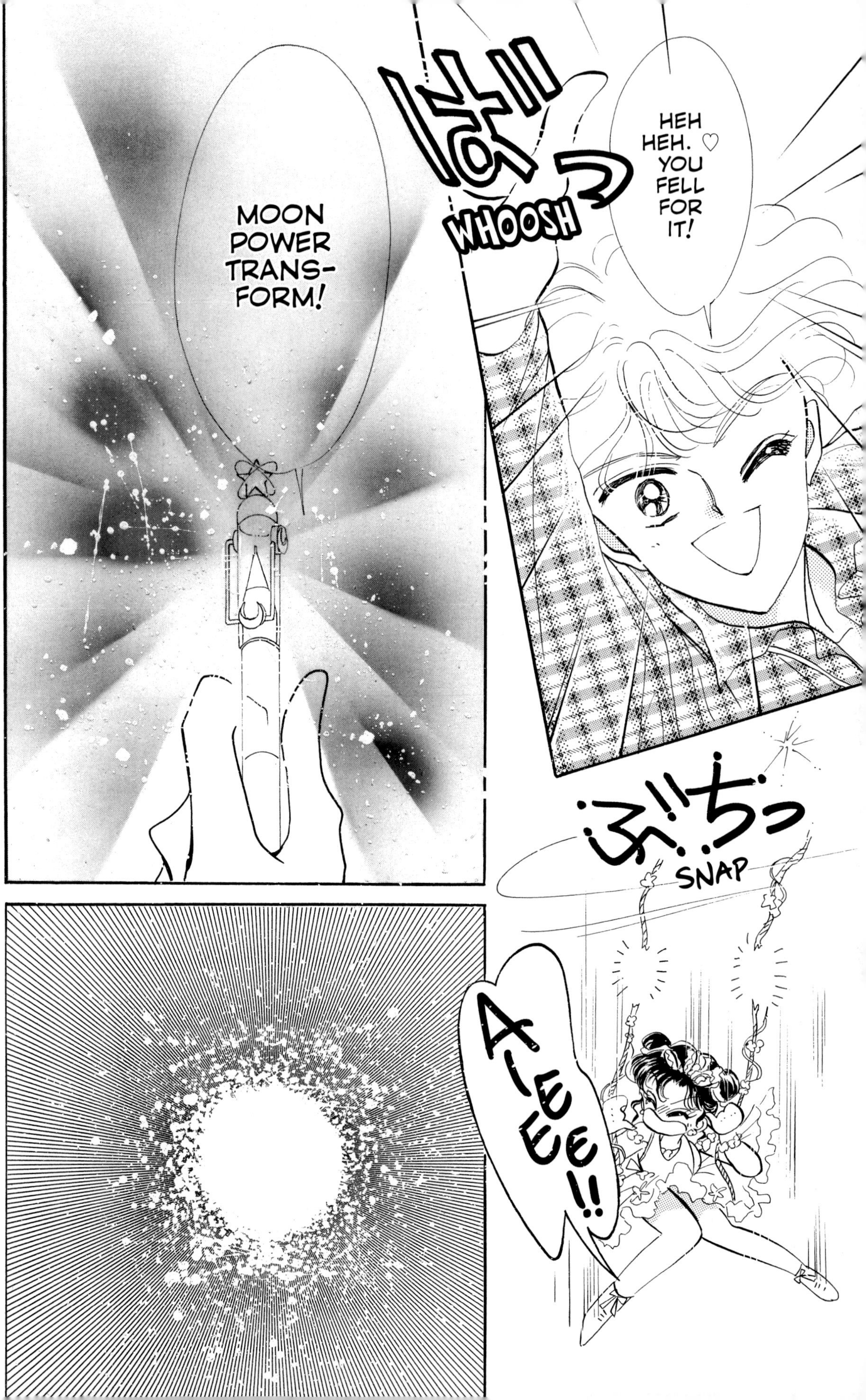
ばっ
WHOOSH
HEH HEH. ♡ YOU FELL FOR IT!
MOON POWER TRANS-FORM!
ぷ!!ちっ
SNAP
AIEEE!!

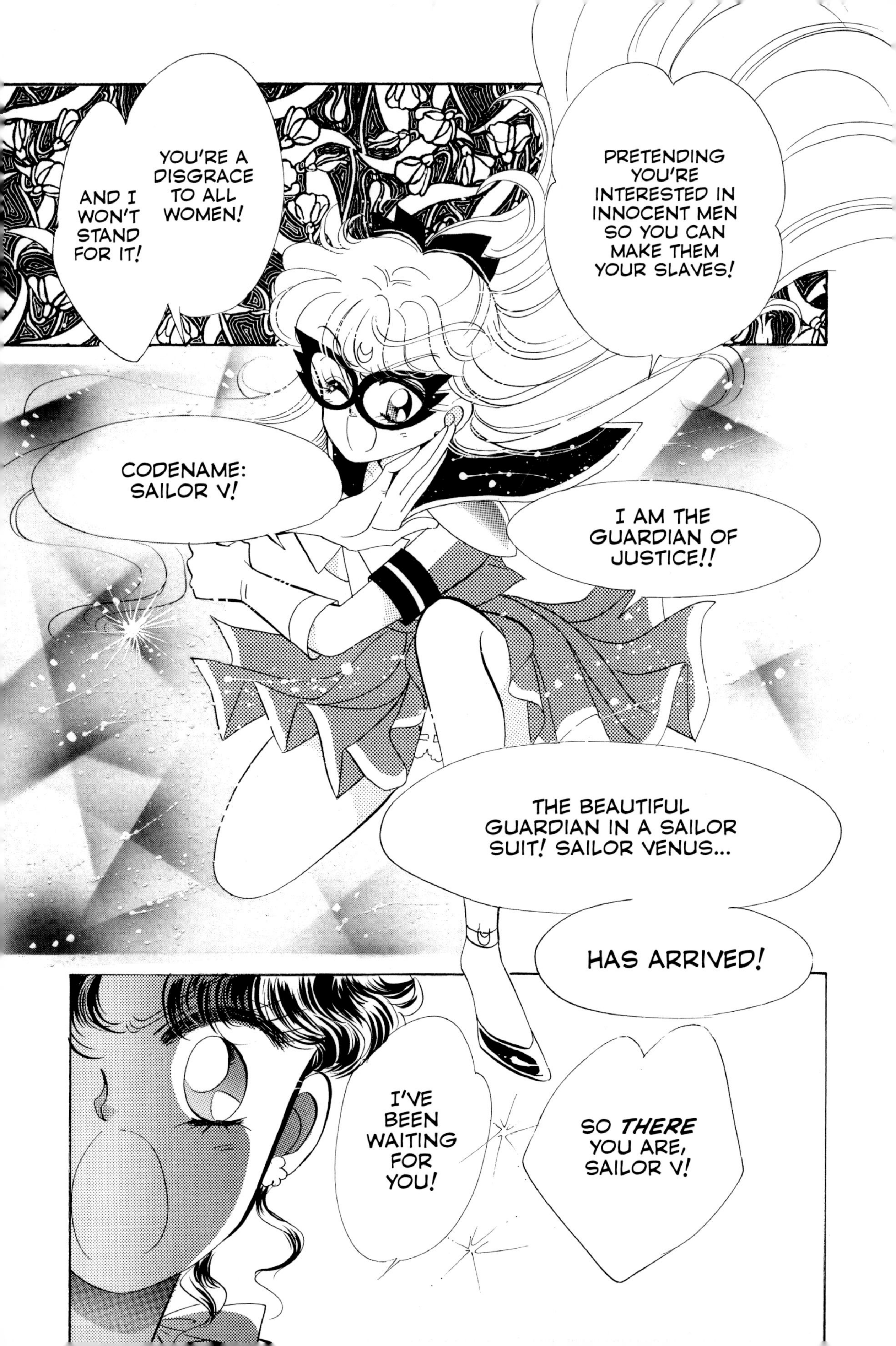
PRETENDING YOU'RE INTERESTED IN INNOCENT MEN SO YOU CAN MAKE THEM YOUR SLAVES!
YOU'RE A DISGRACE TO ALL WOMEN!
AND I WON'T STAND FOR IT!
CODENAME: SAILOR V!
I AM THE GUARDIAN OF JUSTICE!!
THE BEAUTIFUL GUARDIAN IN A SAILOR SUIT! SAILOR VENUS...
HAS ARRIVED!
SO *THERE* YOU ARE, SAILOR V!
I'VE BEEN WAITING FOR YOU!

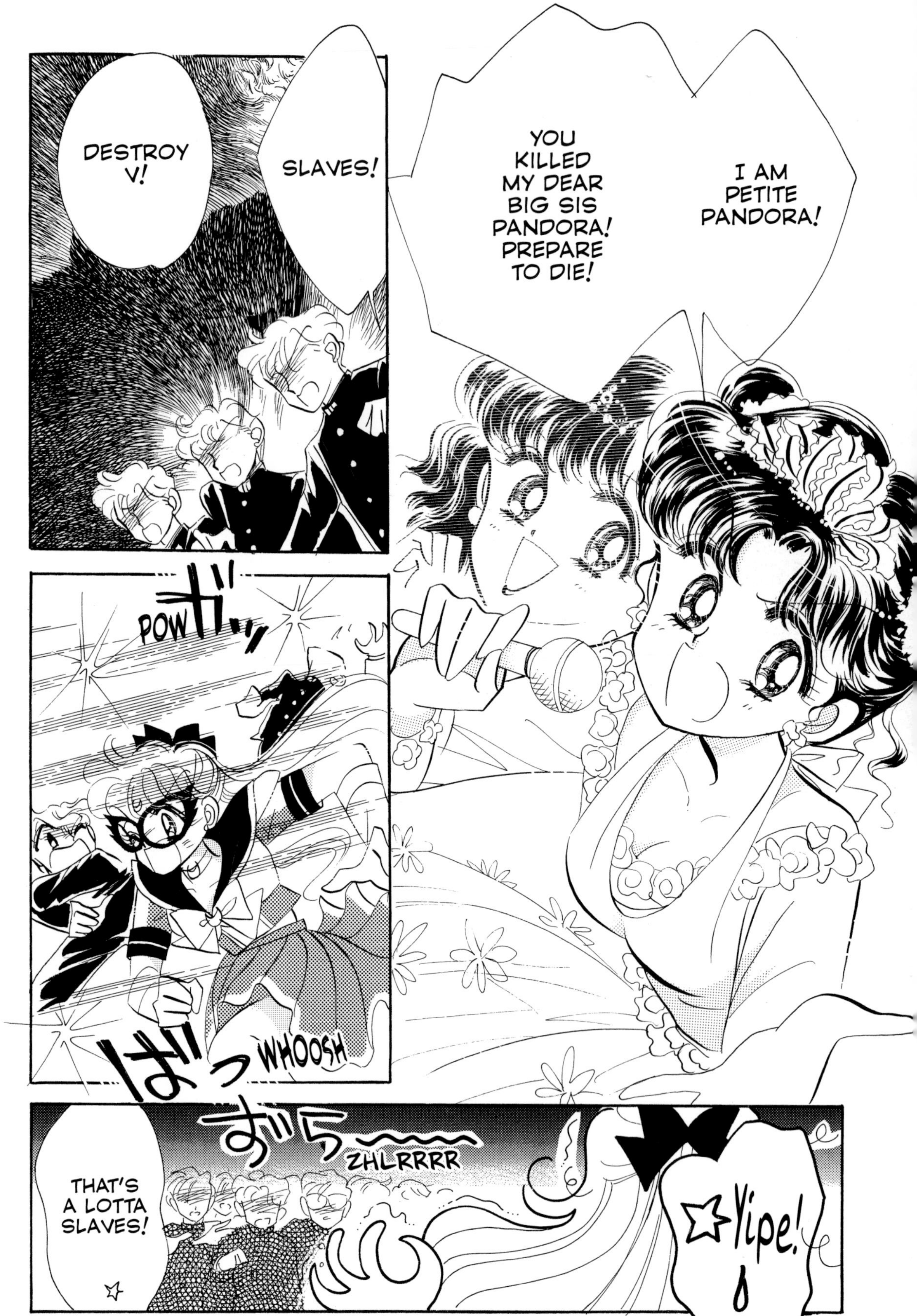
I AM PETITE PANDORA!
YOU KILLED MY DEAR BIG SIS PANDORA! PREPARE TO DIE!
SLAVES!
DESTROY V!
ガッ POW
ばっ WHOOSH
☆Yipe!
ずら ZHLRRRR
THAT'S A LOTTA SLAVES!

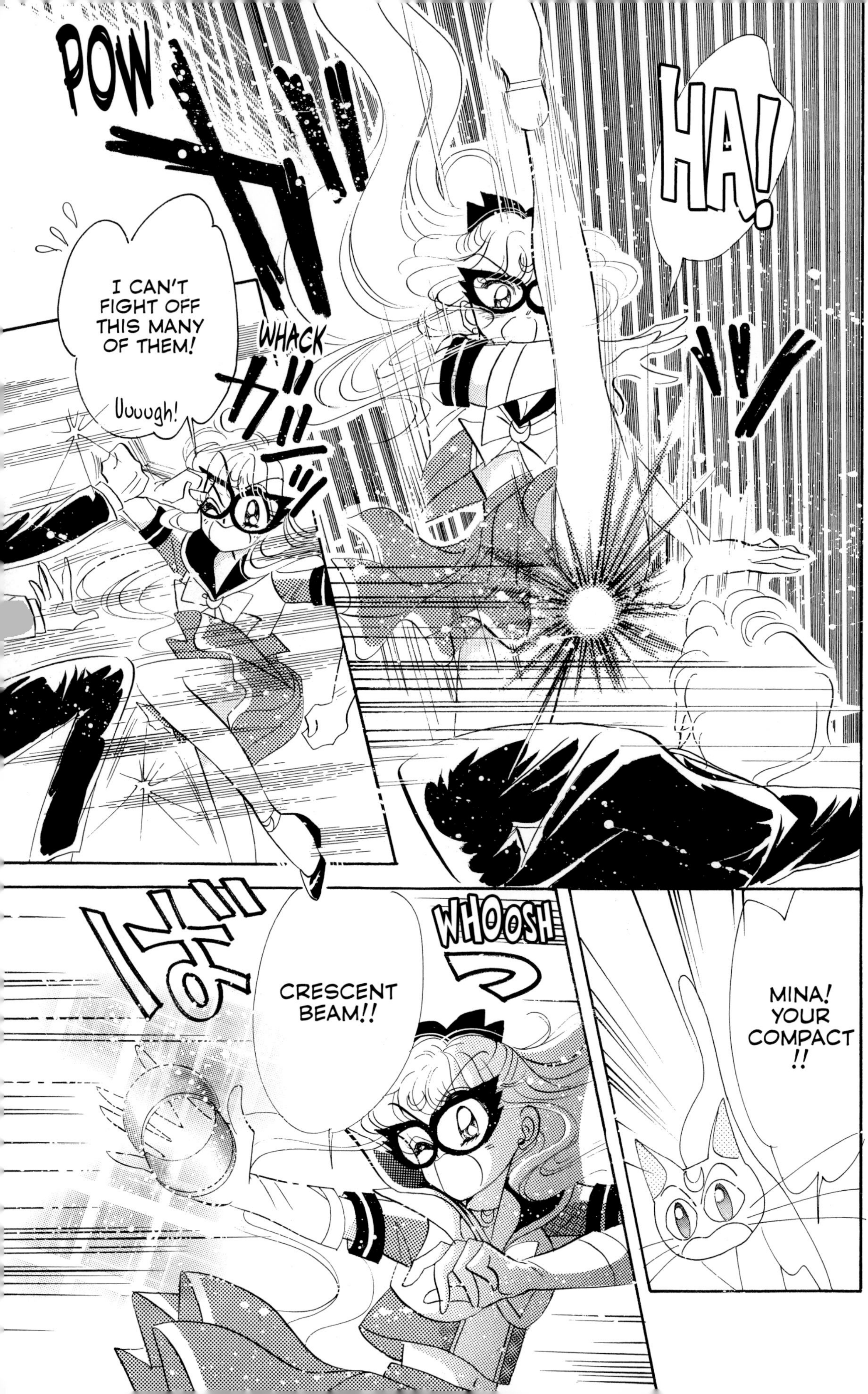

HA!
POW
I CAN'T FIGHT OFF THIS MANY OF THEM!
WHACK
Uuuugh!
MINA! YOUR COMPACT!!
WHOOSH
CRESCENT BEAM!!

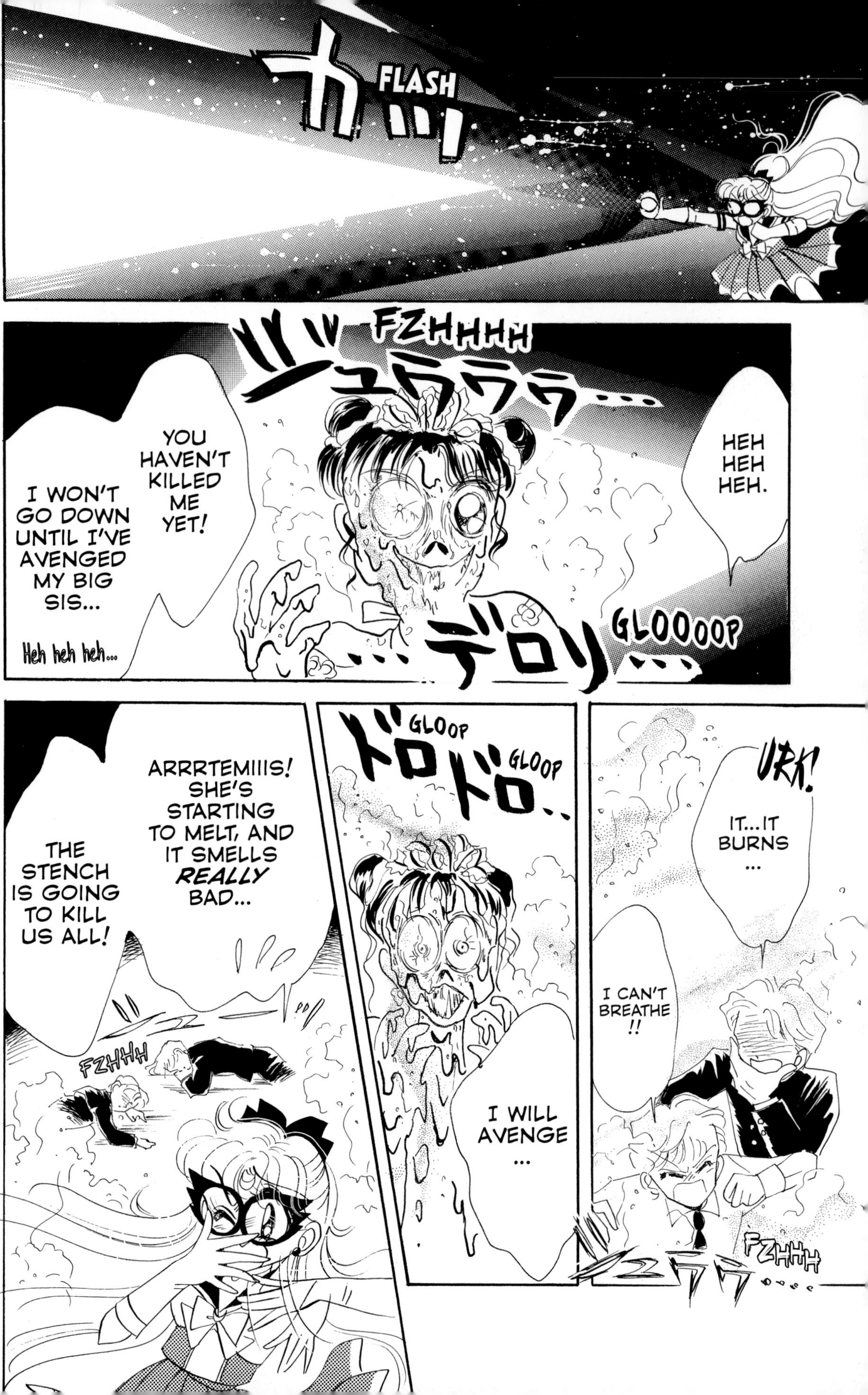

カッ
FLASH
HEH HEH HEH.
ジュラララ...
FZHHHHH
YOU HAVEN'T KILLED ME YET!
I WON'T GO DOWN UNTIL I'VE AVENGED MY BIG SIS...
Heh heh heh...
デロリ...
GLOOOOP
URK!
IT...IT BURNS...
I CAN'T BREATHE!!
FZHHHH
ドロドロ...
GLOOP
GLOOP
I WILL AVENGE...
ARRRTEMIIIS! SHE'S STARTING TO MELT, AND IT SMELLS REALLY BAD...
THE STENCH IS GOING TO KILL US ALL!
FZHHH

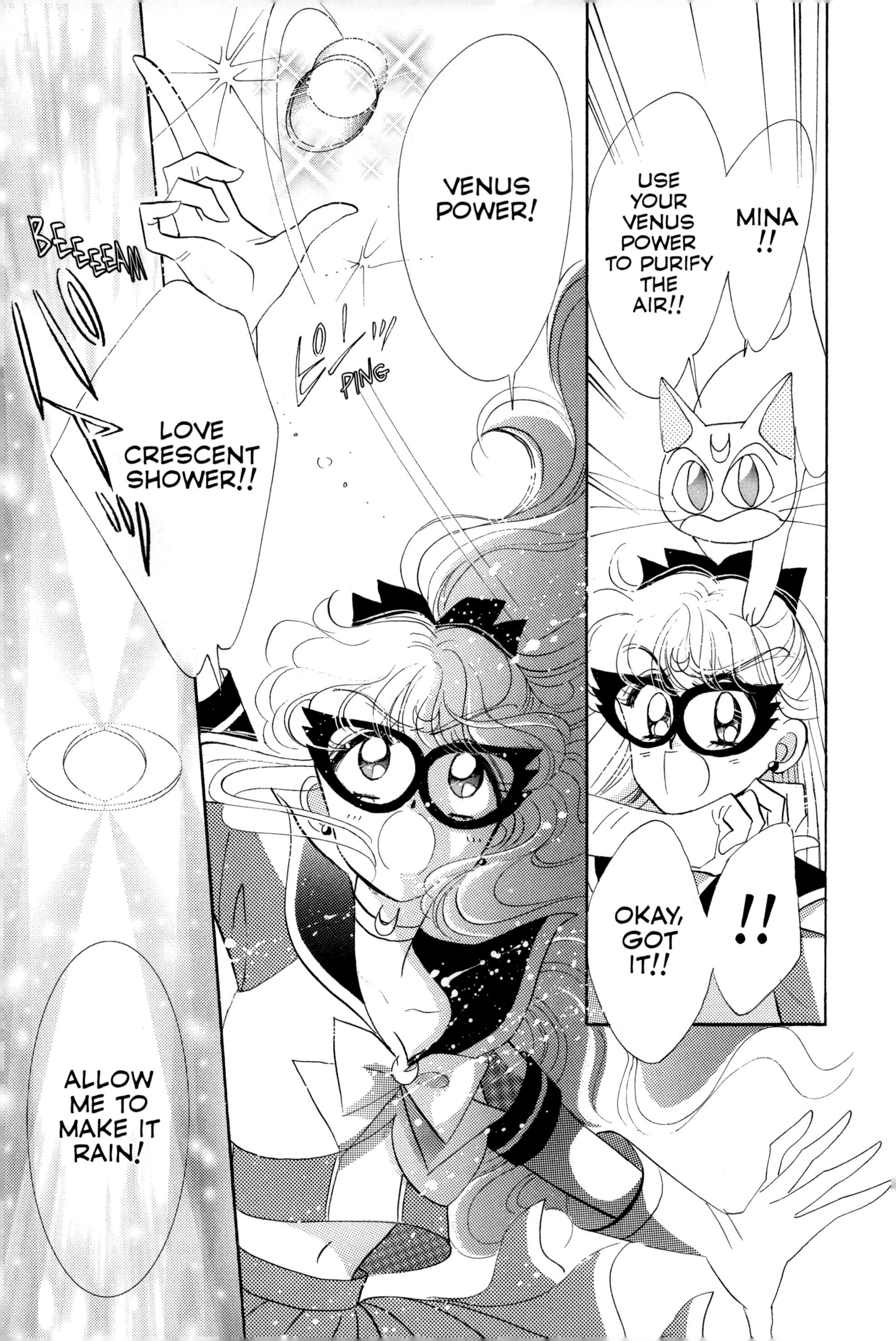
MINA!!
USE YOUR VENUS POWER TO PURIFY THE AIR!!
OKAY, GOT IT!!
!!
VENUS POWER!
PING
LOVE CRESCENT SHOWER!!
BEEEEEAM
ALLOW ME TO MAKE IT RAIN!

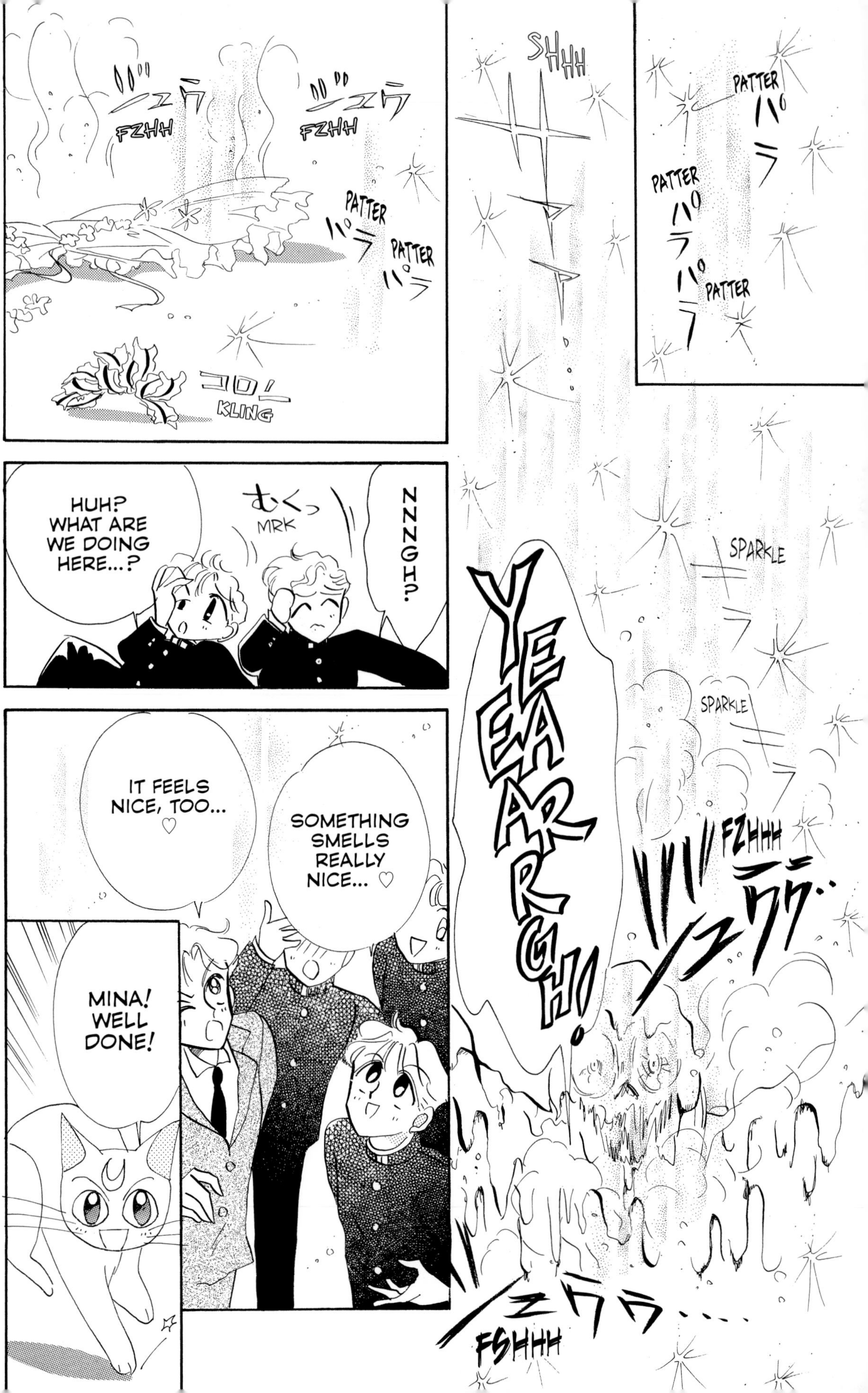
PATTER
パラ
PATTER
パラ
パラ
PATTER
SHHH
SPARKLE
SPARKLE
YEEAARRGH!
FZHHH
FSHHH
ジュワワ
FZHH
FZHH
PATTER
パラ
PATTER
パラ
コロン
KLING
NNNGH?
むくっ
MRK
HUH? WHAT ARE WE DOING HERE...?
SOMETHING SMELLS REALLY NICE... ♡
IT FEELS NICE, TOO... ♡
MINA! WELL DONE!

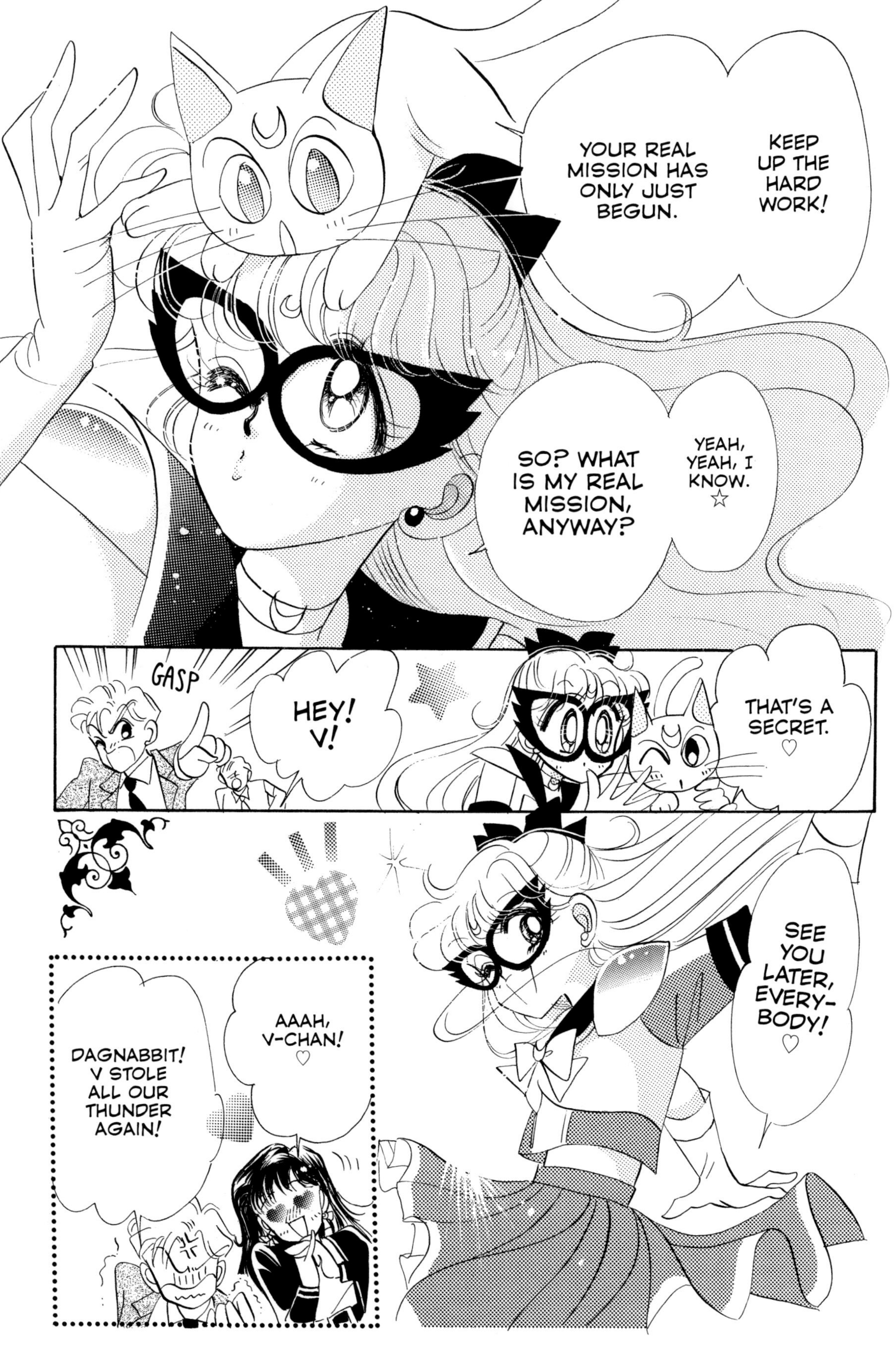
KEEP UP THE HARD WORK!
YOUR REAL MISSION HAS ONLY JUST BEGUN.
YEAH, YEAH, I KNOW. ☆
SO? WHAT IS MY REAL MISSION, ANYWAY?
THAT'S A SECRET. ♡
HEY! V!
GASP
SEE YOU LATER, EVERYBODY! ♡
AAAH, V-CHAN! ♡
DAGNABBIT! V STOLE ALL OUR THUNDER AGAIN!

Codename Sailor V

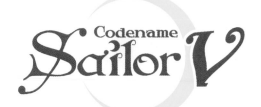

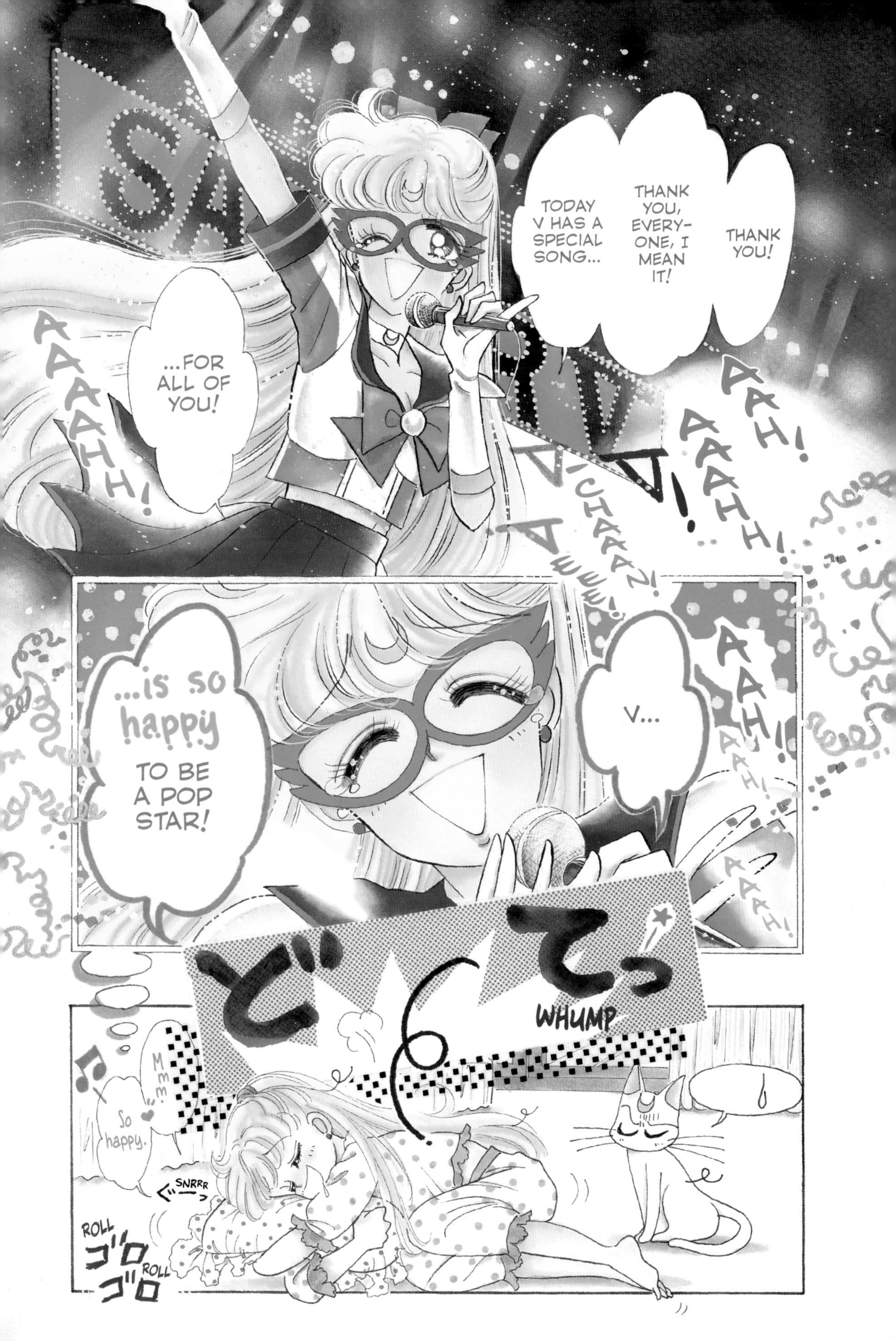
THANK YOU!
THANK YOU, EVERYONE, I MEAN IT!
TODAY V HAS A SPECIAL SONG...
...FOR ALL OF YOU!
AAAAAHH!
AAH!
AAAAHH!!
V-CHAAAN!
AAAAAHH!!
V...
...is so happy TO BE A POP STAR!
AAAH!!
AAAH!
AAAH!
WHUMP
Mmm!
So happy.
SNRRR
ROLL
ゴロ
ROLL
ゴロ

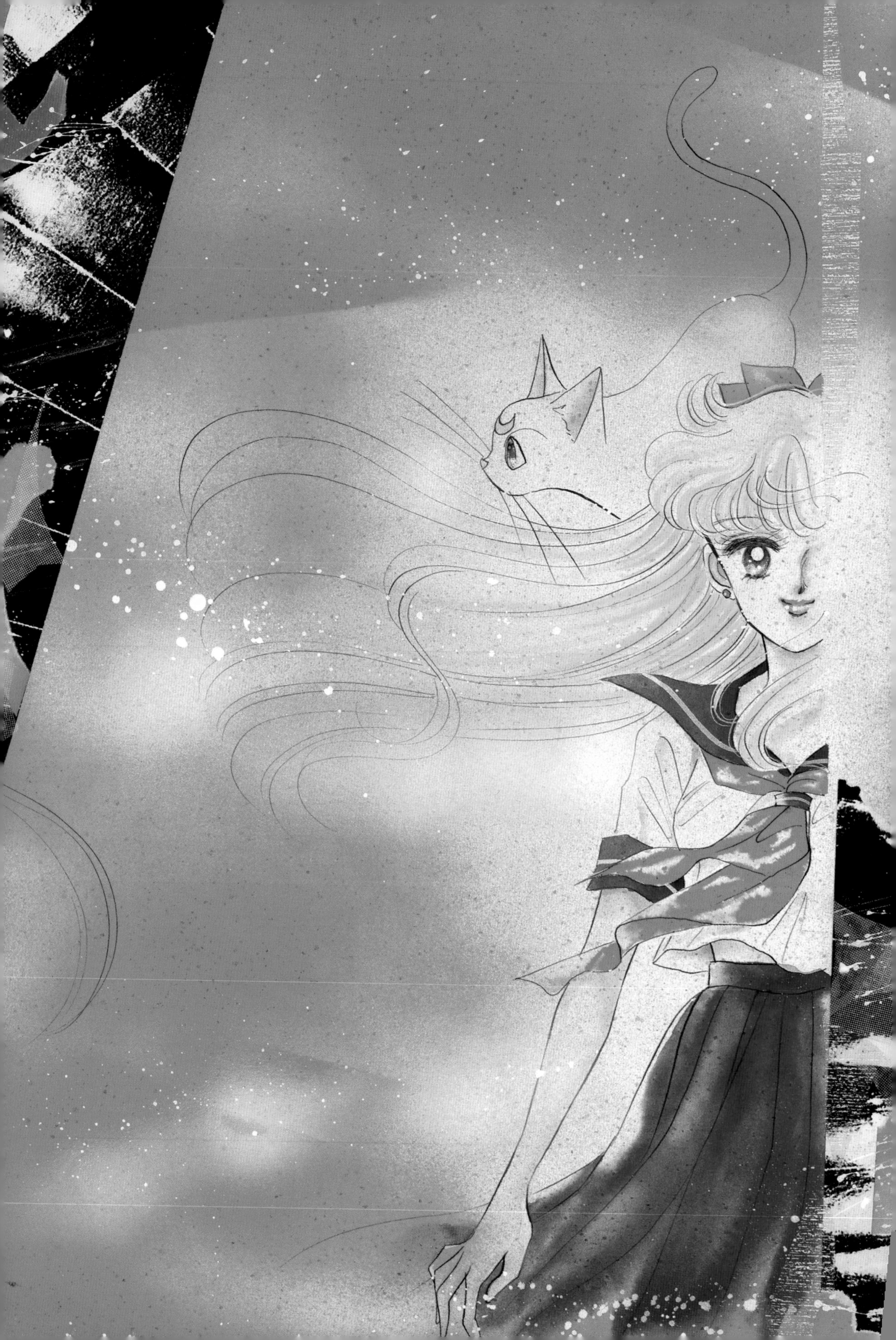

vol.5 The Dark Agency Conspiracy

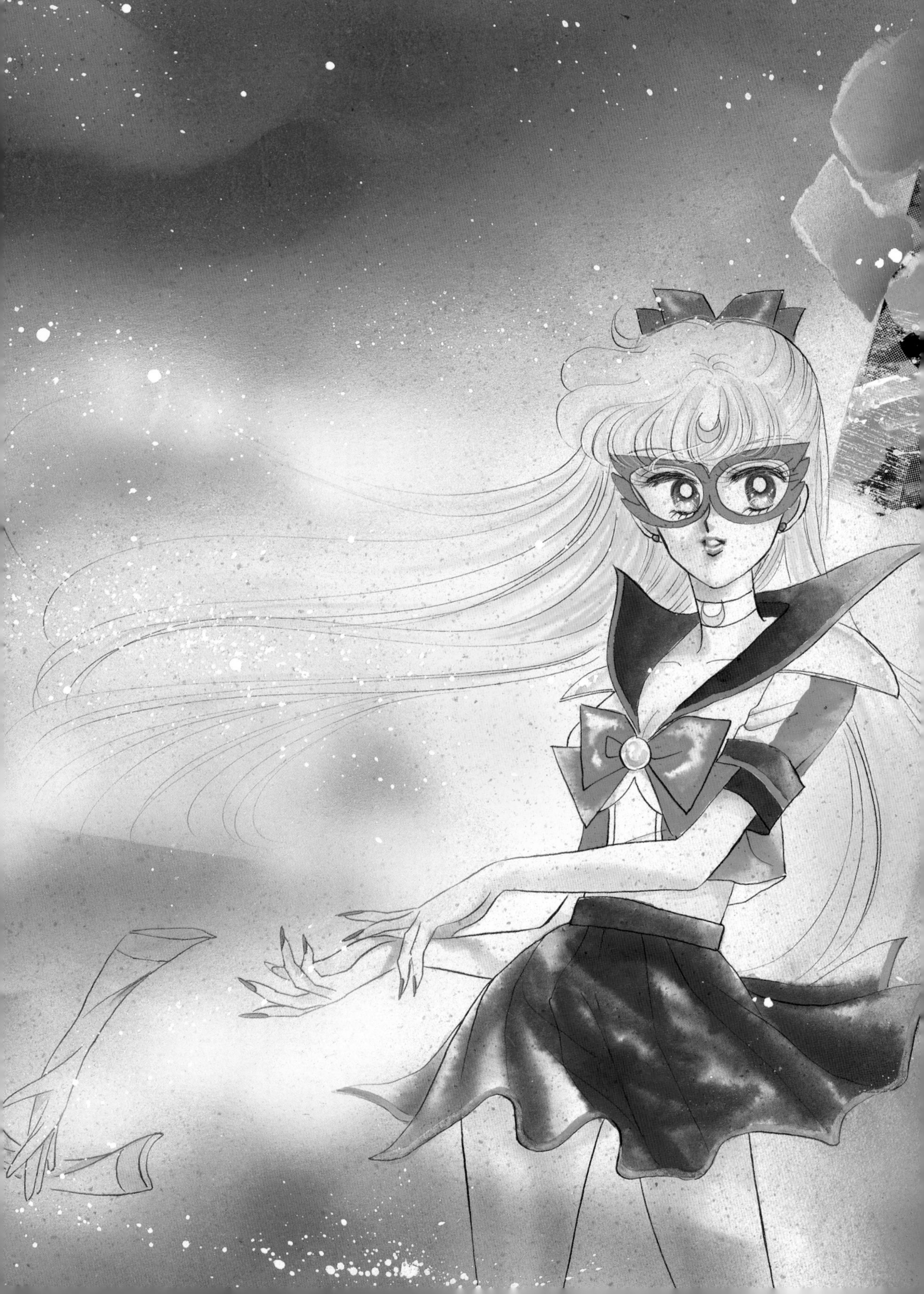

Codename Sailor V

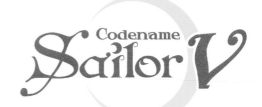

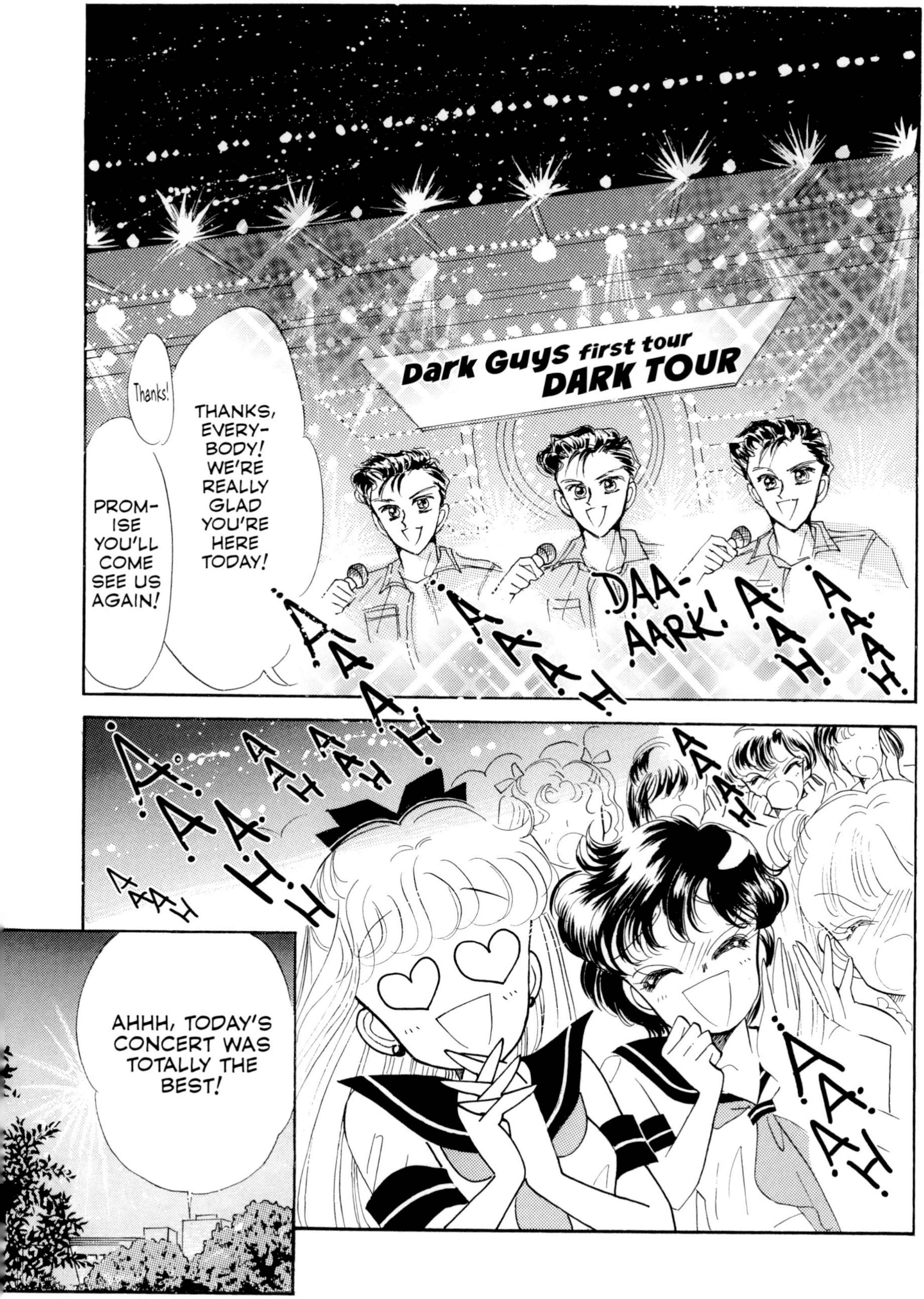
Dark Guys first tour
DARK TOUR
THANKS, EVERYBODY! WE'RE REALLY GLAD YOU'RE HERE TODAY!
Thanks!
PROMISE YOU'LL COME SEE US AGAIN!
AAAH
AAAH
DAA-AARK!
AAAH
AAAH
AAAH
AAAH
AAAH
AAAH
AAAH
AAAH
AAAH
AHHH, TODAY'S CONCERT WAS TOTALLY THE BEST!

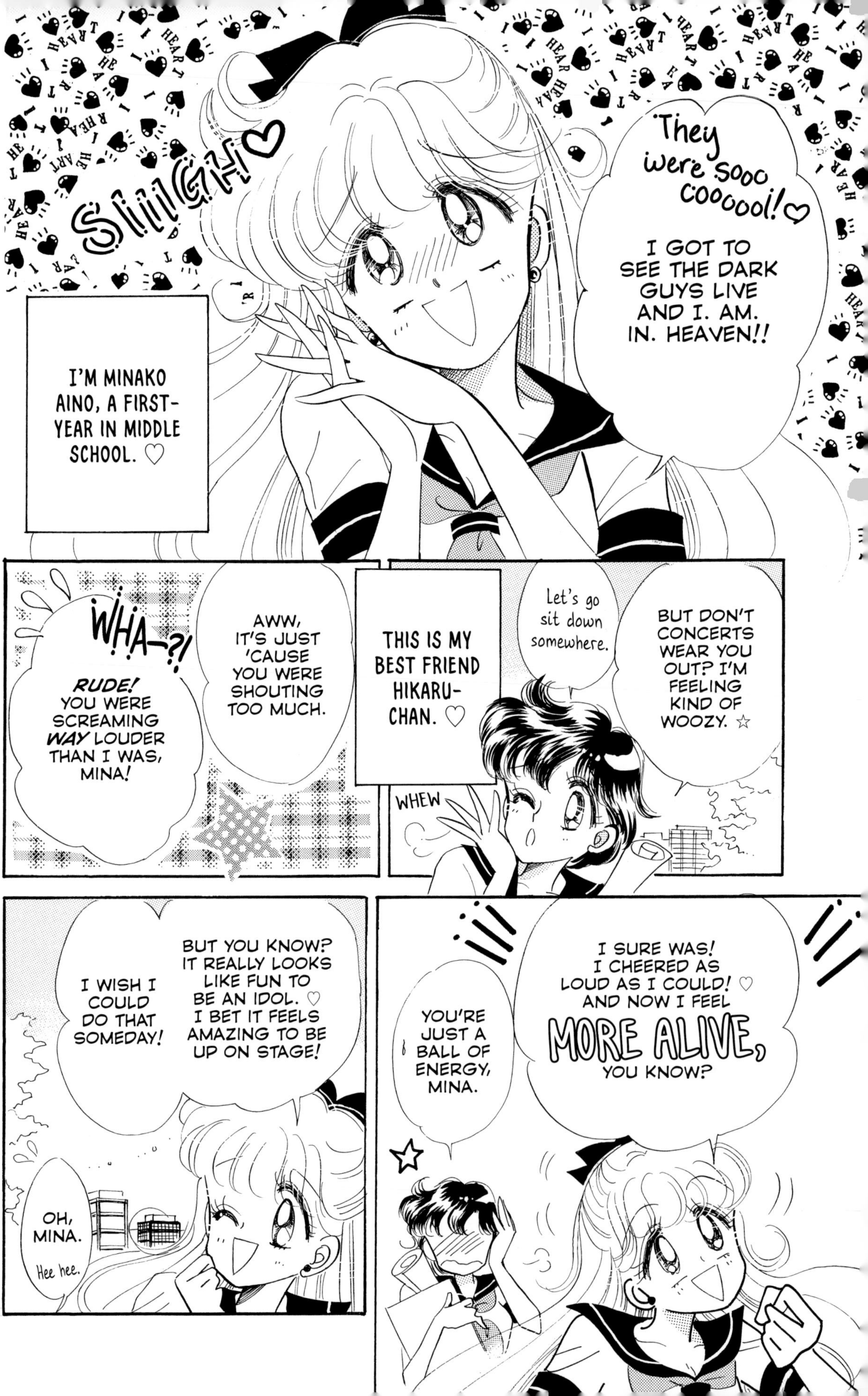
They were sooo cooooool!♡
I GOT TO SEE THE DARK GUYS LIVE AND I. AM. IN. HEAVEN!!
SIIIGH!♡
I'M MINAKO AINO, A FIRST-YEAR IN MIDDLE SCHOOL. ♡
BUT DON'T CONCERTS WEAR YOU OUT? I'M FEELING KIND OF WOOZY. ☆
Let's go sit down somewhere.
THIS IS MY BEST FRIEND HIKARU-CHAN. ♡
WHEW
AWW, IT'S JUST 'CAUSE YOU WERE SHOUTING TOO MUCH.
WHA-?!
RUDE! YOU WERE SCREAMING WAY LOUDER THAN I WAS, MINA!
I SURE WAS! I CHEERED AS LOUD AS I COULD! ♡ AND NOW I FEEL
MORE ALIVE,
YOU KNOW?
YOU'RE JUST A BALL OF ENERGY, MINA.
BUT YOU KNOW? IT REALLY LOOKS LIKE FUN TO BE AN IDOL. ♡ I BET IT FEELS AMAZING TO BE UP ON STAGE!
I WISH I COULD DO THAT SOMEDAY!
OH, MINA.
Hee hee.

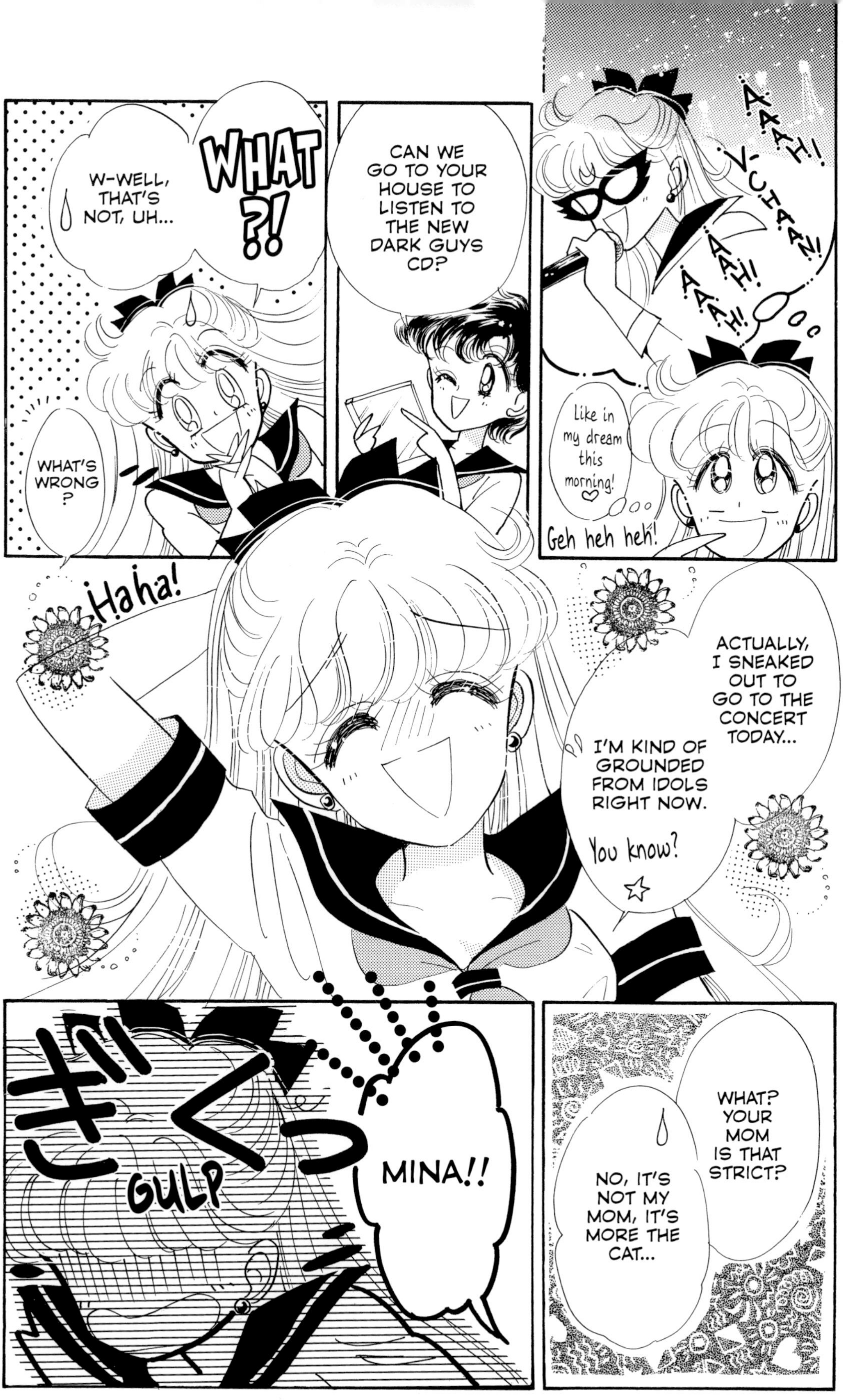
AAAH!
V-CHAAAN!
AAAH!
AAAH!!
Like in my dream this morning! ♡
Geh heh heh!
CAN WE GO TO YOUR HOUSE TO LISTEN TO THE NEW DARK GUYS CD?
WHAT?!
W-WELL, THAT'S NOT, UH...
WHAT'S WRONG?
ACTUALLY, I SNEAKED OUT TO GO TO THE CONCERT TODAY...
I'M KIND OF GROUNDED FROM IDOLS RIGHT NOW.
You know? ☆
Haha!
WHAT? YOUR MOM IS THAT STRICT?
NO, IT'S NOT MY MOM, IT'S MORE THE CAT...
MINA!!
ぎくっ
GULP

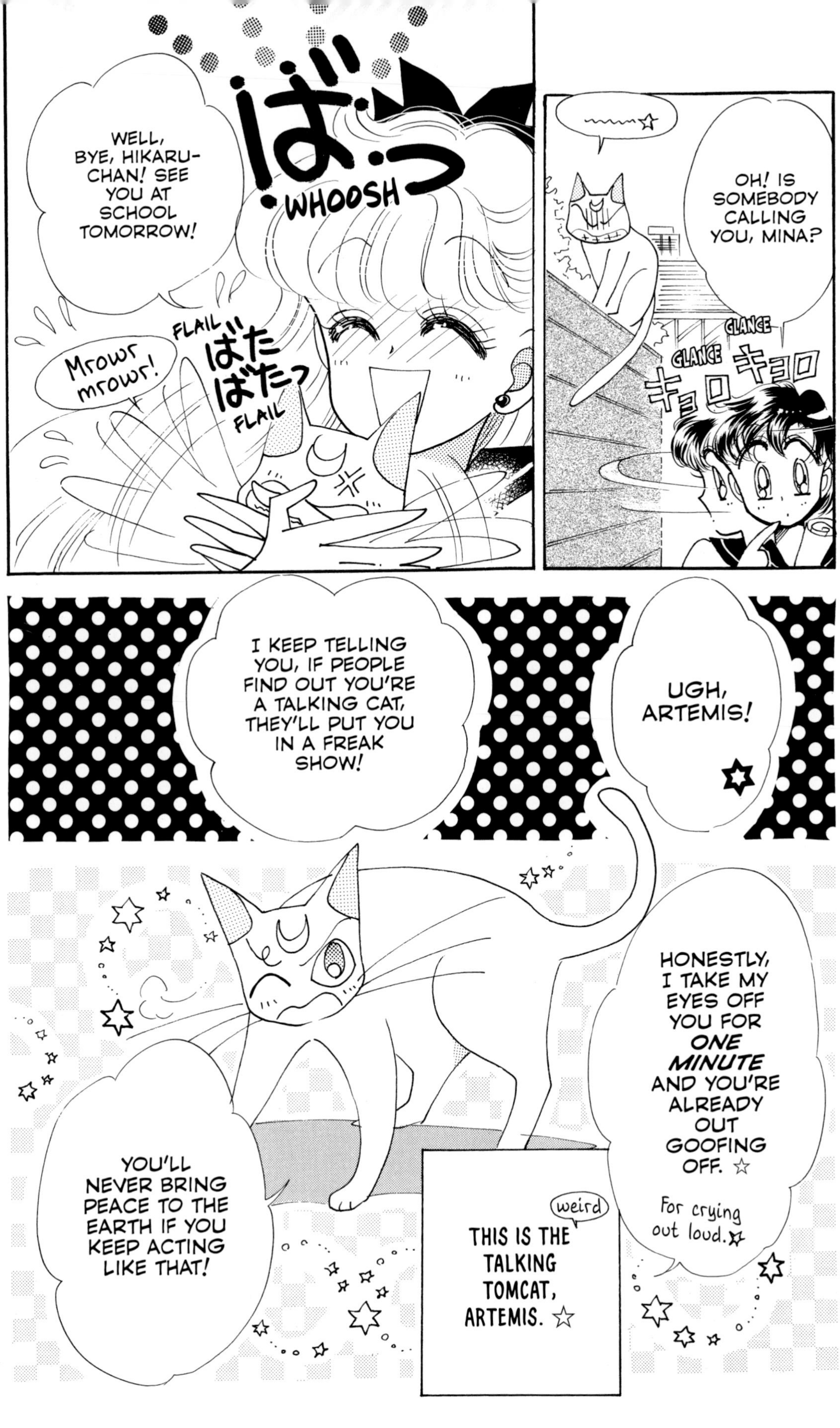
OH! IS SOMEBODY CALLING YOU, MINA?
GLANCE キョロ
GLANCE キョロ
WELL, BYE, HIKARU-CHAN! SEE YOU AT SCHOOL TOMORROW!
ばっ
WHOOSH
FLAIL ばた
ばたっ FLAIL
Mrowr mrowr!
UGH, ARTEMIS!
I KEEP TELLING YOU, IF PEOPLE FIND OUT YOU'RE A TALKING CAT, THEY'LL PUT YOU IN A FREAK SHOW!
HONESTLY, I TAKE MY EYES OFF YOU FOR ONE MINUTE AND YOU'RE ALREADY OUT GOOFING OFF. ☆
For crying out loud.☆
YOU'LL NEVER BRING PEACE TO THE EARTH IF YOU KEEP ACTING LIKE THAT!
THIS IS THE (weird) TALKING TOMCAT, ARTEMIS. ☆

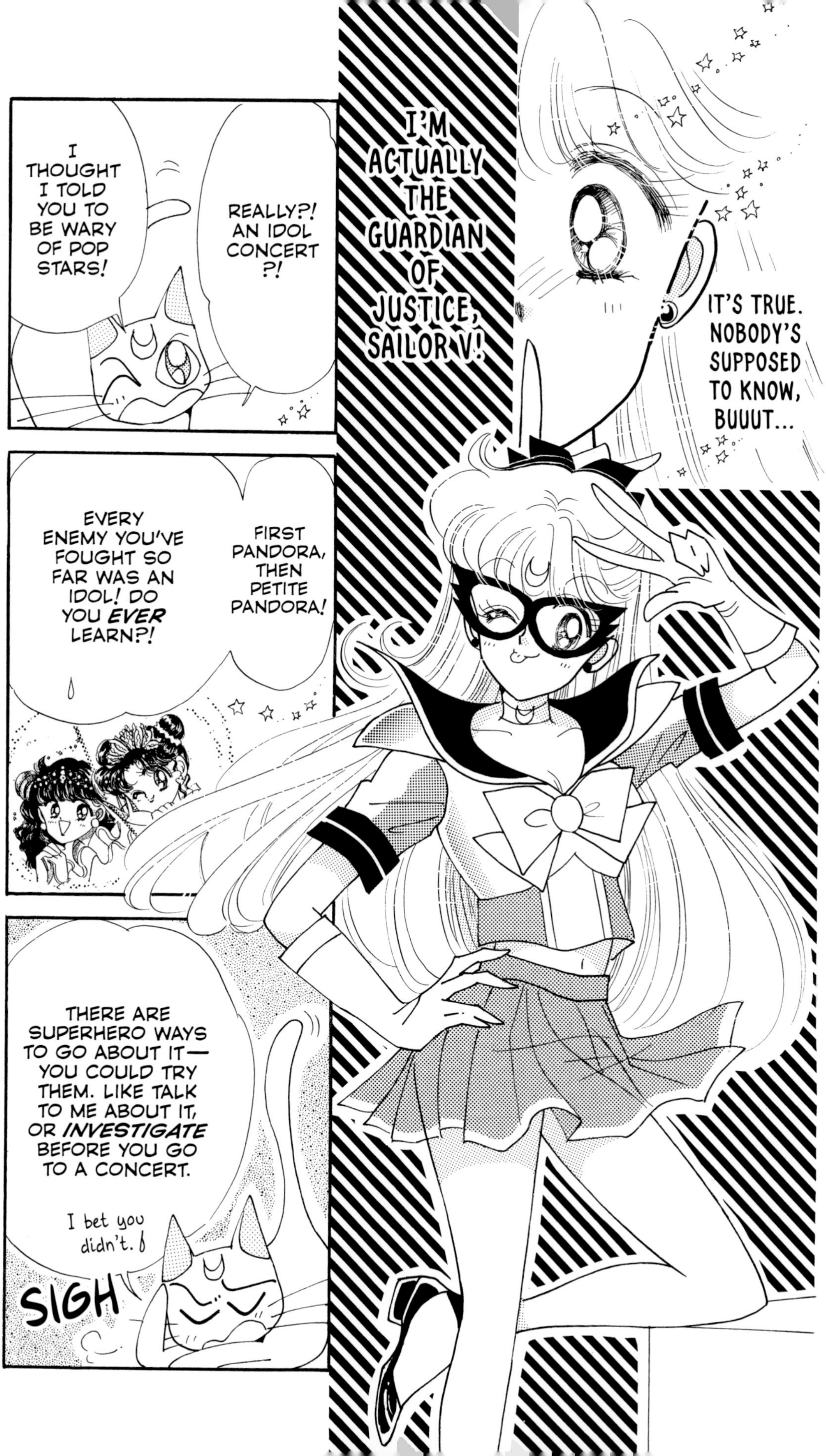
IT'S TRUE. NOBODY'S SUPPOSED TO KNOW, BUUUT...
I'M ACTUALLY THE GUARDIAN OF JUSTICE, SAILOR V!
REALLY?! AN IDOL CONCERT?!
I THOUGHT I TOLD YOU TO BE WARY OF POP STARS!
FIRST PANDORA, THEN PETITE PANDORA!
EVERY ENEMY YOU'VE FOUGHT SO FAR WAS AN IDOL! DO YOU *EVER* LEARN?!
THERE ARE SUPERHERO WAYS TO GO ABOUT IT—YOU COULD TRY THEM. LIKE TALK TO ME ABOUT IT, OR *INVESTIGATE* BEFORE YOU GO TO A CONCERT.
I bet you didn't.
SIGH

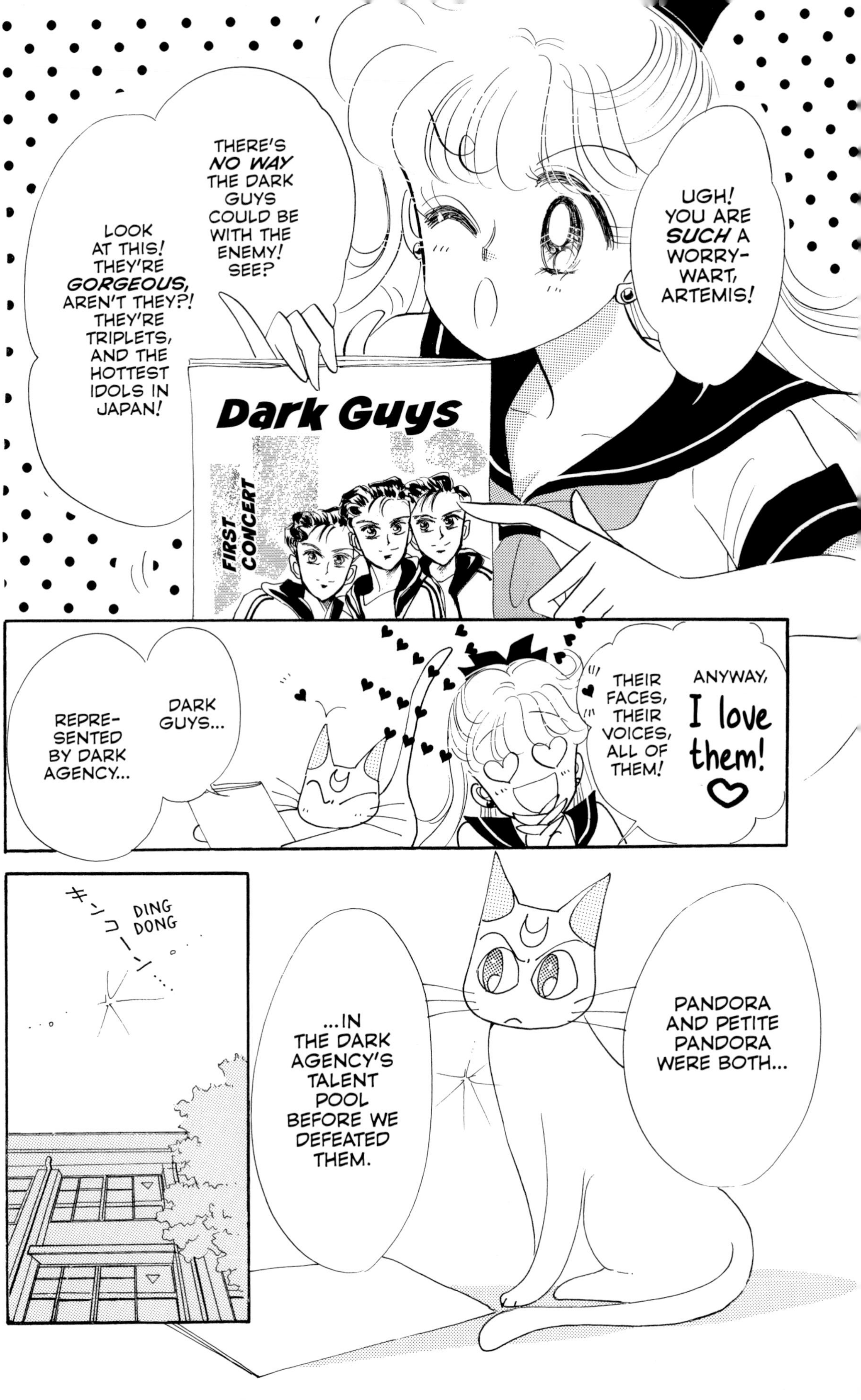
UGH! YOU ARE *SUCH* A WORRY-WART, ARTEMIS!
THERE'S *NO WAY* THE DARK GUYS COULD BE WITH THE ENEMY! SEE?
LOOK AT THIS! THEY'RE *GORGEOUS*, AREN'T THEY?! THEY'RE TRIPLETS, AND THE HOTTEST IDOLS IN JAPAN!
Dark Guys
FIRST CONCERT
ANYWAY, I love them! ♡
THEIR FACES, THEIR VOICES, ALL OF THEM!
DARK GUYS...
REPRE-SENTED BY DARK AGENCY...
PANDORA AND PETITE PANDORA WERE BOTH...
...IN THE DARK AGENCY'S TALENT POOL BEFORE WE DEFEATED THEM.
キーンコーン
DING DONG

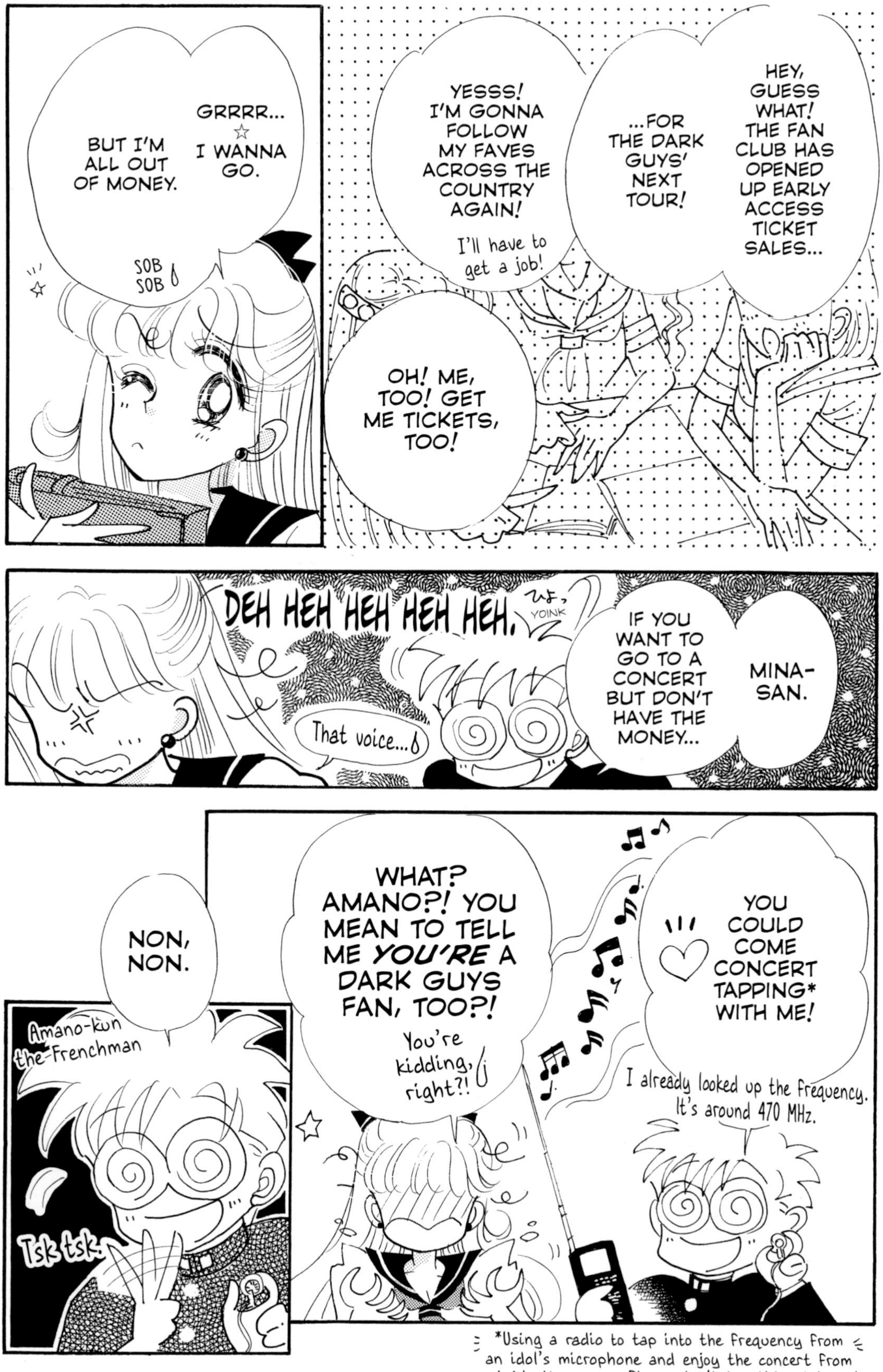
HEY, GUESS WHAT! THE FAN CLUB HAS OPENED UP EARLY ACCESS TICKET SALES...
...FOR THE DARK GUYS' NEXT TOUR!
YESSS! I'M GONNA FOLLOW MY FAVES ACROSS THE COUNTRY AGAIN!
I'll have to get a job!
OH! ME, TOO! GET ME TICKETS, TOO!
GRRRR... ☆ I WANNA GO.
BUT I'M ALL OUT OF MONEY.
SOB SOB
MINA-SAN.
IF YOU WANT TO GO TO A CONCERT BUT DON'T HAVE THE MONEY...
ひょっ YOINK
DEH HEH HEH HEH HEH.
That voice...
YOU COULD COME CONCERT TAPPING* WITH ME!
I already looked up the frequency. It's around 470 MHz.
WHAT? AMANO?! YOU MEAN TO TELL ME *YOU'RE* A DARK GUYS FAN, TOO?!
You're kidding, right?!
NON, NON.
Amano-kun the Frenchman
Tsk tsk.

*Using a radio to tap into the frequency from an idol's microphone and enjoy the concert from outside the venue. Please don't try this at home!

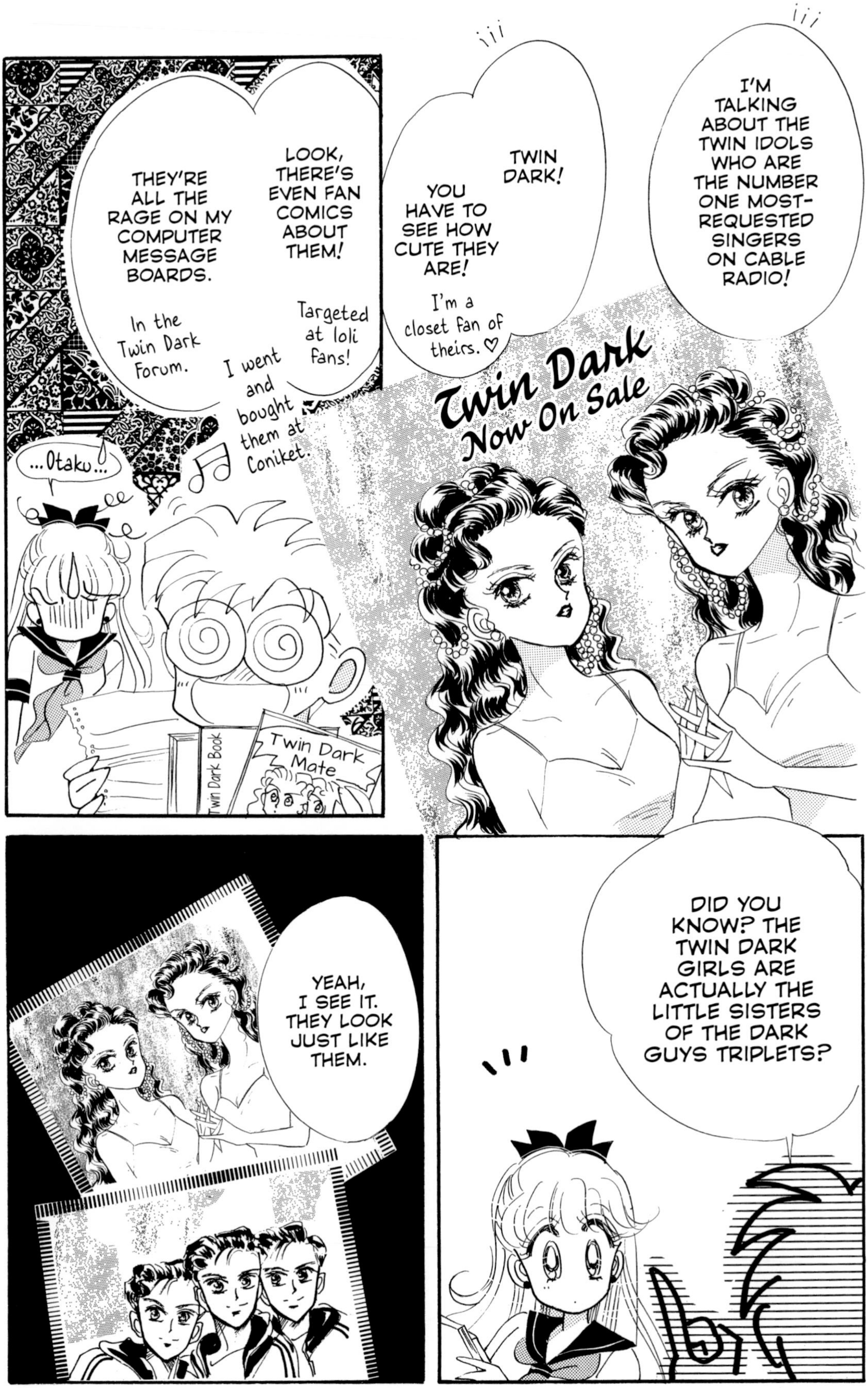
I'M TALKING ABOUT THE TWIN IDOLS WHO ARE THE NUMBER ONE MOST-REQUESTED SINGERS ON CABLE RADIO!
TWIN DARK!
YOU HAVE TO SEE HOW CUTE THEY ARE!
I'm a closet fan of theirs. ♡
Twin Dark Now On Sale
LOOK, THERE'S EVEN FAN COMICS ABOUT THEM!
Targeted at loli fans!
THEY'RE ALL THE RAGE ON MY COMPUTER MESSAGE BOARDS.
In the Twin Dark Forum.
I went and bought them at Coniket.
...Otaku...
Twin Dark Book
Twin Dark Mate
DID YOU KNOW? THE TWIN DARK GIRLS ARE ACTUALLY THE LITTLE SISTERS OF THE DARK GUYS TRIPLETS?
YEAH, I SEE IT. THEY LOOK JUST LIKE THEM.

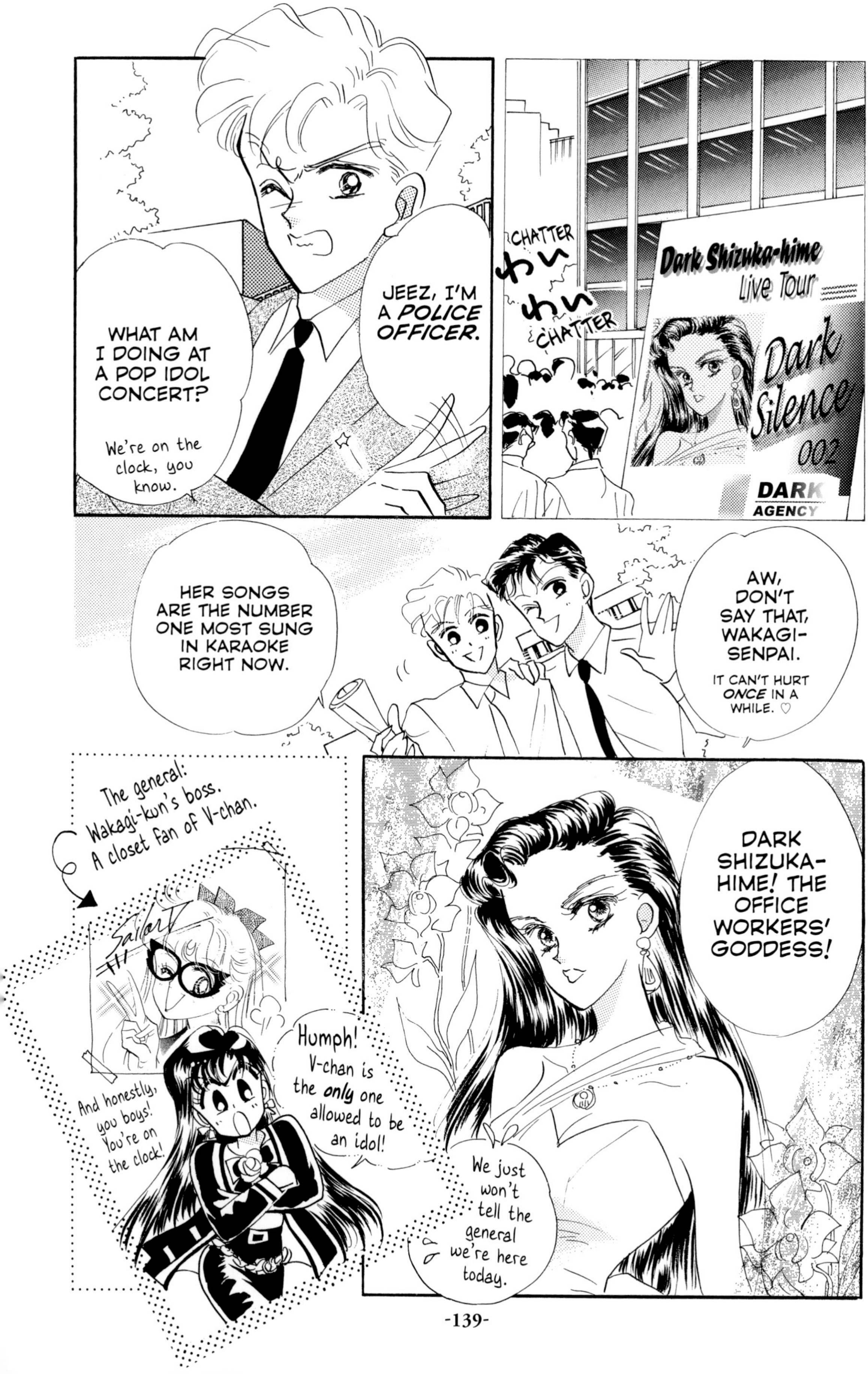
CHATTER
わい
わい
CHATTER
Dark Shizuka-hime Live Tour
Dark Silence 002
DARK AGENCY
JEEZ, I'M A *POLICE OFFICER*.
WHAT AM I DOING AT A POP IDOL CONCERT?
We're on the clock, you know.
AW, DON'T SAY THAT, WAKAGI-SENPAI.
IT CAN'T HURT *ONCE* IN A WHILE. ♡
HER SONGS ARE THE NUMBER ONE MOST SUNG IN KARAOKE RIGHT NOW.
DARK SHIZUKA-HIME! THE OFFICE WORKERS' GODDESS!
We just won't tell the general we're here today.
The general: Wakagi-kun's boss. A closet fan of V-chan.
Sailor V
Humph! V-chan is the *only* one allowed to be an idol!
And honestly, you boys! You're on the clock!

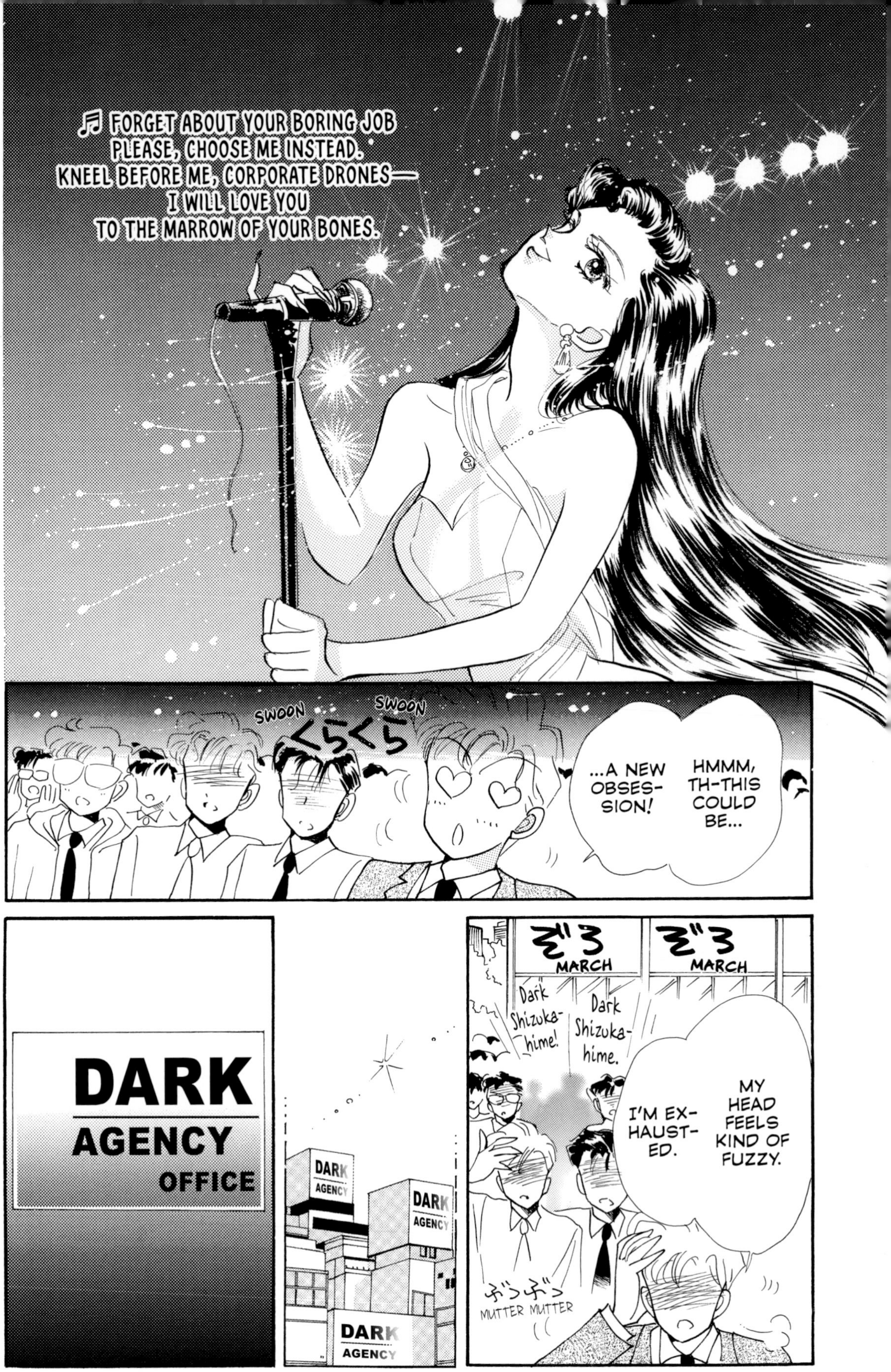
♬ FORGET ABOUT YOUR BORING JOB
PLEASE, CHOOSE ME INSTEAD.
KNEEL BEFORE ME, CORPORATE DRONES—
I WILL LOVE YOU
TO THE MARROW OF YOUR BONES.
HMMM, TH-THIS COULD BE...
...A NEW OBSES-SION!
くらくら
SWOON SWOON
ぞろ MARCH
ぞろ MARCH
Dark Shizuka-hime.
Dark Shizuka-hime!
MY HEAD FEELS KIND OF FUZZY.
I'M EX-HAUST-ED.
ぶつぶつ
MUTTER MUTTER
DARK AGENCY
DARK AGENCY
DARK AGENCY
DARK AGENCY OFFICE

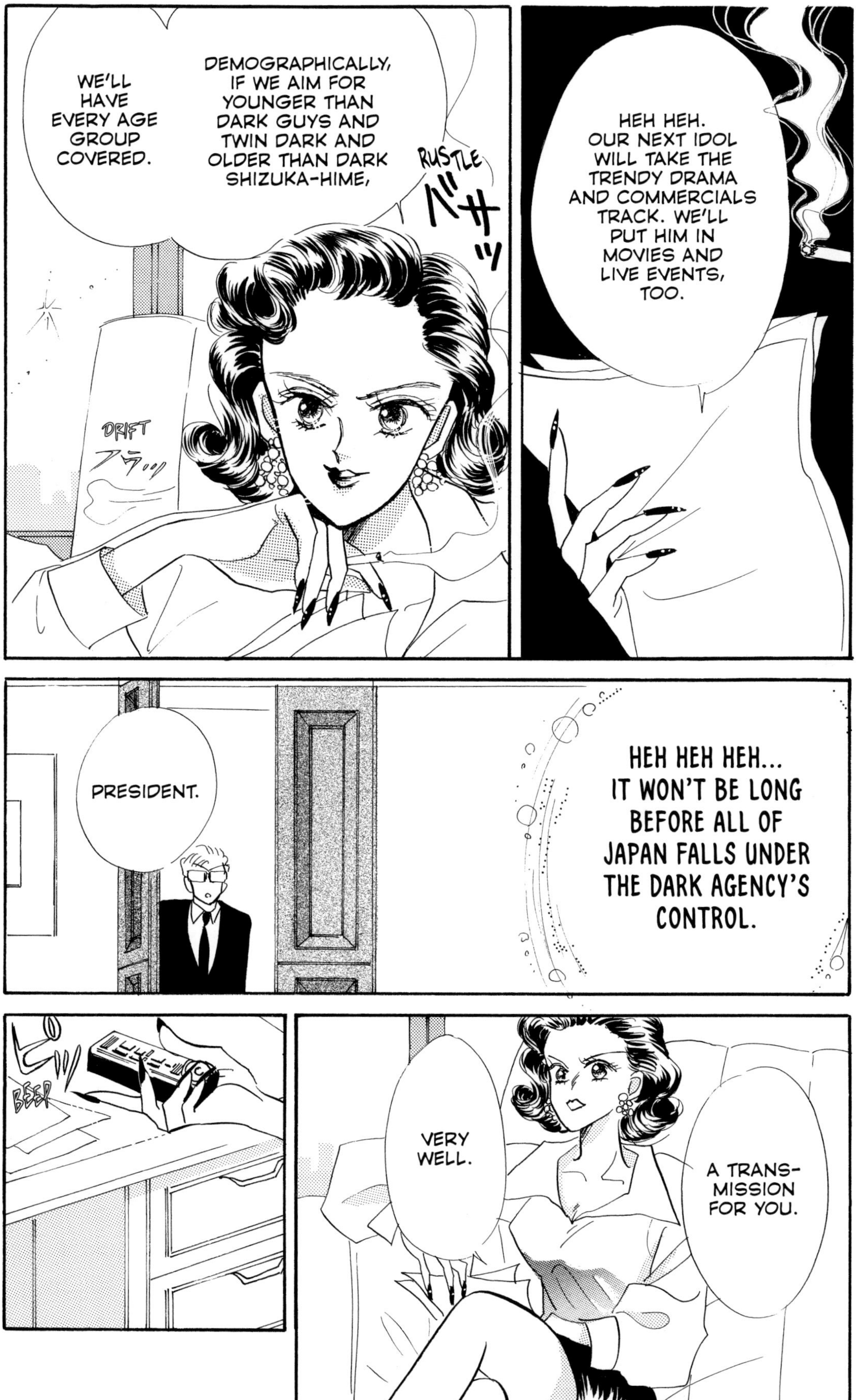
HEH HEH. OUR NEXT IDOL WILL TAKE THE TRENDY DRAMA AND COMMERCIALS TRACK. WE'LL PUT HIM IN MOVIES AND LIVE EVENTS, TOO.
RUSTLE
バサッ
DEMOGRAPHICALLY, IF WE AIM FOR YOUNGER THAN DARK GUYS AND TWIN DARK AND OLDER THAN DARK SHIZUKA-HIME,
WE'LL HAVE EVERY AGE GROUP COVERED.
DRIFT
HEH HEH HEH... IT WON'T BE LONG BEFORE ALL OF JAPAN FALLS UNDER THE DARK AGENCY'S CONTROL.
PRESIDENT.
A TRANS-MISSION FOR YOU.
VERY WELL.
BEEP

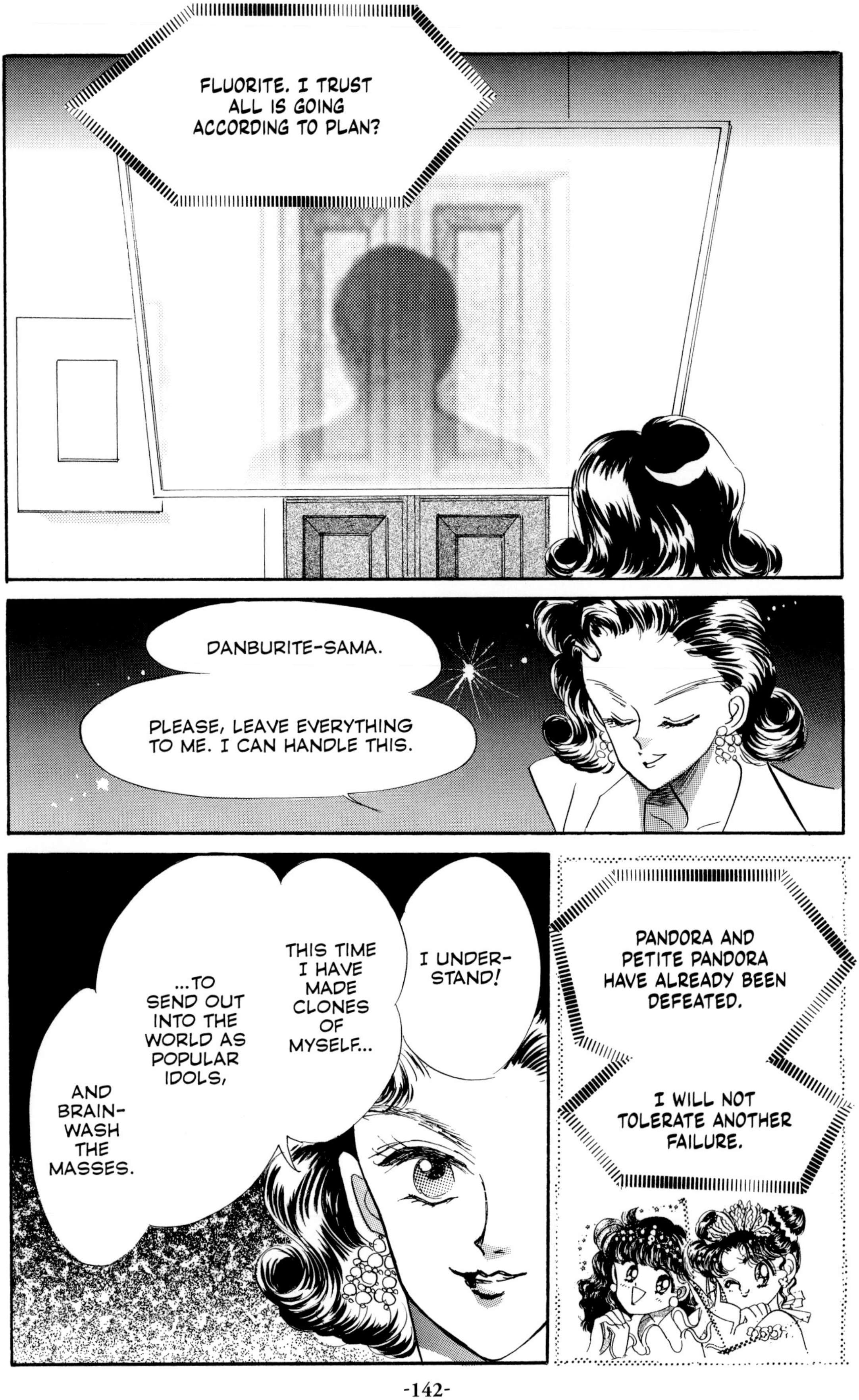
FLUORITE. I TRUST ALL IS GOING ACCORDING TO PLAN?
DANBURITE-SAMA.
PLEASE, LEAVE EVERYTHING TO ME. I CAN HANDLE THIS.
PANDORA AND PETITE PANDORA HAVE ALREADY BEEN DEFEATED.
I WILL NOT TOLERATE ANOTHER FAILURE.
I UNDER-STAND!
THIS TIME I HAVE MADE CLONES OF MYSELF...
...TO SEND OUT INTO THE WORLD AS POPULAR IDOLS,
AND BRAIN-WASH THE MASSES.

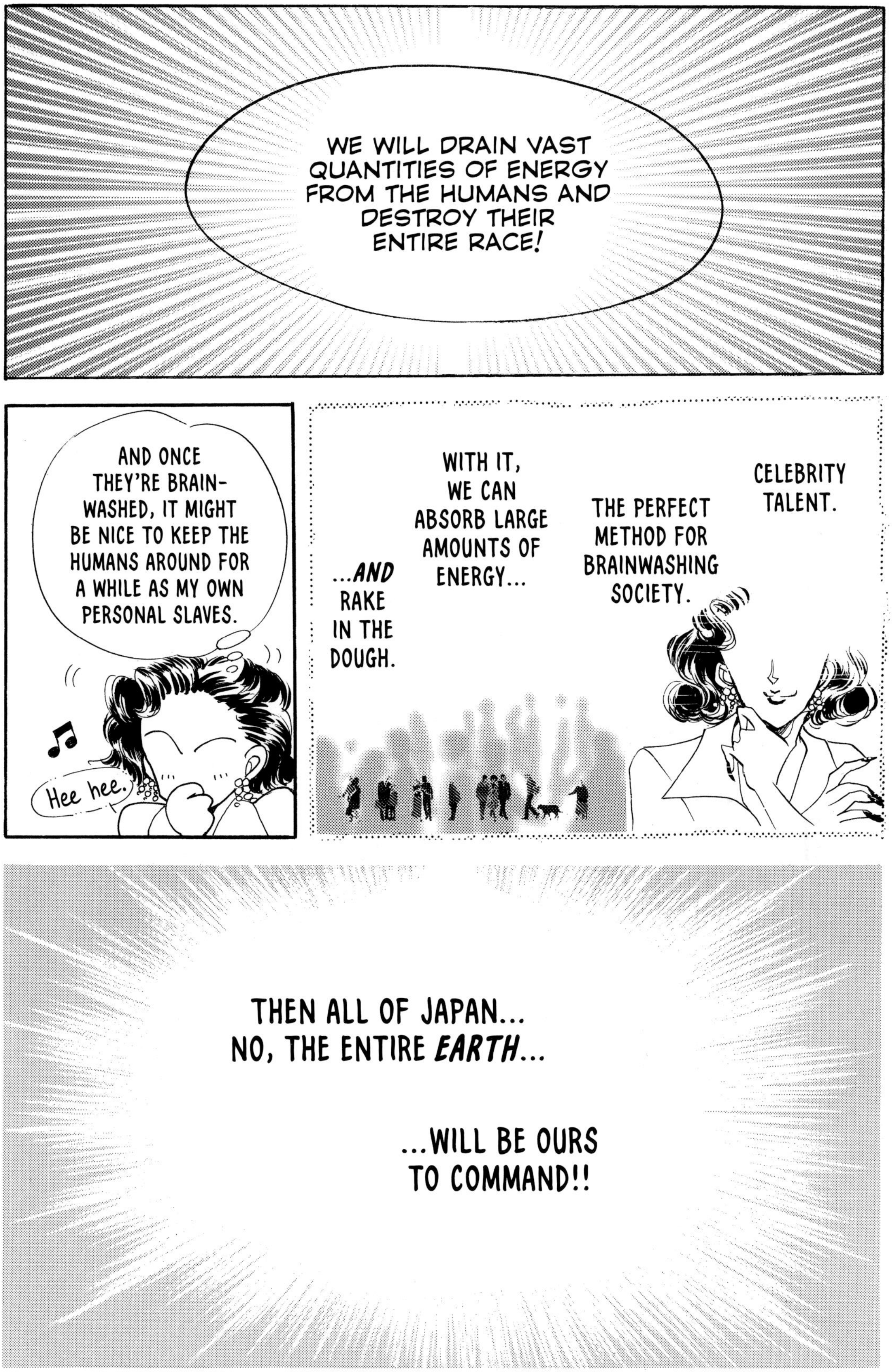
WE WILL DRAIN VAST QUANTITIES OF ENERGY FROM THE HUMANS AND DESTROY THEIR ENTIRE RACE!
CELEBRITY TALENT.
THE PERFECT METHOD FOR BRAINWASHING SOCIETY.
WITH IT, WE CAN ABSORB LARGE AMOUNTS OF ENERGY...
...AND RAKE IN THE DOUGH.
AND ONCE THEY'RE BRAIN-WASHED, IT MIGHT BE NICE TO KEEP THE HUMANS AROUND FOR A WHILE AS MY OWN PERSONAL SLAVES.
Hee hee.
THEN ALL OF JAPAN... NO, THE ENTIRE *EARTH*...
...WILL BE OURS TO COMMAND!!

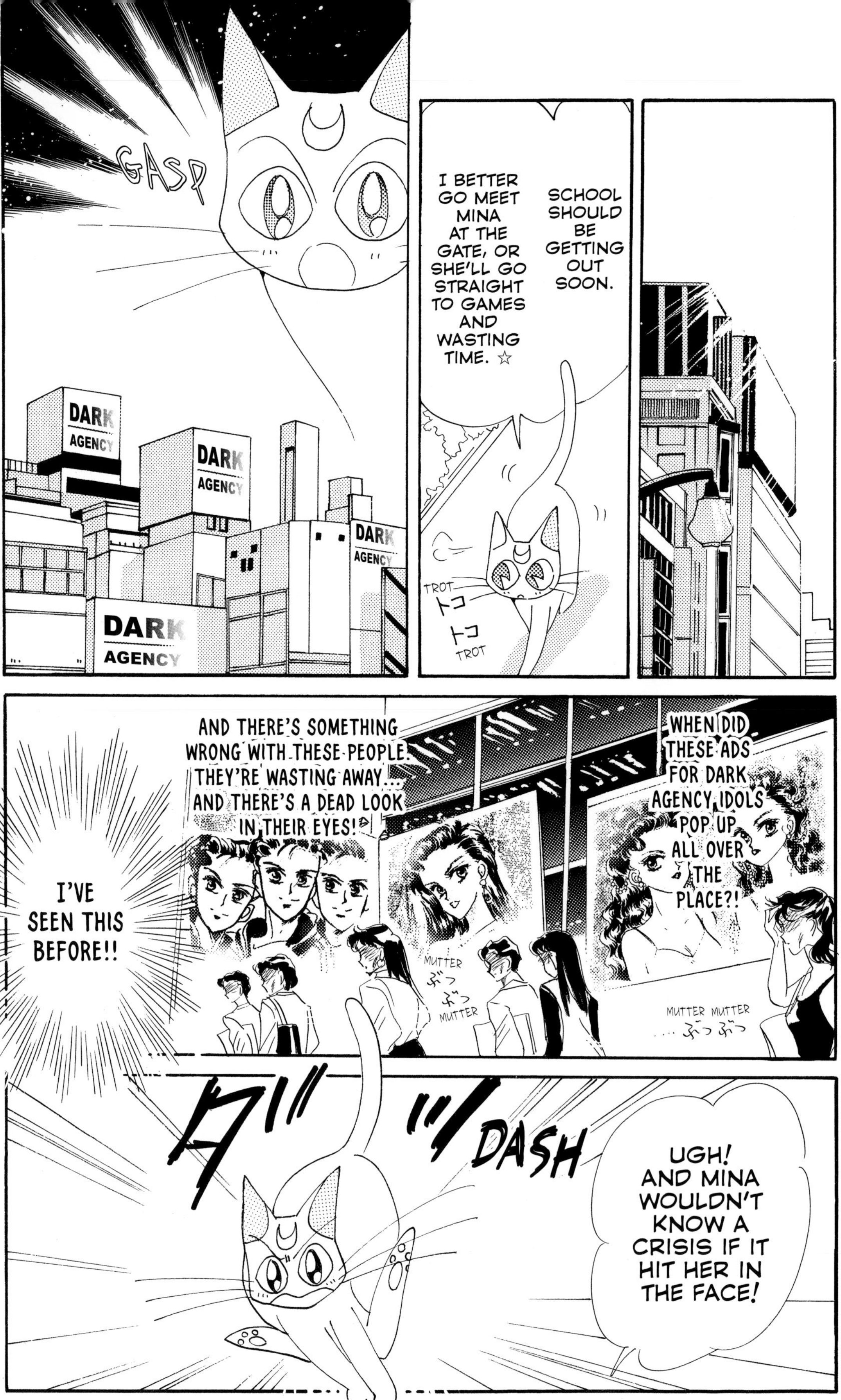
SCHOOL SHOULD BE GETTING OUT SOON.
I BETTER GO MEET MINA AT THE GATE, OR SHE'LL GO STRAIGHT TO GAMES AND WASTING TIME. ☆
TROT トコ
トコ TROT
GASP
DARK AGENCY
DARK AGENCY
DARK AGENCY
DARK AGENCY
WHEN DID THESE ADS FOR DARK AGENCY IDOLS POP UP ALL OVER THE PLACE?!
AND THERE'S SOMETHING WRONG WITH THESE PEOPLE. THEY'RE WASTING AWAY... AND THERE'S A DEAD LOOK IN THEIR EYES!
MUTTER MUTTER ...ぶつぶつ
MUTTER ぶつ ぶつ MUTTER
I'VE SEEN THIS BEFORE!!
UGH! AND MINA WOULDN'T KNOW A CRISIS IF IT HIT HER IN THE FACE!
DASH

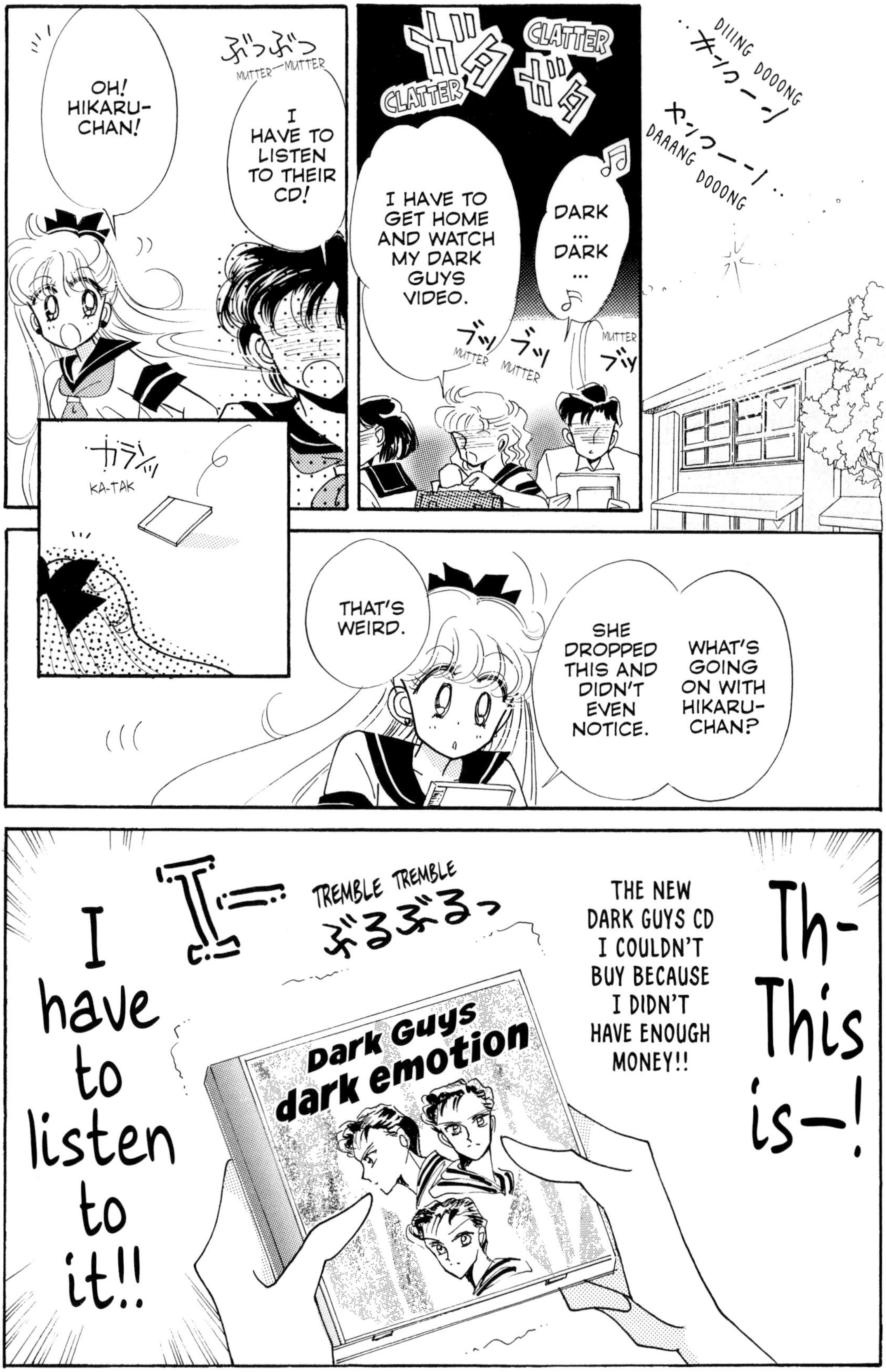
キーンコーン
DIIING DOOONG
カーンコーン
DAAANG DOOONG
ガタ
CLATTER
ガタ
CLATTER
DARK ... DARK ...
I HAVE TO GET HOME AND WATCH MY DARK GUYS VIDEO.
ブツ
MUTTER
ブツ
MUTTER
ブツ
MUTTER
ぶつぶつ
MUTTER—MUTTER
I HAVE TO LISTEN TO THEIR CD!
OH! HIKARU-CHAN!
カランッ
KA-TAK
WHAT'S GOING ON WITH HIKARU-CHAN?
SHE DROPPED THIS AND DIDN'T EVEN NOTICE.
THAT'S WEIRD.
Th-This is—!
THE NEW DARK GUYS CD I COULDN'T BUY BECAUSE I DIDN'T HAVE ENOUGH MONEY!!
TREMBLE TREMBLE
ぶるぶるっ
I—
I have to listen to it!!
Dark Guys
dark emotion

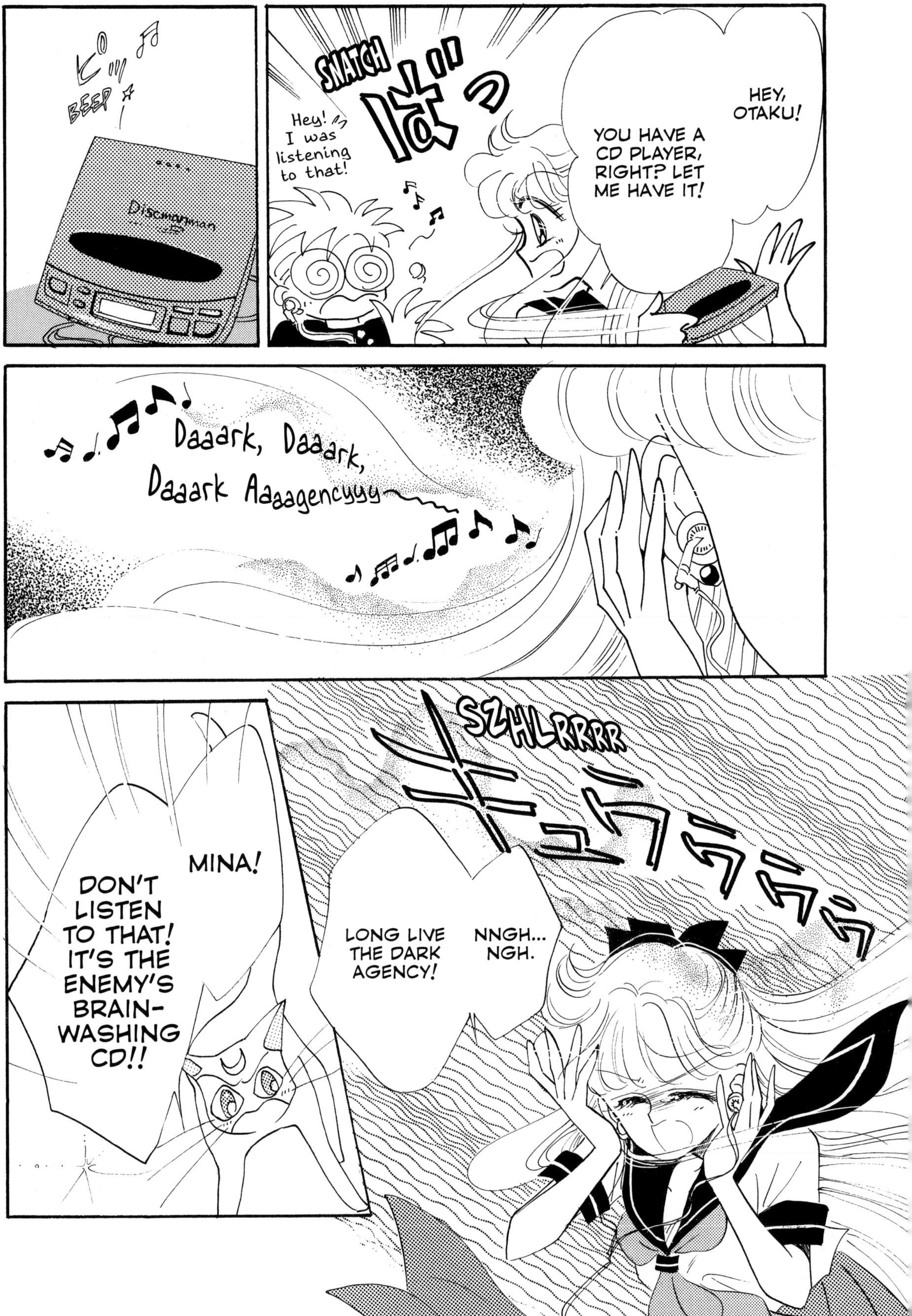
HEY, OTAKU!
YOU HAVE A CD PLAYER, RIGHT? LET ME HAVE IT!
SNATCH
ぱっ
Hey! I was listening to that!
ピッ
BEEP
Discmanman
Daaark, Daaark, Daaark Aaaagencyyy
SZHLRRRR
NNGH... NGH.
LONG LIVE THE DARK AGENCY!
MINA!
DON'T LISTEN TO THAT! IT'S THE ENEMY'S BRAIN-WASHING CD!!

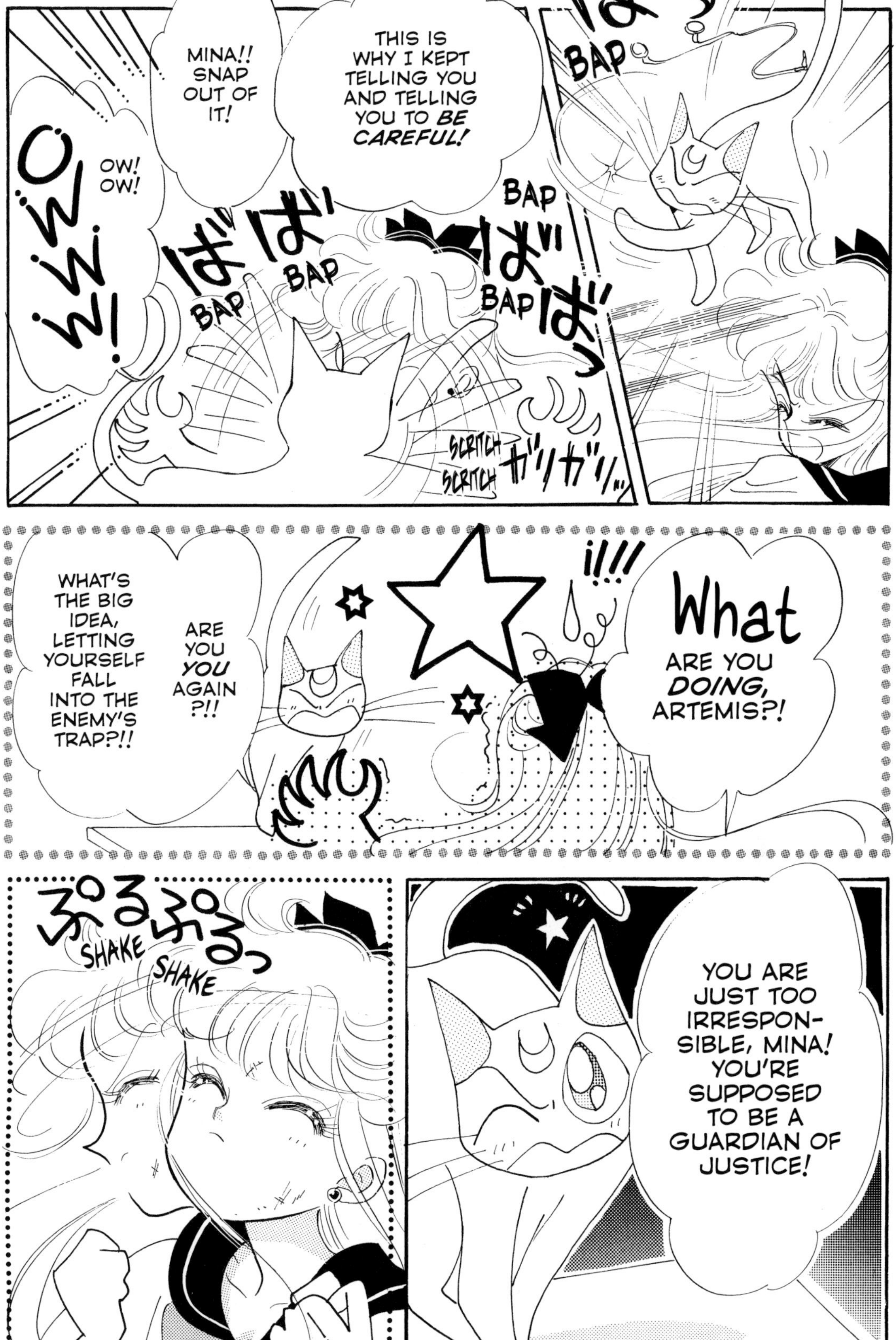
ばっ
BAP
THIS IS WHY I KEPT TELLING YOU AND TELLING YOU TO *BE CAREFUL!*
MINA!! SNAP OUT OF IT!
BAP
ばっ
BAP
ばっ
BAP
ばっ
BAP
OW! OW!
OWWW!
SCRITCH SCRITCH
ガリガリ
What ARE YOU *DOING,* ARTEMIS?!
!!!
ARE YOU *YOU* AGAIN?!!
WHAT'S THE BIG IDEA, LETTING YOURSELF FALL INTO THE ENEMY'S TRAP?!!
YOU ARE JUST TOO IRRESPON-SIBLE, MINA! YOU'RE SUPPOSED TO BE A GUARDIAN OF JUSTICE!
ぷるぷるっ
SHAKE SHAKE

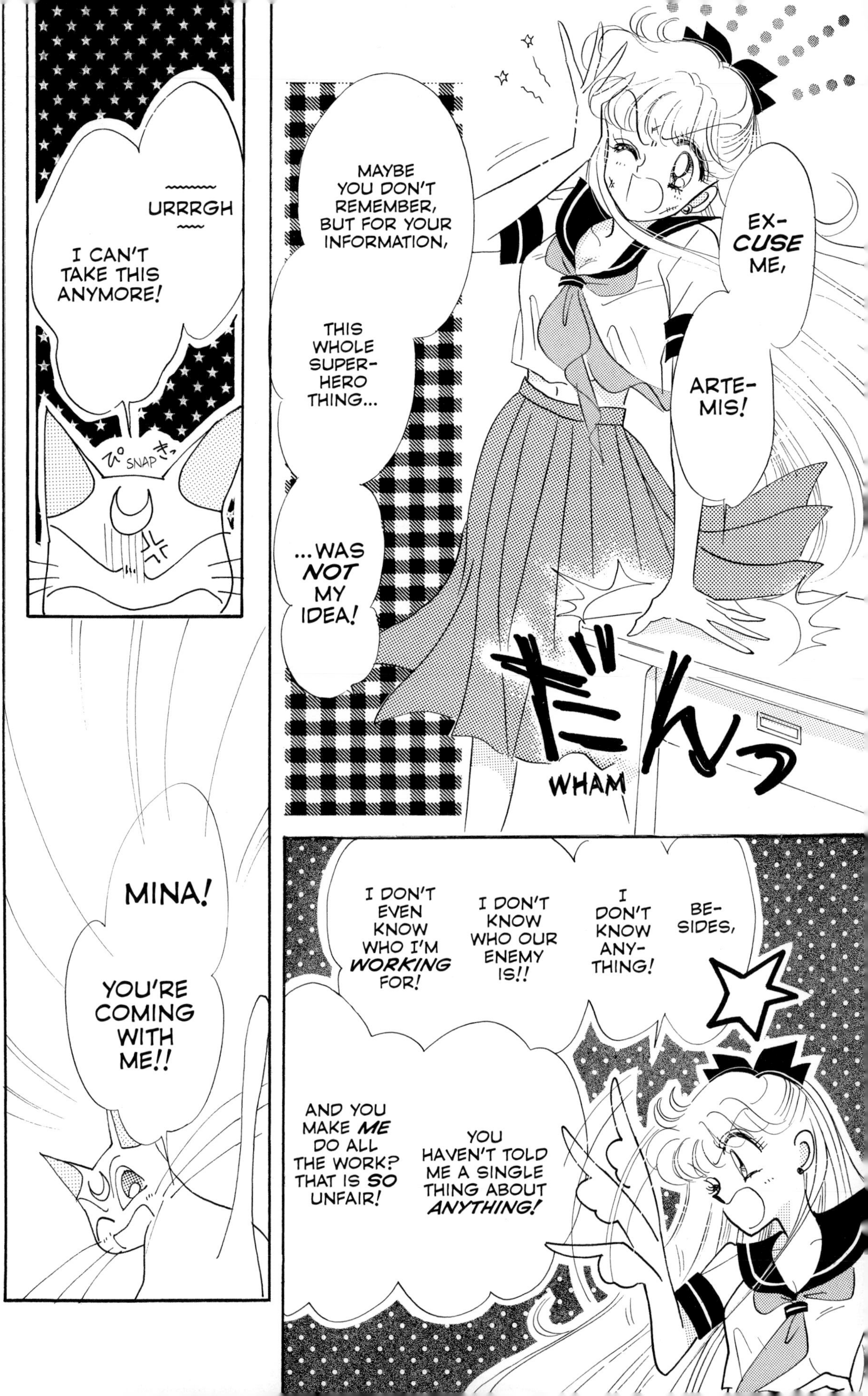
EX-CUSE ME,
ARTE-MIS!
MAYBE YOU DON'T REMEMBER, BUT FOR YOUR INFORMATION,
THIS WHOLE SUPER-HERO THING...
...WAS NOT MY IDEA!
だんっ
WHAM
URRRGH
I CAN'T TAKE THIS ANYMORE!
ぴきっ
SNAP
BE-SIDES,
I DON'T KNOW ANY-THING!
I DON'T KNOW WHO OUR ENEMY IS!!
I DON'T EVEN KNOW WHO I'M WORKING FOR!
YOU HAVEN'T TOLD ME A SINGLE THING ABOUT ANYTHING!
AND YOU MAKE ME DO ALL THE WORK? THAT IS SO UNFAIR!
MINA!
YOU'RE COMING WITH ME!!

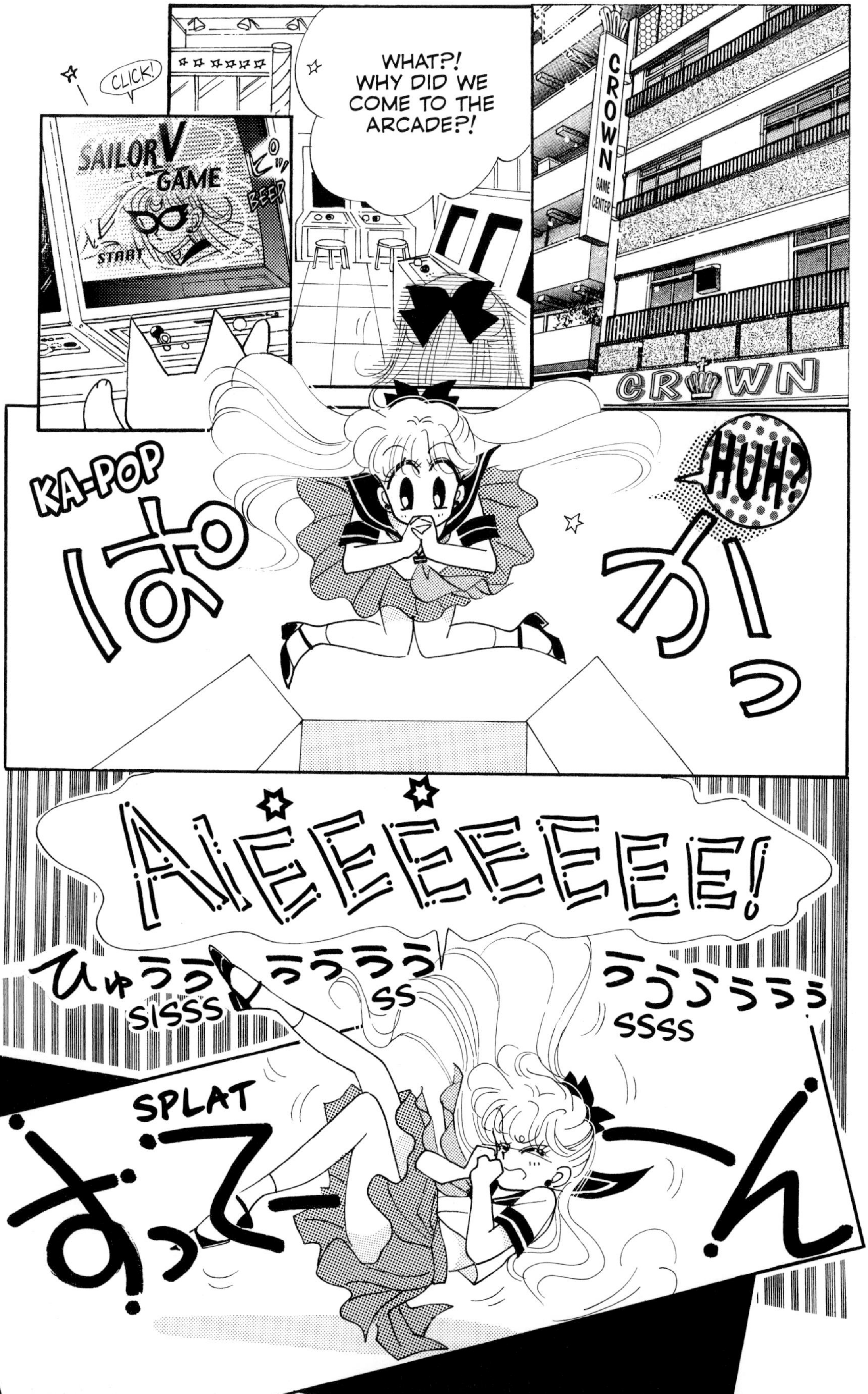
CROWN
GAME CENTER
CROWN
WHAT?! WHY DID WE COME TO THE ARCADE?!
CLICK!
SAILOR V GAME
START
BEEP
HUH?
KA-POP
ぱかっ
AIEEEEEEE!
ひゅううう
SISSS
ううううう
SS
うううううう
SSSS
SPLAT
すってーん

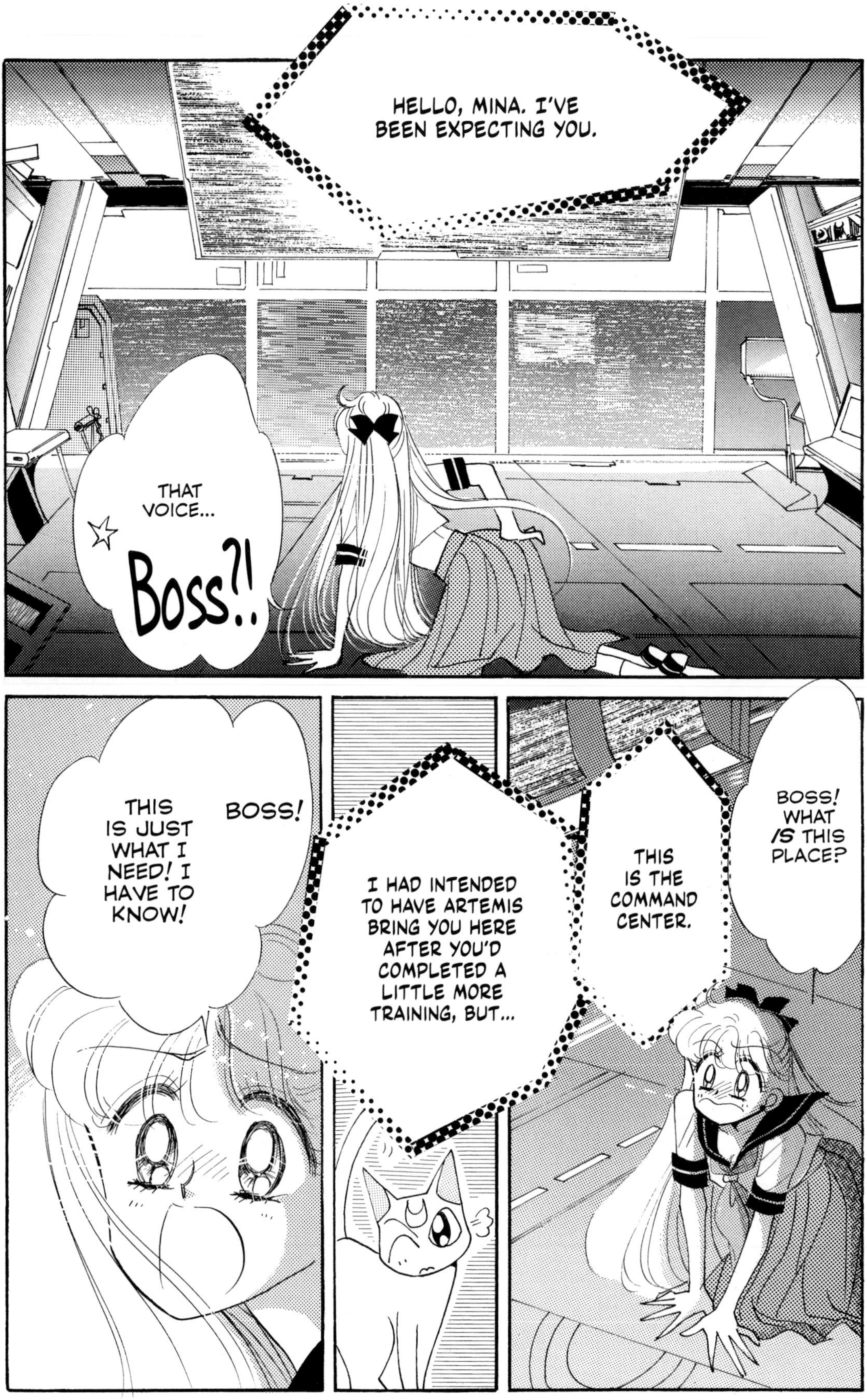
HELLO, MINA. I'VE BEEN EXPECTING YOU.
THAT VOICE...
BOSS?!
BOSS! WHAT *IS* THIS PLACE?
THIS IS THE COMMAND CENTER.
I HAD INTENDED TO HAVE ARTEMIS BRING YOU HERE AFTER YOU'D COMPLETED A LITTLE MORE TRAINING, BUT...
BOSS!
THIS IS JUST WHAT I NEED! I HAVE TO KNOW!

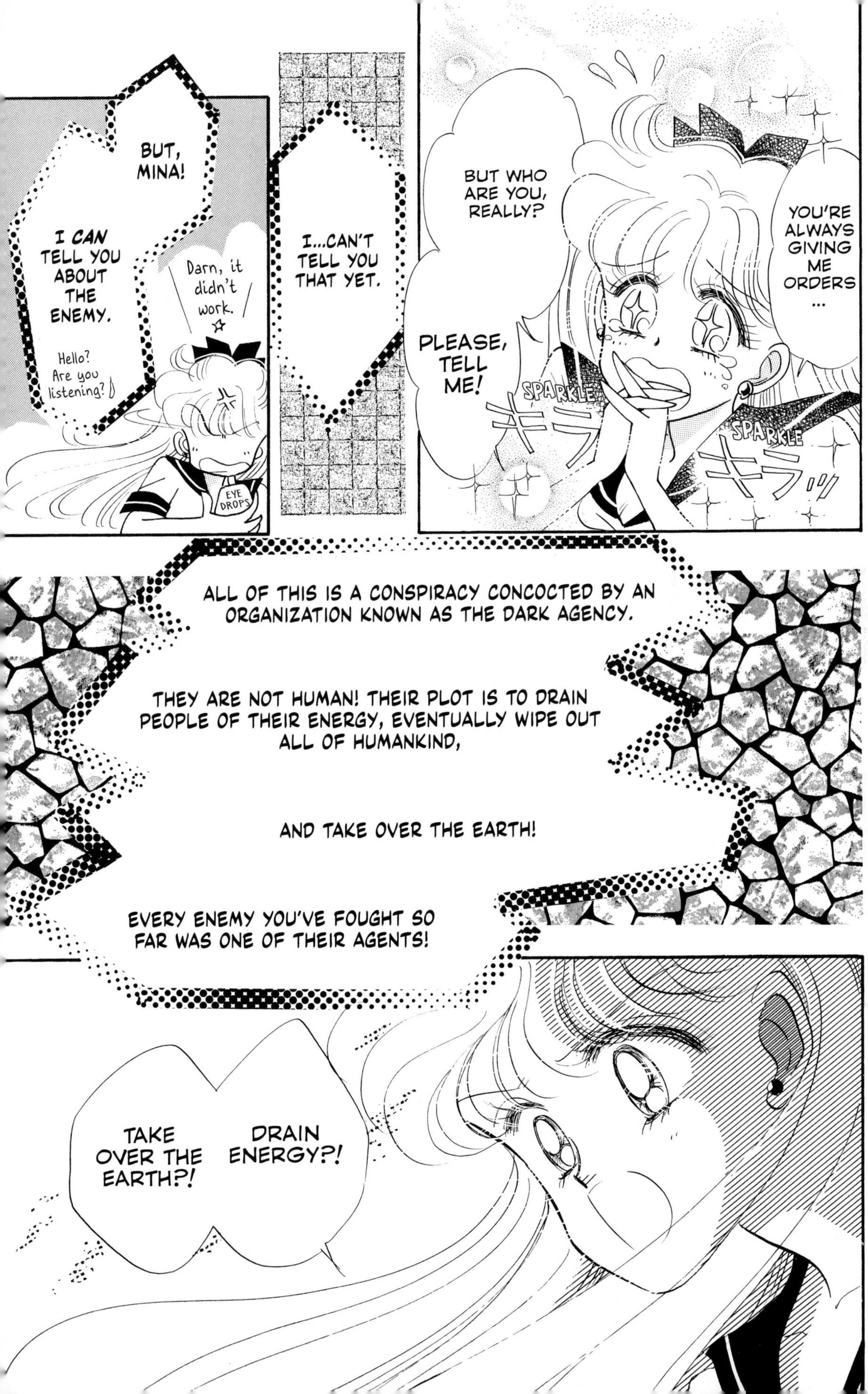
YOU'RE ALWAYS GIVING ME ORDERS...
BUT WHO ARE YOU, REALLY?
PLEASE, TELL ME!
SPARKLE
SPARKLE
I...CAN'T TELL YOU THAT YET.
BUT, MINA!
I *CAN* TELL YOU ABOUT THE ENEMY.
Darn, it didn't work. ☆
Hello? Are you listening?
EYE DROPS
ALL OF THIS IS A CONSPIRACY CONCOCTED BY AN ORGANIZATION KNOWN AS THE DARK AGENCY.
THEY ARE NOT HUMAN! THEIR PLOT IS TO DRAIN PEOPLE OF THEIR ENERGY, EVENTUALLY WIPE OUT ALL OF HUMANKIND,
AND TAKE OVER THE EARTH!
EVERY ENEMY YOU'VE FOUGHT SO FAR WAS ONE OF THEIR AGENTS!
DRAIN ENERGY?!
TAKE OVER THE EARTH?!

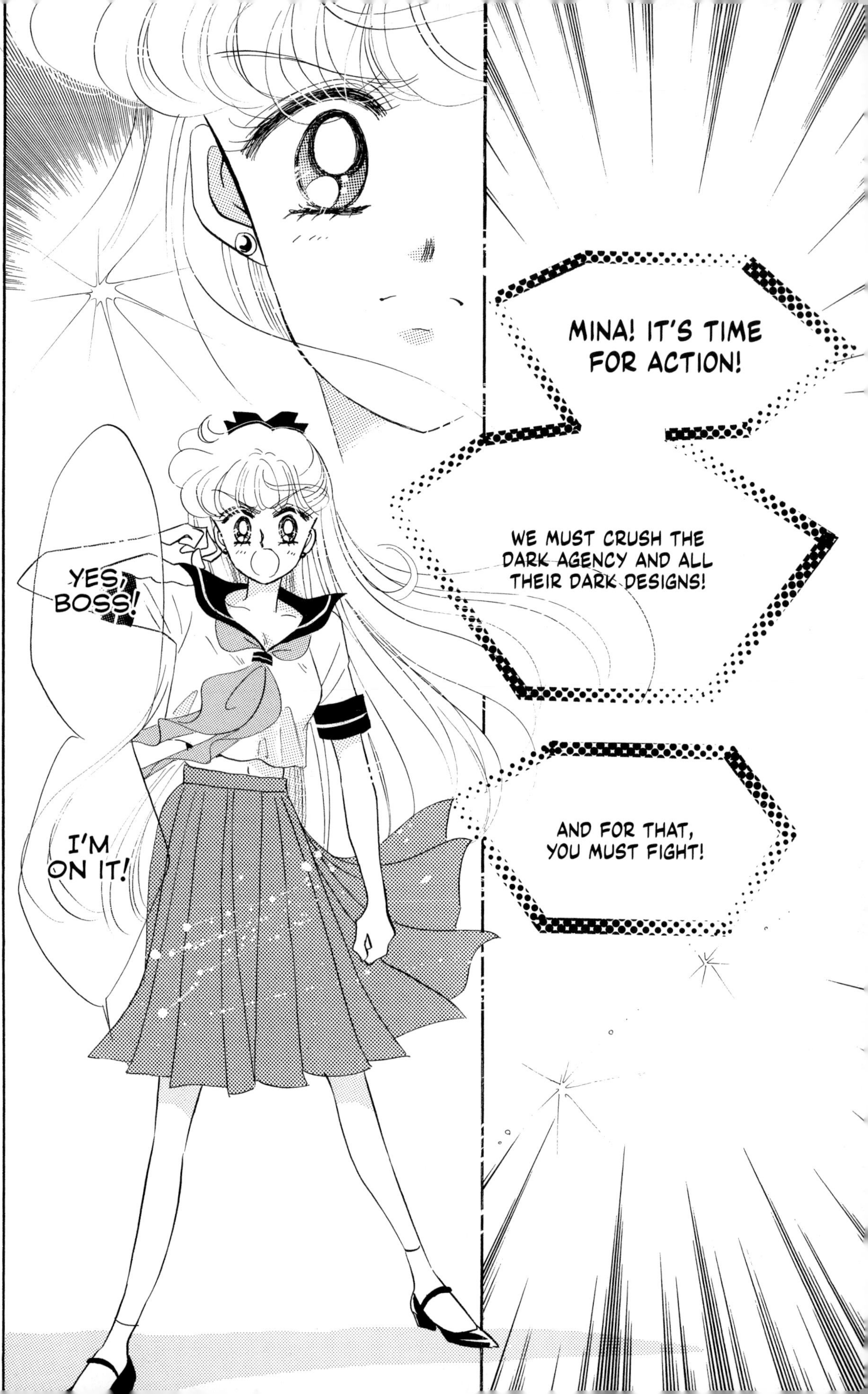
MINA! IT'S TIME FOR ACTION!
WE MUST CRUSH THE DARK AGENCY AND ALL THEIR DARK DESIGNS!
AND FOR THAT, YOU MUST FIGHT!
YES, BOSS!
I'M ON IT!

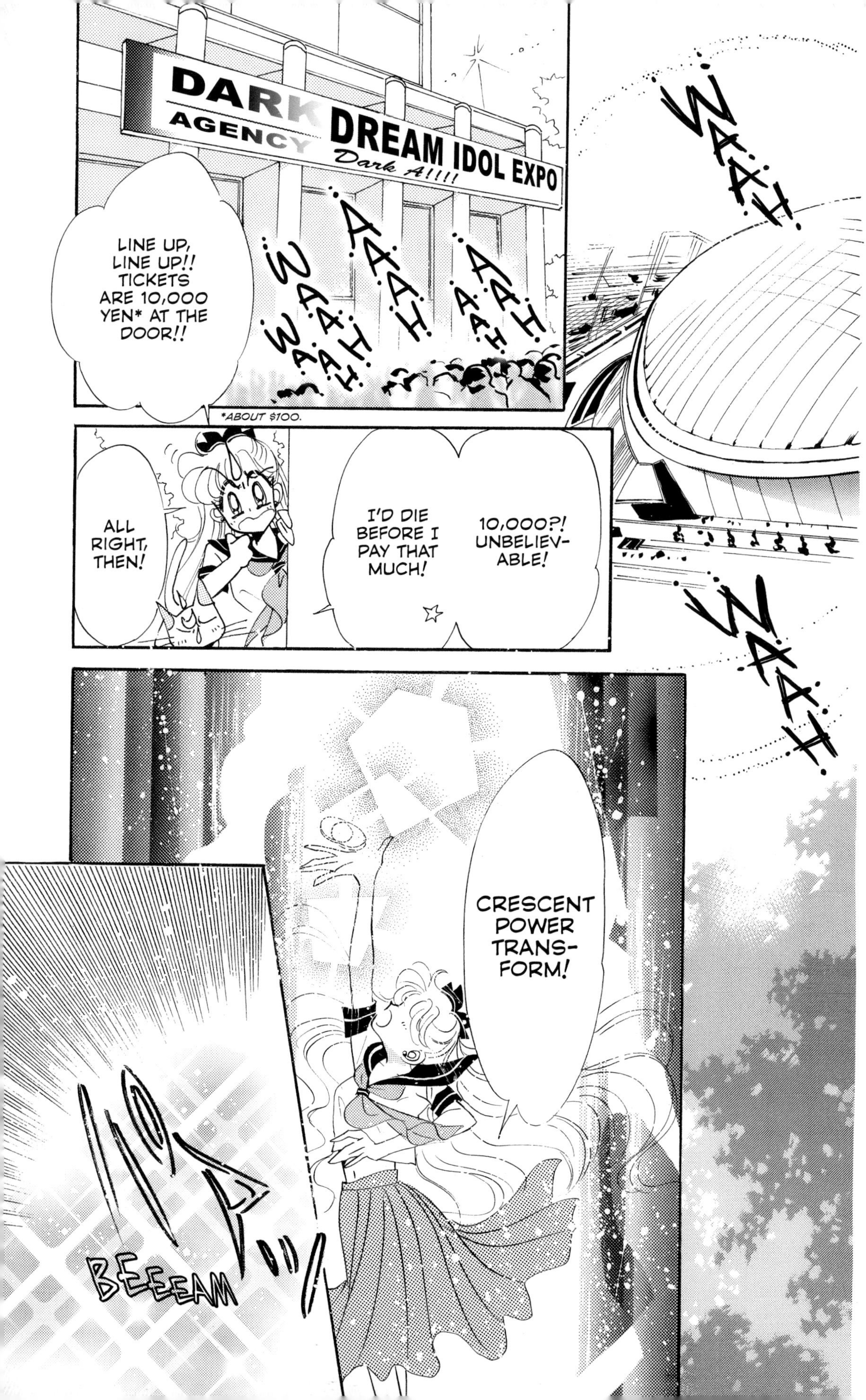
WAAAH!
WAAAH!
DARK AGENCY
DREAM IDOL EXPO
Dark A!!!!
AAAAH
AAAAH
WAAAH
WAAAH
LINE UP, LINE UP!! TICKETS ARE 10,000 YEN* AT THE DOOR!!
*ABOUT $100.
10,000?! UNBELIEV-ABLE!
I'D DIE BEFORE I PAY THAT MUCH!
ALL RIGHT, THEN!
CRESCENT POWER TRANS-FORM!
BEEEEAM

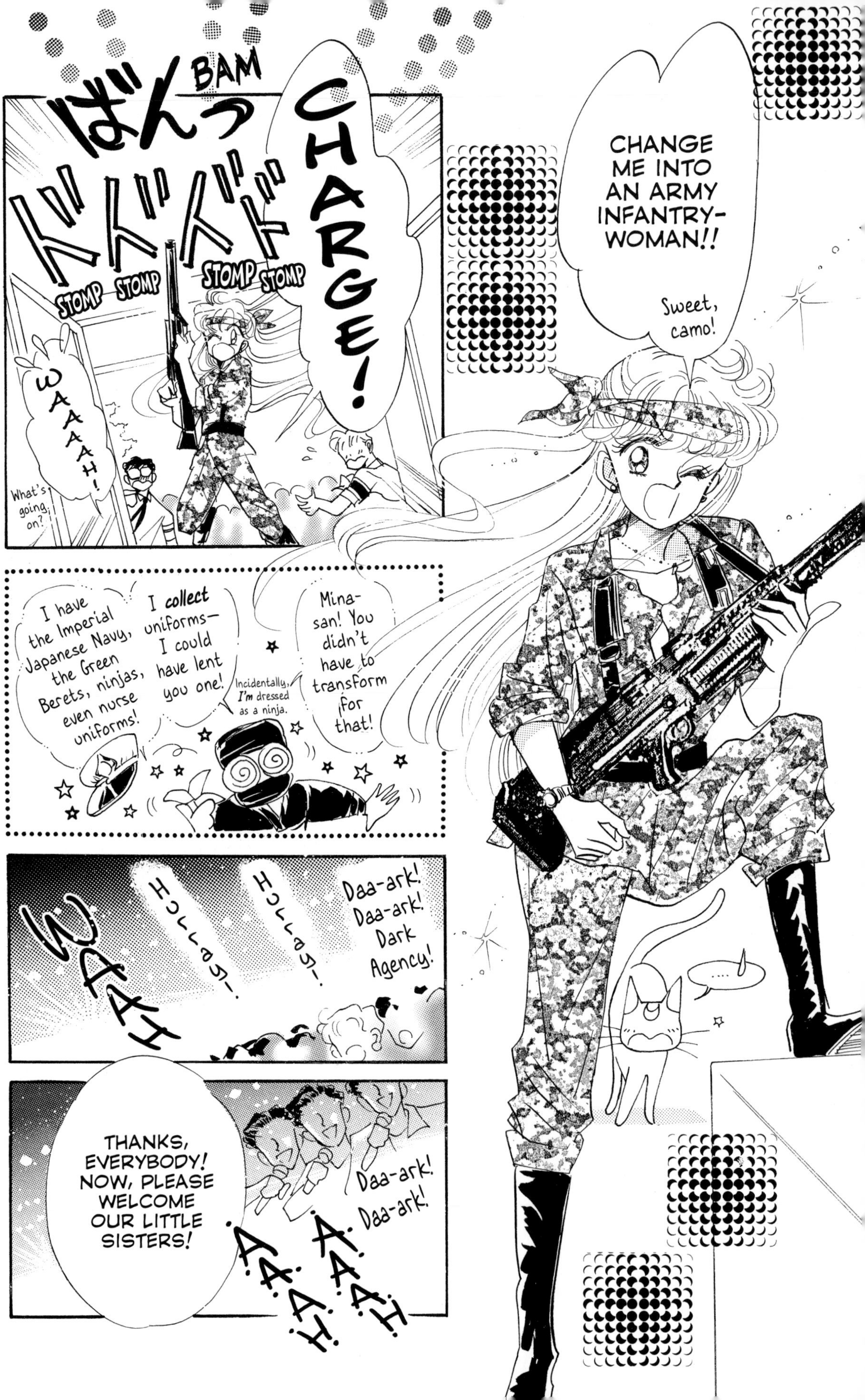

CHANGE ME INTO AN ARMY INFANTRY-WOMAN!!
Sweet, camo!
....
CHARGE!
ばんっ BAM
ドドドド STOMP STOMP STOMP STOMP
WAAAAH!
What's going on?
Mina-san! You didn't have to transform for that!
Incidentally, I'm dressed as a ninja.
I collect uniforms—I could have lent you one!
I have the Imperial Japanese Navy, the Green Berets, ninjas, even nurse uniforms!
Daa-ark! Daa-ark! Dark Agency!
Hurray!..
Hurray!..
WAAH
Daa-ark! Daa-ark!
AAAH
AAAH
THANKS, EVERYBODY! NOW, PLEASE WELCOME OUR LITTLE SISTERS!

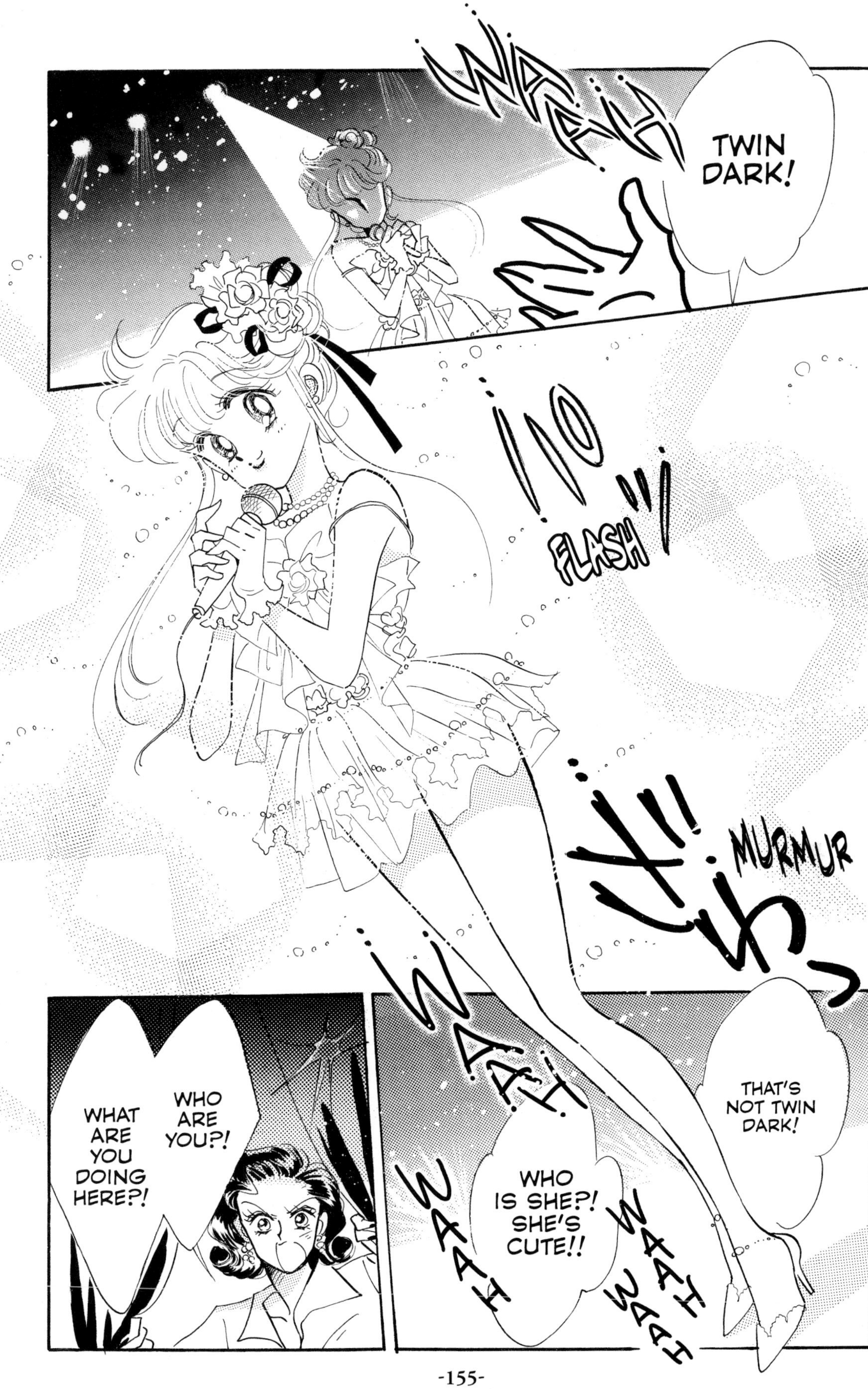

WAAAH!!
TWIN DARK!
FLASH!!
MURMUR
WAAH!
THAT'S NOT TWIN DARK!
WAAH WAAH
WHO IS SHE?! SHE'S CUTE!!
WAAH
WHO ARE YOU?!
WHAT ARE YOU DOING HERE?!

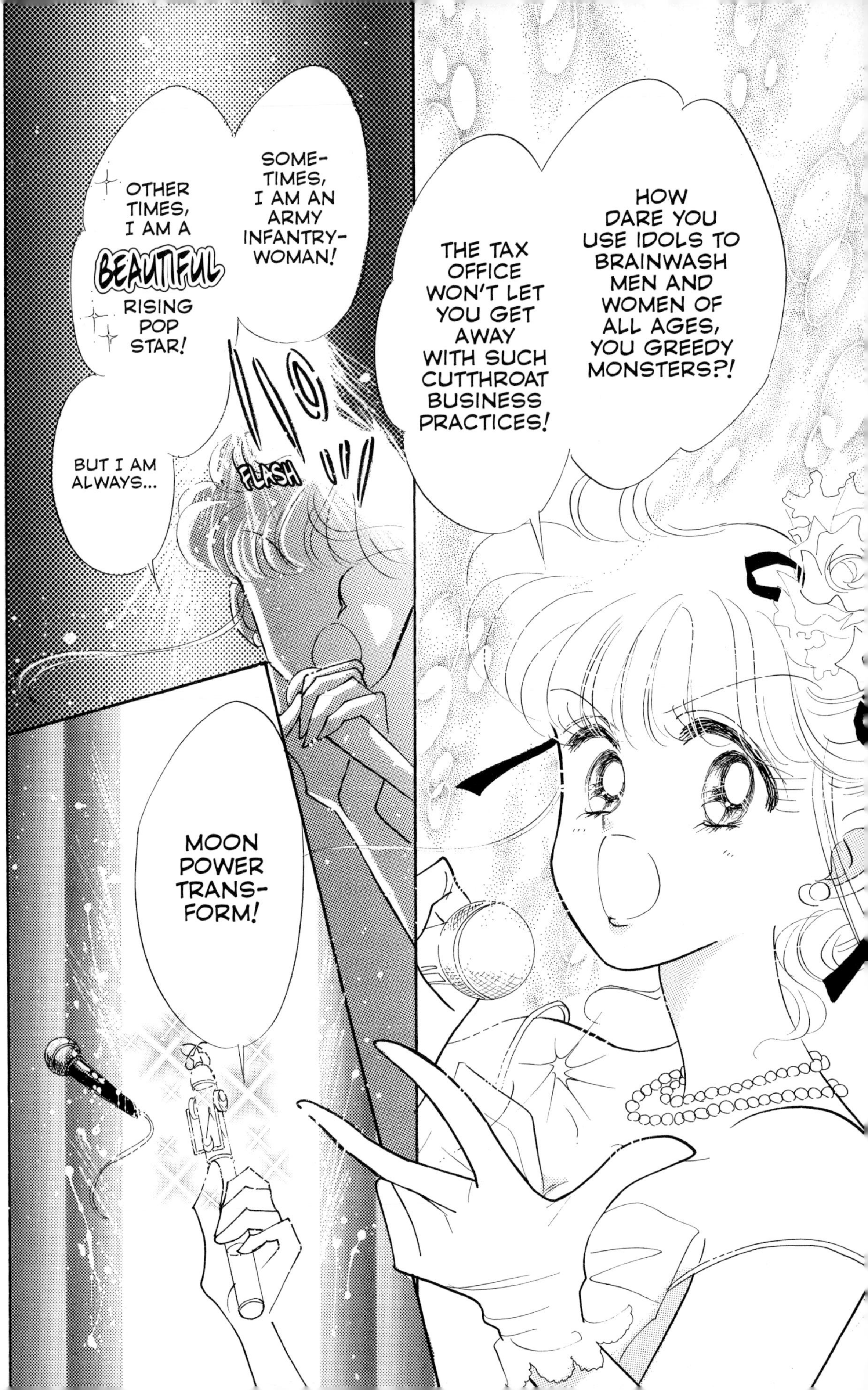
HOW DARE YOU USE IDOLS TO BRAINWASH MEN AND WOMEN OF ALL AGES, YOU GREEDY MONSTERS?!
THE TAX OFFICE WON'T LET YOU GET AWAY WITH SUCH CUTTHROAT BUSINESS PRACTICES!
SOME-TIMES, I AM AN ARMY INFANTRY-WOMAN!
OTHER TIMES, I AM A BEAUTIFUL RISING POP STAR!
BUT I AM ALWAYS...
FLASH
MOON POWER TRANS-FORM!

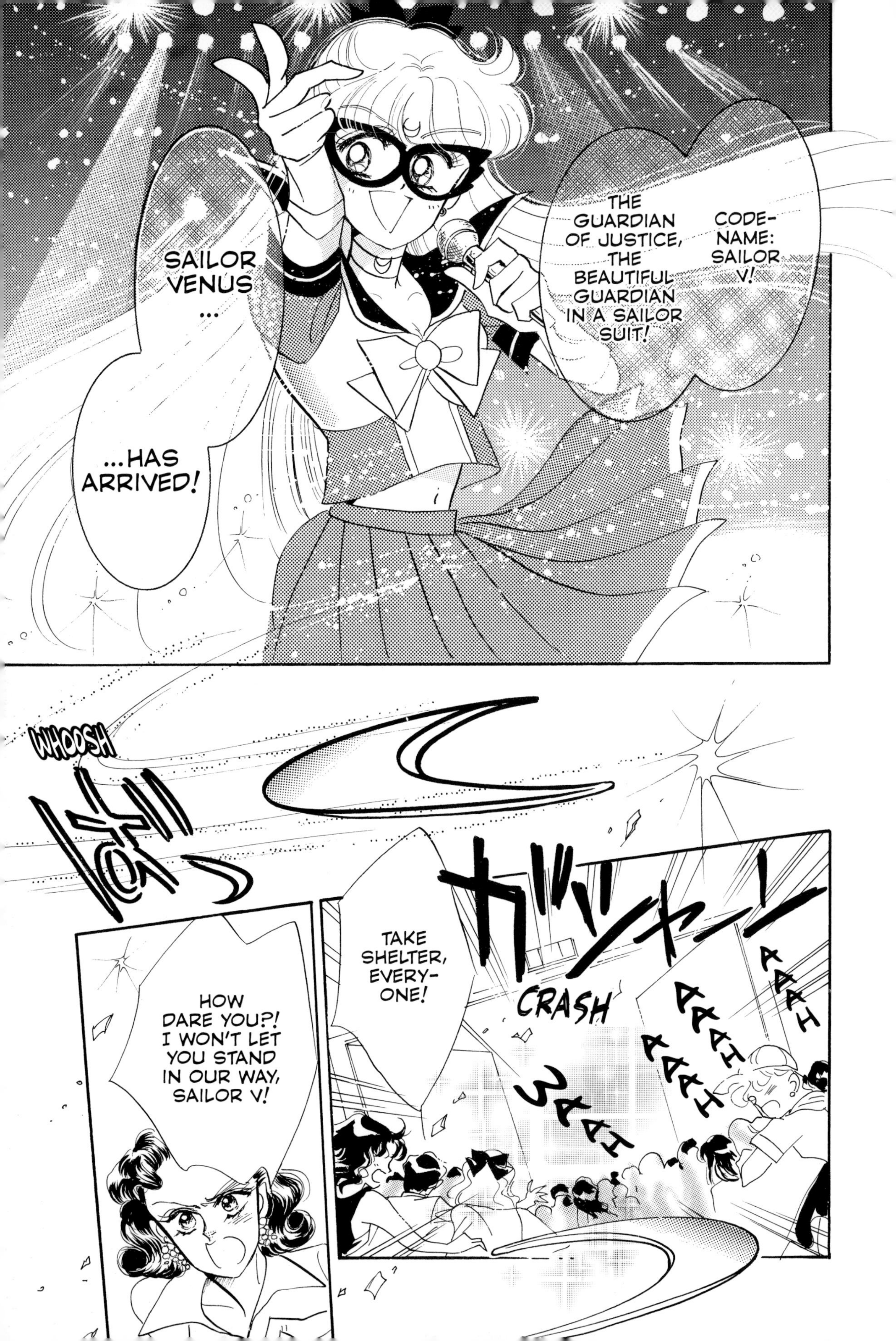
CODE-NAME: SAILOR V!
THE GUARDIAN OF JUSTICE, THE BEAUTIFUL GUARDIAN IN A SAILOR SUIT!
SAILOR VENUS ...
...HAS ARRIVED!
WHOOSH
CRASH
AAAH AAAH AAAH
TAKE SHELTER, EVERY-ONE!
HOW DARE YOU?! I WON'T LET YOU STAND IN OUR WAY, SAILOR V!

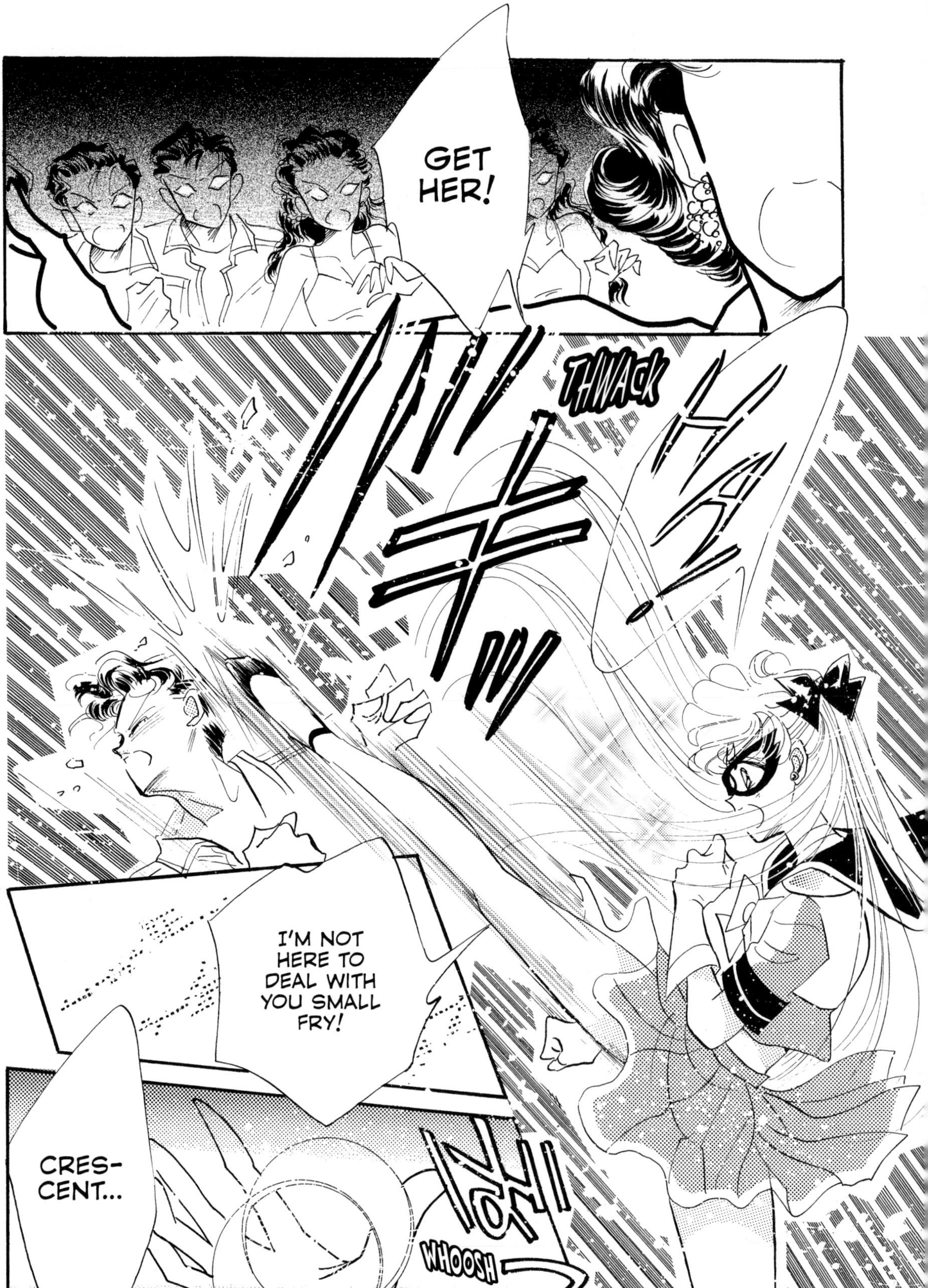
GET HER!
THWACK
I'M NOT HERE TO DEAL WITH YOU SMALL FRY!
CRES-CENT...
WHOOSH

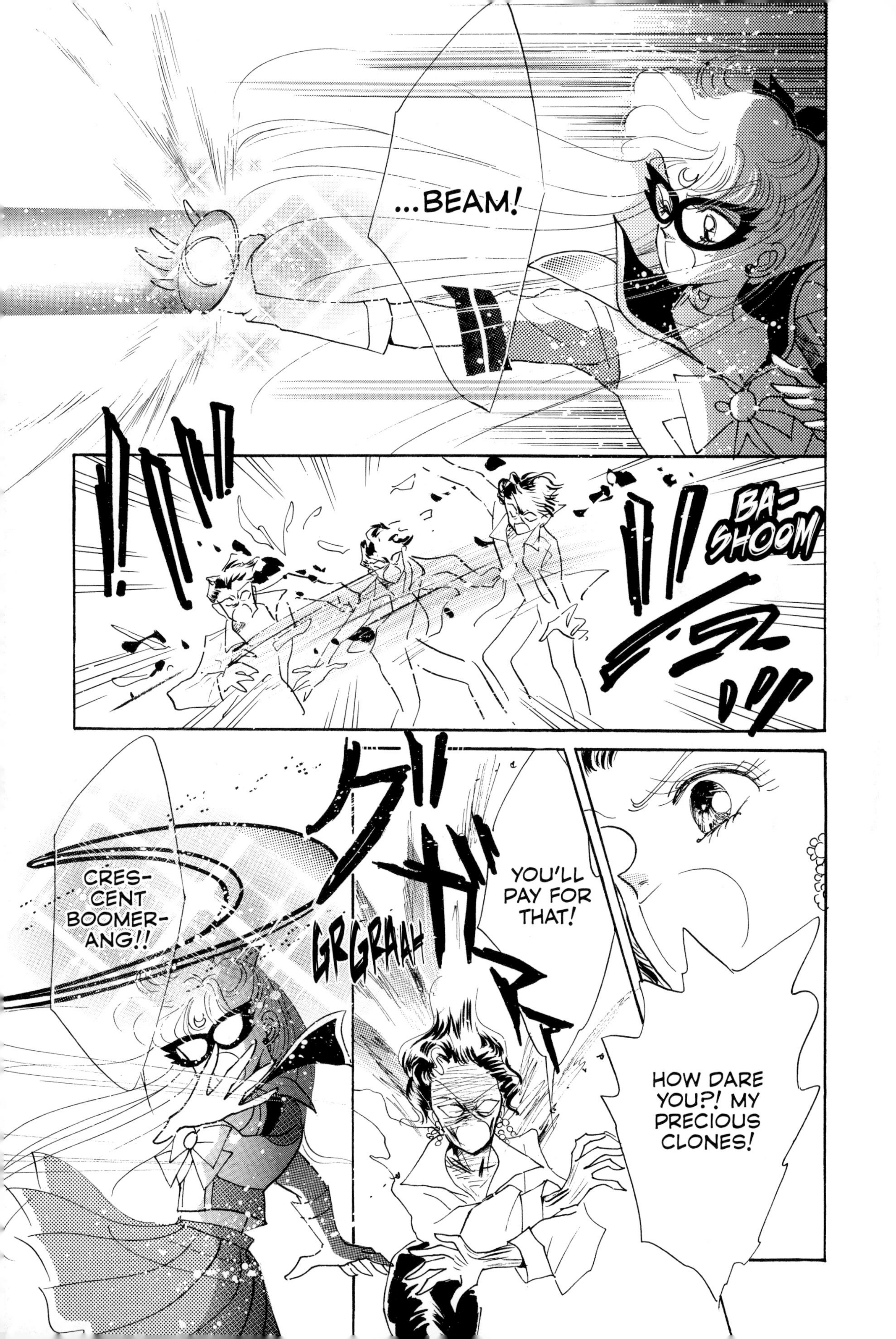
...BEAM!
BA-SHOOM
HOW DARE YOU?! MY PRECIOUS CLONES!
YOU'LL PAY FOR THAT!
GRGRAAH
CRES-CENT BOOMER-ANG!!

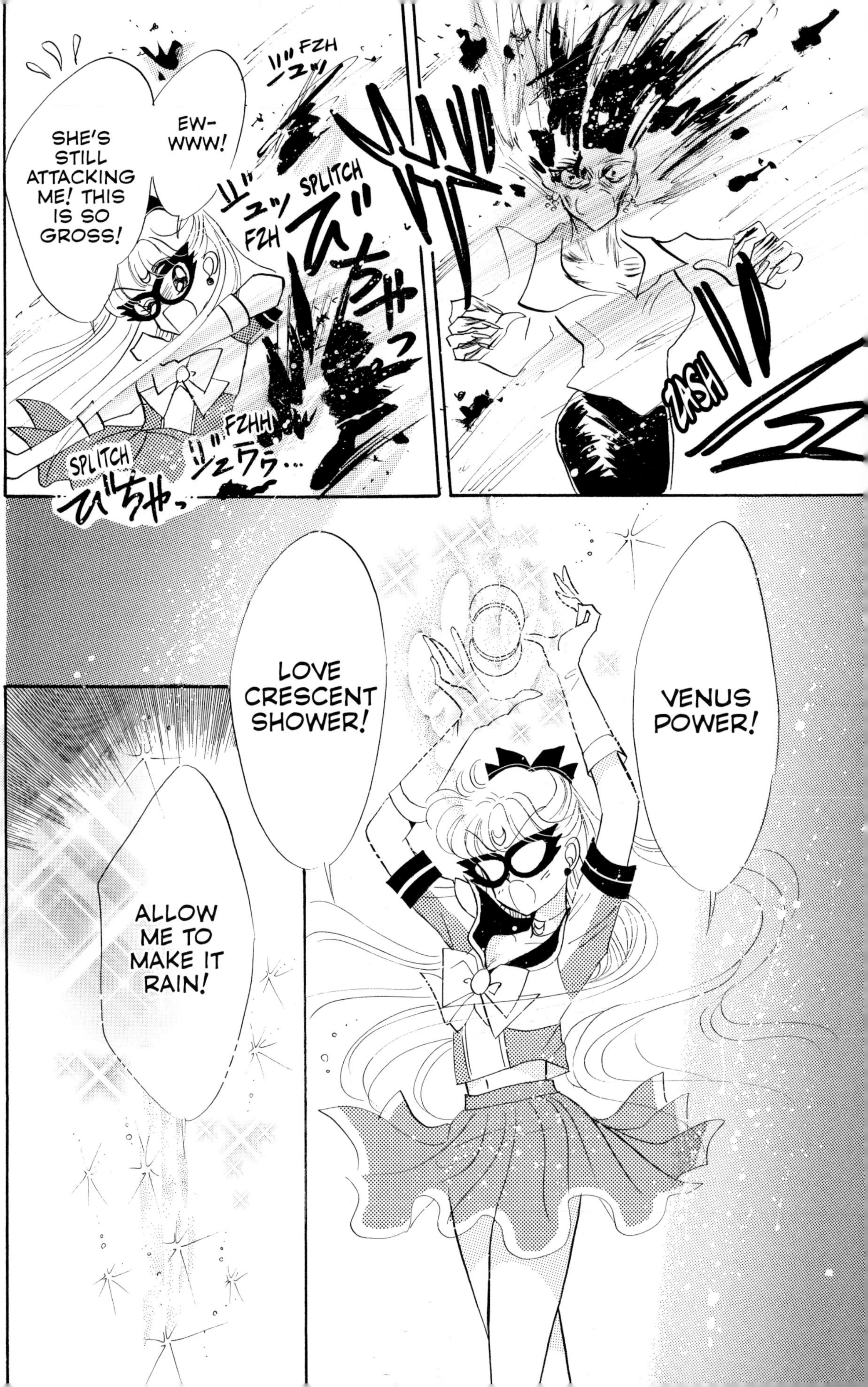
ZASH
ジュッ FZH
EW-WWW!
SHE'S STILL ATTACKING ME! THIS IS SO GROSS!
びちゃっ SPLITCH
ジュッ FZH
ジュワワ… FZHH
びちゃっ SPLITCH
VENUS POWER!
LOVE CRESCENT SHOWER!
ALLOW ME TO MAKE IT RAIN!

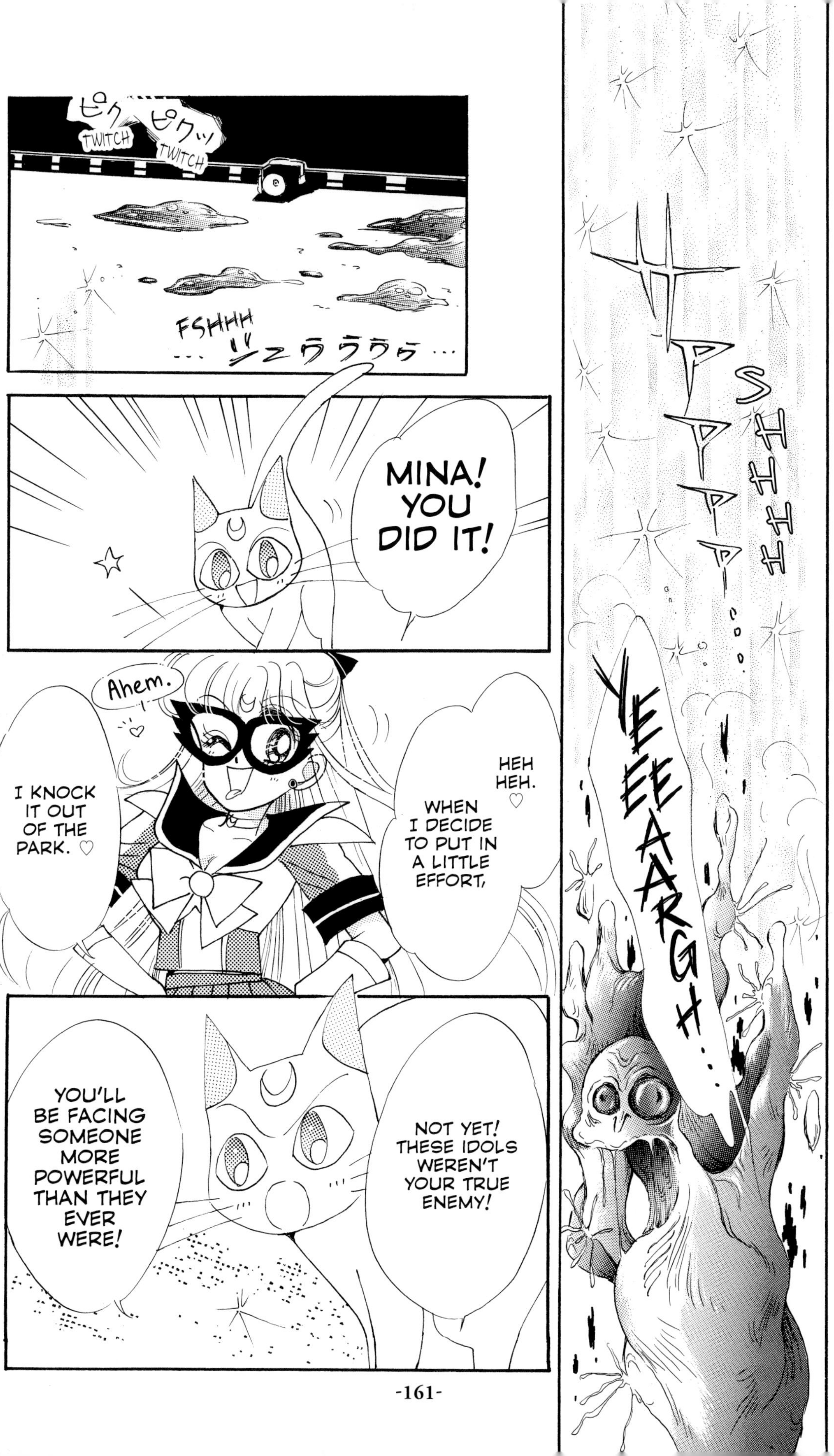
SHHHHH
YEEEAARGH...
ピクッ
TWITCH
ピクッ
TWITCH
FSHHH
...シュワワワワ...
MINA! YOU DID IT!
Ahem.
HEH HEH.
WHEN I DECIDE TO PUT IN A LITTLE EFFORT,
I KNOCK IT OUT OF THE PARK. ♡
NOT YET! THESE IDOLS WEREN'T YOUR TRUE ENEMY!
YOU'LL BE FACING SOMEONE MORE POWERFUL THAN THEY EVER WERE!

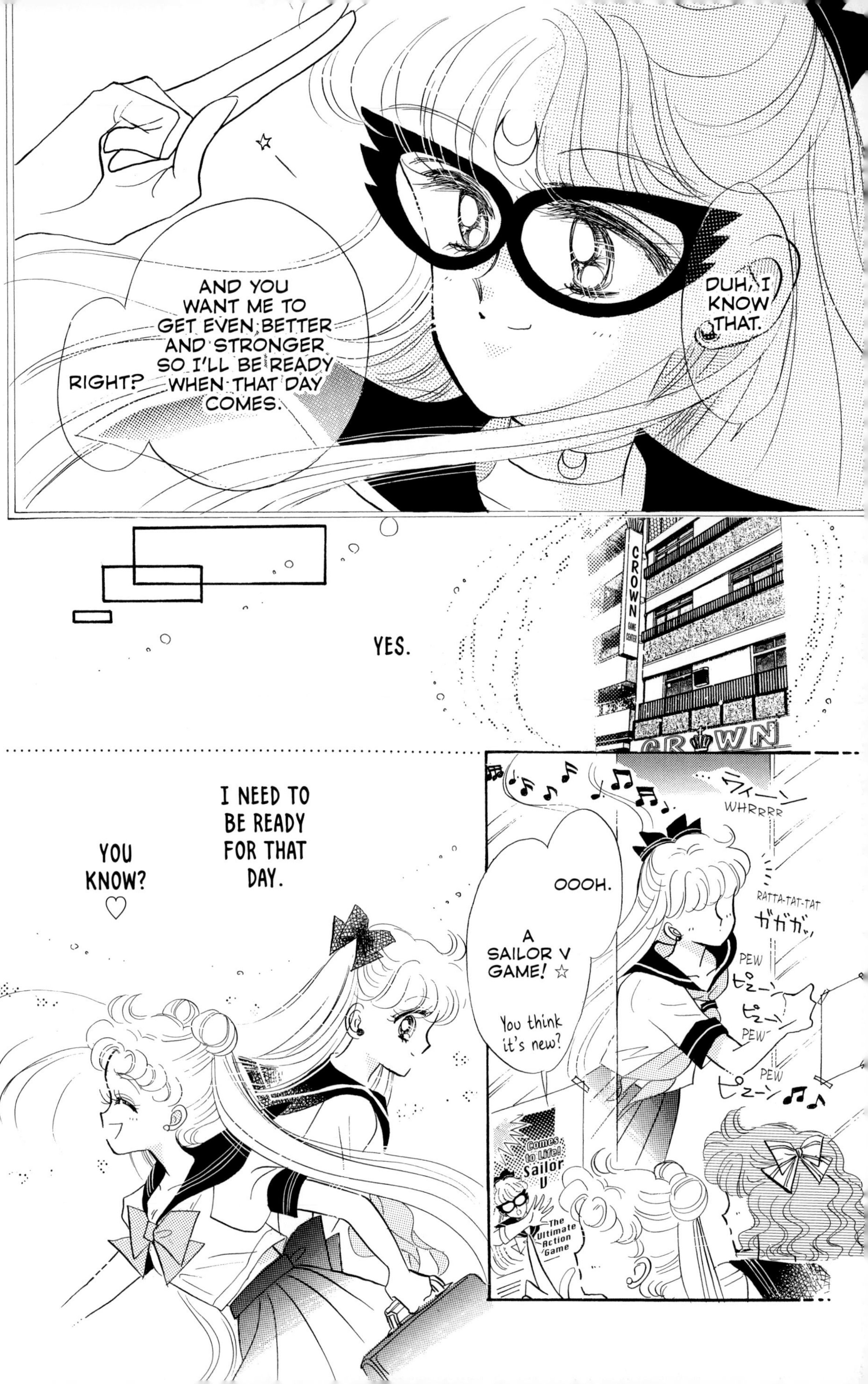

DUH, I KNOW THAT.
AND YOU WANT ME TO GET EVEN BETTER AND STRONGER SO I'LL BE READY WHEN THAT DAY COMES.
RIGHT?
CROWN GAME CENTER
CROWN
YES.
ウィーン
WHRRRR
OOOH.
A SAILOR V GAME! ☆
You think it's new?
RATTA-TAT-TAT
ガガガ
PEW
ピューン
ピューン
PEW
PEW
ピューン
Comes to Life! Sailor V
The Ultimate Action Game
I NEED TO BE READY FOR THAT DAY.
YOU KNOW? ♡

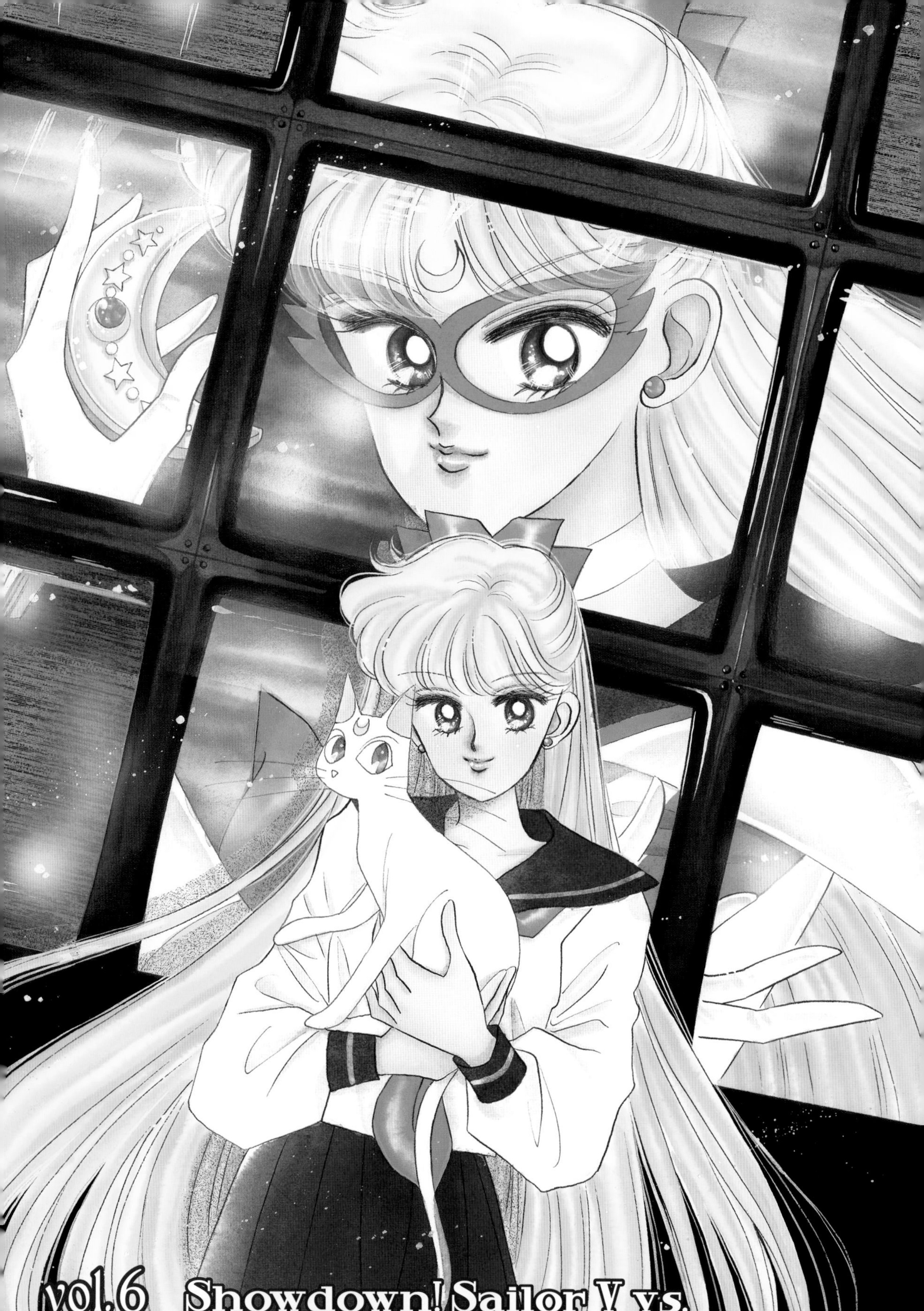

vol.6 Showdown! Sailor V vs. Cyber Gladiatrix Ruga

Codename Sailor V

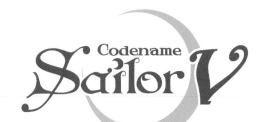

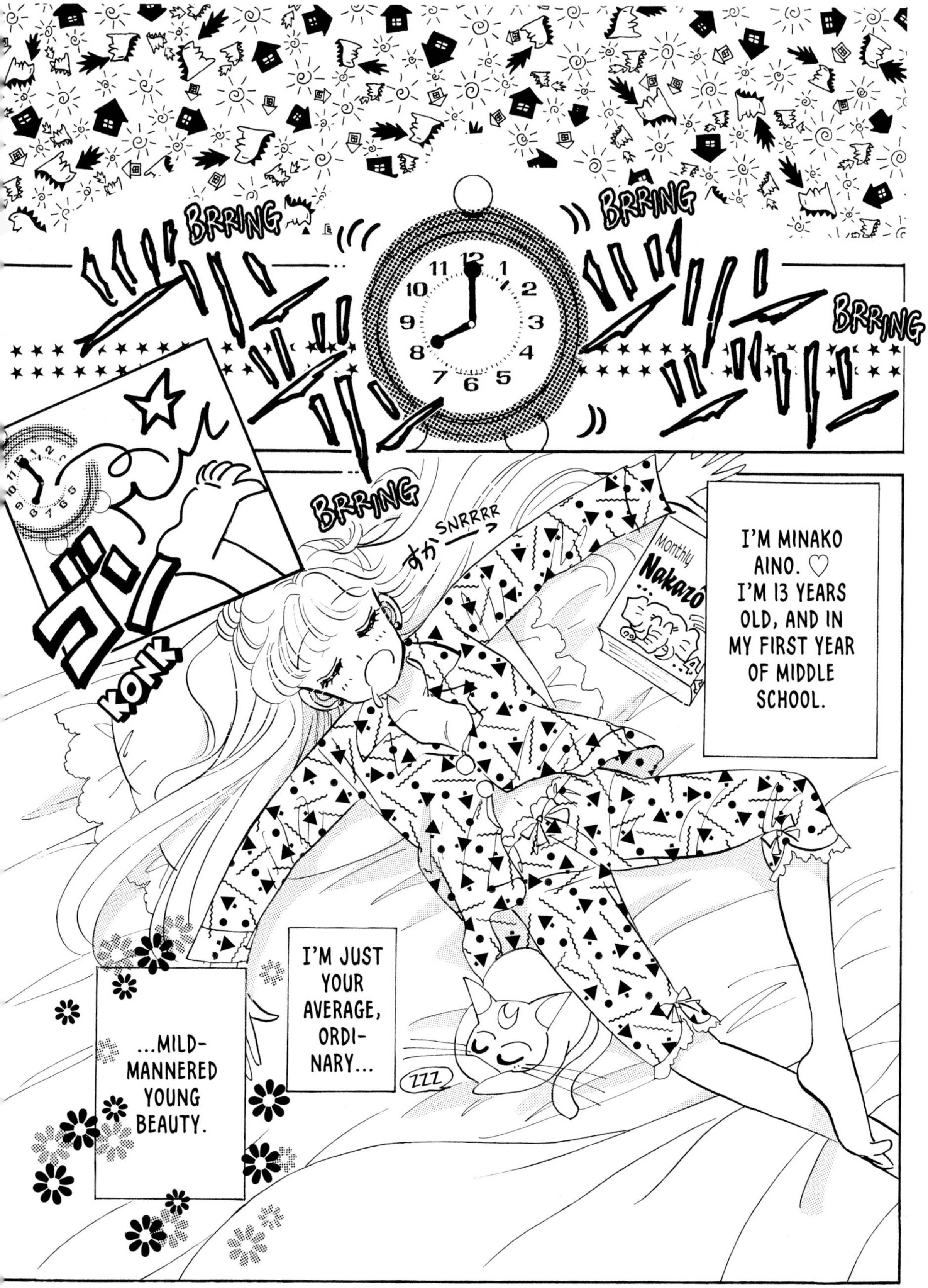
BRRING
BRRING
BRRING
KONK
I'M MINAKO AINO. ♡ I'M 13 YEARS OLD, AND IN MY FIRST YEAR OF MIDDLE SCHOOL.
BRRING
すか SNRRRR
Monthly Nakazō
I'M JUST YOUR AVERAGE, ORDINARY...
ZZZ
...MILD-MANNERED YOUNG BEAUTY.

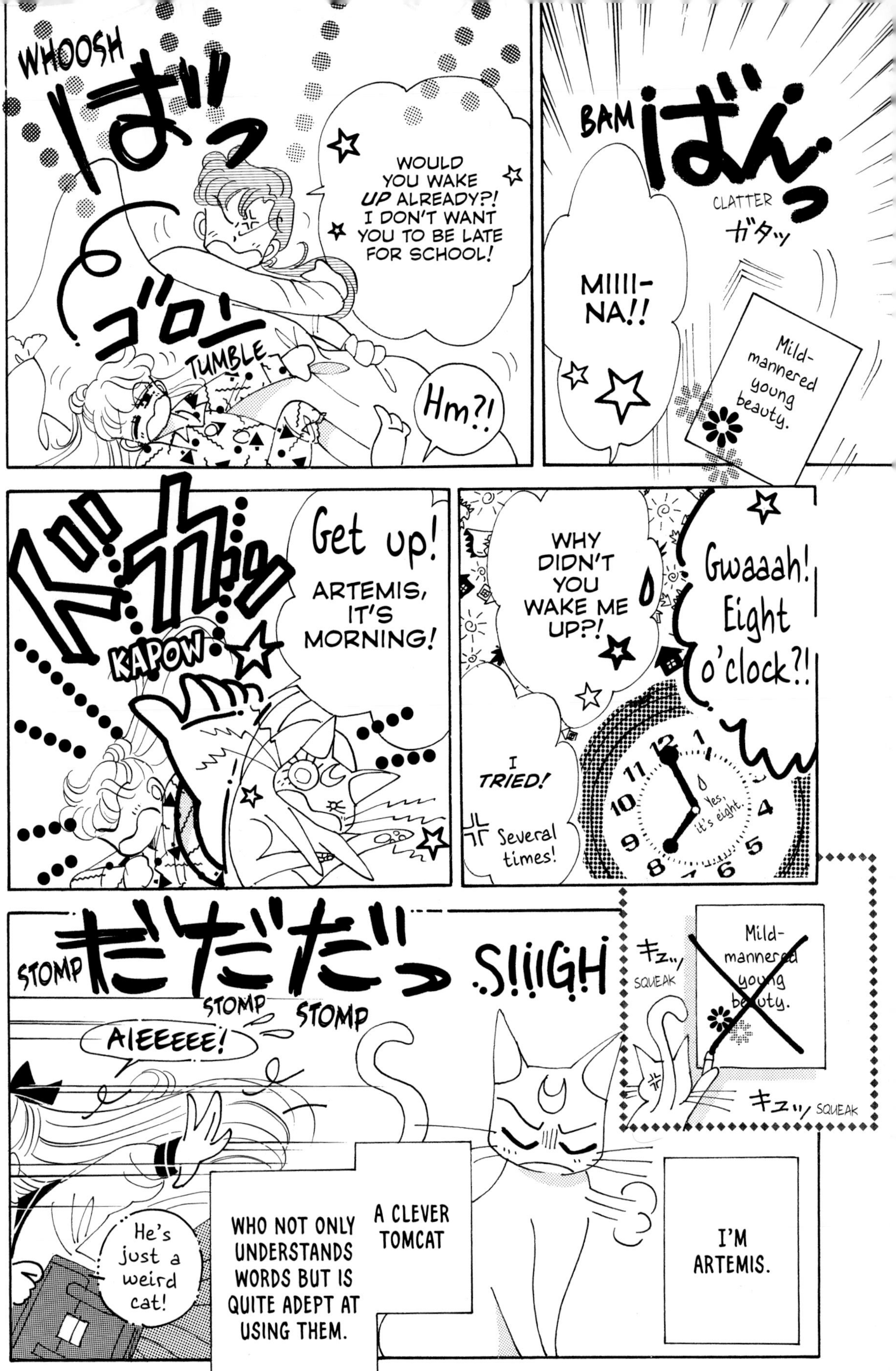
BAM ばんっ
CLATTER ガタッ
MIIIII-NA!!
Mild-mannered young beauty.
WHOOSH ばっ
WOULD YOU WAKE UP ALREADY?! I DON'T WANT YOU TO BE LATE FOR SCHOOL!
ゴロン TUMBLE
Hm?!
Gwaaah! Eight o'clock?!
WHY DIDN'T YOU WAKE ME UP?!
I TRIED!
Several times!
Yes, it's eight.
Get up!
ARTEMIS, IT'S MORNING!
KAPOW
キュッ SQUEAK
Mild-mannered young beauty.
キュッ SQUEAK
I'M ARTEMIS.
A CLEVER TOMCAT
WHO NOT ONLY UNDERSTANDS WORDS BUT IS QUITE ADEPT AT USING THEM.
SIIIGH
STOMP だだだっ
STOMP STOMP
AIEEEEE!
He's just a weird cat!

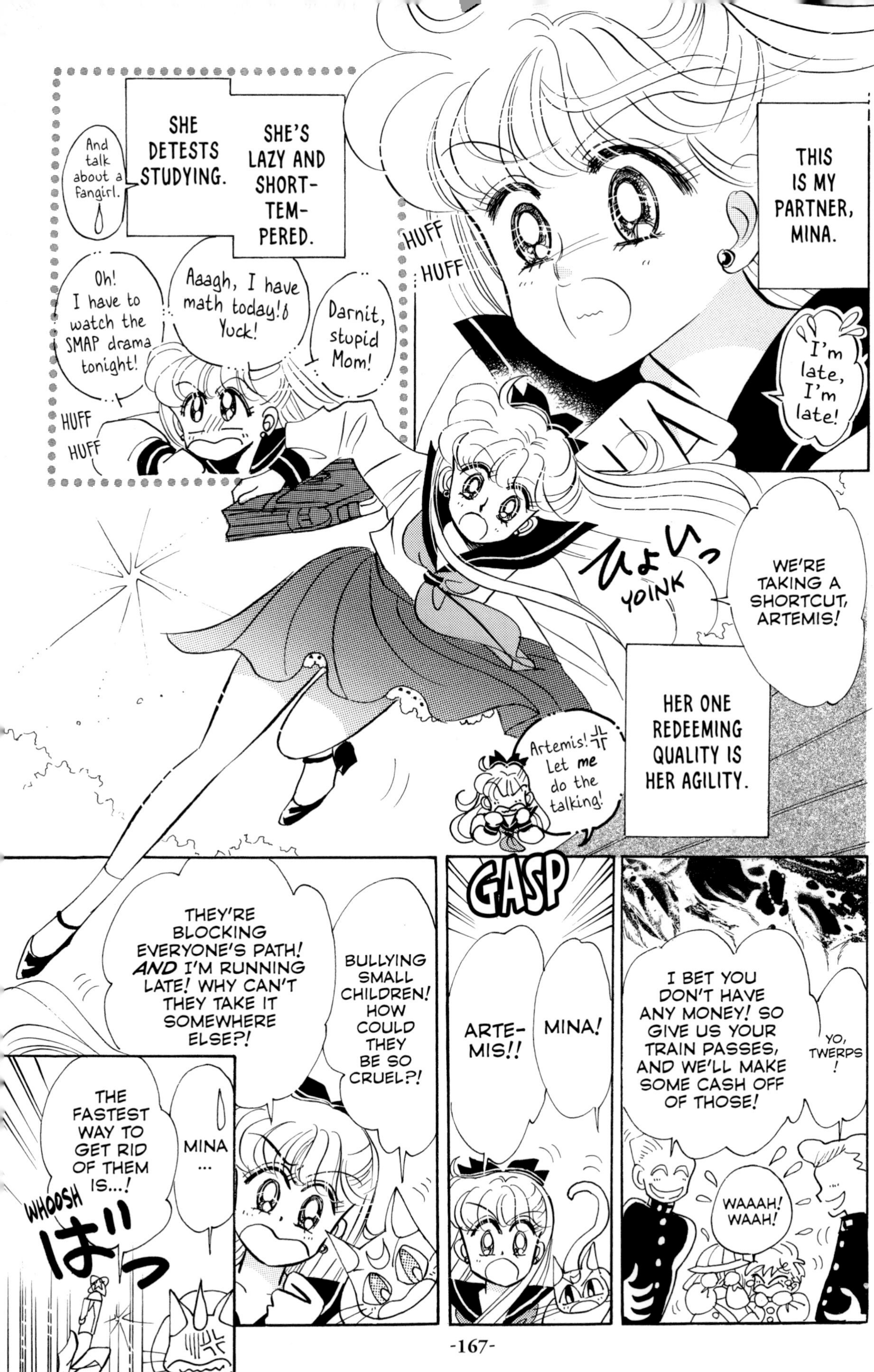
HUFF
HUFF
THIS IS MY PARTNER, MINA.
I'm late, I'm late!
SHE'S LAZY AND SHORT-TEMPERED.
SHE DETESTS STUDYING.
And talk about a fangirl.
Darnit, stupid Mom!
Aaagh, I have math today! Yuck!
Oh! I have to watch the SMAP drama tonight!
HUFF
HUFF
WE'RE TAKING A SHORTCUT, ARTEMIS!
ひょいっ
YOINK
HER ONE REDEEMING QUALITY IS HER AGILITY.
Artemis! Let me do the talking!
YO, TWERPS!
I BET YOU DON'T HAVE ANY MONEY! SO GIVE US YOUR TRAIN PASSES, AND WE'LL MAKE SOME CASH OFF OF THOSE!
WAAAH! WAAH!
GASP
MINA!
ARTE-MIS!!
BULLYING SMALL CHILDREN! HOW COULD THEY BE SO CRUEL?!
THEY'RE BLOCKING EVERYONE'S PATH! AND I'M RUNNING LATE! WHY CAN'T THEY TAKE IT SOMEWHERE ELSE?!
MINA...
THE FASTEST WAY TO GET RID OF THEM IS...!
WHOOSH
はっ

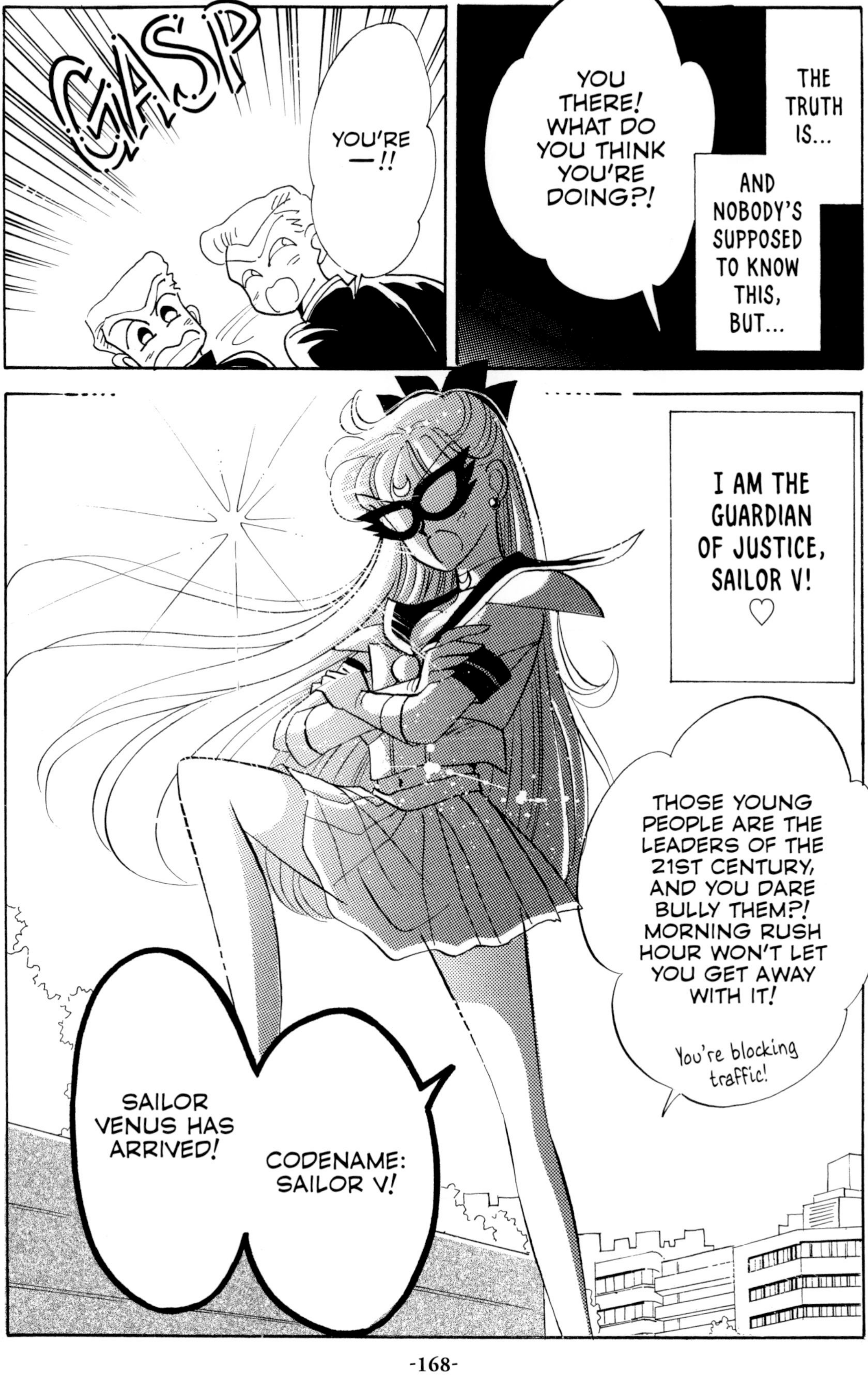
THE TRUTH IS...
AND NOBODY'S SUPPOSED TO KNOW THIS, BUT...
YOU THERE! WHAT DO YOU THINK YOU'RE DOING?!
YOU'RE —!!
GASP
I AM THE GUARDIAN OF JUSTICE, SAILOR V! ♡
THOSE YOUNG PEOPLE ARE THE LEADERS OF THE 21ST CENTURY, AND YOU DARE BULLY THEM?! MORNING RUSH HOUR WON'T LET YOU GET AWAY WITH IT!
You're blocking traffic!
SAILOR VENUS HAS ARRIVED!
CODENAME: SAILOR V!

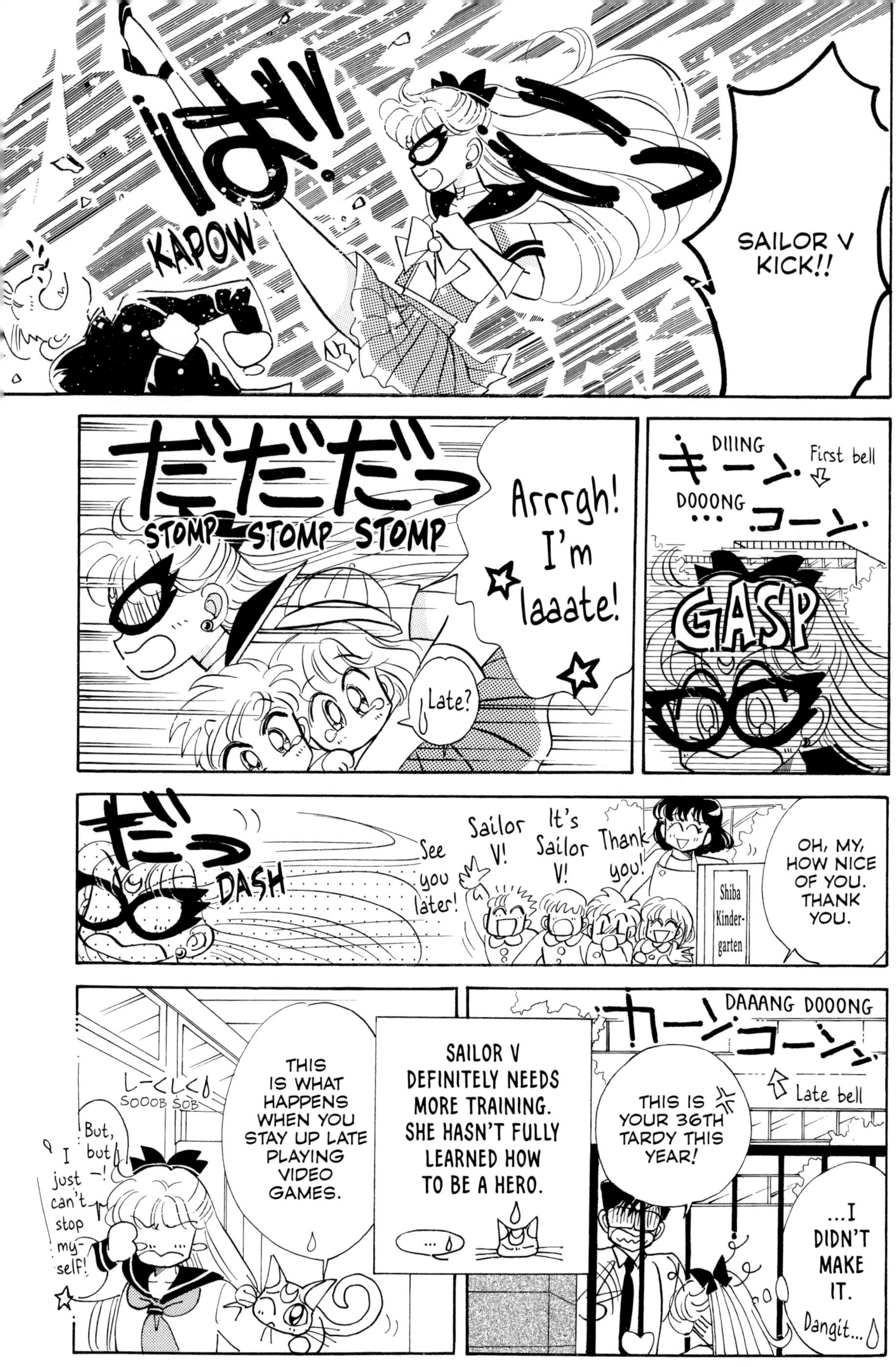

SAILOR V KICK!!
ばっ
KAPOW
キーン
DIIING
First bell
DOOONG…
コーン
GASP
Arrrgh! I'm laaate!
だだだっ
STOMP STOMP STOMP
Late?
OH, MY, HOW NICE OF YOU. THANK YOU.
Shiba Kinder-garten
Thank you!
It's Sailor V!
Sailor V!
See you later!
だっ
DASH
カーンコーン
DAAANG DOOONG
Late bell
THIS IS YOUR 36TH TARDY THIS YEAR!
...I DIDN'T MAKE IT.
Dangit...
SAILOR V DEFINITELY NEEDS MORE TRAINING. SHE HASN'T FULLY LEARNED HOW TO BE A HERO.
...
THIS IS WHAT HAPPENS WHEN YOU STAY UP LATE PLAYING VIDEO GAMES.
しーくしく
SOOOB SOB
But, but—!
I just can't stop my-self!

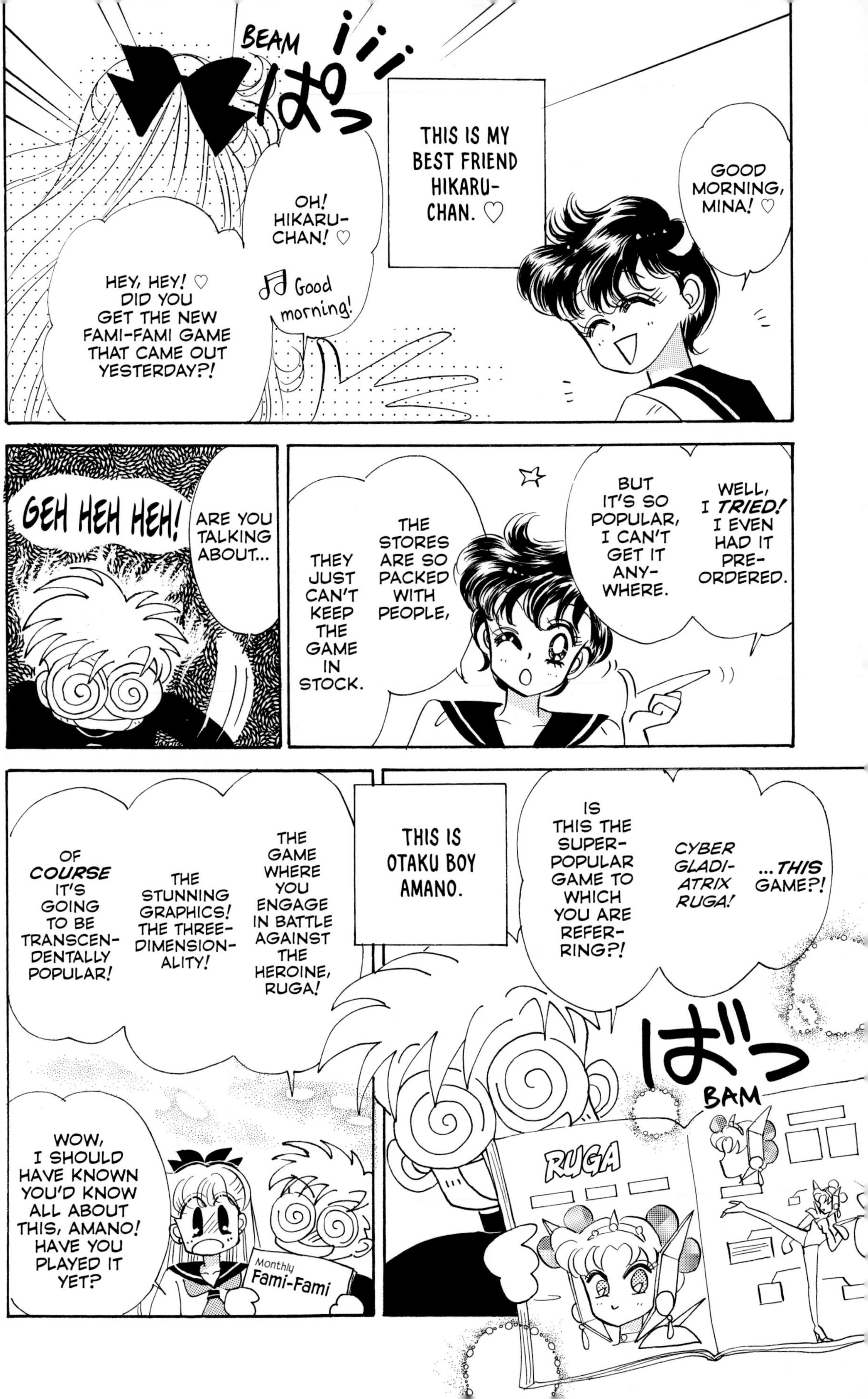
GOOD MORNING, MINA! ♡
THIS IS MY BEST FRIEND HIKARU-CHAN. ♡
ぱっ
BEAM
OH! HIKARU-CHAN! ♡
♫ Good morning!
HEY, HEY! ♡ DID YOU GET THE NEW FAMI-FAMI GAME THAT CAME OUT YESTERDAY?!
WELL, I *TRIED!* I EVEN HAD IT PRE-ORDERED.
BUT IT'S SO POPULAR, I CAN'T GET IT ANY-WHERE.
THE STORES ARE SO PACKED WITH PEOPLE,
THEY JUST CAN'T KEEP THE GAME IN STOCK.
ARE YOU TALKING ABOUT...
GEH HEH HEH!
...*THIS* GAME?!
CYBER GLADI-ATRIX RUGA!
IS THIS THE SUPER-POPULAR GAME TO WHICH YOU ARE REFER-RING?!
THIS IS OTAKU BOY AMANO.
ばっ
BAM
RUGA
THE GAME WHERE YOU ENGAGE IN BATTLE AGAINST THE HEROINE, RUGA!
THE STUNNING GRAPHICS! THE THREE-DIMENSION-ALITY!
OF ***COURSE*** IT'S GOING TO BE TRANSCEN-DENTALLY POPULAR!
WOW, I SHOULD HAVE KNOWN YOU'D KNOW ALL ABOUT THIS, AMANO! HAVE YOU PLAYED IT YET?
Monthly Fami-Fami

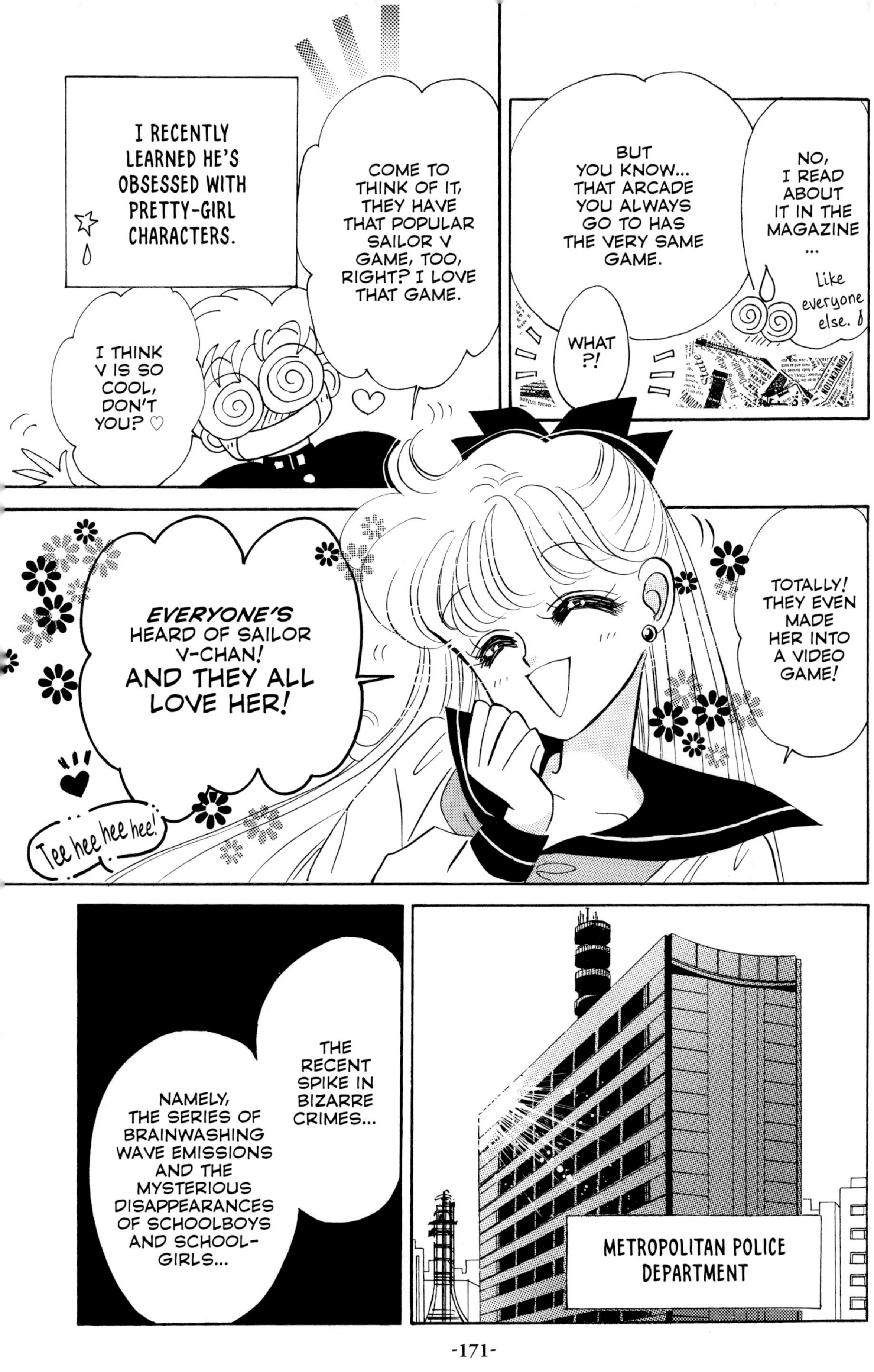

BUT YOU KNOW... THAT ARCADE YOU ALWAYS GO TO HAS THE VERY SAME GAME.
NO, I READ ABOUT IT IN THE MAGAZINE ...
Like everyone else.
WHAT ?!
COME TO THINK OF IT, THEY HAVE THAT POPULAR SAILOR V GAME, TOO, RIGHT? I LOVE THAT GAME.
I RECENTLY LEARNED HE'S OBSESSED WITH PRETTY-GIRL CHARACTERS.
I THINK V IS SO COOL, DON'T YOU? ♡
TOTALLY! THEY EVEN MADE HER INTO A VIDEO GAME!
EVERYONE'S HEARD OF SAILOR V-CHAN! AND THEY ALL LOVE HER!
Tee hee hee hee!
METROPOLITAN POLICE DEPARTMENT
THE RECENT SPIKE IN BIZARRE CRIMES...
NAMELY, THE SERIES OF BRAINWASHING WAVE EMISSIONS AND THE MYSTERIOUS DISAPPEARANCES OF SCHOOLBOYS AND SCHOOL-GIRLS...

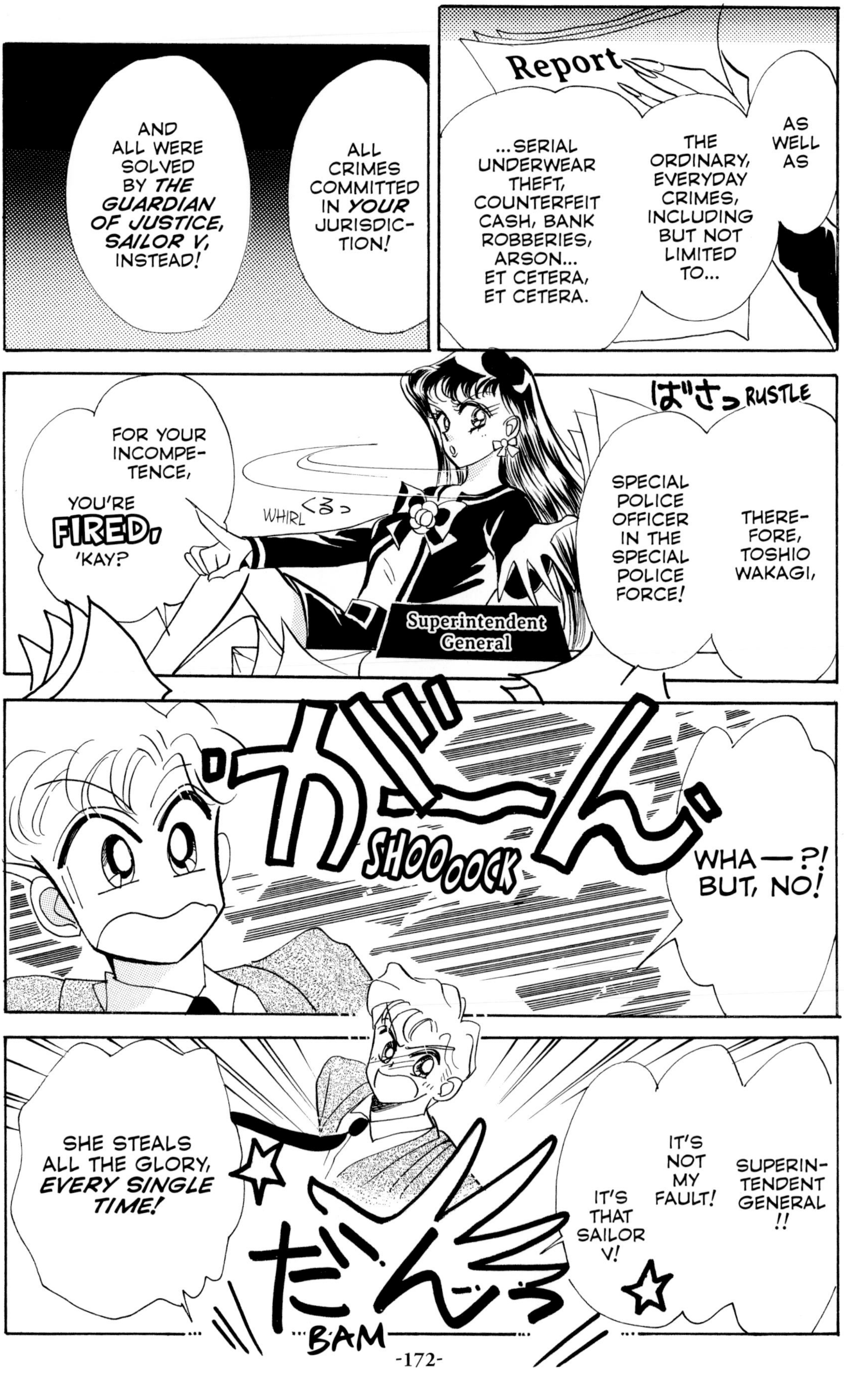
Report
AS WELL AS
THE ORDINARY, EVERYDAY CRIMES, INCLUDING BUT NOT LIMITED TO...
...SERIAL UNDERWEAR THEFT, COUNTERFEIT CASH, BANK ROBBERIES, ARSON... ET CETERA, ET CETERA.
ALL CRIMES COMMITTED IN *YOUR* JURISDICTION!
AND ALL WERE SOLVED BY *THE GUARDIAN OF JUSTICE, SAILOR V,* INSTEAD!
ばさっ RUSTLE
THEREFORE, TOSHIO WAKAGI,
SPECIAL POLICE OFFICER IN THE SPECIAL POLICE FORCE!
Superintendent General
WHIRL くるっ
FOR YOUR INCOMPETENCE,
YOU'RE **FIRED**, 'KAY?
WHA—?! BUT, NO!
がーん SHOOOOCK
SUPERINTENDENT GENERAL!!
IT'S NOT MY FAULT!
IT'S THAT SAILOR V!
SHE STEALS ALL THE GLORY, *EVERY SINGLE TIME!*
だんっ BAM

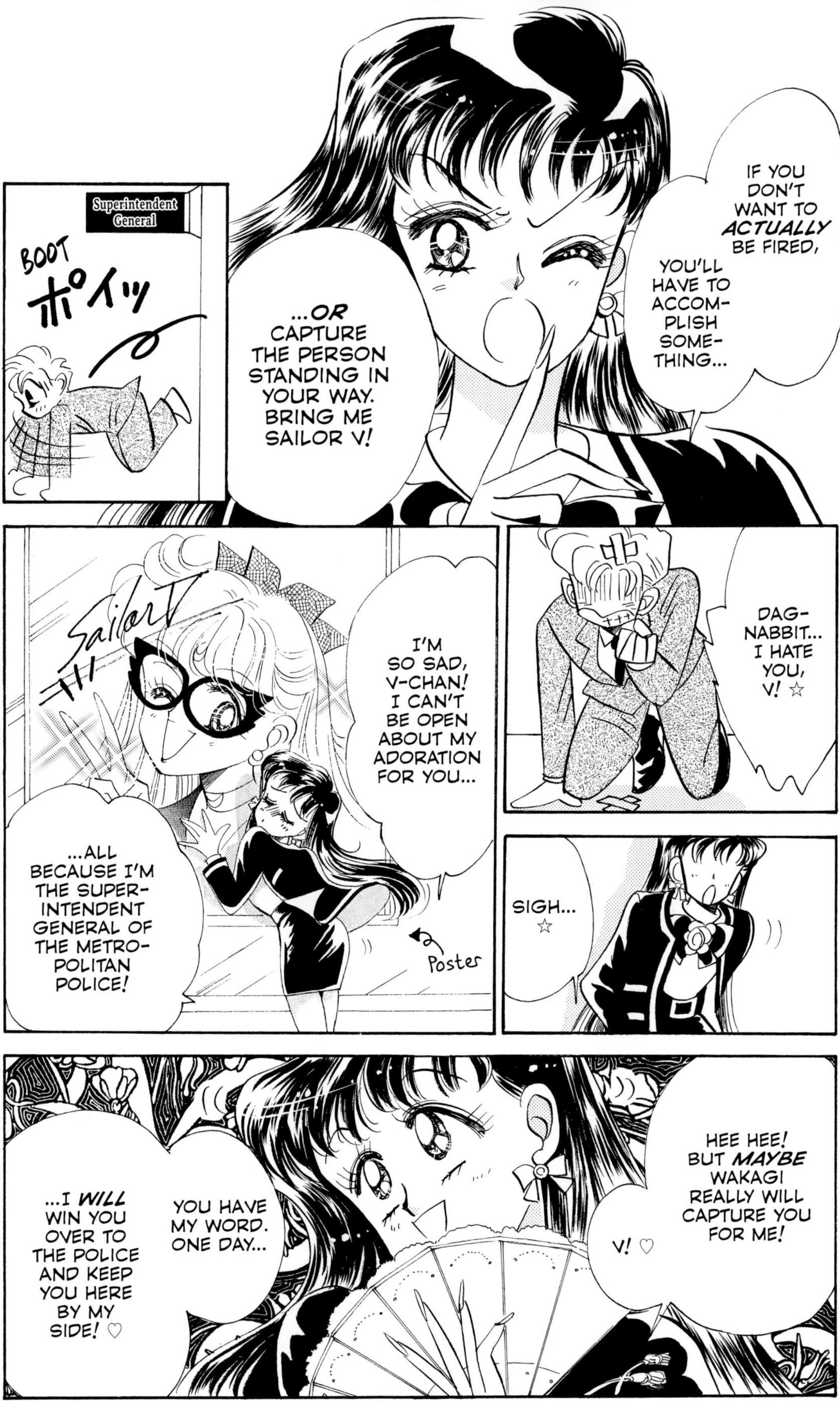
IF YOU DON'T WANT TO ACTUALLY BE FIRED,
YOU'LL HAVE TO ACCOMPLISH SOMETHING...
...OR CAPTURE THE PERSON STANDING IN YOUR WAY. BRING ME SAILOR V!
Superintendent General
BOOT
ポイッ
DAG-NABBIT... I HATE YOU, V! ☆
SIGH... ☆
I'M SO SAD, V-CHAN! I CAN'T BE OPEN ABOUT MY ADORATION FOR YOU...
...ALL BECAUSE I'M THE SUPERINTENDENT GENERAL OF THE METROPOLITAN POLICE!
Sailor V
Poster
HEE HEE! BUT MAYBE WAKAGI REALLY WILL CAPTURE YOU FOR ME!
V! ♡
YOU HAVE MY WORD. ONE DAY...
...I WILL WIN YOU OVER TO THE POLICE AND KEEP YOU HERE BY MY SIDE! ♡

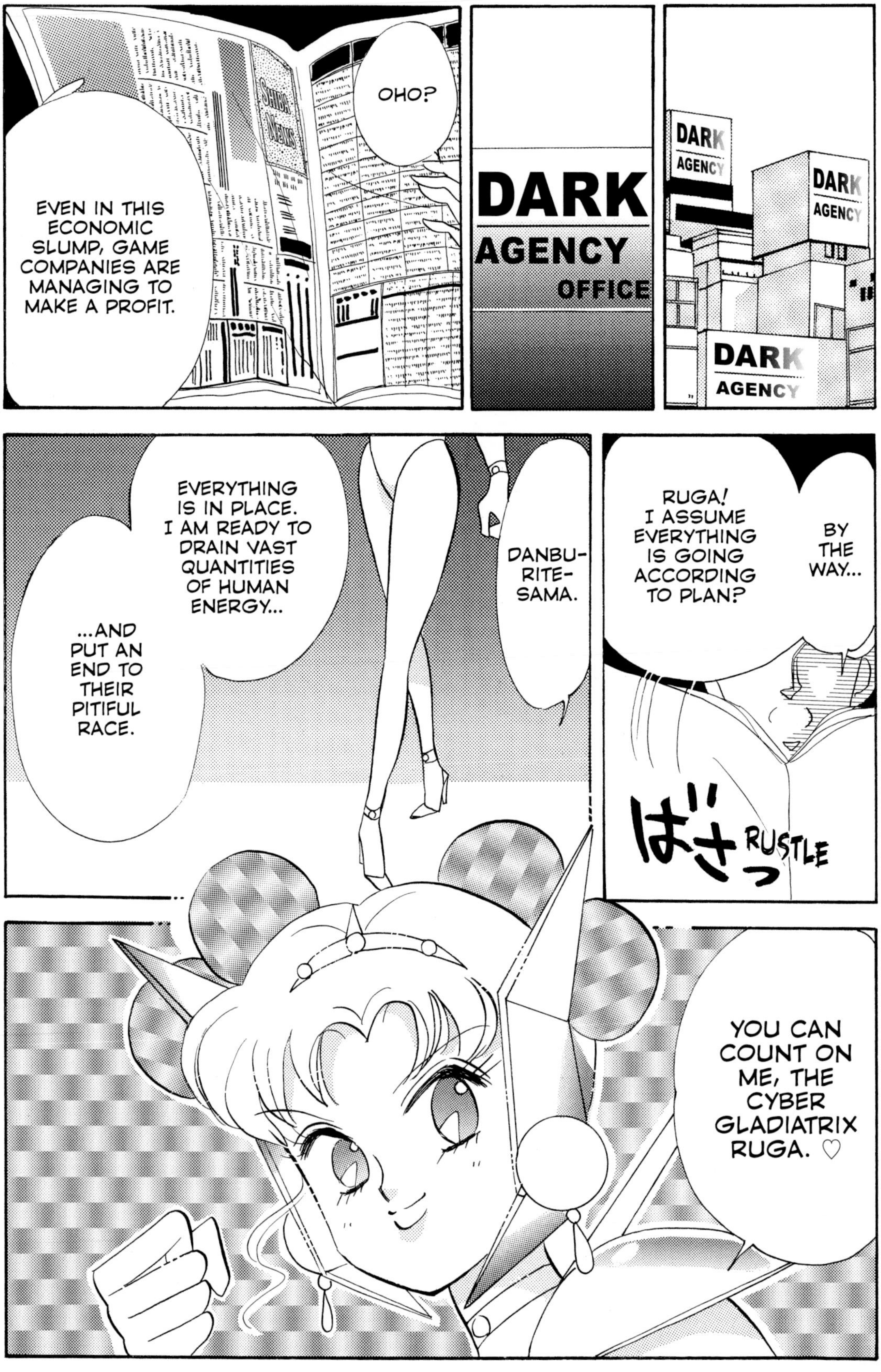
DARK AGENCY
DARK AGENCY
DARK AGENCY
DARK AGENCY OFFICE
OHO?
EVEN IN THIS ECONOMIC SLUMP, GAME COMPANIES ARE MANAGING TO MAKE A PROFIT.
BY THE WAY...
RUGA! I ASSUME EVERYTHING IS GOING ACCORDING TO PLAN?
ばさっ RUSTLE
DANBURITE-SAMA.
EVERYTHING IS IN PLACE. I AM READY TO DRAIN VAST QUANTITIES OF HUMAN ENERGY...
...AND PUT AN END TO THEIR PITIFUL RACE.
YOU CAN COUNT ON ME, THE CYBER GLADIATRIX RUGA. ♡

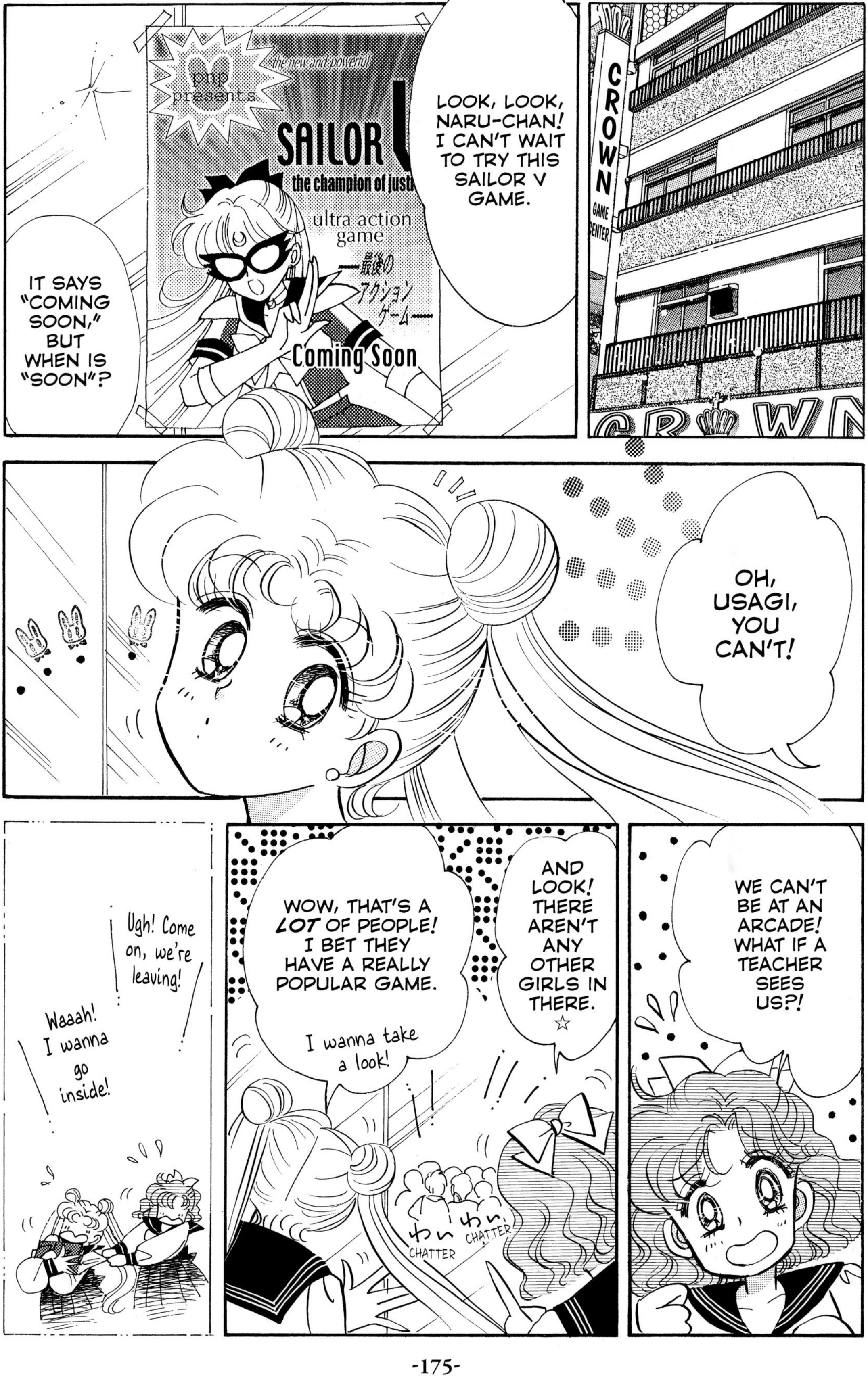
CROWN
GAME CENTER
CROWN
LOOK, LOOK, NARU-CHAN! I CAN'T WAIT TO TRY THIS SAILOR V GAME.
the new and powerful
presents
SAILOR
ultra action game
最後のアクションゲーム
Coming Soon
IT SAYS "COMING SOON," BUT WHEN IS "SOON"?
OH, USAGI, YOU CAN'T!
WE CAN'T BE AT AN ARCADE! WHAT IF A TEACHER SEES US?!
AND LOOK! THERE AREN'T ANY OTHER GIRLS IN THERE. ☆
WOW, THAT'S A *LOT* OF PEOPLE! I BET THEY HAVE A REALLY POPULAR GAME.
I wanna take a look!
わい CHATTER
わい CHATTER
Ugh! Come on, we're leaving!
Waaah! I wanna go inside!

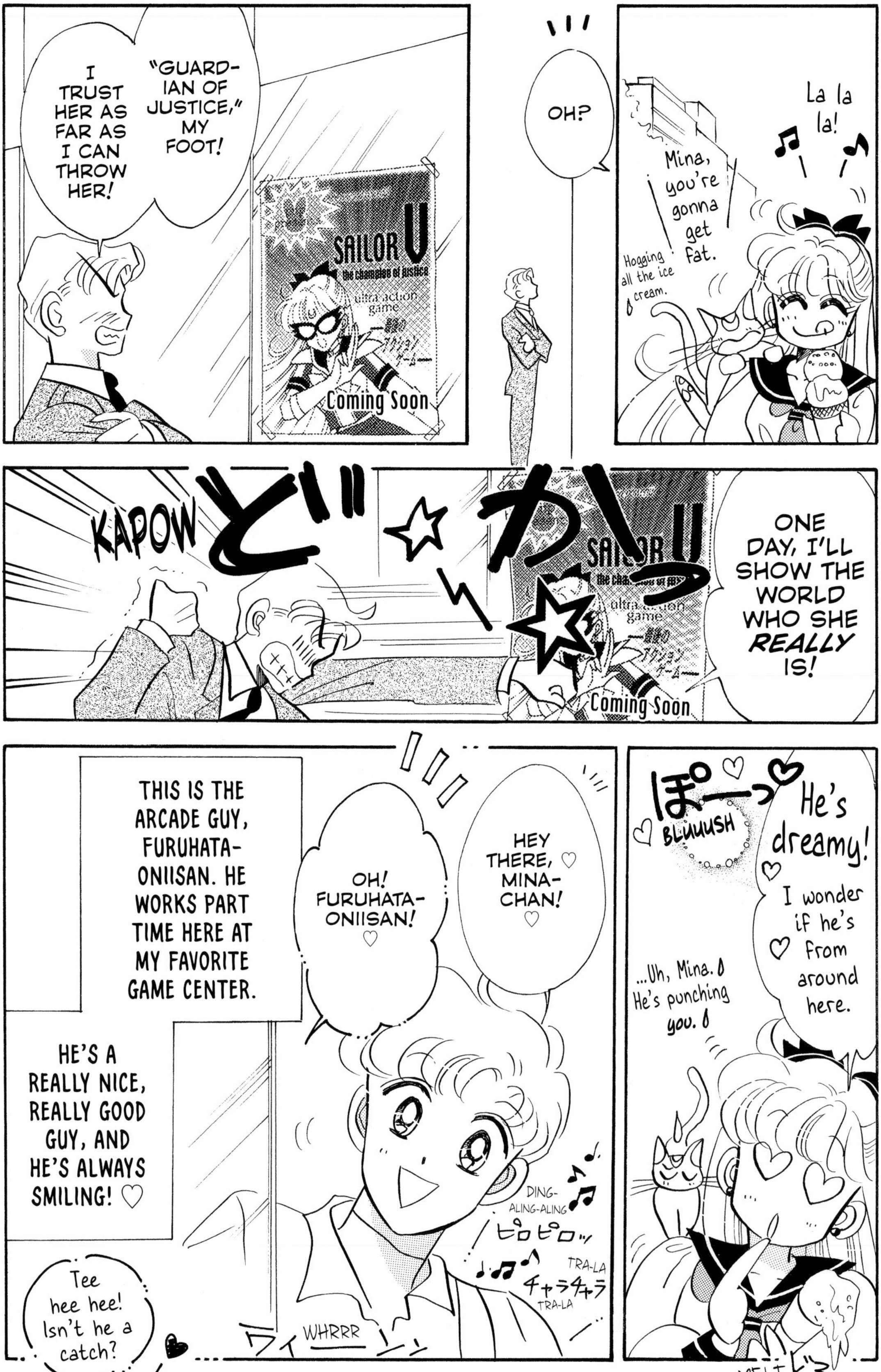
La la la!
Mina, you're gonna get fat.
Hogging all the ice cream.
OH?
"GUARDIAN OF JUSTICE," MY FOOT!
I TRUST HER AS FAR AS I CAN THROW HER!
SAILOR V
the champion of justice
ultra action game
Coming Soon
ONE DAY, I'LL SHOW THE WORLD WHO SHE *REALLY* IS!
KAPOW どかっ
Coming Soon
He's dreamy!
ぽーっ
BLUUUSH
I wonder if he's from around here.
...Uh, Mina. He's punching you.
MELT どろ
HEY THERE, ♡ MINA-CHAN! ♡
OH! FURUHATA-ONIISAN! ♡
THIS IS THE ARCADE GUY, FURUHATA-ONIISAN. HE WORKS PART TIME HERE AT MY FAVORITE GAME CENTER.
HE'S A REALLY NICE, REALLY GOOD GUY, AND HE'S ALWAYS SMILING! ♡
DING-ALING-ALING ピロピロッ
TRA-LA チャラチャラ TRA-LA
WHRRR ウィーン
Tee hee hee! Isn't he a catch?

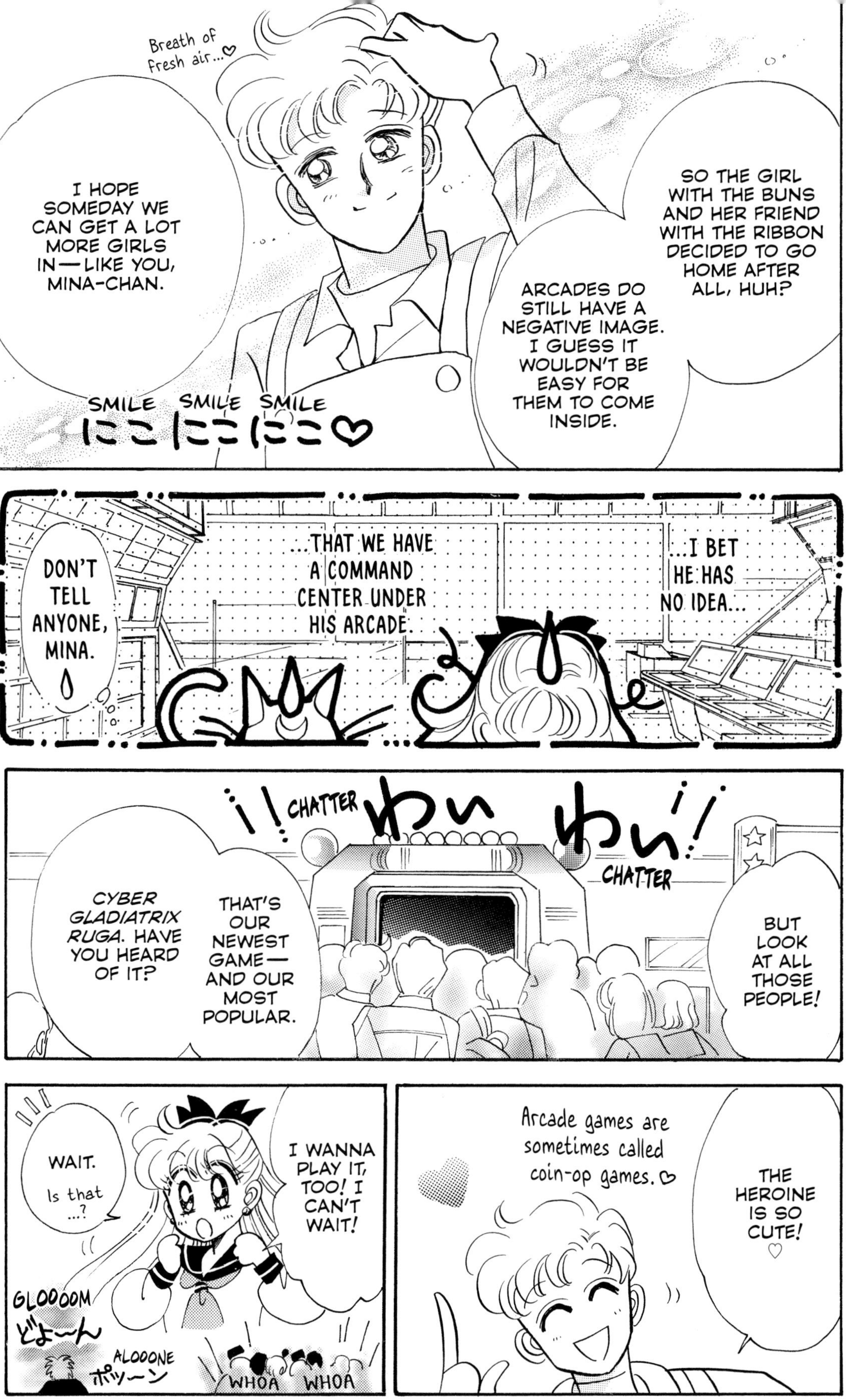
SO THE GIRL WITH THE BUNS AND HER FRIEND WITH THE RIBBON DECIDED TO GO HOME AFTER ALL, HUH?
ARCADES DO STILL HAVE A NEGATIVE IMAGE. I GUESS IT WOULDN'T BE EASY FOR THEM TO COME INSIDE.
Breath of fresh air...♡
I HOPE SOMEDAY WE CAN GET A LOT MORE GIRLS IN—LIKE YOU, MINA-CHAN.
SMILE SMILE SMILE
にこにこにこ♡
...I BET HE HAS NO IDEA...
...THAT WE HAVE A COMMAND CENTER UNDER HIS ARCADE.
DON'T TELL ANYONE, MINA.
CHATTER
わいわい
CHATTER
BUT LOOK AT ALL THOSE PEOPLE!
THAT'S OUR NEWEST GAME—AND OUR MOST POPULAR.
CYBER GLADIATRIX RUGA. HAVE YOU HEARD OF IT?
THE HEROINE IS SO CUTE! ♡
Arcade games are sometimes called coin-op games.♡
I WANNA PLAY IT, TOO! I CAN'T WAIT!
WAIT.
Is that ...?
GLOOOOM
どよ～ん
ALOOONE
ポツーン
WHOA WHOA

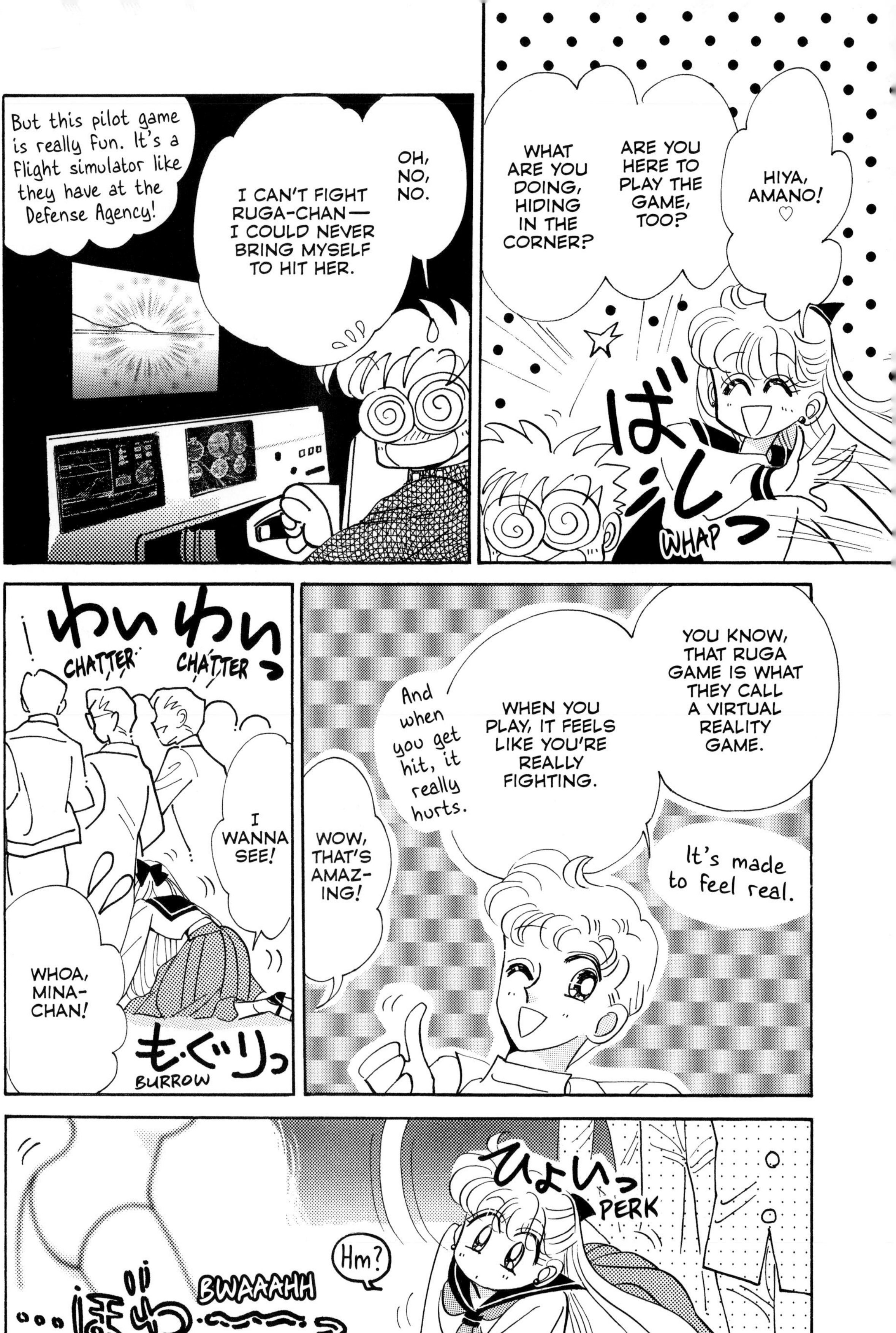
HIYA, AMANO! ♡
ARE YOU HERE TO PLAY THE GAME, TOO?
WHAT ARE YOU DOING, HIDING IN THE CORNER?
ばしっ
WHAP
OH, NO, NO.
I CAN'T FIGHT RUGA-CHAN— I COULD NEVER BRING MYSELF TO HIT HER.
But this pilot game is really fun. It's a flight simulator like they have at the Defense Agency!
YOU KNOW, THAT RUGA GAME IS WHAT THEY CALL A VIRTUAL REALITY GAME.
WHEN YOU PLAY, IT FEELS LIKE YOU'RE REALLY FIGHTING.
And when you get hit, it really hurts.
It's made to feel real.
WOW, THAT'S AMAZING!
わいわいっ
CHATTER
CHATTER
I WANNA SEE!
WHOA, MINA-CHAN!
もぐりっ
BURROW
ひょいっ
PERK
Hm?
...ぼわっ
BWAAAHH

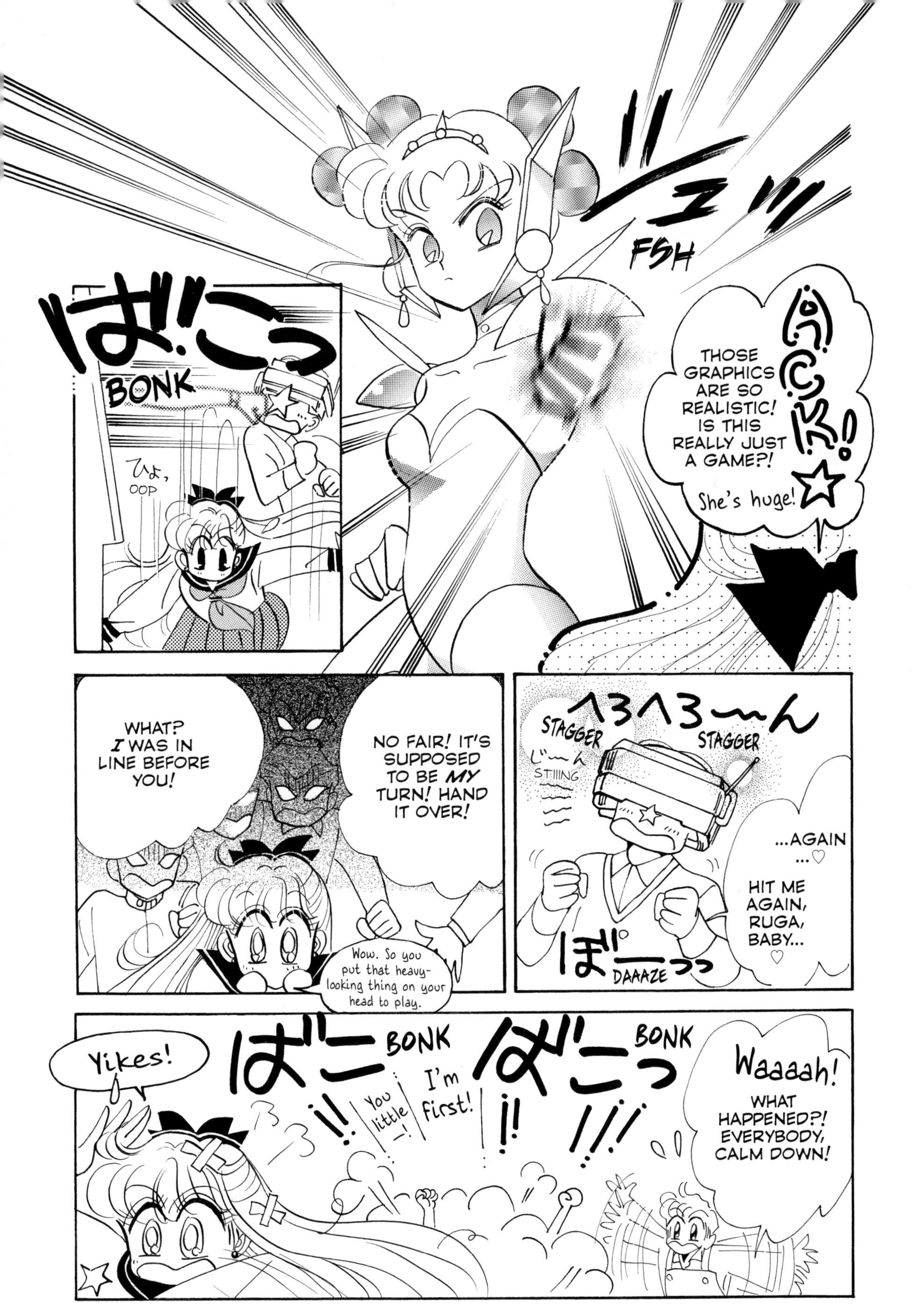

FSH
ACK!☆
THOSE GRAPHICS ARE SO REALISTIC! IS THIS REALLY JUST A GAME?!
She's huge!
ばこっ
BONK
ひょ、
OOP
へろへろ～ん
STAGGER
STAGGER
じ～ん
STIIING
...AGAIN ...♡
HIT ME AGAIN, RUGA, BABY...♡
ぼ～っ
DAAAZE
NO FAIR! IT'S SUPPOSED TO BE *MY* TURN! HAND IT OVER!
WHAT? *I* WAS IN LINE BEFORE YOU!
Wow. So you put that heavy-looking thing on your head to play.
Waaaah!
WHAT HAPPENED?! EVERYBODY, CALM DOWN!
ばこっ
BONK
I'm first!
You little—!
ばこ
BONK
Yikes!

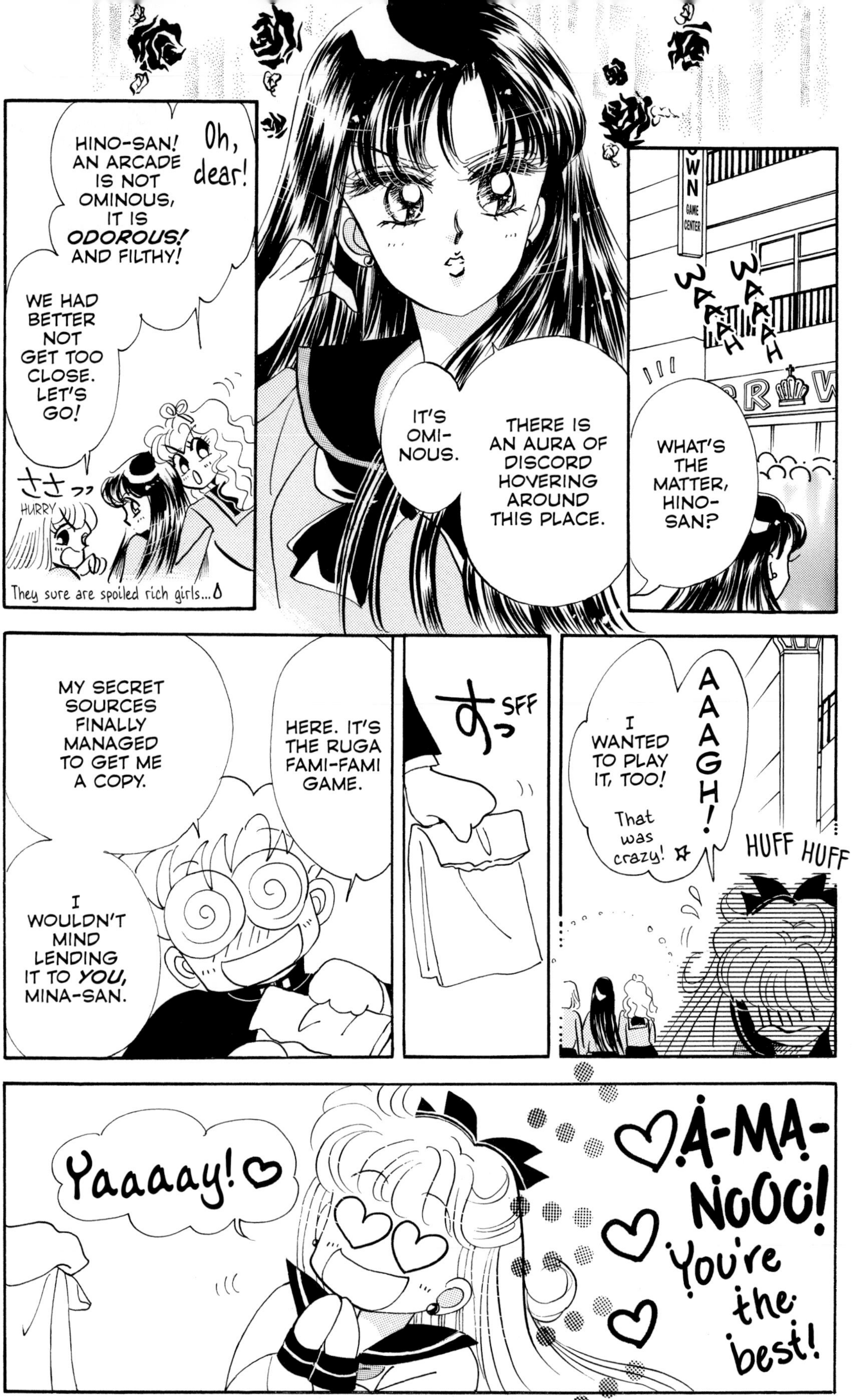
WAAAH WAAAH
WHAT'S THE MATTER, HINO-SAN?
IT'S OMINOUS.
THERE IS AN AURA OF DISCORD HOVERING AROUND THIS PLACE.
Oh, dear!
HINO-SAN! AN ARCADE IS NOT OMINOUS, IT IS ODOROUS! AND FILTHY!
WE HAD BETTER NOT GET TOO CLOSE. LET'S GO!
ささっ HURRY
They sure are spoiled rich girls...
AAAAGH!
I WANTED TO PLAY IT, TOO!
That was crazy!
HUFF HUFF
すっ SFF
HERE. IT'S THE RUGA FAMI-FAMI GAME.
MY SECRET SOURCES FINALLY MANAGED TO GET ME A COPY.
I WOULDN'T MIND LENDING IT TO YOU, MINA-SAN.
A-MA-NOOO! You're the best!
Yaaaay!

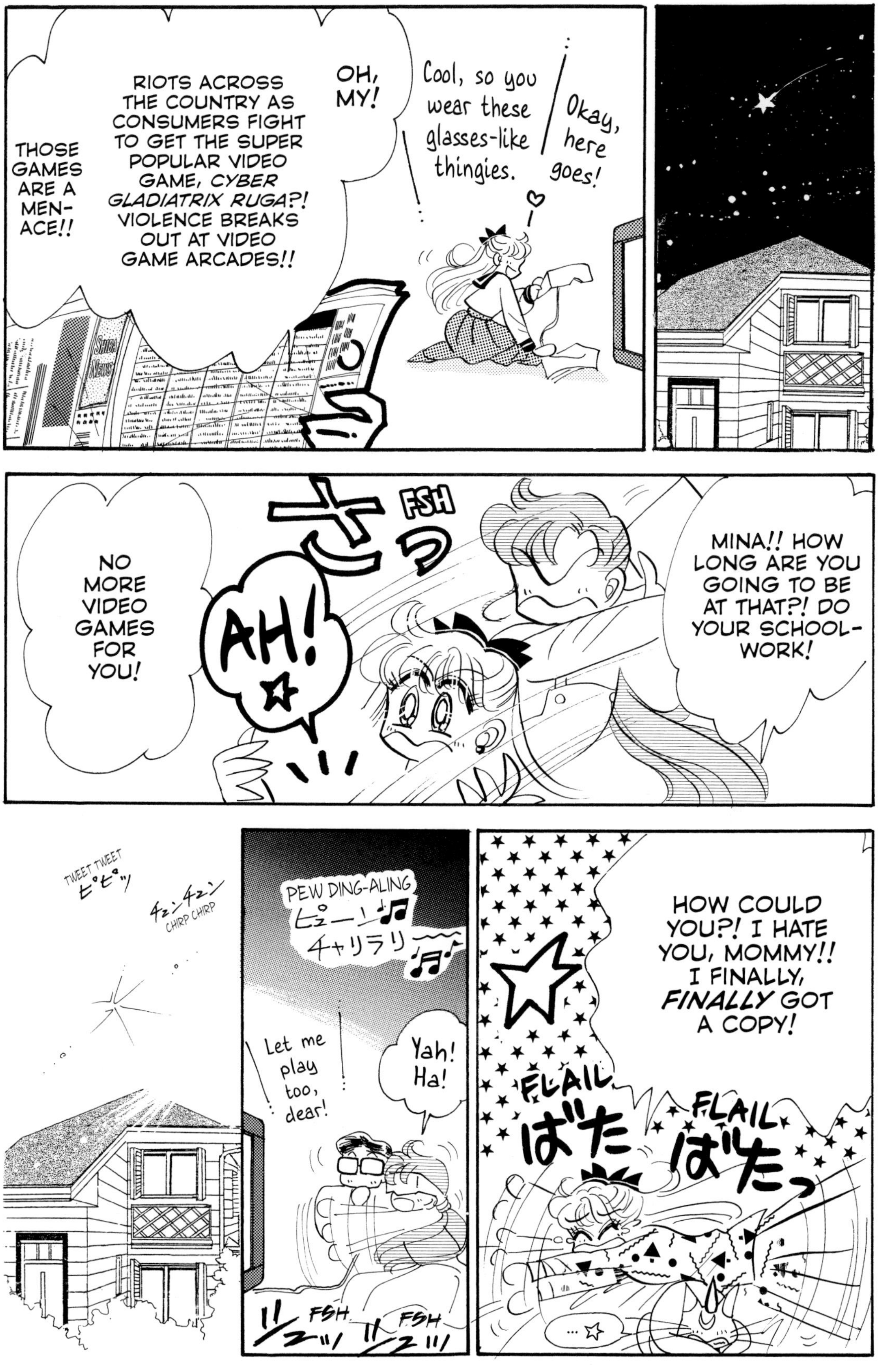
Okay, here goes!
Cool, so you wear these glasses-like thingies.
OH, MY!
RIOTS ACROSS THE COUNTRY AS CONSUMERS FIGHT TO GET THE SUPER POPULAR VIDEO GAME, *CYBER GLADIATRIX RUGA*?! VIOLENCE BREAKS OUT AT VIDEO GAME ARCADES!!
THOSE GAMES ARE A MEN-ACE!!
SHIBA NEWS
MINA!! HOW LONG ARE YOU GOING TO BE AT THAT?! DO YOUR SCHOOL-WORK!
FSH
さっ
AH! ☆
NO MORE VIDEO GAMES FOR YOU!
HOW COULD YOU?! I HATE YOU, MOMMY!! I FINALLY, *FINALLY* GOT A COPY!
FLAIL
ばた
FLAIL
ばたっ
...☆
PEW DING-ALING
ピュー！
チャリラリ
Yah! Ha!
Let me play too, dear!
FSH
FSH
TWEET TWEET
ピピッ
チュンチュン
CHIRP CHIRP

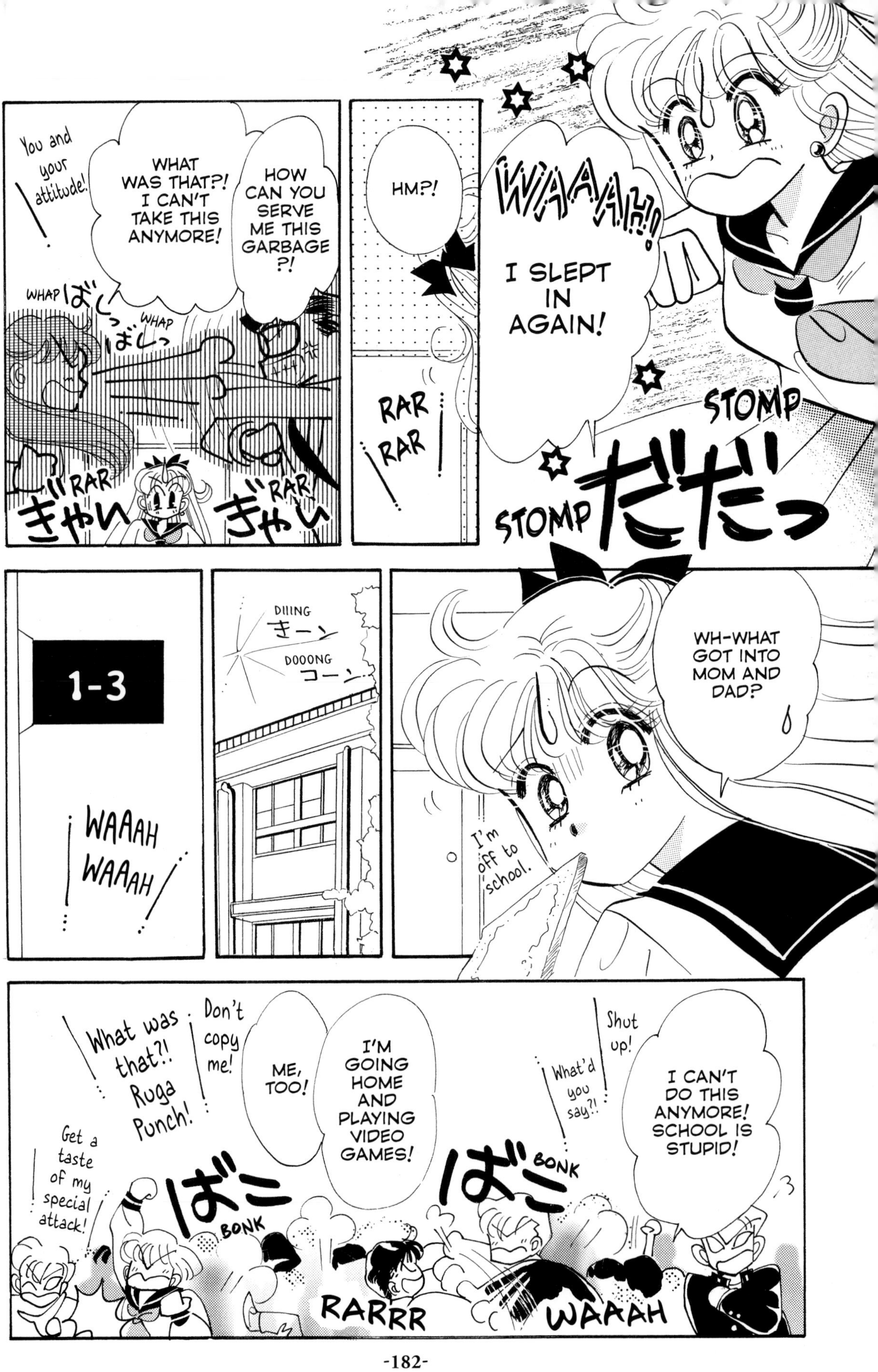
WAAAH!!
I SLEPT IN AGAIN!
STOMP
だだっ
STOMP
HM?!
RAR RAR
HOW CAN YOU SERVE ME THIS GARBAGE?!
WHAT WAS THAT?! I CAN'T TAKE THIS ANYMORE!
You and your attitude!
WHAP ばしっ
WHAP ばしっ
RAR ぎゃい
RAR ぎゃい
WH-WHAT GOT INTO MOM AND DAD?
I'm off to school.
DIIING きーん
DOOONG コーン
1-3
WAAAH WAAAH
I CAN'T DO THIS ANYMORE! SCHOOL IS STUPID!
Shut up!
What'd you say?!
BONK ばこ
I'M GOING HOME AND PLAYING VIDEO GAMES!
ME, TOO!
Don't copy me!
What was that?! Ruga Punch!
Get a taste of my special attack!
ばこ BONK
WAAAH
RARRR

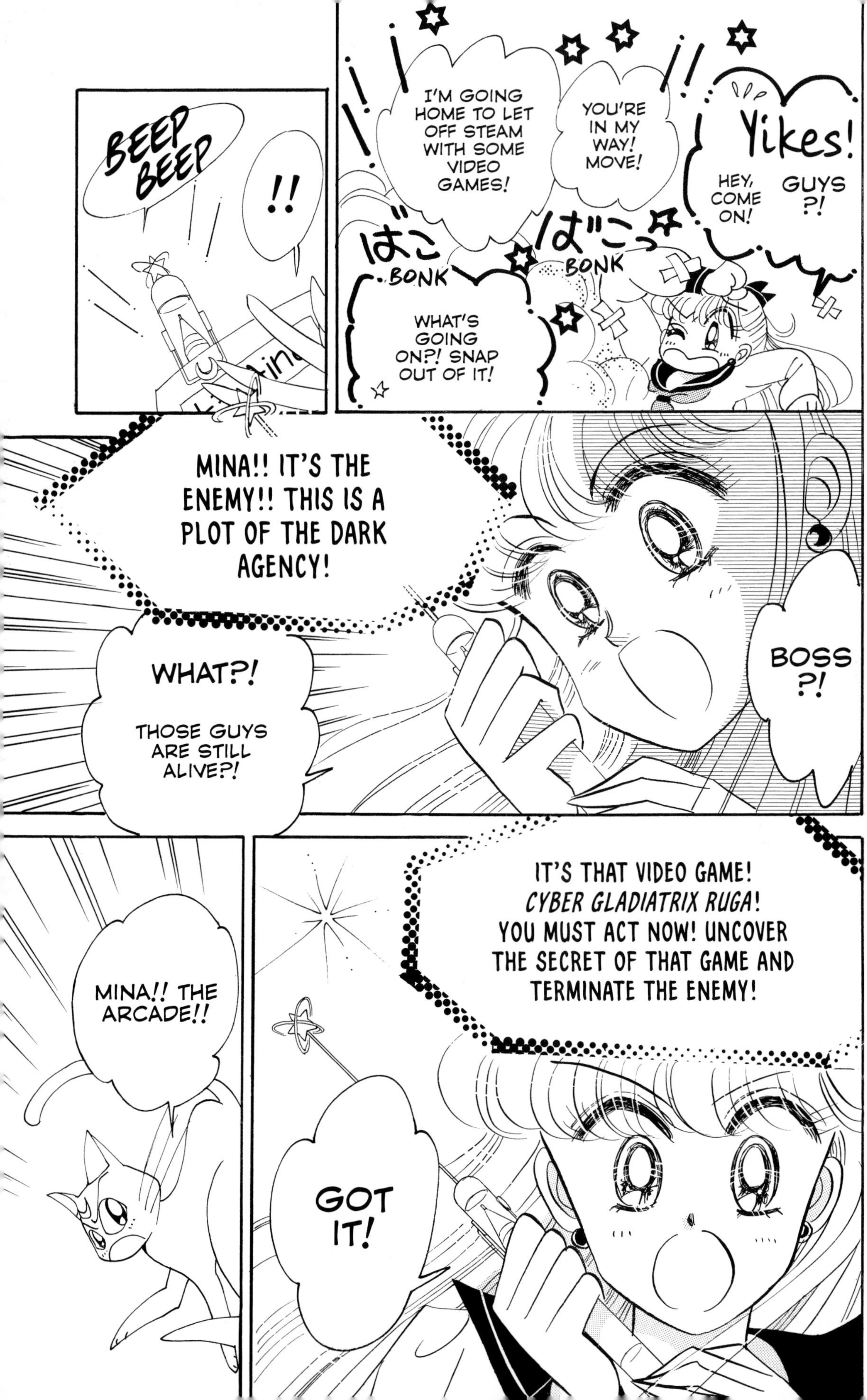
Yikes!
GUYS ?!
HEY, COME ON!
YOU'RE IN MY WAY! MOVE!
I'M GOING HOME TO LET OFF STEAM WITH SOME VIDEO GAMES!
ばこっ
BONK
ばこ
BONK
WHAT'S GOING ON?! SNAP OUT OF IT!
!!
BEEP BEEP
BOSS ?!
MINA!! IT'S THE ENEMY!! THIS IS A PLOT OF THE DARK AGENCY!
WHAT?!
THOSE GUYS ARE STILL ALIVE?!
IT'S THAT VIDEO GAME! *CYBER GLADIATRIX RUGA*! YOU MUST ACT NOW! UNCOVER THE SECRET OF THAT GAME AND TERMINATE THE ENEMY!
GOT IT!
MINA!! THE ARCADE!!

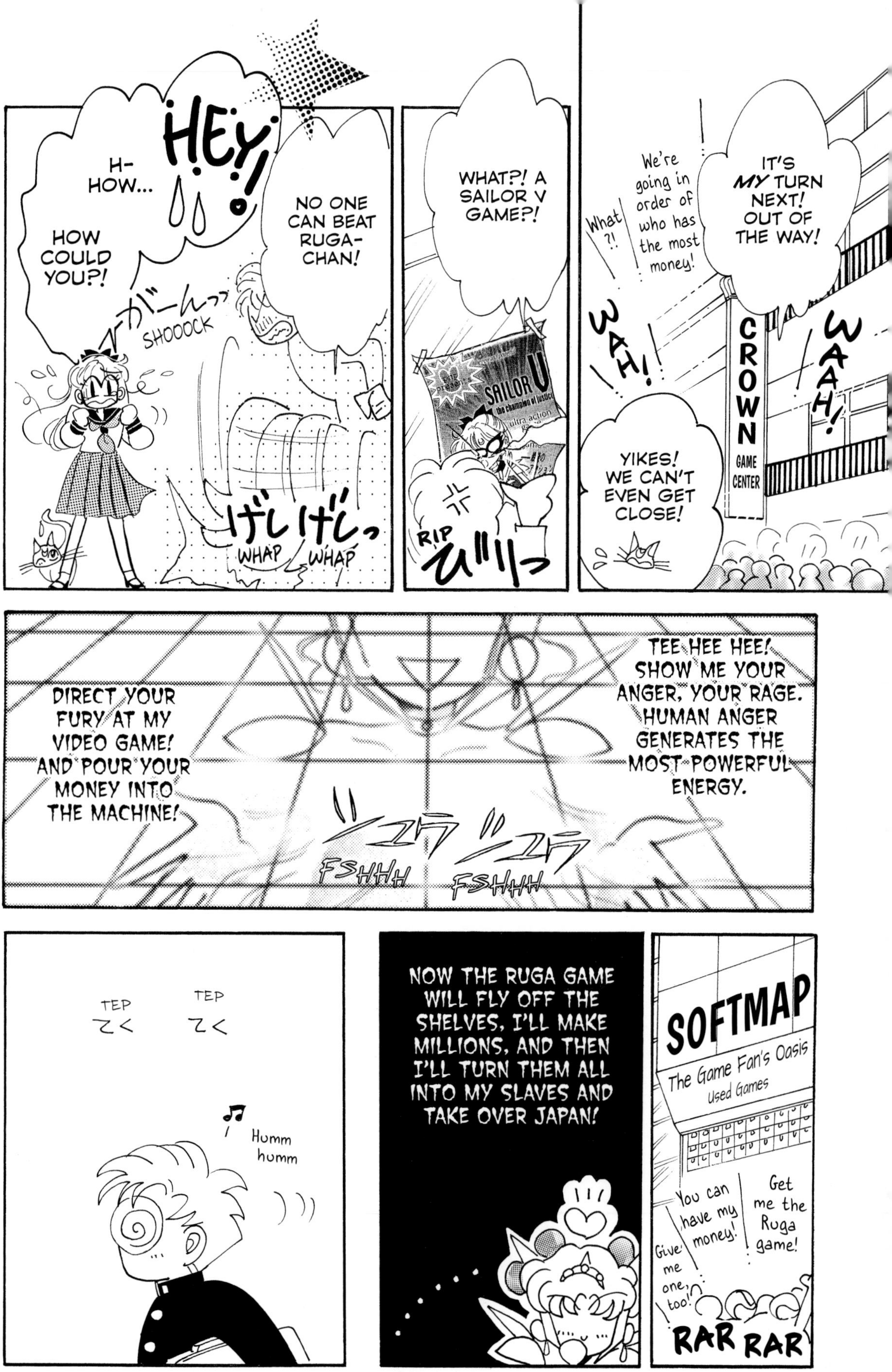
IT'S MY TURN NEXT! OUT OF THE WAY!
We're going in order of who has the most money!
What ?!
WAH!
WAAH!
CROWN GAME CENTER
YIKES! WE CAN'T EVEN GET CLOSE!
WHAT?! A SAILOR V GAME?!
SAILOR V the champion of justice
ultra action
RIP
びりっ
HEY!
H- HOW...
HOW COULD YOU?!
NO ONE CAN BEAT RUGA-CHAN!
ガーんっ
SHOOOCK
げしげしっ
WHAP WHAP
TEE HEE HEE! SHOW ME YOUR ANGER, YOUR RAGE. HUMAN ANGER GENERATES THE MOST POWERFUL ENERGY.
DIRECT YOUR FURY AT MY VIDEO GAME! AND POUR YOUR MONEY INTO THE MACHINE!
FSHHH FSHHH
SOFTMAP
The Game Fan's Oasis
Used Games
Get me the Ruga game!
You can have my money!
Give me one, too!
RAR RAR
NOW THE RUGA GAME WILL FLY OFF THE SHELVES, I'LL MAKE MILLIONS, AND THEN I'LL TURN THEM ALL INTO MY SLAVES AND TAKE OVER JAPAN!
TEP てく
TEP てく
Humm humm

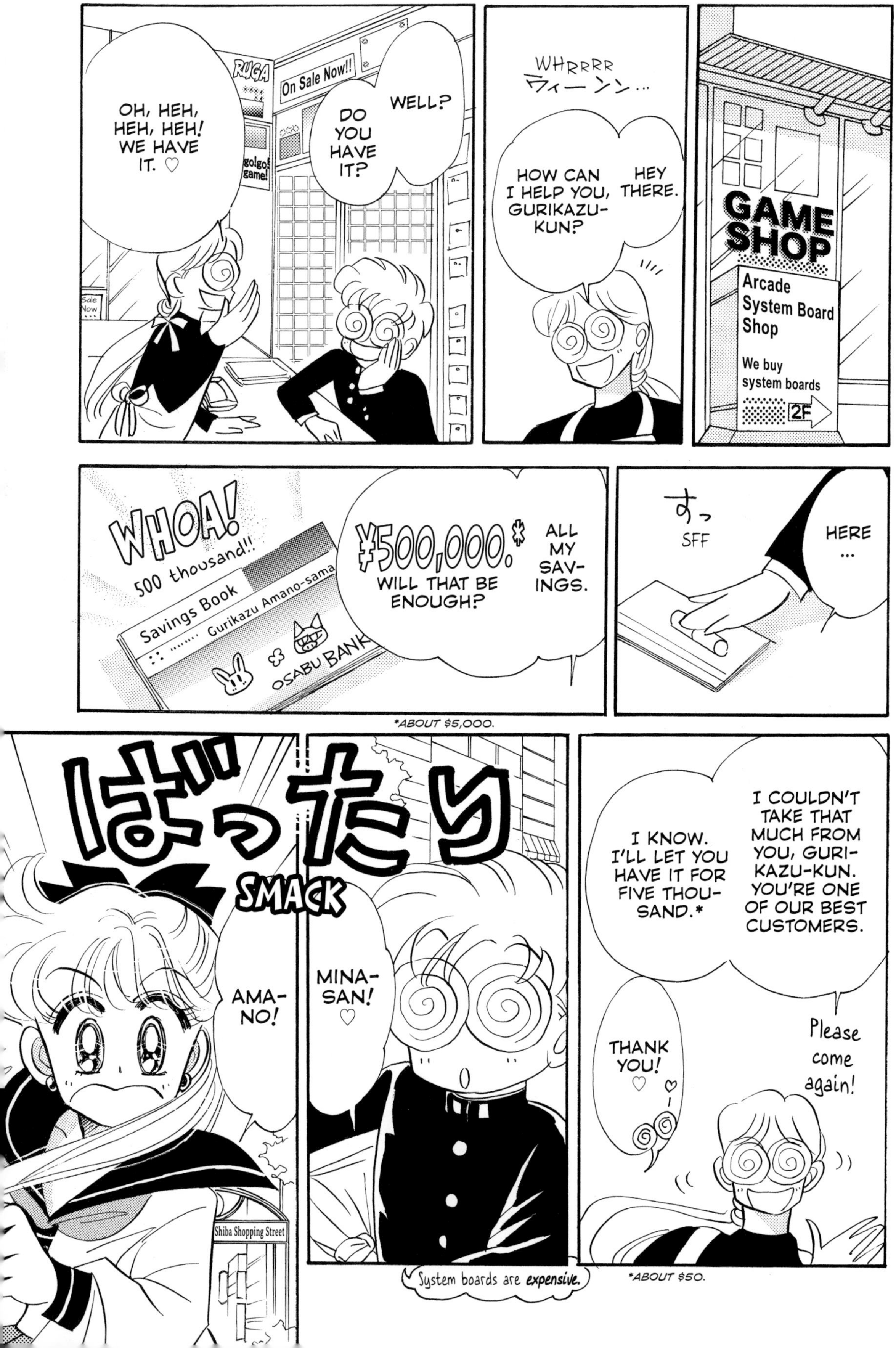
GAME SHOP
Arcade System Board Shop
We buy system boards
2F
WHRRRR ウィーンン…
HEY THERE.
HOW CAN I HELP YOU, GURIKAZU-KUN?
WELL?
DO YOU HAVE IT?
OH, HEH, HEH, HEH! WE HAVE IT. ♡
RUGA
On Sale Now!!
go!go! game!
Sale Now
すっ SFF
HERE …
ALL MY SAVINGS.
¥500,000.* WILL THAT BE ENOUGH?
WHOA!
500 thousand!!
Savings Book
Gurikazu Amano-sama
OSABU BANK
I COULDN'T TAKE THAT MUCH FROM YOU, GURI-KAZU-KUN. YOU'RE ONE OF OUR BEST CUSTOMERS.
I KNOW. I'LL LET YOU HAVE IT FOR FIVE THOU-SAND.*
Please come again!
THANK YOU! ♡
MINA-SAN! ♡
ばったり SMACK
AMA-NO!
Shiba Shopping Street
System boards are expensive.

*ABOUT $5,000.

*ABOUT $50.

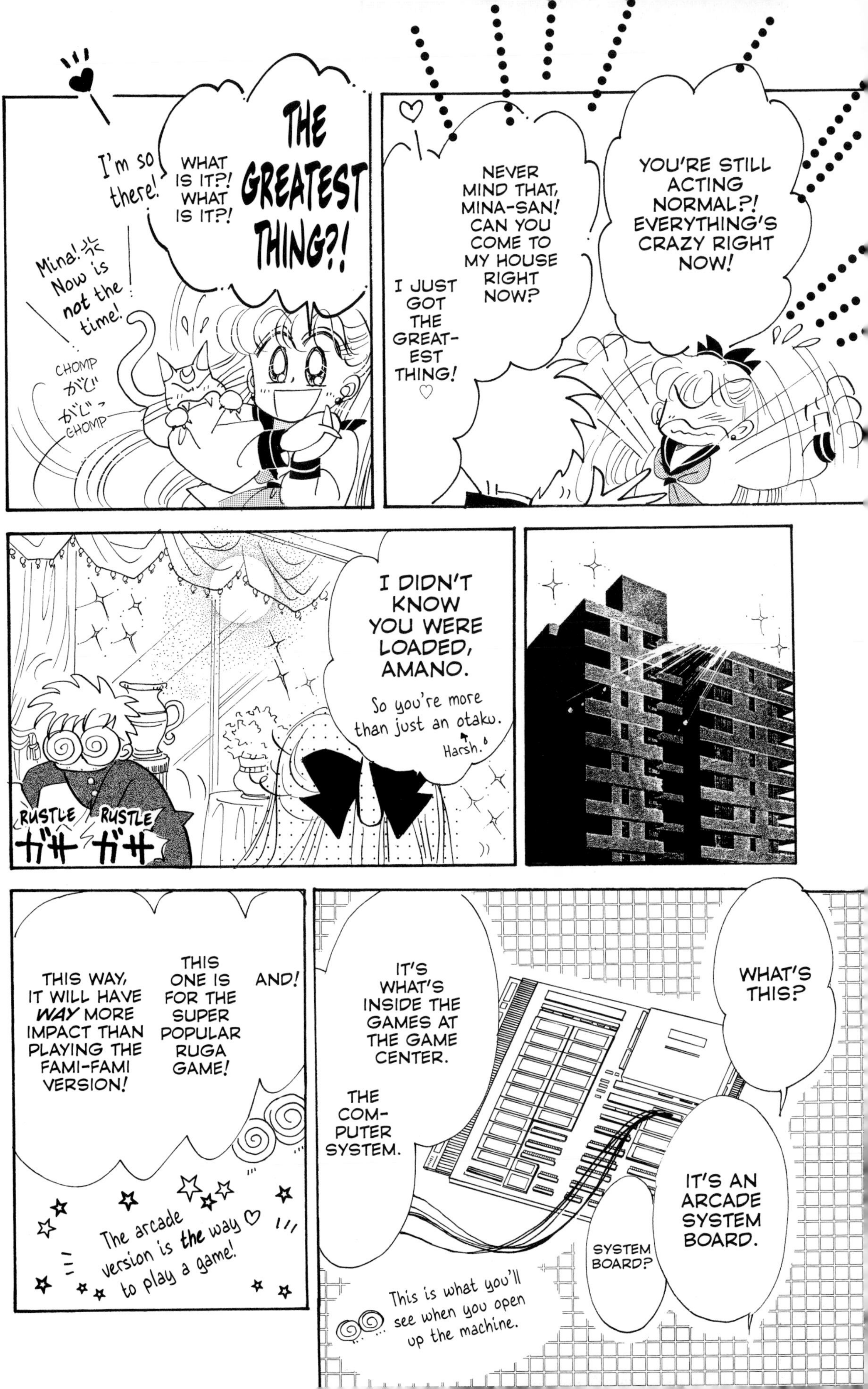
YOU'RE STILL ACTING NORMAL?! EVERYTHING'S CRAZY RIGHT NOW!
NEVER MIND THAT, MINA-SAN! CAN YOU COME TO MY HOUSE RIGHT NOW?
I JUST GOT THE GREATEST THING! ♡
THE GREATEST THING?!
WHAT IS IT?! WHAT IS IT?!
I'm so there!
Mina! Now is **not** the time!
CHOMP がじ
がじっ CHOMP
I DIDN'T KNOW YOU WERE LOADED, AMANO.
So you're more than just an otaku.
Harsh.
RUSTLE ガサ
RUSTLE ガサ
WHAT'S THIS?
IT'S WHAT'S INSIDE THE GAMES AT THE GAME CENTER.
IT'S AN ARCADE SYSTEM BOARD.
SYSTEM BOARD?
THE COMPUTER SYSTEM.
This is what you'll see when you open up the machine.
AND!
THIS ONE IS FOR THE SUPER POPULAR RUGA GAME!
THIS WAY, IT WILL HAVE *WAY* MORE IMPACT THAN PLAYING THE FAMI-FAMI VERSION!
The arcade version is **the** way to play a game! ♡

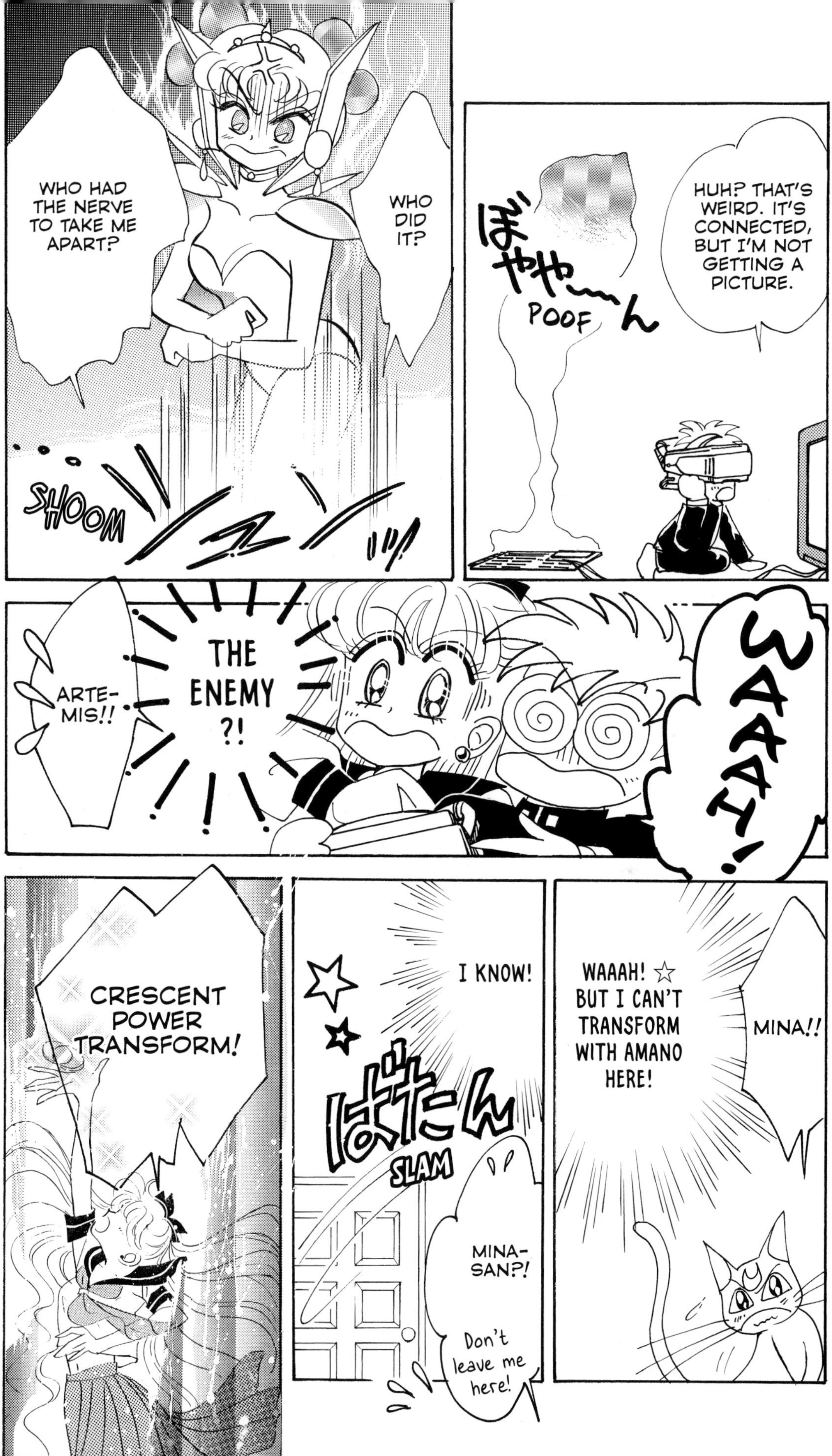
HUH? THAT'S WEIRD. IT'S CONNECTED, BUT I'M NOT GETTING A PICTURE.
ぼややーん
POOF
WHO DID IT?
WHO HAD THE NERVE TO TAKE ME APART?
...
SHOOM
WAAAH!
THE ENEMY?!
ARTE-MIS!!
MINA!!
WAAAH! ☆ BUT I CAN'T TRANSFORM WITH AMANO HERE!
I KNOW!
ばたん
SLAM
MINA-SAN?!
Don't leave me here!
CRESCENT POWER TRANSFORM!

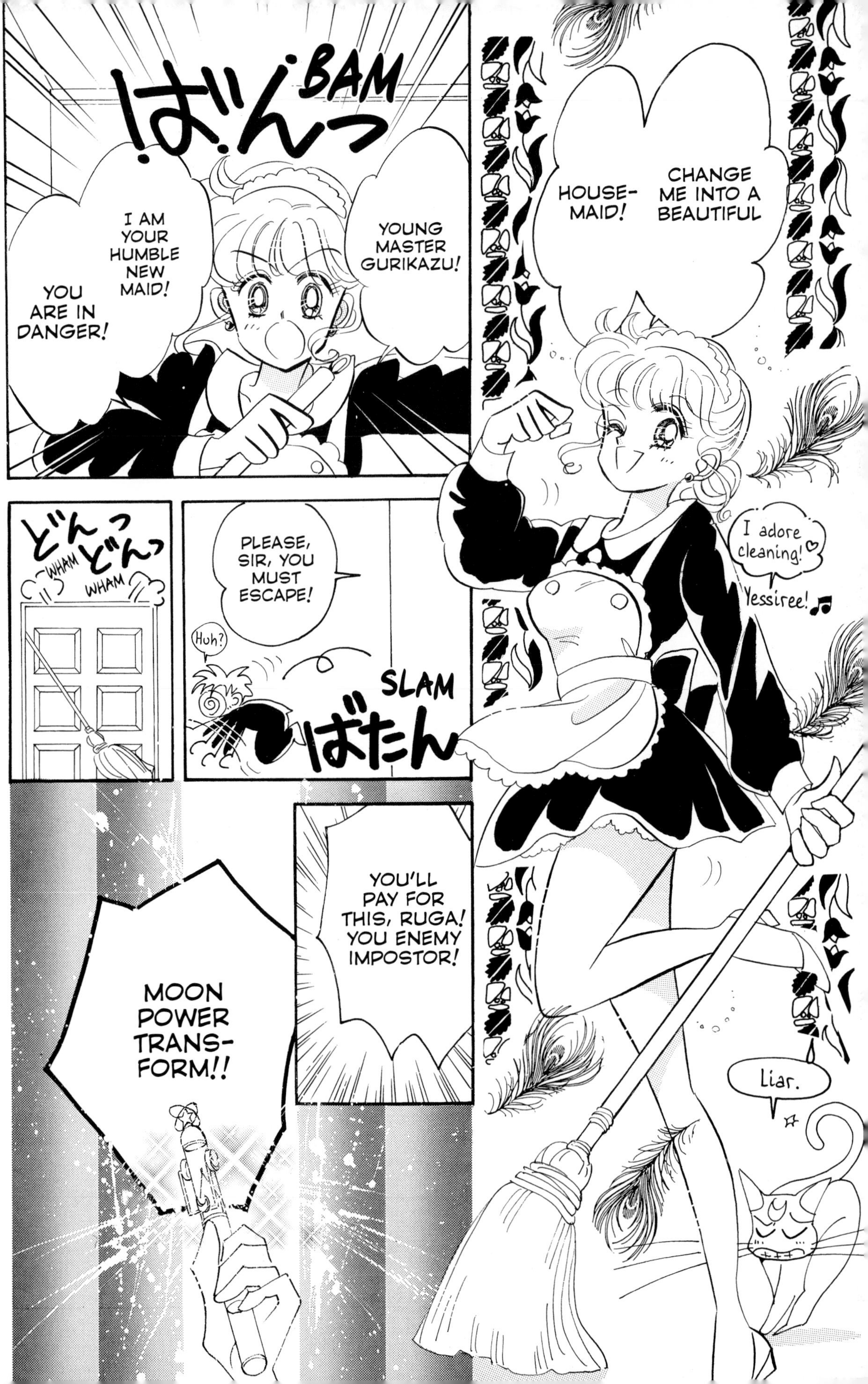
CHANGE ME INTO A BEAUTIFUL HOUSE-MAID!
I adore cleaning!♡
Yessiree!♫
Liar.
ばんっ
BAM
YOUNG MASTER GURIKAZU!
I AM YOUR HUMBLE NEW MAID!
YOU ARE IN DANGER!
PLEASE, SIR, YOU MUST ESCAPE!
Huh?
SLAM
ばたん
どんっどんっ
WHAM
WHAM
YOU'LL PAY FOR THIS, RUGA! YOU ENEMY IMPOSTOR!
MOON POWER TRANS-FORM!!

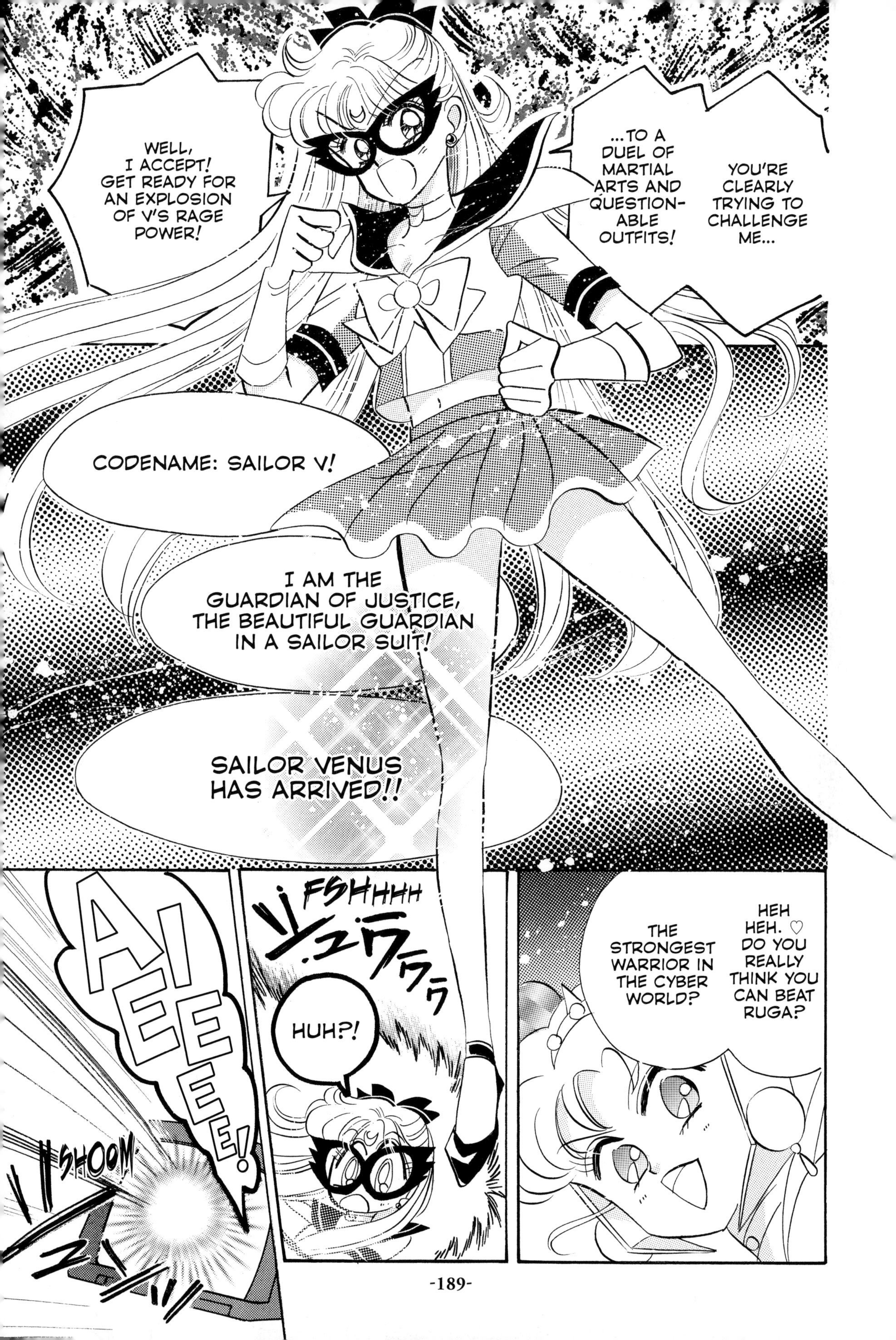
YOU'RE CLEARLY TRYING TO CHALLENGE ME...
...TO A DUEL OF MARTIAL ARTS AND QUESTION-ABLE OUTFITS!
WELL, I ACCEPT! GET READY FOR AN EXPLOSION OF V'S RAGE POWER!
CODENAME: SAILOR V!
I AM THE GUARDIAN OF JUSTICE, THE BEAUTIFUL GUARDIAN IN A SAILOR SUIT!
SAILOR VENUS HAS ARRIVED!!
HEH HEH. ♡ DO YOU REALLY THINK YOU CAN BEAT RUGA?
THE STRONGEST WARRIOR IN THE CYBER WORLD?
FSHHHH
HUH?!
AIEEEEE!
SHOOM

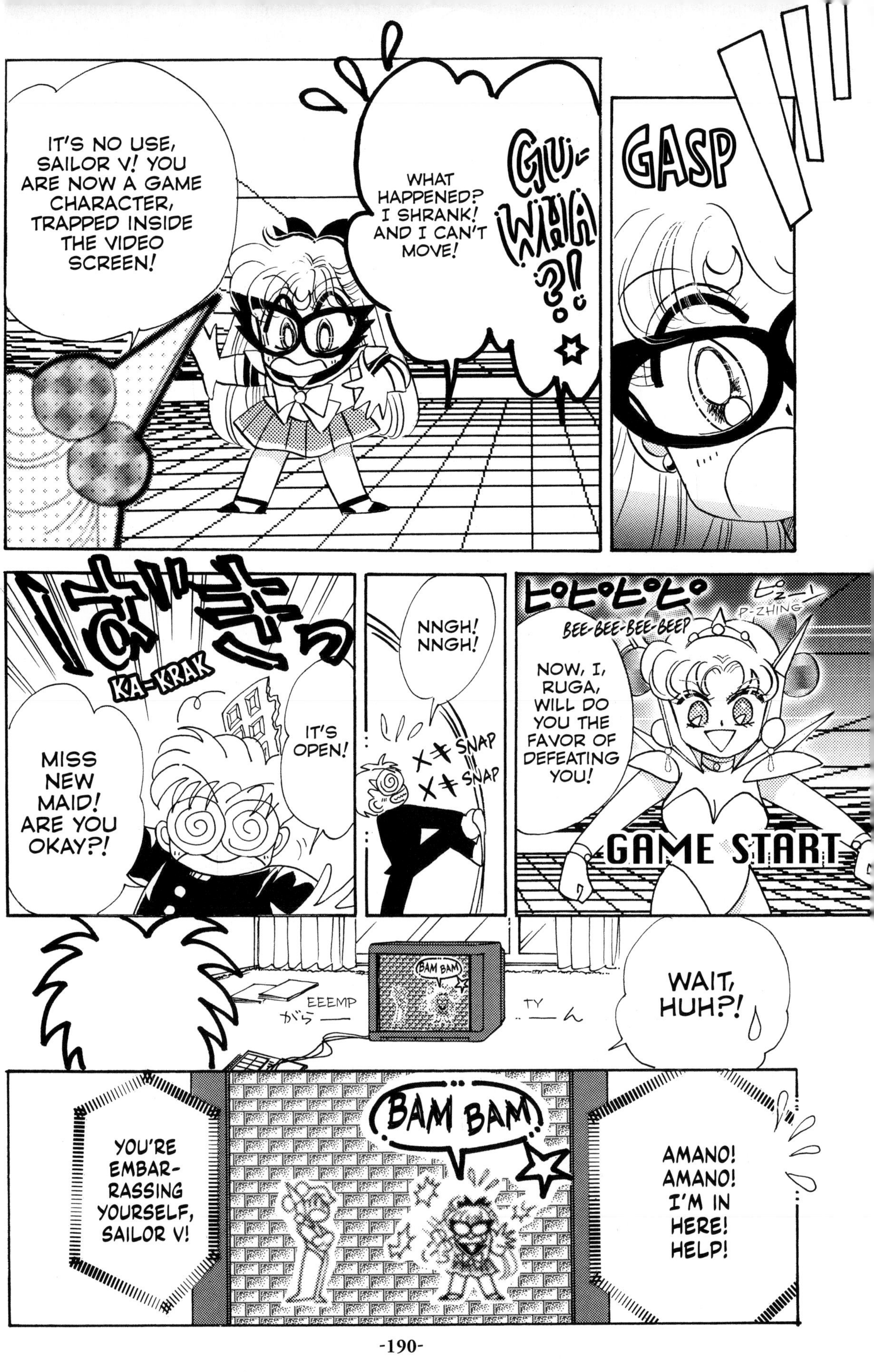
GASP
GU-WHA?!
WHAT HAPPENED? I SHRANK! AND I CAN'T MOVE!
IT'S NO USE, SAILOR V! YOU ARE NOW A GAME CHARACTER, TRAPPED INSIDE THE VIDEO SCREEN!
ピピピピ
BEE-BEE-BEE-BEEP
P-ZHING
NOW, I, RUGA, WILL DO YOU THE FAVOR OF DEFEATING YOU!
GAME START
NNGH! NNGH!
SNAP
SNAP
KA-KRAK
IT'S OPEN!
MISS NEW MAID! ARE YOU OKAY?!
WAIT, HUH?!
TY
BAM BAM
EEEMP
がらーー
AMANO! AMANO! I'M IN HERE! HELP!
BAM BAM
YOU'RE EMBARRASSING YOURSELF, SAILOR V!

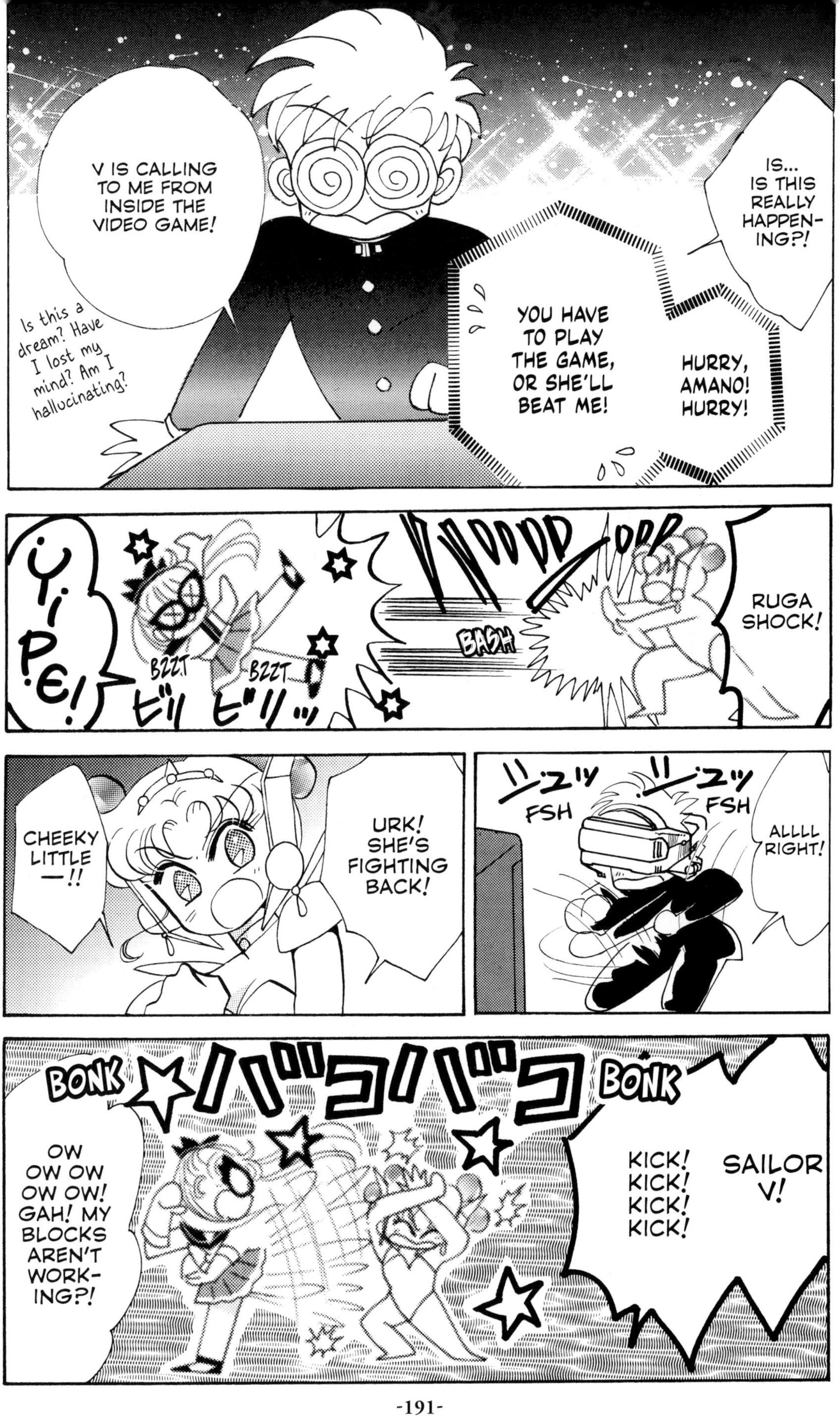
IS... IS THIS REALLY HAPPENING?!
YOU HAVE TO PLAY THE GAME, OR SHE'LL BEAT ME! HURRY, AMANO! HURRY!
V IS CALLING TO ME FROM INSIDE THE VIDEO GAME!
Is this a dream? Have I lost my mind? Am I hallucinating?
RUGA SHOCK!
BASH
BZZT BZZT
YIPE!
ALLLL RIGHT!
FSH FSH
URK! SHE'S FIGHTING BACK!
CHEEKY LITTLE—!!
SAILOR V!
KICK! KICK! KICK! KICK!
BONK BONK
OW OW OW OW OW! GAH! MY BLOCKS AREN'T WORKING?!

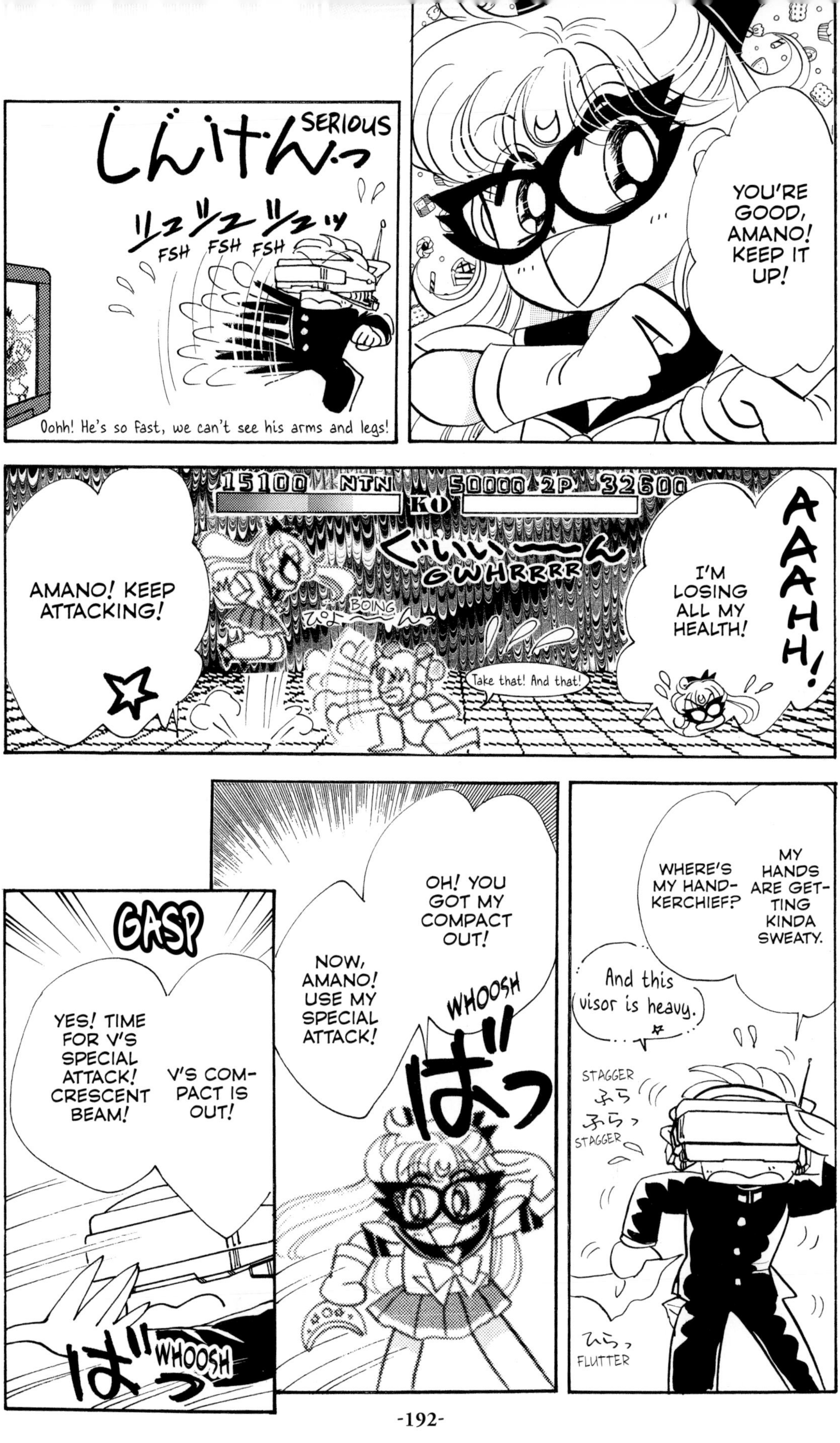
YOU'RE GOOD, AMANO! KEEP IT UP!
しんけんっ
SERIOUS
FSH FSH FSH
Oohh! He's so fast, we can't see his arms and legs!
15100 NTN 50000 2P 32600
KO
AAAAHH!
I'M LOSING ALL MY HEALTH!
Take that! And that!
ぐいいーーん
GWHRRRR
BOING
AMANO! KEEP ATTACKING!
MY HANDS ARE GET-TING KINDA SWEATY.
WHERE'S MY HAND-KERCHIEF?
And this visor is heavy.
STAGGER
ふらふらっ
STAGGER
ひらっ
FLUTTER
OH! YOU GOT MY COMPACT OUT!
NOW, AMANO! USE MY SPECIAL ATTACK!
WHOOSH
ばっ
GASP
V'S COM-PACT IS OUT!
YES! TIME FOR V'S SPECIAL ATTACK! CRESCENT BEAM!
WHOOSH

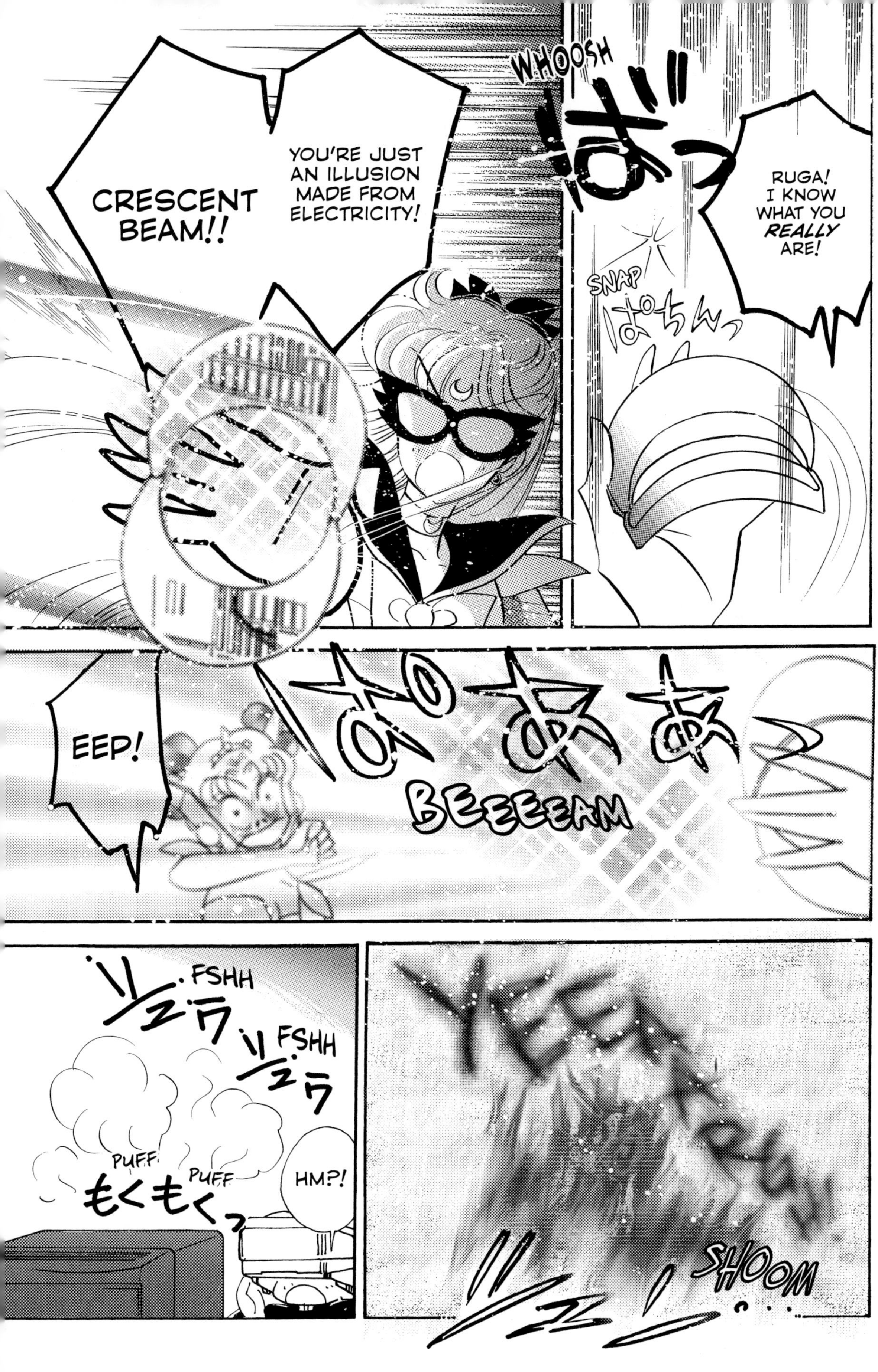
RUGA! I KNOW WHAT YOU *REALLY* ARE!
WHOOSH
ばっ
SNAP
ぱちんっ
YOU'RE JUST AN ILLUSION MADE FROM ELECTRICITY!
CRESCENT BEAM!!
BEEEEAM
EEP!
SHOOM
FSHH
FSHH
PUFF
PUFF
もくもくっ
HM?!

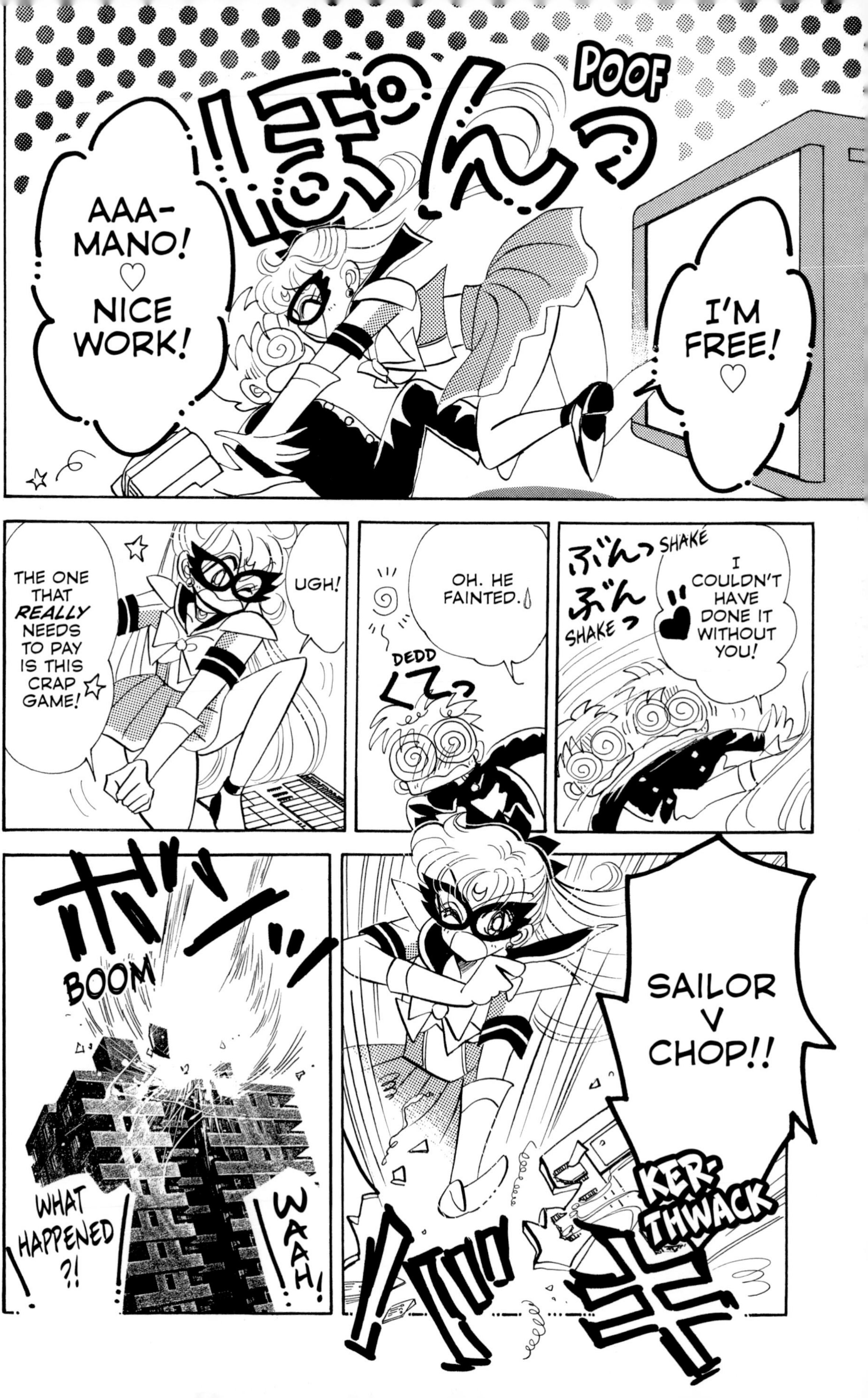
ぽんっ
POOF
I'M FREE! ♡
AAA-MANO! ♡ NICE WORK!
ぶんっ SHAKE
ぶんっ SHAKE
I COULDN'T HAVE DONE IT WITHOUT YOU!
OH. HE FAINTED.
くてっ
DEDD
UGH!
THE ONE THAT *REALLY* NEEDS TO PAY IS THIS CRAP GAME!
SAILOR V CHOP!!
KER-THWACK
ボンッ
BOOM
WAAH!
WHAT HAPPENED?!

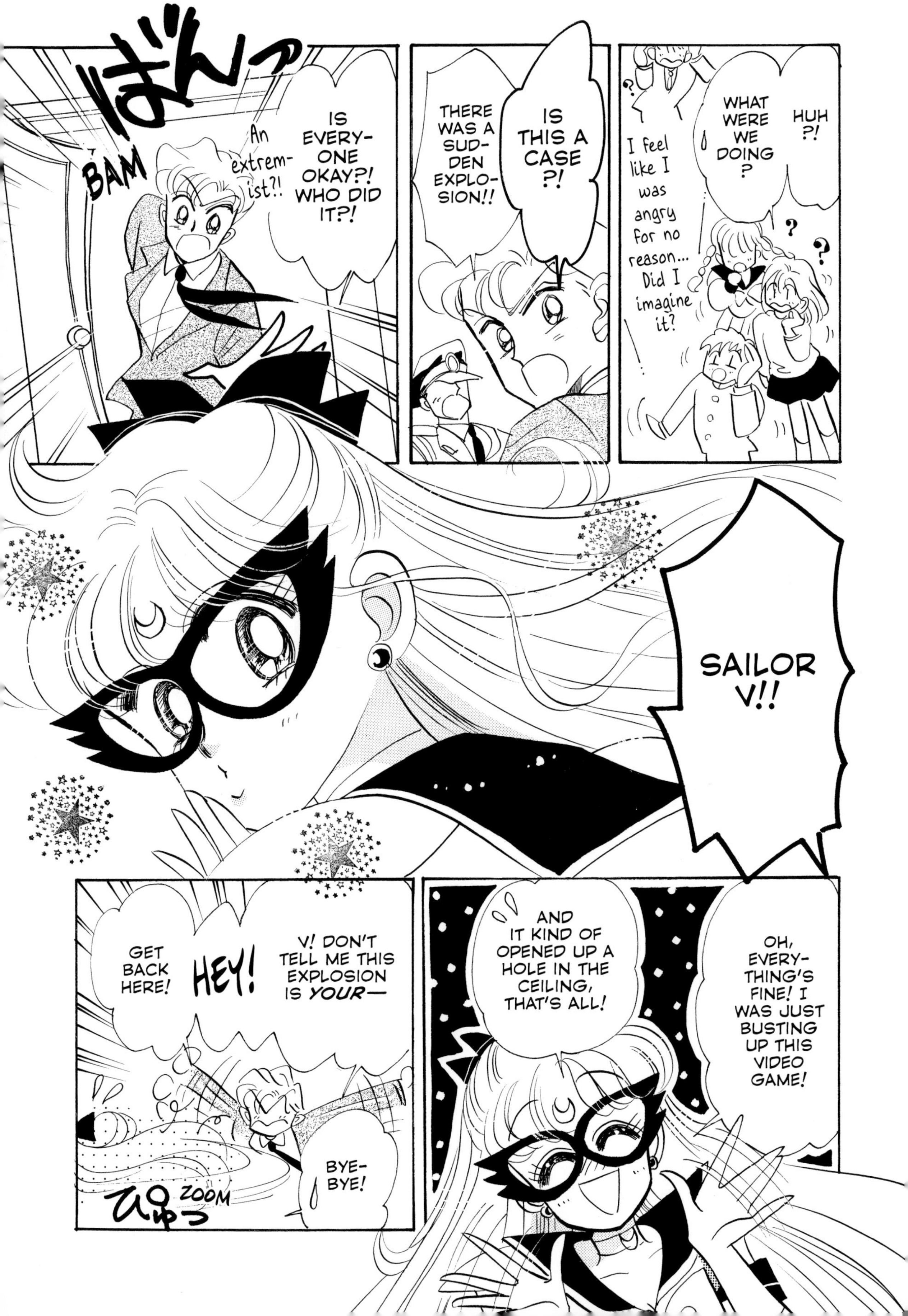
HUH ?!
WHAT WERE WE DOING ?
I feel like I was angry for no reason... Did I imagine it?
IS THIS A CASE ?!
THERE WAS A SUD-DEN EXPLO-SION!!
ばんっ
BAM
IS EVERY-ONE OKAY?! WHO DID IT?!
An extrem-ist?!
SAILOR V!!
OH, EVERY-THING'S FINE! I WAS JUST BUSTING UP THIS VIDEO GAME!
AND IT KIND OF OPENED UP A HOLE IN THE CEILING, THAT'S ALL!
V! DON'T TELL ME THIS EXPLOSION IS *YOUR*—
HEY!
GET BACK HERE!
BYE-BYE!
ひゅっ
ZOOM

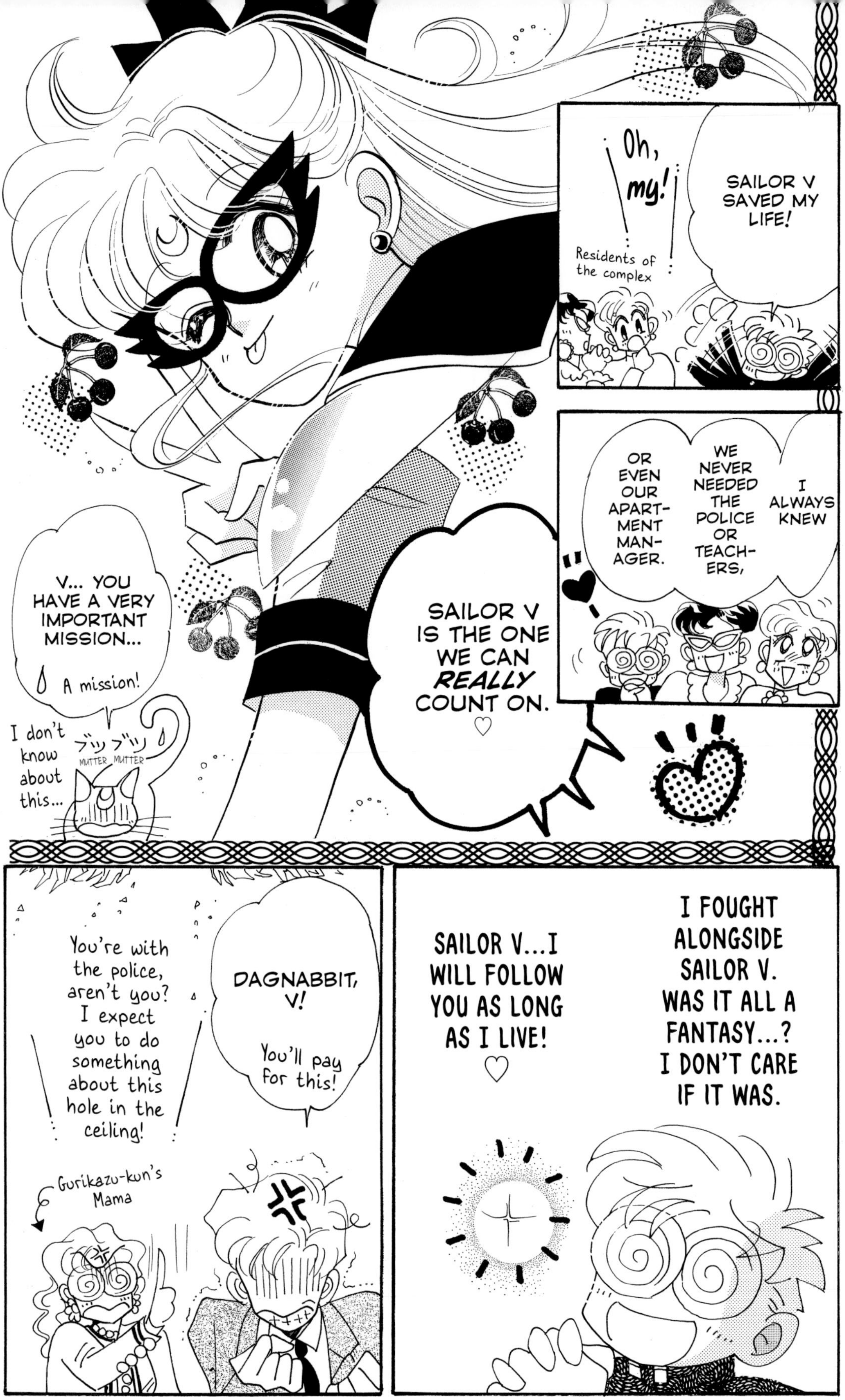

SAILOR V SAVED MY LIFE!
Oh, my!
Residents of the complex
I ALWAYS KNEW
WE NEVER NEEDED THE POLICE OR TEACHERS,
OR EVEN OUR APARTMENT MANAGER.
SAILOR V IS THE ONE WE CAN *REALLY* COUNT ON. ♡
V... YOU HAVE A VERY IMPORTANT MISSION...
A mission!
ブツブツ MUTTER MUTTER
I don't know about this...
I FOUGHT ALONGSIDE SAILOR V. WAS IT ALL A FANTASY...? I DON'T CARE IF IT WAS.
SAILOR V...I WILL FOLLOW YOU AS LONG AS I LIVE! ♡
DAGNABBIT, V!
You'll pay for this!
You're with the police, aren't you? I expect you to do something about this hole in the ceiling!
Gurikazu-kun's Mama

vol. 7 Sailor V on Vacation: Ambitions Toward Hawaii!

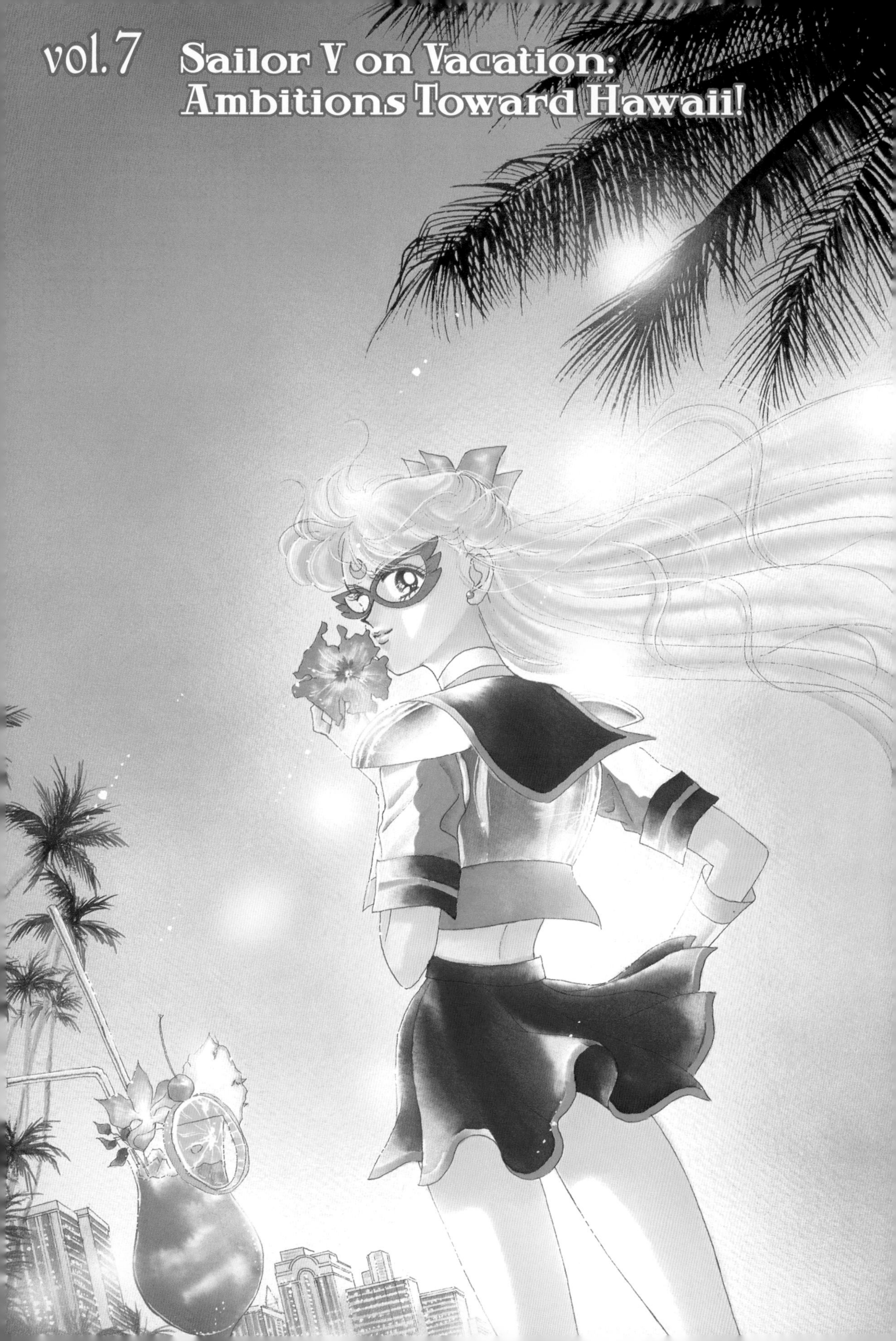

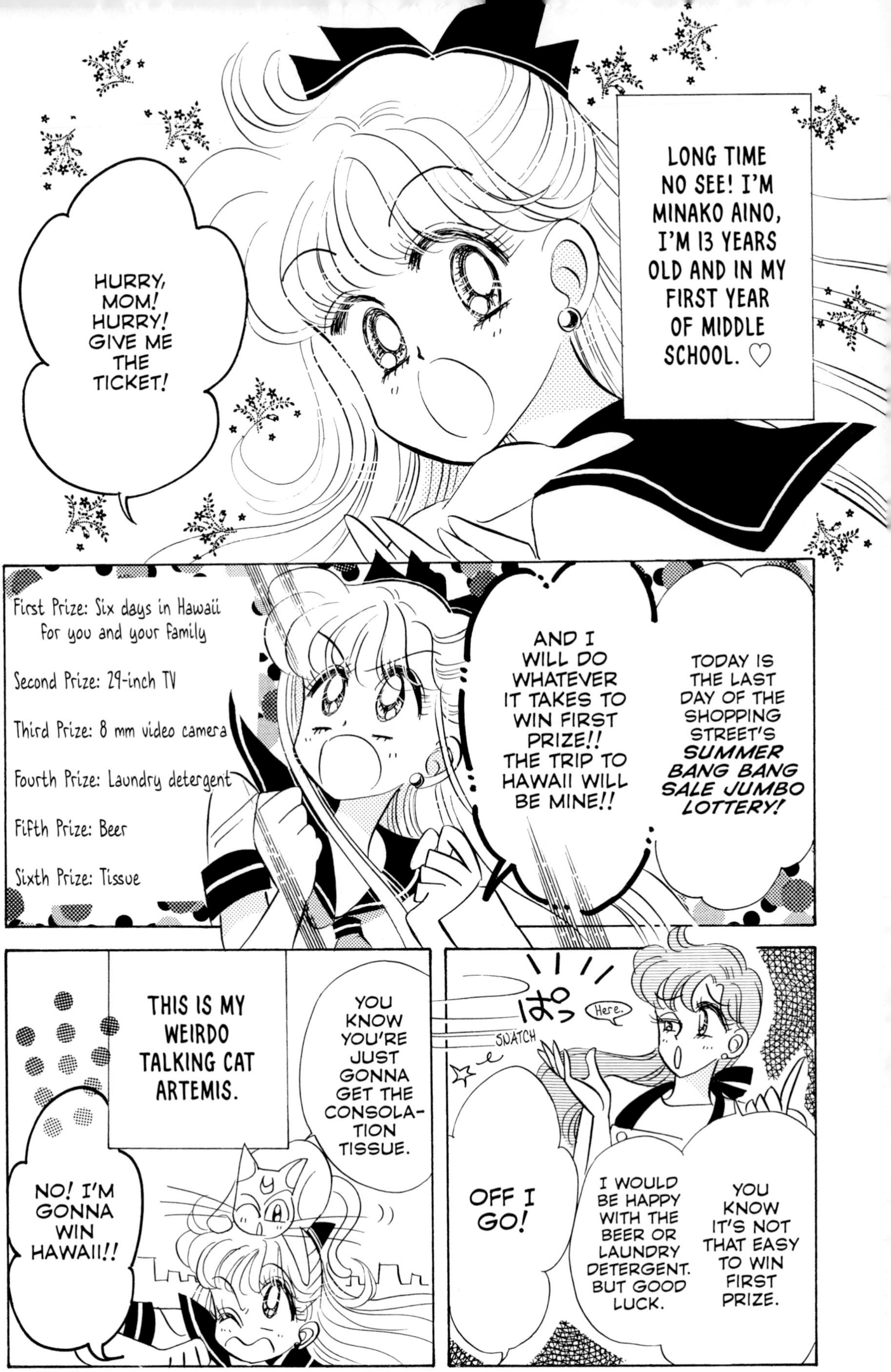
LONG TIME NO SEE! I'M MINAKO AINO, I'M 13 YEARS OLD AND IN MY FIRST YEAR OF MIDDLE SCHOOL. ♡
HURRY, MOM! HURRY! GIVE ME THE TICKET!
TODAY IS THE LAST DAY OF THE SHOPPING STREET'S *SUMMER BANG BANG SALE JUMBO LOTTERY!*
AND I WILL DO WHATEVER IT TAKES TO WIN FIRST PRIZE!! THE TRIP TO HAWAII WILL BE MINE!!
First Prize: Six days in Hawaii for you and your family
Second Prize: 29-inch TV
Third Prize: 8 mm video camera
Fourth Prize: Laundry detergent
Fifth Prize: Beer
Sixth Prize: Tissue
Here.
ぱっ
SNATCH
YOU KNOW IT'S NOT THAT EASY TO WIN FIRST PRIZE.
I WOULD BE HAPPY WITH THE BEER OR LAUNDRY DETERGENT. BUT GOOD LUCK.
OFF I GO!
THIS IS MY WEIRDO TALKING CAT ARTEMIS.
YOU KNOW YOU'RE JUST GONNA GET THE CONSOLATION TISSUE.
NO! I'M GONNA WIN HAWAII!!

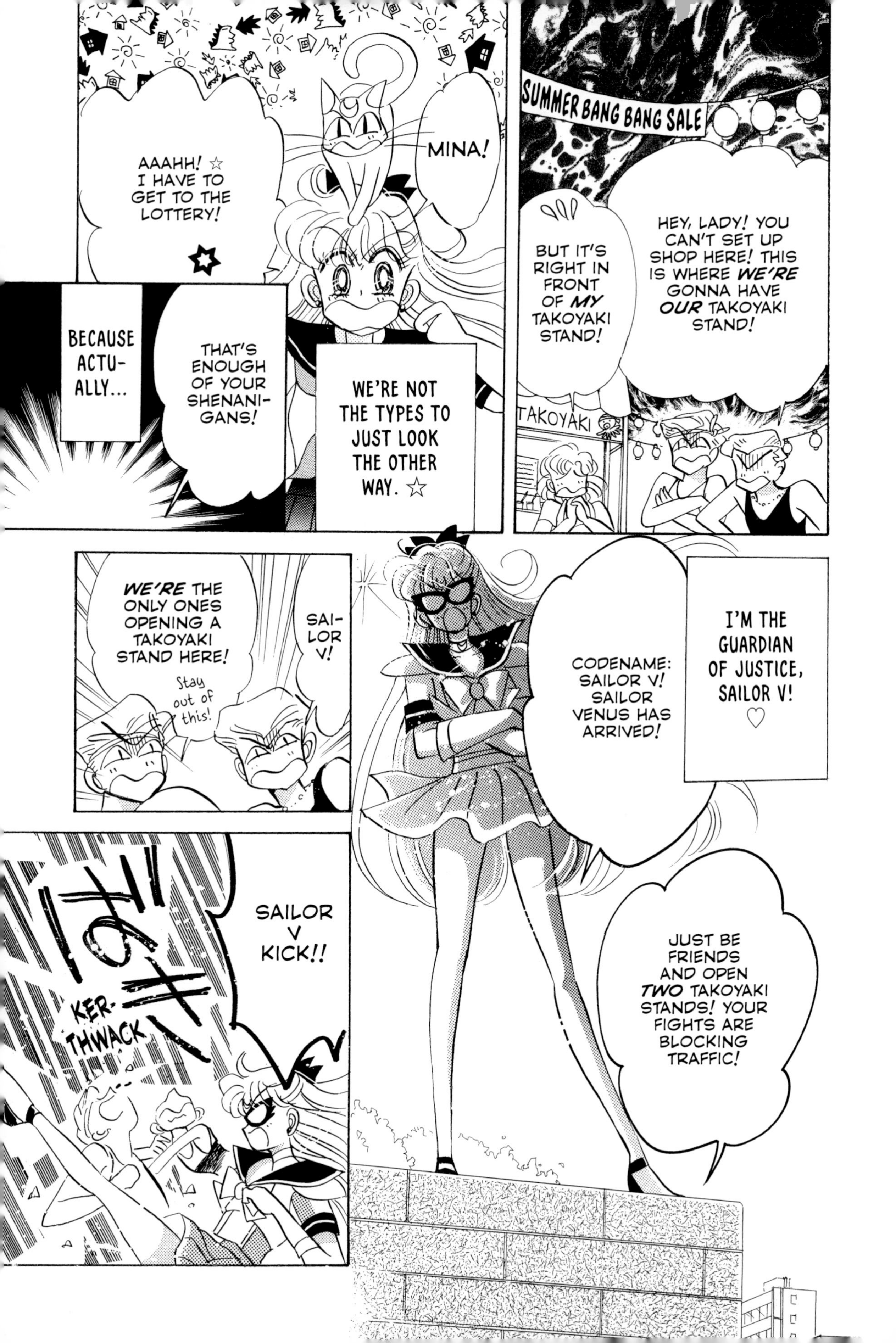
SUMMER BANG BANG SALE
HEY, LADY! YOU CAN'T SET UP SHOP HERE! THIS IS WHERE ***WE'RE*** GONNA HAVE ***OUR*** TAKOYAKI STAND!
BUT IT'S RIGHT IN FRONT OF ***MY*** TAKOYAKI STAND!
TAKOYAKI
MINA!
AAAHH! ☆ I HAVE TO GET TO THE LOTTERY!
WE'RE NOT THE TYPES TO JUST LOOK THE OTHER WAY. ☆
THAT'S ENOUGH OF YOUR SHENANIGANS!
BECAUSE ACTUALLY...
I'M THE GUARDIAN OF JUSTICE, SAILOR V! ♡
CODENAME: SAILOR V! SAILOR VENUS HAS ARRIVED!
JUST BE FRIENDS AND OPEN ***TWO*** TAKOYAKI STANDS! YOUR FIGHTS ARE BLOCKING TRAFFIC!
SAILOR V!
WE'RE THE ONLY ONES OPENING A TAKOYAKI STAND HERE!
Stay out of this!
SAILOR V KICK!!
KER-THWACK

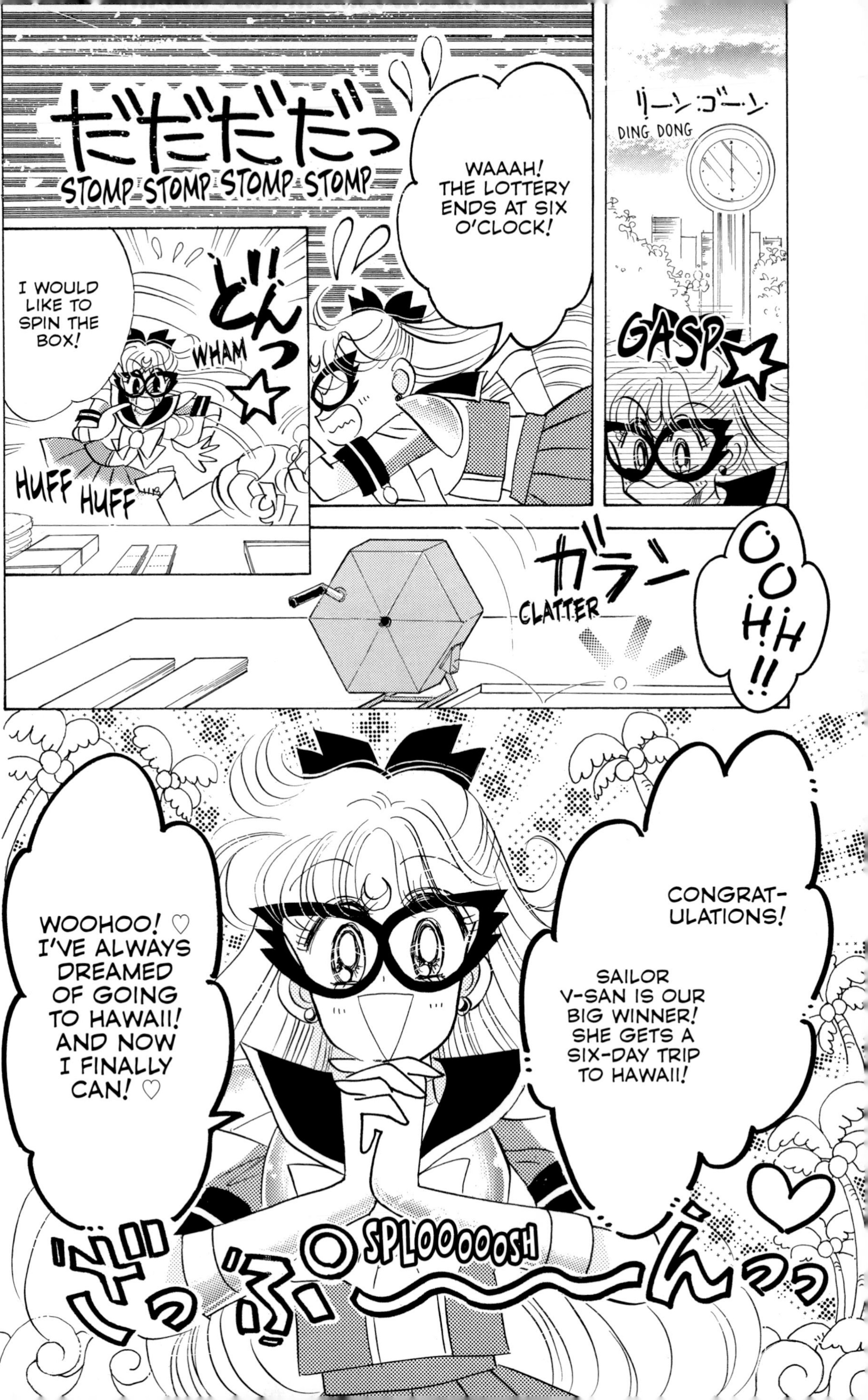
リーンゴーン
DING DONG
GASP
だだだだっ
STOMP STOMP STOMP STOMP
WAAAH! THE LOTTERY ENDS AT SIX O'CLOCK!
どんっ
WHAM
I WOULD LIKE TO SPIN THE BOX!
HUFF HUFF
OOHH!!
ガランッ
CLATTER
CONGRAT-ULATIONS!
SAILOR V-SAN IS OUR BIG WINNER! SHE GETS A SIX-DAY TRIP TO HAWAII!
WOOHOO! ♡ I'VE ALWAYS DREAMED OF GOING TO HAWAII! AND NOW I FINALLY CAN! ♡
ざっぷ〜〜んっっ
SPLOOOOOOSH

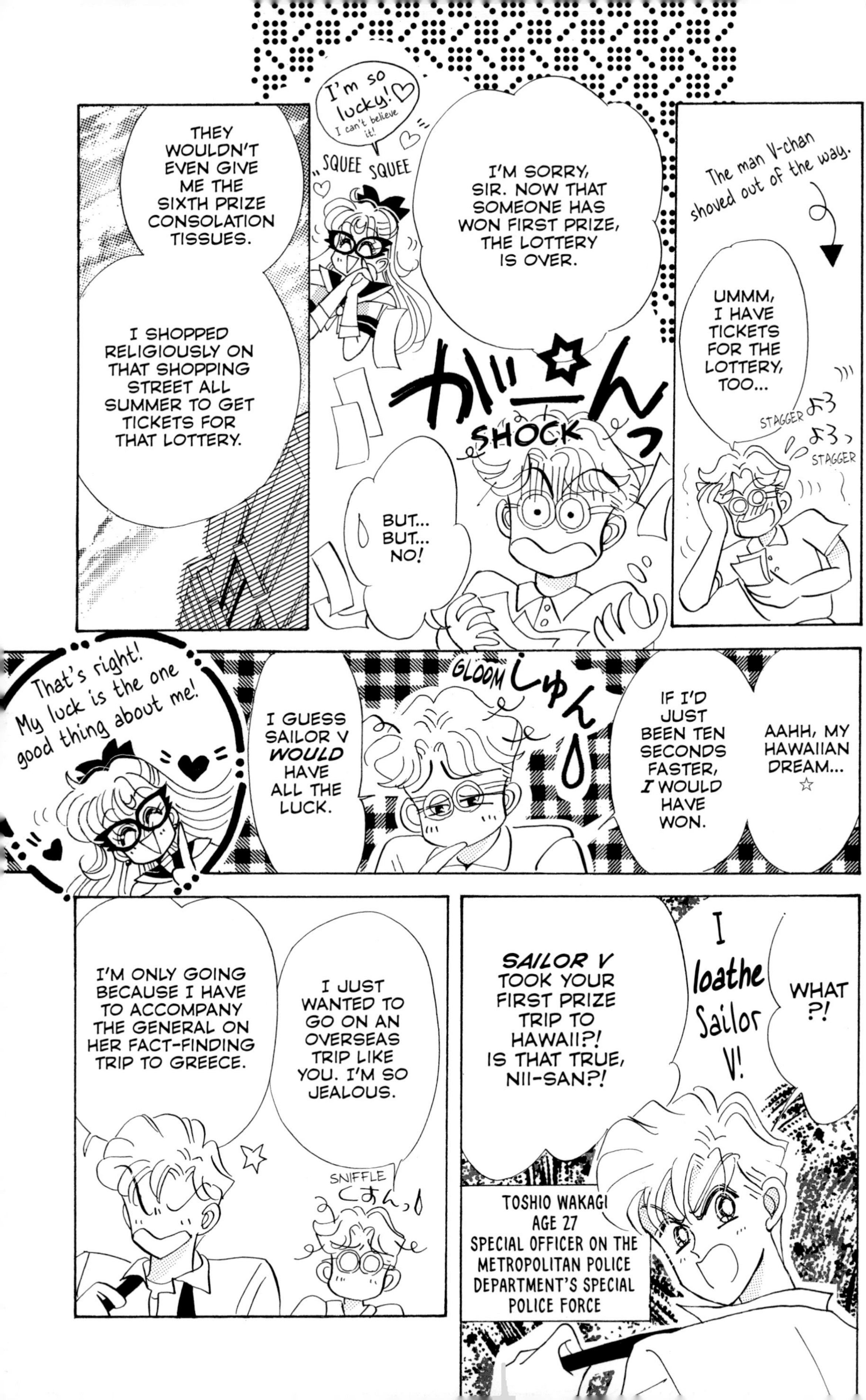

The man V-chan shoved out of the way.
UMMM, I HAVE TICKETS FOR THE LOTTERY, TOO...
STAGGER よろ
よろっ STAGGER
I'M SORRY, SIR. NOW THAT SOMEONE HAS WON FIRST PRIZE, THE LOTTERY IS OVER.
I'm so lucky! ♡ I can't believe it!
SQUEE SQUEE
がーん SHOCK
BUT... BUT... NO!
THEY WOULDN'T EVEN GIVE ME THE SIXTH PRIZE CONSOLATION TISSUES.
I SHOPPED RELIGIOUSLY ON THAT SHOPPING STREET ALL SUMMER TO GET TICKETS FOR THAT LOTTERY.
AAHH, MY HAWAIIAN DREAM... ☆
IF I'D JUST BEEN TEN SECONDS FASTER, *I* WOULD HAVE WON.
GLOOM しゅん
I GUESS SAILOR V *WOULD* HAVE ALL THE LUCK.
That's right! My luck is the one good thing about me!
I loathe Sailor V!
WHAT?!
SAILOR V TOOK YOUR FIRST PRIZE TRIP TO HAWAII?! IS THAT TRUE, NII-SAN?!
TOSHIO WAKAGI AGE 27 SPECIAL OFFICER ON THE METROPOLITAN POLICE DEPARTMENT'S SPECIAL POLICE FORCE
I JUST WANTED TO GO ON AN OVERSEAS TRIP LIKE YOU. I'M SO JEALOUS.
I'M ONLY GOING BECAUSE I HAVE TO ACCOMPANY THE GENERAL ON HER FACT-FINDING TRIP TO GREECE.
SNIFFLE くすん

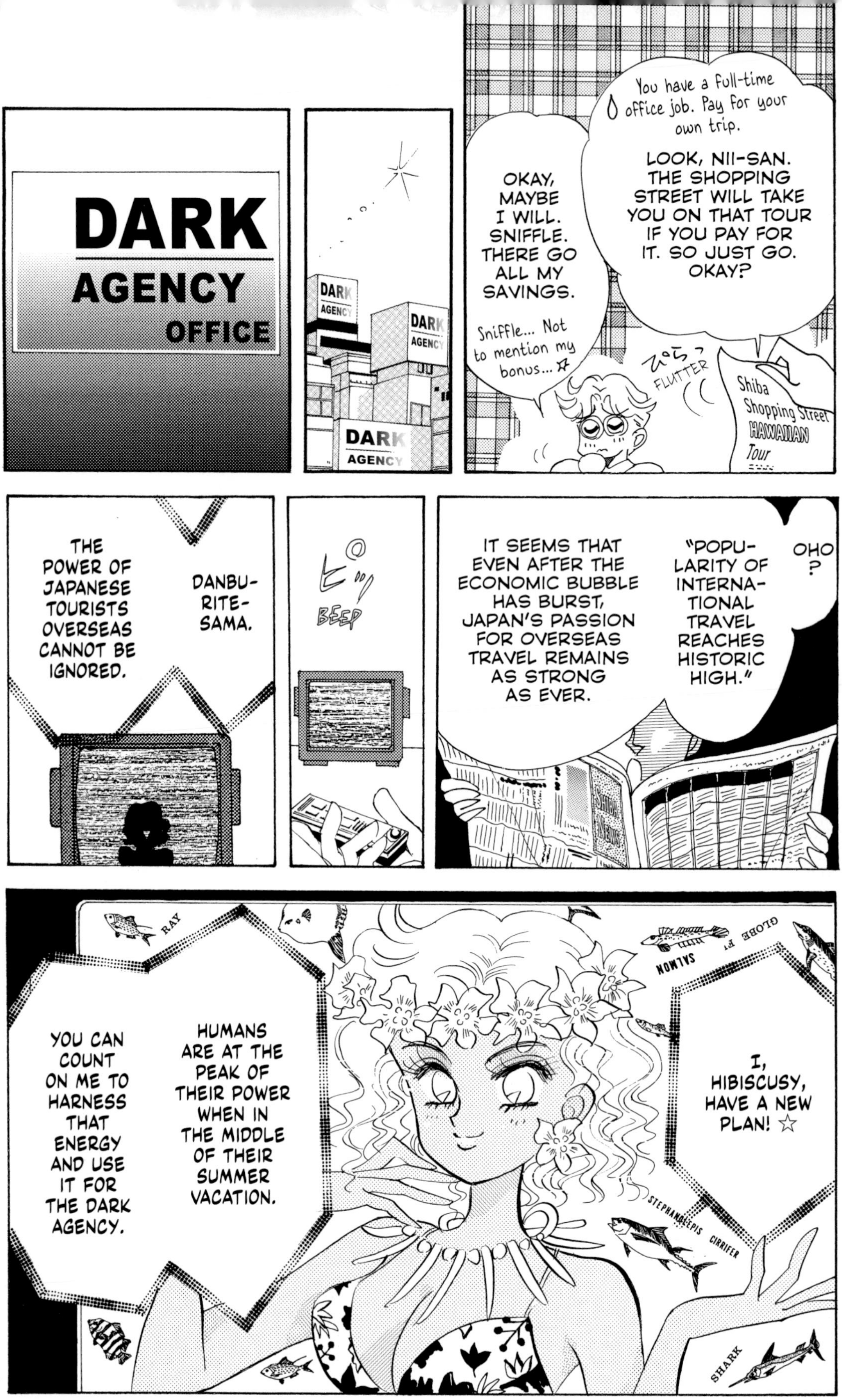
You have a full-time office job. Pay for your own trip.
LOOK, NII-SAN. THE SHOPPING STREET WILL TAKE YOU ON THAT TOUR IF YOU PAY FOR IT. SO JUST GO. OKAY?
OKAY, MAYBE I WILL. SNIFFLE. THERE GO ALL MY SAVINGS.
Sniffle... Not to mention my bonus... ☆
ぴらっ
FLUTTER
Shiba Shopping Street HAWAIIAN Tour
DARK AGENCY
DARK AGENCY
DARK AGENCY
DARK AGENCY OFFICE
OHO?
"POPULARITY OF INTERNATIONAL TRAVEL REACHES HISTORIC HIGH."
IT SEEMS THAT EVEN AFTER THE ECONOMIC BUBBLE HAS BURST, JAPAN'S PASSION FOR OVERSEAS TRAVEL REMAINS AS STRONG AS EVER.
Shiba News
ピッ
BEEP
DANBURITE-SAMA.
THE POWER OF JAPANESE TOURISTS OVERSEAS CANNOT BE IGNORED.
I, HIBISCUSY, HAVE A NEW PLAN! ☆
HUMANS ARE AT THE PEAK OF THEIR POWER WHEN IN THE MIDDLE OF THEIR SUMMER VACATION.
YOU CAN COUNT ON ME TO HARNESS THAT ENERGY AND USE IT FOR THE DARK AGENCY.
RAY
SALMON
STEPHANOLEPIS CIRRIFER
SHARK

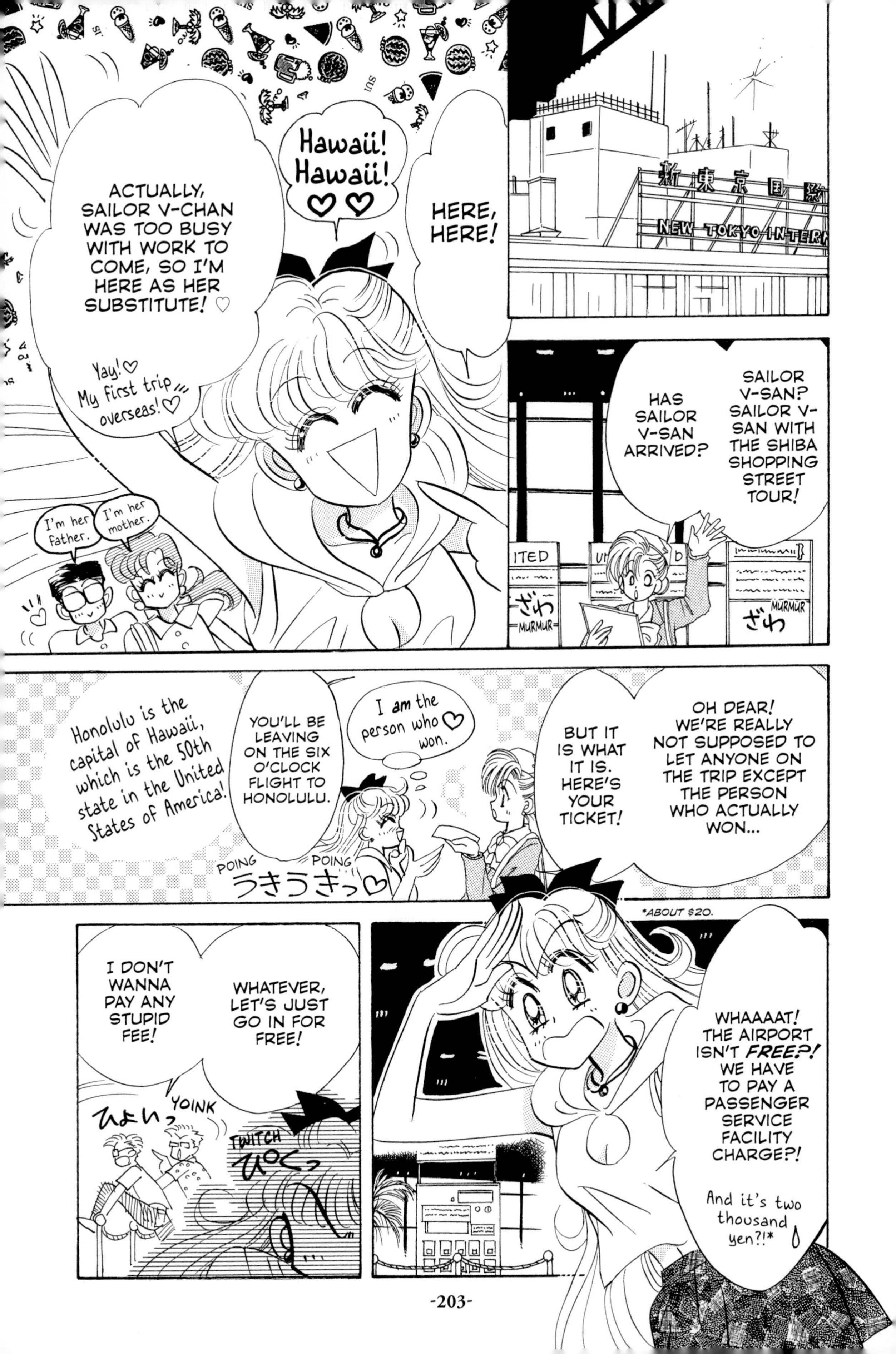

新東京国際
NEW TOKYO INTERN
SAILOR V-SAN? SAILOR V-SAN WITH THE SHIBA SHOPPING STREET TOUR!
HAS SAILOR V-SAN ARRIVED?
ITED
ざわ MURMUR
ざわ MURMUR
HERE, HERE!
Hawaii! Hawaii! ♡♡
ACTUALLY, SAILOR V-CHAN WAS TOO BUSY WITH WORK TO COME, SO I'M HERE AS HER SUBSTITUTE! ♡
Yay! ♡ My first trip overseas! ♡
I'm her mother.
I'm her father.
OH DEAR! WE'RE REALLY NOT SUPPOSED TO LET ANYONE ON THE TRIP EXCEPT THE PERSON WHO ACTUALLY WON...
BUT IT IS WHAT IT IS. HERE'S YOUR TICKET!
I am the person who won. ♡
YOU'LL BE LEAVING ON THE SIX O'CLOCK FLIGHT TO HONOLULU.
Honolulu is the capital of Hawaii, which is the 50th state in the United States of America!
POING POING
うきうきっ♡
WHAAAAT! THE AIRPORT ISN'T *FREE?!* WE HAVE TO PAY A PASSENGER SERVICE FACILITY CHARGE?!
And it's two thousand yen?!*
*ABOUT $20.
WHATEVER, LET'S JUST GO IN FOR FREE!
I DON'T WANNA PAY ANY STUPID FEE!
YOINK
ひょいっ
TWITCH
ぴくっ

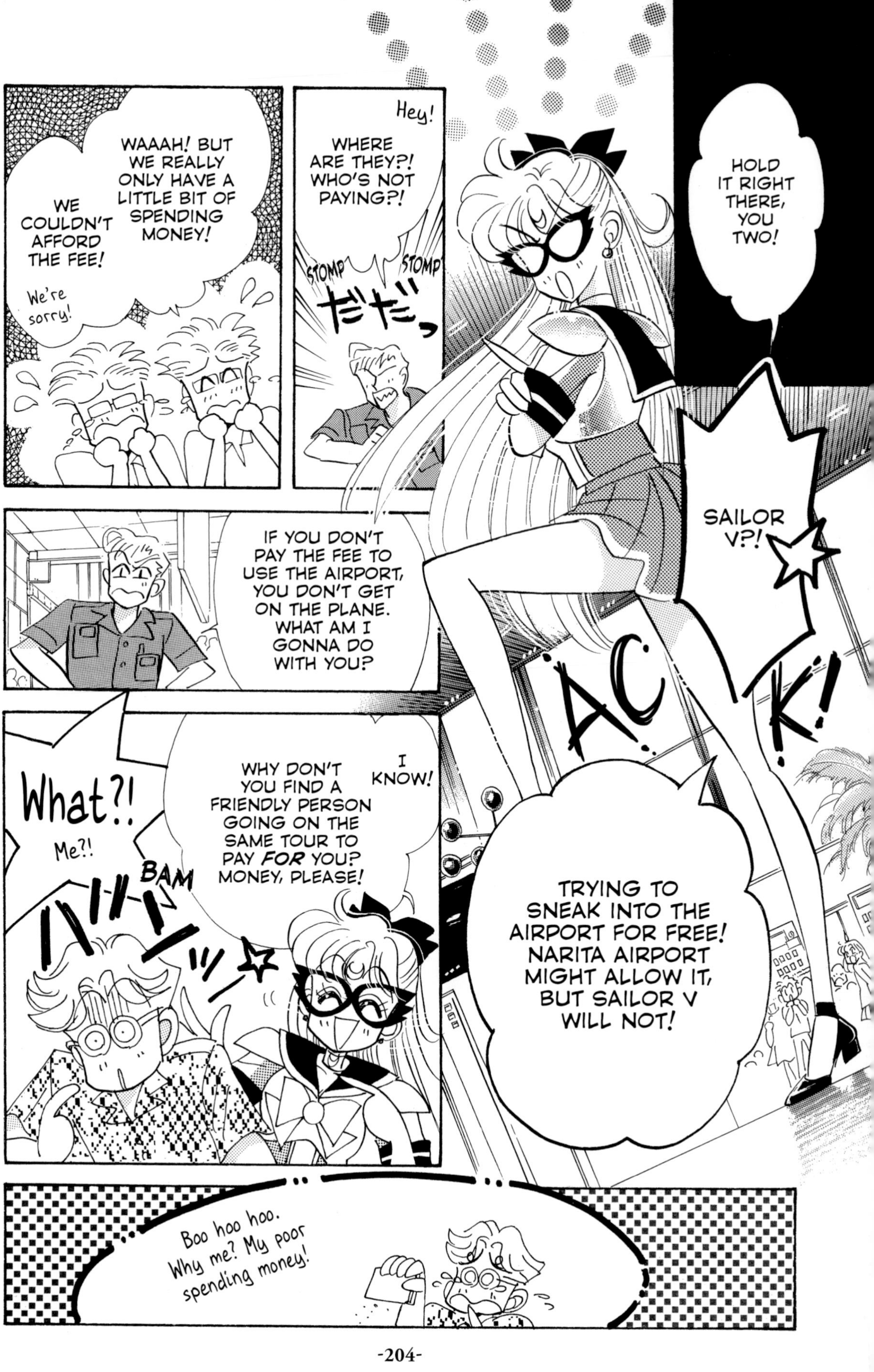
HOLD IT RIGHT THERE, YOU TWO!
SAILOR V?!
ACK!
TRYING TO SNEAK INTO THE AIRPORT FOR FREE! NARITA AIRPORT MIGHT ALLOW IT, BUT SAILOR V WILL NOT!
Hey!
WHERE ARE THEY?! WHO'S NOT PAYING?!
STOMP STOMP
だだっ
WAAAH! BUT WE REALLY ONLY HAVE A LITTLE BIT OF SPENDING MONEY!
WE COULDN'T AFFORD THE FEE!
We're sorry!
IF YOU DON'T PAY THE FEE TO USE THE AIRPORT, YOU DON'T GET ON THE PLANE. WHAT AM I GONNA DO WITH YOU?
I KNOW!
WHY DON'T YOU FIND A FRIENDLY PERSON GOING ON THE SAME TOUR TO PAY *FOR* YOU? MONEY, PLEASE!
What?!
Me?!
BAM
Boo hoo hoo. Why me? My poor spending money!

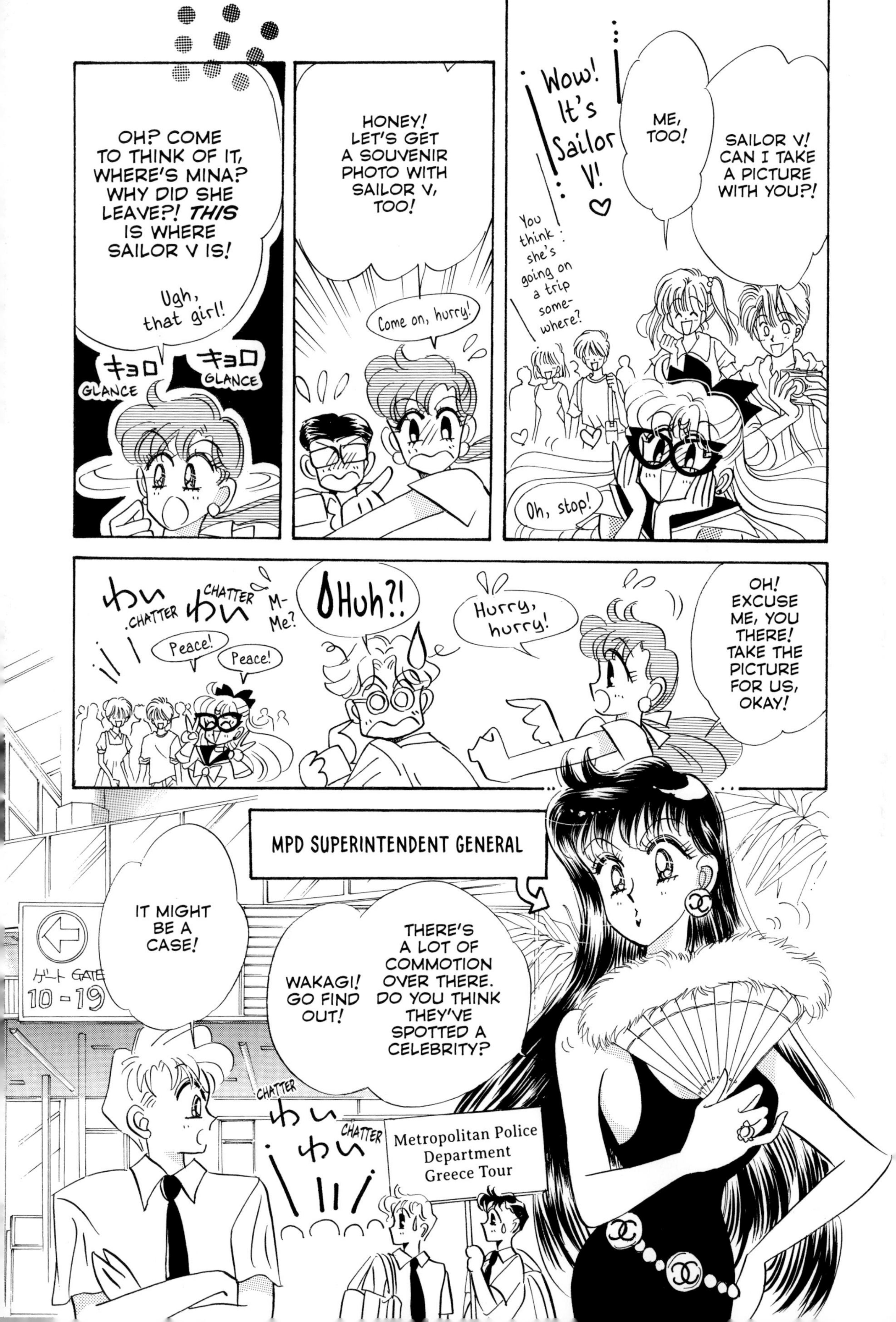
SAILOR V! CAN I TAKE A PICTURE WITH YOU?!
ME, TOO!
Wow! It's Sailor V! ♥
You think she's going on a trip somewhere?
Oh, stop!
HONEY! LET'S GET A SOUVENIR PHOTO WITH SAILOR V, TOO!
Come on, hurry!
OH? COME TO THINK OF IT, WHERE'S MINA? WHY DID SHE LEAVE?! THIS IS WHERE SAILOR V IS!
Ugh, that girl!
キョロ GLANCE
キョロ GLANCE
OH! EXCUSE ME, YOU THERE! TAKE THE PICTURE FOR US, OKAY!
Hurry, hurry!
Huh?!
M-Me?
Peace!
Peace!
わい CHATTER
わい CHATTER
MPD SUPERINTENDENT GENERAL
THERE'S A LOT OF COMMOTION OVER THERE. DO YOU THINK THEY'VE SPOTTED A CELEBRITY?
WAKAGI! GO FIND OUT!
IT MIGHT BE A CASE!
ゲート GATE 10-19
Metropolitan Police Department Greece Tour
わい CHATTER
わい CHATTER

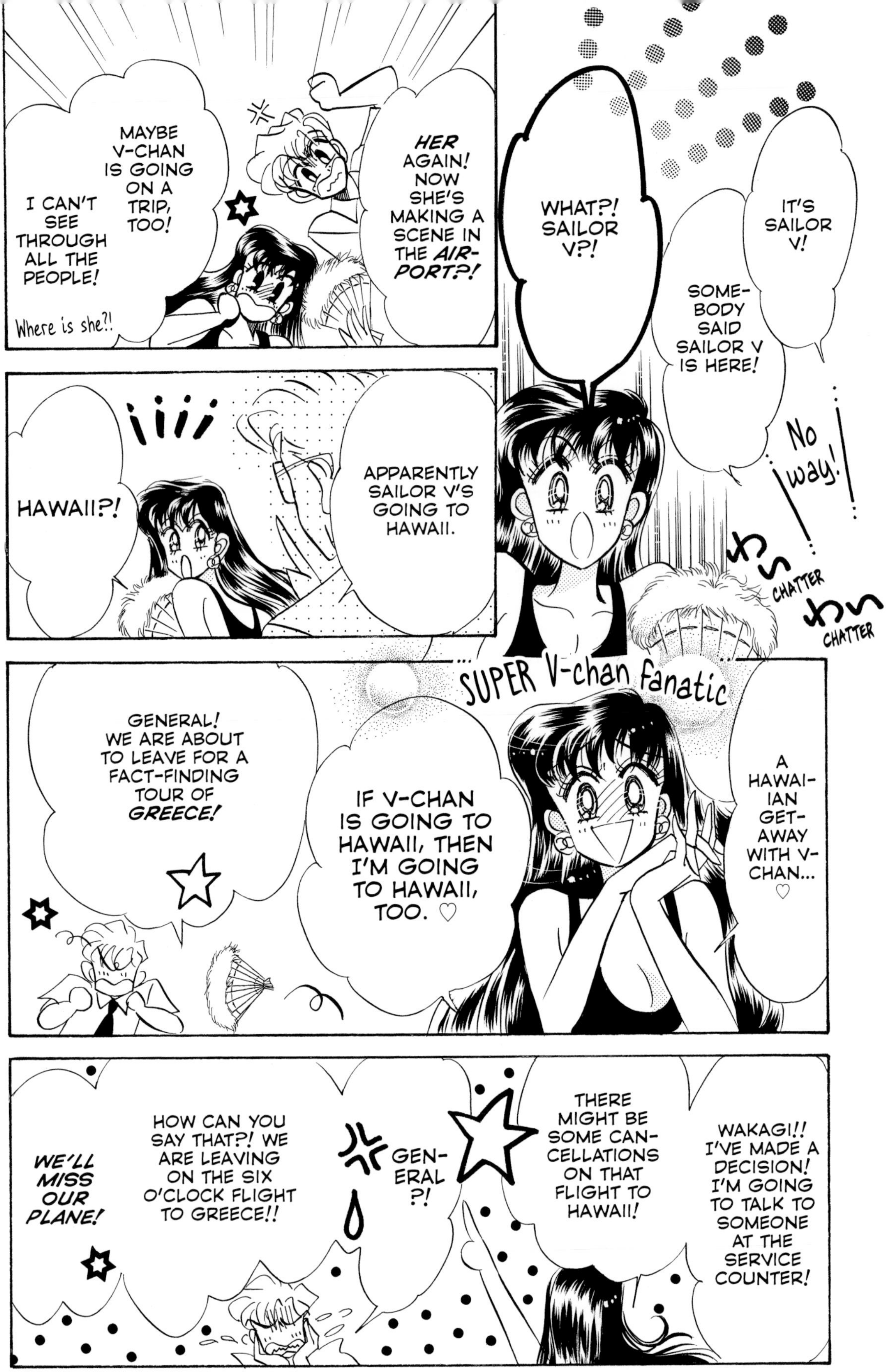
IT'S SAILOR V!
SOME-BODY SAID SAILOR V IS HERE!
WHAT?! SAILOR V?!
No way!
わい CHATTER
わい CHATTER
HER AGAIN! NOW SHE'S MAKING A SCENE IN THE *AIRPORT?!*
MAYBE V-CHAN IS GOING ON A TRIP, TOO!
I CAN'T SEE THROUGH ALL THE PEOPLE!
Where is she?!
APPARENTLY SAILOR V'S GOING TO HAWAII.
HAWAII?!
SUPER V-chan Fanatic
A HAWAIIAN GETAWAY WITH V-CHAN... ♡
IF V-CHAN IS GOING TO HAWAII, THEN I'M GOING TO HAWAII, TOO. ♡
GENERAL! WE ARE ABOUT TO LEAVE FOR A FACT-FINDING TOUR OF *GREECE!*
WAKAGI!! I'VE MADE A DECISION! I'M GOING TO TALK TO SOMEONE AT THE SERVICE COUNTER!
THERE MIGHT BE SOME CANCELLATIONS ON THAT FLIGHT TO HAWAII!
GENERAL?!
HOW CAN YOU SAY THAT?! WE ARE LEAVING ON THE SIX O'CLOCK FLIGHT TO GREECE!!
WE'LL MISS OUR PLANE!

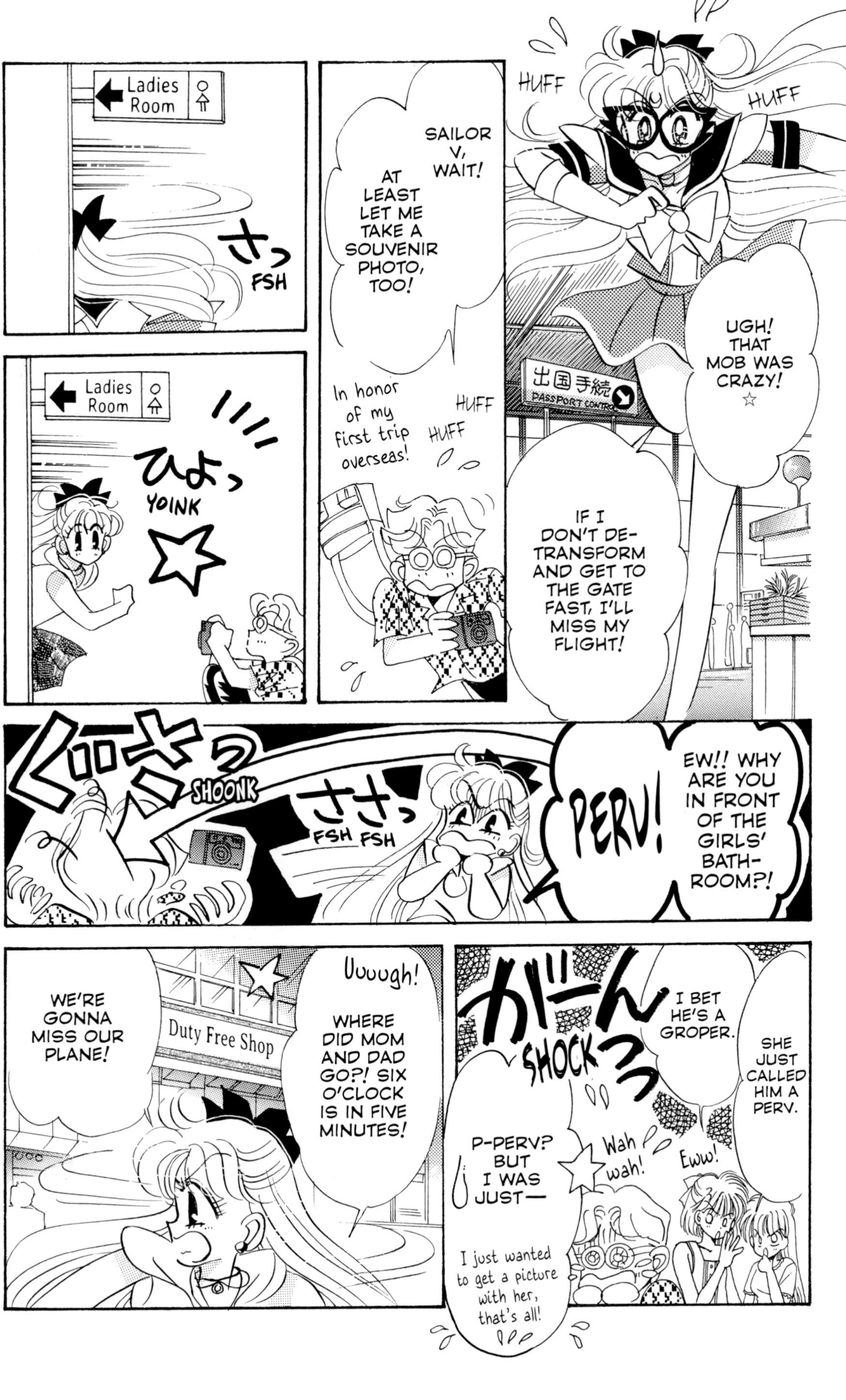
HUFF
HUFF
UGH! THAT MOB WAS CRAZY! ☆
出国手続
PASSPORT CONTR
IF I DON'T DE-TRANSFORM AND GET TO THE GATE FAST, I'LL MISS MY FLIGHT!
SAILOR V, WAIT!
AT LEAST LET ME TAKE A SOUVENIR PHOTO, TOO!
In honor of my first trip overseas!
HUFF
HUFF
Ladies Room
さっ
FSH
Ladies Room
ひょっ
YOINK
EW!! WHY ARE YOU IN FRONT OF THE GIRLS' BATH-ROOM?!
PERV!
ささっ
FSH FSH
SHOONK
SHE JUST CALLED HIM A PERV.
I BET HE'S A GROPER.
がーん
SHOCK
Eww!
Wah wah!
P-PERV? BUT I WAS JUST—
I just wanted to get a picture with her, that's all!
Uuuugh!
WHERE DID MOM AND DAD GO?! SIX O'CLOCK IS IN FIVE MINUTES!
WE'RE GONNA MISS OUR PLANE!
Duty Free Shop

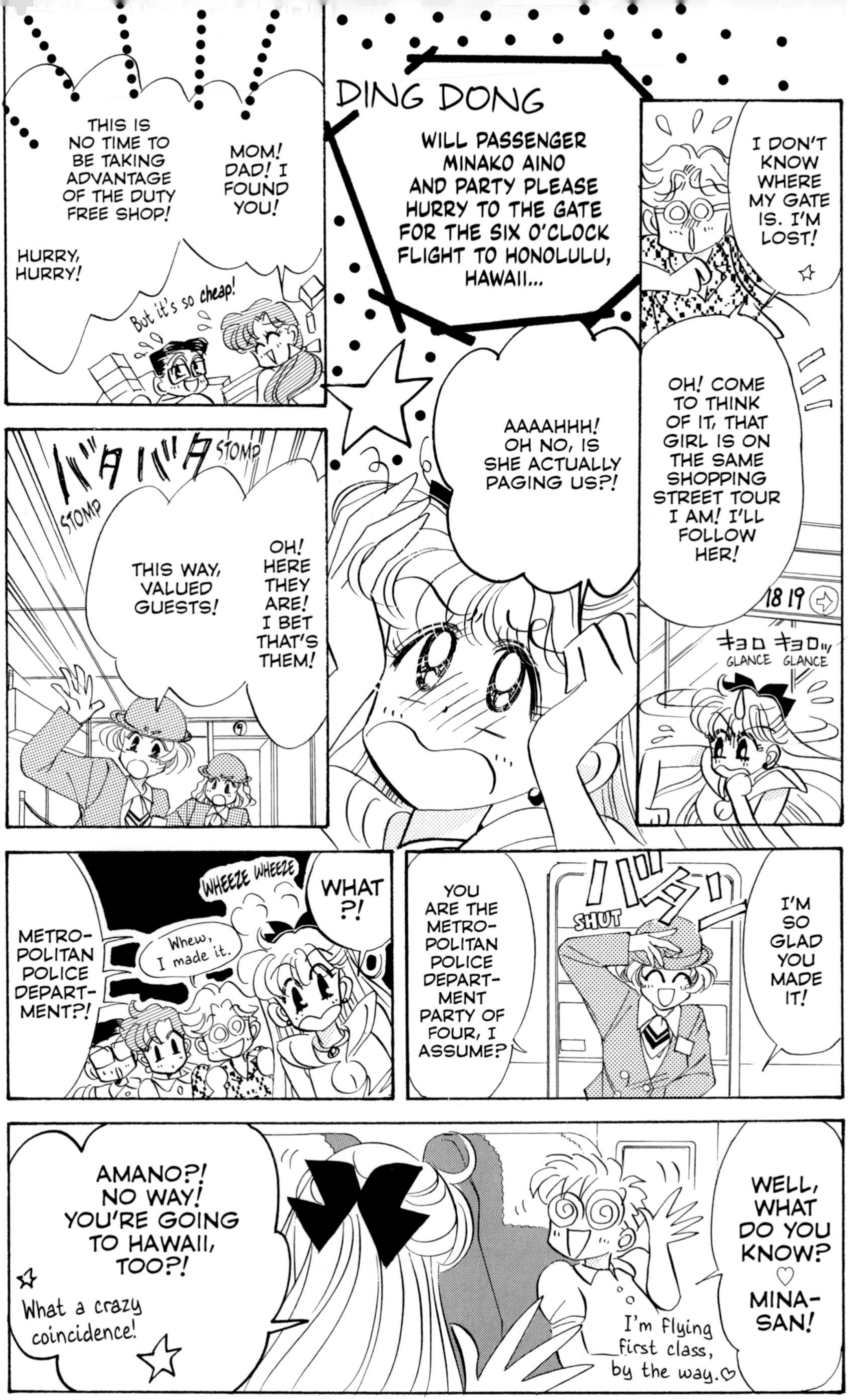
I DON'T KNOW WHERE MY GATE IS. I'M LOST!
OH! COME TO THINK OF IT, THAT GIRL IS ON THE SAME SHOPPING STREET TOUR I AM! I'LL FOLLOW HER!
18 19
キョロ キョロッ
GLANCE GLANCE
DING DONG
WILL PASSENGER MINAKO AINO AND PARTY PLEASE HURRY TO THE GATE FOR THE SIX O'CLOCK FLIGHT TO HONOLULU, HAWAII...
AAAAHHH! OH NO, IS SHE ACTUALLY PAGING US?!
MOM! DAD! I FOUND YOU!
THIS IS NO TIME TO BE TAKING ADVANTAGE OF THE DUTY FREE SHOP!
But it's so cheap!
HURRY, HURRY!
バタバタ
STOMP
OH! HERE THEY ARE! I BET THAT'S THEM!
THIS WAY, VALUED GUESTS!
STOMP
I'M SO GLAD YOU MADE IT!
バタン
SHUT
YOU ARE THE METROPOLITAN POLICE DEPARTMENT PARTY OF FOUR, I ASSUME?
WHAT?!
WHEEZE WHEEZE
Whew, I made it.
METROPOLITAN POLICE DEPARTMENT?!
WELL, WHAT DO YOU KNOW? ♡ MINA-SAN!
I'm flying first class, by the way.♡
AMANO?! NO WAY! YOU'RE GOING TO HAWAII, TOO?!
What a crazy coincidence!

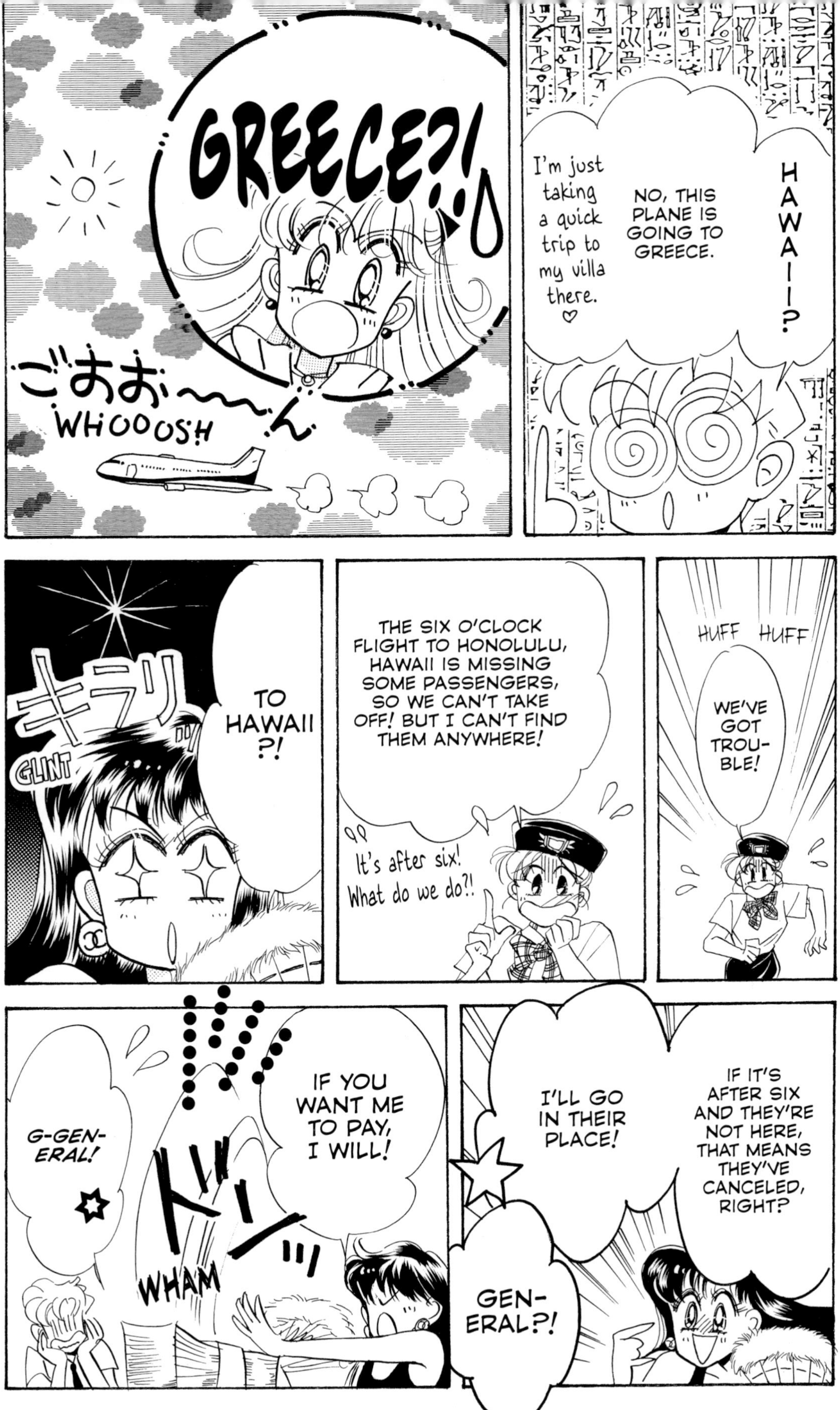
HAWAII?
NO, THIS PLANE IS GOING TO GREECE.
I'm just taking a quick trip to my villa there. ♡
GREECE?!
ごおお〜〜ん
WHOOOSH
HUFF HUFF
WE'VE GOT TROUBLE!
THE SIX O'CLOCK FLIGHT TO HONOLULU, HAWAII IS MISSING SOME PASSENGERS, SO WE CAN'T TAKE OFF! BUT I CAN'T FIND THEM ANYWHERE!
It's after six! What do we do?!
TO HAWAII?!
キラリ
GLINT
IF IT'S AFTER SIX AND THEY'RE NOT HERE, THAT MEANS THEY'VE CANCELED, RIGHT?
I'LL GO IN THEIR PLACE!
GENERAL?!
IF YOU WANT ME TO PAY, I WILL!
ドン
WHAM
G-GENERAL!

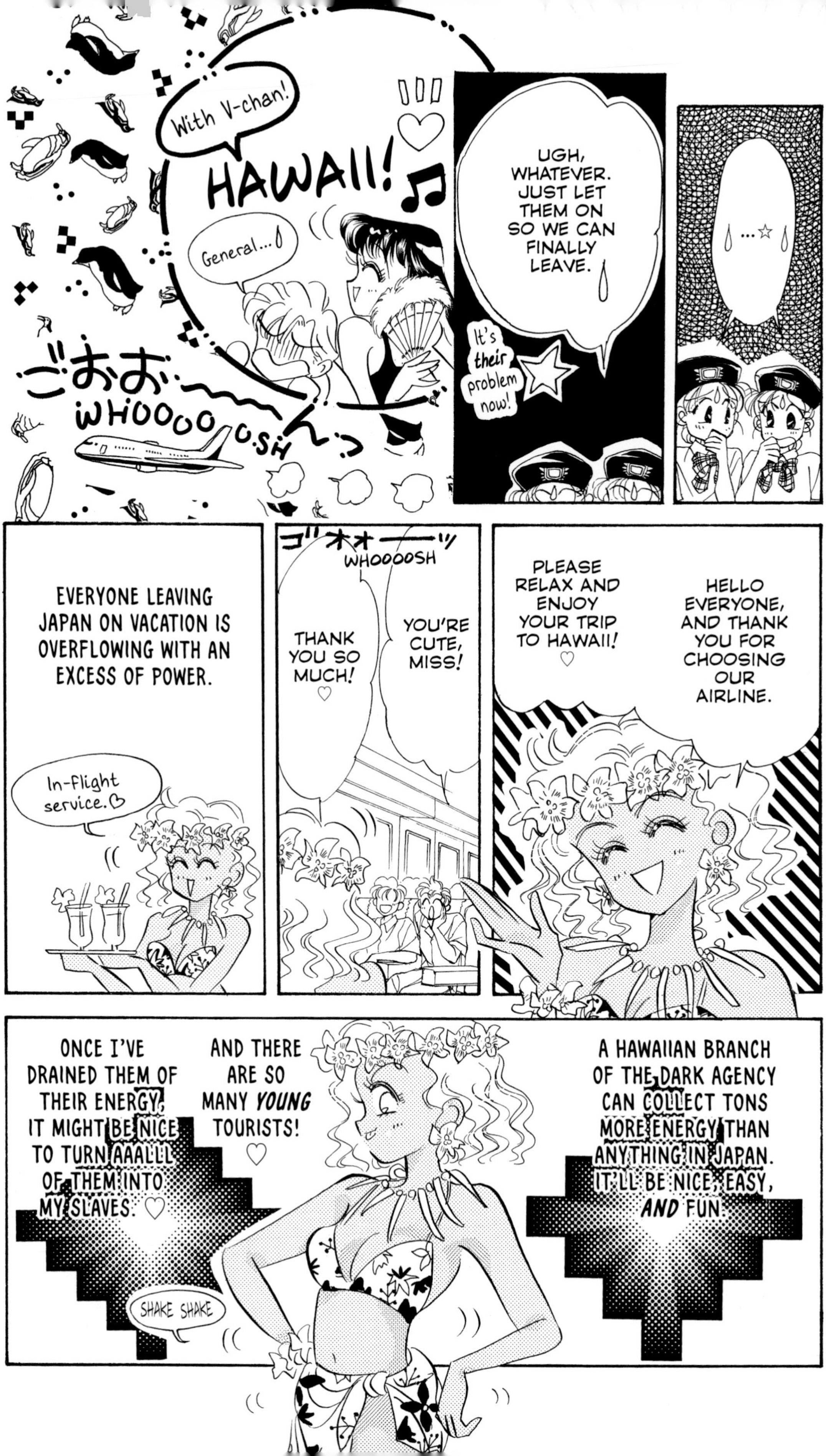

...☆
UGH, WHATEVER. JUST LET THEM ON SO WE CAN FINALLY LEAVE.
It's *their* problem now!
HAWAII!
With V-chan!
General...
ごおお～～ん
WHOOOOOSH
HELLO EVERYONE, AND THANK YOU FOR CHOOSING OUR AIRLINE.
PLEASE RELAX AND ENJOY YOUR TRIP TO HAWAII! ♡
ゴオオーーッ
WHOOOOSH
YOU'RE CUTE, MISS!
THANK YOU SO MUCH! ♡
EVERYONE LEAVING JAPAN ON VACATION IS OVERFLOWING WITH AN EXCESS OF POWER.
In-flight service.♡
A HAWAIIAN BRANCH OF THE DARK AGENCY CAN COLLECT TONS MORE ENERGY THAN ANYTHING IN JAPAN. IT'LL BE NICE, EASY, *AND* FUN.
AND THERE ARE SO MANY *YOUNG* TOURISTS! ♡
ONCE I'VE DRAINED THEM OF THEIR ENERGY, IT MIGHT BE NICE TO TURN AAALLL OF THEM INTO MY SLAVES. ♡
SHAKE SHAKE

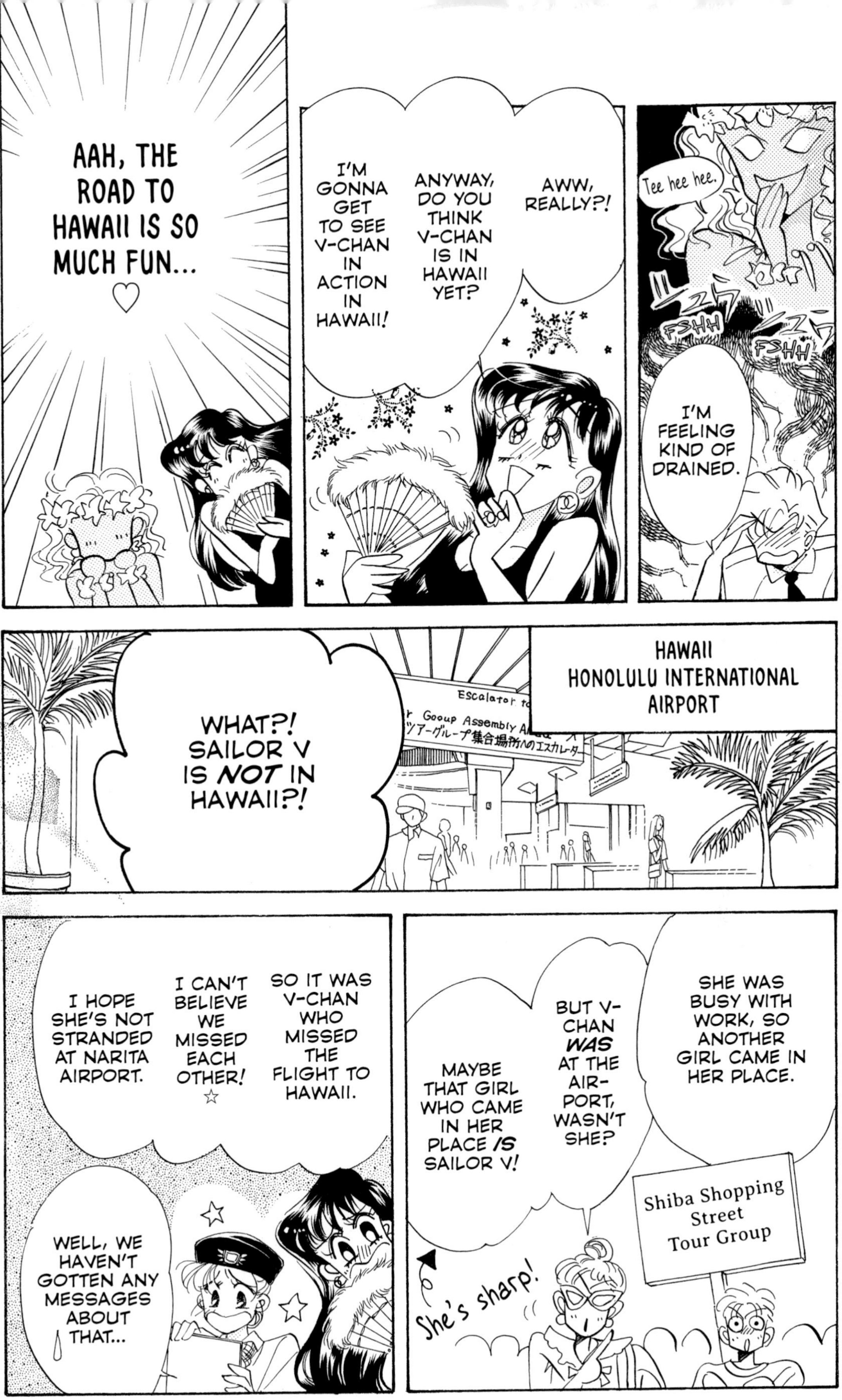

Tee hee hee.
FSHH
FSHH
I'M FEELING KIND OF DRAINED.
AWW, REALLY?!
ANYWAY, DO YOU THINK V-CHAN IS IN HAWAII YET?
I'M GONNA GET TO SEE V-CHAN IN ACTION IN HAWAII!
AAH, THE ROAD TO HAWAII IS SO MUCH FUN... ♡
HAWAII HONOLULU INTERNATIONAL AIRPORT
Escalator to
Gooup Assembly
ツアーグループ集合場所へのエスカレータ
WHAT?! SAILOR V IS *NOT* IN HAWAII?!
SHE WAS BUSY WITH WORK, SO ANOTHER GIRL CAME IN HER PLACE.
BUT V-CHAN *WAS* AT THE AIR-PORT, WASN'T SHE?
MAYBE THAT GIRL WHO CAME IN HER PLACE *IS* SAILOR V!
She's sharp!
Shiba Shopping Street Tour Group
SO IT WAS V-CHAN WHO MISSED THE FLIGHT TO HAWAII.
I CAN'T BELIEVE WE MISSED EACH OTHER! ☆
I HOPE SHE'S NOT STRANDED AT NARITA AIRPORT.
WELL, WE HAVEN'T GOTTEN ANY MESSAGES ABOUT THAT...

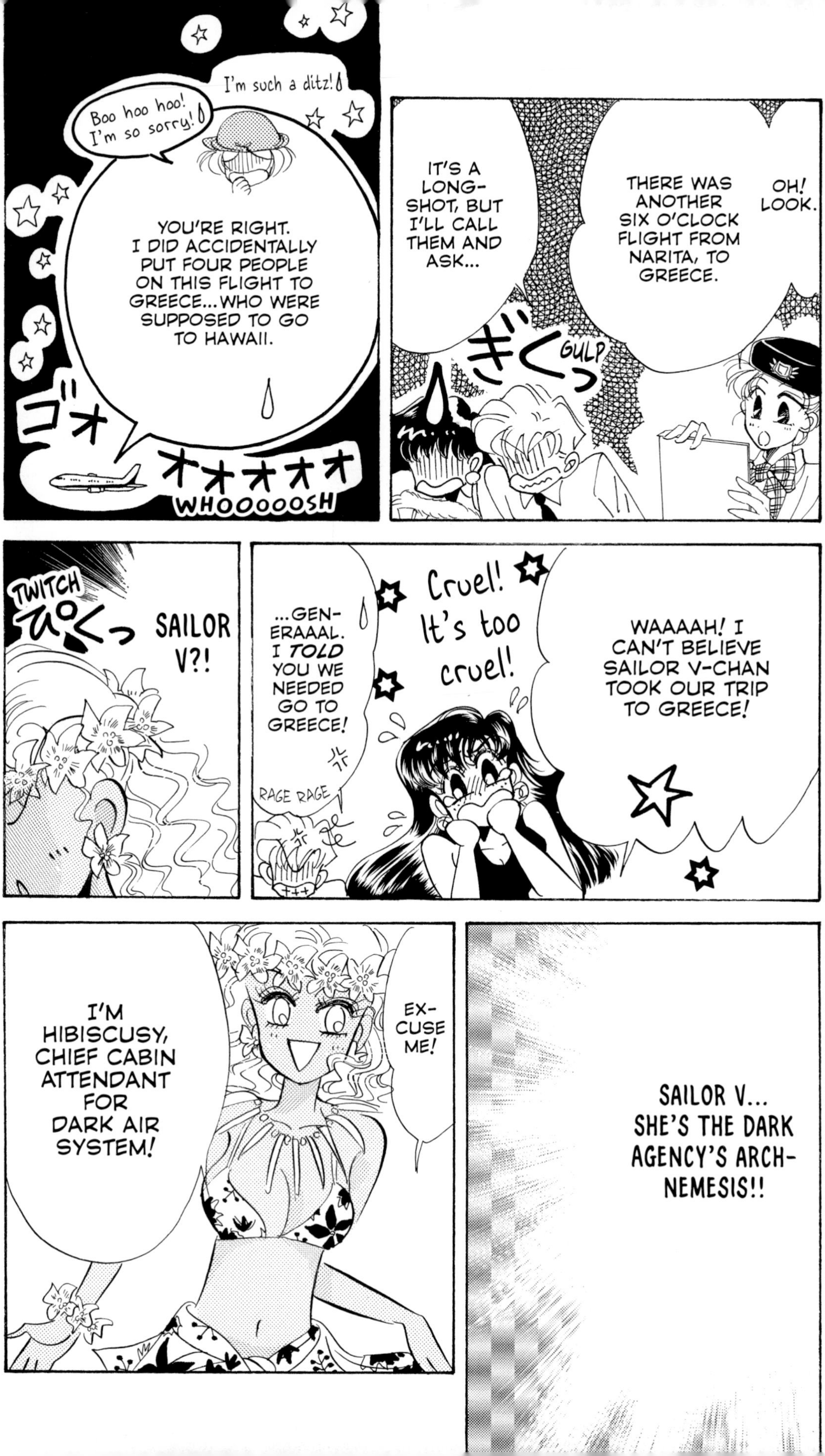
OH! LOOK.
THERE WAS ANOTHER SIX O'CLOCK FLIGHT FROM NARITA, TO GREECE.
IT'S A LONG-SHOT, BUT I'LL CALL THEM AND ASK...
ぎくっ GULP
I'm such a ditz!
Boo hoo hoo! I'm so sorry!
YOU'RE RIGHT. I DID ACCIDENTALLY PUT FOUR PEOPLE ON THIS FLIGHT TO GREECE...WHO WERE SUPPOSED TO GO TO HAWAII.
ゴオオオオオオ
WHOOOOOOSH
WAAAAH! I CAN'T BELIEVE SAILOR V-CHAN TOOK OUR TRIP TO GREECE!
Cruel! It's too cruel!
...GEN-ERAAAL. I *TOLD* YOU WE NEEDED GO TO GREECE!
RAGE RAGE
TWITCH ぴくっ
SAILOR V?!
SAILOR V... SHE'S THE DARK AGENCY'S ARCH-NEMESIS!!
EX-CUSE ME!
I'M HIBISCUSY, CHIEF CABIN ATTENDANT FOR DARK AIR SYSTEM!

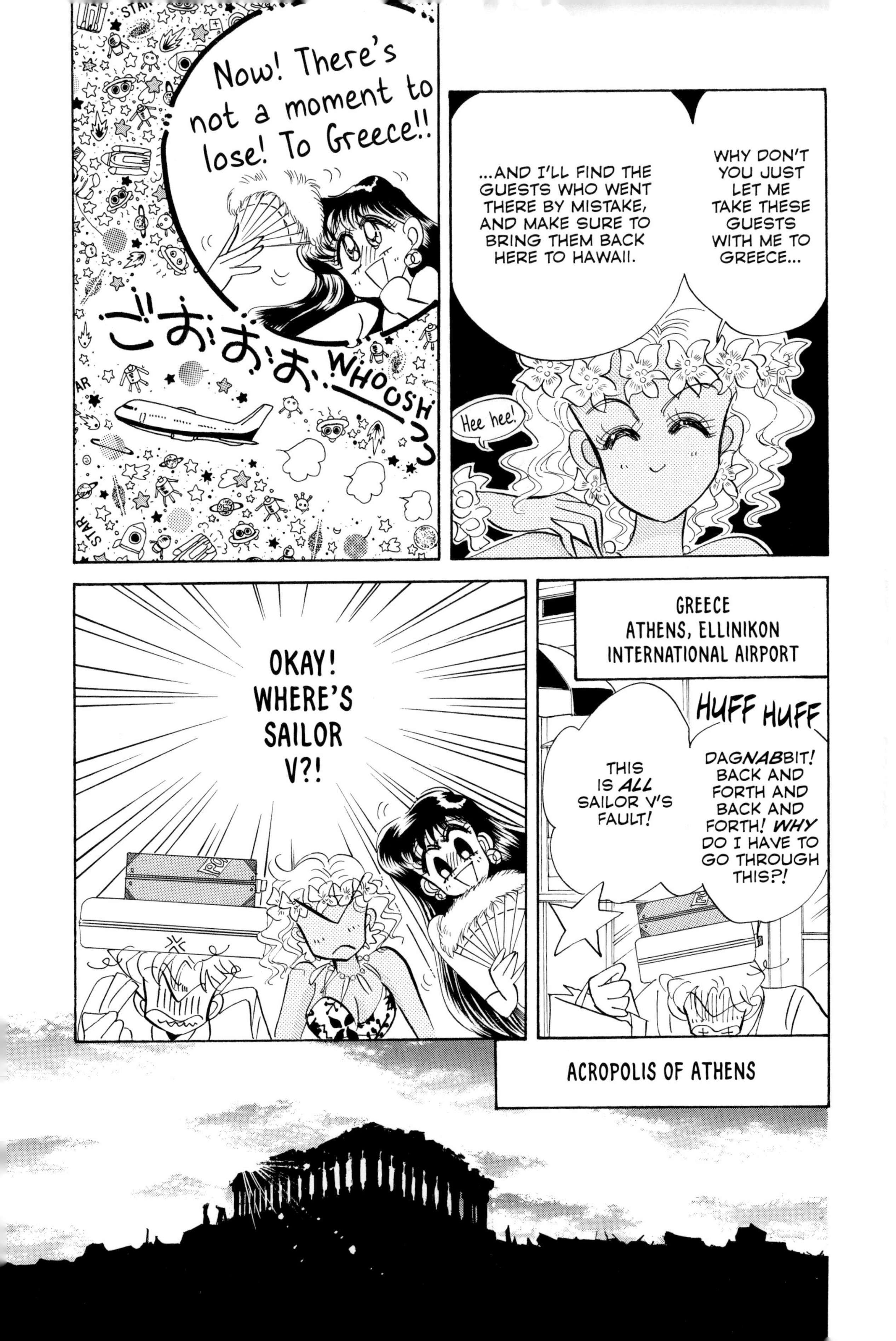
WHY DON'T YOU JUST LET ME TAKE THESE GUESTS WITH ME TO GREECE...
...AND I'LL FIND THE GUESTS WHO WENT THERE BY MISTAKE, AND MAKE SURE TO BRING THEM BACK HERE TO HAWAII.
Hee hee!
Now! There's not a moment to lose! To Greece!!
ごおおお
WHOOSH
GREECE ATHENS, ELLINIKON INTERNATIONAL AIRPORT
HUFF HUFF
DAGNABBIT! BACK AND FORTH AND BACK AND FORTH! WHY DO I HAVE TO GO THROUGH THIS?!
THIS IS ALL SAILOR V'S FAULT!
OKAY! WHERE'S SAILOR V?!
ACROPOLIS OF ATHENS

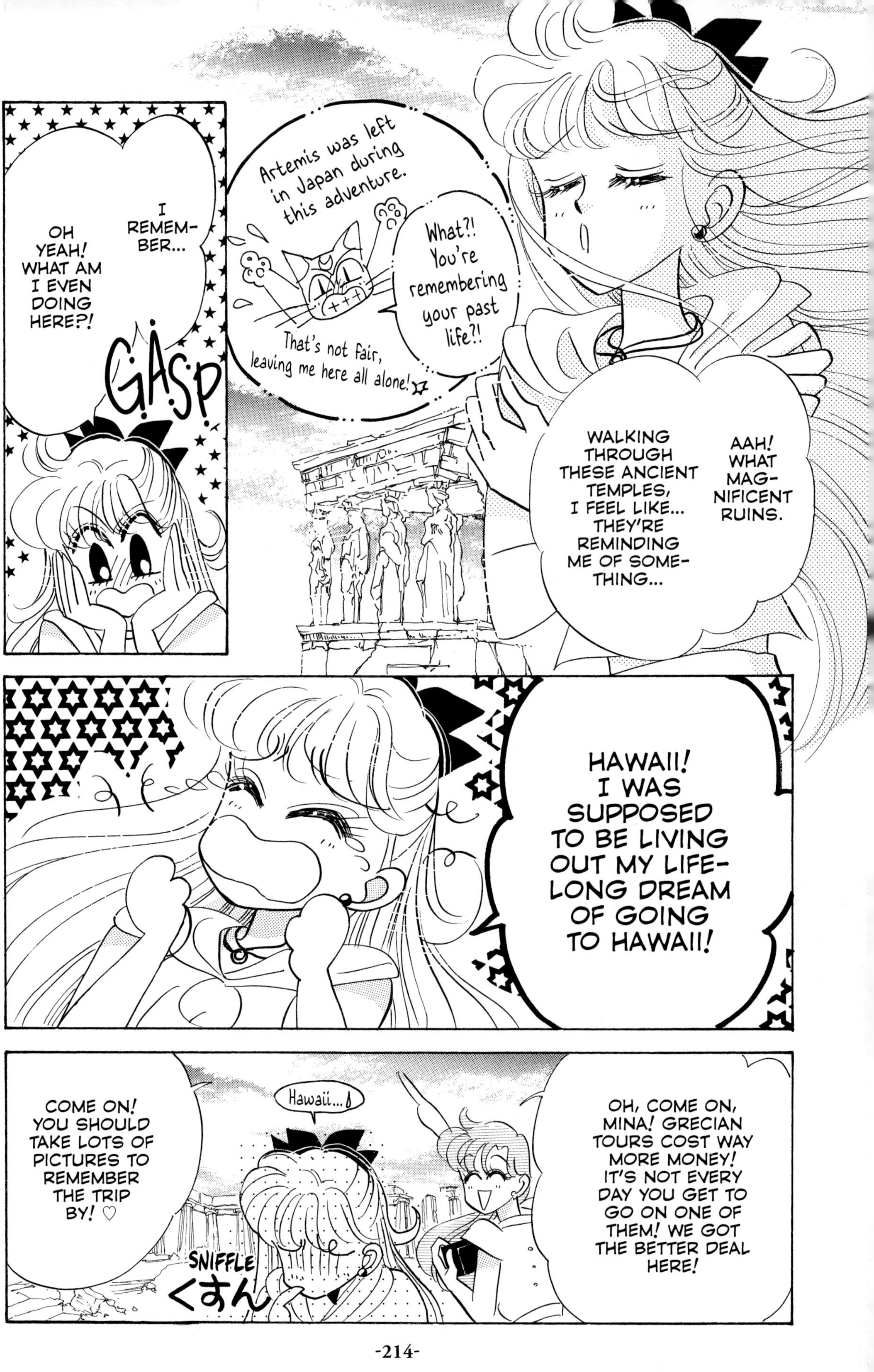
AAH! WHAT MAGNIFICENT RUINS.
WALKING THROUGH THESE ANCIENT TEMPLES, I FEEL LIKE... THEY'RE REMINDING ME OF SOMETHING...
Artemis was left in Japan during this adventure.
What?! You're remembering your past life?!
That's not fair, leaving me here all alone!
I REMEMBER...
OH YEAH! WHAT AM I EVEN DOING HERE?!
GASP
HAWAII! I WAS SUPPOSED TO BE LIVING OUT MY LIFE-LONG DREAM OF GOING TO HAWAII!
OH, COME ON, MINA! GRECIAN TOURS COST WAY MORE MONEY! IT'S NOT EVERY DAY YOU GET TO GO ON ONE OF THEM! WE GOT THE BETTER DEAL HERE!
Hawaii...
SNIFFLE
くすん
COME ON! YOU SHOULD TAKE LOTS OF PICTURES TO REMEMBER THE TRIP BY! ♡

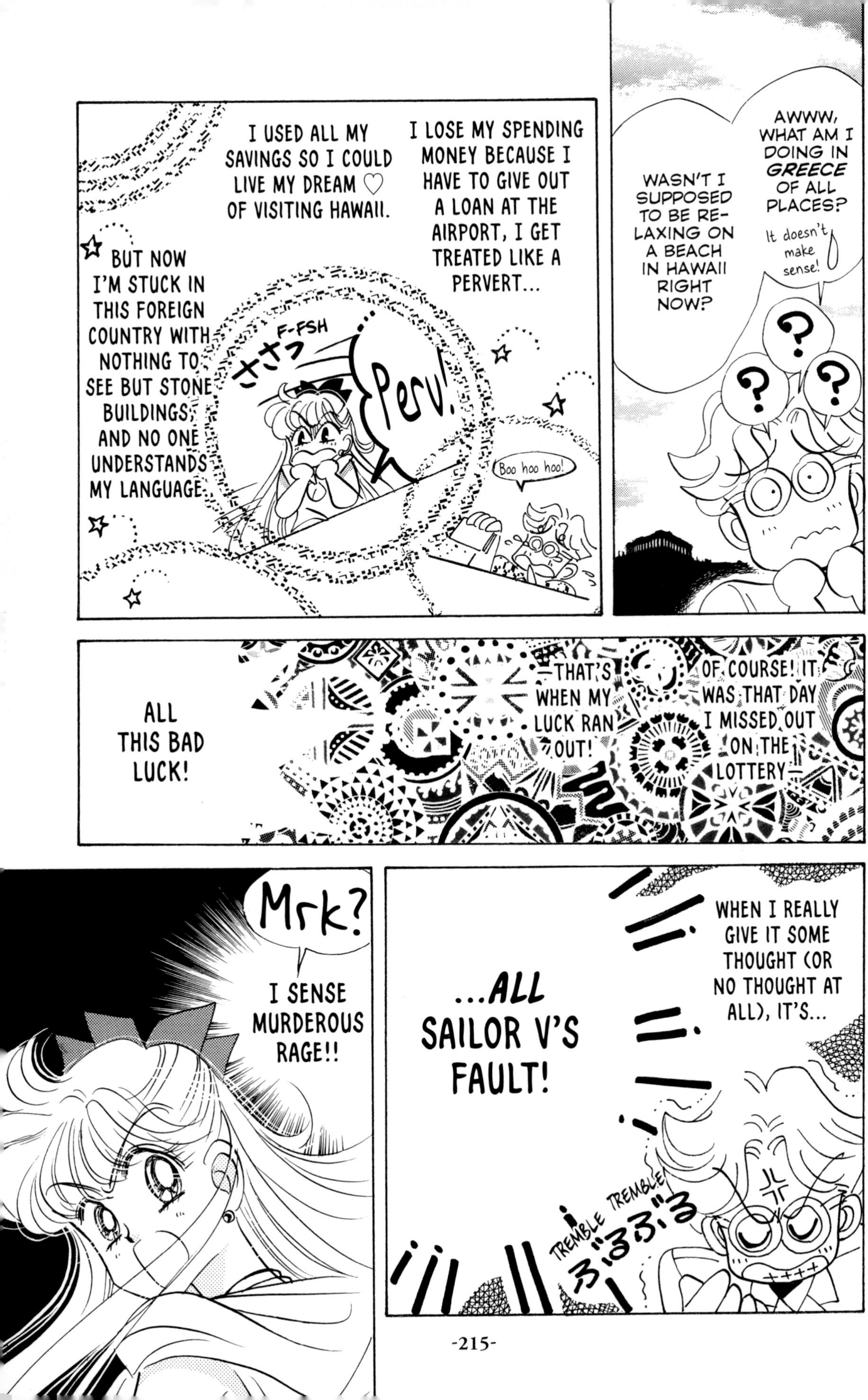
AWWW, WHAT AM I DOING IN GREECE OF ALL PLACES?
It doesn't make sense!
WASN'T I SUPPOSED TO BE RE-LAXING ON A BEACH IN HAWAII RIGHT NOW?
?
?
?
I LOSE MY SPENDING MONEY BECAUSE I HAVE TO GIVE OUT A LOAN AT THE AIRPORT, I GET TREATED LIKE A PERVERT...
I USED ALL MY SAVINGS SO I COULD LIVE MY DREAM ♡ OF VISITING HAWAII.
Perv!
F-FSH
ささっ
BUT NOW I'M STUCK IN THIS FOREIGN COUNTRY WITH NOTHING TO SEE BUT STONE BUILDINGS, AND NO ONE UNDERSTANDS MY LANGUAGE.
Boo hoo hoo!
OF COURSE! IT WAS THAT DAY I MISSED OUT ON THE LOTTERY.
THAT'S WHEN MY LUCK RAN OUT!
ALL THIS BAD LUCK!
WHEN I REALLY GIVE IT SOME THOUGHT (OR NO THOUGHT AT ALL), IT'S...
...ALL SAILOR V'S FAULT!
TREMBLE TREMBLE
ぶるぶる
Mrk?
I SENSE MURDEROUS RAGE!!

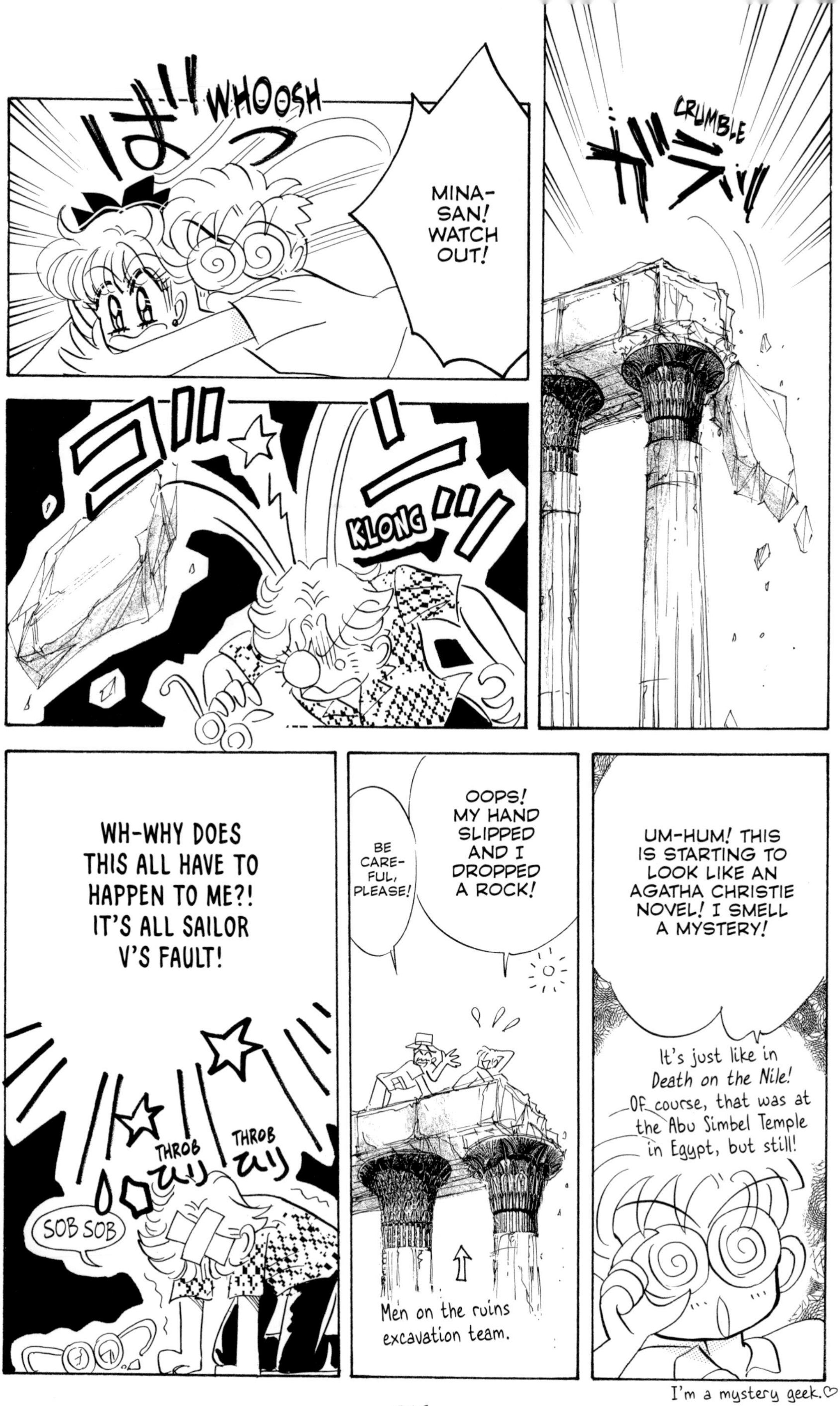
CRUMBLE
WHOOSH
MINA-SAN! WATCH OUT!
KLONG
UM-HUM! THIS IS STARTING TO LOOK LIKE AN AGATHA CHRISTIE NOVEL! I SMELL A MYSTERY!
It's just like in *Death on the Nile!* Of course, that was at the Abu Simbel Temple in Egypt, but still!
OOPS! MY HAND SLIPPED AND I DROPPED A ROCK!
BE CARE-FUL, PLEASE!
Men on the ruins excavation team.
WH-WHY DOES THIS ALL HAVE TO HAPPEN TO ME?! IT'S ALL SAILOR V'S FAULT!
THROB
THROB
SOB SOB

I'm a mystery geek.♡

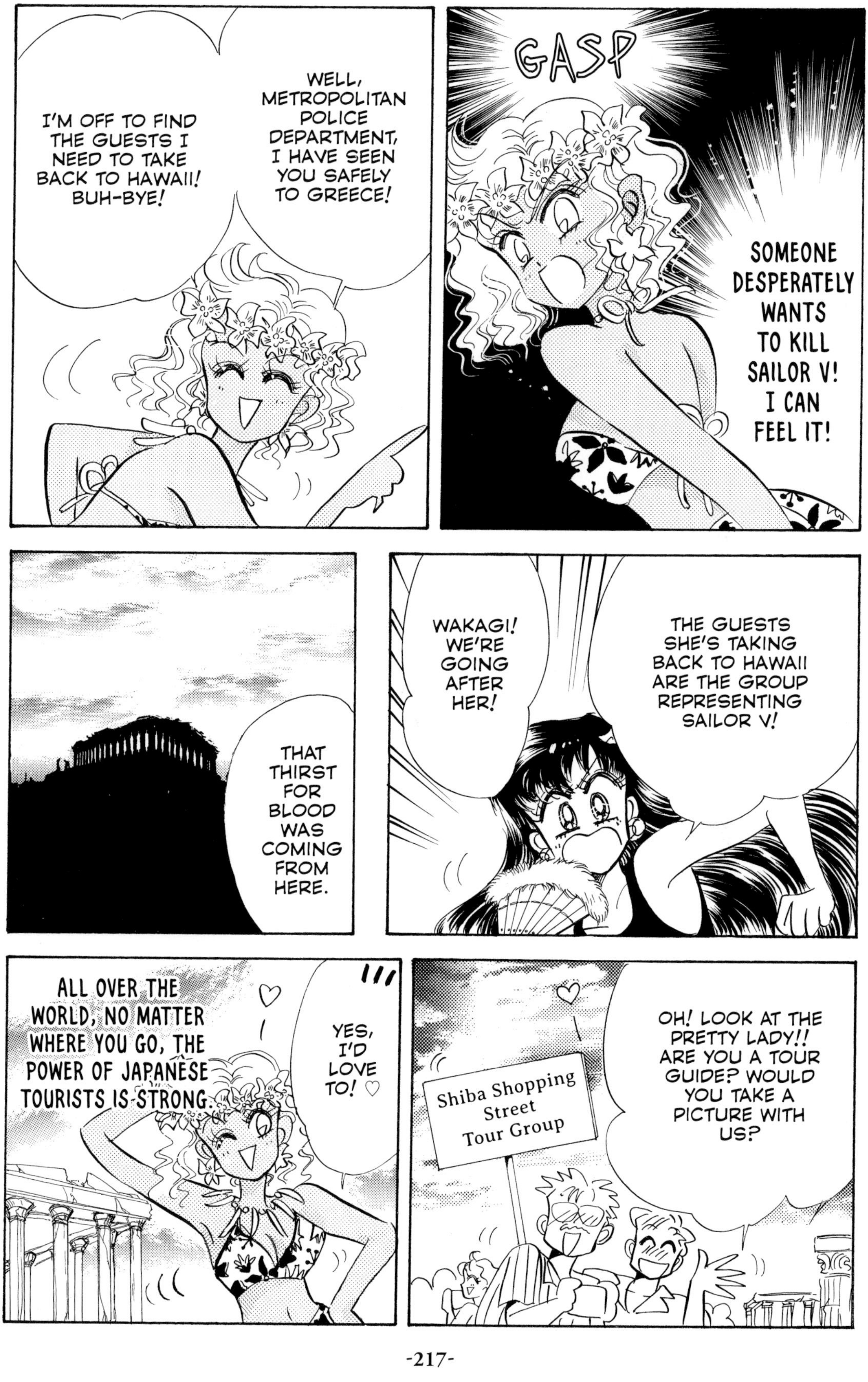
GASP
SOMEONE DESPERATELY WANTS TO KILL SAILOR V! I CAN FEEL IT!
WELL, METROPOLITAN POLICE DEPARTMENT, I HAVE SEEN YOU SAFELY TO GREECE!
I'M OFF TO FIND THE GUESTS I NEED TO TAKE BACK TO HAWAII! BUH-BYE!
THE GUESTS SHE'S TAKING BACK TO HAWAII ARE THE GROUP REPRESENTING SAILOR V!
WAKAGI! WE'RE GOING AFTER HER!
THAT THIRST FOR BLOOD WAS COMING FROM HERE.
OH! LOOK AT THE PRETTY LADY!! ARE YOU A TOUR GUIDE? WOULD YOU TAKE A PICTURE WITH US?
Shiba Shopping Street Tour Group
YES, I'D LOVE TO! ♡
ALL OVER THE WORLD, NO MATTER WHERE YOU GO, THE POWER OF JAPANESE TOURISTS IS STRONG.

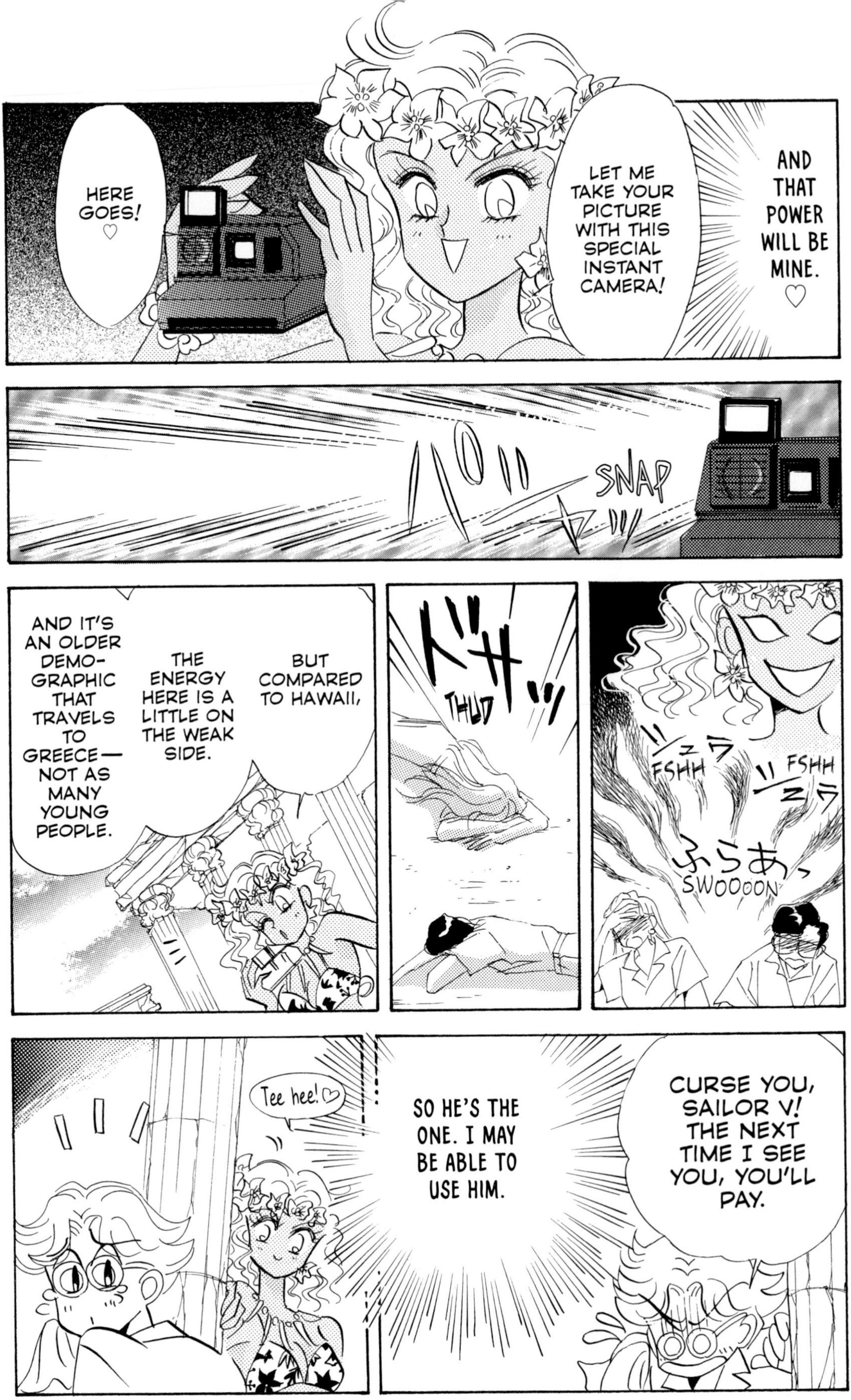
AND THAT POWER WILL BE MINE. ♡
LET ME TAKE YOUR PICTURE WITH THIS SPECIAL INSTANT CAMERA!
HERE GOES! ♡
SNAP
ドサッ
THUD
FSHH
FSHH
ふらあっ
SWOOOON
BUT COMPARED TO HAWAII,
THE ENERGY HERE IS A LITTLE ON THE WEAK SIDE.
AND IT'S AN OLDER DEMO-GRAPHIC THAT TRAVELS TO GREECE—NOT AS MANY YOUNG PEOPLE.
CURSE YOU, SAILOR V! THE NEXT TIME I SEE YOU, YOU'LL PAY.
SO HE'S THE ONE. I MAY BE ABLE TO USE HIM.
Tee hee! ♡

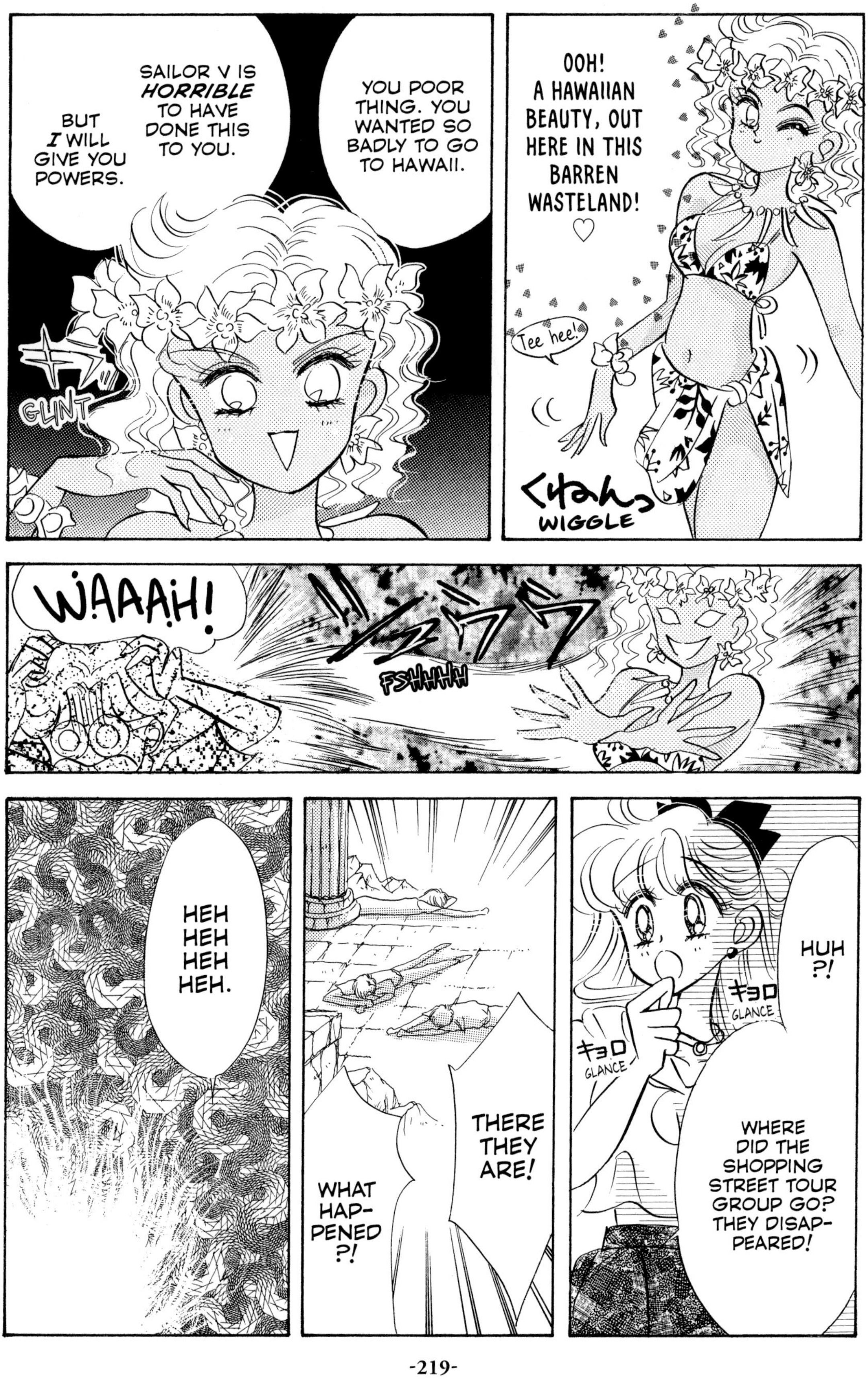

OOH! A HAWAIIAN BEAUTY, OUT HERE IN THIS BARREN WASTELAND! ♡
Tee hee!
くねんっ
WIGGLE
YOU POOR THING. YOU WANTED SO BADLY TO GO TO HAWAII.
SAILOR V IS HORRIBLE TO HAVE DONE THIS TO YOU.
BUT I WILL GIVE YOU POWERS.
GLINT
FSHHHH
WAAAH!
HUH?!
キョロ
GLANCE
キョロ
GLANCE
WHERE DID THE SHOPPING STREET TOUR GROUP GO? THEY DISAPPEARED!
THERE THEY ARE!
WHAT HAPPENED?!
HEH HEH HEH HEH.

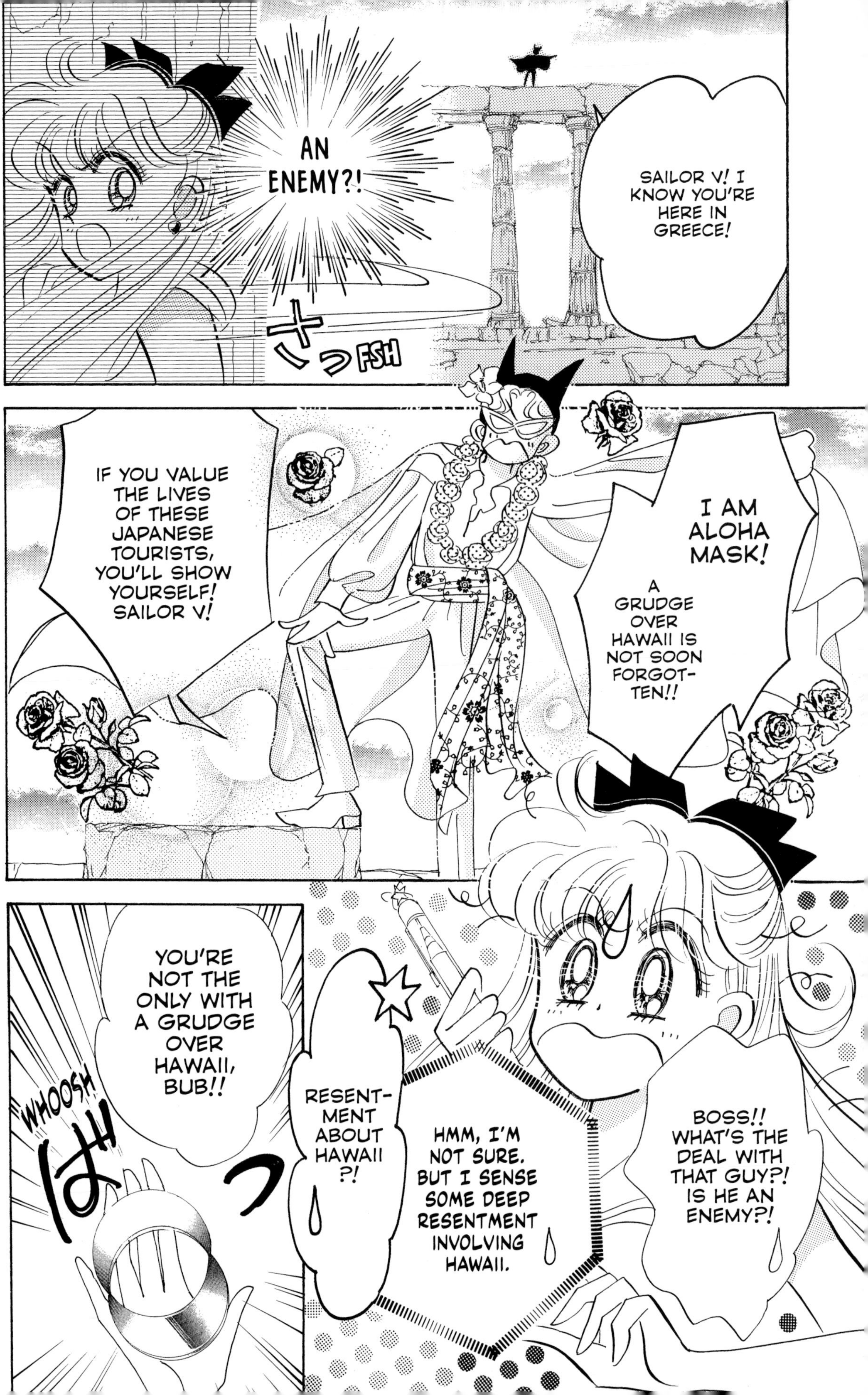
SAILOR V! I KNOW YOU'RE HERE IN GREECE!
AN ENEMY?!
さっ FSH
I AM ALOHA MASK!
A GRUDGE OVER HAWAII IS NOT SOON FORGOT-TEN!!
IF YOU VALUE THE LIVES OF THESE JAPANESE TOURISTS, YOU'LL SHOW YOURSELF! SAILOR V!
BOSS!! WHAT'S THE DEAL WITH THAT GUY?! IS HE AN ENEMY?!
HMM, I'M NOT SURE. BUT I SENSE SOME DEEP RESENTMENT INVOLVING HAWAII.
RESENT-MENT ABOUT HAWAII?!
YOU'RE NOT THE ONLY WITH A GRUDGE OVER HAWAII, BUB!!
WHOOSH
ばっ

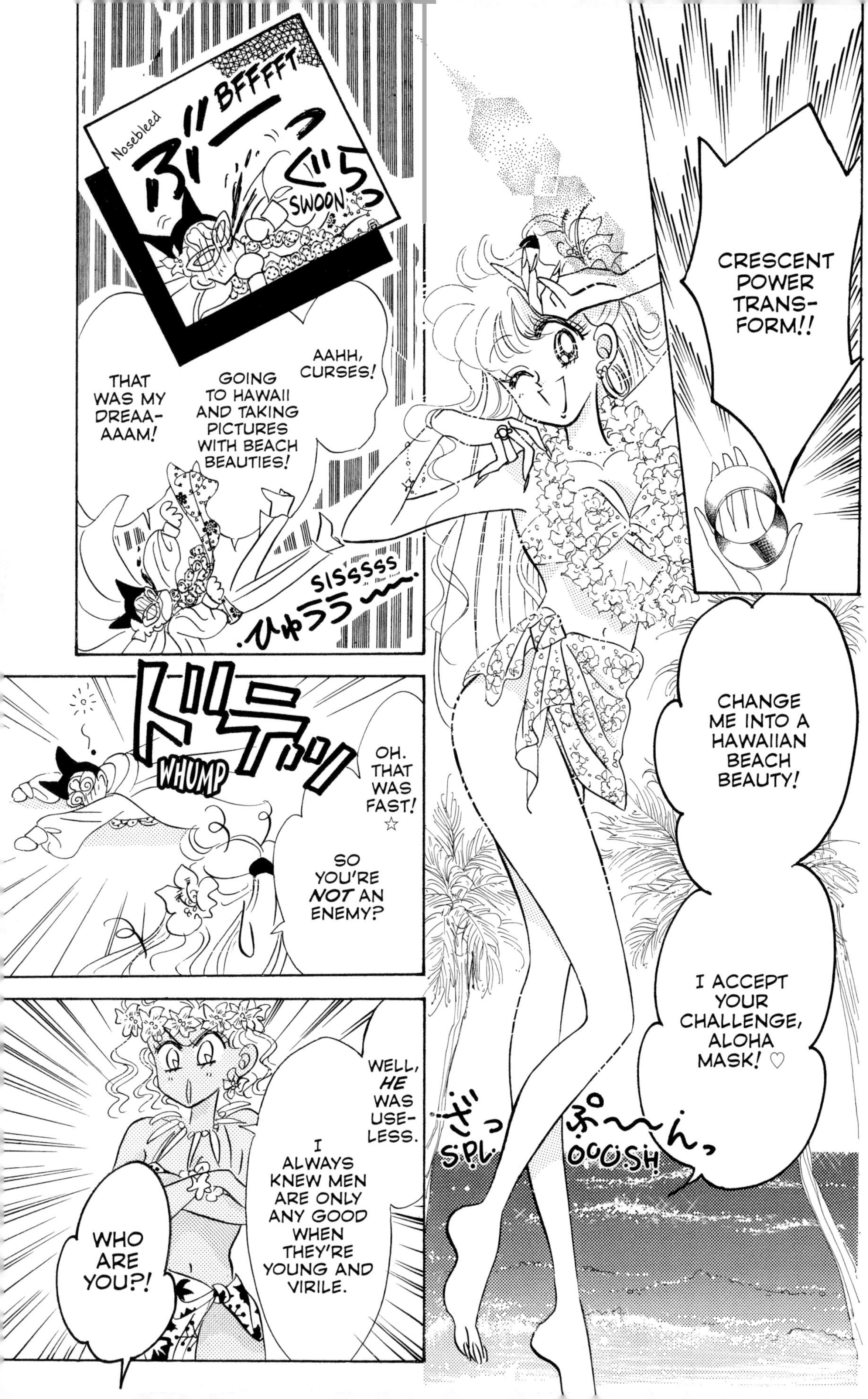
CRESCENT POWER TRANS-FORM!!
CHANGE ME INTO A HAWAIIAN BEACH BEAUTY!
I ACCEPT YOUR CHALLENGE, ALOHA MASK! ♡
ざっ SPL
ぷ〜〜んっ OOOSH
Nosebleed
ぶ——っ BFFFFT
ぐらっ SWOON
AAHH, CURSES!
GOING TO HAWAII AND TAKING PICTURES WITH BEACH BEAUTIES!
THAT WAS MY DREAA-AAAM!
ひゅううう〜 SISSSSS
ドテッ WHUMP
OH. THAT WAS FAST! ☆
SO YOU'RE *NOT* AN ENEMY?
WELL, *HE* WAS USE-LESS.
I ALWAYS KNEW MEN ARE ONLY ANY GOOD WHEN THEY'RE YOUNG AND VIRILE.
WHO ARE YOU?!

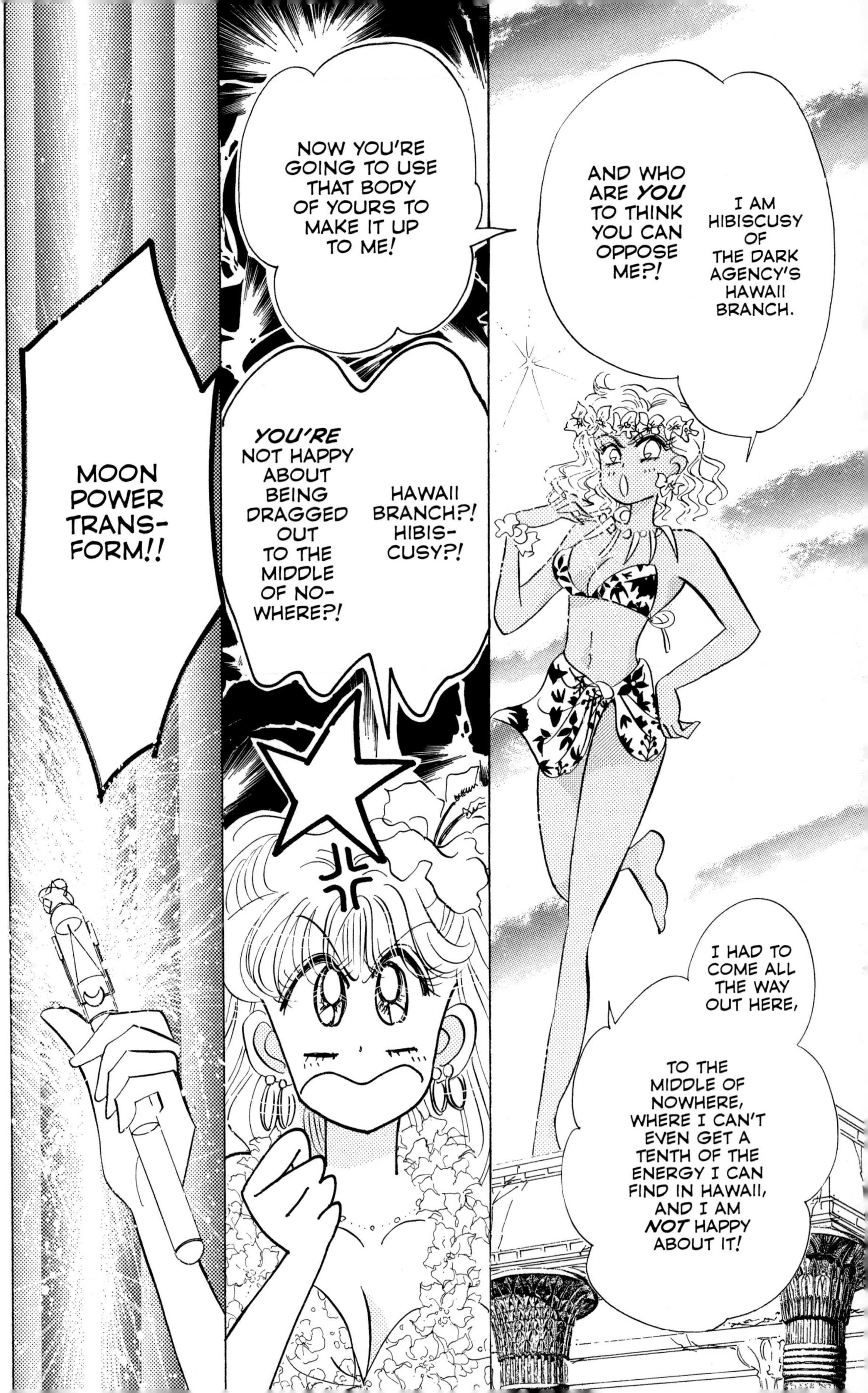
I AM HIBISCUSY OF THE DARK AGENCY'S HAWAII BRANCH.
AND WHO ARE *YOU* TO THINK YOU CAN OPPOSE ME?!
I HAD TO COME ALL THE WAY OUT HERE,
TO THE MIDDLE OF NOWHERE, WHERE I CAN'T EVEN GET A TENTH OF THE ENERGY I CAN FIND IN HAWAII, AND I AM *NOT* HAPPY ABOUT IT!
NOW YOU'RE GOING TO USE THAT BODY OF YOURS TO MAKE IT UP TO ME!
HAWAII BRANCH?! HIBISCUSY?!
YOU'RE NOT HAPPY ABOUT BEING DRAGGED OUT TO THE MIDDLE OF NOWHERE?!
MOON POWER TRANSFORM!!

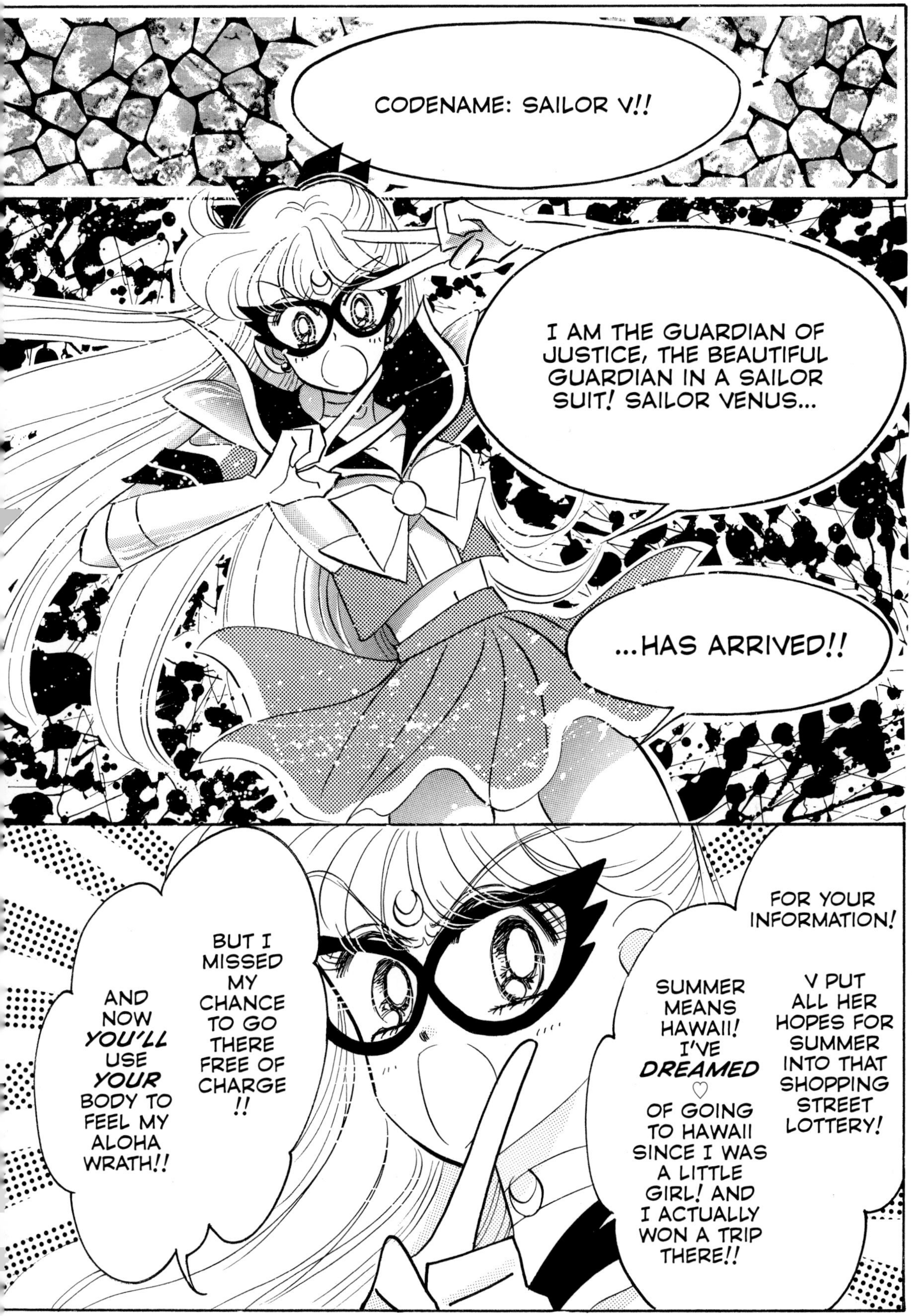
CODENAME: SAILOR V!!
I AM THE GUARDIAN OF JUSTICE, THE BEAUTIFUL GUARDIAN IN A SAILOR SUIT! SAILOR VENUS...
...HAS ARRIVED!!
FOR YOUR INFORMATION!
V PUT ALL HER HOPES FOR SUMMER INTO THAT SHOPPING STREET LOTTERY!
SUMMER MEANS HAWAII! I'VE DREAMED ♡ OF GOING TO HAWAII SINCE I WAS A LITTLE GIRL! AND I ACTUALLY WON A TRIP THERE!!
BUT I MISSED MY CHANCE TO GO THERE FREE OF CHARGE!!
AND NOW YOU'LL USE YOUR BODY TO FEEL MY ALOHA WRATH!!

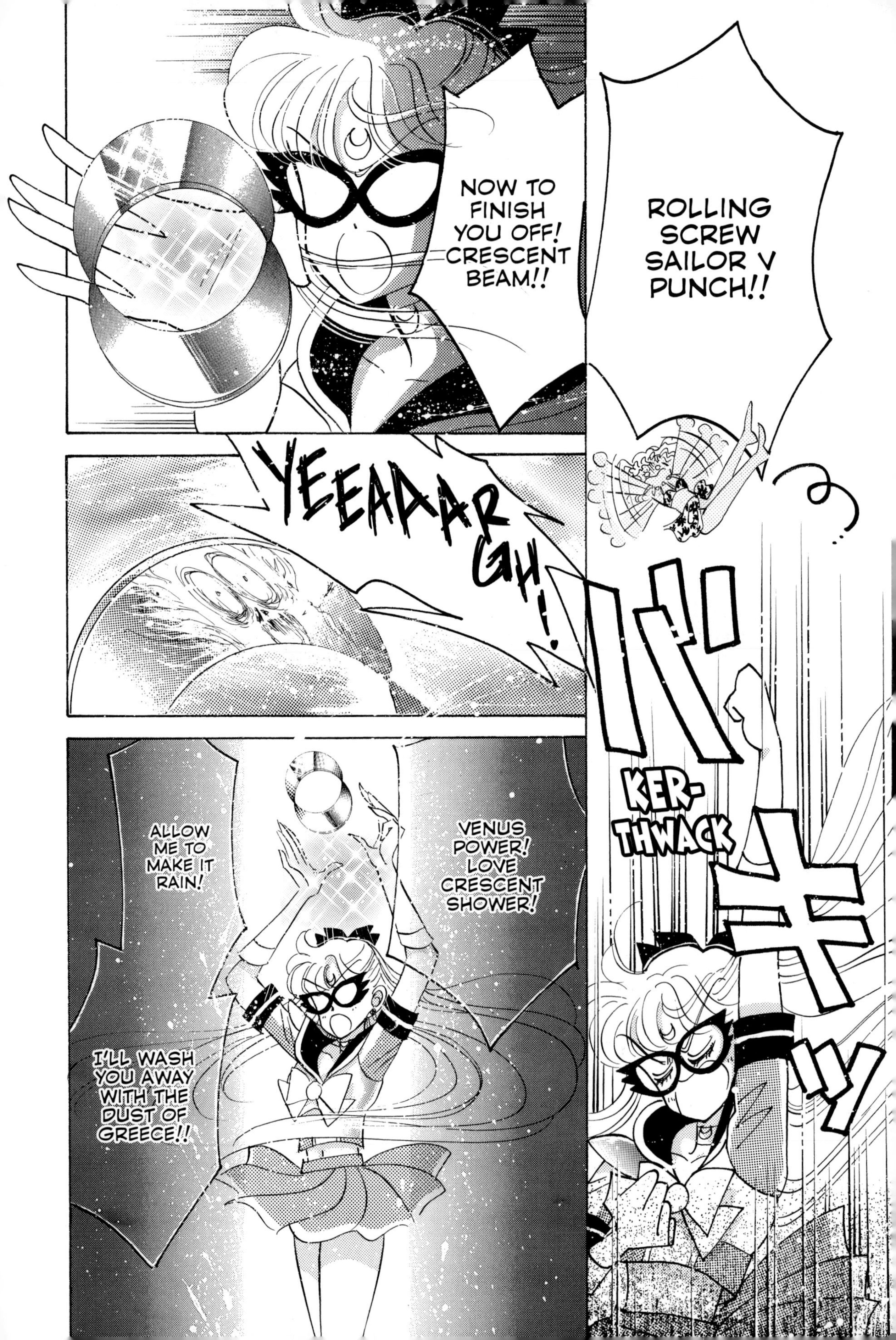
ROLLING SCREW SAILOR V PUNCH!!
バキッ
KER-THWACK
NOW TO FINISH YOU OFF! CRESCENT BEAM!!
YEEAAARGH!!
VENUS POWER! LOVE CRESCENT SHOWER!
ALLOW ME TO MAKE IT RAIN!
I'LL WASH YOU AWAY WITH THE DUST OF GREECE!!

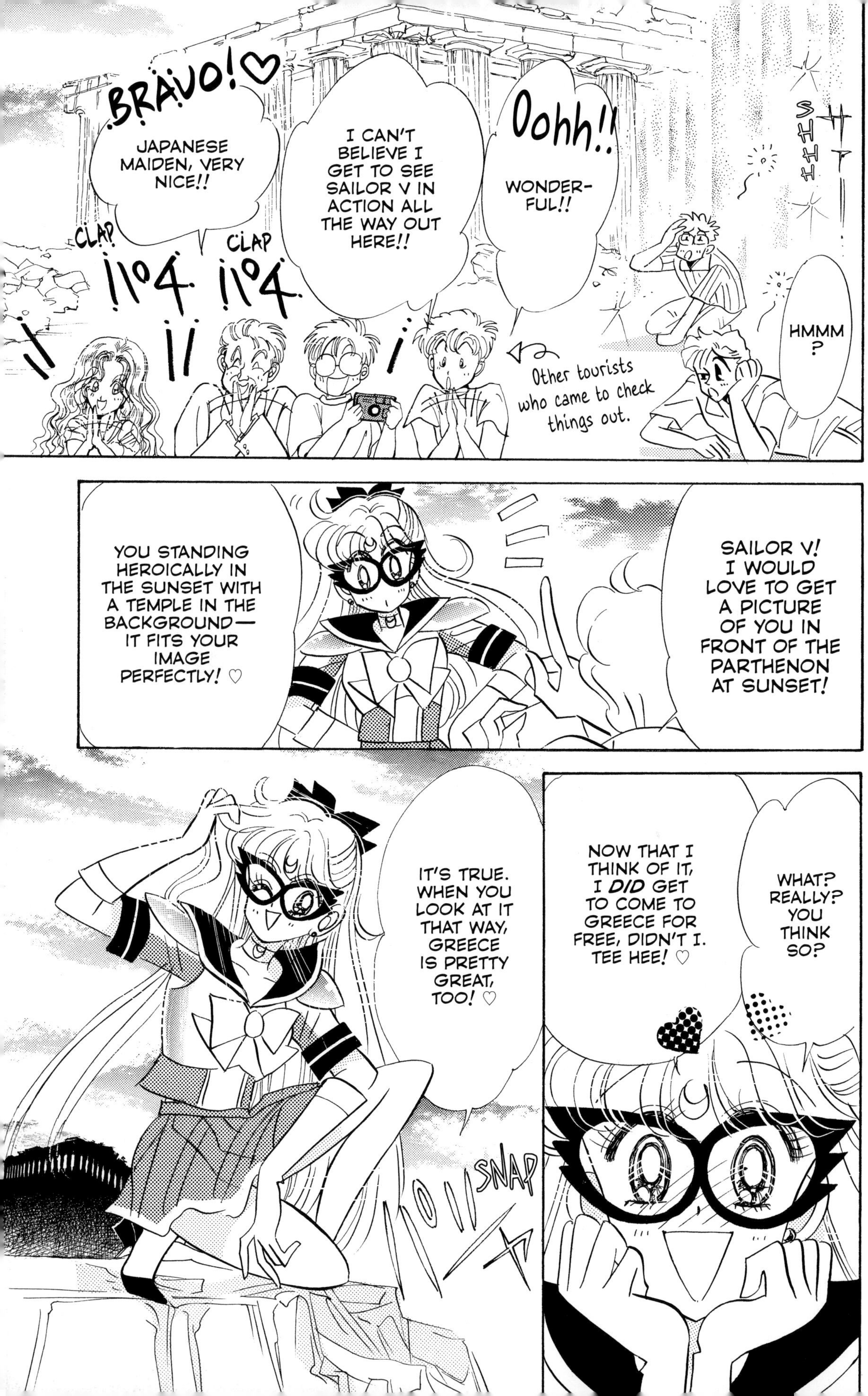
SHHH
HMMM?
Oohh!! WONDERFUL!!
I CAN'T BELIEVE I GET TO SEE SAILOR V IN ACTION ALL THE WAY OUT HERE!!
BRAVO! JAPANESE MAIDEN, VERY NICE!!
CLAP
CLAP
Other tourists who came to check things out.
SAILOR V! I WOULD LOVE TO GET A PICTURE OF YOU IN FRONT OF THE PARTHENON AT SUNSET!
YOU STANDING HEROICALLY IN THE SUNSET WITH A TEMPLE IN THE BACKGROUND— IT FITS YOUR IMAGE PERFECTLY! ♡
WHAT? REALLY? YOU THINK SO?
NOW THAT I THINK OF IT, I ***DID*** GET TO COME TO GREECE FOR FREE, DIDN'T I. TEE HEE! ♡
IT'S TRUE. WHEN YOU LOOK AT IT THAT WAY, GREECE IS PRETTY GREAT, TOO! ♡
SNAP

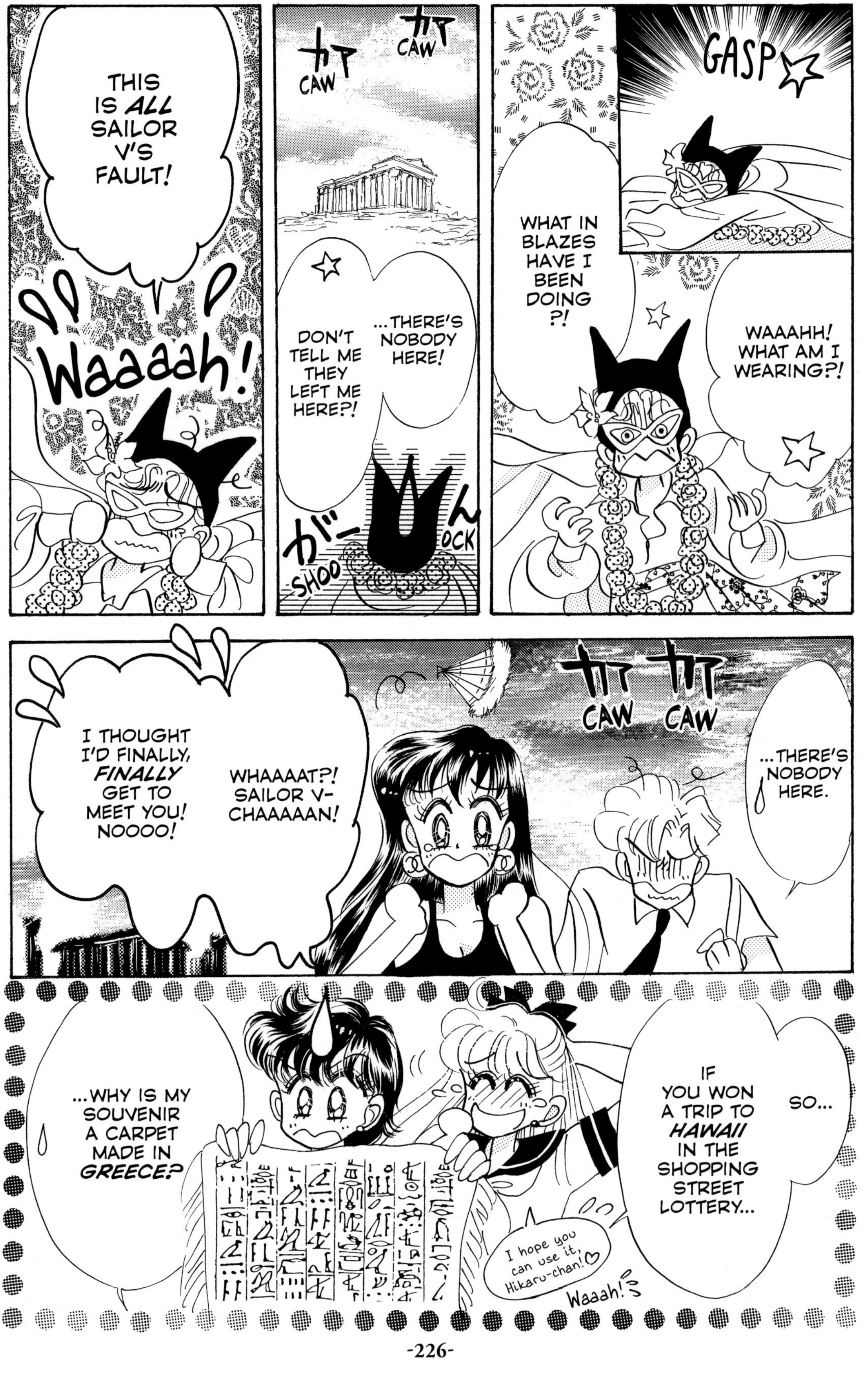
GASP
WAAAHH! WHAT AM I WEARING?!
WHAT IN BLAZES HAVE I BEEN DOING?!
CAW
CAW
...THERE'S NOBODY HERE!
DON'T TELL ME THEY LEFT ME HERE?!
SHOO
OCK
THIS IS ALL SAILOR V'S FAULT!
Waaaah!
CAW CAW
...THERE'S NOBODY HERE.
WHAAAAT?! SAILOR V-CHAAAAAN!
I THOUGHT I'D FINALLY, FINALLY GET TO MEET YOU! NOOOO!
SO...
IF YOU WON A TRIP TO HAWAII IN THE SHOPPING STREET LOTTERY...
I hope you can use it, Hikaru-chan! ♡
Waaah!
...WHY IS MY SOUVENIR A CARPET MADE IN GREECE?

Codename
Sailor V

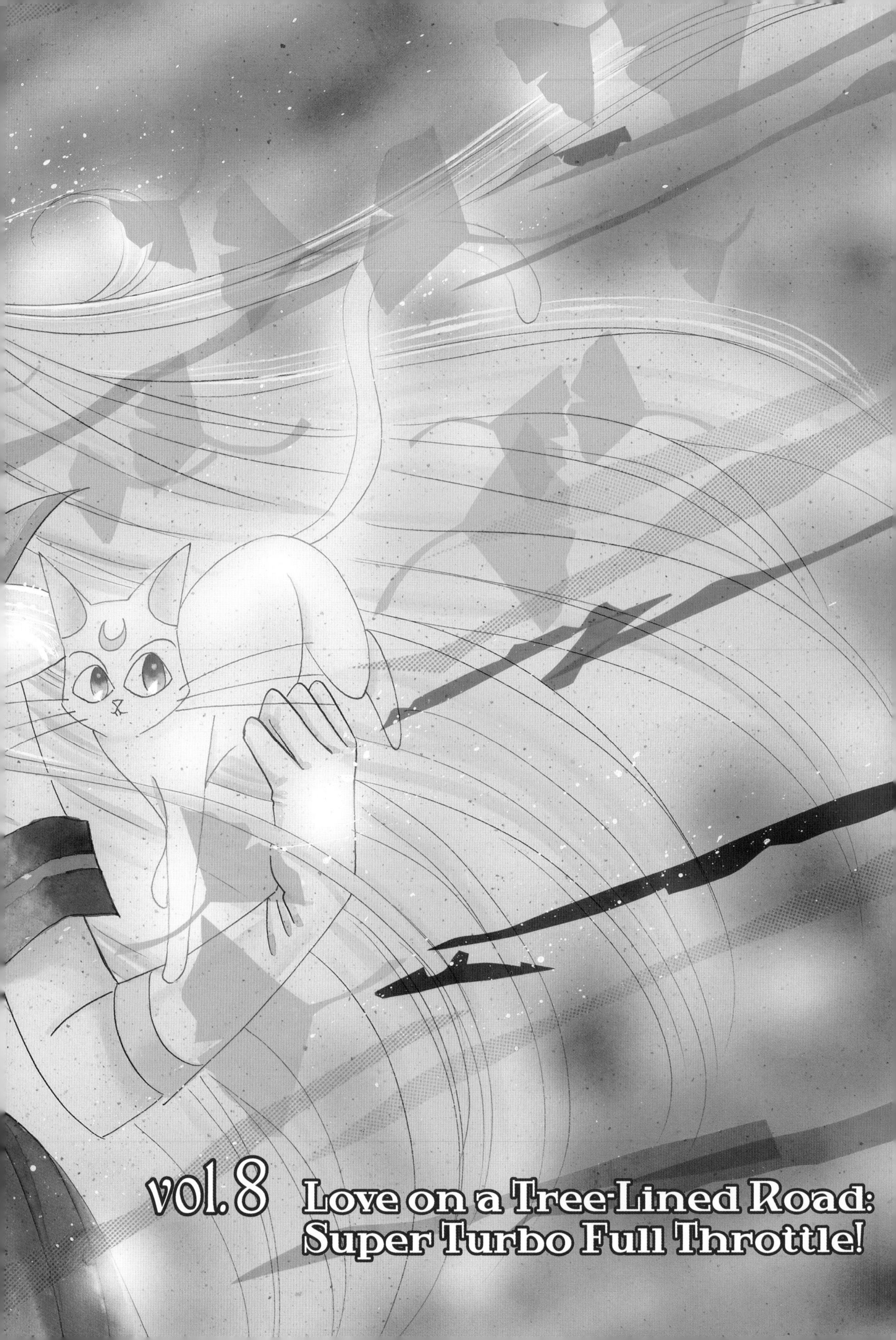

vol. 8 Love on a Tree-Lined Road: Super Turbo Full Throttle!

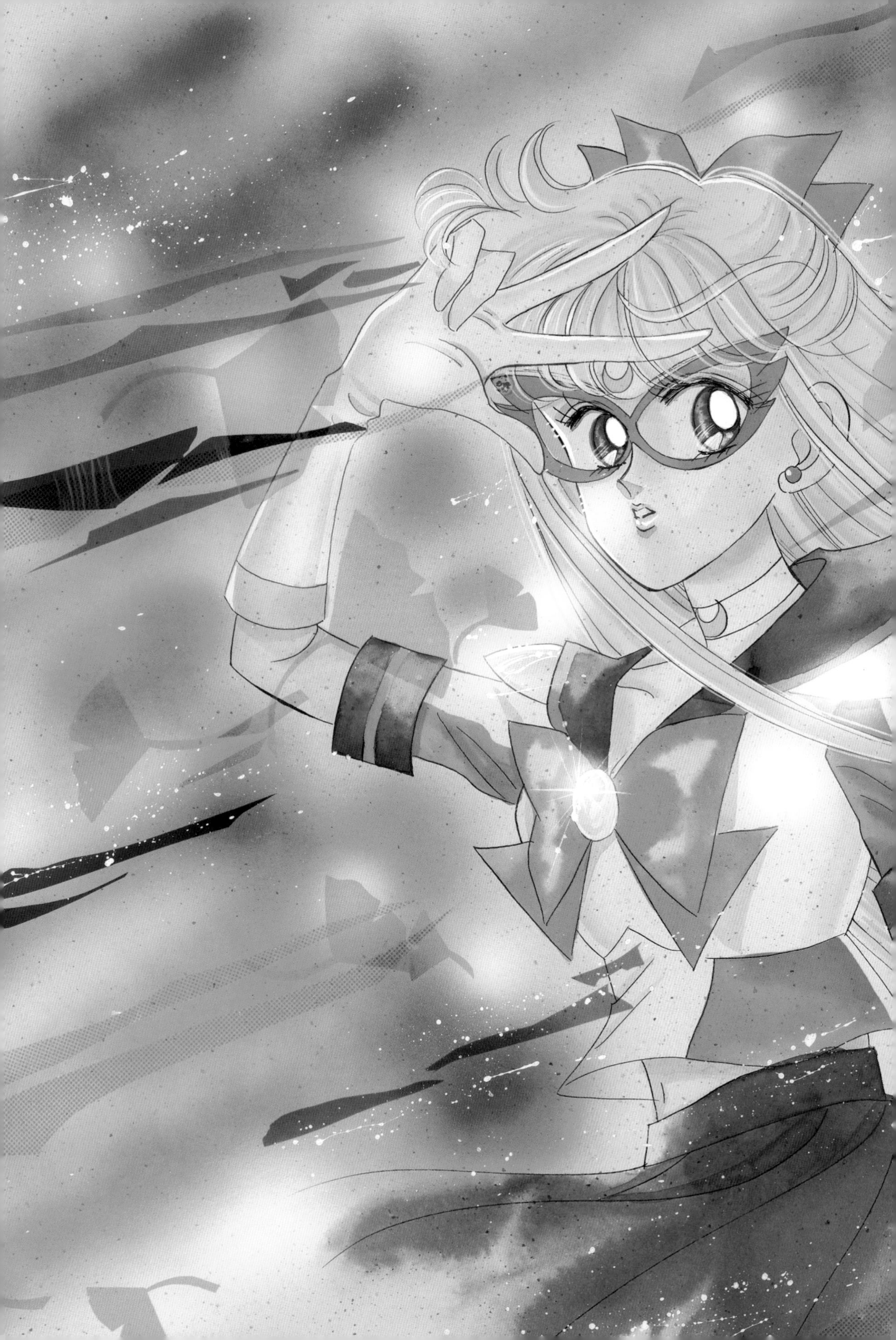

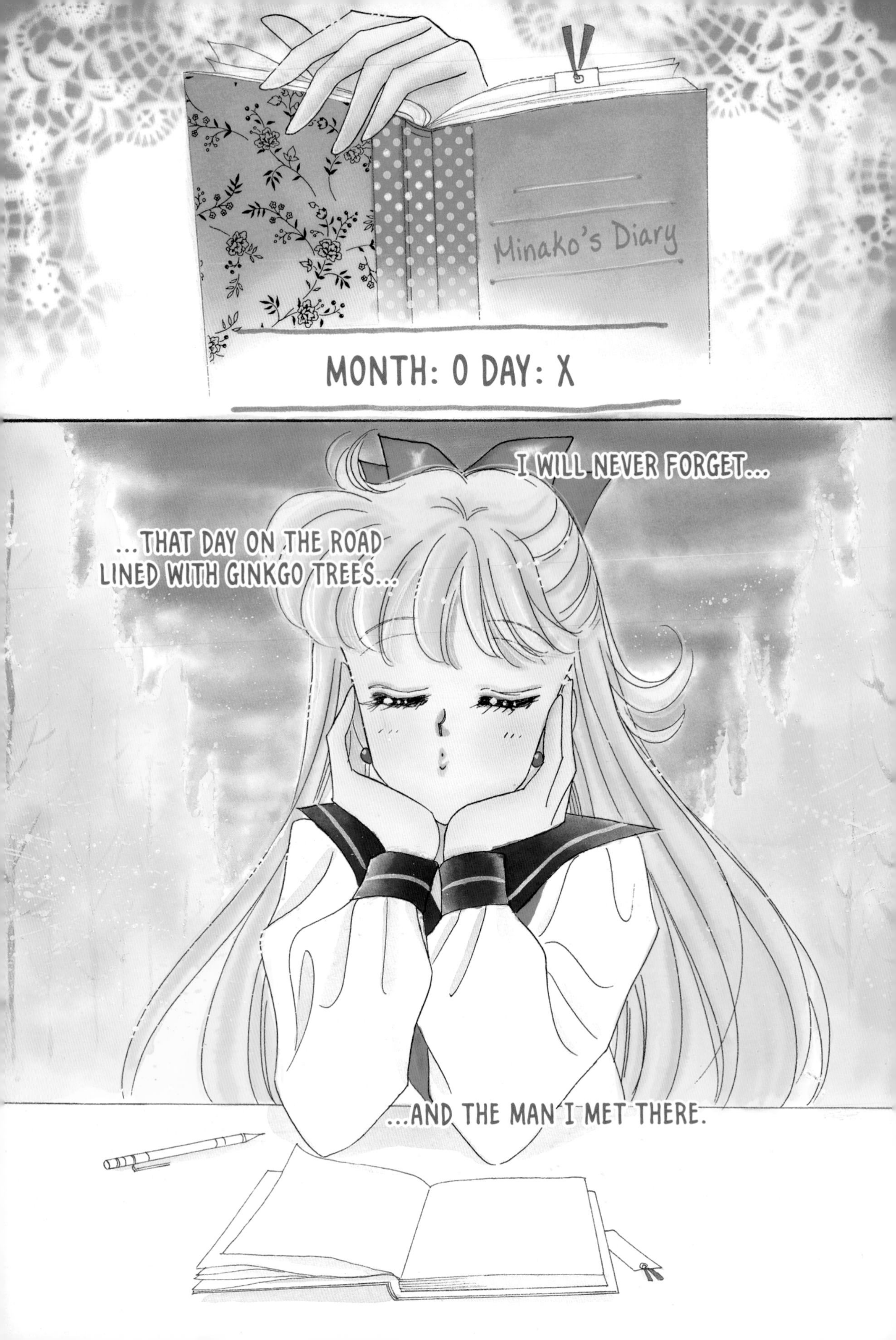
Minako's Diary
MONTH: 0 DAY: X
I WILL NEVER FORGET...
...THAT DAY ON THE ROAD LINED WITH GINKGO TREES...
...AND THE MAN I MET THERE.

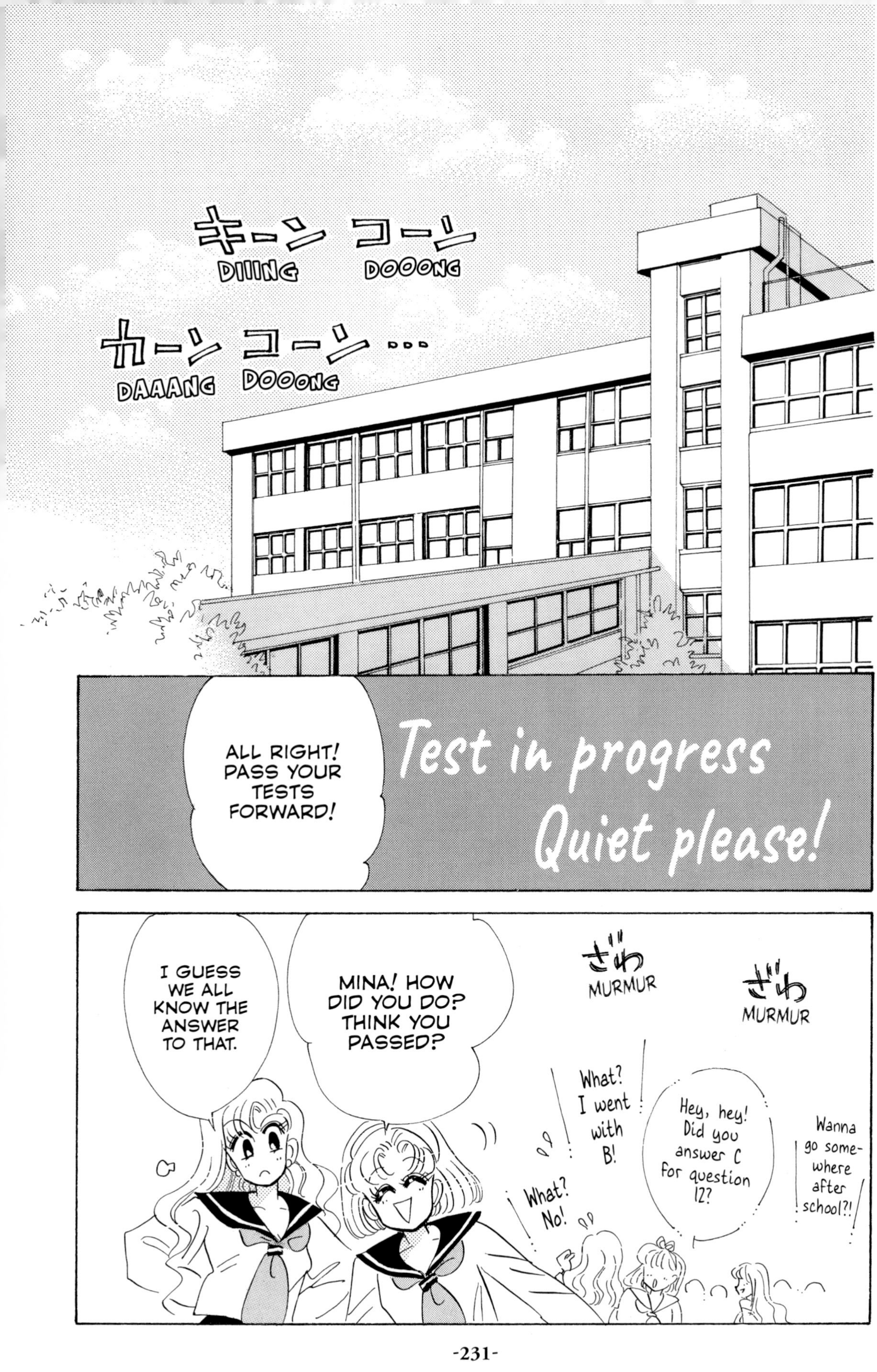
キーン コーン
DIIING DOOONG
カーン コーン…
DAAANG DOOONG
Test in progress Quiet please!
ALL RIGHT! PASS YOUR TESTS FORWARD!
ざわ
MURMUR
ざわ
MURMUR
Wanna go some-where after school?!
Hey, hey! Did you answer C for question 12?
What? I went with B!
What? No!
MINA! HOW DID YOU DO? THINK YOU PASSED?
I GUESS WE ALL KNOW THE ANSWER TO THAT.

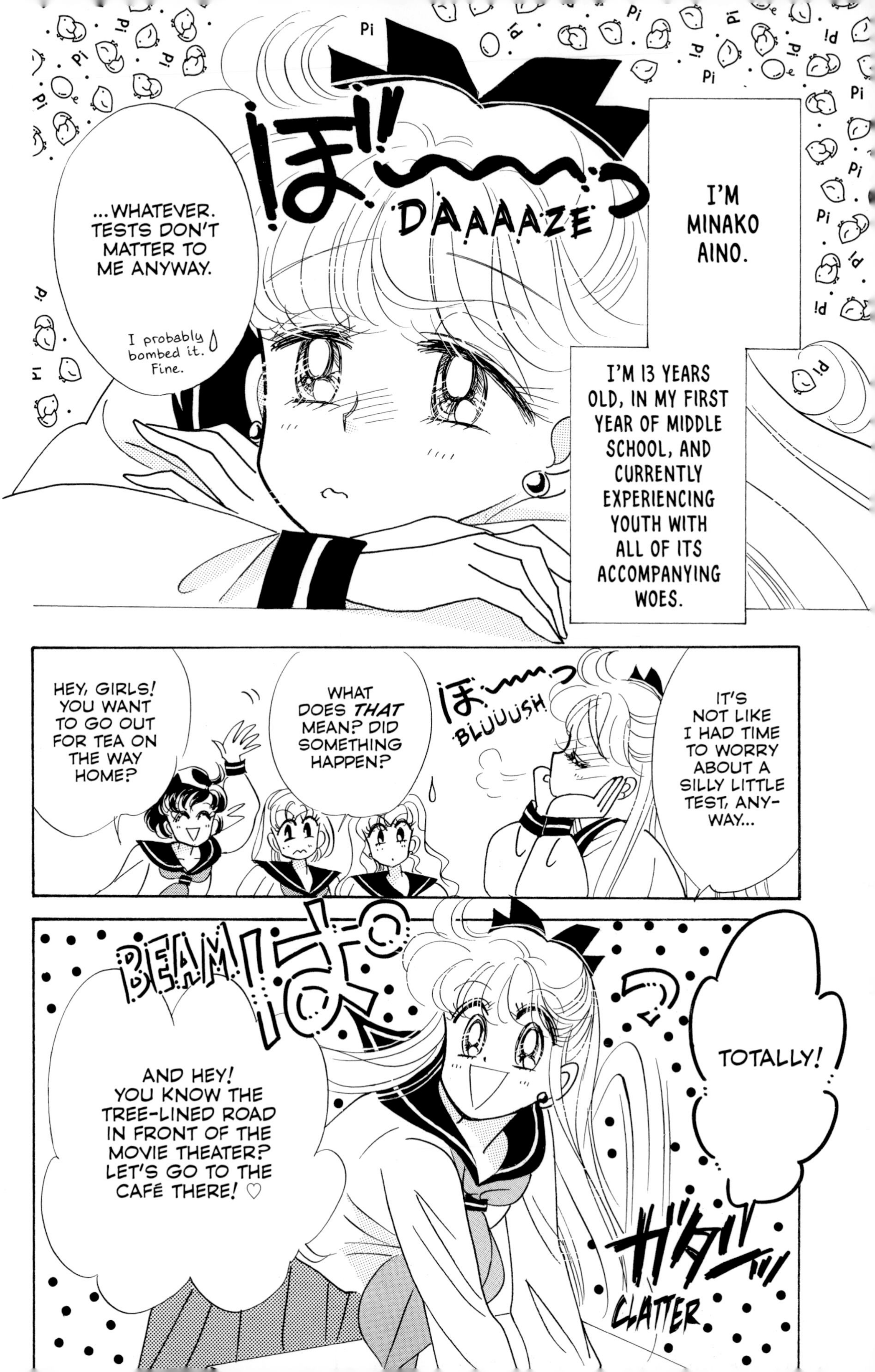
I'M MINAKO AINO.
I'M 13 YEARS OLD, IN MY FIRST YEAR OF MIDDLE SCHOOL, AND CURRENTLY EXPERIENCING YOUTH WITH ALL OF ITS ACCOMPANYING WOES.
ぼ!!〜〜っ
DAAAAZE
...WHATEVER. TESTS DON'T MATTER TO ME ANYWAY.
I probably bombed it. Fine.
IT'S NOT LIKE I HAD TIME TO WORRY ABOUT A SILLY LITTLE TEST, ANYWAY...
ほ〜〜っ
BLUUUSH
WHAT DOES *THAT* MEAN? DID SOMETHING HAPPEN?
HEY, GIRLS! YOU WANT TO GO OUT FOR TEA ON THE WAY HOME?
TOTALLY!
はっ
BEAM!
AND HEY! YOU KNOW THE TREE-LINED ROAD IN FRONT OF THE MOVIE THEATER? LET'S GO TO THE CAFÉ THERE! ♡
ガタッ
CLATTER

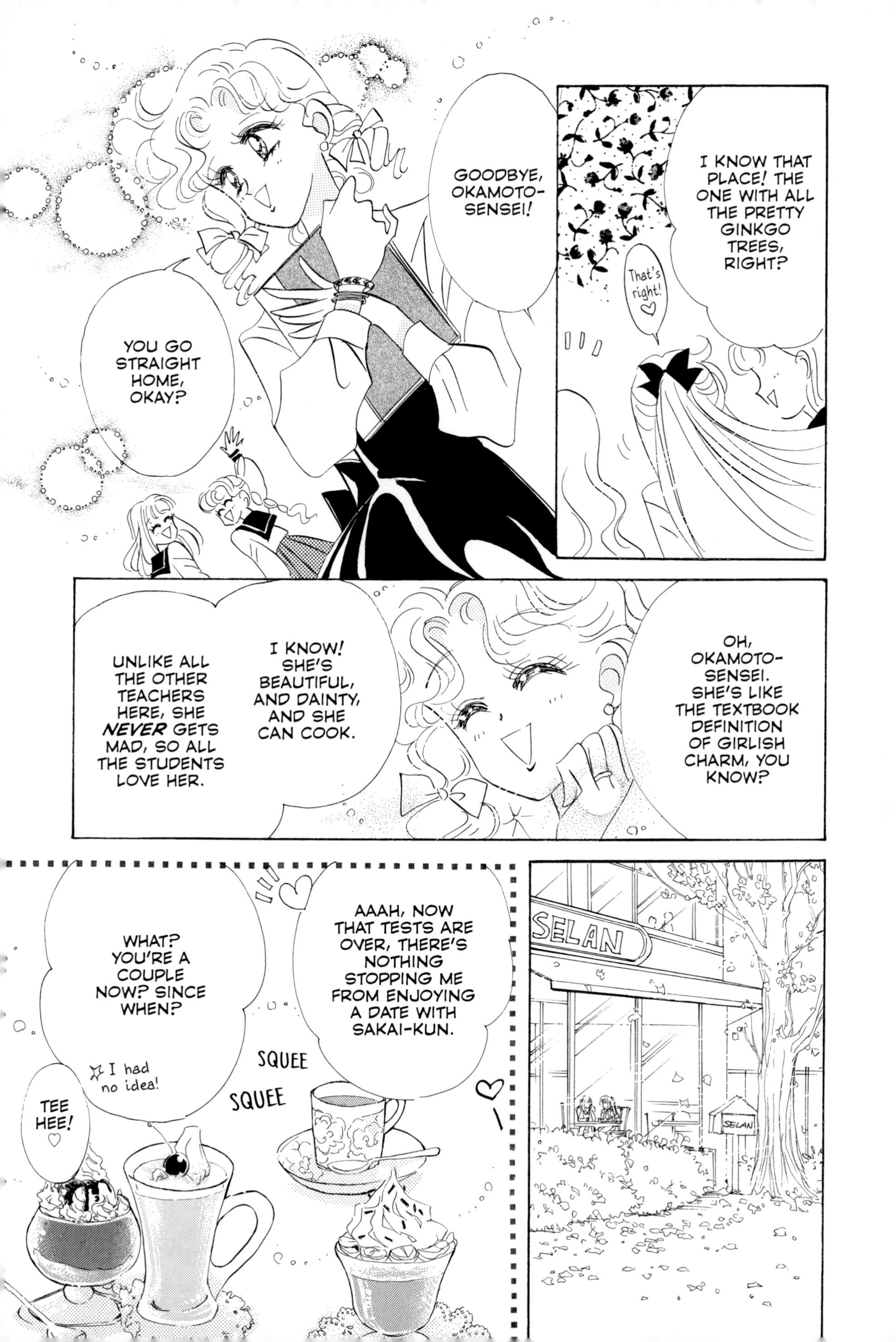
I KNOW THAT PLACE! THE ONE WITH ALL THE PRETTY GINKGO TREES, RIGHT?
That's right! ♡
GOODBYE, OKAMOTO-SENSEI!
YOU GO STRAIGHT HOME, OKAY?
OH, OKAMOTO-SENSEI. SHE'S LIKE THE TEXTBOOK DEFINITION OF GIRLISH CHARM, YOU KNOW?
I KNOW! SHE'S BEAUTIFUL, AND DAINTY, AND SHE CAN COOK.
UNLIKE ALL THE OTHER TEACHERS HERE, SHE ***NEVER*** GETS MAD, SO ALL THE STUDENTS LOVE HER.
SELAN
SELAN
AAAH, NOW THAT TESTS ARE OVER, THERE'S NOTHING STOPPING ME FROM ENJOYING A DATE WITH SAKAI-KUN.
SQUEE
SQUEE
WHAT? YOU'RE A COUPLE NOW? SINCE WHEN?
I had no idea!
TEE HEE! ♡

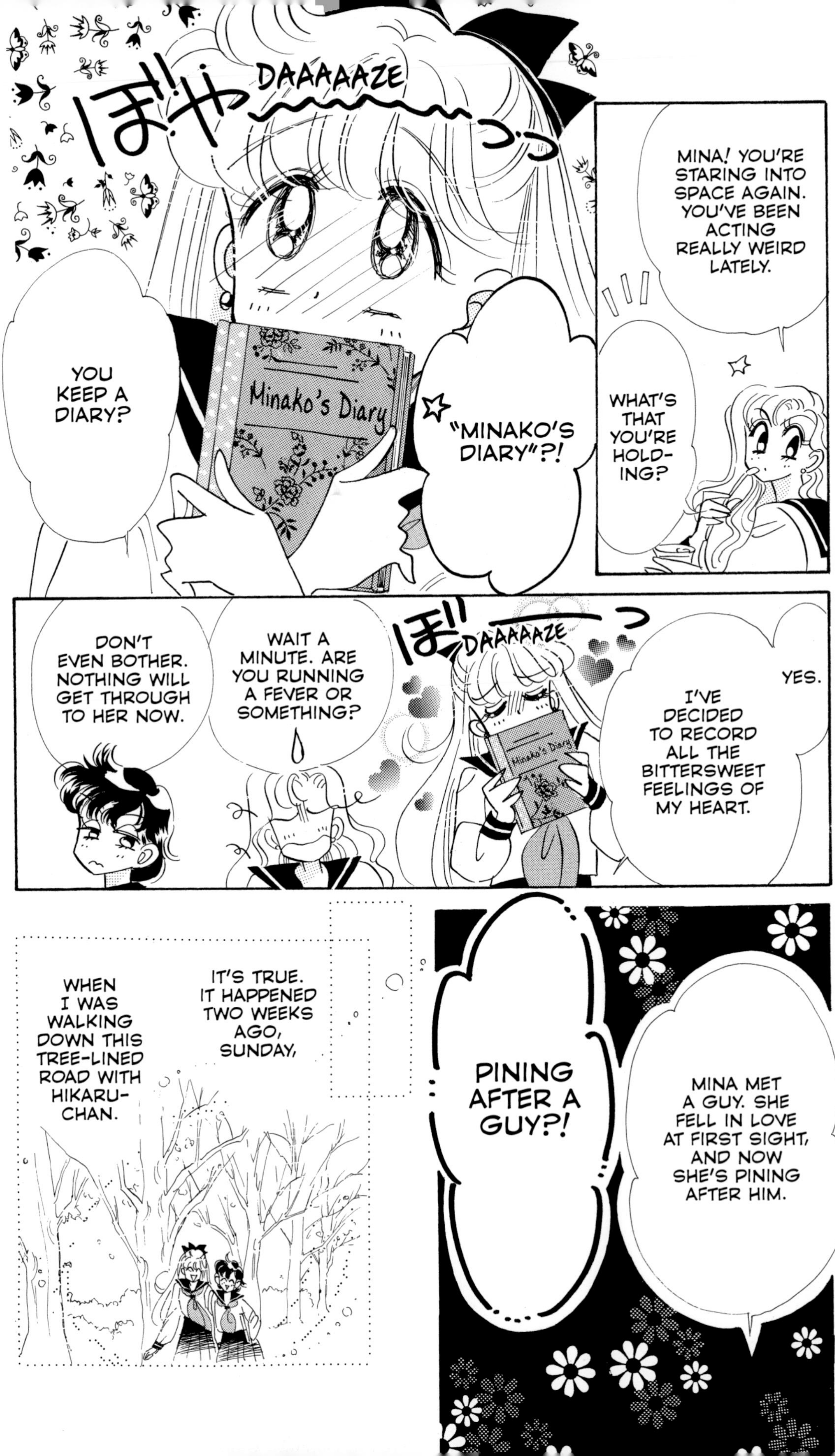
MINA! YOU'RE STARING INTO SPACE AGAIN. YOU'VE BEEN ACTING REALLY WEIRD LATELY.
WHAT'S THAT YOU'RE HOLD-ING?
ぼや
DAAAAAZE
"MINAKO'S DIARY"?!
YOU KEEP A DIARY?
Minako's Diary
YES.
I'VE DECIDED TO RECORD ALL THE BITTERSWEET FEELINGS OF MY HEART.
ぼ
DAAAAAZE
WAIT A MINUTE. ARE YOU RUNNING A FEVER OR SOMETHING?
DON'T EVEN BOTHER. NOTHING WILL GET THROUGH TO HER NOW.
MINA MET A GUY. SHE FELL IN LOVE AT FIRST SIGHT, AND NOW SHE'S PINING AFTER HIM.
PINING AFTER A GUY?!
IT'S TRUE. IT HAPPENED TWO WEEKS AGO, SUNDAY,
WHEN I WAS WALKING DOWN THIS TREE-LINED ROAD WITH HIKARU-CHAN.

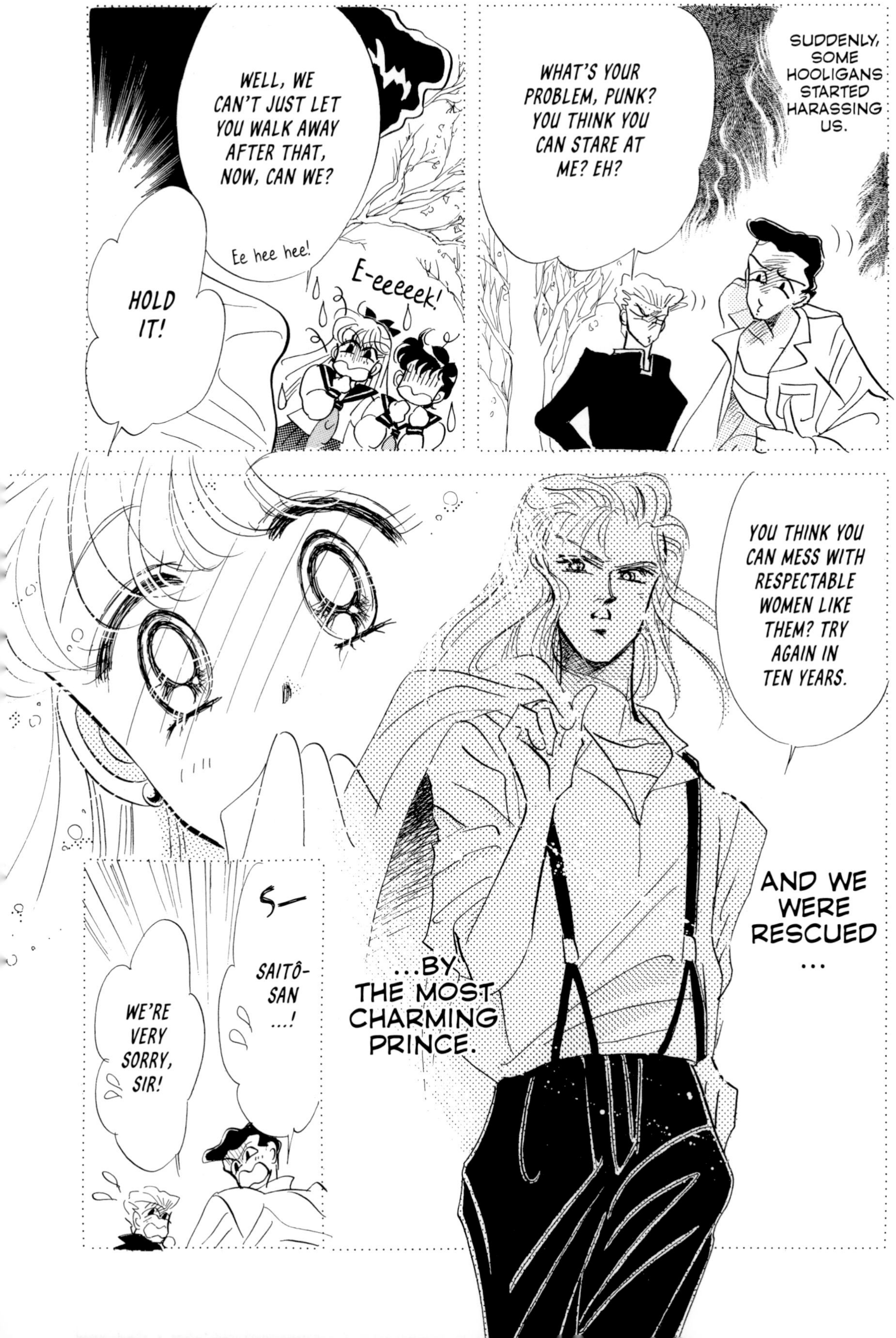
SUDDENLY, SOME HOOLIGANS STARTED HARASSING US.
WHAT'S YOUR PROBLEM, PUNK? YOU THINK YOU CAN STARE AT ME? EH?
WELL, WE CAN'T JUST LET YOU WALK AWAY AFTER THAT, NOW, CAN WE?
Ee hee hee!
E-eeeeek!
HOLD IT!
YOU THINK YOU CAN MESS WITH RESPECTABLE WOMEN LIKE THEM? TRY AGAIN IN TEN YEARS.
AND WE WERE RESCUED...
...BY THE MOST CHARMING PRINCE.
S—
SAITÔ-SAN ...!
WE'RE VERY SORRY, SIR!

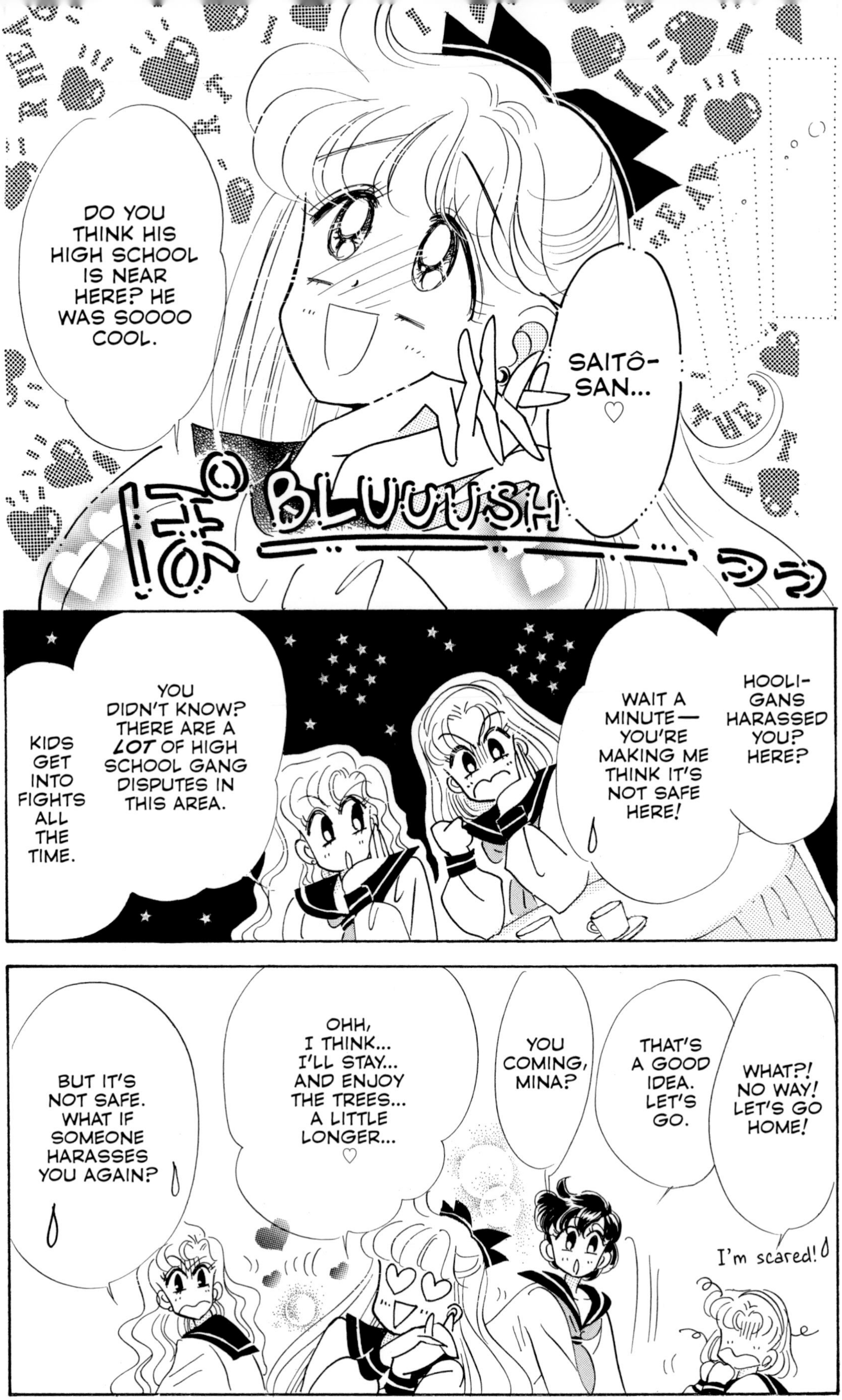
SAITÔ-SAN... ♡
DO YOU THINK HIS HIGH SCHOOL IS NEAR HERE? HE WAS SOOOO COOL.
BLUUUSH
HOOLI-GANS HARASSED YOU? HERE?
WAIT A MINUTE— YOU'RE MAKING ME THINK IT'S NOT SAFE HERE!
YOU DIDN'T KNOW? THERE ARE A *LOT* OF HIGH SCHOOL GANG DISPUTES IN THIS AREA.
KIDS GET INTO FIGHTS ALL THE TIME.
WHAT?! NO WAY! LET'S GO HOME!
I'm scared!
THAT'S A GOOD IDEA. LET'S GO.
YOU COMING, MINA?
OHH, I THINK... I'LL STAY... AND ENJOY THE TREES... A LITTLE LONGER... ♡
BUT IT'S NOT SAFE. WHAT IF SOMEONE HARASSES YOU AGAIN?

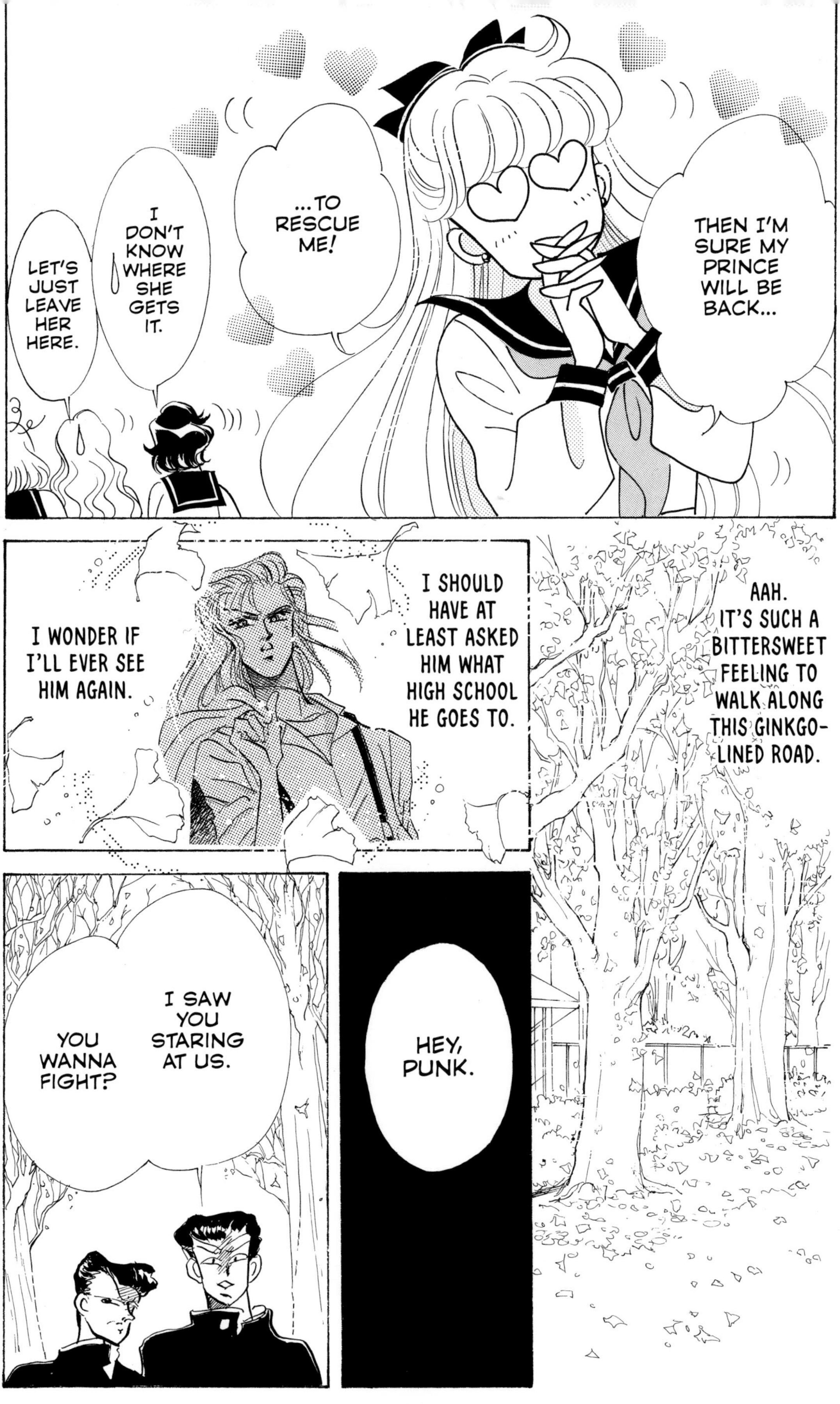
THEN I'M SURE MY PRINCE WILL BE BACK...
...TO RESCUE ME!
I DON'T KNOW WHERE SHE GETS IT.
LET'S JUST LEAVE HER HERE.
AAH. IT'S SUCH A BITTERSWEET FEELING TO WALK ALONG THIS GINKGO-LINED ROAD.
I SHOULD HAVE AT LEAST ASKED HIM WHAT HIGH SCHOOL HE GOES TO.
I WONDER IF I'LL EVER SEE HIM AGAIN.
HEY, PUNK.
I SAW YOU STARING AT US.
YOU WANNA FIGHT?

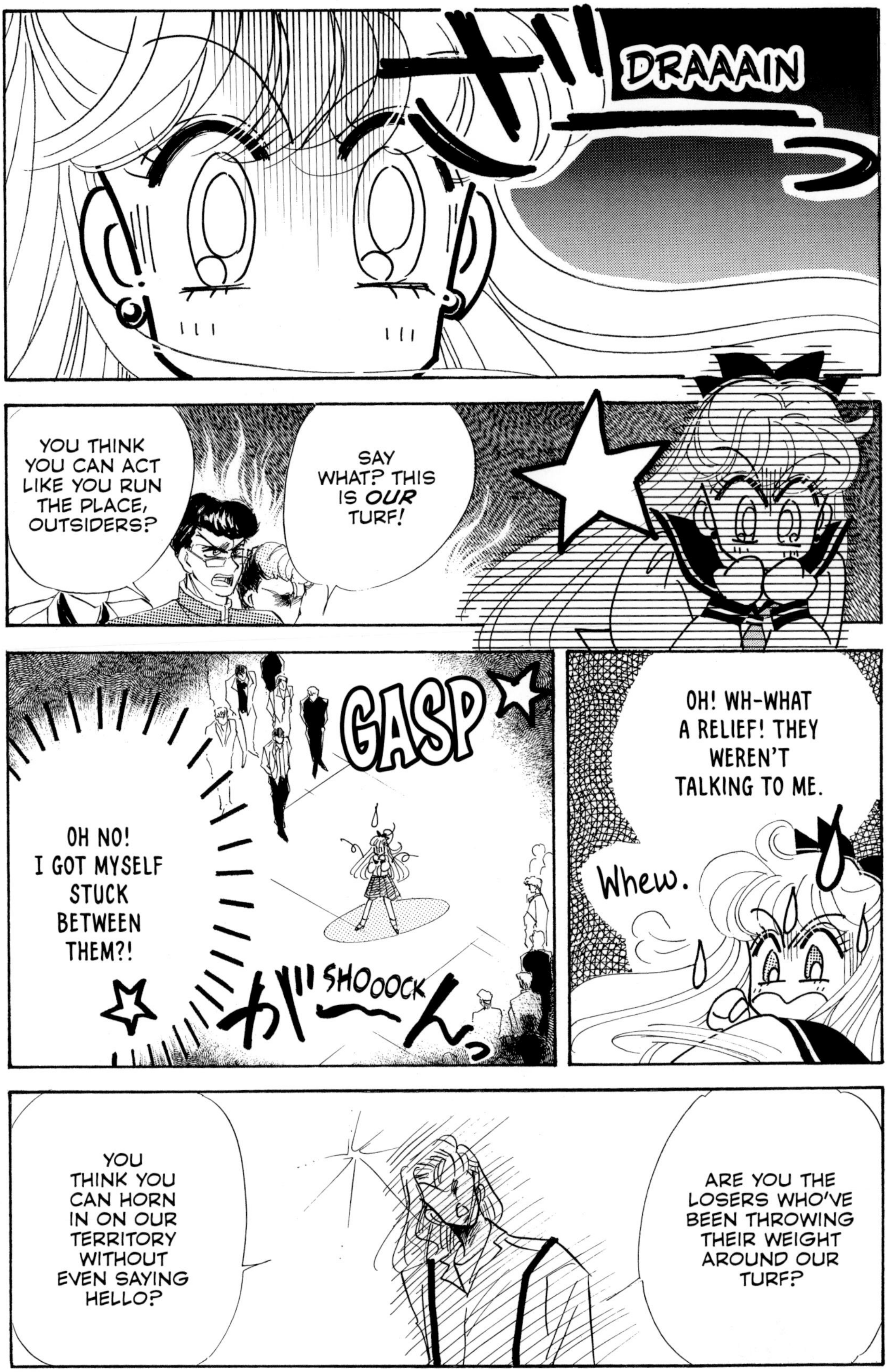
ザーっ
DRAAAIN
SAY WHAT? THIS IS *OUR* TURF!
YOU THINK YOU CAN ACT LIKE YOU RUN THE PLACE, OUTSIDERS?
OH! WH-WHAT A RELIEF! THEY WEREN'T TALKING TO ME.
Whew.
GASP
OH NO! I GOT MYSELF STUCK BETWEEN THEM?!
がーんっ
SHOOOCK
ARE YOU THE LOSERS WHO'VE BEEN THROWING THEIR WEIGHT AROUND OUR TURF?
YOU THINK YOU CAN HORN IN ON OUR TERRITORY WITHOUT EVEN SAYING HELLO?

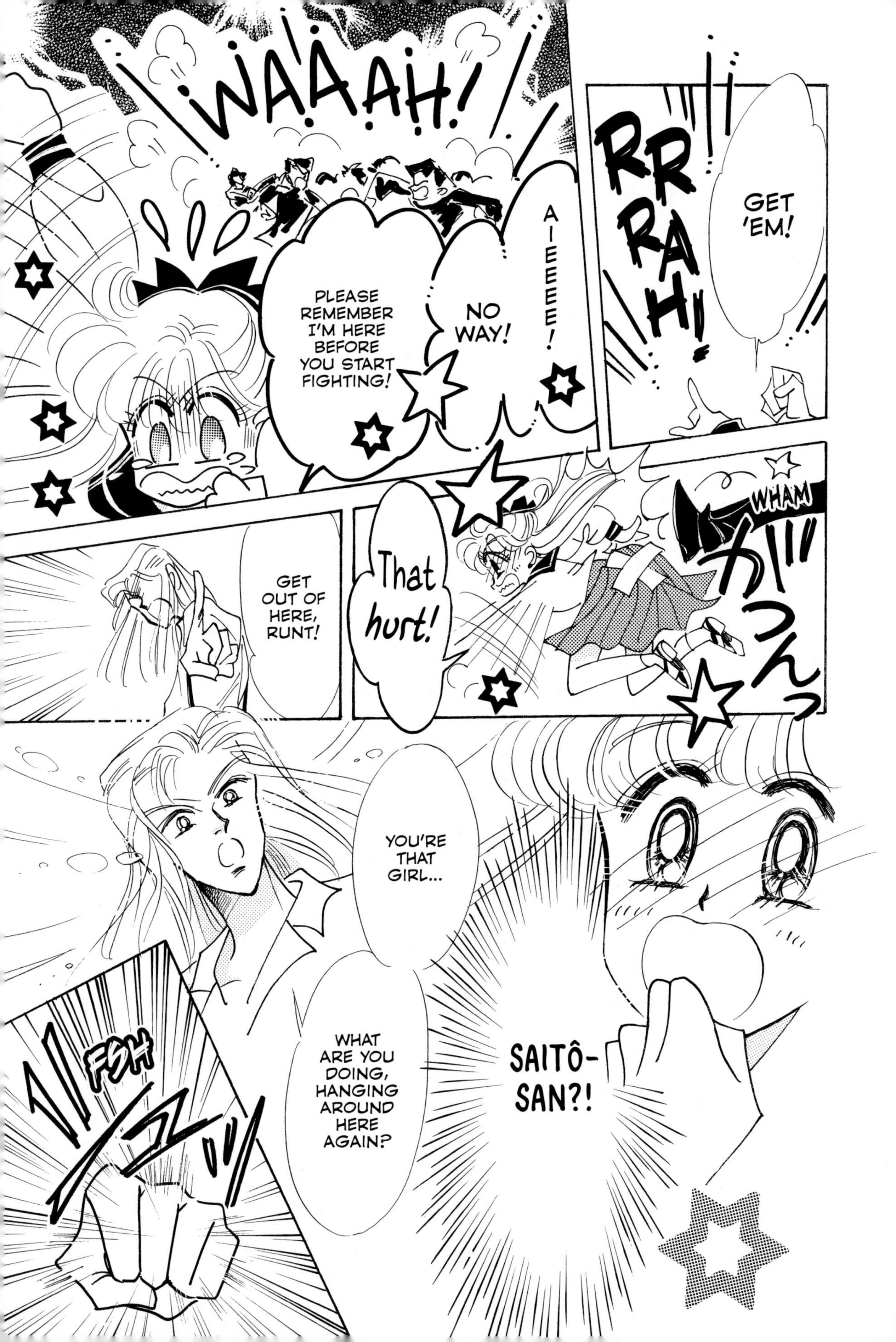
RRRAH!
GET 'EM!
WAAAH!
AIEEEE!
NO WAY!
PLEASE REMEMBER I'M HERE BEFORE YOU START FIGHTING!
WHAM
がつんっ
That hurt!
GET OUT OF HERE, RUNT!
SAITÔ-SAN?!
YOU'RE THAT GIRL...
WHAT ARE YOU DOING, HANGING AROUND HERE AGAIN?
FSH

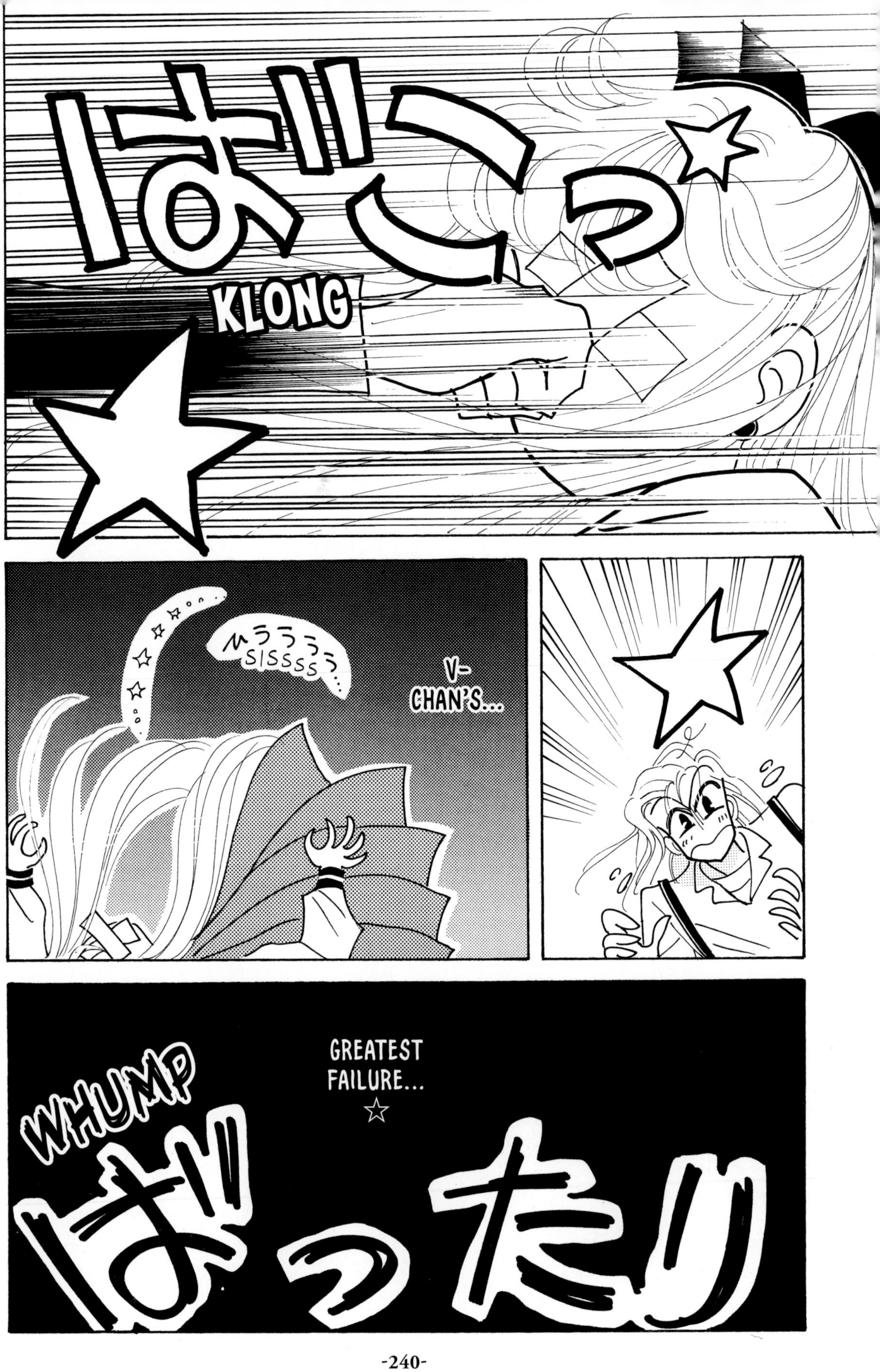

ばごっ☆
KLONG
V-CHAN'S...
ひうううう
SISSSS...
GREATEST FAILURE... ☆
WHUMP
ばったり

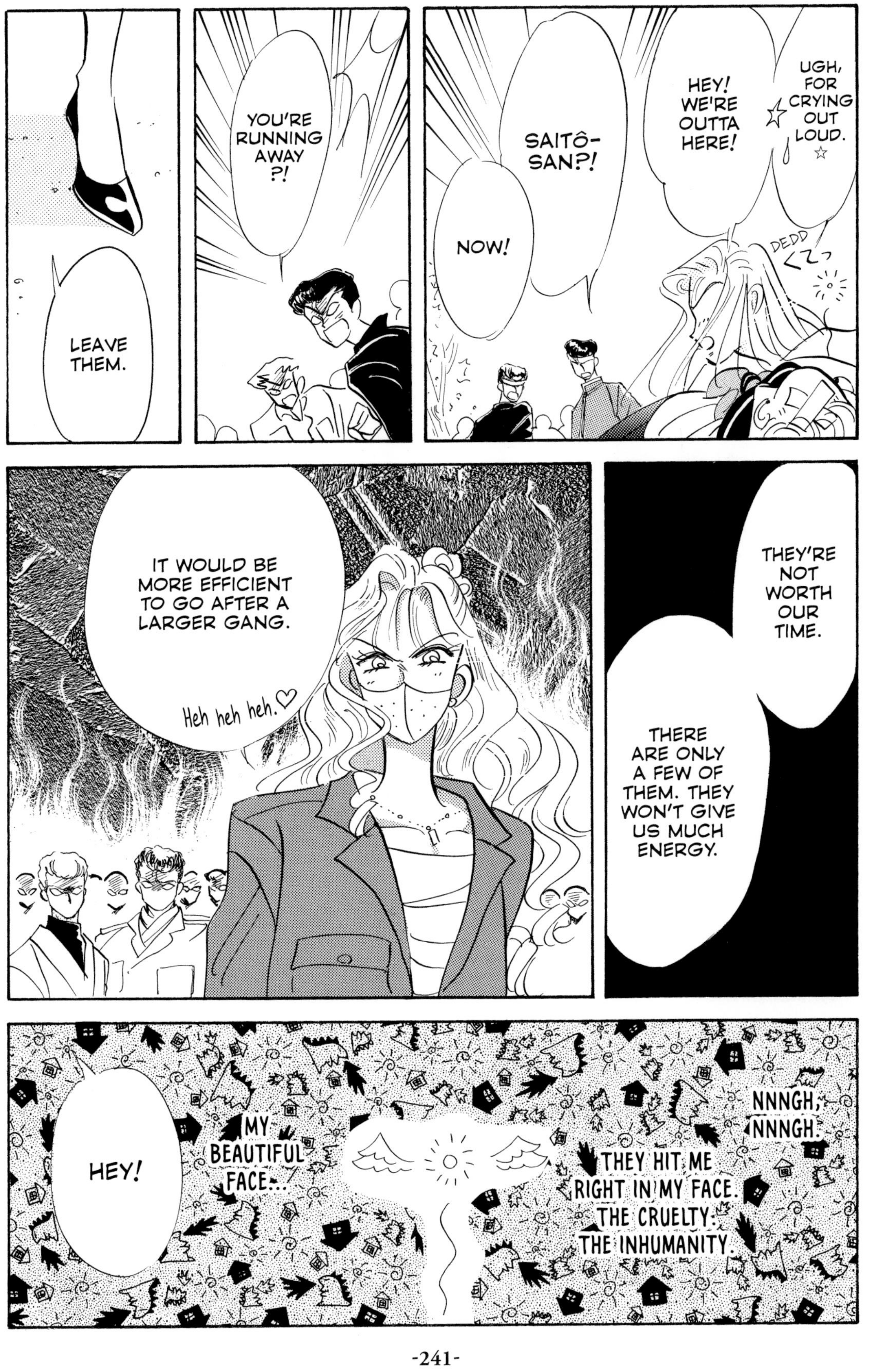
UGH, FOR CRYING OUT LOUD.
HEY! WE'RE OUTTA HERE!
DEDD
SAITÔ-SAN?!
NOW!
YOU'RE RUNNING AWAY ?!
LEAVE THEM.
THEY'RE NOT WORTH OUR TIME.
THERE ARE ONLY A FEW OF THEM. THEY WON'T GIVE US MUCH ENERGY.
IT WOULD BE MORE EFFICIENT TO GO AFTER A LARGER GANG.
Heh heh heh.♡
NNNGH, NNNGH.
THEY HIT ME RIGHT IN MY FACE. THE CRUELTY. THE INHUMANITY.
MY BEAUTIFUL FACE...
HEY!

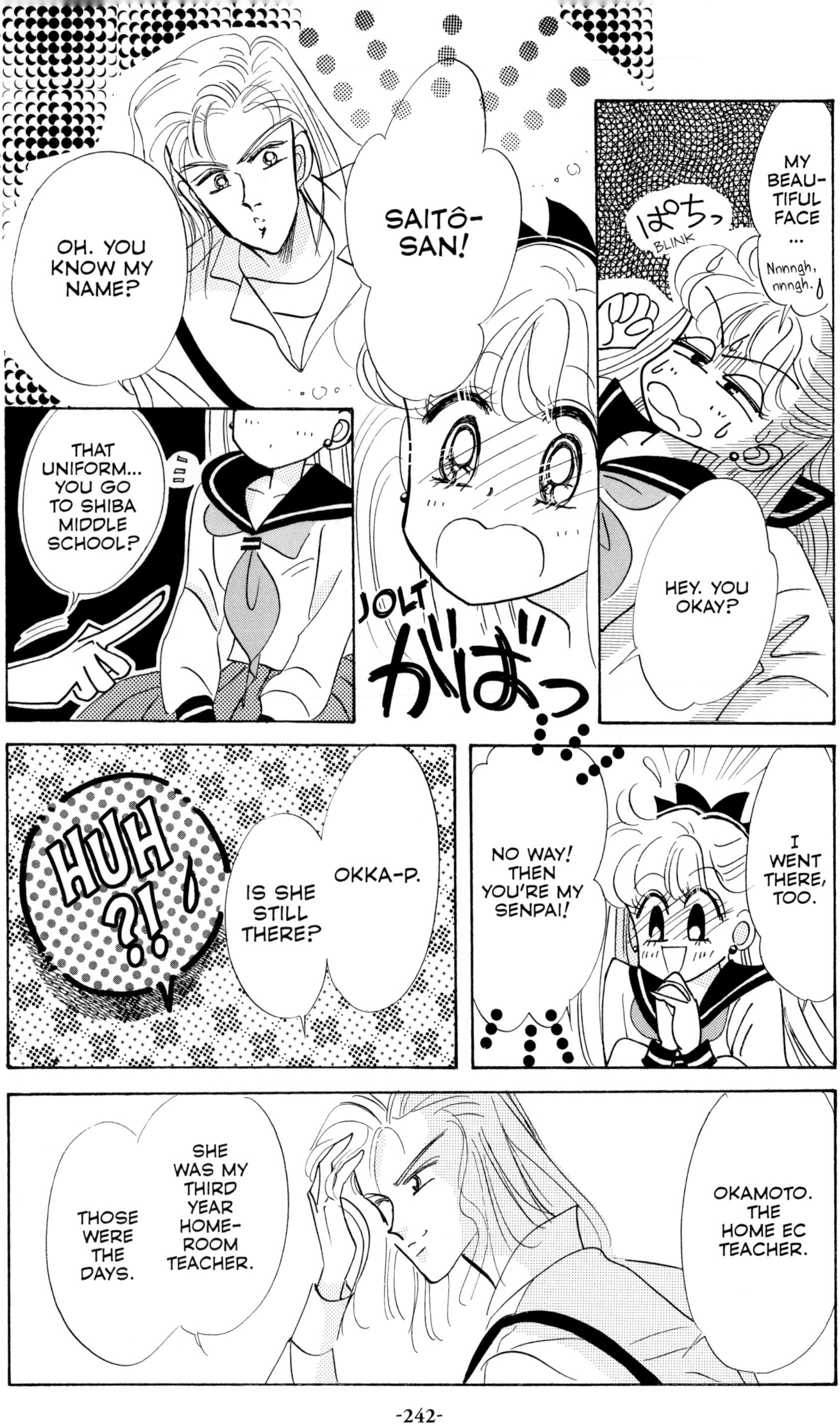
MY BEAUTIFUL FACE ...
Nnnngh, nnngh.
ぱちっ
BLINK
HEY. YOU OKAY?
SAITÔ-SAN!
JOLT
がばっ
OH. YOU KNOW MY NAME?
THAT UNIFORM... YOU GO TO SHIBA MIDDLE SCHOOL?
I WENT THERE, TOO.
NO WAY! THEN YOU'RE MY SENPAI!
OKKA-P.
IS SHE STILL THERE?
HUH?!
OKAMOTO. THE HOME EC TEACHER.
SHE WAS MY THIRD YEAR HOME-ROOM TEACHER.
THOSE WERE THE DAYS.

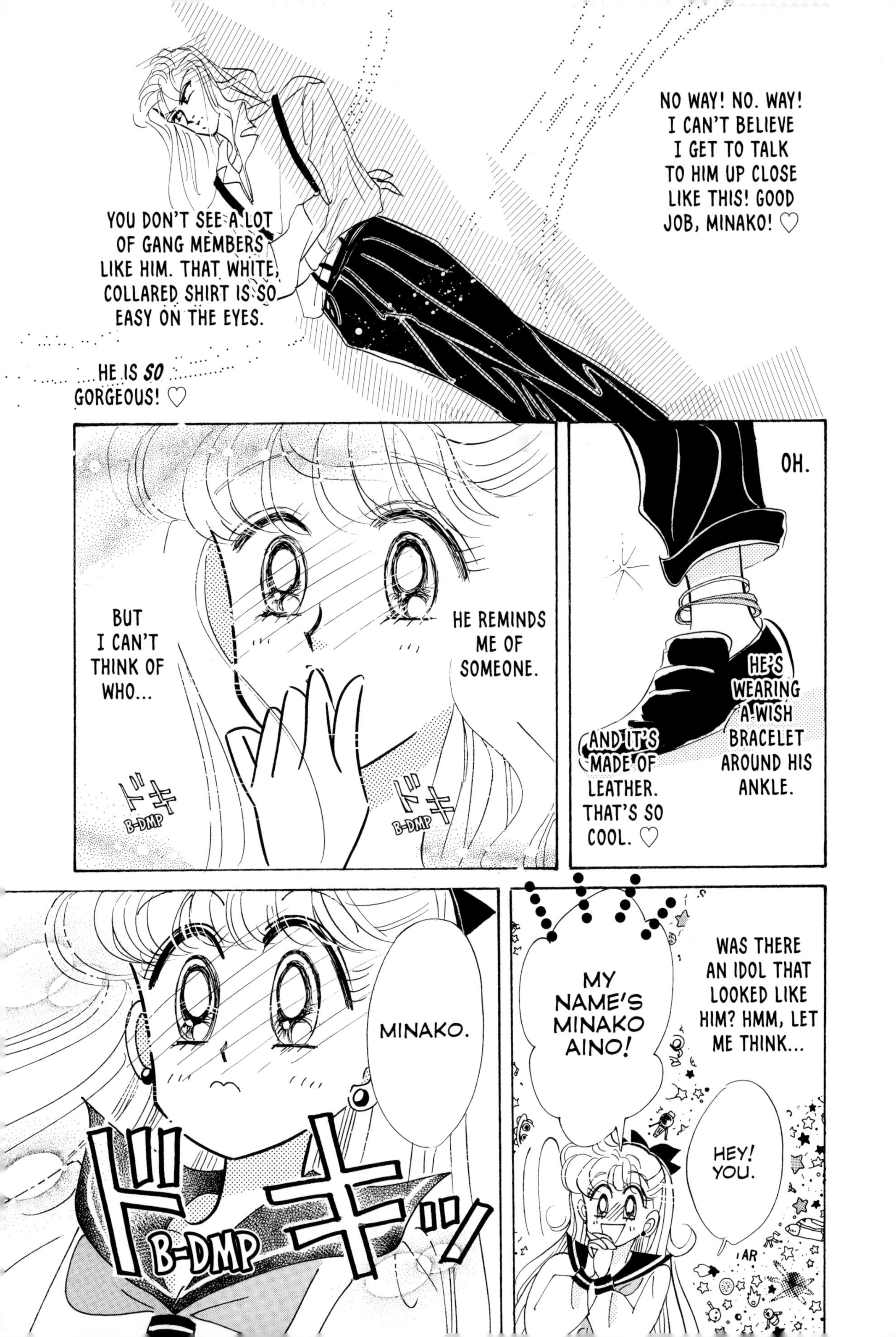
NO WAY! NO. WAY! I CAN'T BELIEVE I GET TO TALK TO HIM UP CLOSE LIKE THIS! GOOD JOB, MINAKO! ♡
YOU DON'T SEE A LOT OF GANG MEMBERS LIKE HIM. THAT WHITE, COLLARED SHIRT IS SO EASY ON THE EYES.
HE IS *SO* GORGEOUS! ♡
OH.
HE'S WEARING A WISH BRACELET AROUND HIS ANKLE.
AND IT'S MADE OF LEATHER. THAT'S SO COOL. ♡
HE REMINDS ME OF SOMEONE.
B-DMP
BUT I CAN'T THINK OF WHO...
B-DMP
WAS THERE AN IDOL THAT LOOKED LIKE HIM? HMM, LET ME THINK...
MY NAME'S MINAKO AINO!
HEY! YOU.
MINAKO.
B-DMP

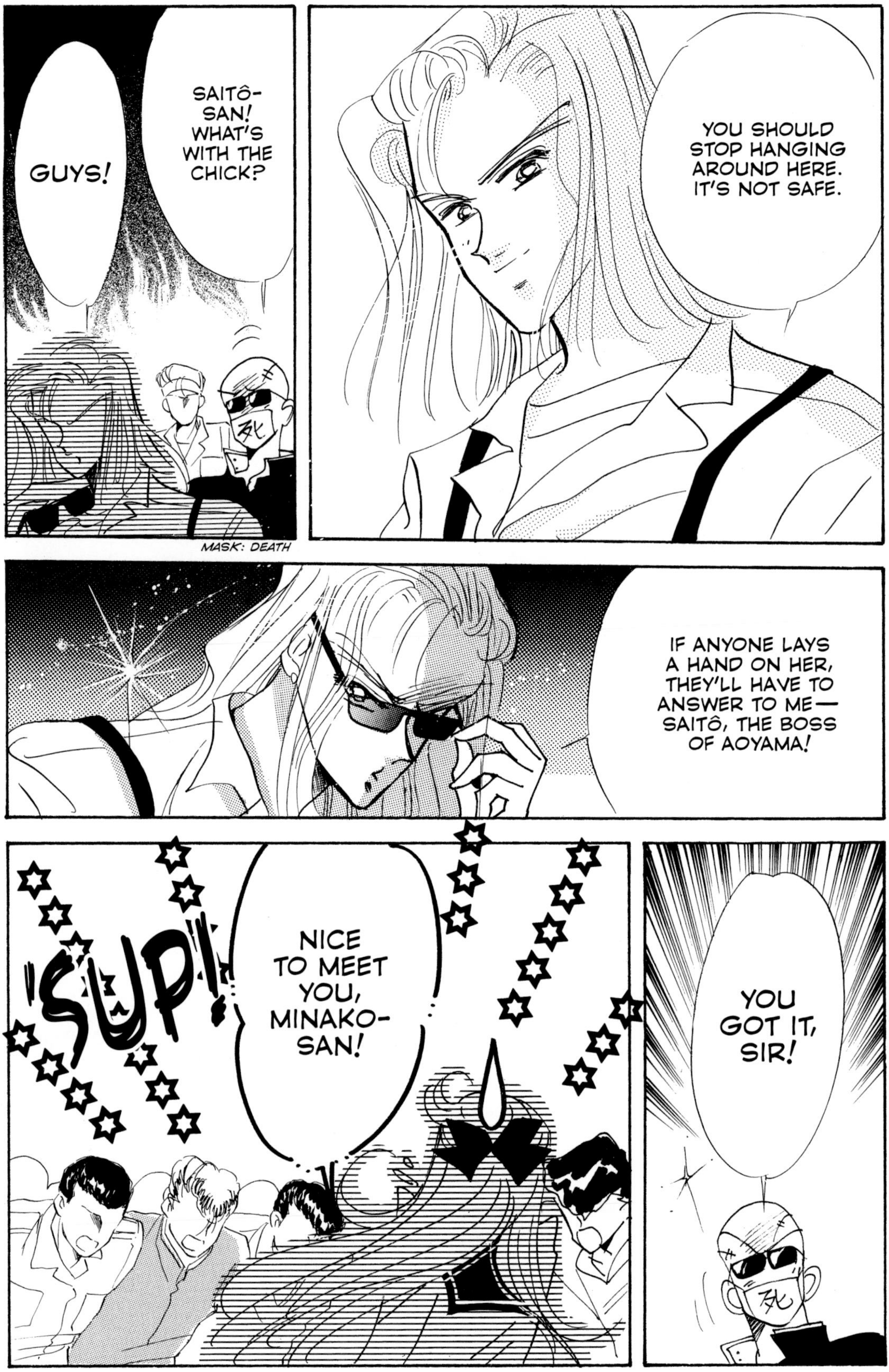
YOU SHOULD STOP HANGING AROUND HERE. IT'S NOT SAFE.
SAITÔ-SAN! WHAT'S WITH THE CHICK?
GUYS!
MASK: DEATH
IF ANYONE LAYS A HAND ON HER, THEY'LL HAVE TO ANSWER TO ME—SAITÔ, THE BOSS OF AOYAMA!
YOU GOT IT, SIR!
NICE TO MEET YOU, MINAKO-SAN!
'SUP!

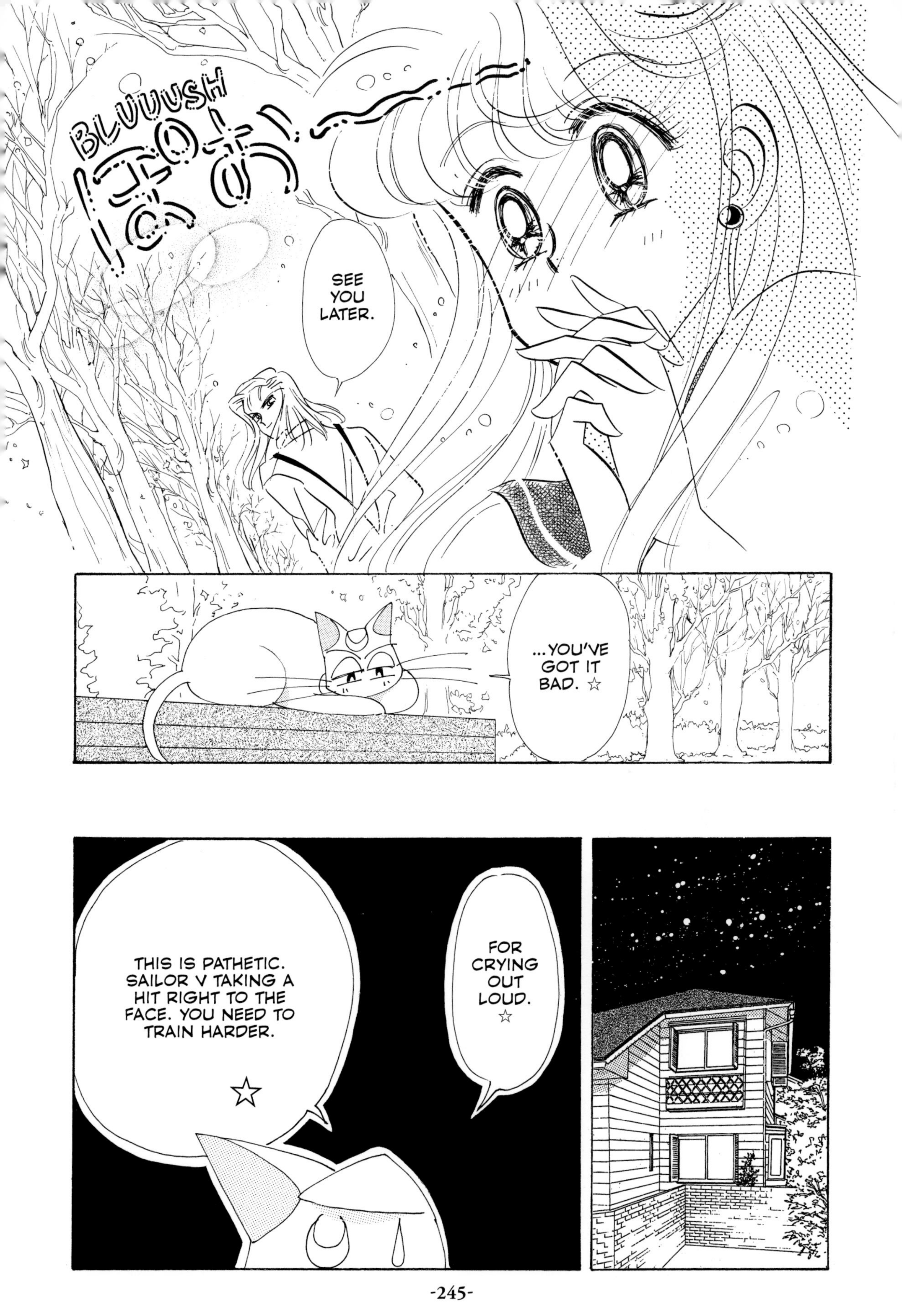
BLUUUSH
SEE YOU LATER.
...YOU'VE GOT IT BAD. ☆
FOR CRYING OUT LOUD. ☆
THIS IS PATHETIC. SAILOR V TAKING A HIT RIGHT TO THE FACE. YOU NEED TO TRAIN HARDER. ☆

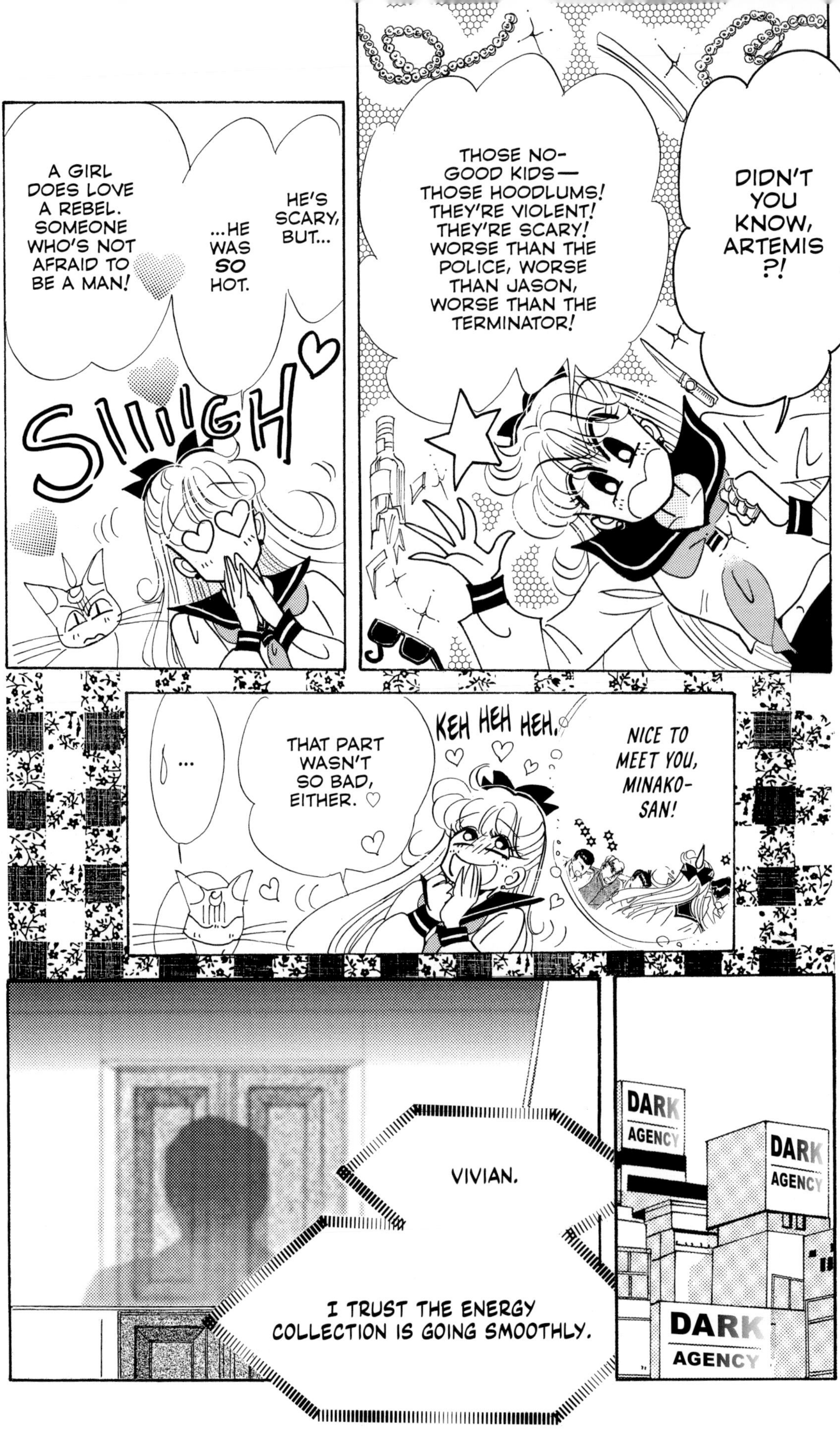
DIDN'T YOU KNOW, ARTEMIS?!
THOSE NO-GOOD KIDS—THOSE HOODLUMS! THEY'RE VIOLENT! THEY'RE SCARY! WORSE THAN THE POLICE, WORSE THAN JASON, WORSE THAN THE TERMINATOR!
HE'S SCARY, BUT...
...HE WAS SO HOT.
A GIRL DOES LOVE A REBEL. SOMEONE WHO'S NOT AFRAID TO BE A MAN!
SIIIGH
NICE TO MEET YOU, MINAKO-SAN!
KEH HEH HEH.
THAT PART WASN'T SO BAD, EITHER.
...
DARK AGENCY
DARK AGENCY
DARK AGENCY
VIVIAN.
I TRUST THE ENERGY COLLECTION IS GOING SMOOTHLY.

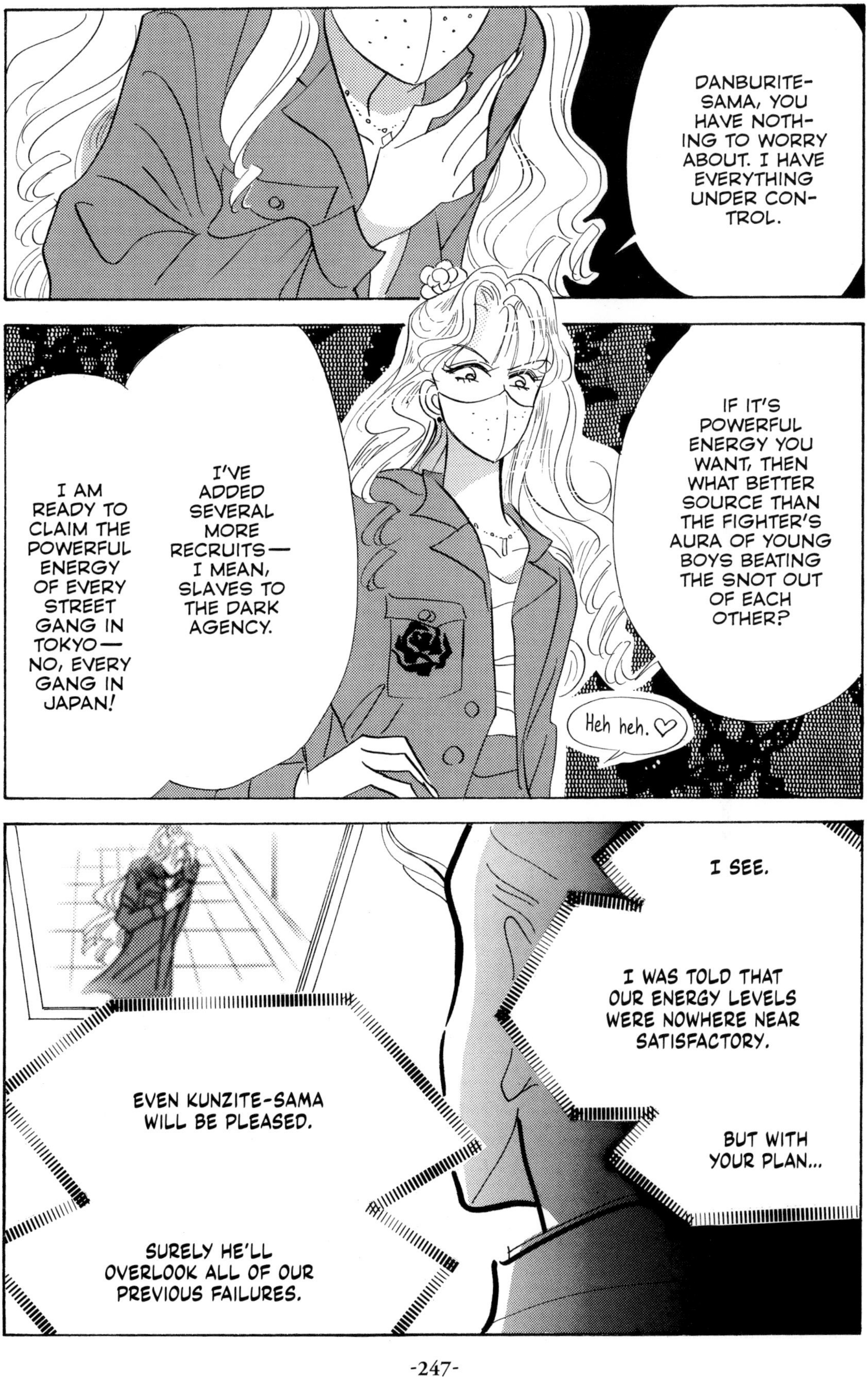
DANBURITE-SAMA, YOU HAVE NOTHING TO WORRY ABOUT. I HAVE EVERYTHING UNDER CONTROL.
IF IT'S POWERFUL ENERGY YOU WANT, THEN WHAT BETTER SOURCE THAN THE FIGHTER'S AURA OF YOUNG BOYS BEATING THE SNOT OUT OF EACH OTHER?
Heh heh. ♡
I'VE ADDED SEVERAL MORE RECRUITS— I MEAN, SLAVES TO THE DARK AGENCY.
I AM READY TO CLAIM THE POWERFUL ENERGY OF EVERY STREET GANG IN TOKYO— NO, EVERY GANG IN JAPAN!
I SEE.
I WAS TOLD THAT OUR ENERGY LEVELS WERE NOWHERE NEAR SATISFACTORY.
BUT WITH YOUR PLAN...
EVEN KUNZITE-SAMA WILL BE PLEASED.
SURELY HE'LL OVERLOOK ALL OF OUR PREVIOUS FAILURES.

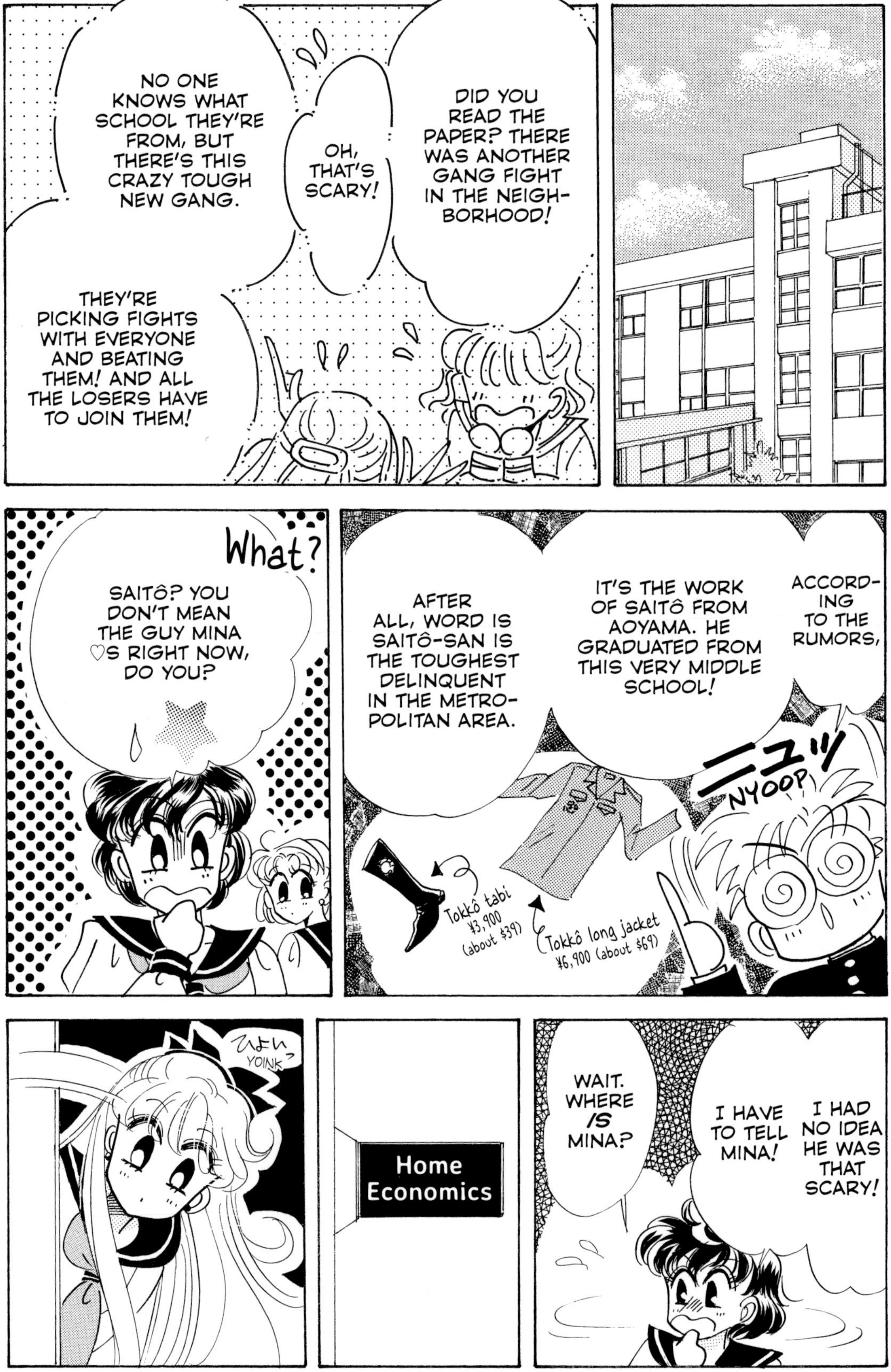
DID YOU READ THE PAPER? THERE WAS ANOTHER GANG FIGHT IN THE NEIGHBORHOOD!
OH, THAT'S SCARY!
NO ONE KNOWS WHAT SCHOOL THEY'RE FROM, BUT THERE'S THIS CRAZY TOUGH NEW GANG.
THEY'RE PICKING FIGHTS WITH EVERYONE AND BEATING THEM! AND ALL THE LOSERS HAVE TO JOIN THEM!
ACCORDING TO THE RUMORS,
IT'S THE WORK OF SAITÔ FROM AOYAMA. HE GRADUATED FROM THIS VERY MIDDLE SCHOOL!
AFTER ALL, WORD IS SAITÔ-SAN IS THE TOUGHEST DELINQUENT IN THE METROPOLITAN AREA.
ニュッ
NYOOP
Tokkô long jacket ¥6,900 (about $69)
Tokkô tabi ¥3,900 (about $39)
What?
SAITÔ? YOU DON'T MEAN THE GUY MINA ♡S RIGHT NOW, DO YOU?
I HAD NO IDEA HE WAS THAT SCARY!
I HAVE TO TELL MINA!
WAIT. WHERE *IS* MINA?
Home Economics
ひょい
YOINK

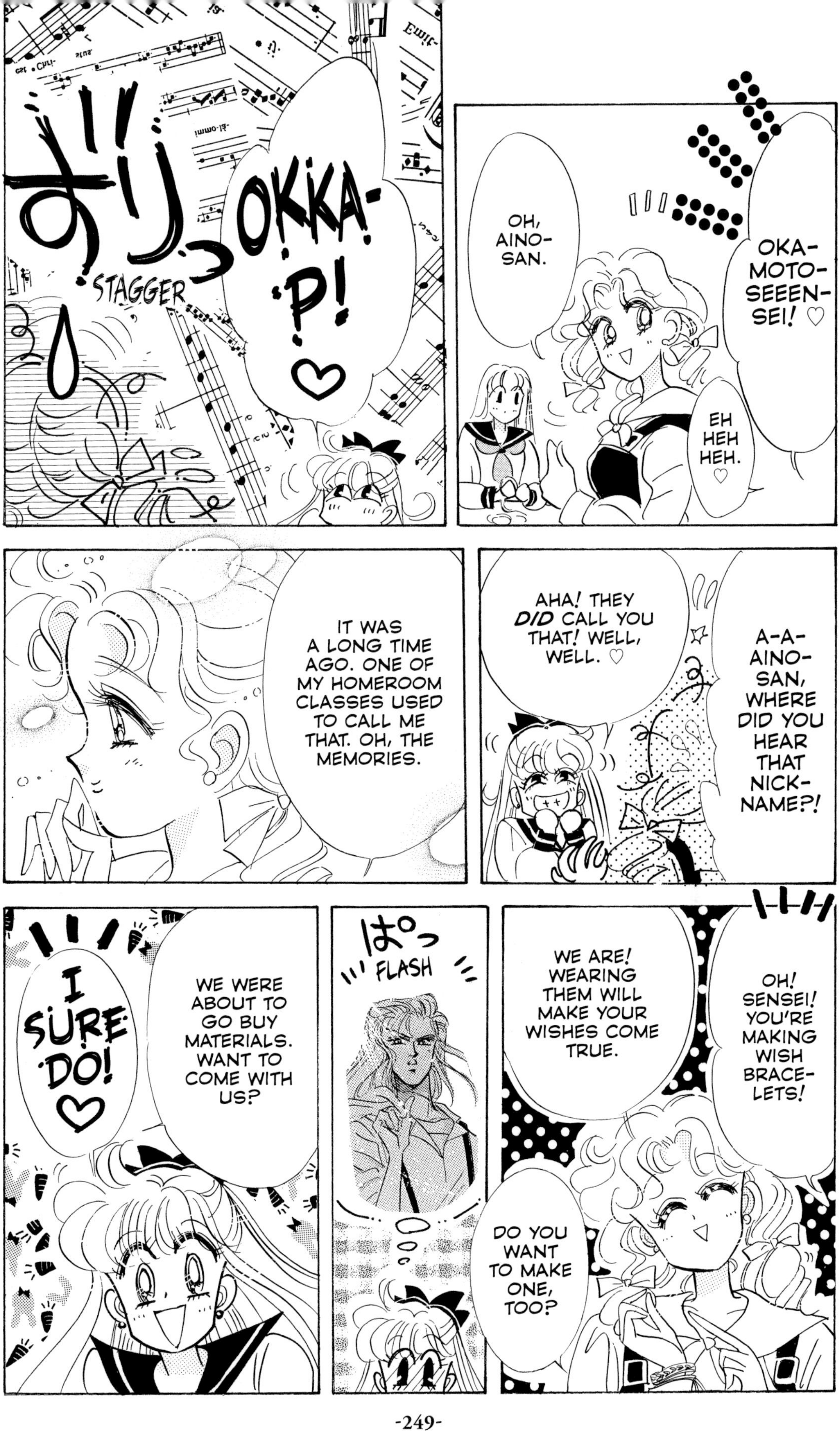
OKA-MOTO-SEEEN-SEI! ♡
OH, AINO-SAN.
EH HEH HEH. ♡
OKKA-P! ♡
ずりっ
STAGGER
A-A-AINO-SAN, WHERE DID YOU HEAR THAT NICK-NAME?!
AHA! THEY *DID* CALL YOU THAT! WELL, WELL. ♡
IT WAS A LONG TIME AGO. ONE OF MY HOMEROOM CLASSES USED TO CALL ME THAT. OH, THE MEMORIES.
OH! SENSEI! YOU'RE MAKING WISH BRACE-LETS!
WE ARE! WEARING THEM WILL MAKE YOUR WISHES COME TRUE.
DO YOU WANT TO MAKE ONE, TOO?
ぱっ
FLASH
WE WERE ABOUT TO GO BUY MATERIALS. WANT TO COME WITH US?
I SURE DO! ♡

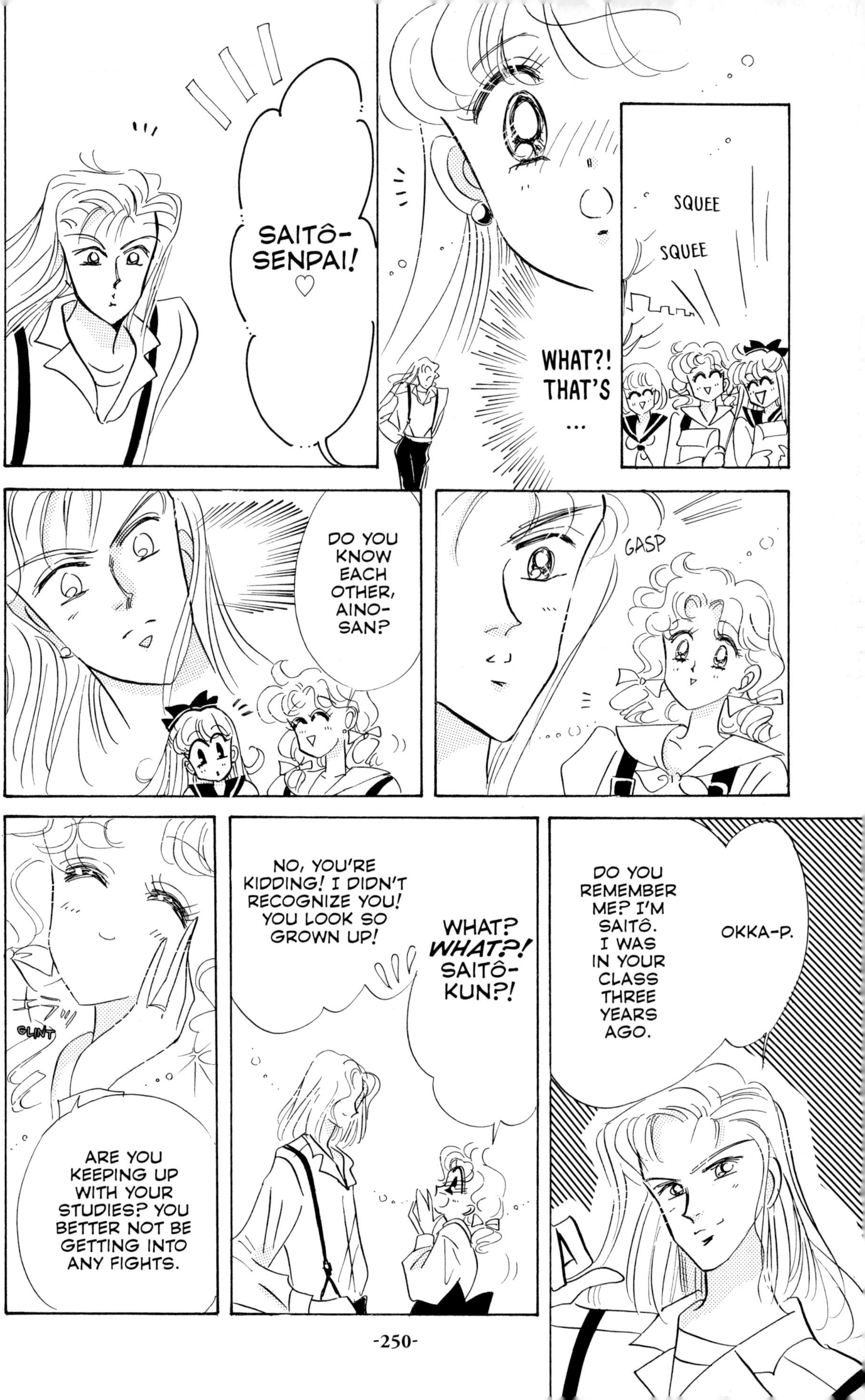
SQUEE
SQUEE
WHAT?! THAT'S ...
SAITÔ-SENPAI! ♡
GASP
DO YOU KNOW EACH OTHER, AINO-SAN?
DO YOU REMEMBER ME? I'M SAITÔ. I WAS IN YOUR CLASS THREE YEARS AGO.
OKKA-P.
WHAT? *WHAT?!* SAITÔ-KUN?!
NO, YOU'RE KIDDING! I DIDN'T RECOGNIZE YOU! YOU LOOK SO GROWN UP!
GLINT
ARE YOU KEEPING UP WITH YOUR STUDIES? YOU BETTER NOT BE GETTING INTO ANY FIGHTS.

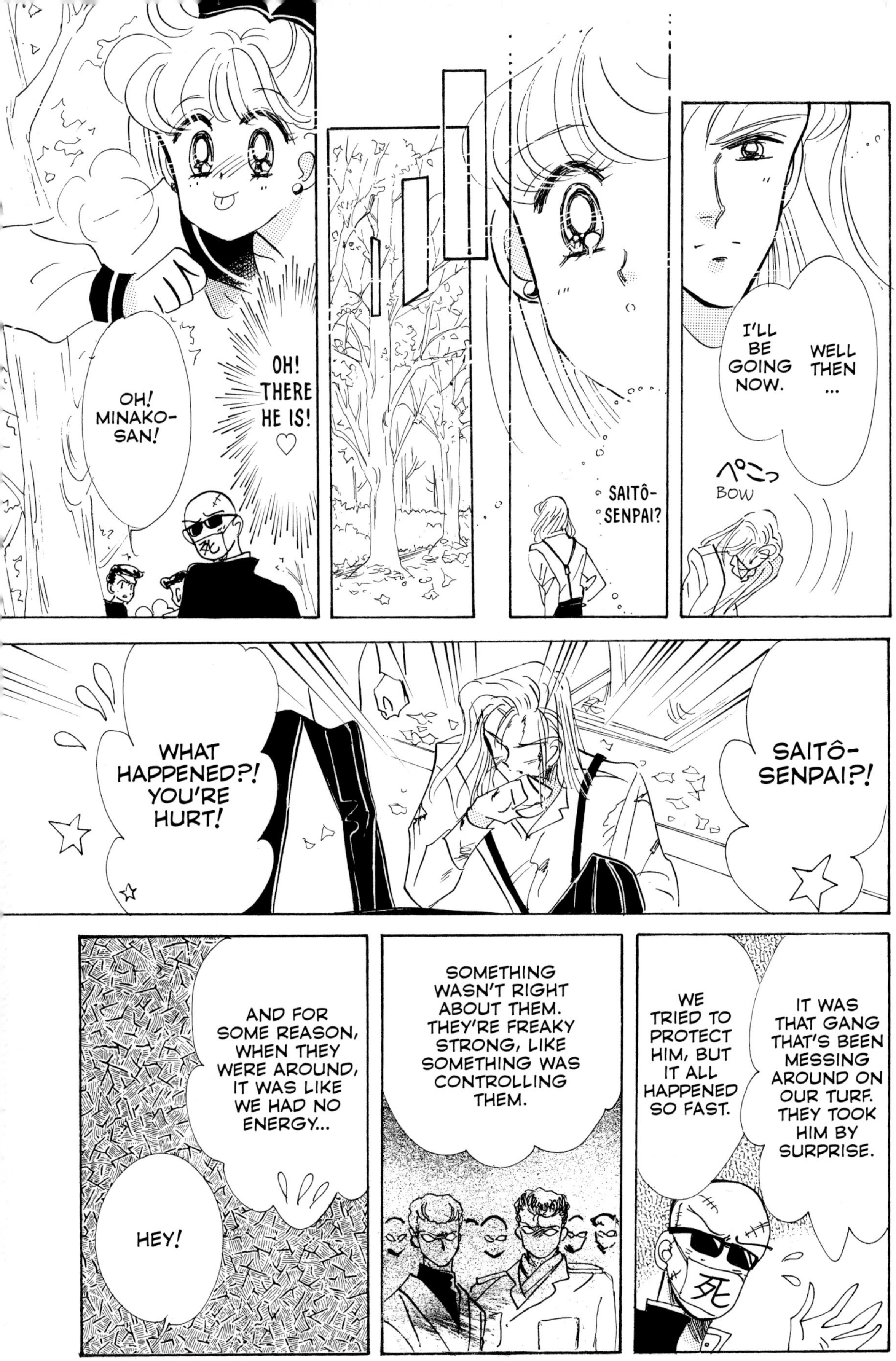
WELL THEN ...
I'LL BE GOING NOW.
ぺこっ
BOW
SAITÔ-SENPAI?
OH! THERE HE IS! ♡
OH! MINAKO-SAN!
SAITÔ-SENPAI?!
WHAT HAPPENED?! YOU'RE HURT!
IT WAS THAT GANG THAT'S BEEN MESSING AROUND ON OUR TURF. THEY TOOK HIM BY SURPRISE.
WE TRIED TO PROTECT HIM, BUT IT ALL HAPPENED SO FAST.
SOMETHING WASN'T RIGHT ABOUT THEM. THEY'RE FREAKY STRONG, LIKE SOMETHING WAS CONTROLLING THEM.
AND FOR SOME REASON, WHEN THEY WERE AROUND, IT WAS LIKE WE HAD NO ENERGY...
HEY!

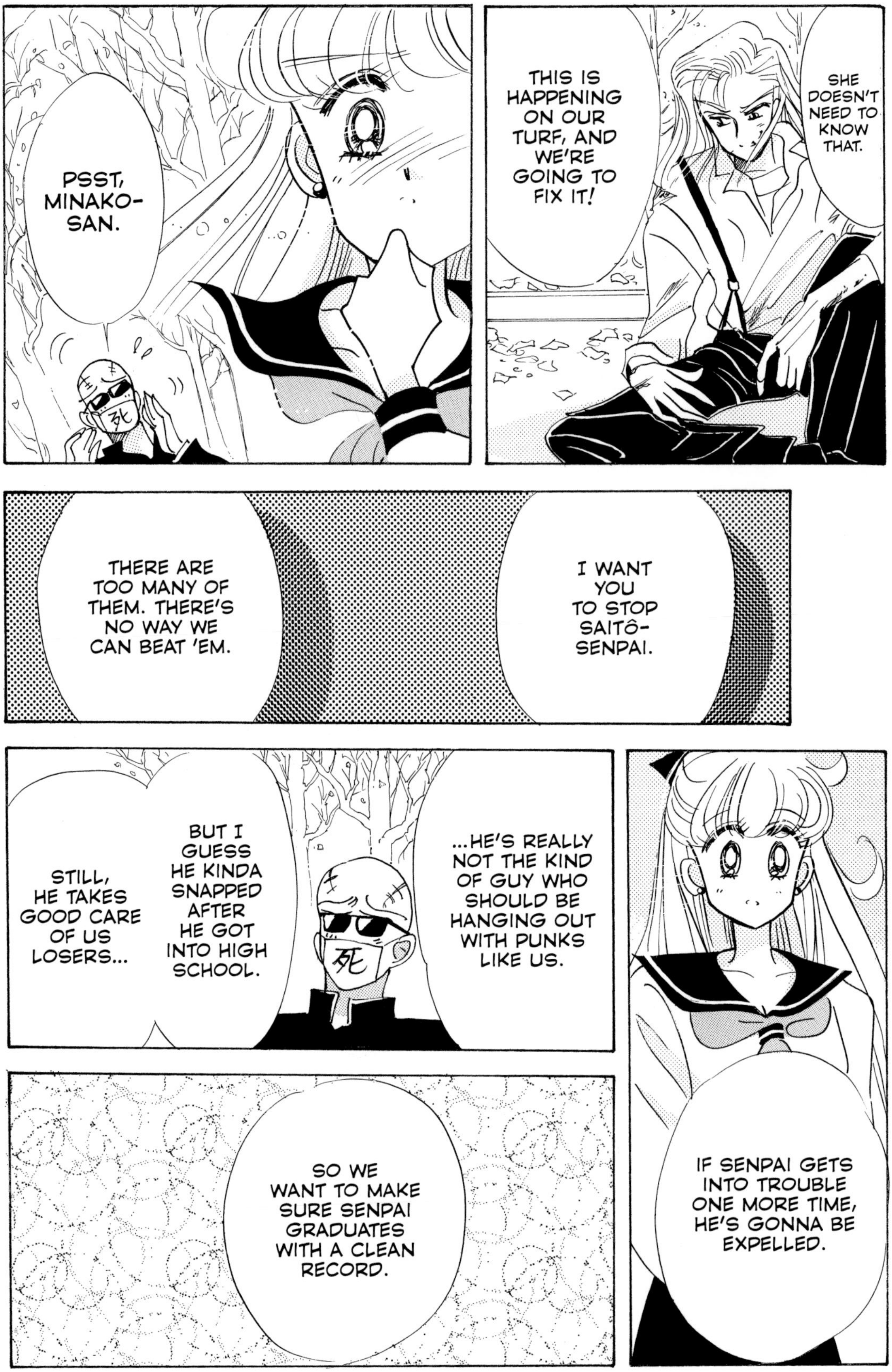
SHE DOESN'T NEED TO KNOW THAT.
THIS IS HAPPENING ON OUR TURF, AND WE'RE GOING TO FIX IT!
PSST, MINAKO-SAN.
I WANT YOU TO STOP SAITÔ-SENPAI.
THERE ARE TOO MANY OF THEM. THERE'S NO WAY WE CAN BEAT 'EM.
IF SENPAI GETS INTO TROUBLE ONE MORE TIME, HE'S GONNA BE EXPELLED.
...HE'S REALLY NOT THE KIND OF GUY WHO SHOULD BE HANGING OUT WITH PUNKS LIKE US.
BUT I GUESS HE KINDA SNAPPED AFTER HE GOT INTO HIGH SCHOOL.
STILL, HE TAKES GOOD CARE OF US LOSERS...
SO WE WANT TO MAKE SURE SENPAI GRADUATES WITH A CLEAN RECORD.

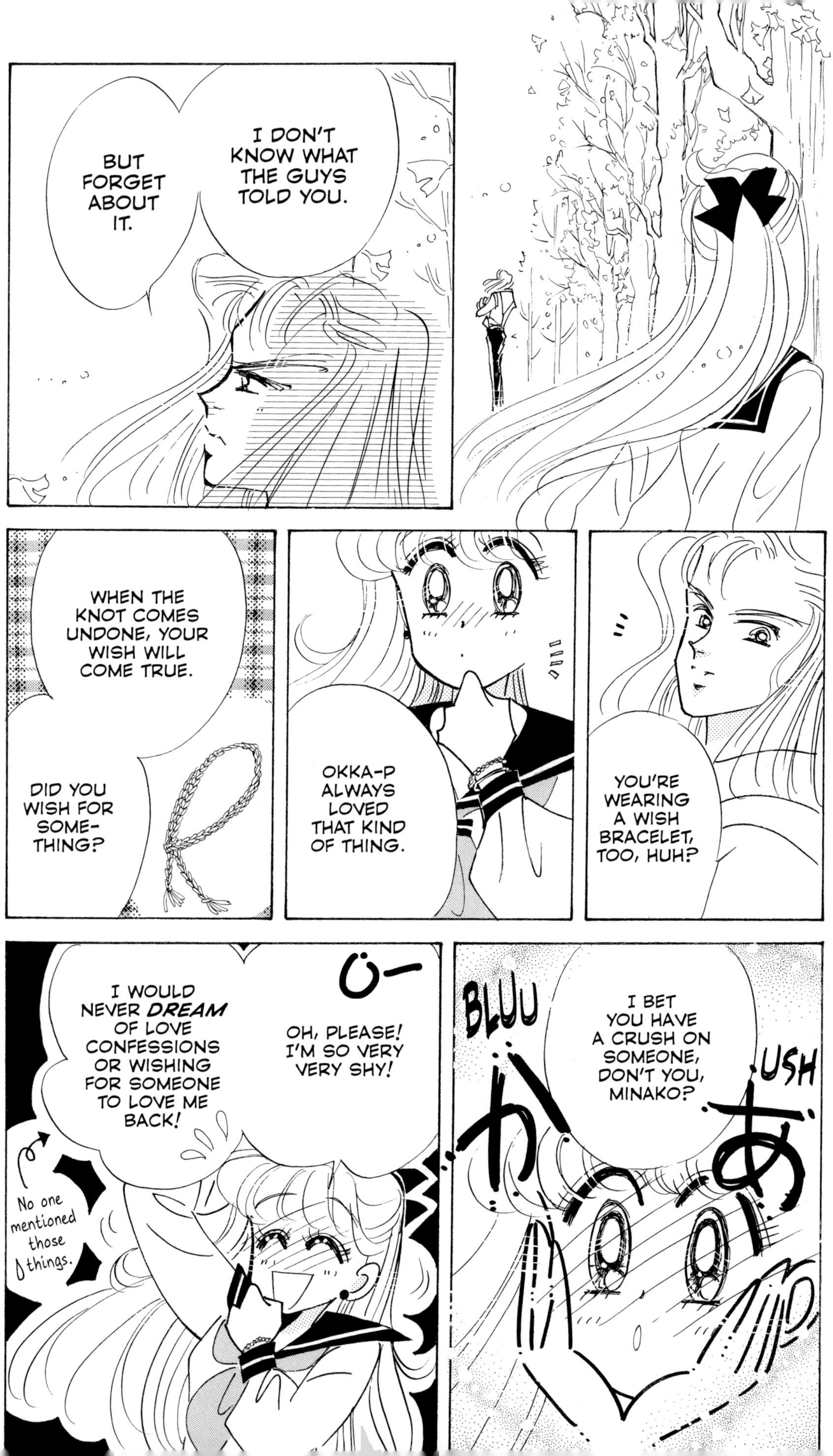
I DON'T KNOW WHAT THE GUYS TOLD YOU.
BUT FORGET ABOUT IT.
YOU'RE WEARING A WISH BRACELET, TOO, HUH?
OKKA-P ALWAYS LOVED THAT KIND OF THING.
WHEN THE KNOT COMES UNDONE, YOUR WISH WILL COME TRUE.
DID YOU WISH FOR SOME-THING?
I BET YOU HAVE A CRUSH ON SOMEONE, DON'T YOU, MINAKO?
BLUU
USH
OH, PLEASE! I'M SO VERY VERY SHY!
I WOULD NEVER DREAM OF LOVE CONFESSIONS OR WISHING FOR SOMEONE TO LOVE ME BACK!
No one mentioned those things.

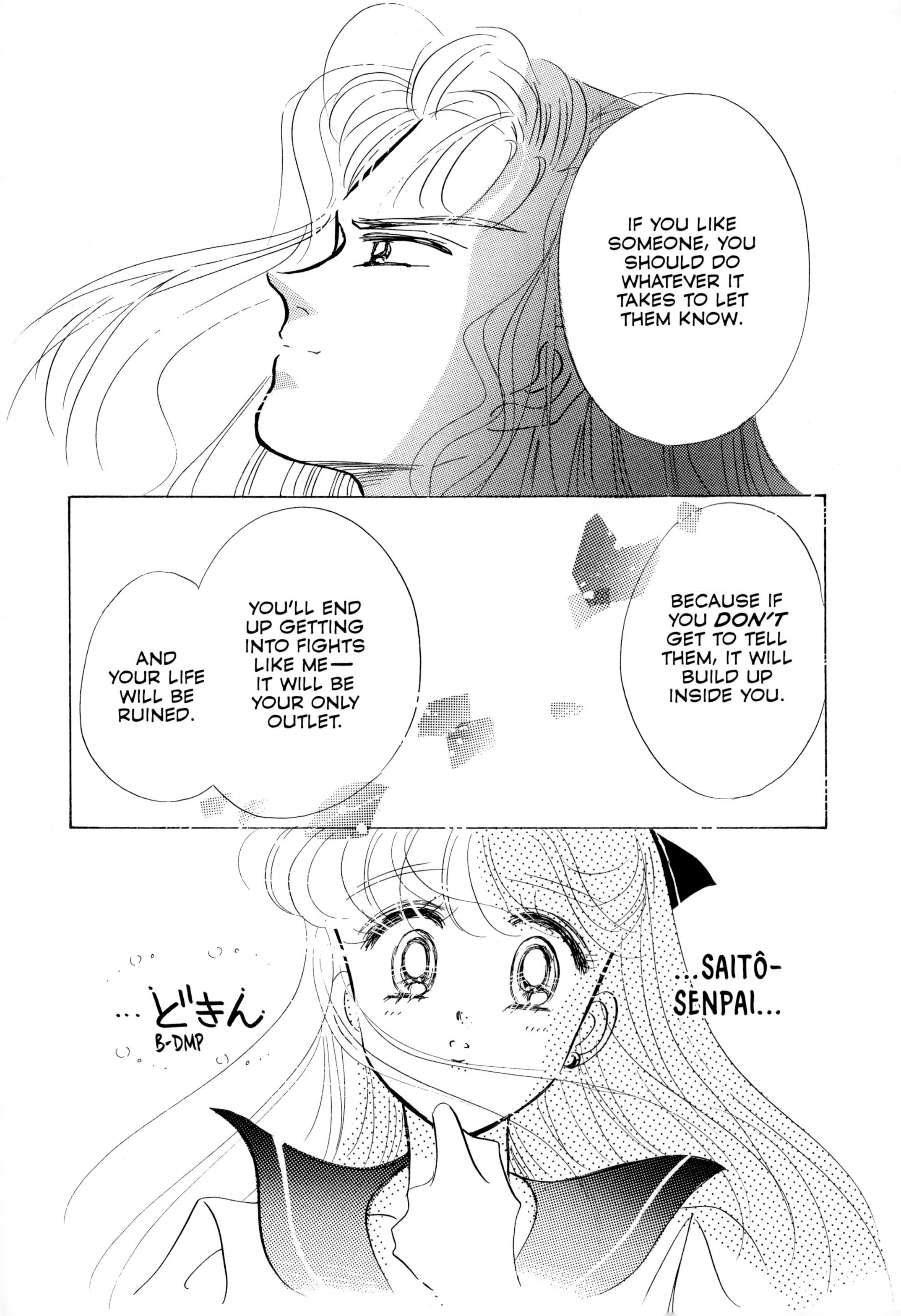
IF YOU LIKE SOMEONE, YOU SHOULD DO WHATEVER IT TAKES TO LET THEM KNOW.
BECAUSE IF YOU *DON'T* GET TO TELL THEM, IT WILL BUILD UP INSIDE YOU.
YOU'LL END UP GETTING INTO FIGHTS LIKE ME— IT WILL BE YOUR ONLY OUTLET.
AND YOUR LIFE WILL BE RUINED.
...SAITÔ-SENPAI...
...どきん
B-DMP

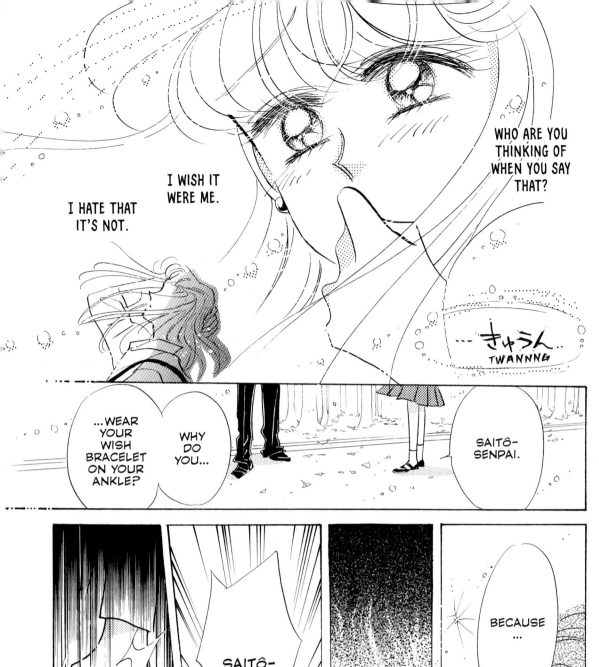

WHO ARE YOU THINKING OF WHEN YOU SAY THAT?

I WISH IT WERE ME.

I HATE THAT IT'S NOT.

きゅうん
TWANNNG

...WEAR YOUR WISH BRACELET ON YOUR ANKLE?

WHY DO YOU...

SAITÔ-SENPAI.

SAITÔ-SENPAI!!

ZSH

BECAUSE...

CLAK

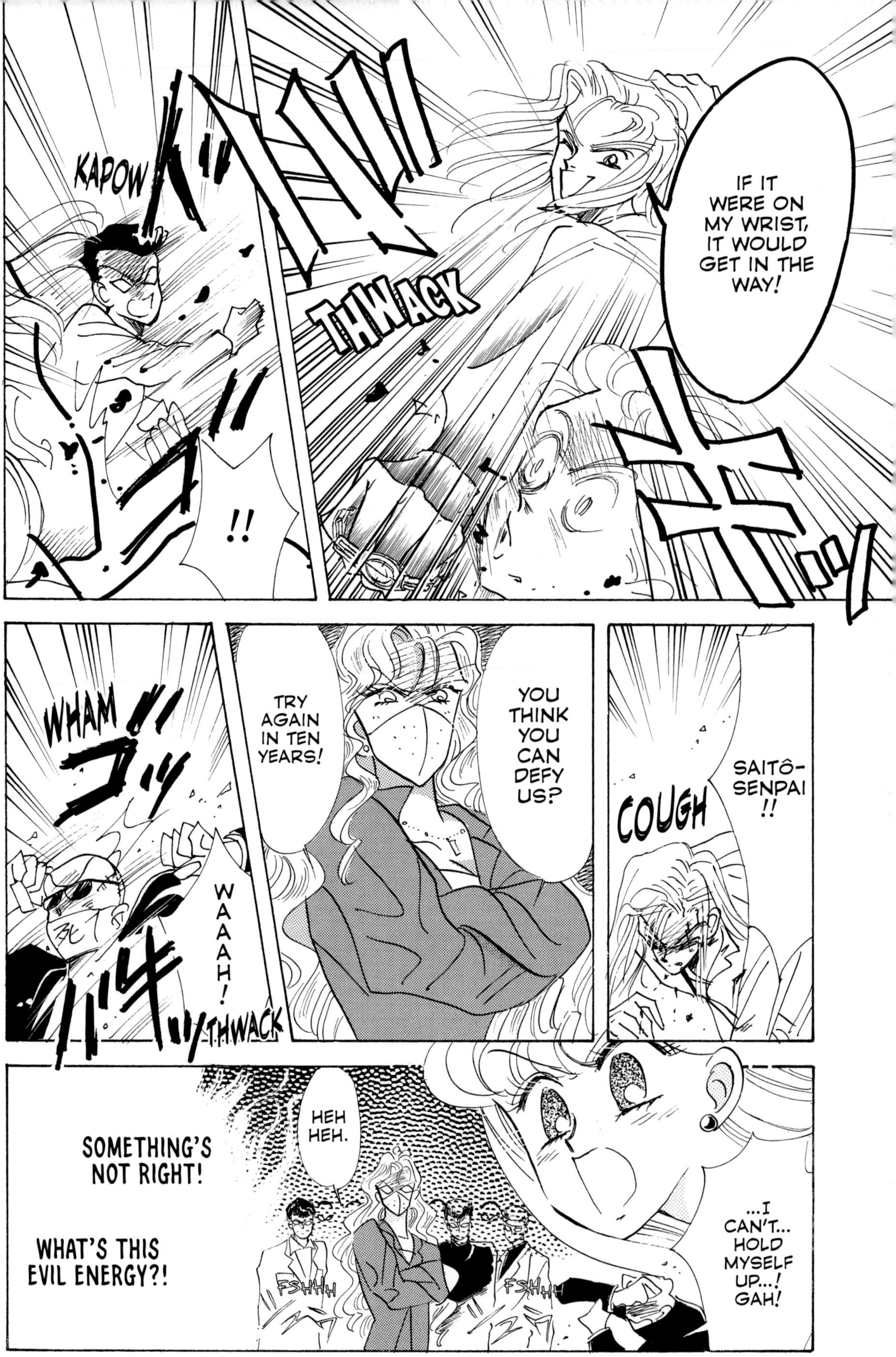
IF IT WERE ON MY WRIST, IT WOULD GET IN THE WAY!
THWACK
KAPOW
!!
SAITÔ-SENPAI!!
COUGH
YOU THINK YOU CAN DEFY US?
TRY AGAIN IN TEN YEARS!
WHAM
WAAAAH!
THWACK
HEH HEH.
...I CAN'T... HOLD MYSELF UP...! GAH!
SOMETHING'S NOT RIGHT!
WHAT'S THIS EVIL ENERGY?!
FSHHH
FSHHH

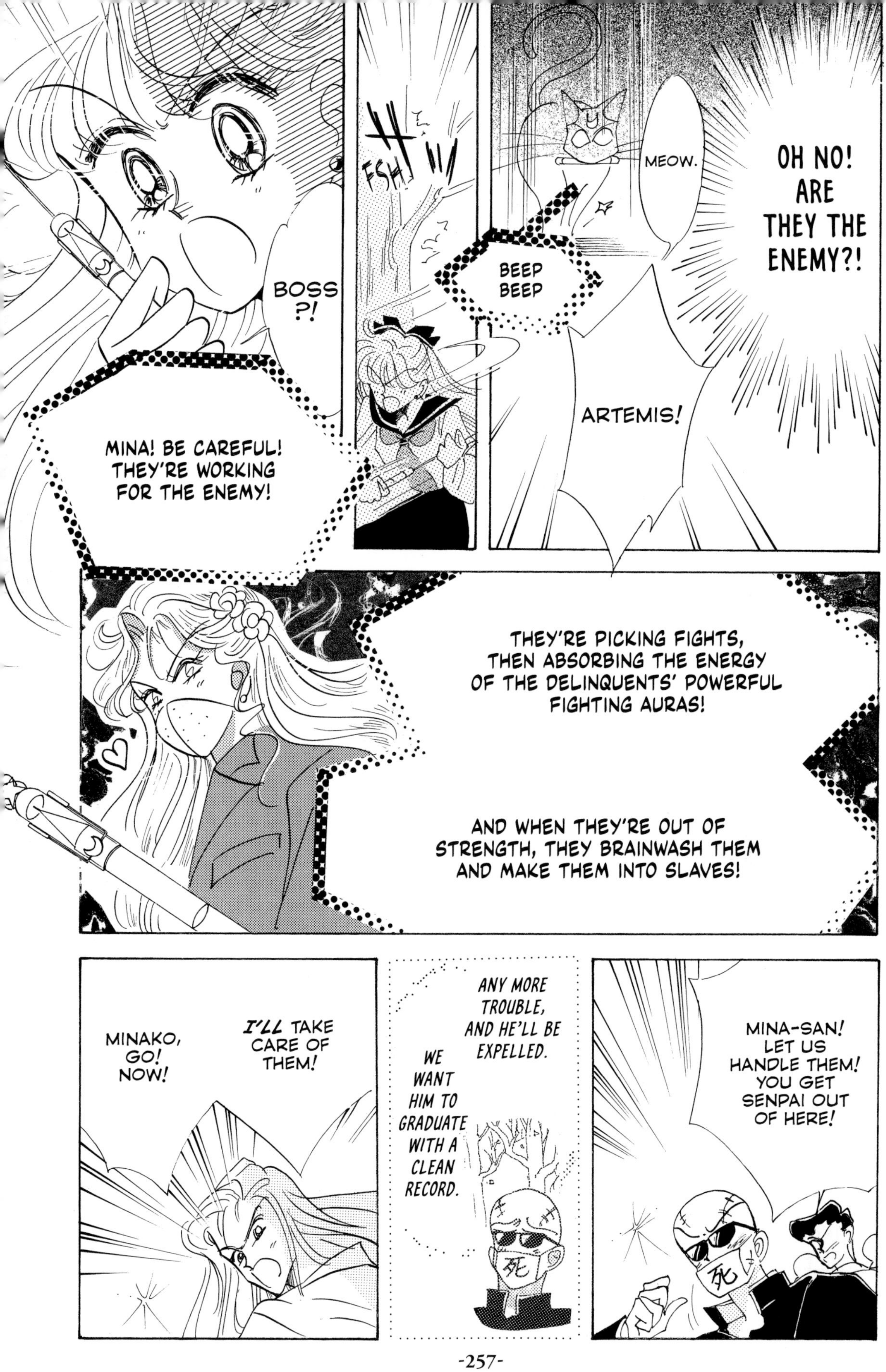
OH NO! ARE THEY THE ENEMY?!
MEOW.
ARTEMIS!
FSH
BEEP BEEP
BOSS?!
MINA! BE CAREFUL! THEY'RE WORKING FOR THE ENEMY!
THEY'RE PICKING FIGHTS, THEN ABSORBING THE ENERGY OF THE DELINQUENTS' POWERFUL FIGHTING AURAS!
AND WHEN THEY'RE OUT OF STRENGTH, THEY BRAINWASH THEM AND MAKE THEM INTO SLAVES!
MINA-SAN! LET US HANDLE THEM! YOU GET SENPAI OUT OF HERE!
ANY MORE TROUBLE, AND HE'LL BE EXPELLED.
WE WANT HIM TO GRADUATE WITH A CLEAN RECORD.
I'LL TAKE CARE OF THEM!
MINAKO, GO! NOW!

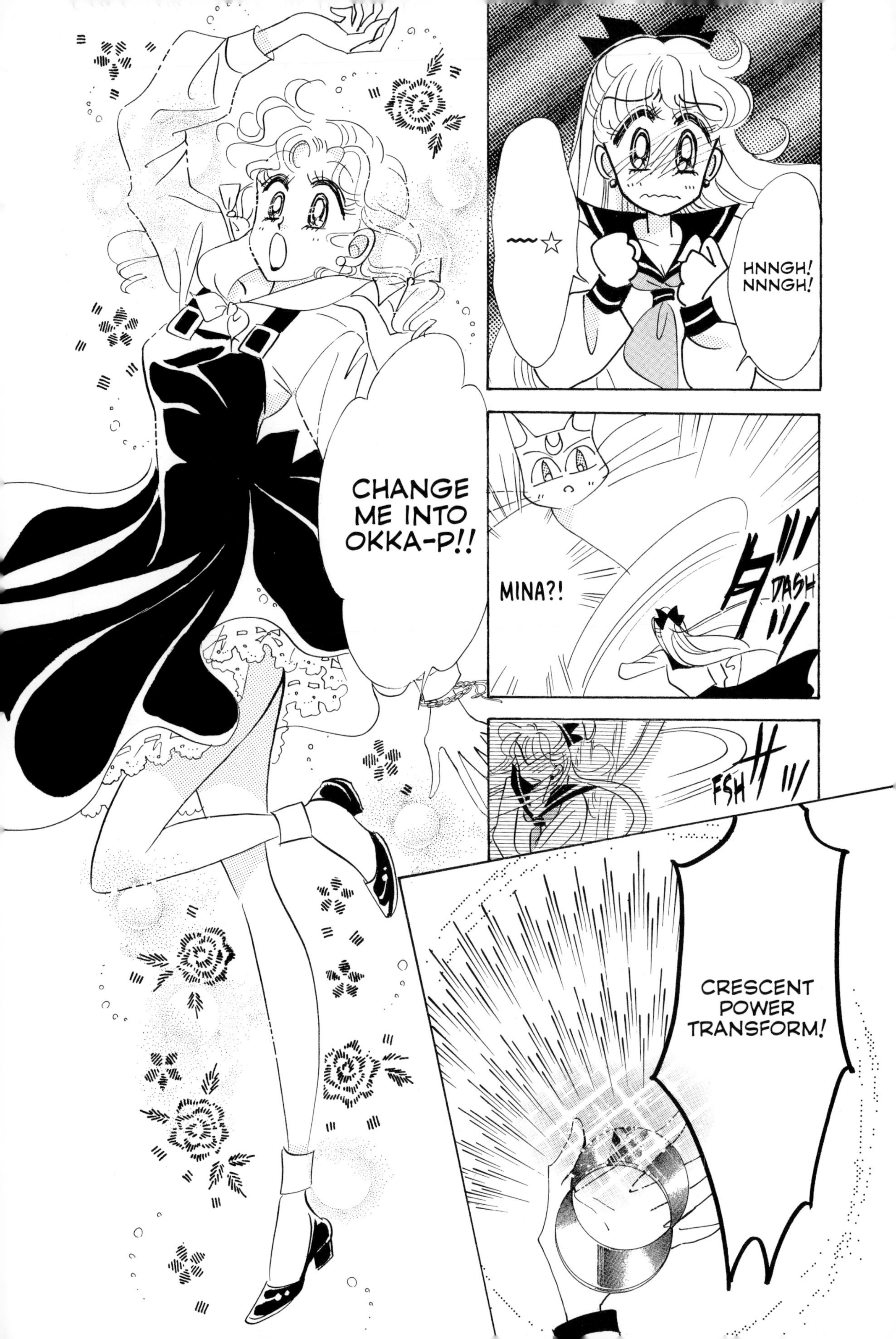
HNNGH! NNNGH!
~☆
DASH
MINA?!
FSH
CRESCENT POWER TRANSFORM!
CHANGE ME INTO OKKA-P!!

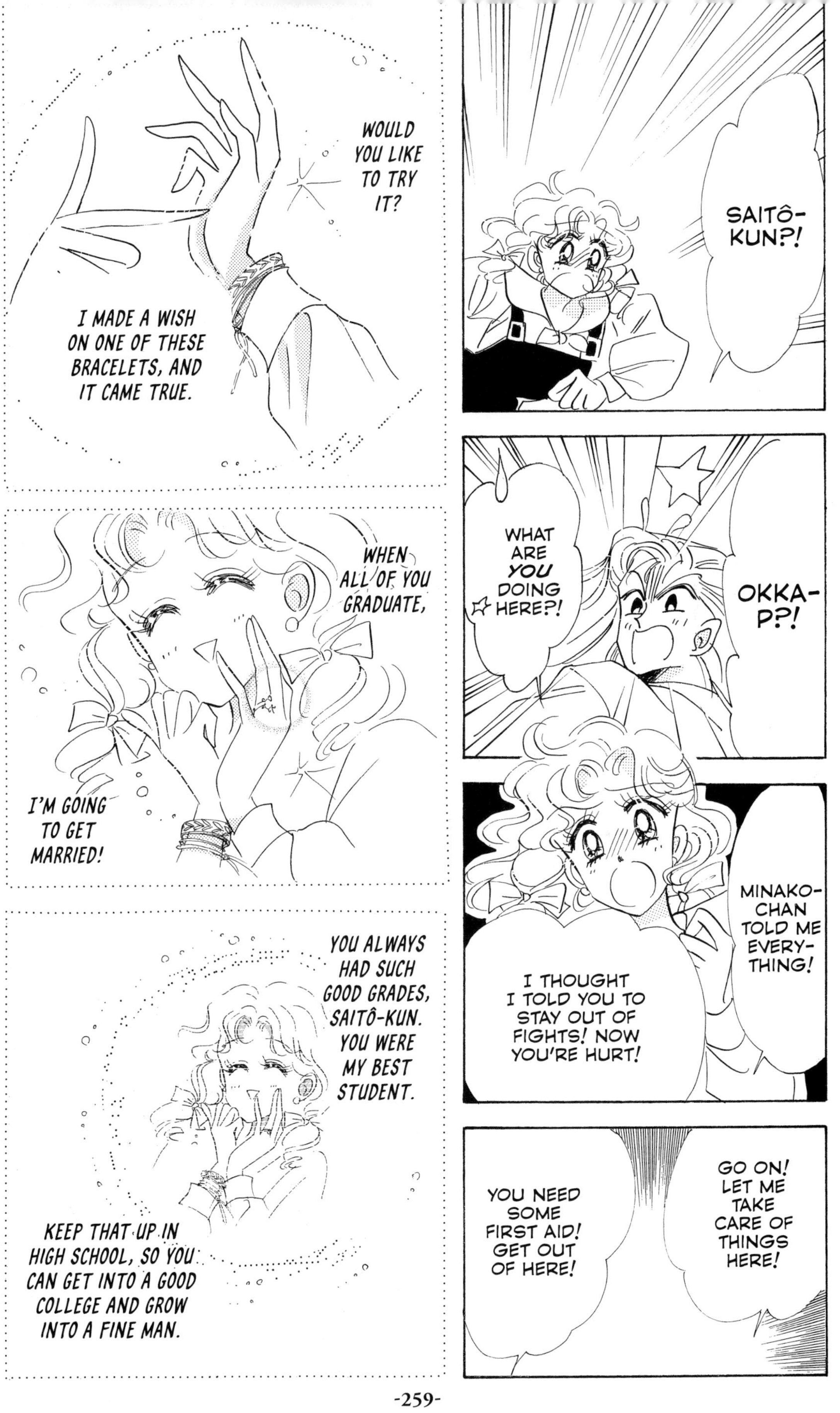
SAITÔ-KUN?!
OKKA-P?!
WHAT ARE *YOU* DOING HERE?!
MINAKO-CHAN TOLD ME EVERYTHING!
I THOUGHT I TOLD YOU TO STAY OUT OF FIGHTS! NOW YOU'RE HURT!
GO ON! LET ME TAKE CARE OF THINGS HERE!
YOU NEED SOME FIRST AID! GET OUT OF HERE!
WOULD YOU LIKE TO TRY IT?
I MADE A WISH ON ONE OF THESE BRACELETS, AND IT CAME TRUE.
WHEN ALL OF YOU GRADUATE,
I'M GOING TO GET MARRIED!
YOU ALWAYS HAD SUCH GOOD GRADES, SAITÔ-KUN. YOU WERE MY BEST STUDENT.
KEEP THAT UP IN HIGH SCHOOL, SO YOU CAN GET INTO A GOOD COLLEGE AND GROW INTO A FINE MAN.

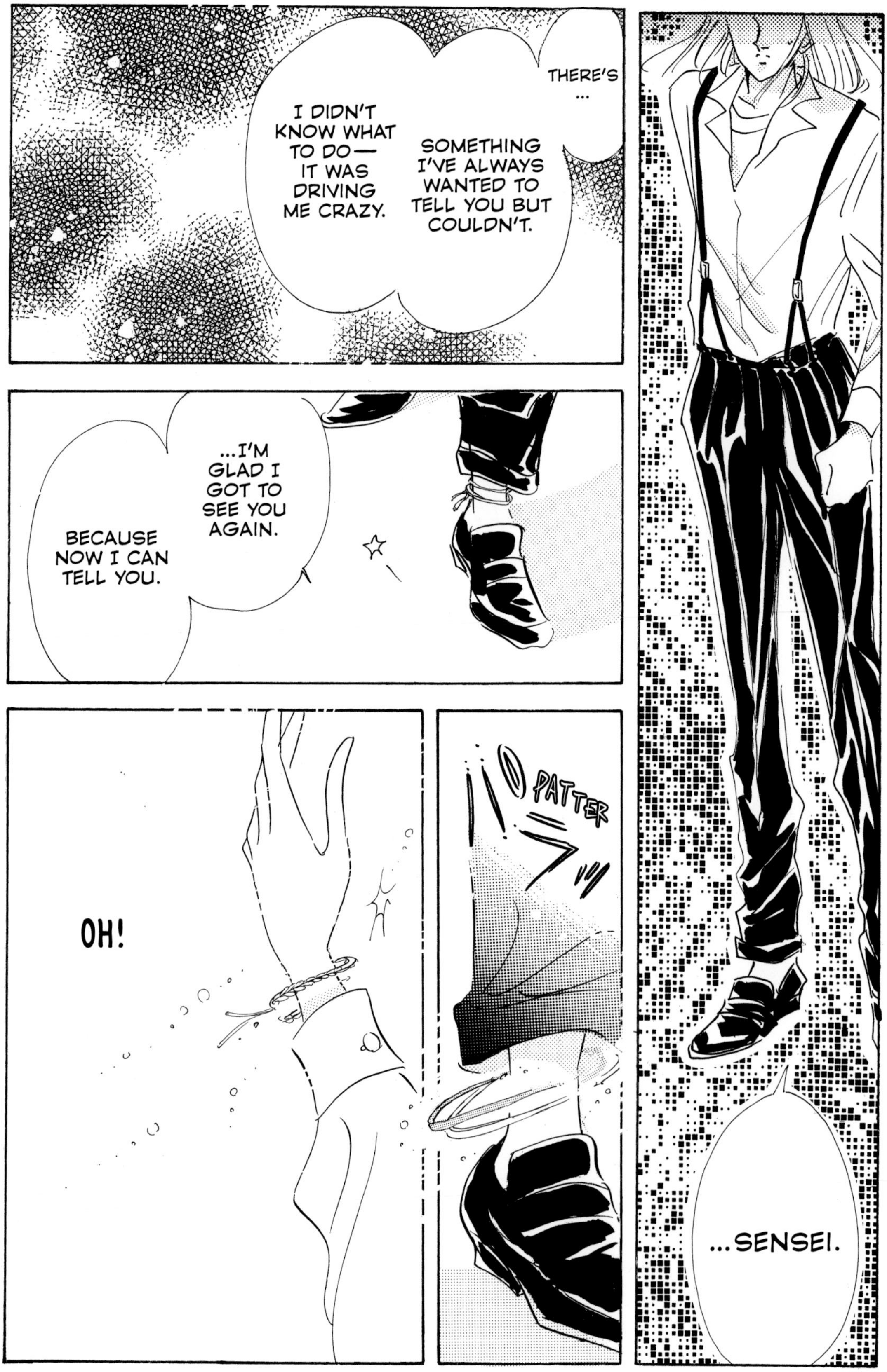
...SENSEI.
THERE'S ...
SOMETHING I'VE ALWAYS WANTED TO TELL YOU BUT COULDN'T.
I DIDN'T KNOW WHAT TO DO— IT WAS DRIVING ME CRAZY.
...I'M GLAD I GOT TO SEE YOU AGAIN.
BECAUSE NOW I CAN TELL YOU.
PATTER
OH!

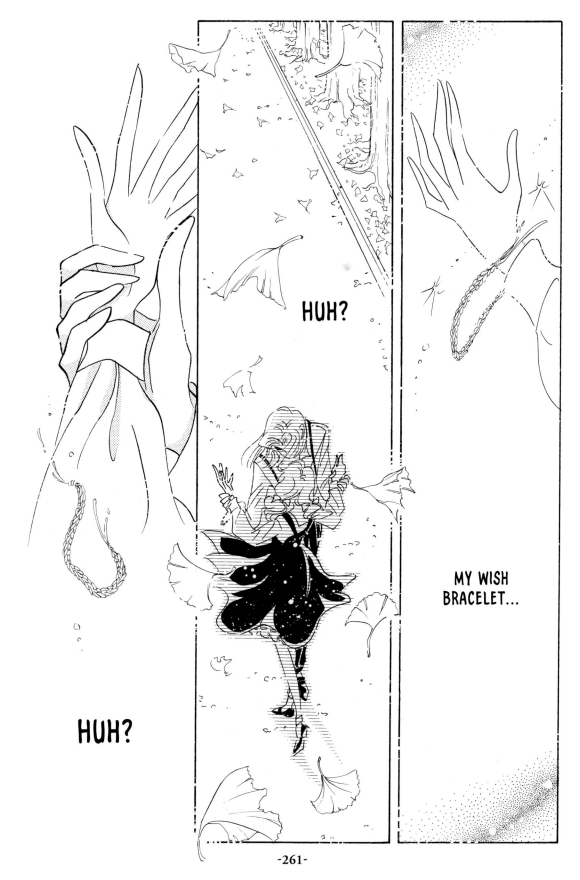

HUH?

MY WISH
BRACELET...

HUH?

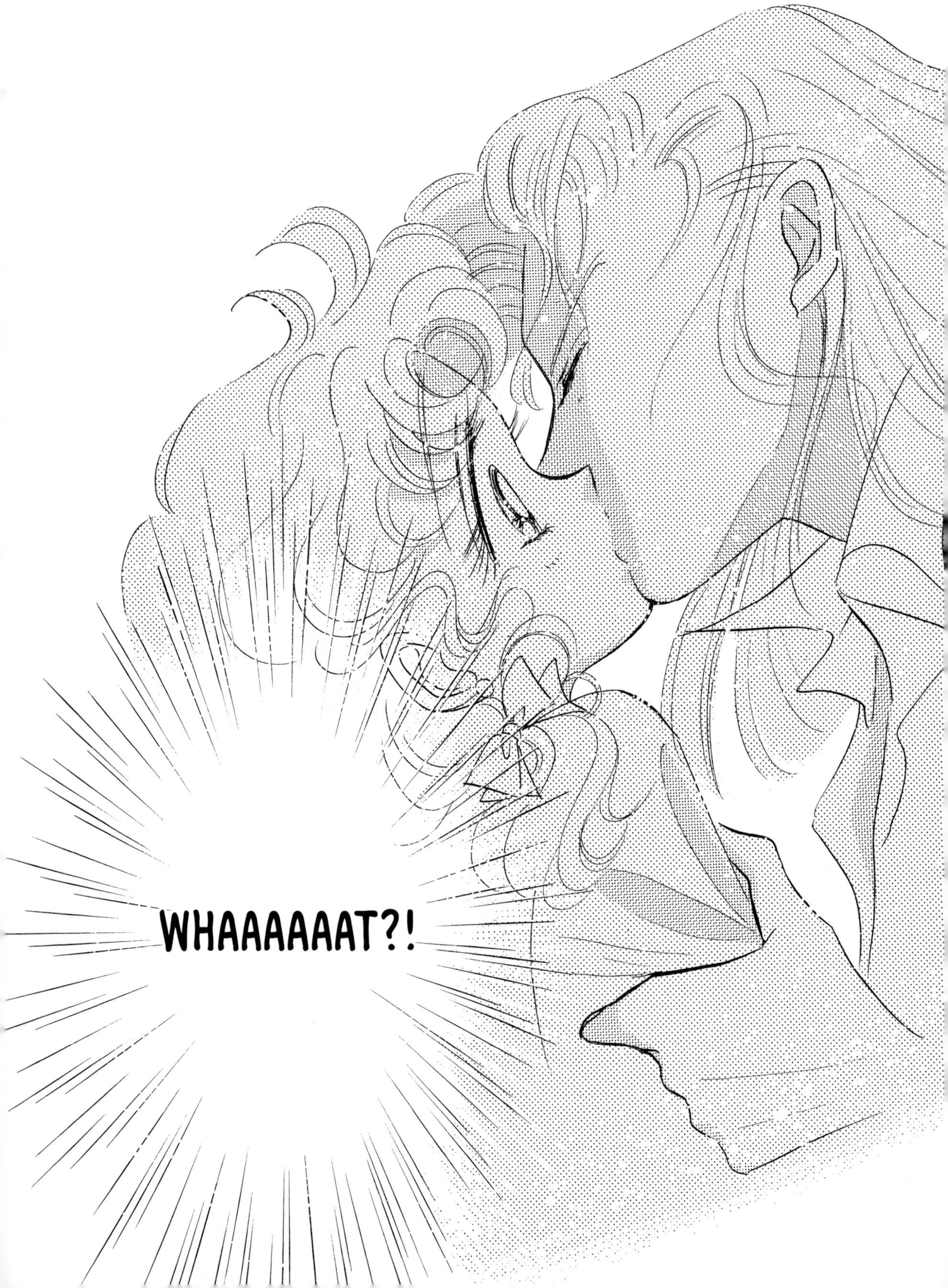
WHAAAAAAT?!

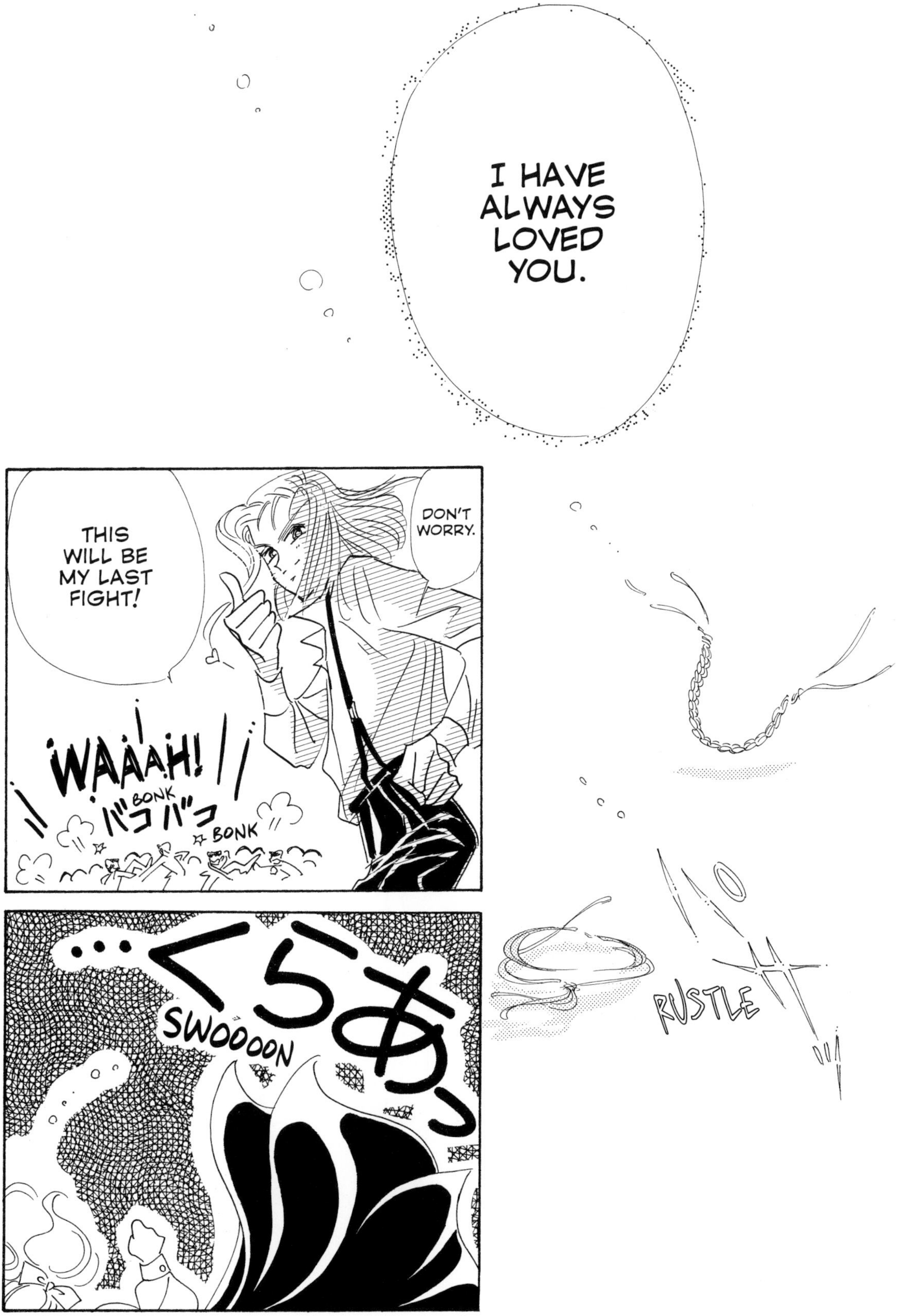
I HAVE ALWAYS LOVED YOU.
RUSTLE
DON'T WORRY.
THIS WILL BE MY LAST FIGHT!
WAAAH!
BONK
バコバコ
BONK
…くらあっ
SWOOOON

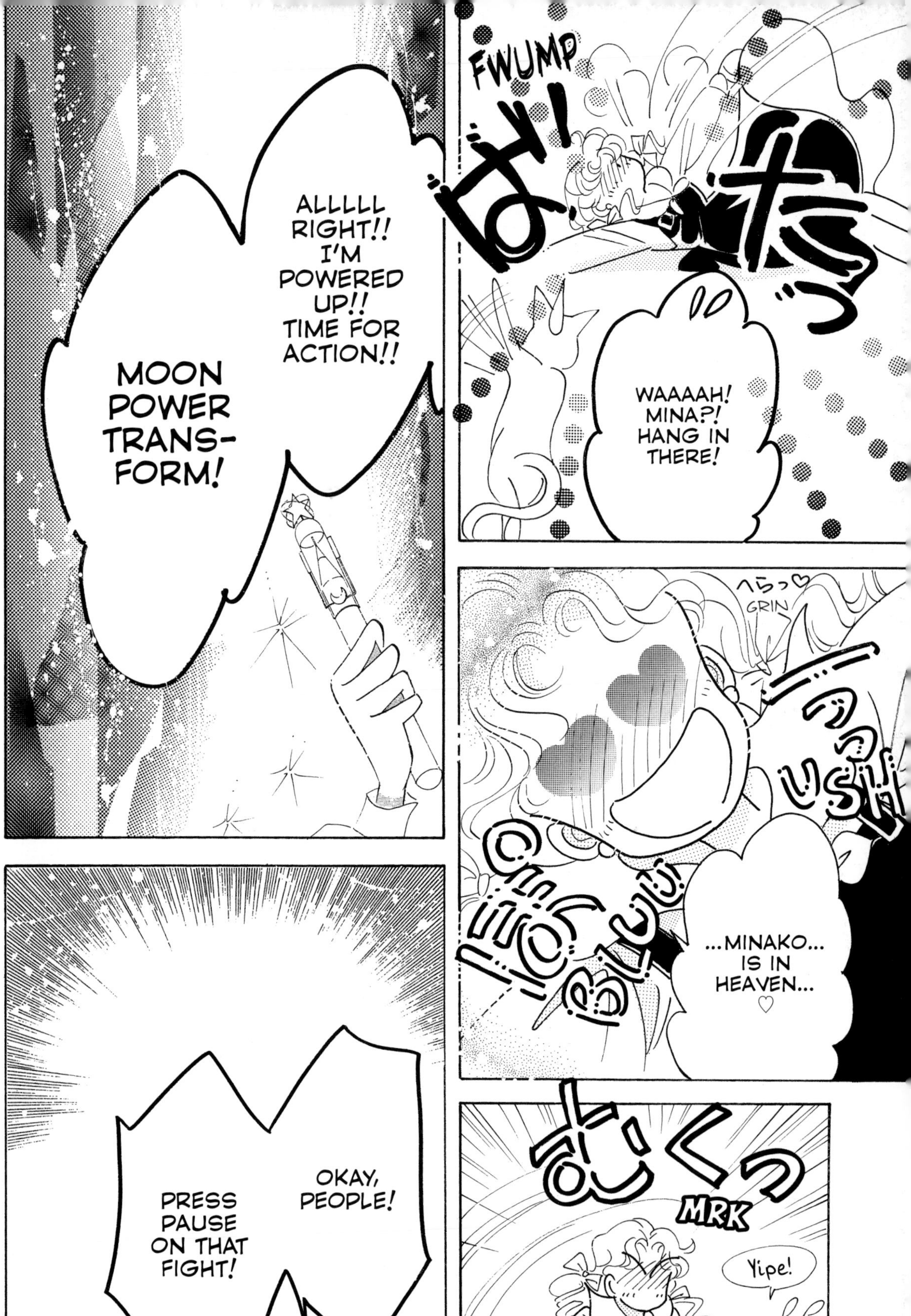
FWUMP
ばたっ
WAAAAH! MINA?! HANG IN THERE!
へらっ♡
GRIN
...MINAKO... IS IN HEAVEN... ♡
ALLLLL RIGHT!! I'M POWERED UP!! TIME FOR ACTION!!
MOON POWER TRANS-FORM!
むくっ
MRK
Yipe!
OKAY, PEOPLE!
PRESS PAUSE ON THAT FIGHT!

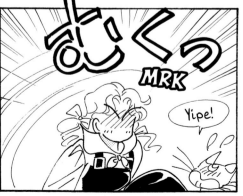

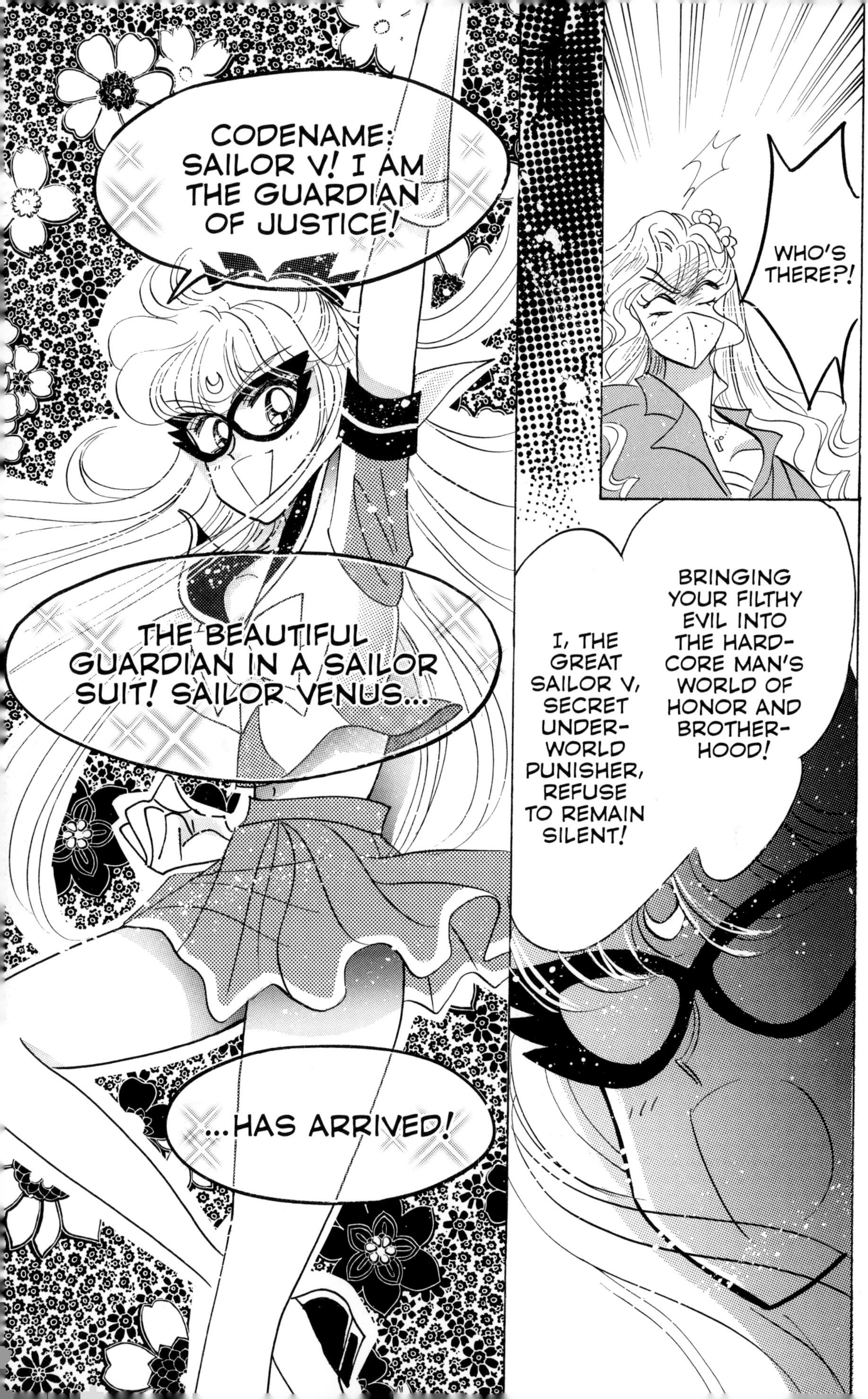
WHO'S THERE?!
BRINGING YOUR FILTHY EVIL INTO THE HARD-CORE MAN'S WORLD OF HONOR AND BROTHER-HOOD!
I, THE GREAT SAILOR V, SECRET UNDER-WORLD PUNISHER, REFUSE TO REMAIN SILENT!
CODENAME: SAILOR V! I AM THE GUARDIAN OF JUSTICE!
THE BEAUTIFUL GUARDIAN IN A SAILOR SUIT! SAILOR VENUS...
...HAS ARRIVED!

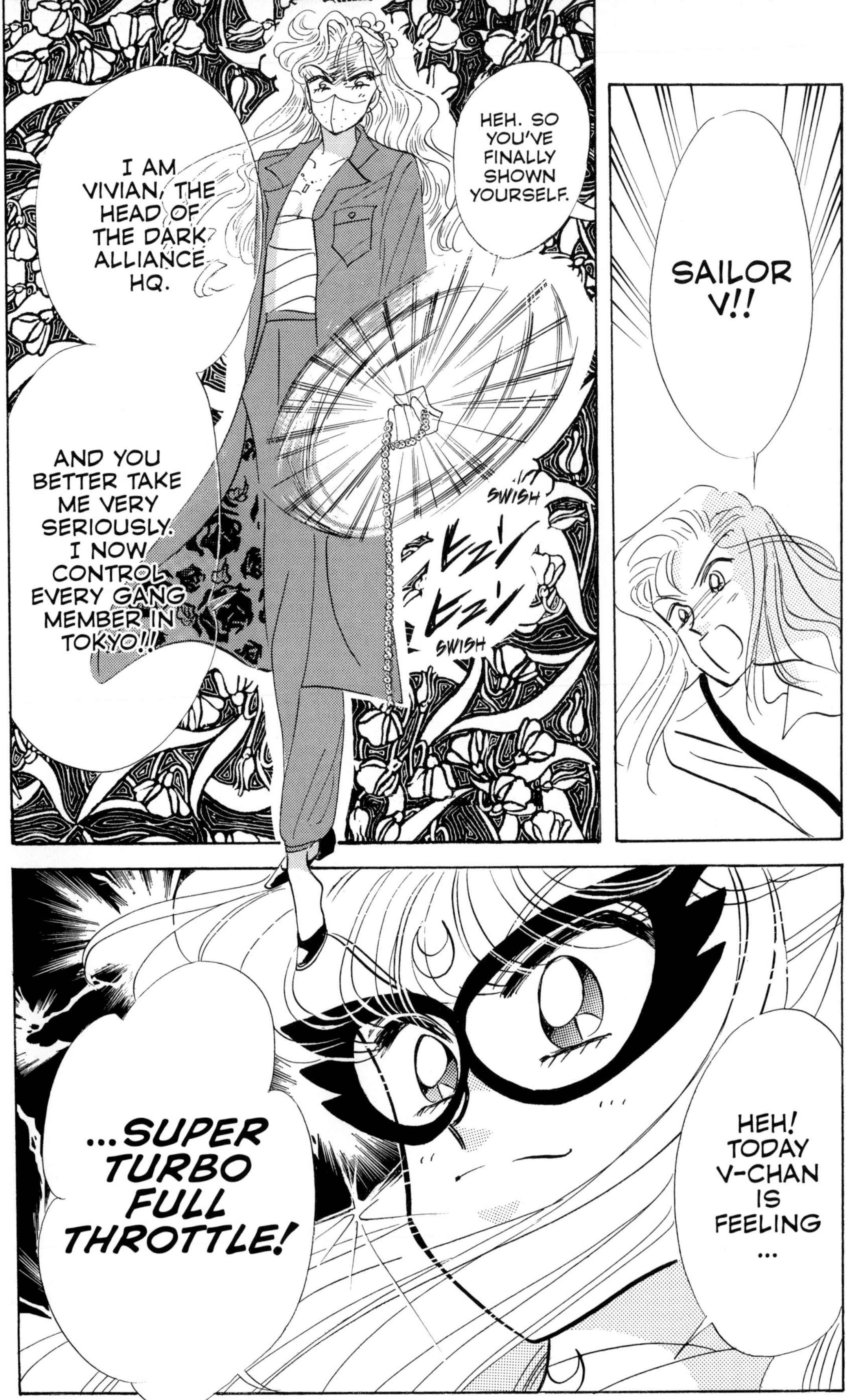
SAILOR V!!
HEH. SO YOU'VE FINALLY SHOWN YOURSELF.
I AM VIVIAN, THE HEAD OF THE DARK ALLIANCE HQ.
SWISH
SWISH
AND YOU BETTER TAKE ME VERY SERIOUSLY. I NOW CONTROL EVERY GANG MEMBER IN TOKYO!!
HEH! TODAY V-CHAN IS FEELING ...
...SUPER TURBO FULL THROTTLE!

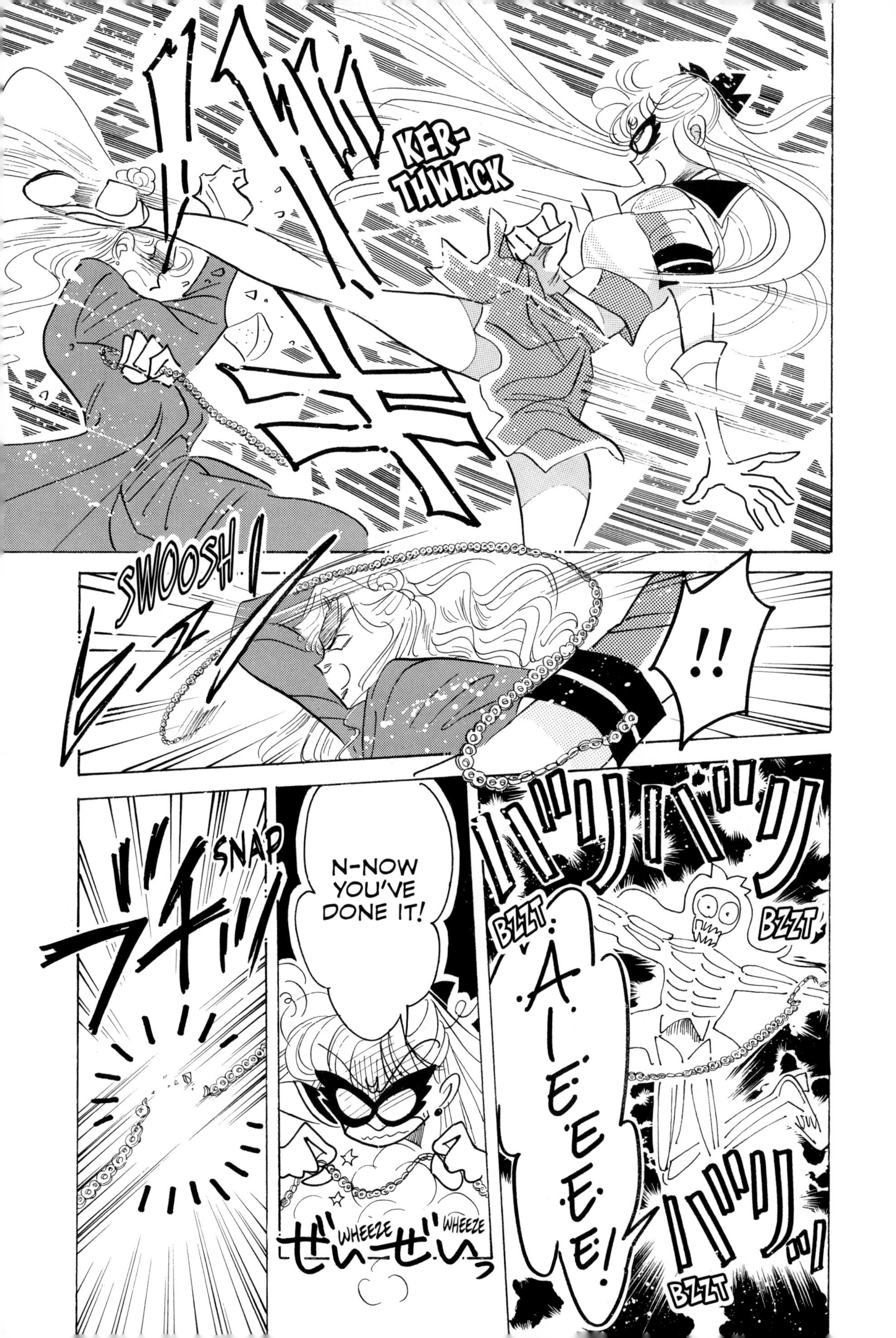
KER-THWACK
!!
SWOOSH
BZZT
BZZT
AIEEEEE!
BZZT
N-NOW YOU'VE DONE IT!
WHEEZE WHEEZE
ぜいぜいっ
SNAP

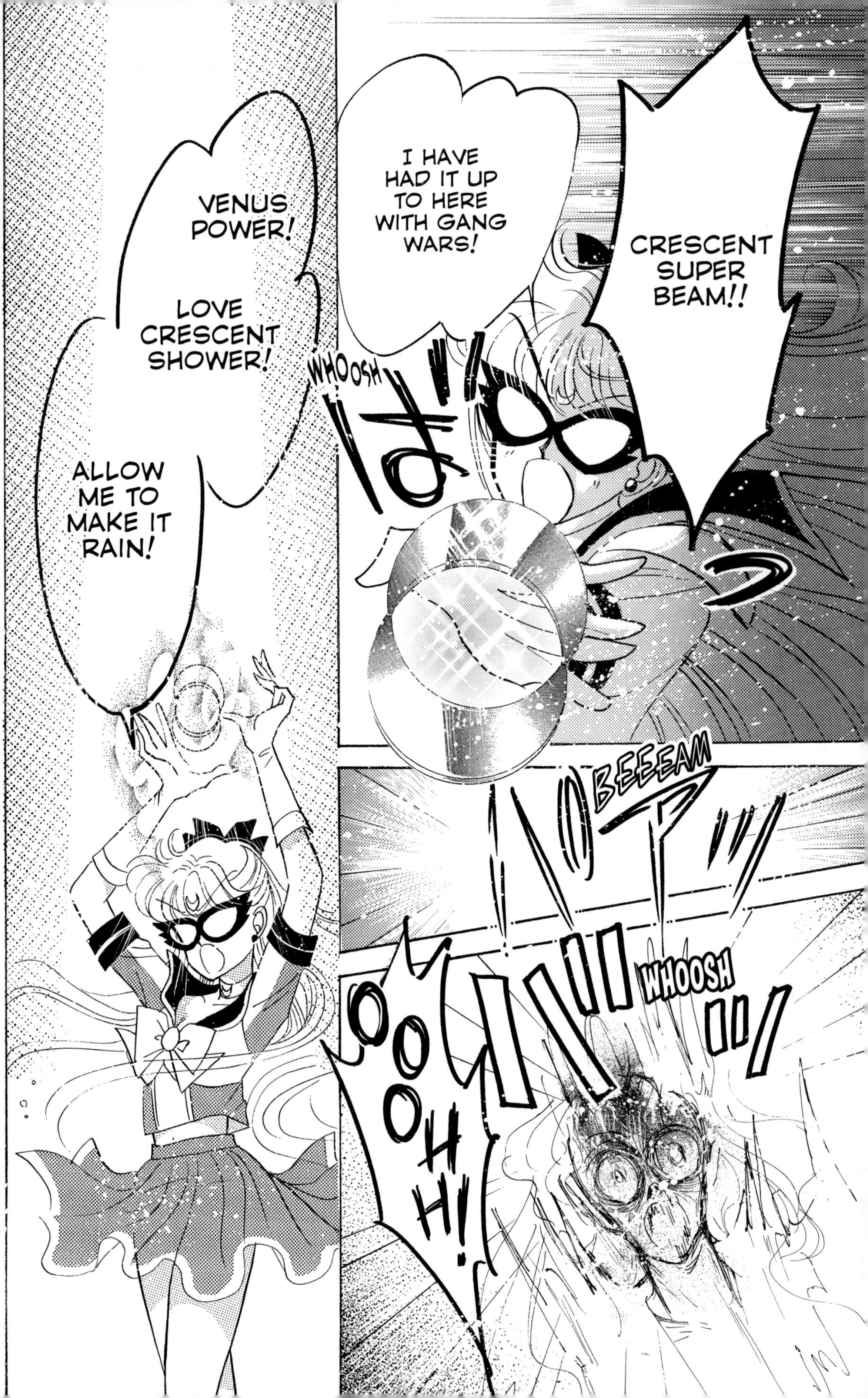
CRESCENT SUPER BEAM!!
I HAVE HAD IT UP TO HERE WITH GANG WARS!
WHOOSH
BEEEAM
WHOOSH
OOOOHH!!
VENUS POWER!
LOVE CRESCENT SHOWER!
ALLOW ME TO MAKE IT RAIN!

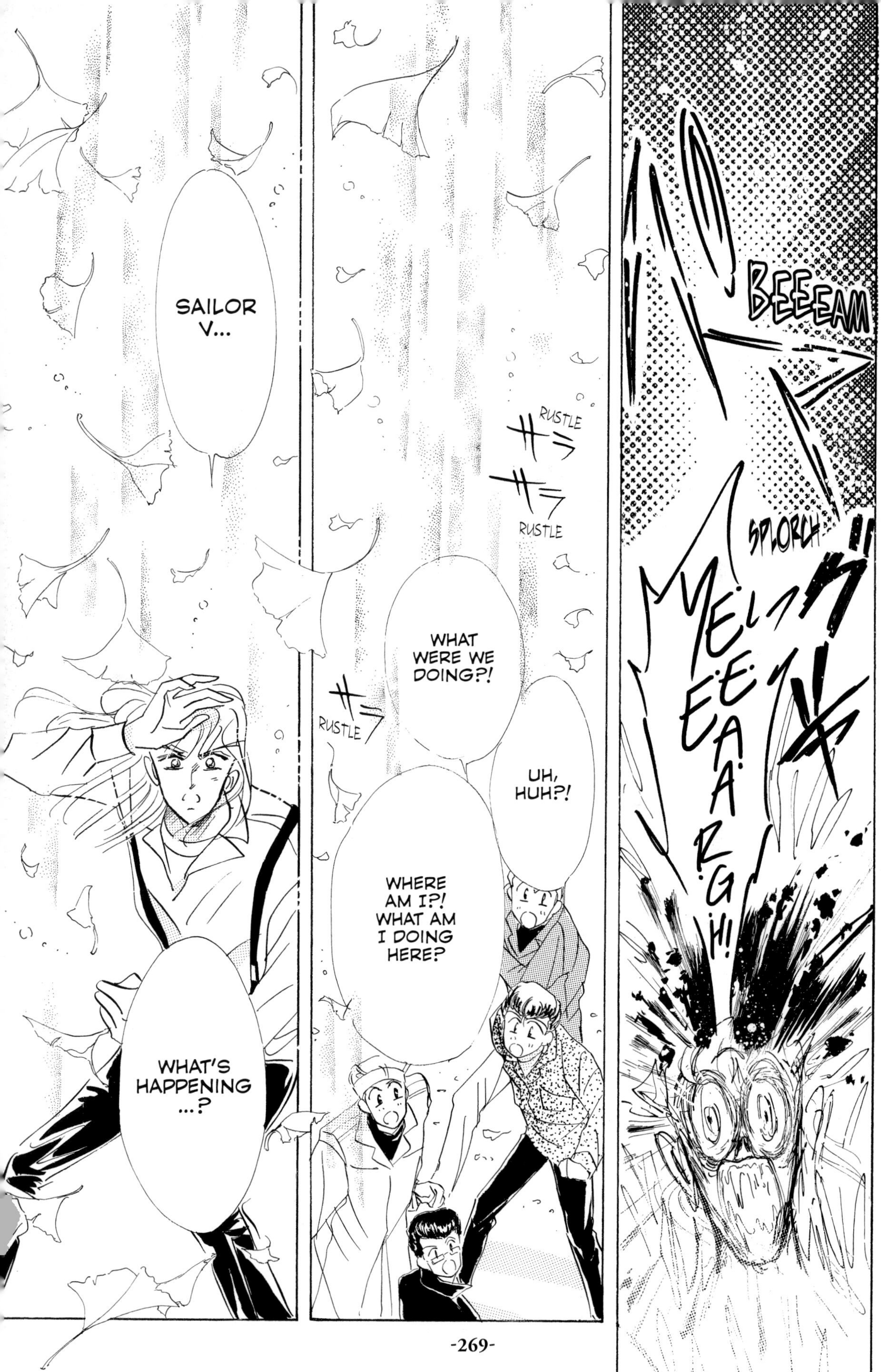
BEEEAM
SPLORCH
MEEEAARGH!
RUSTLE
RUSTLE
WHAT WERE WE DOING?!
UH, HUH?!
RUSTLE
WHERE AM I?! WHAT AM I DOING HERE?
SAILOR V...
WHAT'S HAPPENING ...?

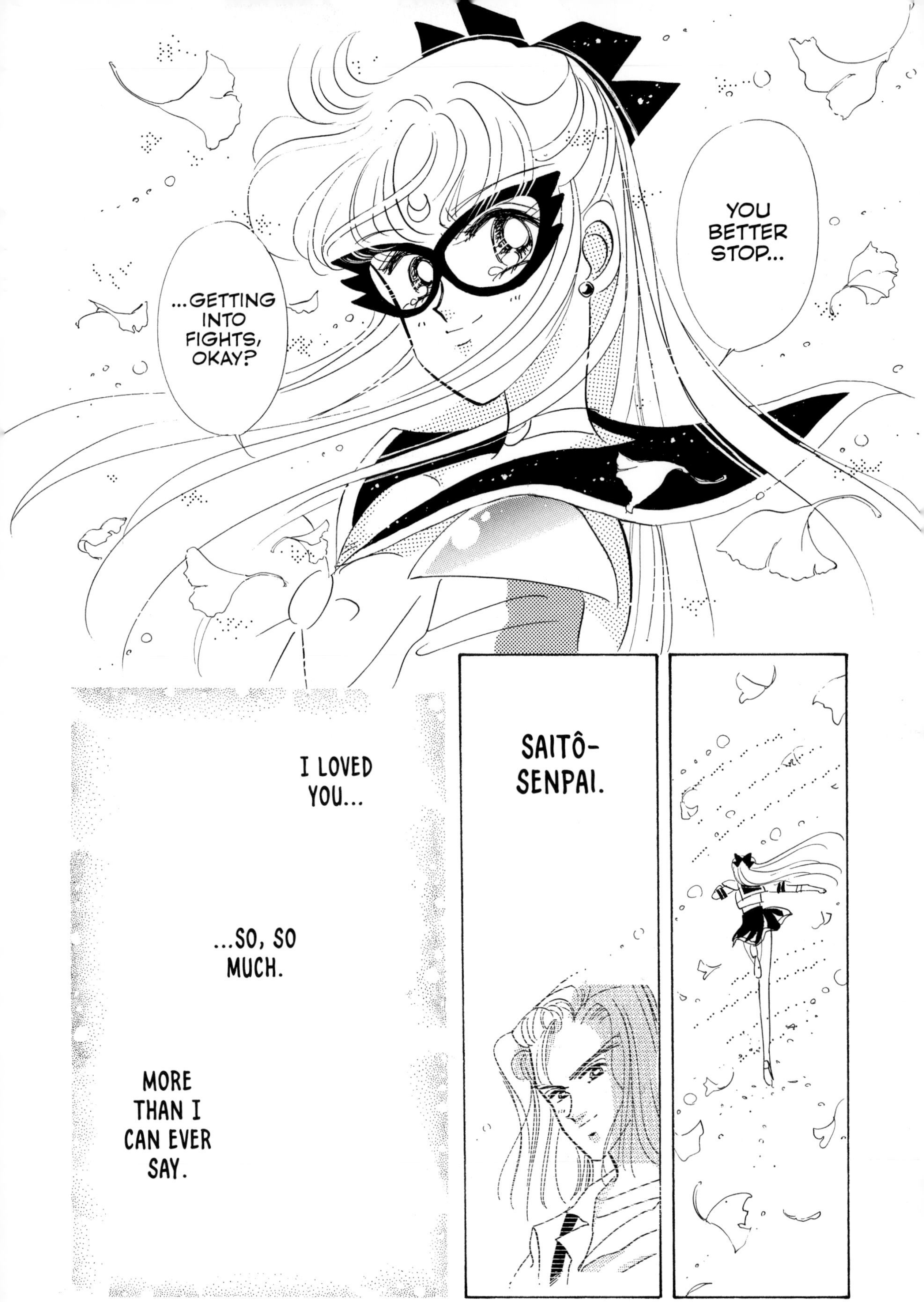
YOU BETTER STOP...
...GETTING INTO FIGHTS, OKAY?
SAITÔ-SENPAI.
I LOVED YOU...
...SO, SO MUCH.
MORE THAN I CAN EVER SAY.

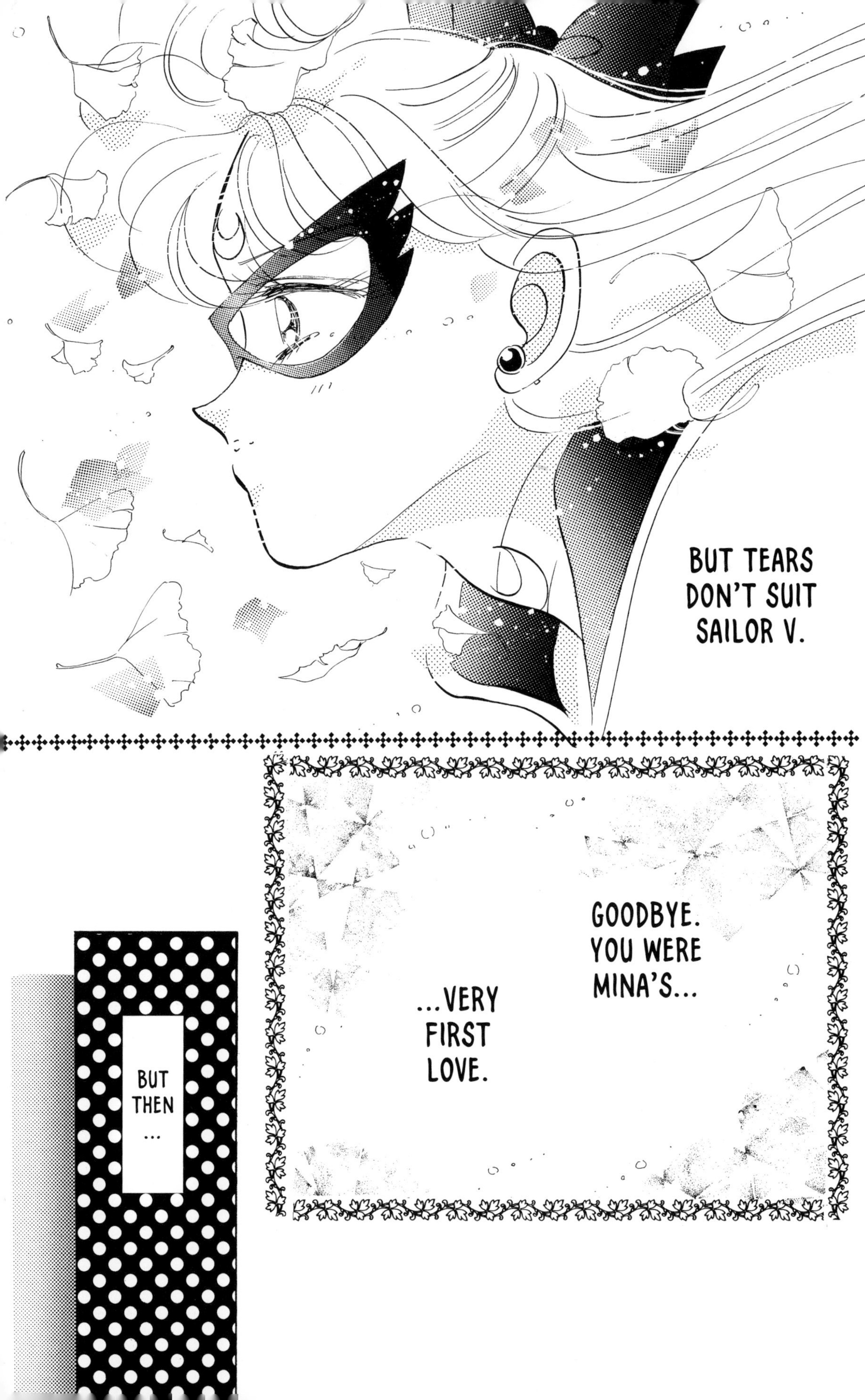
BUT TEARS DON'T SUIT SAILOR V.
GOODBYE. YOU WERE MINA'S...
...VERY FIRST LOVE.
BUT THEN ...

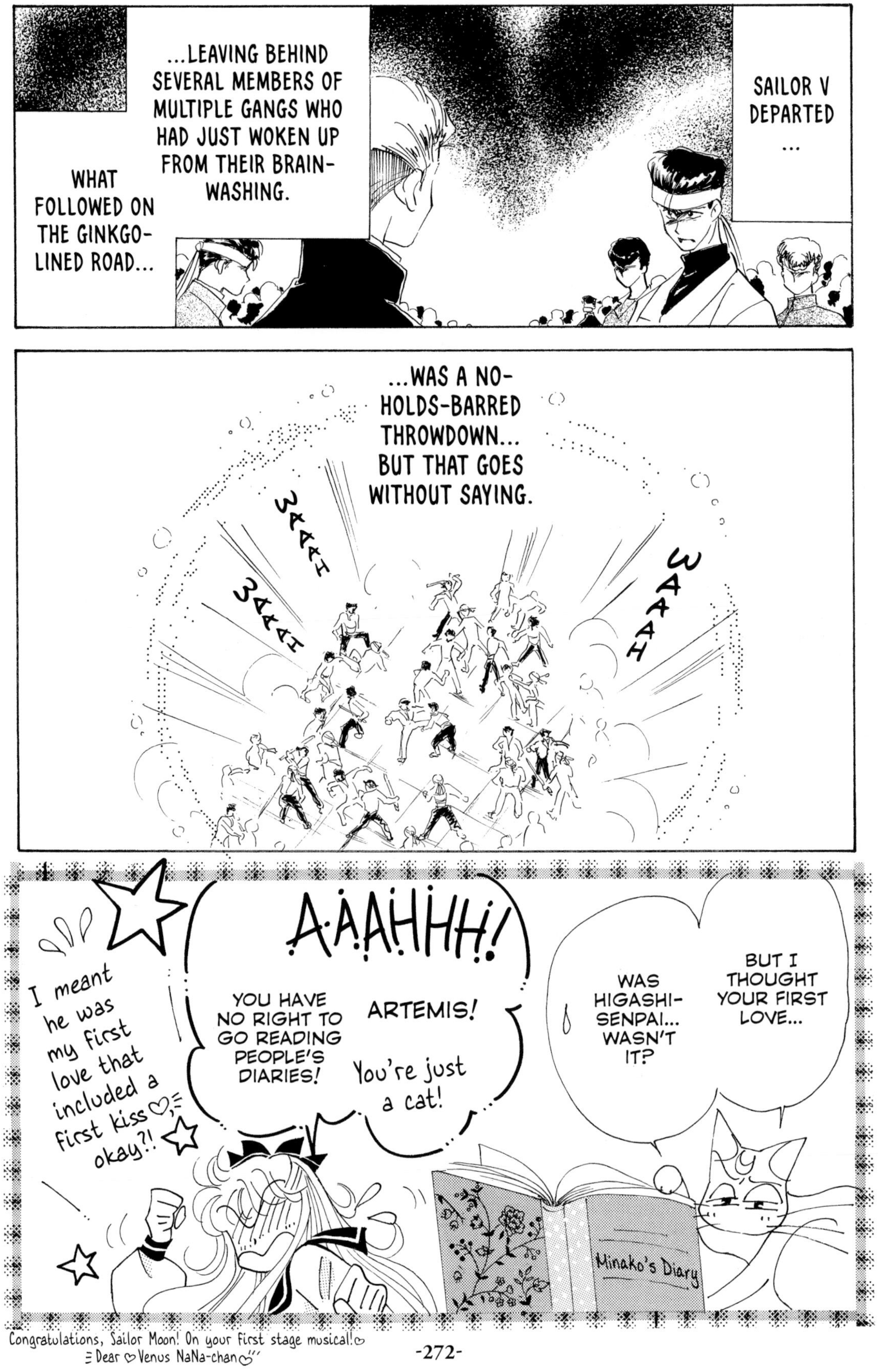
SAILOR V DEPARTED ...
...LEAVING BEHIND SEVERAL MEMBERS OF MULTIPLE GANGS WHO HAD JUST WOKEN UP FROM THEIR BRAIN-WASHING.
WHAT FOLLOWED ON THE GINKGO-LINED ROAD...
...WAS A NO-HOLDS-BARRED THROWDOWN... BUT THAT GOES WITHOUT SAYING.
WAAAH
BUT I THOUGHT YOUR FIRST LOVE...
WAS HIGASHI-SENPAI... WASN'T IT?
Minako's Diary
AAAHHH!
ARTEMIS!
YOU HAVE NO RIGHT TO GO READING PEOPLE'S DIARIES!
You're just a cat!
I meant he was my first love that included a first kiss♡, okay?!

Congratulations, Sailor Moon! On your first stage musical!♡
Dear ♡ Venus NaNa-chan♡

Codename Sailor V

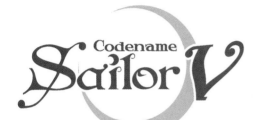

Translation Notes

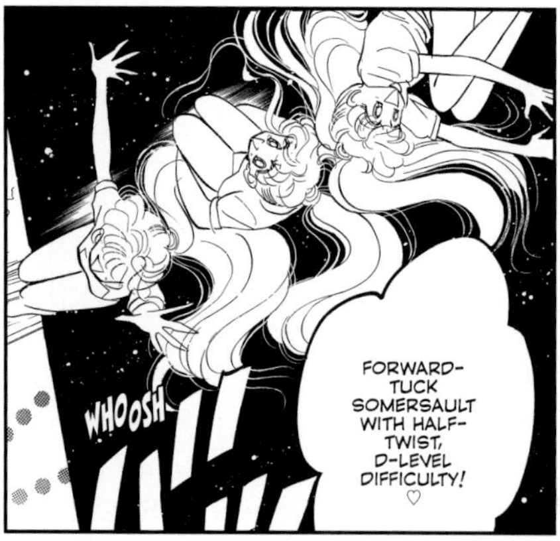
FORWARD-TUCK SOMERSAULT WITH HALF-TWIST, D-LEVEL DIFFICULTY! ♡
WHOOSH

D-level difficulty, page 7

In competitive gymnastics, the different moves are given different difficulty ratings. Before 2006, the ratings started at A for the easiest, and Super E for the hardest. In other words, Minako is trying a rather advanced move.

Honorifics, page 9

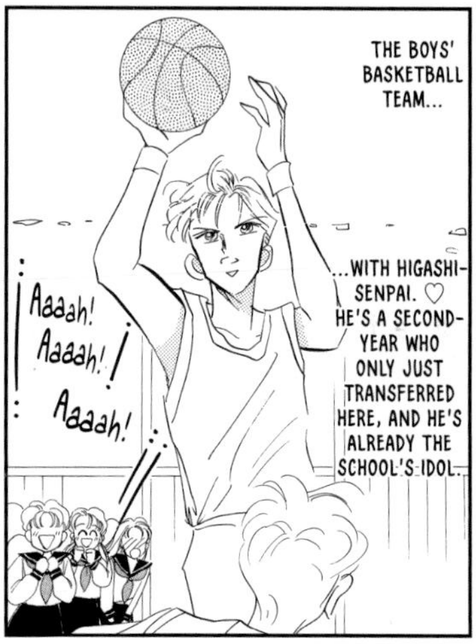
THE BOYS' BASKETBALL TEAM...
...WITH HIGASHI-SENPAI. ♡ HE'S A SECOND-YEAR WHO ONLY JUST TRANSFERRED HERE, AND HE'S ALREADY THE SCHOOL'S IDOL...
Aaaah!
Aaaah!
Aaaah!

The Japanese language uses a number of honorifics which change depending on the relationships of the speakers. Here are the most commonly used suffixes:

-san: This is the polite default, and is used when greeting strangers or others one may not know particularly well (colleagues, etc). It is generally used after the last name: Aino-san.

-chan: This is used by young children, by female friends (often who have grown up together), by parents to (often female) children, and by family members or couples to denote closeness: Hikaru-chan.

-kun: This is often used when speaking to boys, but can also be used to refer to younger colleagues, including women: Amano-kun.

-senpai: This is used when speaking to someone who is a higher rank or who has spent more time than the speaker in an institution (school or work) or a club/hobby, and is a polite way to denote rank and a mentoring relationship. The counterpart for the younger party is *-kohai*. *Senpai* and *Kohai* can also be used as nouns. Example: Higashi-senpai.

-sama: Once used to denote those of lordly rank, it is now often used (especially in manga) to refer to someone the speaker idolizes and greatly respects: Higashi-sama.

-oniichan/-oneechan: These refer to "older brother" and "older sister," respectively, but don't necessarily correlate to a blood relation. They can also be used when referring to a somewhat older boy or girl: Furuhata-oniisan.

-sensei: Used for teachers, doctors, and masters of craft. Anyone who has become an expert can be called *sensei*, not just instructors: Okamoto-sensei.

No honorifics: Sometimes, no honorifics are used at all. Only people who are extremely close tend to omit honorifics entirely...unless they're trying to pick a fight. While Mina doesn't use honorifics for Artemis, that may just be because he's a cat!

Eikô Juku, page 12

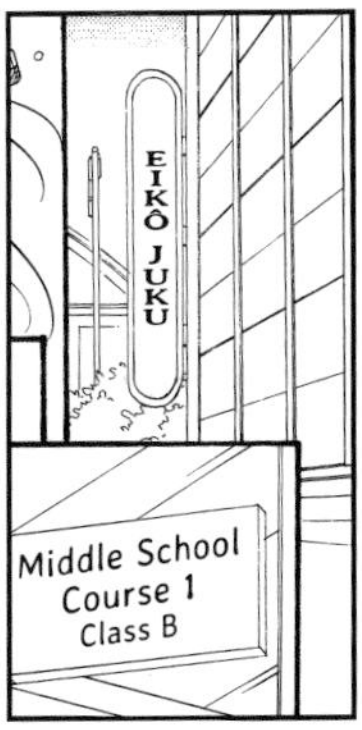
EIKÔ JUKU
Middle School
Course 1
Class B

In Japan, many high schools require their potential students to pass an entrance exam before they can enroll. The more elite the school, the harder the exam. To prepare for these tests, students can attend *juku*, a type of supplementary test-prep school specifically geared to help them get into the high school, and eventually college, of their choice.

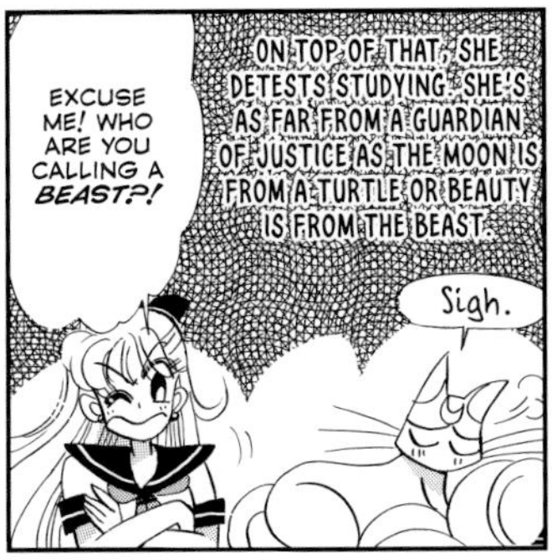
ON TOP OF THAT, SHE DETESTS STUDYING. SHE'S AS FAR FROM A GUARDIAN OF JUSTICE AS THE MOON IS FROM A TURTLE OR BEAUTY IS FROM THE BEAST.
EXCUSE ME! WHO ARE YOU CALLING A *BEAST?!*
Sigh.

Moon and turtle, page 45

This Japanese idiom expresses how two objects may seem similar at first, but are actually so different, they cannot be compared. Though the moon and a turtle (specifically a soft-shelled one) are both round in shape, one is considered a symbol of beauty while the other is mud-stained and ugly. The mention of Beauty and the Beast also serves the purpose of highlighting the mismatch between Minako and her role as guardian.

Shôryuken, Hadouken, Yakyuken, page 46

The reader may have realized that one of these things is not like the others. *Shôryuken* (Rising Dragon Fist) and *Hadouken* (Surge Fist), were made famous as special attacks in the *Street Fighter* video game series. *Yakyuken*, on the other hand, is something very different. Literally meaning "baseball fist," *Yakyuken* is the name of the strip version of rock-paper-scissors—played like regular rock-paper-scissors, but the loser has to remove an article of clothing.

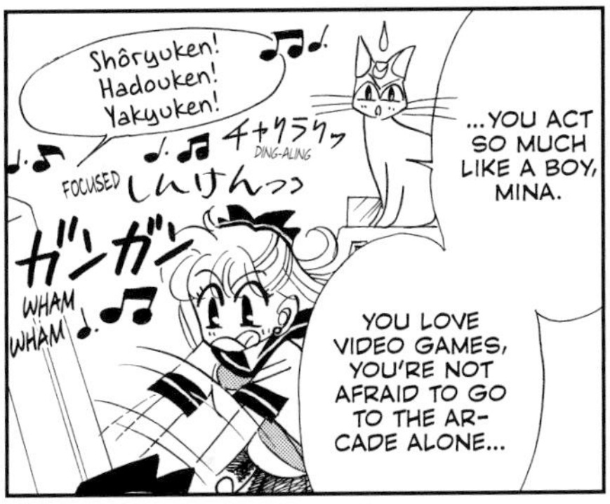
...YOU ACT SO MUCH LIKE A BOY, MINA.
YOU LOVE VIDEO GAMES, YOU'RE NOT AFRAID TO GO TO THE AR-CADE ALONE...
Shôryuken! Hadouken! Yakyuken!
DING-ALING
FOCUSED
WHAM WHAM

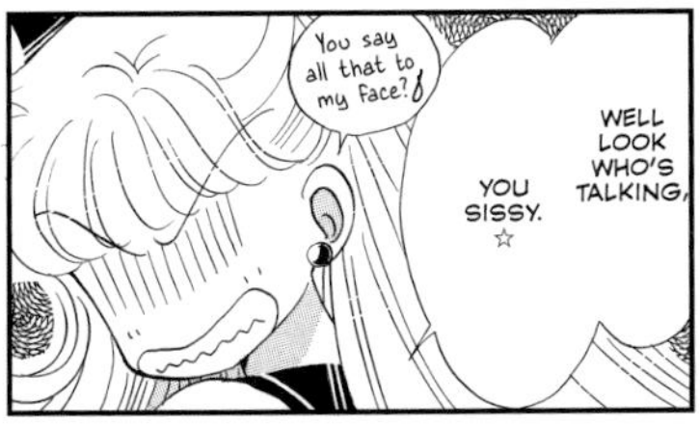
WELL LOOK WHO'S TALKING,
YOU SISSY. ☆
You say all that to my face?

Sissy, page 46

In this panel, Minako calls Artemis an *okama*-cat, where *okama* is the most commonly used Japanese term referring to gay men. It is not always an insult, for many people self-identify as *okama*, too. The definition itself has changed throughout the years—in the early 2000s, the term connoted more of a gendered performance, not just a specific sexuality or romantic interest. Since then, and today, *okama* has come to refer to people in male-to-male relationships more broadly.

A forbidden sailor uniform, page 49

In Japan, most high schools and junior high schools require their students to wear uniforms. It is generally encouraged to at least go home and change clothes, and perhaps finish one's homework, before indulging in such frivolities as goofing off at the arcade.

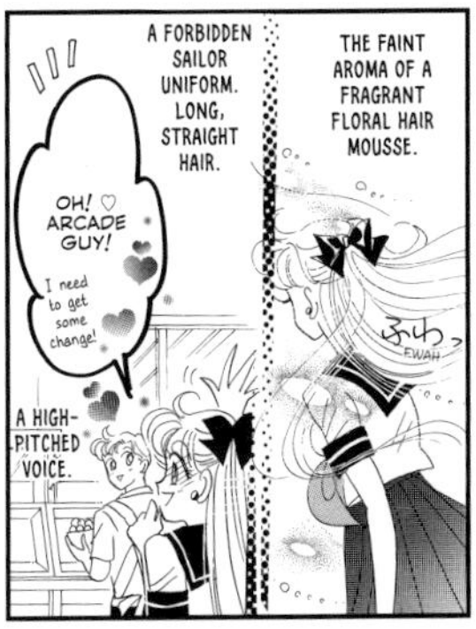
THE FAINT AROMA OF A FRAGRANT FLORAL HAIR MOUSSE.
A FORBIDDEN SAILOR UNIFORM. LONG, STRAIGHT HAIR.
FWAH
OH! ♡ ARCADE GUY!
I need to get some change!
A HIGH-PITCHED VOICE.

Takurô "Taku" Ôtaku, page 54
While Taku's full name literally means "large home home wave," colloquially, *otaku* is the word for someone with a surpassing love of whatever inspires their enthusiasm, such as anime, trains, or video games. In other words, an English rendition of his name might be something like Geeky McGeekerson.

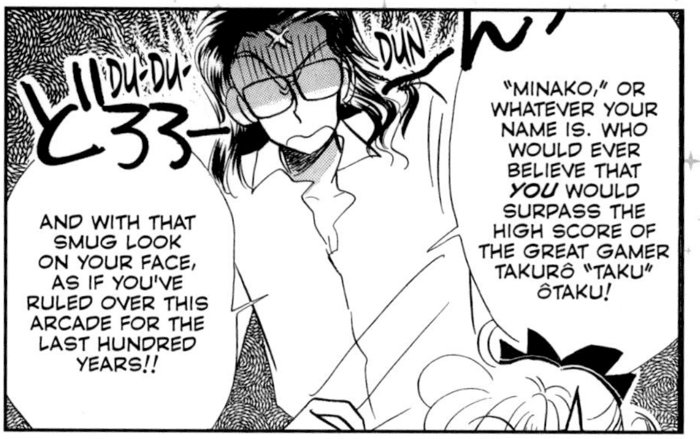
DUN
DU-DU-
"MINAKO," OR WHATEVER YOUR NAME IS. WHO WOULD EVER BELIEVE THAT *YOU* WOULD SURPASS THE HIGH SCORE OF THE GREAT GAMER TAKURÔ "TAKU" ÔTAKU!
AND WITH THAT SMUG LOOK ON YOUR FACE, AS IF YOU'VE RULED OVER THIS ARCADE FOR THE LAST HUNDRED YEARS!!

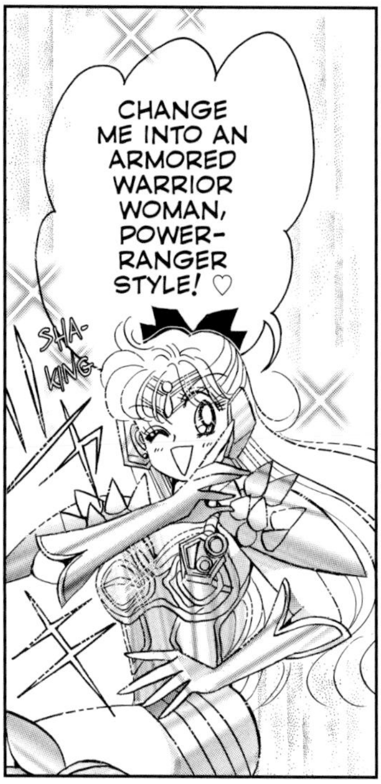
CHANGE ME INTO AN ARMORED WARRIOR WOMAN, POWER-RANGER STYLE! ♡
SHA-KING

Power Ranger-style!, page 56
In the original Japanese, Minako asks to be changed into a "*sentai* heroine-style" warrior woman. *Sentai* means "squadron," but is often a reference to the genre of children's programming known in English as Super Sentai. This genre began in Japan in 1975, and came to America in 1993 as *Mighty Morphin Power Rangers*, which was an adapted version of *Kyôryû Sentai Jyûrenger (Dinosaur Squadron Beast Rangers)*, the sixteenth installment of the series. It involves heroes who transform into new forms and fight, in groups, against new evil threats every week.

BS vs CS, page 68
The difference between a broadcast satellite and a communication satellite is that the former is used for broadcasts of radio and TV programs, while the latter was originally used by businesses for communication that was not specifically entertainment. That changed in 1989, when the Japanese broadcast laws were changed and CS broadcasts became more generally available. These days, the main difference between the two is that BS programming is available to all, while CS programming requires extra fees.

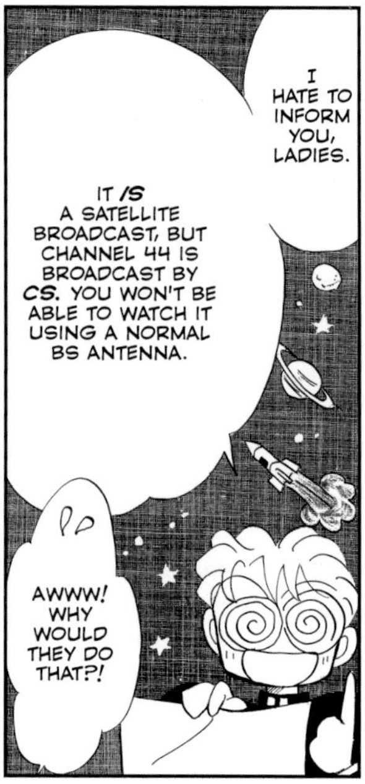
I HATE TO INFORM YOU, LADIES.
IT *IS* A SATELLITE BROADCAST, BUT CHANNEL 44 IS BROADCAST BY *CS*. YOU WON'T BE ABLE TO WATCH IT USING A NORMAL BS ANTENNA.
AWWW! WHY WOULD THEY DO THAT?!

MMMM?
TUMBLE

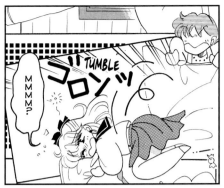

Minako's uniform, page 96
If Minako is waking up on a Sunday morning after going to sleep in her uniform, that means she was wearing her school uniform on a Saturday. Students in Japan will occasionally have extra classes or club or team activities on the weekend, and would be expected to wear their uniforms to school in those cases. Minako is on the volleyball team, and may have gone to school for practice, or she may have worn her uniform to test-prep school.

LOOK, THERE'S EVEN FAN COMICS ABOUT THEM!
THEY'RE ALL THE RAGE ON MY COMPUTER MESSAGE BOARDS.
Targeted at loli fans!
In the Twin Dark Forum.
I went and bought them at Coniket.
...Otaku...
Twin Dark Mate

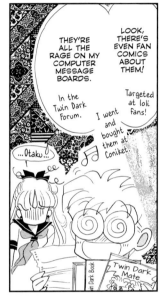

Computer message boards and Coniket, page 138
The World Wide Web went live in 1991, but it was not easily available to most of the public until a few years later. Nevertheless, people could still connect one computer to another using phone lines. The process wasn't nearly as easy as it is now, and so generally only major enthusiasts availed themselves of this technology.

Coniket is the Sailor V world's equivalent of Comiket, a nickname for Comic Market. Starting in 1975, Comic Market is a big convention where artists get together and sell their comics—including original comics, fan comics (*dôjinshi*), and other fan art and fan works based on their favorite anime, manga, video game, or pop star.

CHATTER
わい
わい
CHATTER
Dark Shizuka-hime
Live Tour
Dark Silence
002
DARK

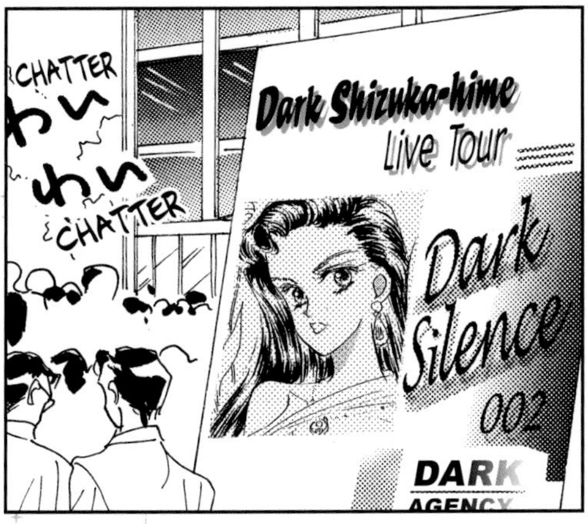

Dark Shizuka-hime, page 139
In Japanese, *hime* is a suffix attached to the name Shizuka to indicate that she is beautiful and elegant like a princess (*hime* is often translated as "princess," though it does not refer exclusively to royalty). The suffix is also attached to Snow White's Japanese name in translations of that fairy tale.

HEH HEH. OUR NEXT IDOL WILL TAKE THE TRENDY DRAMA AND COMMERCIALS TRACK. WE'LL PUT HIM IN MOVIES AND LIVE EVENTS, TOO.

Trendy drama, page 141
"Trendy drama" is a genre of Japanese television programming from the '80s and early '90s. It focused on daily life and romance, and was popular among women in their 20s.

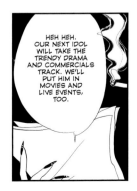

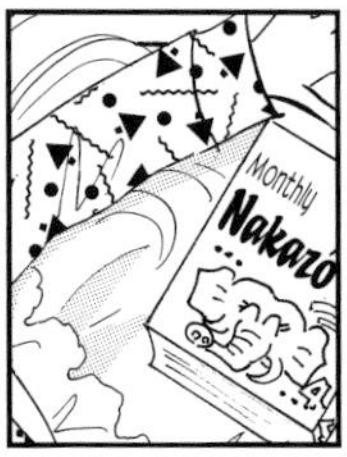
Monthly Nakazô

Monthly Nakazô, page 165
Codename Sailor V has a somewhat complex publishing history, but it started with what is now the third chapter in the series in a magazine that came out three to four times a year, *Nakayosi Zôkan: Nakazô* (in English, *Nakayoshi Special (Edition)*). The monthly version of *Nakazô* featured here has an elephant on it, because *zô* is also the Japanese pronunciation for "Elephant."

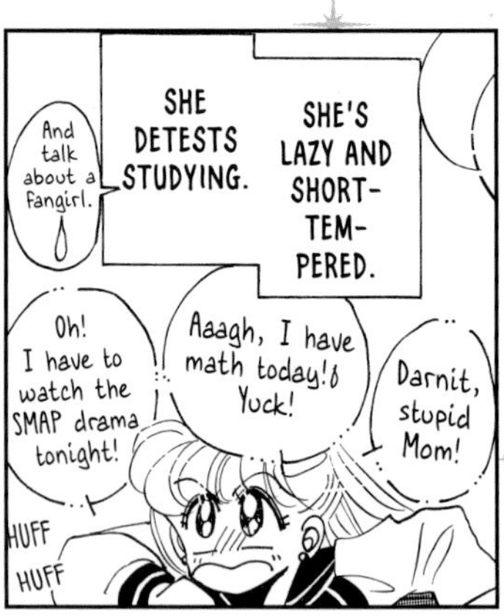
SHE'S LAZY AND SHORT-TEMPERED.
SHE DETESTS STUDYING.
And talk about a fangirl.
Darnit, stupid Mom!
Aaagh, I have math today! Yuck!
Oh! I have to watch the SMAP drama tonight!
HUFF HUFF

The SMAP drama, page 167
SMAP is a popular Japanese boy band—the most successful boy band of the Japanese Heisei Era (1989-2019)—that was active from 1988 through 2016. By 1991, their music was already topping the charts, and the band's members were appearing on Japanese variety shows and television dramas. Minako is most likely referring to *Hatachi no Yakusoku (Promise of 20-Year-Olds)*, starring Goro Inagaki.

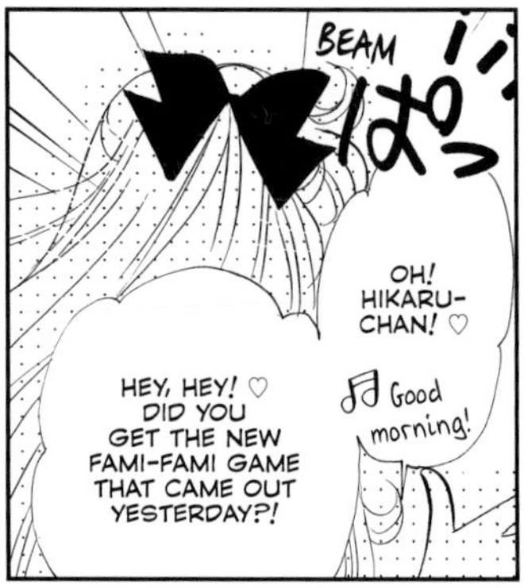
BEAM
ぱっ
OH! HIKARU-CHAN! ♡
Good morning!
HEY, HEY! ♡ DID YOU GET THE NEW FAMI-FAMI GAME THAT CAME OUT YESTERDAY?!

Fami-Fami, page 170
Fami-Fami is the Sailor V world version of a Famicom. Famicom, short for "Family Computer," was the game console that was marketed overseas as the Nintendo Entertainment System back in the dark ages. In those days, a gamer could not buy a digital copy of a game, so if a store was sold out of the physical cartridge, they were doomed to wait until a new shipment came in.

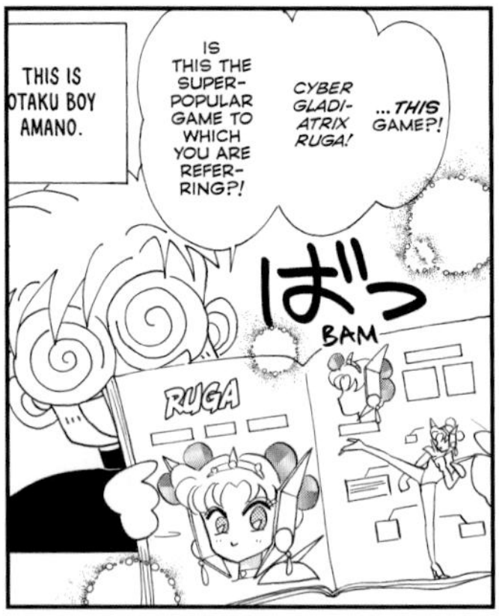
...THIS GAME?!
CYBER GLADIATRIX RUGA!
IS THIS THE SUPER-POPULAR GAME TO WHICH YOU ARE REFERRING?!
THIS IS OTAKU BOY AMANO.
ばっ
BAM
RUGA

***Cyber Gladiatrix Ruga*, page 170**
Ruga likely gets her name from a Japanese TV show that started in 1992 called *Ugo Ugo Ru-ga*, which was a children's variety show that used computer animation. The title comes from reversing the Japanese characters used to spell *gou gou ga-ru*, or "go go girl." In other words, Ruga is the Japanese pronunciation of the English word "girl" spelled backwards.

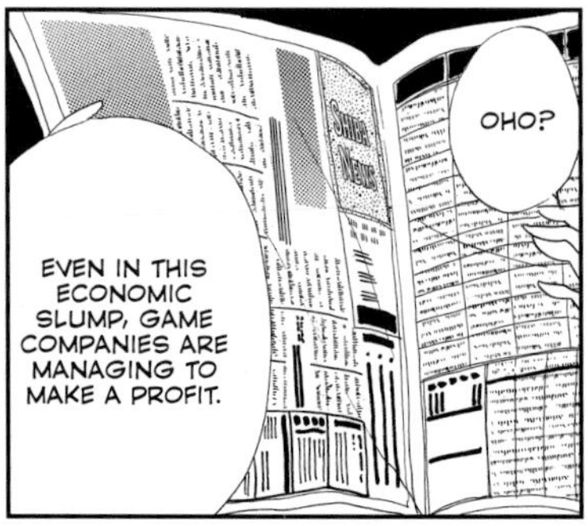
OHO?
EVEN IN THIS ECONOMIC SLUMP, GAME COMPANIES ARE MANAGING TO MAKE A PROFIT.

Economic slump, page 174
The events in this scene take places in 1993, towards the beginning of what is sometimes referred to in Japan as "the Lost Decade." Japan experienced great prosperity in the late '80s until the stock market crashed in 1991. It took years for Japan's economy to recover—so many, in fact, that the reason this period is only sometimes referred to as the Lost Decade is that the recession went on so long that now it is referred to as the Lost 20 Years.

Defense Agency, page 178
The Defense Agency was the government body in charge of Japan's defense. They were responsible for the Japan Self-Defense forces. In 2007, these responsibilities were taken over by the newly formed Ministry of Defense.

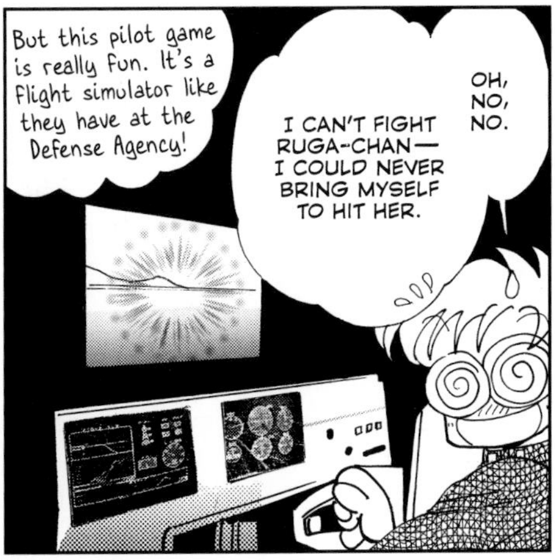
OH, NO, NO.
I CAN'T FIGHT RUGA-CHAN—I COULD NEVER BRING MYSELF TO HIT HER.
But this pilot game is really fun. It's a flight simulator like they have at the Defense Agency!

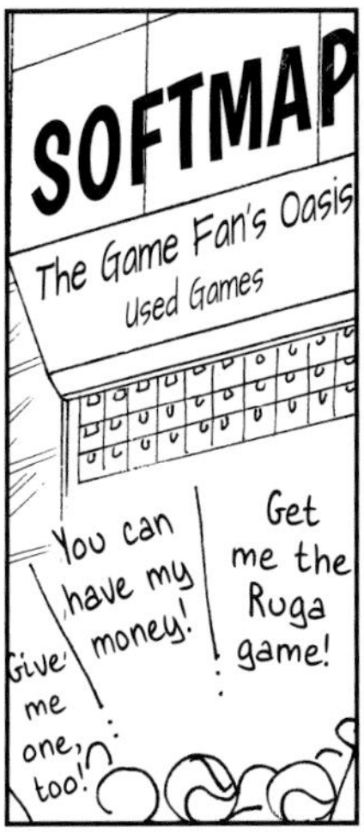
SOFTMAP
The Game Fan's Oasis
Used Games
Get me the Ruga game!
You can have my money!
Give me one, too!

Softmap, page 184
The Sailor V world's equivalent of Sofmap, a popular video game retailer.

Passenger service facility charge, page 203
In order to cover the costs of running an airport smoothly, many airports charge a service fee. In the United States, this fee is usually included in the ticket price, but in Japan, it is paid separately. As of this writing, the fee at Narita Airport for international travelers is still around 2,000 yen, or approximately $20, but with the added security fee that is also required, it comes to about 2,600 yen, or about $26.

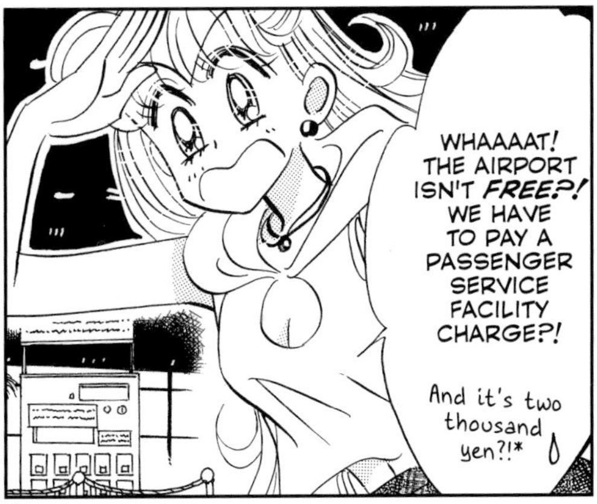
WHAAAAT! THE AIRPORT ISN'T *FREE?!* WE HAVE TO PAY A PASSENGER SERVICE FACILITY CHARGE?!
And it's two thousand yen?!*

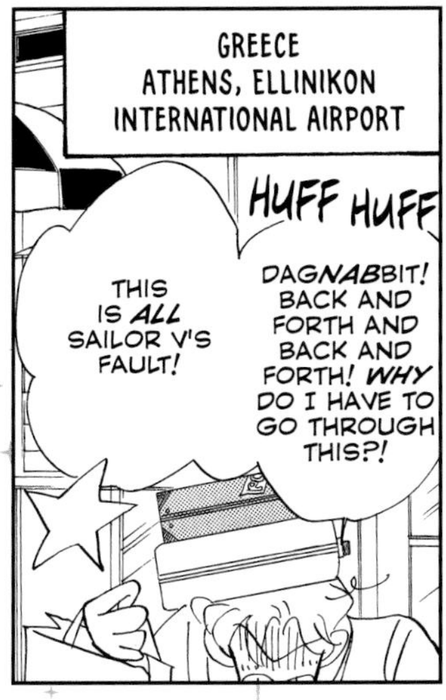
GREECE
ATHENS, ELLINIKON
INTERNATIONAL AIRPORT
HUFF HUFF
DAG*NAB*BIT! BACK AND FORTH AND BACK AND FORTH! *WHY* DO I HAVE TO GO THROUGH THIS?!
THIS IS *ALL* SAILOR V'S FAULT!

Ellinikon International Airport, page 213
This is the name of the international airport that served Athens, Greece at the time this chapter took place. In 2001, it was replaced by the new Athens International Airport *Eleftherios Venizelos.*

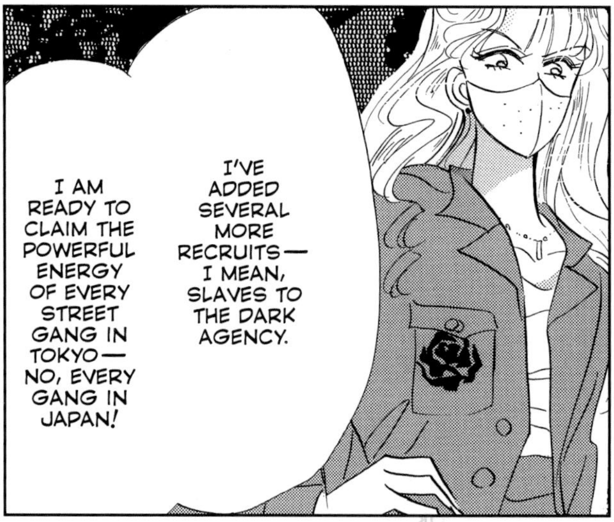
I'VE ADDED SEVERAL MORE RECRUITS— I MEAN, SLAVES TO THE DARK AGENCY.
I AM READY TO CLAIM THE POWERFUL ENERGY OF EVERY STREET GANG IN TOKYO— NO, EVERY GANG IN JAPAN!

Recruits, page 247
Vivian actually refers to her brainwashees as *shatei*, which literally means "younger brother," and is how mid-level gang leaders refer to their younger underlings.

Tokkô, page 248
Tokkô means "special attack" or "suicide squad," and is the adjective used to describe the typical Japanese youth gang uniform. This uniform includes the long coat (as seen on Vivian) which is often covered in intricate embroidery.

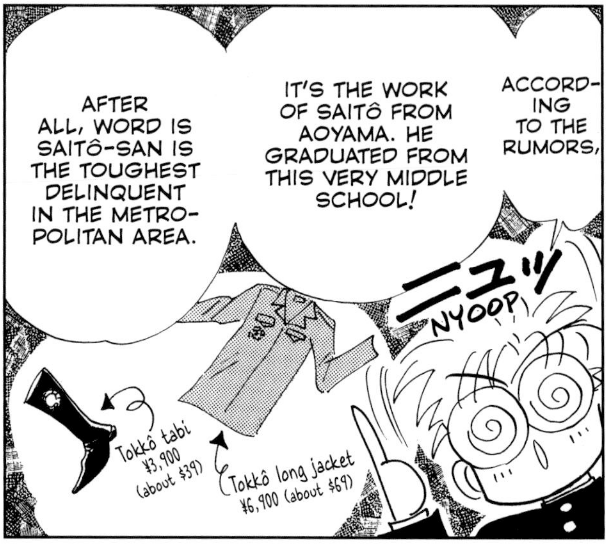
ACCORD-ING TO THE RUMORS,
IT'S THE WORK OF SAITÔ FROM AOYAMA. HE GRADUATED FROM THIS VERY MIDDLE SCHOOL!
AFTER ALL, WORD IS SAITÔ-SAN IS THE TOUGHEST DELINQUENT IN THE METRO-POLITAN AREA.
ニュッ
NYOOP
Tokkô tabi ¥3,900 (about $39)
Tokkô long jacket ¥6,900 (about $69)

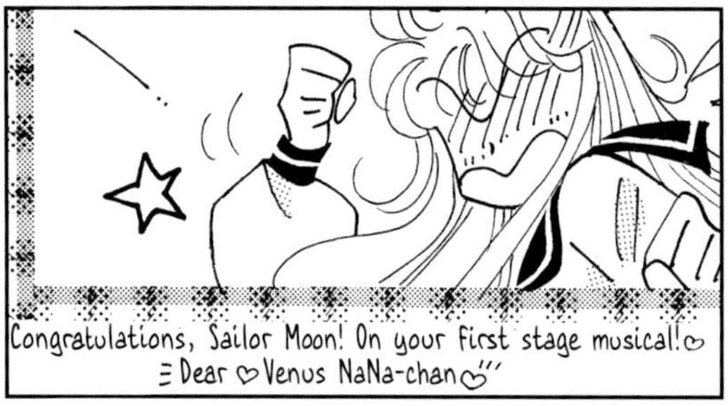
Congratulations, Sailor Moon! On your first stage musical!
Dear Venus NaNa-chan

Sailor Moon Musical, page 272
This chapter of *Codename: Sailor V* was inspired by the very first Sailor Moon musical. It featured a number called *Namikimichi no Koi* (Love on a Tree-Lined Road), sung by Nana Suzuki as Minako. The song tells of how she saw a young man on a tree-lined road and instantly fell in love. The young man in question was one "Saitô-kun," who subsequently admits that he loves Minako, too. However, later on, he reveals that his name was a code! When "Saitô-kun" is flipped around, it becomes "Kun-saito," or Kunzite, one of the Dark Kingdom's Four Heavenly Kings!

A Kodansha Comics Trade Paperback Original
Codename: Sailor V Eternal Edition 1 copyright © Naoko Takeuchi
English translation copyright © Naoko Takeuchi

Published in the United States by Kodansha Comics, an imprint of
Kodansha USA Publishing, LLC, New York.

Publication rights for this English edition arranged through
Kodansha Ltd., Tokyo.

First published in Japan in 2014 by Kodansha Ltd., Tokyo
as *Codename wa Sailor V*, volume 1.

ISBN 978-1-64651-143-3

Printed in China.

www.kodanshacomics.com

9 8 7 6 5 4 3 2 1
Translation: Alethea Nibley & Athena Nibley
Lettering: Lys Blakeslee
Editing: Lauren Scanlan
Kodansha Comics edition cover design by Phil Balsman

Publisher: Kiichiro Sugawara

Director of publishing services: Ben Applegate
Associate director of operations: Stephen Pakula
Publishing services managing editor: Noelle Webster
Assistant production manager: Emi Lotto, Angela Zurlo